Deaf Persons
in the
Arts and Sciences

DEAF PERSONS
IN THE
ARTS AND SCIENCES

A Biographical Dictionary

Harry G. Lang
and
Bonnie Meath-Lang

GREENWOOD PRESS
Westport, Connecticut • London

Library of Congress Cataloging-in-Publication Data

Lang, Harry G.
   Deaf persons in the arts and sciences : a biographical dictionary
/ Harry G. Lang and Bonnie Meath-Lang.
    p. cm.
   ISBN 0–313–29170–5 (alk. paper)
   1. Deaf—Biography. I. Meath-Lang, Bonnie. II. Title.
HV2372.L36   1995
920'.0087'1—dc20   94–24206

British Library Cataloguing in Publication Data is available.

Library of Congress Catalog Card Number: 94–24206
ISBN: 0–313–29170–5

First published in 1995

Greenwood Press, 88 Post Road West, Westport, CT 06881
An imprint of Greenwood Publishing Group, Inc.

Printed in the United States of America

∞

The paper used in this book complies with the
Permanent Paper Standard issued by the National
Information Standards Organization (Z39.48–1984).

10 9 8 7 6 5 4 3 2 1

Contents

Illustrations

Preface

Over the past thirty years, the number of deaf persons studying in colleges and universities has increased from several hundred to more than twelve thousand. Several factors have contributed to this dramatic change. Organizations of deaf people have worked tirelessly to challenge attitudes and break down the communication barriers. Federally funded colleges such as the National Technical Institute for the Deaf at the Rochester Institute of Technology in Rochester, New York, and Gallaudet University in Washington, D.C., are now graduating large numbers of deaf students in pursuit of professional careers, and federal legislation such as the Americans with Disabilities Act (ADA) has facilitated entry and advancement of deaf professionals in the work force. The past few decades have also seen educational interpreting grow into a profession, assisting deaf and hearing students in courses and programs, while new information technologies are rapidly being developed to accommodate the ever-growing numbers of deaf persons receiving quality academic preparation. Other deaf students continue to matriculate in schools without any such support.

Yet despite these changes, attitudes, in particular, continue to make it difficult for deaf individuals to enter various programs of study. One result is the low representation of deaf people in certain fields, such as science, medicine, engineering, and mathematics. In *Silence of the Spheres: The Deaf Experience in the History of Science*, Lang (1994) identified more than 670 deaf women and men in scientific professions. An analysis of the barriers these persons faced led to several recommendations, including increased availability of information about the successes of deaf people in these careers. There is a similar need for information about successful deaf artists and writers, not only to help increase awareness of the contributions deaf people have made, but to serve in motivating aspiring young deaf artists and writers. *Deaf Persons in the Arts and Sciences: A Biographical Dictionary* is a reference for both students and scholars, providing information about people whose deafness occurred at a point in their lives where it played a significant role in influencing their choices and/or the direction of their careers. In addition to their accomplishments, we share relevant biographical data illustrating how individuals challenged attitudes, communication, and other barriers to foster relationships and to achieve in a field of science or the arts.

While the emphasis in this collection focuses largely on the traditional disciplines associated with the arts and sciences, particularly the physical sciences, selected individuals are included for their leadership in associated fields, such as education or politics. In some cases, these women and men were the first deaf persons to hold certain positions. In other instances, they gained esteem by virtue of their unceasing dedication to creating opportunities for deaf people to achieve in the arts and sciences. In so doing, these persons distinguished themselves in their pioneering efforts to effect a major change in shaping the cultural, social, and intellectual landscape.

As with any field, certain uses of terminology related to deaf people and deafness are complex and varied from individual to individual. We use the term ''deaf'' in a broad and inclusive sense to embrace cultural and functional deafness. The capitalized term ''Deaf'' is used herein to indicate cultural and community constructs defined by use of American Sign Language (ASL), affiliation with particular organizations, and specific cultural events and disciplines. Many individuals prefer to describe themselves as Deaf; we do not apply that usage to particular people in these entries, because we believe that it is not our place to make that selective determination for others.

The reader will see the archaic terms ''deaf and dumb'' and ''deaf-mute'' in certain quotations and the former names of schools and institutions. We do not insert ''[sic]'' after each of these; it would be visually distracting; but these are obsolete and inappropriate terms. There are also numerous references to Gallaudet College in the context of the time when persons attended the college. In 1988, Gallaudet officially became Gallaudet University. Within a number of biographical entries, it is noted that individuals interacted with or were influenced by others whose lives are also documented in this book. These cross-references are indicated with an asterisk (*).

A wide range of literary sources was used to collect biographical data for *Deaf Persons in the Arts and Sciences*, including the periodicals of the Deaf community, archival information in the United States and abroad, and books and journals on the education of deaf students, as well as those in the sciences and arts. There were, of course, discrepancies and contradictions in secondary information, so every effort was made to consult multiple sources. In the case of many contemporaries, interviews and correspondence assisted in the development of the biographical sketches. Certainly, the reader will agree that any such project is a selective endeavor, and that there are many other deaf women and men who deserve to be included in such a volume. An appendix lists some of these, in the hope that future volumes will detail their accomplishments.

Our research and writing were made slightly less formidable by the unstinting generosity and phenomenal skill of some talented individuals. Gail Kovalik—henceforth to be known as "Sherlock"—of the Staff Resource Center of the National Technical Institute for the Deaf (NTID) at Rochester Institute of Technology (RIT) hunted down obscure journals, searched the Internet for dates, made phone calls to organizations, and was generally intrepid. She sets a standard of excellence for library services. Puck Winqvist and Anne-Marie Bégin are also to be commended. Ulf Hedberg, Michael Olsen, Marguerite Glass-Englehart, and Carolyn Jones of Gallaudet University Merrill Learning Center also were enthusiastic, helpful, humorous, and highly trained resource specialists. We also appreciate the assistance of the reference and interlibrary loan staff at the Wallace Memorial Library at RIT for their kind assistance, especially Richard Squires, Melanie Norton, Linda Coppola, and Barbara Polowy. Librarians and archivists from the United States, Canada, and abroad responded to our numerous requests expeditiously. Our friends on the editorial staff of the Greenwood Publishing Group—Karen Davis, Cynthia Harris, Maureen Melino, and Leslie Treff—are skilled, sensitive, and supportive communicators. We are grateful, too, to Gayle Meegan and Kim Singer at NTID for their help with correspondence and duplicating.

A gifted and sensitive graduate student from the People's Republic of China, Yufang Liu, worked tirelessly on eleventh-hour manuscript preparation. Another graduate student and English teacher, Anne Kingston, assisted in the initial library research. Mark Benjamin of NTID applied creativity and problem-solving skill to photograph preparation with uncommon devotion. Thanks also to Susan Cergol and Deborah Waltzer for helping us locate photographs in NTID's department of public affairs.

Professor Robert F. Panara, outstanding teacher he is, read and critiqued every biography with care and exuberance. His life is a story we tell herein with great joy and respect. Critiques and moral support from our colleagues Marc Marschark and John Albertini were also sincerely appreciated.

This project was supported, in part, by the Gallaudet University Laurent Clerc Cultural Fund, and we are grateful to Mary Ann Pugin and her colleagues for the funds to defray some manuscript preparation costs. Barbara McKee and NTID's Dean Jim DeCaro took the time to write in support of the application for the grant.

There is a saying, which varies slightly across many languages, to the effect that those who ensure human progress and a better world are the people who build up, rather than tear down, others. This book is dedicated to the memory of those chroniclers of the Deaf community who have gone before us, among them Yvonne Pitrois, Corrine Rocheleau, Felix Kowalewski, Kelly H. Stevens, Guilbert C. Braddock, James E. Gallaher, and Ferdinand Berthier. We are even more happy to dedicate this work to those who continue to write and celebrate other people's stories, in particular, Loy Golladay, Frank Bowe, Jack Gannon, Francis Higgins, Linda Levitan, Tom Willard, and Matthew Moore.

Introduction

As schoolchildren, we learn one of our earliest lessons in the genres of literature when we are taught the distinction between biography and autobiography. When asked to parrot back the difference, as students invariably are requested to do, we embellish this rite of passage by highlighting our understanding of the three Greek roots involved, reasoning through a process of elimination that the distinctive feature "auto" means that autobiography is writing one's own life, the life of the self, as opposed to poor, plain biography, the life written by just anyone. The exercise is probably more valuable for its contribution to our cognitive development and budding logic than to our understanding of the genres themselves. It is some time before we come to know, usually as adults, that the complicated act of representing a life is often viewed with puzzlement at best and suspicion at worst.

The writing of biographies, especially brief ones for reference work, is made more complex when a particular area of life is emphasized for the purpose of presenting a powerful influence and/or connection to a common theme. This is the case for this collection, *Deaf Persons in the Arts and Sciences: A Biographical Dictionary*. Like all biographers writing our version of other people's lives, we identify with some of our subjects. We frankly love some of these men and women, both known to us and imagined by us. Others disturb us, and we disagree with their choices. We are distressed by the relative lack of minority deaf citations, despite innumerable hours of searching and inquiry, as a sad commentary on how much needs yet to be accomplished. Fortunately, the lives and accomplishments of these individuals and the multiple ways the deaf experience speaks to the human condition are strikingly self-evident. While we, a deaf and a hearing biographer, have endeavored to be as fair, thorough, and careful in the writing and research as possible, the ultimate trust should be placed in the lives and examples that emerge from these pages. In the end, for us, the powerful argument for biography is in its demonstration that the individual *can* make a difference.

Nicholas Mirzoeff (1992) reminds us of Leonardo da Vinci's advice to artists—to observe and learn from deaf persons: "Do not laugh at me because I propose a teacher without speech to you, for he will teach you better through facts than will all the other masters through words." Such learning from the lives of some remarkable deaf persons is the desired outcome of this biographical work.

DEAF PERSONS' EMERGENCE IN THE ARTS AND SCIENCES

One of the earliest historical records of a deaf person entering the arts or sciences is found as a singular, obscure anecdote in the thirty-seven volume encyclopedia *Historia Naturalis* by the Roman scholar Pliny the Elder (23–79A.D.), a work of natural science with especial emphasis on how science touches life. This anecdote mentions Quintus Pedius, a deaf son of the Consul and co-heir of Augustus, who is said to have had the approval of Augustus to receive instruction in painting. Although little else is known about Quintus Pedius and his contribution to the world of art, the report of his instruction is intriguing for many reasons. First, it illustrates the relative invisibility of deafness and deaf people in ancient history. Fifteen hundred years pass after Pliny's writing with hardly any deaf people mentioned by name. Yet, the brief story of Quintus Pedius may also be viewed as an exciting clue to a new generation of historians in search of the "Deaf Experience." We are presently in the midst of a revolutionary period in historical writing where deaf people are being discovered and credited for their work. Traditionally, there has been a great focus in published histories on the "deficiencies" associated with deafness. This is particularly true with regard to concern for majority language development and spoken communication skills. Histories have for too long emphasized the controversies over communication methods and the accomplishments of hearing people in the education of deaf students, with inadequate attention paid to those deaf individuals who created communication bridges and distinguished themselves as change agents in their respective fields of endeavor.

Most histories of the education of deaf students, for example, emphasize the importance of the hearing mathematician Jerome Cardan's (1501–1576) report of Agricola's observation of a deaf person who could hear by reading and speak by writing. With appropriate credit due these two hearing scholars, one wonders why there is little mention of the success stories of both congenitally and adventitiously deafened people in the same era. There were, for example, the two bright stars of the Pléiade, Joachim Du Bellay (about 1525–1560) and Pierre de Ronsard (1524–1585), both deaf, who brought new life to French Renaissance poetry. Henry Gurney (1548–1616), a late-deafened writer and the head of a well-known Quaker family, adjusted to deafness and went on to complete *The Commonplace Book or Register*, which records such historical events as the defeat of the Spanish Armada off the Norfolk coast. Charles Butler (?–1647), a British naturalist, published, among other works, *The Feminine Monarchie, Or a Treatise Concerning Bees and the Due Ordering of Them* (1609). At this time, there were also many distinguished artists born deaf or deafened at a very early age, including Bernardino di Betto Biagi (1454–1513), who studied with Raphael under Pietro Vanucci and painted frescoes of Moses' life in the Sistine Chapel; and Ambrosio de Predis, a student of Da Vinci, who became a talented painter. De Predis' deaf father, Christoforo, was a respected illuminator. Juan Fernandez Navarrete (1526–1579) earned the title of the "Spanish Titian" for his masterpieces in the Escorial, and Jaime Lopez decorated the sixteenth-century Hermitage of Notre Dame (the Prado). Fray Gaspar of Burgos, a deaf pupil of Pedro Ponce, the pioneer educator of Spain, became a talented deaf illuminator as well. These are but a few of the great artists of this period, who were characterized invariably as "El Mudo," "El Surdillo," "Il Fornaretto," and other appellations that sometimes stigmatized them and sometimes conveyed their effect as deaf persons in a world unready to acknowledge their essential humanity. In the tradition of emphasizing the importance of spoken language, there has also been an absence of discussion in these historical contexts of the rich forms of gestural communication and sign language observed among deaf persons through time, although Socrates himself touched upon this in Plato, and Da Vinci celebrated gesture in his writing.

Buried in Thomas Fuller's quaint 1602 document entitled *The Worthies of England* is a reference to Edward Bone. Bone, deaf from the cradle, could "express to his master any news that was stirring in the Country." When he met with his deaf friend, Kempe, "there were often such earnest tokenings, as such hearty laughters and other passionate gestures, that their want of a tongue seemed rather an hindrance to others conceiving them, than to their conceiving one another." Similarly, the deaf knight Sir John Gawdy, a pupil of Lely who had intended to follow portraiture as a profession and who became heir to his family's estates upon his brother's death, was described by the diarist John Evelyn as having communicated through gestures and signs without difficulty with his family. These and other sixteenth-century anecdotes reveal that gestural communication systems and sign languages prevailed as an accepted form of intelligent communication even before Cardano published Agricola's observation of a deaf person who could hear by reading and speak by writing. Yet, the belief in speech as a defining feature of humanity itself, possibly influenced by interpretations of Aristotle's own writings on the subject, greatly delayed formal efforts to educate deaf people for centuries—and delayed an emphasis on academic content over communication in that education for centuries more.

Deafness as an essentially human condition is a thread that is woven throughout *Deaf Persons in the Arts and Sciences*. Most of the individuals in this volume may be described as "functionally deaf," that is, unable to hear or understand spoken language with the eyes closed. While many were born deaf or lost their hearing very early in life, we also include some biographies of women and men with progressive deafness, or late-deafness. As much as possible, we include the individuals' own perspectives on being deaf, and how being a deaf person may have transformed their lives and influenced the work they pursued in the arts and sciences.

Many late-deafened people, as well as hearing people, have wondered what the world of the congenitally deaf is like, while those born deaf must wonder, in turn, what it is like to have once heard. Some individuals in both categories consider being deaf a blessing; others have found it a burden. Such diverse attitudes pervade the biographies in the present volume. Writing about the musical composers Beethoven and Smetana, we describe the profound effects of deafness not only on their music careers, but on their compositions. To a lesser extent, Gabriel Fauré's sensori-neural deafness, which began at about the age of fifty-eight, uniquely affected his hearing of instruments having a higher range of harmonics. Fauré viewed his deafness as a cruel fate in which sounds were "so wildly distorted that I thought I was going mad." The tragic element of deafness for some persons may be seen in such statements. On the other hand, being a deaf person was cause for rejoicing for others, such as the French novelist and dramatist Alain René Le Sage, who was unable to hear without an ear trumpet. Le Sage habitually and mischievously took advantage of his deafness. "It is my benefactor," he said. "I am invited to an evening party. I find many new faces. I hope to encounter a congenial spirit. I make use of my cherished trumpet. I see here a guest who might prove interesting. I annex myself to him and say 'I defy you to bore me!' Voila!" Le Sage apparently became more selective through time. As Count de Tressan drily remarked about the dramatist in his final years, "nothing would induce him to put his ear trumpet to his ear when persons he disliked were his interlocutor, though it went up readily enough when any one he liked approached."

The lesson in the lives of the deaf persons whose stories we document has not been lost on the very fields in which these individuals have made their mark. The biographies of the astronomers Annie Jump Cannon and Henrietta Swan Leavitt are punctuated by the comments of their scientifically oriented colleagues, who observed and remarked upon their powers of concentration and meticulous recording of detail. The anthropologist Margaret Mead discussed how her great friend and colleague Ruth Benedict transformed cultural field work as a whole by shifting the emphasis of her own studies from oral interviews, which were difficult for Benedict to conduct, to methods of deep ethnography using carefully recorded visual observation.

Another lesson is that life and art, in truth, follow one another alternately. The emphasis in many of these biographies is, of course, on the creation of works of art by deaf persons, some of whom have been mentioned above. But a number of these lives have also become the subject of art. Helen Keller comes to mind—in the autobiographical film *Deliverance*, the wildly successful, albeit sensationalistic, play *The Miracle Worker*, and numerous television dramas. But other real-life deaf personalities have also inspired many writers to develop semi-biographical literary works. "El Sordo," a guerrilla leader in the Spanish

Civil War, emerges in Ernest Hemingway's *For Whom the Bell Tolls.* The Biblical scholar John Kitto's autobiography, *The Lost Senses,* influenced Wilkie Collins' development of the character ''Madonna'' in *Hide and Seek,* in another example.

All of this points the reader to what we, the authors, have found—that the study of biographies, even viewed through the filters and limits of our own experiences, allows the reader access to other people's ways of knowing and appreciating the universe. As deaf people have accomplished notable achievements and forged important relationships, we are further educated in the unique understanding that the human condition of deafness brings to a view of the world. This worldview has contributed to the advancement of scientific knowledge, the creation of art in multiple forms, and the formulation of political positions. The people of this book have served as inspirations for works of art and as ideals for fellow professionals and students. Yet, for us, the most interesting and unromantic part of many of these stories is the resourcefulness of these individuals in making the connections they did to live their lives and to do their work. For resourcefulness is born of hope. And our position in that ancient debate to define humanity is the belief that it is *hope*—not the ear, nor eye, nor hand, nor voice—that makes us fully human.

Deaf Persons
in the
Arts and Sciences

A

ROBERT GRANT AITKEN (1864–1951), American Astronomer.

Robert Grant Aitken was born on December 31, 1864, in Jackson, California. His father came to America from Scotland, and his mother was the daughter of German immigrants. Aitken was encouraged to enter the ministry as a young man, and had that in mind when he began his studies at Williams College in 1883. His fascination with courses in biology and astronomy, however, led him to change his mind about the ministry. After graduating in 1887, he married Jessie L. Thomas and took a position at Livermore College in California. In 1891, he accepted a professorship in mathematics at the University of the Pacific. The observatory there included a 6-inch refractor telescope built by Alvin Clark's firm. Aitken then spent forty years at the Lick Observatory at the University of California at Santa Cruz, and he was the director during the last five years before his 1935 retirement.

Aitken's progressive deafness began in early childhood. With the help of a hearing aid, he was able to enjoy music somewhat, but communication was more challenging. A copy of his "Record of Family Traits," which he completed for the Eugenics Record Office, indicated that the cause of his deafness was catarrhal otitis media (middle ear hearing loss). In 1922, at the first Astronomical Union Assembly in Rome, Aitken relied primarily on speechreading, not responding to a message even when it was shouted at him. Dr. C. Donald Shane, in an unpublished autobiography, "Life of Mt. Hamilton, 1914–1920," described Aitken's voice as rather hollow and resonant, a result of a "considerable degree of deafness." Aitken's career—and life—were once almost cut short when he did not hear the approach of an automobile.

Aitken began his astronomy work with a 12-inch refractor telescope, under the direction of Edward E. Barnard at Lick Observatory. At first, he observed comets, asteroids, and other objects, but was quickly attracted to binary stars. It was as a double star astronomer that he distinguished himself. Aitken's first publication on "Double Star Measures" appeared in an 1895 issue of the *Publication of the Astronomical Society of the Pacific*. In 1899, he began a careful survey of double stars, working closely with William Joseph Hussey. Many of his measurements were made on 12-inch and 36-inch telescopes, and he established as a limit the magnitude 9.0 of the Bonn Durchmusterung. When Hussey left in 1905, Aitken took over the unfinished work himself, completing the survey in 1915. His discovery of over 3,000 double star systems during this survey is particularly important, since many of these stars were so close to each other that measurements of their orbits were quite challenging. It is for the accuracy with which he made these measurements that Aitken is well remembered. His book *The Binary Stars* was published in 1918, with a revised edition published in 1935 and a reprinted edition in 1964. In this work, he provided a historical sketch of binary stars, including the 1782 discovery of the variability of brightness of Algol by the deaf astronomer John Goodricke*, and Goodricke's advancement of the theory that the bright star was periodically eclipsed by a relatively dark companion. Aitken also reported on the statistical analyses of the data from his own orbital measurements of many binary stars. He recognized the importance of longitudinal studies of these stars in providing a critical mass of observational data for astronomers. Such information is gleaned from repeated observations, including periodicity, eccentricity of orbit, and the orientation of orbit planes in stellar space. Importantly, he emphasized to the student of double stars the precaution of taking measurements only when the observing conditions are good; for if this advice is not followed, the investigator may be misled.

In 1920, Aitken combined the observational data given to him by Eric Doolittle with his own. With these data, Aitken completed Doolittle's update of S. W. Burnham's 1906 catalogue. In 1932, he published *A New General Catalogue of Double Stars Within 120° of the North Pole*. In preparing this volume, he compared his list of 5,400 double stars with the great *Henry Draper Catalogue* developed by the deaf astronomer Annie Jump Cannon* at Harvard College Observatory. This *New General Catalogue* is considered a lasting monument to Aitken's work.

Aitken was a prolific writer with more than 175 articles on this subject, including about twenty-five lists of his own discoveries. In addition, he published nearly 100 reports on comets and on his observations of satellites of various planets, and more than 135 reports on miscellaneous topics, including obituaries and reviews. A crater on our moon is named after him.

Among Aitken's awards were honorary doctoral degrees from the University of the Pacific (1903), Williams College (1917), University of Arizona (1923), and University of California at Los Angeles (1935). He was awarded the Lalande Gold Medal from the French Academy of Sciences (1906), the Bruce Gold Medal from the Astronomical Society of the Pacific (1926), and the Royal Astronomical Society's Gold Medal (1932). He held membership and offices in many professional societies, most notably as president of the Astronomical Society of the Pacific in both 1898 and 1915, vice president of the American

Astronomical Society from 1924 to 1931 (and president from 1937 to 1940), and president of the Pacific Division of the American Association for the Advancement of Science in 1925. He was the first president of the Commission on Double Stars in the International Astronomical Union. One of the gestures of appreciation from his colleagues that greatly pleased him was his selection as "Honorary President" of this commission upon his retirement. As editor of publications for the Astronomical Society of the Pacific for many years, Aitken had opportunities to bypass the frustration of face-to-face communication and converse with the general public through writing about the wonders of the heavens.

Aitken died on October 29, 1951, in Berkeley, California.

References

Aitken, R. G. (1964). *The binary stars*. New York: Dover.
Van Den Bos, W. H. (1952). *Monthly Notices of the Royal Astronomical Society, 112,* 271–273.
Van Den Bos, W. H. (1958). Robert Grant Aitken. In *National Academy of Sciences biographical memoirs* (Vol. 32, pp. 1–30). Washington, DC: National Academy of Sciences.

Information on Aitken's deafness was also obtained from the Mary Lea Shane Archives of the Lick Observatory.

GUSTINUS AMBROSI (1893–1975), Austrian Sculptor.

Gustinus Ambrosi was born near Vienna on February 24, 1893. His father was a descendent of an Italian family prominent during the Renaissance. An accomplished pianist and violinist at the age of seven, total deafness due to meningitis was a devastating blow to him and his family. Throughout his professional life, he described how the melodies of his childhood resurfaced in the form of sculpture, and his many sculpted portraits of Beethoven* attest to the recollected love for music he held as a child. Despite its noble lineage, Ambrosi's family was poor; and at the age of thirteen, he was apprenticed to learn a trade. In the evenings, he studied at the Academy of Fine Arts, working late into the night by candlelight on his first sculptured figures. He also visited Berlin, Amsterdam, and Switzerland to study the work of masters. Ambrosi's earliest work of note, *Man with the Broken Neck*, which he completed at the age of sixteen, remains among his best. It was a haunting recreation of an accident he had witnessed; and this work is representative of how the deaf artist sculpted his emotions into the bronze and marble pieces he produced.

As a youth, Ambrosi spent his leisure time studying faces and other features of many people around him, especially the characteristic play of muscles. Among the strangers he asked to pose for his sculptures, there were, as he described, cold faces with intensely smoldering eyes, energetic demeanors, and mask-like, empty profiles. Ambrosi noted often how a face reflects character. He spoke with his models so he could observe the movement in the muscles as they varied expression, urging them to move around his studio naturally so he could study them. He quoted Jules Dupré, describing how he felt that an artist was like a sponge, absorbing nature and expressing it in creations.

Before he was twenty years old, he had completed a bronze bust of the Swiss painter Arnold Böcklin and one of the Belgian artist Constantin Meunier in terracotta. His prodigious work commanded immediate attention. In 1912, he won both the National Prize for sculpture and the Felix von Weingartner Prize for sculpture. In 1916, Ambrosi first exhibited in Vienna; this was followed by an exhibit at the Secession in 1918 and a show at the State Museum in 1923. By the age of thirty-three, he had completed more than 250 works; and he had received the highest praise from art critics. "There is a young man in Vienna," wrote Kineton Parkes in *Apollo* in 1927, "who is possessed of the pristine tyranny which Michelangelo and Rodin shared. Like the former, this young Austrian artist is precipitated by this original and titanic power into poetic as well as plastic form-creation."

The Bible was one of Ambrosi's greatest sources of inspiration. He sculpted many biblical subjects such as his nine-foot-high *Creation of Adam*, which shows God's hand drawing the figure of Adam out of the earth. Ambrosi did not attempt to illustrate the Scriptures literally, but interpreted them visually. *Abel* and *Cain* each expressed emotion symbolic of the horror of fratricide in the tragic tone that is characteristic of many of Ambrosi's works. Greek myth was also inspiring to him. In each of his mythical works, the muscles, bones, and swollen veins help to heighten the emotion, as in the fall of "Icarus," a sculpture three meters high. His *Prometheus* is both frightening and lyrical. Other works of note include *Genius and Idea*, *The Evil Conscience*, *Eve after the Fall*, *Orpheus and Eurydice*, and the marble group of *Spring*.

In Paris, Ambrosi sculpted busts of notables, including the politician Paul Painlevé, the ex-Premier Georges Clemenceau, and the statesman Aristide Briand. He was commissioned to complete a portrait of Admiral Horthy de Nagybánya, in celebration of his fifty years as regent of Hungary. In Rome, he had simultaneous commissions for busts of Pope Pius XI and Benito Mussolini, each confiding to the deaf sculptor his candid opinion of the other. Pleased with the expression of radiant serenity given him by Ambrosi, the Pope awarded him a sizable honorarium, a letter of appreciation, and appointed him to the Artistic Council of the Vatican. Mussolini ordered eight duplicates of his bust and gave Ambrosi a pension for life. The original bust was kept by Il Duce in his study in the Chigi Palace. Ambrosi also sculpted busts of the German philosopher Friedrich Nietzsche, whom he considered a master "sculptor of thoughts." His interest in poets and great thinkers led him to sculpt such subjects as Johann Wolfgang von Goethe, Richard Strauss, August Strindberg, and Gerhart Hauptmann; the latter read Kant's *Critique of Pure Reason* while sitting for Ambrosi. He sculpted the bust of the Austrian architect Otto Wagner in the last years of his life and incorporated the shadow of approaching death.

Ambrosi worked for several decades in an official studio in Prater Park as-

Gustinus Ambrosi, Austrian sculptor. Photo from *The Silent Worker*, 41, (5), 1929, courtesy of Gallaudet University Archives.

signed to him by ministerial decree. By the 1920s, when he exhibited at the Vienna Seccession and State Museum, his works were already to be found in private collections in Chicago, New York, and Ohio. Although people thought him rich, he had no orders for many years after the Depression, and he never accepted monetary favors from friends. Happiness for him, he said, was to live in Vienna—Beethoven's city. During World War II, however, in his beloved city, he was confined by the Nazis to work as a stonemason. He sabotaged every assignment given him.

Although he seldom associated with other deaf (or, for that matter, hearing) people, Ambrosi valued the deaf workmen whom he employed in his foundry. Tacked to the door of his studio was a sign, "If you love me, let me work!" At one time, he maintained studios in Vienna, Rome, Paris, London, and Brussels.

In 1963, the District of Columbia chapter of the Gallaudet College Alumni Association commissioned Ambrosi to make a sculpture of Edward Miner Gallaudet for the hundredth anniversary of the college (now Gallaudet University). His thousands of other works are scattered throughout the world in both museums and private collections.

Ambrosi also published several volumes of poems in German, including sonnets to Michelangelo, Beethoven, Shakespeare, and Savonarola, whom he referred to as "familiar spirits." *Sonnets to God* and *Sonnets at the Tomb of One Beloved* are vivid and philosophical. The *Sonnets to God* is divided into several parts: "Concerning the Conception of God," "Concerning Love," and "Concerning Work and Toil." In his poetry, Ambrosi described how, through the talents God had granted him, he was able to merge the real and the supernatural in a new and beautiful form.

Gustinus Ambrosi committed suicide on July 2, 1975, as he perceived his mental and physical powers beginning to fail him. He had once remarked to a deaf visitor that the two of them were better off not having to deal with the noise of everyday living. He listened instead to inner Muses and expressed his genius in multiple forms throughout a productive life.

References

Halbertstam, L. (1929). Gustinus Ambrosi: The celebrated deaf sculptor and poet of Vienna. *The Silent Worker, 51* (5), 3–4.
Halbertstam, L. (1937). Sculpture, philosophy and deafness: An interview with Gustinus Ambrosi. *The Volta Review, 39*, 406–408, 423–424.
Parkes, K. (1927). Gustinus Ambrosi: Sculptor and poet. *Apollo, 2*, 152–157.
McClave, E. (1987). Gustinus Ambrosi. In J. V. Van Cleve (Ed.), *Gallaudet encyclopedia of deaf people and deafness* (Vol. 1, pp. 14–15). New York: McGraw-Hill.
Vance, Y. W. (1948). Triumphant soul of Austria. *The American Era, 35* (3), 1–2.

GUILLAUME AMONTONS (1663–1705), French Physicist.

Guillaume Amontons was born on August 31, 1663, in a time of turmoil and excitement. Before he was five years old, his country would invade the Spanish Netherlands, and the War of Revolution would end with France maintaining its conquests in Flanders. While Amontons was an adolescent, the Royal Academy of Sciences in Paris celebrated twenty-five years in the pursuit of knowledge. It was in this Academy that Amontons would demonstrate many great inventions developed in his quest to understand the phenomena associated with heat, temperature, and barometric pressure.

Profoundly deafened as a young adolescent, he refused medical treatment for his deafness throughout his life, preferring the world of silence and its beneficial effects when conducting scientific experiments. His father, a lawyer from Normandy, did not encourage him when he expressed interest in science. He first became interested in mechanics, attempting fruitlessly to develop a perpetual motion machine. After experimenting with architectural drawing, Amontons studied celestial mechanics and optical telegraphy. As a young physicist, he demonstrated a form of long-distance communication to the royal family. When he realized the French government was not interested in this work, he began to investigate the construction of instruments to measure temperature, atmospheric pressure, and humidity, an area that became a primary focus of investigation for the remainder of his career. In his early work to improve on Galileo's air thermometers, Amontons used a glass tube with a closed bulb at one end. The bulb was filled with air at the upper end, and the lower end was open. The device measured temperature by the change in pressure of the gas instead of by the change in volume. In 1688, at the age of twenty-five, Amontons produced an air thermometer in which the readings were regularly corrected for changes in atmospheric pressure.

Amontons conducted some remarkable experiments on heat in a prism. His proposal for a thermic motor included the principle of external combustion with direct rotation. This work was published in *Mémoires de l'Académie des Sciences* on June 20, 1699, under the title, "A commodious way of substituting the action of fire, instead of the force of men and horses to move machines." Over the next six years, he published numerous reports through the Academy, including his observations of an increase in volume of air by about one third when water is heated from the freezing point to the temperature at which it boils. He also published the results of his investigation into the frictional losses in machines and on the relationship between friction forces and the pressure of the bodies in contact. Amontons confirmed Leonardo da Vinci's estimate of the force needed to turn a crank.

In 1702, Amontons further improved upon Galileo's air thermometer by using a constant-volume, U-shaped tube. Temperature was measured by the height of a mercury column in a 45-inch-long arm of the thermometer. Although Amontons had difficulty in attaining great accuracy, his thermometer was more accurate than Galileo's, and he used it to study the boiling points of liquids.

Amontons laid the foundations for Gabriel Daniel Fahrenheit's work in the following decades. Newton, Halley, and Huygens had all previously noted the constancy of the boiling point of water, but it was Amontons' observations that inspired Fahrenheit in his investigations on the fixed boiling points of other liquids. With these, he noted the relationship of the fixed points to atmospheric pressure and made the practice of thermometry more exact. Amontons' observations that the temperature of water ceases to increase at its boiling point led him to propose that this be a fixed thermometric point. Fahrenheit apparently used alcohol as the thermometric fluid for his own early instruments, but by 1721, he had constructed his first mercury thermometer; this was the instrument he used to confirm Amontons' observations that water boils at a specific temperature.

Amontons also contributed to the science of meteorology, particularly with his research on the construction of barometers. At the time of his experimentation with barometers, he was well aware that the readings were influenced by a number of factors that had nothing to do with atmospheric pressure, including the lack of uniformity of the bore of the glass tube, temperature, and corresponding changes in the density of mercury. By 1704, he had developed a table of corrections for temperature to be used with the barometer. Other physicists ignored these corrections until their importance was once again emphasized by Jean André De Luc. Along with other scientists, Amontons labored to make the original form of the barometer developed by Torricelli more precise, compact, and portable.

Amontons conducted some of the earliest investigations that led to the concept of "ideal gas." Nearly a century passed, however, before Jacques Charles found Amontons' observations and repeated the work of the deaf physicist. But Charles did not publish his experiments. Around 1802, Joseph Louis Gay-Lussac duplicated the work of Charles and Amontons and published his results. This was one of Amontons' most significant accomplishments. The deaf scientist had established a relationship between the temperature and volume of gases (which led others to further discoveries). The Roman Catholic priest Edme Mariotte had previously shown that the volume of gases changed with temperature. Amontons went beyond this. Examining a variety of gases, he concluded that the volume of each gas changed by the same amount for a given increment in temperature. Amontons may have envisioned the notion of a temperature at which gases could contract no more ("absolute zero"). Although Amontons barely implied this in his memoir of 1703, it is believed that this conclusion presented Johann Heinrich Lambert with a basis for his more detailed investigation of this idea. When Lambert analyzed the experiments of Amontons and those of Isaac Newton, he found them reasonably consistent. Lambert added his own experimental results to these analyses, and when he repeated Amontons' experiments on absolute temperature, he estimated the temperature at -270.3 degrees Celsius. Today the accepted value is -273.15 degrees Celsius. The significance of this concept was shown in the work of Lord Kelvin, who, in about 1850, designated the absolute thermodynamic scale of temperature that is independent of the physical properties of any substance.

In 1705, Amontons warned his contemporaries of the possibility of error in reading the thermometers of his time. He cautioned them that the glass tubes expand as well as their contents. In his last experiment before the Royal Academy of Sciences, Amontons demonstrated an error in measurement due to the expansion of the apparatus. He used the barrel of a gun, well-soldered at one end, instead of a glass tube. His fellow scientists were able to observe that the quicksilver stood much lower in the metal barrel than in the glass. This caution was published on February 11, 1705.

Amontons may have been the first deaf person to contribute to the science of geology through his experimental work in meteorology and the physics of heat. His research helped others formulate theories relative to the earth's composition and history, and he also proposed an explanation for such natural catastrophes as earthquakes.

Information about Amontons' deafness and how he communicated with fellow members of the Academy is meager. It is known that he was a close associate of the hearing scientists Louis Joblot (1645–1723), the first French microscopist who held an interest in physics, and the chemist Wilhelm Homberg. By the sheer number of his presentations to the Academy, it appears that his profound deafness posed no serious barrier for him. He lived long before a Deaf community was established in France, and likely had no interactions with others who were deaf. His friend Fontenelle (1705) wrote of him respectfully:

The qualities of his heart were even greater than those of his mind, an honesty so innocent and so spontaneous that one sensed therein the impossibility of hypocrisy, an artlessness, a sincerity and a candor which his infrequent dealings with men had helped to preserve. He could only perceive of his own worth in terms of the fruit of his labor, nor could he leave his mark in any way other than through his own merit.

Amontons's death at the age of forty-two, on October 11, 1705, was a tragic loss to both his family and the scientific community. He left behind a loving wife and a two-month-old son. In his relatively short life he had contributed significantly to the foundations of what became thermodynamic research.

References

Fontenelle, Bernard Le Bovier de. (1705). Éloge De M. Amontons. *Histoire de l'Académie Royale des Sciences*, 150–154.

Lang, H. G. (1994). *Silence of the spheres: The deaf experience in the history of science.* Westport, CT: Bergin & Garvey.

Middleton, W.E.K. (1968). *The history of the barometer.* Baltimore: The Johns Hopkins Press.

Payen, J. (1970). Guillaume Amontons. In C. C. Gillispie (Ed.), *Dictionary of scientific biography* (Vol. 1, pp. 138–139). New York: Charles Scribner's Sons.

GLENN B. ANDERSON (1945–   ), American Educator/Deaf Community Advocate.

Glenn B. Anderson was born deaf on October 16, 1945, in Chicago, Illinois. He was enrolled in a day class program with about 150 deaf students, and later in Parker High School, a large public school where he was one of about fifteen deaf students and several thousand hearing students. Anderson and his parents had decided against a vocational school program, even though he was interested in drafting, because it would have meant several hours of bus travel each day. One afternoon in his homeroom at Parker, Anderson saw a brochure advertising Gallaudet College, a college of which he had not heard. The volunteer teacher in the room at the time, however, crumpled up the flyer and told him such an opportunity was not meant for him. Anderson disregarded the affront, went on to enroll in honors classes, graduated from Parker High School, and enrolled the following fall at Northern Illinois University. After a semester there, he transferred to Gallaudet College, where he graduated with a bachelor's degree in psychology in 1968. Yet, even at Gallaudet in the 1960s, he had to continue to ignore the advice of those who did not see his full potential. In the turbulence of the 1960s, feelings of mistrust surfaced and people became polarized at Gallaudet, as on most American campuses. Anderson recalled a disagreement with a teacher who felt his only opportunities would be teaching in segregated black schools in the South. Anderson had higher professional goals. He went on to earn a master's degree in rehabilitation counseling at the University of Arizona in 1970 and a Ph.D. in rehabilitation counseling from New York University in 1982.

In 1970, Anderson became the first deaf person to be hired for a vocational rehabilitation position in Michigan. He served as a vocational rehabilitation counselor for the Michigan Rehabilitation Services in Detroit. From 1975 until 1982, he was the program director of the Continuing Education Program for Deaf Adults at Laguardia Community College of the City University of New York. Since 1982, he has served as director of training for the Rehabilitation and Research Training Center for Deaf and Hard of Hearing Persons at the University of Arkansas in Little Rock. During this period, he has taught many university courses on such topics as supervised practice in rehabilitation case management, principles and techniques of counseling deaf persons, deafness rehabilitation, and hearing impairment and human behavior. He also served as the national program chairperson for the National Conference on the Habilitation and Rehabilitation of Hearing-Impaired Adolescents, the Biennial Conference of the American Deafness and Rehabilitation Association, and the First National Forum on Employment of Deaf and Hard of Hearing People.

Anderson's professional activities took an increasingly multicultural theme and dimension as he served on the National Advisory Committee for the Project on Black Deaf Children and Their Families, the Arkansas Governor's Commission on People With Disabilities (which he chaired for several years), and the National Advisory Committee for the Rehabilitation Cultural Diversity Initiative at San Diego State University. He is a member of the American Association for

Counseling and Development, American Deafness and Rehabilitation Association, National Rehabilitation Association, and National Black Deaf Advocates.

Anderson has published more than forty chapters in books, articles, and research reports on such topics as multicultural diversity, mental health services for deaf persons, the black deaf experience, empowerment of black deaf persons, standards for the training of sign language interpreters, and enhancing the employability of deaf persons. In addition, he has presented over 100 conference papers and commencement addresses. His work is imbued with a consciousness of the serious lack of opportunity and mentoring for young, black deaf children aspiring to higher education. Anderson has presented numerous talks with such titles as "Straight Talk About Being Black and Deaf in America," "Becoming a Successful Black Deaf American," "Learning Black History Through a Study of African Coins," and "Role and Contributions of African-Americans to the American West." He has also demonstrated through personal example that there is no barrier to pursuing excellence in both academics and athletics. Anderson joined Gallaudet University's "1,000 Points Club" for basketball, scoring over a thousand points in two and one-quarter seasons. He was an all-star for many teams in tournaments around the country, was selected Scholar-Athlete of the Year by Gallaudet College in 1968, and subsequently elected to the American Athletic Association of the Deaf Hall of Fame. Over the years, he has served as a basketball coach in numerous tournaments, sharing his athletic skills and leadership abilities with many young deaf people.

In 1994, Anderson made history when he was selected as the chairman of the Board of Trustees of Gallaudet University, the first African-American and the second deaf person to hold this position. He has served as a member of the Board since 1989. In choosing him, Gallaudet University cited Anderson for his "broad understanding of issues in higher education, commitment to strengthening undergraduate education, excellence in research and scholarship, [and] outstanding leadership qualities." One of his first formal activities in this role was to read the citation on the Honorary Doctor of Laws degree to U.S. President Bill Clinton at Gallaudet University's 125th commencement in May, 1994.

References

Puckett, P. (1988, Spring). Dr. Glenn Anderson: RT–31 training director. *The Deaf Arkansan.*

Strassler, B. (1994, April). Sports was his launching pad. *Silent News*, pp. 43–44.

Uyttebrouck, O. (1993, February 10). LR professor committed to helping black deaf children beat harsh odds. *Arkansas Democrat Gazette.*

N. HILLIS ARNOLD (1906–1988), American Sculptor.

Hillis Arnold was born on a wheat farm in Beach, North Dakota, on June 10, 1906, and was totally deafened by meningitis at the age of six months. With only a small country school nearby, his chances for a good education were slim. Even at the age of three, he had demonstrated artistic talents; and within a few years, his mother had taken him to Milwaukee and made arrangements to have him placed in a school while under the care of Mrs. Walter W. Howe. Although he made progress, an illness prevented him from returning to school the following year, and he remained on the family farm, learning from his mother, a former teacher. By the time he was ten years old, Arnold's molded mud sculptures so impressed his mother that she bought him modeling clay and, with remarkable foresight, started him on a career of international renown. At the age of eleven, Arnold's family moved to Minneapolis, where he received an education at a day school for deaf children. He then graduated with honors from the Minneapolis Central High School, where he first expressed aspirations to be a magazine illustrator. Because of the disruptions in his education, he was almost twenty-two years old when he graduated.

Arnold graduated from the University of Minnesota in 1933. This success was particularly noteworthy in view of the fact that the dean of the School of Architecture was reluctant to admit him because of his deafness. After some reconsideration, Arnold enrolled in the art school; and, after three years of studying painting, a professor noticed his talents in three-dimensional work and encouraged him to pursue sculpture. Arnold never lost his enthusiasm for the study of architecture, however. With his proven success in art, he was finally accepted to the School of Architecture, where he studied under S. Chatwood Burton and graduated *cum laude*. He also was elected to the honorary architectural fraternity, won the Keppel prize in sculpture, and finished first in a class competition for the design of murals for the School of Architecture. The impressive mural he had completed consisted of eighteen panels illustrating the erection of a building, celebrating the dignity of work.

Supported by scholarships, Arnold attended the Minneapolis School of Art for three years. There he specialized in sculpture and mural painting. He then enrolled at the Cranbrook Academy of Art at Bloomfield Hills, Michigan, where he continued to develop his talent as an artist and gained his first teaching experience as a sculpture instructor. His companion at the Cranbrook Academy was the imaginative Swedish sculptor Carl Milles, whom Arnold assisted in the production of *The Wedding of the Rivers* fountain display at the Union Station park in St. Louis. Reviews of his work already referred to him as a "distinguished sculptor," and he received commissions from Thomas Ellerbe, the architect for the Mayo Clinic, for sculpted figures for the Minnesota Terrace of the Hotel Nicollet and the Book Cadillac Hotel in Detroit.

An important commission Arnold received at this time was for deep-relief panels for the façade of the new University of Minnesota Public Health Building, designed by William Ingemann. Allegorical in nature, the large panels are visual metaphors for the fields of study housed in that building, including such subjects as water sanitation, water inspection, medical care, milk inspection, nursing, and immunization. With the commissions he received, he was able to travel throughout Europe the following summer.

In 1938, Arnold was offered a position as instructor in sculpture and ceramics at Monticello College in Godfrey, Illinois; he remained there for thirty-four years. During his early years at Monticello, he realized the need for further professional training, enrolling in summer classes to study ceramics for four years, as well as attending adult night classes at the Central Institute for the Deaf, where he took additional speechreading courses to assist in his communication with hearing students at Monticello. He also took an interest in advising parents whose deaf children showed early talent in art, publishing in the periodicals for educators of deaf students on the challenges facing deaf artists, and advising those who were precocious to consider a combination of teaching and free-lancing. He also won an Education Press All-American Award for an article he authored in 1967. His sculpture *Deaf Given a Voice* reflected his belief in Total Communication, an educational philosophy advocating use of appropriate combinations of communication modes and languages—signing, speaking, writing, graphics, etc.—in teaching deaf children. The sculpture has a large eye form at the top, which Arnold explained represents the eye of the deaf person, necessary for sign and spoken communication skills. The arm with mobile fingers at the bottom of the sculpture signifies the use of sign languages.

Arnold's wood, stone, metal, and ceramics sculptures are found in churches, schools, and homes throughout the midwest. Rudolf Torrini, a fellow sculptor, felt that this versatility in all the traditional media made Arnold unique. During a one-year leave of absence from Monticello, Arnold pursued experimental studies in polyester resin. With a chemist at Wallace Pencil Company of St. Louis, he developed a new plastic aluminum casting process that included the use of metal pipes, rods, galvanized mesh screen and brass screen, with plastic aluminum material applied over the mesh. The U.S. Information Agency in Washington, D.C., chose one of his works made from polyester resin for the "Plastics, USA" exhibit on tour throughout Europe. In 1939, his statue *Burden* gained critical attention in a New York City exhibit. In this piece, he stressed the responsibility of educated and skilled workers to those who have had fewer opportunities. In *The Joy of Freedom*, Arnold defined freedom as both a physical and a mental construct. Arnold was a symbolist, and it is not always easy to interpret his abstract works. He strove for emotional as well as visual responses. He considered *The American Dream* a more transparent work, one of his best. Two ebony figures, a husband and wife, stand on a cracked base, their backs turned to one another. They represent spouses who put possessions and external recognition above love and communication, symbolized by the cracks in the marble pedestal. Arnold's wife had her own interpretation of this piece. She saw it as representing the frustration the deaf sculptor experienced at the obligatory exhibit openings and cocktail parties, where few people made the small extra effort needed to converse with him.

Throughout Arnold's career he exhibited at museums, galleries, colleges, and fairs. He collaborated with architects in national competitions, such as the Roosevelt Memorial project for Washington, D.C., and the Jefferson National Memorial project, receiving honorable mention in both. One of his popular works is the World War II Memorial in the Aloe Plaza near Kiel Auditorium in St. Louis, a 32-foot-high limestone shaft portraying soldiers and sailors on either side of the shaft, leaving home, engaging in combat, and emerging from death. A second work of note is a giant wooden eagle with a 5-foot wingspread, the symbol of *Manifest Destiny*, which was part of the Museum of Westward Expansion on the riverfront in downtown St. Louis. His 16-foot-tall limestone statue of St. Anne, *Mother and Child Mary*, for St. Ann's Catholic Church in Normandy, Missouri, was highlighted in *Time* and *Life* magazines. His *Abraham and Isaac*, two-and-a-half feet tall and polychromed in mahogany, was selected as one of sixteen examples of American liturgical art for the International Biennale of Contemporary Christian Art in Salzburg, Austria, in 1948. It was later purchased by Cardinal Joseph Ritter in St. Louis. In *The Lord is My Shepherd*, located in Cardinal Ritter's garden in St. Louis, Missouri, the Lord is represented by a symbolic and mystic form which, Arnold explained, "cannot be interpreted by naturalistic or realistic elements of art." In his abstract sculptures, he saw two purposes. First, he strove for simplicity of form and contour in order to create a silhouette against the natural forms and lines of a garden setting. Second, the effort to evoke plasticity in marble suggested, to him, a divine form. He tried to create very different perspectives from each side of the statue: from one side a caring protection, from another an expression of admiration, and from a third, the expression of "judgment of the lamb by the Lord." Arnold's other works of note include *The Heritage Sculpture* on the Monticello College campus, *Rhapsody* at Southeast Missouri State College campus, and *I am the Vine, You are the Branches*, a 15-foot-long altar panel for Grace Episcopal Church in Kirkwood, Missouri.

For many years, Arnold sculpted miniature portrait heads, and proceeds from these were donated to charity. After retiring from teaching in 1975, he continued to do commissioned sculptures in the large studio beside his home in Kirkwood. In 1975, he sculpted *The Learners* to be presented to the Central Institute for the Deaf by Artists' Sponsors, Incorporated. In white Georgia marble, it is an abstract, simple form of a teacher and deaf child. By 1979, he was commissioned to sculpt fifty additional copies to be given to persons for distinguished service to that institute. The inspiration for this work was the appreciation he felt for his own mother, who helped him develop communication skills when he was a child.

Arnold died of cancer at his home on November 18, 1988. Among his honors was selection as a Live Fellow of the International Institute of Arts and Letters; he joined such other noted members as Aldous Huxley, Thornton Wilder, William Steinberg, and William Saroyan. He considered this a crowning achievement of his career. His works can be found in more than ten major cities.

References

Arnold, N. H. (1967). A deaf sculptor. *The Volta Review, 69* (6), 378–381.

Herweg, J. (1979, November/December). Hillis Arnold: Sculptor of silence. *Missouri Life*, 41–43.

Kowalewski, F. (1972). Hillis Arnold: American deaf sculptor. *The Deaf American, 25* (3), 3–5.

Montague, H. (1939). Promise and fulfillment: Hillis Arnold—Sculptor. *The Volta Review, 41* (12), 677–681, 723.

JACK ASHLEY (1922–   ), British Politician/Writer.

Jack Ashley was born on December 6, 1922, in Widnes, England, on the banks of the Mersey River. His father, a night watchman, died of pneumonia at the age of thirty-five, when Ashley was only five; his mother was left with the prospect of raising a family alone. Ashley's early schooling ended at the age of fourteen, when he obtained a job as laborer at Imperial Chemical Industries in Widnes, hammering corks into carboys. After two years, he found employment delivering coal and ladling molten metal at a copper-smelting works. When World War II began, he joined the Royal Army Service Corps, but was discharged in his first year as a result of his noticeable hearing loss. He returned to the copper factory where he advocated the establishment of a union, calling a strike when the management resisted negotiations, and, in time, becoming a leading spokesman for the union, advancing to its Executive Council.

Meanwhile, in the local community, Ashley fought for the rights of tenants in slums, urging them to complain about neglected repairs and dumped rubbish, prompting one local reporter to write of him as "the knight errant of the dustbins." Within a short time, he held a seat on the Town Council and had earned a national reputation. In 1946, Ashley ended his industrial experience when he was awarded a scholarship at Oxford University's Ruskin College. He received a diploma in Economics and Political Science and was awarded a scholarship for further study at Cambridge (Gonville and Caius College). He graduated in 1951. While a student, Ashley's love for community politics never waned. He aligned himself with numerous campaigns and increased his social activism as he absorbed economic and political theory.

After returning to Widnes for a short time, Ashley moved to London, where he took a position first in the National Union of General and Municipal Workers, then later at the British Broadcasting Corporation as a radio producer. His first attempt to enter Parliament with the Labor party was unsuccessful, the prevailing support at that time being strongly for Conservative candidates. Ashley then toured broadcasting stations in the United States for several months, studying the influence of sponsors on television standards. He transferred to television as a producer upon his return to London. His subsequent work covering and writing on political issues for BBC programs brought back his yearning for Parliament, however, and his next campaign with the Labor Party was successful.

Ashley spent his first year in Parliament addressing issues of social services, industrial relations, broadcasting, and a growing interest in foreign affairs. His speech on behalf of thalidomide-deformed babies presented to a packed Chamber made headlines all over England, helping to increase compensation from 3.5 million pounds to 25 million. He campaigned for battered wives, old age pensioners, mentally retarded persons, and even moving a bus stop closer to the home of an elderly man. Ashley received an average of 1,200 letters a month from as far away as Asia. He came further into the limelight of British politics when he argued for the right of a soldier accused of desertion to be released, pending the results of the inquiry.

Ashley's popularity was at a high point, after just fifteen months as Member of the Parliament for Stoke-on-Trent, when he was deafened in 1966. He had turned down an invitation to become a Government Whip and accepted an offer to serve as Parliamentary Private Secretary to Michael Stewart, Minister for Economic Affairs, when, first, his left eardrum perforated, probably a result of a childhood infection. His right ear was also failing, and he underwent three surgeries in an effort to salvage his hearing. A virus infection and a final, unsuccessful operation left him nearly completely deaf. During the following months, he consulted with a series of specialists, nevertheless continuing to remain abreast of the Parliamentary debates through reading. He also took a crash course in speechreading at the Institute for Further Education for the Deaf in London. While he was at first buoyed by visits from supportive colleagues, he soon became discouraged not only by the loss of hearing, but also by the accompanying tinnitus (head noises) and eyestrain. He decided to resign the post of Parliamentary Private Secretary to Stewart. Ashley returned to the House of Commons on April 23, 1968, however, after four months of rehabilitation. One of his primary frustrations was that opposition speakers were too far away to allow him to speechread. As he wrote in his autobiography, *Journey Into Silence* (1973), even a wisp of hearing had once given him a sense of reality, and the silence was eerie: "Had I been alone, I would almost certainly have despaired because the exhaustion was exacerbated by unfathomable depths of depression. I felt isolated, but I was not alone." Ashley credited his wife, Pauline, for providing him with support and advice. When his premature decision to resign from Parliament was made, the London editor Will Stewart said that it was the saddest exclusive he had ever had to write. Stewart later became the person who first interested Ashley to campaign for persons with disabilities.

Many MPs argued for Ashley's return, believing that the barriers presented by his deafness could be circumvented; and Professor Peter Townsend, an eminent sociologist, publicly encouraged Ashley not only to return but to advocate for persons with disabilities. In a letter to the *London Times*, Townsend argued that a disabled MP would have more persuasive power sitting in the actual debates. Further letters and telegrams from constitutents and advocacy groups were overwhelmingly encouraging. Prime Minister Harold Wilson invited the Ashleys to his office, offering to help him in any way if he decided to remain. His constituents voted overwhelmingly in favor of his return as well. His decision to return to Parliament was a formidable one. Communication through speechreading was tedious. Some MPs shied away from him; others appeared friendly, but Ashley believed "the warmth had vanished." He felt a demoralizing sense of isolation in the crowded enclaves of the House of Commons, where few Members came to talk to him. A small group of colleagues became a dependable support to him. Soon, he was able to have a dry objectivity about his situation. "Whenever I walked into the Chamber I was struck by the absolute silence of the greatest debating forum in the land."

Ashley was tested early when he was asked to propose a Ten-Minute Rule Bill requesting the establishment of a Commission to investigate the problems of people with disabilities. He had campaigned for people with disabilities in the House of Commons prior to his complete loss of hearing, but never did he realize the extent of the need for Government action until he received an avalanche of letters. Based on this correspondence and his own personal experiences, he fought hard for change that eventually led to the formation of the All-Party Disablement Group, which he chaired. A fellow Member assisted him by signaling when his voice was too loud or soft during debates. Ashley led the battle for the Chronically Sick and Disabled Persons Bill, a struggle that not only greatly improved conditions for persons with disabilities in England, but convinced him that he could indeed be an effective MP despite profound deafness.

In the 1970s, Dr. Alan Newell, with the support of the National Research Development Corporation, adapted the Palantype machine, which produced phonetic symbols and entered them into a decoder. A stenotypist located in the Press Gallery of the House of Commons transcribed the debates for him. Prime Minister Callaghan considered Ashley to be one of the most effective Members of the Parliament. Affectionately called "the man for all minorities," by Minister for the Disabled Alf Morris, Ashley was publicly honored by Queen Elizabeth, who made him a Companion of Honour. He became a privy councillor in 1979 and has received numerous honorary degrees.

References

Ashley, J. (1973). *Journey into silence*. London: William Clowes & Sons Ltd.
Green, F. (1979). Man for all minorities. *The Deaf American, 31* (10), 5–6.

B

CHARLES CRAWFORD BAIRD (1947–), American Painter.

Charles Crawford Baird was born deaf in Kansas City, Missouri, on February 22, 1947, the youngest of five children. His parents were hearing, but three of his four siblings were deaf. American Sign Language (ASL) and English were the languages of his home, and Baird grew up in a natural and supportive early communication environment. ASL was always a part of the landscape of his mind, and he immediately began to connect his visual language to his visual world, a motif to appear in much of his mature artistic work. Like his older deaf sisters, he attended the Kansas School for the Deaf (KSD) where, also like his sisters and an older hearing brother, a photographer, he displayed an unusual early aptitude for art.

At that time, the Kansas School for the Deaf had on faculty a well-known watercolorist, Grace Bilger, who became an early mentor to Baird. With her connections to local galleries and the Kansas City Art Institute, she opened doors to the delight and wonder of the visual arts for many students. She paid particular attention to the promising young Baird, who attributes his precocious passion for painting to her guidance.

His budding talent would be quickly validated. At the age of thirteen, he submitted an oil painting to the highly competitive Scholastic Magazine Art Contest. It won the regional competition and, two years later, the same painting won the National Scholastic Art Award. For the next five years, Baird won regional competitions and was a finalist for the national award. While still in high school, he mastered the essential techniques of watercolors, oil painting, and drawing. At this time, he also put together a portfolio that would demonstrate the repertoire of his skills.

As he was preparing to go to Gallaudet College following his graduation from KSD, he heard of a position for apprentice Deaf artists designing and executing scenery at Lincoln Center in New York City. Intrigued by this possibility and testing himself, he sent his application to David Hays, who would later become Executive Director of the National Theatre of the Deaf (NTD). To his pleasure, and immediate consternation, he was accepted by Hays. Reasoning that leaving Kansas for Washington, D.C., would be less like going to Oz than leaving Kansas for New York City, Baird informed Hays that he had reconsidered; that it would be more prudent for him to begin his studies at Gallaudet. He remained there for two years.

The National Technical Institute for the Deaf (NTID) had just been established at the Rochester Institute of Technology (RIT), and Baird heard about the program from a recruiter at Gallaudet. While not enamoured of the commercial and industrial focus of most applied arts programs, he was also aware of the strong fine arts program and intense studio work at RIT. How intense came as something of a shock to the shy, unassuming, but at the time largely unchallenged, young artist. The competitive environment and grueling critique typical of this national program sent him into a crisis of the soul. He was more than willing to face the challenges to his assumptions and to his technique, and he painted his way out of self-doubt and easy stylization. He graduated with a B.F.A. in Painting in 1974.

During his time at NTID at RIT, the intensity of the academic pace was alleviated for Baird by participation in theatre. Robert F. Panara,* who had been a professor of English and drama at Gallaudet and was a founding member of NTD, directed the theatre program at NTID. He immediately saw Baird's fluency in theatrical ASL and his excellent design skills. Baird performed in *Rashomon*, *The Madwoman of Chaillot*, and other productions.

Following his college graduation, Baird worked at the New York State School for the Deaf in Rome and became artist-in-residence at the Margaret Sterck School for the Hearing Impaired. In 1975, with his sister Liz and a collective of Deaf artists, he joined SPECTRUM, a nonprofit educational center for deaf visual and performing artists in Austin, Texas. He was originally a staff photographer, but later became Visual Coordinator, documenting the work of hundreds of Deaf artists and fundraising for related educational programs. During this time, he designed sets for NTD, and, when SPECTRUM folded for lack of support, he joined NTD full time as both an innovative set designer and a gifted actor. He was actually able to combine the two in playing the Painter in *King of Hearts*, where he literally painted scenes in the course of the play, a tour de force that received impressive reviews. After leaving NTD, he toured with the Milwaukee Repertory Theatre and was appointed artist-in-residence at the California School for the Deaf, Fremont.

Baird had been painting throughout his peripatetic teaching, administrating, and theatrical career, but felt the need to return to his art full time. He had received a number of commissions, including one for a striking mural at the historic Deaf Way conference in 1989, and his work is displayed prominently at a number of institutions. Still, he found the ''business'' end of producing fine art a wearing and depressing proposition, which pointed to the rifts in communication that can occur around such transactions. He seized upon the opportunity to join Dawn Sign Press, a publisher devoted to the promotion of Deaf culture and art, to paint full time and collect a volume of his work for publication.

Baird's work is marked by vivid plays of color and light. *Blue Hens* (1983) depicts the strikingly blue birds picking their way among the shadows on the ground in the early morning light. *Tyger, Tyger*, a 1992 acrylic, which hangs in the office of President Albert J. Simone at the Rochester Institute of Technology, juxtaposes the innocent young man dressed in yellow signing "tiger" against the ominous head of the tiger emerging from darkness. Baird's incorporation of sign imagery is a delightful, and often thought-provoking, feature of his work. The sign-name of the first deaf teacher in the United States, Laurent Clerc,* for example, animates the staid traditional bust in *America's First Deaf Teacher* (1993) and reminds us of the action and vitality of Clerc's continued contribution to Deaf heritage.

Chuck Baird lives and works in San Diego, California.

References

Elion, L. K. (1993). Introduction. In C. Baird (Ed.), *Chuck Baird*. San Diego: Dawn Sign Press.

Leamon, E. (1983, Spring/Summer). Chuck Baird: Creating art on stage and canvas. *NTID Focus*, 30–31.

DONALD L. BALLANTYNE (1922–   ), Professor of Experimental Surgery.

Donald L. Ballantyne, an eminent scientist and internationally known authority on transplantation techniques, was born on November 8, 1922, in Peking, China, where his father served as Far Eastern representative of an American bank. He became deaf a few months after birth, due to complications from pneumonia developed while recovering from a stomach operation.

His parents decided to send him to the United States at the age of thirteen because of the few opportunities for American students in Asia. Ballantyne attended the Archmere Academy in Delaware and the Canterbury Preparatory School in Connecticut. The headmaster of the latter school was reluctant to take him as a student, but his dedicated mother convinced the school to give the boy a chance. In the years prior to the Pearl Harbor attack, Ballantyne traveled back to Hong Kong by ocean-going ships each summer; and the experiences during his many trips helped him to develop a strong independence. One experience Ballantyne would not forget occurred on August 30, 1937, which he described in detail in a paper he wrote for Archmere entitled "The Bombing of the *S.S. President Hoover*." While he was aboard the American liner that afternoon, four Chinese military planes bombed the ship. The Chinese claimed they had mistaken it for a Japanese vessel carrying troops. One American was killed. When the first bomb struck, the unfazed Ballantyne, profoundly deaf, had thought someone was pounding on his cabin door.

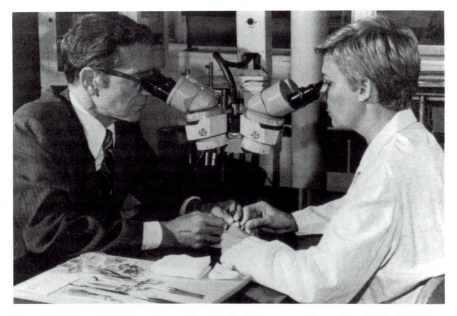

Donald L. Ballantyne, American professor of microsurgery. Photo from S. Phyllis Stearner (1984) *Able Scientist—Disabled Persons: Careers in Science* (Oakbrook, IL: John
Racila Associates), courtesy of S. Phyllis Stearner.

After graduating from Archmere, Ballantyne went on to receive a bachelor's
degree in chemistry from Princeton, and a master's degree in biology and a
Ph.D. in animal biology from the Catholic University of America in Washington,
D.C. He also studied French, German, and Russian. Ballantyne had many friends
in college and acquired excellent notes by giving carbon papers to the best
notetakers in each class.

Despite his superb credentials as a premedical student at Princeton, he was
unable to gain acceptance to any medical school. The repeated rejections were
because of his deafness.

Ballantyne never met another deaf person until he was twenty-five years old.
While studying at Catholic University between 1946 and 1948, he applied for
a position as part-time chemistry instructor at Gallaudet College; at this time,
he learned sign language. After completing his Ph.D. studies and getting married
in 1952, he began his career as a research assistant in parasitology with Squibb
Laboratories in New Brunswick, New Jersey. Later, he was employed at the
Illinois State Psychopathic Institute in Chicago where he helped conduct studies
on the effects of parasites in pregnant women.

In 1954, he began working for Dr. John Marquis Converse, the founder and
director of the Institute of Reconstructive Plastic Surgery at New York University Medical Center. Ballantyne worked there for over thirty-five years, involved

in important research on skin and organ transplants. He also was a visiting investigator at the Roscoe B. Jackson Memorial Laboratories in Bar Harbor, Maine, in 1958; and between 1966 and 1969, he was awarded several Milbank Memorial Fund Teaching Fellowships in Transplantation Biology.

Ballantyne developed a unique pedagogical subspecialty. Because many of the foreign students coming to the Institute for training in research and residency had accents, Converse realized that Ballantyne's superb speechreading skills put him at an advantage. Ballantyne was assigned responsibility for instructing many of these students, residents, fellows, and visiting surgeons or professors. Speechreading, as difficult as it is, may sometimes be helpful when spoken communication is not understood. Ironically, despite his own rejection by medical schools, Ballantyne became an instructor of physicians and surgeons in the principles as well as the methods of plastic and microvascular surgery.

Through his experiments on laboratory animals, Ballantyne also developed new methods of transplanting human skin grafts and kidneys. In the 1970s, with the advent and spread of microsurgical techniques in the field of plastic surgery, he acquired an international reputation for his expertise in these techniques. Using powerful microscopes and delicately scaled, miniature instruments, Ballantyne trained doctors in revolutionary techniques that enabled thousands of people to regain use of limbs. His techniques are also used to reduce blindness caused by diabetes and to remove tumors. During his tenure as the Professor of Experimental Surgery and Director of the Microsurgical Research and Training Laboratories of the Institute of Reconstructive Plastic Surgery at New York University Medical Center, he was frequently invited to Europe and Israel to give lectures and conduct seminars. He has authored and co-authored four books and over 120 scientific articles in American, British, and German medical journals on such topics as skin grafts, vascularization of skin, silicone fluid research, and kidney transplants. His major research interests in transplantation biology, wound healing, and parasitology led him to active involvement in the American Association of Plastic and Reconstructive Surgery, the American Association for the Advancement of Science, the Transplantation Society, and the Society for Cryobiology (in which he served on the editorial board). He was also active in community organizations, collaborating with other deaf scientists in the American Professional Society of the Deaf (APSD). He held the office of vice president and chaired the Scholarship Committee in APSD, and served on steering committees for the New Jersey Council of Organizations Serving the Deaf and the New Jersey State Department of Education Planning Program for Mental Health Serving the Deaf.

In 1981, Ballantyne became the first recipient of the Edmund Lyon Memorial Lecturer Award, given at the National Technical Institute for the Deaf at Rochester Institute of Technology. He was also the first recipient of the Amos Kendall Award presented by the Laurent Clerc Cultural Fund Committee of Gallaudet College in 1979. In 1983, he received the Outstanding Achievement Award in the field of Medical Research presented by the Catholic University of America Alumni Association.

On September 1, 1990, Ballantyne became Professor Emeritus at New York University Medical Center, and has continued to write articles and to train residents, physicians, and surgeons in the operative techniques of microvascular surgery.

References

Ballantyne, D. L. (1938). The bombing of the S.S. President Hoover. Washington, DC, Gallaudet University archives.

Bowe, F. (1973). Bob Harris interviews Dr. Donald Ballantyne. *The Deaf American, 26* (3), 5–9.

Carr, S. (1979, August 23). Bloomfielder probes the small world of microsurgery. *Essex Journal,* 4.

Milner, L. B. (1965). Dr. Donald Ballantyne—Deaf researcher in transplants. *The Deaf American, 18* (3), 3–4.

ALBERT BALLIN (1861–1932), American Artist/Silent Film Actor.

Albert Ballin was born on March 12, 1861, in New York. His father, also deaf, held a successful lithographing business in that city. Ballin was deafened in early childhood and entered the institution that is now the New York School for the Deaf, where he was a bright and enthusiastic student for several years. After he realized his talents in art, he left school to study under the deaf artist H. Humphrey Moore,* who was then rapidly gaining an international reputation for his portrait and landscape paintings. Based on Moore's advice in designing a course of study for him, Ballin traveled to Paris and Rome. During Ballin's three years of study, his talents were recognized at the Paris Salon, where he had several paintings exhibited. In Rome he studied under José Villegas, whose influence has been recognized in his work. In 1882, he won a silver medal for a Venetian scene at that city. The following year he received an honorable mention for a painting of Arab life exhibited in Munich. Ballin became a close associate of Juan Luna, a Philippino who won many prizes in the salons of Paris and Madrid. In the process, Ballin acquired a working command of Italian and French and studied at universities while producing lifelike portraits of Jean-Louis Meissonier, Benjamin Constant, Carolus, Duran, Ristori, and others.

Upon returning to the United States, Ballin produced many portraits, landscapes, and genre pictures. His oil portrait of the Reverend Thomas Gallaudet earned him great praise in the *New York Tribune.* The subject of this painting was the son of Thomas Hopkins Gallaudet, one of the cofounders of the first formal school for deaf pupils in the United States (the American School for the Deaf in Hartford). Ballin also painted portraits of other individuals who had distinguished themselves in the education of deaf persons, including Isaac Lewis Peet of the New York Institution. This life-size oil painting of Peet was presented to the New York Institution in 1890 at the National Association of the Deaf convention. Ballin's former teachers, however, were puzzled when he took a temporary hiatus from his art work, establishing a lithographing business. Thereafter, he did not further his reputation on the level he had established in Europe. Ballin also became increasingly involved in supporting the political campaign of President Cleveland. With the financial backing of Josiah Quincy, Jr., Ballin launched a campaign for Cleveland within the Deaf community. He further strengthened his ties to the American Deaf community by serving as an American representative to the 1889 World Congress of the Deaf in Paris.

After returning from the World Congress, Ballin lectured on his "Personal Impressions of Paris." He settled with his wife in Pearl River, New York, and for years he focused on miniature painting on ivory. His work has been frequently praised for its delicate qualities. His miniatures for the Deaf community included works for Thomas Hopkins Gallaudet and James Dennison of Washington. Portraits of women with such titles as *Listening*, *Contemplation*, and *Dreaming*, and landscapes including *At the Creek* and *The Orchard* were highlighted in the periodicals of the Deaf community.

In the 1920s, Ballin became interested in the roles deaf people and sign language played in silent films. In 1924, he traveled to Los Angeles to supervise a production that he had written. J. Parker Read, Jr., his friend, learned sign language and fingerspelling and became Ballin's business manager. As often happens, artists suffer during periods of war, and Ballin was forced to turn to designing advertising calendars, which Parker helped him market. During this time, he enrolled in the Palmer Photoplay Corporation, where he learned scriptwriting. The great sculptor Douglas Tilden* believed one of Ballin's scripts, "Sardanapolus," had the potential to be filmed. But, by then, Ballin was interested in getting into film as an actor himself. After unsuccessfully seeking employment at the Ince Studio, he turned to painting again. It was while painting in the middle of the William Fox Studio, completing a portrait of Thomasina Mix, the three-year-old daughter of the cowboy actor Tom Mix, that Ballin attracted much attention with his artistic talents. Among those who subsequently commissioned him for portraits were the great director John Ford and such actors and actresses as Alice Calhoun, Jacqueline Logan, and Cullen Landis. While Ballin watched Ford's production of *Lightnin'*, the beautiful child star Madge Bellamy sat next to him and described on his sketching pad what was happening. At the studio, he also made friends with such film stars as Laura La Plante, May McAvoy, George O'Brien, Edmund Lowe, and Neil Hamilton; he taught sign language to the latter. The wife of Cecil B. DeMille was so enraptured with Ballin's rendition of the French anthem, "Marseillaise," in sign language that she invited him to perform it at a party in her home. Thomas Ince once threw away a story he had spent $50,000 on, based on Ballin's criticism.

Ballin also contributed to such trade journals as *Hollywood Filmgraph*. In "Motion Picture Making as Seen from A Deaf Man's View," he proposed the use of sign language as a viable solution to communicating across heights and distances on platforms and on noisy sets. Such communication also would be accessible to deaf colleagues. His vocal desire to be a major player rather than an extra, however, antagonized some of the motion picture people. In "The Life of a Lousy Extra" published in *The Silent Worker,* Ballin described to the American Deaf community his experiences in attempting to get into films, most of the time lost in the crowds, but other times easily recognized, such as in *Silk Stockings, The Man Who Laughs, Michigan Kid,* and *The Woman Disputes.* Other deaf film stars were then appearing in more significant roles, including Granville Redmond,* Tommy Albert (Emerson Romero),* and Paul Waddell. Ballin recognized the challenge of realizing his dream, feeling fortunate he could fall back on portrait painting when necessary.

In 1930, Ballin published a book, *The Deaf Mute Howls,* that contained a statement elaborating on his conviction that deaf people would contribute to the culture as actors and that sign language could facilitate communication in the movie industry. Sadly, Ballin's major break in film, *His Busy Hour,* in which he appeared as a hermit, was never distributed. With thousands of other nitrate-based films, it was eventually lost to chemical decomposition. *His Busy Hour* was noteworthy in its attempt, with support by *New York Times* movie editor James O. Spearing, to establish a film company of and by deaf artists and shareholders. *The Deaf Mute Howls* also takes on educational practices, and Ballin lashed out at the ignorance of self-interested administrators and rigid teachers in educational institutions for deaf children.

Ballin died of heart complications in Los Angeles on November 2, 1932. In his final years, he enjoyed visiting schools as he enthralled students with his stories of his meetings with such movie legends as Mary Pickford and Douglas Fairbanks.

References

Ballin, A. V. (1925). A New York deaf artist in Hollywood. *The Silent Worker, 38* (1), 27–29.

Ballin, A. V. (1930). *The deaf mute howls.* Los Angeles, CA: Grafton.

Jenkins, W. (1904). Albert Victor Ballin, artist. *The Silent Worker, 16* (3), 53–56.

Schuchman, J. S. (1987). Silent Films. In J. V. Van Cleve (Ed.), *Gallaudet encyclopedia of deaf people and deafness* (Vol. 3, pp. 275–279). New York: McGraw-Hill.

FREDERICK A. P. BARNARD (1809–1889), American Scientist/Educator.

Frederick Augustus Porter Barnard was born in Sheffield, Massachusetts, on May 5, 1809, and began his formal schooling at the Saratoga Academy in New York while staying with his grandfather. He acquired further education at the academy in Stockbridge. His early interest in science is indicated in one of the two preserved letters written by him as a child—a thirteen-year-old's request to one of his cousins for the purchase of a microscope. Throughout his life, his dedication to science was evident, not only in his scientific endeavors but also in his approach to other fields of study.

The onset of his deafness while at Yale led Barnard to pursue teaching deaf children as a profession. His experience at Yale was a particularly difficult time for him, and he had wide mood swings. Observant friends noted that Barnard would sit discouraged for a half hour at a time with his head bowed on his desk. At other times his bravado and good humor were intense and seemingly forced. And as his friend Fulton (1896) wrote:

> The hereditary character of his infirmity forbade him to hope that it could ever be cured. It might indeed stop short of an entire loss of hearing; but even partial deafness would incapacitate him for the legal profession for which he had been preparing himself, and he closed his Blackstone "with a feeling of gloom bordering on despair." It was no light affliction to a youth of twenty to find himself thus compelled to abandon the profession he had chosen and the well-grounded hopes of distinction he had cherished. (p. 55)

Teaching deaf children seemed to Barnard an occupation where he could acquire experience and earn a living without having to be overly preoccupied with the challenge of communicating with those unused to working with deaf people. Barnard became a devoted teacher and developed fluency in American Sign Language, on which he published eloquently. He metaphorically tapped his interest in astronomy by introducing his treatise on the education of deaf children in a publication titled "Existing State of the Art of Instructing the Deaf and Dumb" in the *Literary and Theological Review* (1835). He made the case for the uniqueness of individual institutions as necessary and proper.

Barnard's devotion to teaching deaf children did not diminish his interest in science and mathematics while on the faculty of institutions in Connecticut and New York. In 1830, he published *A Treatise on Arithmetic*, and in 1831, another treatise on the property of conic sections. While at the New York Institution, he prepared a report for the *American Journal of Science* titled "On the Aurora Borealis of 14 November 1837"; the report was published in 1838. In 1837, he accepted a position as professor of mathematics and natural philosophy at the University of Alabama; Barnard taught chemistry for six of his seventeen years there. Barnard built an astronomical observatory at Alabama, erected a Foucault pendulum with ninety feet of piano wire, and experimented with stereoscopic photography, which he is credited as having invented.

Barnard moved to the University of Mississippi at Oxford in 1854. As chair of astronomy and mathematics, he impressed his superiors, advancing in a few years to President of the University. Under his leadership, astronomical and magnetic observatories were built at the University. Barnard remained fascinated by optical phenomena, publishing an article on the theory describing the Zodiacal Light. His order of a 19-inch lens from the noted instrument maker Alvan Clark of Cambridge, however, was never delivered. As the tensions of the Civil War increased, Barnard found it harder to continue his scientific pursuits. Still, in 1860, he managed to join A. D. Bache, the great-grandson of Benjamin

Franklin, on an expedition to view a total eclipse of the sun in Labrador; and he published a report on this phenomenon in an issue of the *American Journal of Science* in that year. Returning from Labrador, Barnard held the office of president of the American Association for the Advancement of Science.

When the tensions of the War flared up, it became very difficult for Barnard, a northerner, not only to function in his capacity as a scientist, but particularly in his role as Chancellor. When in 1861 the students of the University of Mississippi organized the University Greys, Barnard's loyalty to the Union made it hard to remain. Jefferson Davis pleaded with him to stay and assist as investigator of the natural resources of the Confederate States, but Barnard left with his wife for Norfolk, Virginia. That city was then captured by Federal troops, and he moved to Washington where he directed the office that prepared war maps. When Barnard and his wife paid a visit to the White House, Abraham Lincoln interrupted a meeting to extend his greeting, telling Barnard that he was familiar with the deaf scientist's work. Lincoln introduced his guests without ceremony into the midst of the assembled Cabinet.

Barnard denounced slavery in his thirty-two-page-long "Letter to the President of the United States by a Refugee," published in 1863, a work for which he is remembered most. This declamatory letter against the Confederate States argued for the support of Lincoln. It aroused great public interest and immediately attracted the attention of the trustees of Columbia College (later, Columbia University) to his worth as a scholar.

In his inaugural address as President of Columbia College, Barnard, who was ordained in the Episcopal Church in 1854, took for his topic the absence of conflict between science and religion. He continued a strong interest in the education of deaf people and personally coached deaf students pursuing courses of study at Columbia. In a report that followed his death, the Deaf community periodical *The Silent Worker* recognized Barnard's efforts in making special arrangements for R. B. Lloyd, in particular, so that Lloyd could make all his recitations at Columbia in writing.

Barnard continued as president of Columbia for twenty-five years, resigning in May, 1888. His writings covered a span of fifty-eight years. His versatility was well illustrated in his ability in science as well as in literature and history. Besides his publications on arithmetic and analytic grammar, with a symbolic system he designed for use with deaf children, Barnard wrote on a wide variety of topics, especially physics, including the expenditure of heat in engines, pendulum motion, voltaic circuits, optics, hydraulics, gun powder, the metric system, chemistry of metals, meteorology, and his various studies in astronomy.

Barnard received many honorary degrees. He succeeded Professor Agassiz as corresponding secretary of the National Academy of Sciences, and he was an active member of the American Academy of Arts and Sciences and the Royal Society of Liège, Belgium. He also served as President of the Microscopical Society and the Board of Experts of the American Bureau of Mines. The French Government conferred upon him the high honor of an Officer of the Legion of

Honor for his work as chairman of the Committees on Machinery and on the Apparatus of the Exact Sciences at the Paris Exposition in 1867.

With such a full and productive life, only a small part here mentioned, it is strange to read his friend Nicholas Murray Butler's description of his activities as limited by his deafness. While Fulton's descriptions of Barnard's life as a lonely one are understandable, it is especially important to balance them against the fact that Barnard accomplished formidable work as president of a college during a period when technology and other communication support (sign language interpreters, for example) had not yet been made available. He nevertheless attempted to devise his own ways to make use of any residual hearing he had left. This was obviously not much, as seen in Butler's description of the difficulty encountered in communicating with the deaf president:

In his office, he had standing on his desk a large wooden sound receiver, perhaps two feet square, into which one spoke when conversing with him. When himself speaking, his voice was naturally affected by his deafness and was neither clear nor pleasant. On the other hand, he had great charm of personality, manifested by his facial expression, by the character and cordiality of his speech and by his generous and kindly interest in those with whom he was associated. (Davenport, 1939, p. 265)

Of this homemade amplifier, Professor James C. Egbert of Columbia College sighed that it "was very awkward when one was particularly anxious to make an impression on him."

Barnard died on April 27, 1889. He carved a distinguished career as university president at two colleges over a course of fifty-one years, 1837–1888. He wrote on educational administration in addition to his scientific work. One hundred years later, in 1988, in a college founded primarily for deaf students (Gallaudet University), the controversy raged over the world's readiness for a deaf college president. Barnard had resolved the argument a century before.

References

Barnard, F.A.P. (1835). Existing state of the art of instructing the deaf and dumb. *Literary and Theological Review, 2* (7), 367–398.

Davenport, C. B. (1939). Frederick Augustus Porter Barnard. *National Academy of Sciences Biographical Memoirs* (Vol. 20, pp. 259–272). Washington, DC: National Academy of Sciences.

Elliott, C. A. (Ed.). (1979). Frederick Augustus Porter Barnard. *Biographical dictionary of American science: The seventeenth through the nineteenth centuries* (pp. 23–24). Westport, CT: Greenwood Press.

Fulton, J. (1896). *Memoirs of Frederick A. P. Barnard, D.D., L.L.D., L.H.D., D.C.L., Etc., tenth president of Columbia College in the city of New York.* New York: Macmillan.

LUDWIG VAN BEETHOVEN (1770–1827), German Composer.

Ludwig Van Beethoven was born in December, 1770, in the town of Bonn on the Rhine river. His family was poor. His mother, Mary Magdalena, was a kind woman whom Beethoven fondly remembered. His father, a singer and instrumentalist in the court orchestra of the Elector of Cologne, saw Beethoven's talent for music surface early and instructed him on the piano and the violin. By the age of fifteen, Beethoven held the position of assistant organist and violist to Christian Neefe at the Court Chapel. There, he impressed the Elector of Cologne enough to garner support for further study in Vienna, where he intended to take lessons from Mozart. He was seventeen years old when his mother's death deeply saddened him, and he left Vienna to help provide for his two younger brothers. Back in Bonn, Beethoven spent several years teaching, which he disliked. Neefe introduced him to the work of J. S. Bach and Mannheim; and, in 1792, at the age of twenty-two, he again travelled to Vienna, this time for lessons in music theory under the great master Franz Joseph Haydn. After many disagreements, however, Beethoven and his mentor Neefe parted ways. Beethoven then turned to Johann Albrechtsberger and Antonio Salieri, and gained a name as a concert pianist. His nontraditional technique quickly attracted the attention of the Viennese public, and his genius was matched only by his devotion to music. At the age of twenty-five, he published his first work. This period of his life was also marked by a series of love affairs, but Beethoven never married. For several years, he performed as a pianist and composer for such nobles as Count Waldstein, Prince Lichnowsky, and Archduke Rudolf.

It was around 1798 that Beethoven first began to notice a loss of hearing, possibly caused by dysentery, although there is no agreement among experts. Some believe Beethoven's deafness may have been associated with his mother's tuberculosis, of which his brother had also died. Others have ascribed it to venereal disease. Beethoven himself once attributed the origin to a "terrible typhus," and another time he reported it to be related to "troubles with his abdomen." Regardless of the origin, high-pitched sounds and murmured conversation were the first to be lost. At the time his deafness began to be noticeable, he had completed ten piano sonatas, six string quartets, two symphonies, two piano concertos, and the ballet *The Creatures of Prometheus.*

Beethoven attempted to hear sounds better by placing a wooden stick between his teeth and resting the other end on the piano. He went from one doctor to another who plied useless treatments, including tepid baths in the Danube River, cold baths, vesicatory ointment on the arms, and various medications. He began to feel somewhat paranoid, and he begged his closest friends not to betray the "secret" of his diminishing hearing. But, by the age of thirty, he realized that total deafness was his fate. In subsequent years, a mechanic named Melzl assisted him with various ear trumpets and other aids, but these helped Beethoven very little. Tinnitus and earaches haunted him further, yet he passionately hoped that others might interpret his behaviors as due to absentmindedness.

Beethoven began to isolate himself more and more from society, his heart heavy with grief as he described in a letter to his friend, Dr. Franz Wegeler: "My poor hearing haunted me everywhere like a ghost; and I avoided—all human society." The torment of a musical genius deafened for life is also revealed in his letters to his brother written during a country retreat in Heiligenstadt in 1802. He wrote, continuing to characterize his deafness as a "demon" or a "spectre," that awareness of what he was missing drove him close to suicide—but that his art held him in check.

Like Mozart, Beethoven chose a life primarily as a freelance musician, even turning down the post of *Kapellmeister* at the court of Jerome Bonaparte at Kassel in 1808. His masterpieces fell into a variety of categories. His music reflected a wide range of emotions and experiences, particularly as a man who repeatedly failed in love and long suffered with deafness. The sonata *Pathétique* is believed to have especially reflected the sorrows of his life.

Musicologists have offered diverse interpretations of how Beethoven's deafness influenced his work. Some actually believe that his hearing loss drew him away from writing with the assumption that he, the composer, would be the sole interpreter of that work. In that view, the history of music benefitted from Beethoven's deafness. Beethoven may also be the first composer to establish his art for its own sake. He stopped playing the piano in performance and writing conventional virtuoso pieces for himself. In a more clinical vein, musicologists and physicians have suggested that Beethoven's head noises may have led to bold, creative effects.

In the July, 1909 issue of *Current Literature*, in an article entitled, "Beethoven's Malady and Its Influence Upon His Music," a writer in the *Boston Musician* named J. Ermoloff similarly concluded:

The wild, uncanny cries . . . he converted into that eery [sic], weird music that suggests almost the preternatural—passionate utterances of joy, triumph, surprise, pain, supplication. As he could live a life withdrawn in a world peopled by his own imaginings, the easier, doubtless, for his deafness, he may have missed the lesser comforts of life, but reward came in ways reserved for the select few. The "moaning" within, whether in the form of poignant complaints, sorrowful sighs, tender emotions, or poetic cries, took shape and form in imperishable works of art. (p. 86)

Others believe that much of Beethoven's music is excessively loud, if explosive in feeling, possibly the result of his straining to hear the compositions in face of progressive hearing loss. In his chamber music, secular vocal music, and choral works, as well as his symphonies and concertos, Beethoven revealed a soulful humanity. In the last decade of his life, Beethoven's deafness must have influenced to some degree his final sonatas and quartets as well. His later music reflects realism and employs mysterious harmonies that are believed to have emanated from an interior voice. It is generally agreed that Beethoven's depth of feeling was heretofore unknown in music, and that his work provided the transition to the dramatic character of the Romantic movement.

The German conductor Anton Felix Schindler, Beethoven's friend, described the tragic evening when Beethoven attempted to direct a rehearsal of his only opera, *Fidelio*, unable to hear the orchestra or voices of those singing. Several times there was embarrassing confusion led by Beethoven's baton until, with all looking on in awkward silence, the composer left, troubled and heartbroken. His remarkable inner strength nevertheless led him to complete such masterpieces as the *Ninth Symphony* (1823), during which it is said that a chorus member gently turned the deaf composer toward the audience so that he might see the enthusiastic ovation of hats and hands.

Never careful with his own finances and always charitable to others, Beethoven lived without adequate means during a period when he was an honored citizen of Vienna. Through a benefit concert of his work, a friend in London raised $500 for him shortly before his last illness, for which he was grateful. Conversation books helped him to communicate during the last decade of his life. All through his life he never gave up hope of having his hearing restored. Only a few months before his death, he recorded his excitement over a discovery of a new restorative consisting of green nut-rinds crushed in lukewarm oil, a few drops of which were to be inserted into the ears.

Beethoven lived a remarkable life as a deaf composer. He completed thirty-two piano sonatas and seventeen string quartets. He wrote nine symphonies, the *Fifth Symphony*—with its haunting theme of "fate knocking at the door"—being the most popular today. Deaf, in generally poor health, never married yet having to raise a nephew while struggling financially, he also wrote five sonatas for the cello and piano, ten for violin and piano, five piano concertos, one violin concerto, one concerto for piano, violin and cello, ten overtures, two masses, one opera, and a ballet. In addition, he composed chamber and occasional music.

On March 26, 1827, Beethoven lay unconscious and dying. He had been administered the last rites and a fierce thunderstorm momentarily aroused him. It is recorded that Beethoven looked at those near his bedside and defiantly declared, "I shall hear in heaven!"

References

Anderson, E. (1961). *The letters of Beethoven*. New York: St. Martin's Press.

Forbes, E. (Ed.). (1967). *Thayer's life of Beethoven*. Princeton: Princeton University Press.

Lloyd, N. (1968). *The encyclopedia of music* (pp. 57–60). New York: Golden Press.

Rolland, R. (1929). *Beethoven the creator* (E. Newman, Trans.). New York: Harper & Brothers.

Schauffler, R. H. (1936). *Beethoven: The man who freed music*. Garden City, NY: Doubleday, Doran & Company.

RUTH FULTON BENEDICT (1887–1948), American Anthropologist.

Ruth Fulton Benedict was born on June 5, 1887, in the Shenango Valley of northern New York. When she was two years old, her father, a physician, died of an undiagnosed disease. Her family moved to various cities where her mother found employment as a teacher and librarian. As a child, she was continually corrected. Her deafness was at first so mild that it was not recognized; and, in comparison to her younger sister, she simply appeared less responsive. Both the trauma associated with her father's death, especially in its effect on her mother, as well as the experience of progressively losing her hearing, profoundly saddened the child. The stress and alienation she experienced eventually became manifest in isolation and seizure-like tantrums. In her personal journal, Benedict wrote about this alienation: "Happiness was a world I lived in all by myself, and for precious moments." In regard to her hearing loss, Benedict also wrote that her hearing was worsening; tonsillectomies and other means to keep her eardrums intact were tried. Benedict's deafness also exacerbated her tendency to withdraw after her father's death. Discipline became a problem, as relatives only gradually realized that they would need to use different strategies to communicate and get Ruth's attention. The entire family's adjustment became a source of confusion to her for some time.

In the late nineteenth century, there was inadequate technology to determine exactly the extent of Ruth Benedict's deafness. Ruth's mother resorted to available texts on childrearing and deafness. She learned to talk slowly and form her words clearly. Facial expressions became crucial in the household and communicating through sight as much as sound became habitual. However, talking continued to be exhausting. Conversations between Ruth and her mother, while improved from a communication strategies standpoint, were psychologically fraught. Often, shouting and outbursts of anger were the outcome of everyday interactions.

Writing was an escape from the struggles of Ruth's youth, including the financial difficulties resulting from her father's death. She won scholarships to St. Margaret's, an Episcopal preparatory school in Buffalo, New York, and to Vassar College, where she majored in English literature. At Vassar, she appeared attracted to other lonely people. Despite this shyness, she attained both Phi Beta Kappa and an A.B. degree in 1909. In 1911, she began to teach young girls in California and continued for about three years until she married a young biochemist, Stanley Rossiter Benedict. The marriage was unsatisfying and, although they lived together, Ruth's need for independence and Stanley's strong feelings about her role in their relationship were sources of emotional conflict. They finally separated in 1931, after years of struggling. Neither ever remarried.

In 1919, Benedict came under the influence of Columbia University's eminent anthropologist Franz Boas. She studied anthropology diligently, completing her doctorate in 1923. At Columbia, she found herself missing a good deal in group discussions, which frustrated her.

The early part of her career was spent studying various Indian tribes, including the Serrano Indians of southern California in 1922, the Pueblo Indians of Zuñi and Cochiti in 1924 and 1925, and the Pima in 1926. She helped to train student anthropologists with the Mescalero Apache in 1931 and the Blackfoot of Montana in 1939, and throughout these years published numerous works about the folklore she had collected. *Tales of the Cochiti Indians*, for example, was published in 1931; *Zuñi Mythology* in 1935.

At Barnard College, Benedict inspired Margaret Mead to enter the field of anthropology. Together they shared teaching responsibilities and a lifelong friendship. As Benedict's confidante, Mead is the most knowledgeable source with regard to how deafness influenced Benedict's personal and professional life. In her biography *Ruth Benedict: A Humanist in Anthropology* (1974), Mead elaborated on how the hearing loss made it difficult for Benedict to do field work with a tribe of native Americans; for example

Although she respected field work and emphasized the great importance of the field methods taught by Boas, including meticulous, verbatim recording of informants' words, field work for her was always arduous. Her deafness made learning a language or even taking linguistic texts impracticable. The bulk of her work was with individual informants who, hour after hour, dictated in English or through an interpreter the endless, repetitious pueblo folktales. . . . Nevertheless she did enough field work to understand very well many of the problems of modern field research. . . . In spite of the handicaps under which she worked and the uncertainties of field work in the pueblos, her responses to the field situation were vivid and visually acute and her relations with her informants were lively and realistically appreciative. (pp. 30–32)

But Benedict's deafness also brought advantages. She was led to an interest in the more *visual* products of culture, particularly literature, poetry, architecture, and painting. Instead of relying on sound patterns, she wrote of cultures as works of art. Benedict's poetic verses at times revealed the interplay between her personal life, including her deafness, and her anthropological work. Following her experience with the Pima tribe she wrote a series of verses; and, in "This is my Body," the reader can observe Benedict's self-positioning between silence, or the unknown, and the concrete representation of symbols.

Benedict began to postulate a theory that many cultures could be described according to a single dominant type of personality that they appeared to foster. Fleming (1971), Mead (1974), and others believed Benedict's deafness may have given her the benefit of a different perspective on the cultures she studied, because, in addition to direct observation, the patterns she recorded were often filtered through others or related by third parties.

Benedict's theory was presented in 1934 in *Patterns of Culture*, which for many years was the major introductory anthropology text.

Mead described Benedict as shy and tentative. She also commented about the effects the deafness had on class discussions, but she may not have known that Benedict had experimented with a hearing aid. In her journal for Monday, January 11, 1926, Benedict wrote, "Shopping for earphones!" However, she found the aids cumbersome and disturbing and soon returned them. In her view, they interfered with her natural pedagogical style.

Benedict's students reacted differently to her deafness. Some, including Mead, appreciated the attentiveness with which she communicated, particularly in the way she watched each student's facial expressions to avoid missing important information. They also appreciated the repetition and careful rewording of questions. Yet, some students disliked the repetitiveness and waited impatiently for her to make a point during her ethnographic descriptions, and more than Benedict's meandering, they found some of her speech patterns hard to follow.

In 1936, Benedict was considered for the position of chairperson of the Department of Anthropology by Howard Lee McBain, Dean of the Graduate School at Columbia. Before the appointment process could be completed, however, McBain died of a heart attack. Benedict never received an offer.

During World War II, she was asked to help prepare documents on Asian and European cultures for the Office of War Information. In this situation—a noisy office plagued by gossip, committee demands, and government-bureau infighting—she found deafness to be an advantage, and enjoyed the singular opportunity to concentrate on her work.

Through the 1940s, she published extensively on the subject of race. During a leave of absence from Columbia following her work with the Office of War Information, she published her classic work, *The Chrysanthemum and the Sword: Patterns of Japanese Culture* (1946), which subsequently brought a large government grant to Columbia for supporting similar studies of cultures.

Benedict died of a coronary thrombosis on September 17, 1948. She is considered by many to have been the first American woman to become the preeminent leader of an academic discipline.

References

Caffrey, M. M. (1989). *Ruth Benedict: Stranger in this land*. Austin: University of Texas Press.

Fleming, D. (1971). Ruth Fulton Benedict. In *Notable American women, 1607–1950: A biographical dictionary* (Vol. 1, pp. 128–131). Cambridge, MA: Harvard University Press.

Mead, M. (1966). *An anthropologist at work: Writings of Ruth Benedict*. Boston: Houghton Mifflin.

Mead, M. (1974). *Ruth Benedict: A humanist in anthropology*. New York: Columbia University Press.

EUGENE BERGMAN (1932–), American Writer/Educator.

Eugene Bergman was born in Posnan, Poland, in 1932, the son of a fabric store owner. He lived in a Jewish neighborhood in Posnan until he was seven years old, when the Germans invaded Poland. The Bergman family lost their home and business within a month of the invasion and were forced to move from Posnan to Lodz, designated as a resettlement. On one of his first days in the Lodz Ghetto, Bergman encountered a group of German soldiers, one of whom clubbed him in the head with a rifle. Five days later, he woke from a coma completely deaf.

After a while, the Bergman family moved to Warsaw. Within a few months, they were again crowded into a ghetto. His father, Pesakh, managed to acquire false identification papers and continued to live outside the ghetto as a non-Jew, smuggling in food once a week to keep his wife and three sons alive as the Nazis attempted to starve them. Tens of thousands of their neighbors died within a few months' time. Bergman recollected that his mother managed to keep him and his brothers relatively free of fear during the next year. In July 1942, Bergman's father learned of the Reich's plan to send the people in the Warsaw Ghetto to the Treblinka Extermination Camp. He sent a message concealed in a loaf of bread that the family should attempt to escape. After bribing a German soldier, the Bergmans joined Pesakh and escaped the subsequent murder of over 310,000 Jews that followed within a few months.

The Bergman family was fortunate to similarly escape the Czestochowa Ghetto a few months later, returning to Warsaw, where they lived until August 1944. While his family stayed in the Wola quarter, Eugene Bergman, now twelve years old, assisted a detachment of insurgents fighting the Nazis. Living in bombed-out buildings for several months, he rummaged for food to supply the soldiers until he was captured in October when the Poles surrendered. From the Lamsdorf prison camp in Silesia, he was moved to a factory in Brochwitz. He was liberated by the Russians in May 1945. His father and older brother were never found, although a fellow tenant later told his brother that he saw them shot. After two years in a displaced persons' camp in Germany, he and his family were sent by his uncle to the United States.

In Brooklyn, New York, Bergman managed to complete public high school. In 1951, he was one of eight foreign and 235 American students at Gallaudet College. He completed his bachelor's degree in Literature and Languages in 1953, followed by his master's degree in English from Georgetown University in 1971 and a Ph.D. in English from George Washington University in 1978. His dissertation focused on the "divided self" in the fiction of Hawthorne and Dostoevsky. He has been on the faculty of Gallaudet College (University) since 1970.

As a scholar, Bergman has a working knowledge of five languages. He taught himself English at the age of sixteen by attempting to read Thomas Mann's *The Magic Mountain* with the help of a German-English dictionary. He learned French in the Warsaw Ghetto, borrowing books from a library.

Having directly experienced the worst inhumanity, Bergman has a particular interest in the Absurdist dramatists Eugene Ionesco and Samuel Beckett and an affinity for their central themes of estrangement and rootlessness. In his own creative work, he has chosen to deal with alienation in a more comic vein. In 1981, with the actor Bernard Bragg,* Bergman wrote *Tales from a Clubroom,* a play which describes what he called the "heart of the deaf world." The play was written primarily for and about deaf people, and has been performed throughout the Deaf community. Enormously popular in its treatment of community, success, and class, it has become part of the repertoire of many Deaf theatre companies. Bergman also coedited *The Deaf Experience* with Trenton Batson in 1977, an anthology of deaf characters and deafness in literature. Bernard Bragg's autobiography, *Lessons in Laughter* (1989), was signed in ASL to Bergman who then translated it into English. He authored *Art for the Deaf and Hearing Impaired*, and has published and lectured on such topics as "Autonomous and Unique Features of American Sign Language" and "Images of the Deaf in Literature." Bergman has served as editor or coeditor of various periodicals and publications, including *Teaching English to the Deaf*, the *Proceedings* of the First Gallaudet College symposium on Research in Deafness, and the thematic periodical *Directions*.

References

Beck, E. (1982). Eugene Bergman: Deaf Survivor. *The Deaf American, 35* (3), 4–6.
Walter, V. (1987–88). Inside the madness: A deaf survivor remembers the Holocaust. *Gallaudet Today, 18* (3), 2–4.

JEAN-FERDINAND BERTHIER (1803–1886), French Writer/Deaf Community Advocate.

Jean-Ferdinand Berthier was born in 1803 at Louhans, France. He attended the famous National Institute for Deaf-Mutes, considered by many historians to be the birthplace of the education of deaf persons. His primary teacher was Auguste Bébian, a hearing teacher, who was fluent in French Sign Language (FSL). It was Bébian who first proposed replacing "methodical signs" with sign language. This sparked one of Berthier's own lifelong causes: the movement to teach deaf children through the natural sign language used in Deaf communities (e.g., FSL) rather than artificial, "methodical" signs invented purely for pedagogical purposes. Berthier was a star pupil, being appointed to a professorship at the age of twenty-six.

Simultaneously, Berthier rapidly ascended as leader of the large and influential Deaf community in Paris. He was a skilled politician and tactician, urging better public information about deafness. He also continued Bébian's argument for educational methods that used natural sign language to teach content subjects and to promote the learning of written French. He published numerous papers and books in defense of a Deaf "nation."

In 1834, Berthier instituted a tradition of celebrating the anniversary of the birth of the Abbé de l'Epée with conferences and galas. The elegant banquets were open to a cross-section of French Deaf society. They ironically excluded women and foreign leaders. However, in later years, deaf foreigners and women traveled to Paris for what was an international reunion of deaf people. Berthier was the preeminent leader and charismatic president of these banquets, which were active with reports and entertainments notable for their attention to sign language. There was a period of controversy in later years over how often invitations to these banquets should be extended to hearing people. After some time and much debate, government officials and the press were invited, and interpreters hired.

The umbrella organization that sponsored these events, the Société Centrale des Sourds-Muets, was established to organize the banquets and promote the welfare of deaf people. Chartered in 1838, its goals included the formulation of strategies for influencing public policy on deafness, citizenship, and advocacy training for all Deaf community members, and serving as an educational "watchdog" group.

Berthier addressed numerous research papers to the French parliament on the subject of legal procedures and codes, and their impact on deaf people. He appeared before the Academy of Moral and Political Sciences and the Academy of Medicine at various times. His testimony addressed the constraints of medical and clinical approaches to deafness and the assurance of civil rights of deaf persons. He also continued to present prolifically on sign language.

Though the elite of the Deaf community had won recognition and respect, Berthier would never be able to cease fighting the negative attitudes toward deaf people, not only in the general public but even from within the Paris Institute where he was a recognized senior faculty member. In the wake of the Milan Conference, several attempts to change the language policy of the institute to oral-only methods were defeated by Berthier and a cadre of teachers under his leadership. Berthier was an idealist but also a pragmatist, who emphasized the need for Deaf citizens to act in unity and not to disempower themselves through factions. One of the themes that he and Claudius Forestier, another influential deaf teacher, repeated at the banquets and monthly meetings of the Société Centrale was the need to become a Deaf nation coexistent with hearing allies. They urged deaf people to think of themselves as educators of hearing people and counseled them to know their friends among the hearing.

Berthier was devoted to the memory of the man he considered to be the greatest hearing ally, the Abbé de l'Epée. He led drives to erect memorials to Epée in Versailles, at the church of Saint-Roch in Paris, and at the Paris Institute. He was clearsighted and not uncritical of his mentor, however. Berthier criticized openly the system of methodical pedagogical signs created by the Abbé de l'Epée and his successor, the Abbé Sicard. Where Berthier genuinely loved the Abbé de l'Epée, who had innocently developed his method as a classroom tool and studied FSL in the Deaf community, he was equally contemptuous of Sicard for his rigidity, opportunism, and avoidance of deaf people.

Berthier was also one of the first deaf biographers, publishing summaries of the lives of his hearing instructors, *Notice sur la Vie et les Ouvrages d'Auguste Bébian* (1839), *L'Abbé de l'Epée* (1859), and *L'Abbé Sicard* (1873). His *Le Code Napoleon mis a la portée des Sourds-Muets* (1868) assisted the deaf people of France in understanding clearly their rights and duties as French citizens. In this handbook and in his other writings, he exhibited clarity and analytical brilliance. His writings on the education of deaf students and communication illuminate the issues of his time. His most notable works were *Histoire et statistique de l'Education des Sourds-Muets* (1839), *Les Sourds-Muets avant et depuis l'Abbé de l'Epée* (1840), *Observations sur la Mimique* (1852), and *Examen Critique de l'opinion de feu le Docteur Itard* (1852). Berthier also was documented, in the writings of contemporaries, as having an elegant and intellectual signing style.

Unfortunately, Berthier's lifework, which was characterized by a brief Deaf Renaissance in Paris during his career, lost considerable ground. As Moody (1987) notes, the year after Berthier's death, the last students taught in sign language graduated from the Paris Institute, and the last deaf teachers at the Institute were forced into early retirement.

Perhaps Berthier's crowning achievement was his being the first deaf man to receive the medal of the Legion of Honor. In 1849, he was also elected to the Société des Gens des Lettres, an exclusive and esteemed literary society.

Berthier died in Paris on July 12, 1886.

References

Lane, H. (Ed.). (1984). *The deaf experience: Classics in language and education.* Cambridge, MA: Harvard University Press.

Moody, W. (1987). Jean-Ferdinand Berthier. In J. V. Van Cleve (Ed.), *Gallaudet Encyclopedia of deaf people and deafness* (Vol. 1, pp. 141–143). New York: McGraw-Hill.

DAVID LUDWIG BLOCH (1910–   ), American Artist.

David Ludwig Bloch was born in 1910 in Floss, Bavaria, and orphaned soon after birth. Raised by his grandmother, Bloch was deafened in his first year. He began his formal education in a school for deaf children in Munich at the age of five, attended a second school in Jena, and then the Technical School of Porcelain Industry in Selb. By the age of fifteen, he had demonstrated considerable artistic talent and for three years was apprenticed to a porcelain director in Selb. In 1934, he received a scholarship for study at the State Academy of Applied Arts.

In 1938, however, the Reich was firmly established, and Nazi legislation was enacted to discourage Jews from study and work. This led to Bloch being expelled from the Academy. He was then imprisoned in the Dachau Concentration Camp, where he remained until 1940 when an American cousin bought him passage to Shanghai. There, he lived for nine years, meeting a deaf Chinese woman, whom he married in 1946. During some of this time, Bloch lived under and observed the Japanese occupation. Bloch nevertheless was able to produce many fine pieces in graphics and oil, exhibiting and selling his works to diplomats. Many of his black-and-white and colored woodcuts were satirical pieces on Chinese life, such as a rickshaw series later published in book form with commentary. Others, however, were compelling illustrations of the destitute Shanghai refugees, other victims of the war. That his own wife was unable to view these illustrations without distress revealed to him the emotional impact of his work. The experience served as a prelude to his later translation into art of his own personal experiences as a Holocaust survivor.

In 1949, Bloch and his wife settled in Mt. Vernon, New York, where he worked as a lithographic artist for twenty-six years. They raised two sons. His major decorative project of note was a service of china for the Lyndon Baines Johnson White House, depicting flowers from each state of the Union. Many of his watercolors, woodcuts, china designs, and book illustrations were exhibited at the Washburn Arts Center at Gallaudet College in October, 1975. Included in this exhibit was a set of playing cards, a result of five years of work on his own time, based on watercolor paintings depicting historical American events and personalities.

In 1976, Bloch returned to Dachau, an experience that started him on an intense and critical period of his life. Drawing on his recollections as a Dachau inmate, he began to portray the Nazi legacy of suffering, despair, and death. "My pictures are my language," he explained. "I can't find the words. It is my duty not to forget. These paintings are my dissertation. My hands are my degree."

"Never Again" was Bloch's answer to Hitler's "Jewish Question." Each of his paintings represented a story, and each painting measured 48 inches by 13 inches, symbolizing the endless train of boxcars that carried prisoners to the death camps. Bloch held many exhibits of his Holocaust art at galleries, public libraries, and Jewish community centers across the United States.

Not only did he portray the Holocaust in general, but he participated in numerous exhibits and projects that revealed the stories of deaf victims, in particular. In May, 1942, at the Israelite Institute for the Deaf in Berlin, for example, 146 deaf Jewish citizens were dragged from the building and murdered. Thousands of other deaf people were put to death, and tens of thousands sterilized as the Nazis attempted to eradicate the "defect" of deafness. Stories have been told about how, in the concentration camps, hearing friends risked their lives by answering for the deaf prisoners when their names were called. In his paintings and sketches, Bloch presented these and other stories, as well as his own as a deaf prisoner who heard the screams with his eyes. His "Crying Hands" program was a moving testimony to deaf Holocaust victims and their efforts to recover their heritage. "Crying Hands," which often closed with a memorial service, has been praised by critics around the world. Along with Bloch's art, the three-hour program included Yiddish songs and poems of the Warsaw Ghetto, interpreted in sign.

Bloch's lithographic work was also exhibited in "In Der Nacht," which premiered at the Los Angeles World Games for the Deaf in July 1985. The documentary exhibit included the film *All the People Saw the Voices*, a photo-narrative, and an art portion featuring selections from the works of Bloch and the deaf painter Morris Broderson's* well-known series on Anne Frank. "In Der Nacht" toured the world for several years, including stops in Bonn, Frankfurt, Berlin, Tel Aviv, Jerusalem, London, and Paris; exhibits were also held at the Federation of Jewish Philanthropies in New York, Congregation Rodef Shalom in Pittsburgh, Judas Magnes Museum in San Francisco, and the American Jewish Historical Society at Brandeis University.

"The Holocaust Images of David Ludwig Bloch" exhibit has touched the hearts of thousands upon thousands of people over the years. Many of the titles of his paintings completed since 1977 need no explanation—*No Place to Go*, *The Gate to Hell*, *The Showers*, *Death Factory*, *Reception-Deception*, *Waiting*, *Why*? The paintings include prisoners as skeletal phantoms, images of Hitler, and the horrors of torture and death. Bloch's work accomplished much more than evoking emotion. His exhibits led to literary contests for students and prompted others to establish museums on the Holocaust. In one gallery exhibit in 1987, visitors recorded their reactions as they left. The comments revealed the intensity of the feelings of those who saw the paintings. "Devastating—I can see my grandparents being taken away," wrote one person. "I pray that mankind will never let such horror exist again," summarized another. And, in a youthful handwriting, one naive viewer remarked, "I now believe it did happen!"

Bloch's work has also been exhibited at the National Gallery of Art, where several pieces are on permanent display. His paintings are held in many other collections, including the Leo Baeck Institute, the Holocaust Library and Research Center of San Francisco, Gallaudet University, and Temple Beth Solomon of the Deaf. In April 1983, Stella Wieseltier, Associate Director of the Center for Holocaust Studies, wrote to him and thanked him for his magnificent exhibit: "All of us should be grateful that there is a 'David Bloch' who has the genius to preserve our suffering on canvas for future generations."

References

Bloch's one-man show. (1975). *Gallaudet Today, 6* (1), 18–19.
David Bloch: Bilder sind seine Sprache. (1983, November 10). *Weser-Kurier.*
Kritzwiser, K. (1987, April 1). Looking back through the eyes of Holocaust survivors. *Globe and Mail.*
Tugend, T. (1983, May 13). Deaf were special victims of the Nazis. *Heritage.*

CHARLES BONNET (1720–1793), Swiss Naturalist.

Born on March 13, 1720, in Geneva, three years before the naturalist Anton van Leeuwenhoek died, Charles Bonnet was the son of Pierre Bonnet and Anne-Marie Lullin. We do not know how much hearing Charles Bonnet retained during his childhood, but it was clearly not enough to understand speech in the classroom. Throughout Bonnet's life, he struggled to communicate with others. As a child he did not initially do well in school. When it was discovered that his peers teased him about his deafness, his father withdrew Charles and hired a private tutor. The child's confidence was in jeopardy; and with it, his happiness and chances for success. This was long before the establishment of special schools and formal procedures for parents of deaf children advocating for them, but Bonnet's parents' decision was probably a correct one. Because of both his deafness and his frail health, however, this decision became the first episode in a lifelong pattern of withdrawal and isolation. Considering the quality of schooling that existed for deaf children at that time, though, it was a blessing for the world of science that Bonnet was assigned to Dr. Laget, who taught him devotedly in Greek and Latin, and stimulated his interest in the natural sciences. In particular, he read with great excitement Abbé Pluches' *Spectacle de la Nature*, becoming so interested in the history of the ant lion (an insect of the family Myrmeleontidae) that he searched the countryside until he had found one to study himself.

In 1735, he entered the Auditoire de Belles-Lettres, followed by the Auditoire de Philosophie in 1736, where he was instructed by Jean Louis Calandrini and Gabriel Cramer. The latter professor, whom, with Réaumur, he considered as one of his "oracles," taught him to read the works of Swammerdam, Malpighi, Fontenelle, Voltaire, and others. After reading *Histoire des Insectes*, Bonnet began a correspondence with Réaumur, asking the naturalist to suggest subjects for investigation.

Bonnet's greatest discovery was made in 1740, after several years of study. On May 20th of that year, he filled a flower pot with earth and soaked it with water. A newborn aphid was placed on a plant, which was then covered by a bell jar. Bonnet kept an exact diary of his observations, made hourly, sometimes more often. The aphid under observation changed its skin four times and came to maturity on June 1st, when the first young one was born. By June 21st, the unfertilized female had produced ninety-five aphids, all born alive. This led to his discovery of reproduction without fertilization, a process biologists call parthenogenesis. His work at the age of twenty won him an appointment as a corresponding member of the French Academy of Sciences.

Bonnet's father, ever-watchful and concerned, did not wish for him to pursue science as a career and discouraged him from doing so. The son first entered into a study of law, passing the public examination for his doctorate in 1743. There is little information on how he communicated with his professors, but reading and writing appeared to be his passions. During the time that he studied law, Bonnet did not give up his interest in science, however. In fact, in 1743 he was elected a fellow of the Royal Society for his work on regeneration in lower animals, particularly the rainwater worm, and for his investigations of breathing pores in butterflies and caterpillars. His entomological interests included a continuation of his early study of the locomotion of ants.

Among his many writings, Bonnet published *Traité d'Insectologie* (1745), a comprehensive work which entitles him the honor of being called one of the first experimental entomologists. The first volume reports his study of the aphids. The second volume describes his experiments with a long aquatic worm, Lumbriculus, which he had cut into twenty-six parts, most of which had become complete individual worms.

Bonnet published *Essai analytique sur les Facultés de l'Ame (Analytical Es-*

say on the Powers of the Soul) in 1760. His *Memoires* were written as a series
of letters to the Swiss physiologist Albrecht von Haller; Bonnet's cousin Abraham Trembley, also a naturalist; and his adopted son, Horace Bénédict de Saus-
sure, a nephew of Madame Bonnet's, who eventually became a notable physicist
and explorer.

Bonnet's deafness was challenge enough for a young man. To complicate
matters, he became almost completely blind in his youth, and severe asthma
attacks troubled him in his later years. He often referred to his deafness in his
memoirs. As early as 1743, at the age of twenty-three, he began to curtail his
investigations, not only because of his failing eyesight (which was greatly exacerbated by his continuous microscopical analyses and voluminous correspondence with Réaumur—some letters thirty to forty pages long); but also his
deafness made him fearful of committing mistakes that would embarrass and
frustrate him. In discussing his retreat, he wrote, "As for my life, it has been
as routine as the course of the stars in the heavens, although touched by experiences that affect the heart and exert Christian fortitude." Bonnet continued:
"But, in truth, is it worth it for the public to be interested in me? I have almost
always lived in a kind of isolation; At least I have never lived in what one calls
big society: My own tastes, my domestic circumstances, and especially my deafness contrasted too much with the life of society's people. Normally, I lived in
the country during most of the year and for about ten years, I have not left it,
even in Winters.

Bonnet also recalled the grief he experienced as other children teased him
about his deafness: "It was my deafness, which had already begun to manifest
itself, that frequently made me the object of scorn in the lessons and lectures
and exposed me without stop to ridicule." In one part of his autobiography, he
recounted a humorous anecdote pertaining to his deafness. It was 1754 and
Voltaire, the satirical French author, had arrived in Délices. All of Geneva was
excited over his visit. Tronchin, the future Attorney General, and his friend
Beaumont convinced Bonnet to join them in visiting the house of the celebrated
writer whose pen would help arouse the emotions of the French masses. Dressed
in nightclothes, Voltaire greeted the three of them at his door and invited them
inside. Once in the house, Bonnet noticed a copy of Etienne Bonnot de Condillac's *Traité des Sensations*, which had just been published in Paris. He attempted awkwardly to lead a conversation about the book. Voltaire appeared
embarrassed and said he didn't occupy himself with such matters. A short while
later, however, having taken Bonnet to the next room, Voltaire began to talk
profusely and wisely on Condillac's work, "as only the best philosopher would
have done." Bonnet was surprised and intrigued by this sudden change in his
host. It was only after returning to the parlor that his friend Beaumont gave him
the key to the riddle. Voltaire, standing close to the door, had followed the
conversation on Condillac's book held between Beaumont and Tronchin in the
next room, and he had repeated the exchange to Bonnet. Because of his deafness,

however, Bonnet had not heard a word spoken by his friends. He was a victim of playful deception by the great Voltaire.

To accommodate his disabilities, Bonnet employed assistants to conduct his research. His blindness, which he considered the more serious difficulty, forced him to change from microscopic examination of insects to the grosser investigation of plants. He followed Malpighi's work on the functions of different leaf surfaces, and these investigations culminated in *L'Usage des Feuilles dans les Plants*, published in 1754.

Bonnet's contributions to botany included his pioneering investigations of photosynthesis. He carefully examined the movements of leaves, their position on the axis of the stalk, and the movement of sap; many of his observations are found in *L'Usage des Feuilles dans les Plants*. When he was no longer able to study the specimens with his own eyes, Bonnet recruited collaborators, many of whom, like Jean Senebier, distinguished themselves in plant and animal science in the years to follow.

Bonnet published a number of theoretical and philosophical papers, some of which were quite controversial at the time. His description of the structure and function of the cell was 100 years ahead of his time. He wrote voluminously—treatises, notes, monographs, and hundreds of letters. It may have been a result of his deafness that he resorted to extensive and prolific correspondence. The many letters he wrote to the notable scientists of his day provide evidence of his far-reaching imagination. Since his blindness prevented him from experimenting, he suggested investigations to others. He encouraged Lazzaro Spallanzani to conduct experiments that led to artificial insemination of a dog. He acknowledged the importance of observation in scientific research. He is recognized as one of the founding fathers of modern biology.

Bonnet responded to fossil evidence of extinct species in the last of his principal works, *La Palingenesie philosophique*, published in 1769. He put forth his belief in the catastrophism theory later adopted by Georges Cuvier, which greatly influenced geological thinking until the 1820s. The argument found in this theory is that periodic catastrophes are responsible for destroying many forms of life on earth and explain the evolution of others. Bonnet was one of the first persons to use the term "evolution" in a biological context. He proposed a chain of living beings that was not definitive, but put forward the idea as a metaphor and explanation of natural interdependence among the creatures of the world.

Bonnet died on May 20, 1793, during the French Revolution.

References

Anderson, L. (1982). *Charles Bonnet and the order of the known*. Dordrecht, Holland: D. Reidel.
de Caraman, Le Duc. (1859). *Charles Bonnet, Philosophe et naturaliste: Sa vie et ses oeuvres*. Paris: A. Vaton.

Lang, H. G. (1994). *Silence of the spheres: The deaf experience in the history of science.* Westport, CT: Bergin & Garvey.

Savioz, R. (1848). *Mémoires autobiographiques de Charles Bonnet de Genève.* Paris: Librairie Philosophique J. Vrin.

EDMUND BOOTH (1810–1905), American Editor/Writer.

Edmund Booth was born on a farm in Chicopee, Massachusetts, on August 24, 1810. His father died of meningitis when Edmund was about four years old; this same illness left Edmund blind in one eye, totally deaf in one ear, and with very little hearing in the other. He lost the remainder of his hearing when he was about seven years old. With the help of his mother, Booth learned to read and this prepared him well for school. The only two teachers who made an effort to speak to him were nevertheless unsuccessful at communicating, and Booth usually stayed out of school to help his stepfather work in the tobacco field. At the age of sixteen, while living with his uncle, Booth was encouraged to enter what is now the American School for the Deaf in Hartford, Connecticut. The school was then near the end of its first decade under the eminent educators Thomas Hopkins Gallaudet and Laurent Clerc,* the latter being the first deaf teacher in the United States.

Since the quota of students from Massachusetts had been reached, Booth had to wait until the following year to enter the school. Under Clerc, Gallaudet, and Lewis Weld, who filled the superintendent's position when Gallaudet resigned, Booth learned well. He graduated in 1830 and, by 1832, he was serving as a substitute teacher when Frederick A. P. Barnard* fell ill. The following year, he was appointed to a full-time position there, serving not only as an instructor, but also traveling with Weld to South Carolina and Georgia to recruit deaf students to Hartford from these two states that had yet to establish their own schools.

In 1839, Booth left Connecticut for Iowa. Had the salary at the American School been better, Booth, a very good teacher, would likely have remained, although an attack of pneumonia had also left him with a need for a more active, outdoor life. Iowa was also where one of his former students, Mary Ann Walworth, then lived. During the adventurous sixteen-day trip by railroad, stage, and horseback, he was detained in Chicago, then a town of about two dozen houses, when he was mistaken for a fugitive murderer whose picture appeared on a handbill—a tall man with one eye.

Booth experienced a decade of frontier life in Iowa, working at mills and dambuilding. After his mother and his brother's family joined him in Iowa, he built the first frame house in Anamosa, in which he married Miss Walworth. All the other houses in the town were log cabins. In 1841, he was elected County Recorder, fulfilling the responsibilities so well that he was twice re-elected. In 1844, he was made Enrollment Clerk to the Iowa House of Representatives.

In 1849, Booth left his wife and two children with relatives to join the forty-niners in the California gold rush. For five years, he mined for gold near Sonora, sending home enough money for his wife to purchase a five-acre tract of land for a home. Filling his lonely hours with reading, Booth wrote home regularly, encouraging his wife to instill a love for reading in their children as well. "I am staying here chiefly for the children," he wrote from Sonora on September 1, 1850. "They must have as good an education as possible." In his autobiographical notes and gold rush diary, which includes many personal letters (*Edmund Booth, Forty Niner: The Life Story of a Deaf Pioneer*, 1953), Booth described the trials and tribulations of a gold miner. He encouraged his children to write, then offered writing lessons to them by mail. Booth also recommended specific history books for his son to read. He came down with smallpox at one point and was fortunate to survive. Then, one of his partners, a lawyer, committed suicide while drunk. When he finally returned to Iowa in 1854, he had brought with him a "considerable sum of money" he had gained from mining.

In 1856, Booth began his career as a writer and newspaper editor with the *Anamosa Eureka*. Asked to contribute an article for the first issue, he had responded; and, as one of the few people in the county with any literary skills, his regular writings became leading editorials. Booth also regularly helped his own and other people's children with their schooling, using a well-stocked library he had brought with him from Hartford. In 1858, he bought a half share of the newspaper from Matthew Parrott; and four years after that, he purchased the remaining half with money he made by selling the family farm. In 1868, his son, Thomas, joined him as a partner under a new firm name, "E. Booth & Son." The *Anamosa Eureka* soon became a prosperous, leading official weekly of Jones County—printed on the first Hoe Power Press ever used in Northern Iowa, an 1866 Booth purchase. In addition to contributions to the *American Annals of the Deaf* and other periodicals of the Deaf community, Booth published a number of poems, nearly always anonymously.

During his many years in Iowa, Booth continued his early interest in social programs and advocacy. In 1848, after Iowa entered statehood, he encouraged the Iowa legislature to financially support and send its deaf children to the school established in Jacksonville, Illinois, for the purpose of education. He also helped to establish the Iowa School for the Deaf in Council Bluffs. When John J. Flournoy began to advocate vehemently for a Deaf commonwealth in the 1850s, Booth was one of the Deaf community leaders who opposed Flournoy's efforts, arguing against the idea mainly for economic reasons. An abolitionist, he published an antislavery poem in 1858 and, in an article in the *Annals of Iowa* in 1871, he attacked the U.S. census for a bias in favor of slavery. He was so fierce in labeling Northern men who favored the South "copperheads" that he often engaged them in debate on the streets. The emotion in his message would cause his voice to rise to such a high pitch that his son could hear it from a distance; and Booth's antagonists found it useless to reply to a deaf man. In 1879, the Chicago Historical Society gave Booth an honorable mention and his portrait was included in a history of Jones County.

In 1880, Booth helped found the National Association of the Deaf (NAD).

He traveled to Cincinnati, and received the nomination as its first president; but feeling that his age was problematic, he served as chairman *pro tempore*. He consented to chair the National Executive Committee of the NAD, and he helped launch its far-reaching programs. In a large hall in a building overlooking the city, Booth called to order the meeting that was to organize the NAD, which would serve a vital role in advocating for the rights of deaf persons in the United States.

Booth's powerful presence and style were emulated for many years by Deaf community leaders such as George T. Dougherty,* a young Gallaudet student interested in the NAD when the organization held its first convention.

In 1893, Booth attended the World's Fair in Chicago, where the World Congress of the Deaf was also convening. "There stood father in the midst [of the many teachers who respectfully greeted him]," wrote his son Frank, "six feet, two and a half inches tall, and of massive frame, and, like King Saul of old, 'higher than any of the people from his shoulders and upward'—a veritable patriarch among the representatives of his class from the four quarters of the globe."

Booth retired as the editor of the *Anamosa Eureka* in 1895. His wife died three years later. He continued to travel and give speeches in his old age. In 1901, during a visit to his son in Philadelphia, he accepted an invitation to address the Clerc Literary Association. As probably the oldest living pioneer educator of deaf persons in the United States who could boast of having personally known Laurent Clerc and Thomas Hopkins Gallaudet, he was able to pay a moving personal tribute to them.

Edmund Booth died on March 24, 1905, in Anamosa, at the age of ninety-five. All of the businesses and the District Court there closed for his funeral. Upon learning of Booth's death, the editor of the *Deaf-Mutes' Journal* paid tribute: "To him is accorded the unique distinction of being the first man to preside at a gathering of the representative deaf from all parts of the United States."

References

Booth, E. (1953). *Edmund Booth (1810–1905) Forty-Niner: The life story of a deaf pioneer*. Stockton, CA: San Joaquin Pioneer and Historical Society.

Booth, F. W. (1905). Edmund Booth: A life sketch. *The Association Review, 7* (3), 225–237.

Edmund Booth, M.A. (1881). *The Silent World, 2* (8), 1–2.

Edmund Booth [Obituary]. (1905). *The Silent Worker, 17* (8), 123.

LINDA BOVE (1945–), American Actress.

Linda Bove was born on November 30, 1945, in Garfield, New Jersey. Both of her parents were also deaf. Bove began her education at St. Joseph's School for the Deaf in the Bronx, New York, and then attended the Marie Katzenbach School for the Deaf in Trenton, New Jersey, graduating in 1963. Her interest in theater began while she was a library science student at Gallaudet College. At Gallaudet she participated in feature roles in the university theatre repertoire, including the role of the character "Polly Peachum" in *The Three Penny Opera* and the poetic characterizations of the *Spoon River Anthology*. She was also the stage manager for the college's first all-student cast-and-crew production of *The Man Who Came to Dinner*. During her senior year at Gallaudet, Bove studied in the Summer School Program of the National Theatre of the Deaf (NTD). After graduating from Gallaudet in 1968, she joined NTD. There, she performed with Edmund Waterstreet, Jr.,* whom she married two years later.

NTD's repertoire afforded Bove the opportunity to demonstrate the versatility of her acting skills. In multiple touring productions across the United States and abroad, she performed classic roles, such as "Mrs. Webb" in *Our Town*, "Canina" in *Volpone*, and "Belissa" in *The Love of Don Perlimplin and Belissa in the Garden*. Her Broadway debut was as "Lauretta" in *Gianni Schicchi* at the Longacre Theatre. She could also, however, play "camp" roles, such as that of "Priscilla," the superheroine wonder woman in *Priscilla, Princess of Power*. Under Director David Hays, she performed with Phyllis Frelich,* Bernard Bragg,* Freda Norman,* Dorothy Miles, and other actors on NTD's fourth tour through Yugoslavia, Israel, Holland, France, Argentina, and other countries.

In the early 1970s, Bove joined other deaf actors, including Bernard Bragg, Mary Beth Miller, and Richard Kendall to establish the Little Theatre of the Deaf, a company with the goal of making a theatre of deaf persons accessible and relevant to children. The company gained the attention of the national and international press. Under a contract from Media Services and Captioned Films, McCay Vernon at the Western Maryland College and NTD collaborated to produce a series of films at the O'Neill Theater Center in Waterford, Connecticut, and at Western Maryland College. Bove starred with Nanette Fabray and other actors to address issues of communication, language, and development of other skills in deaf children through these films.

At approximately the same time, Bove joined the CBS-TV soap opera *Search for Tomorrow*, becoming one of the first deaf actors to play a regular role in a series. Sign language education and issues in communication were woven into the scripts centering on her character, "Melissa Hayley." There was also a romantic subplot concerning Melissa and a young doctor at Henderson Hospital where she worked. The episodes spanned twenty-six weeks and elicited positive public response. Soon, Bove was making appearances on prime time television, such as *Omnibus* with Meryl Streep on PBS. She starred in *A Child's Christmas in Wales*, a Christmas special first broadcast in 1973 and repeated in subsequent years. In 1974, Bove and Marlo Thomas were both given the AMITA award for outstanding work on television.

In 1976, Bove joined the *Sesame Street* program as a regular. The role was a significant milestone in that her deafness was only one facet of her character, "Linda the Librarian," who worked and educated with the other adults on *Sesame Street*. The role reconnected her to her college major as well; her degree

Linda Bove, ''Sesame Street'' star. Photo courtesy of the National Technical Institute for the Deaf.

in library science allowed her to bring an authenticity to the part. Her experience with Jim Henson's Muppets has been the source of humorous stories in her interviews. Initially, producers and writers assumed she could read lips—or an approximation of lips—on such characters as Oscar the Grouch, Bert, Ernie, and Cookie Monster. Bove traveled with *Sesame Street* on the road, visiting both deaf and hearing schoolchildren and playing in touring productions, teaching young audiences to sign along with her. In 1978, Bove starred as ''Linda the Librarian'' in the Emmy Award-winning program *Christmas Eve on Sesame Street*.

In the fall of 1979, Bove played a major role in the NTD's 30,000-mile world tour. The theater's visit to Japan was a major triumph. David Hays, the founder and artistic director of the NTD, and Bove were invited to come to Japan and appear on a television show. Later, the NTD company's performance was attended by the Crown Prince, his wife, and Prince Hitachi. During the intermission, Bove and Hays met with the royal family. Within two years, the deaf people of Japan established their own professional theater and a successful cultural exchange resulted.

In 1980, Bove appeared on ABC-TV's serial *Happy Days* as "Allison," the deaf girlfriend of its leading star, Fonzie. Throughout this period, she also continued to be very active on the stage. During 1980–1982, she was the understudy and stand-in for her NTD colleague, Phyllis Frelich, as "Sarah Norman" in *Children of a Lesser God*, the Tony Award–winning Broadway play. When the National Tour Company was formed, Bove was given top billing.

In addition to *Sesame Street*, Bove appeared in the movie *Follow That Bird!* She authored two popular Sesame Street books, *Sign Language Fun* and *Sign Language ABC*, and the video *Sign-Me-A-Story*, the latter of which won both the Action for Children's Television Award and the Parents Choice Video Award in 1988.

Bove also did freelance work for Beyond Sound, a deaf television production company, performing in a documentary honoring the Greater Los Angeles Council on Deafness. In 1991, working with her husband Artistic Director Ed Waterstreet, she directed *The Gin Game*, which starred Phyllis Frelich and Patrick Graybill.* *The Gin Game* received international coverage on CNN. The Pulitzer Prize–winning play by D. L. Coburn was particularly praised in Bove's version for its intense and psychologically compelling translation into American Sign Language.

In 1992, Bove was honored with the Bernard Bragg Artistic Achievement Award for her many contributions to the world of theatrical arts and the advancement of deaf people in that world. Her sixteen years as "Linda the Librarian" on *Sesame Street* were cited as a landmark in creating access for deaf children to children's educational television, promoting greater awareness in all children, and building the case for consistent use of Deaf talent in the mass media.

References

Brown, R. (1977). Linda Bove: Sesame Street star. *The Deaf American, 30* (4), 4–6.
Deaf West's "Gin Game" scores aces in Hollywood!!! (1991, July). *Silent News, 23* (7), 1, 31.
Hall, S. (1992, June 12). Linda Bove takes "Sesame Street" on the road. *Indianapolis Star.*
Panara, R. F., & Panara, J. (1983). *Great deaf Americans.* Silver Spring, MD: T. J. Publishers.
Stratton, J. (1976). The "eye-music" of deaf actors fills stage eloquently. *Smithsonian, 6* (12), 67–73.

BERNARD BRAGG (1928–   ), American Actor.

Bernard Bragg was born deaf on September 27, 1928, in Brooklyn, New York. Both of his parents were also deaf. As a child, Bragg had theater in his blood, since his father, Wolf Bragg, managed and acted in an amateur theater company in New York. In 1933, Bragg enrolled in the Fanwood School for the Deaf, now known as the New York School for the Deaf at White Plains, graduating in 1947. His first deaf teacher at the New York School for the Deaf was Robert F. Panara,* who mentored him further in the performing arts. They sat down together and planned the school performance of *The Christmas Bell*, followed by Dickens' *Christmas Carol* the next year. Bragg entered Gallaudet College in 1952, majoring in English and education; and he was the editor of the *Buff and Blue* when it attained status with the American Association of Collegiate Press. His dramatic roles at Gallaudet grounded him in a classical repertoire, as he played lead roles in *The Miser*, *The Merchant Gentleman*, and *Tartuffe*, earning him "Best Actor of the Year" awards twice. In his senior year, he directed John Galsworthy's *Escape*. Panara's influence on Bragg also extended to poetry; and Bragg was honored with the Teegarden Award for poetry in his senior year.

For fifteen years, Bragg taught at the California School for the Deaf in Berkeley, emphasizing to his students that in the art of mime, it was not the formation of sign, but the feeling that was of utmost importance. This he demonstrated in his own performances in night clubs and on stage as well. In 1956, he met the great French mime Marcel Marceau, who immediately invited the deaf actor to study with him in Paris that summer. Following his training with Marceau, Bragg traveled to London, where, with the deaf American artist Robert Freiman,* he ventured into a backstage cocktail party at the Palladium. Among the more than one hundred stars gathered there was Sir Laurence Olivier who, impressed with the young deaf actor's ambitious summer with Marceau, introduced Bragg to other prominent persons, including producer David Miller. Miller subsequently attempted to hire Bragg as a technical advisor for the filming of *The Story of Esther Costello*, a movie about a young deaf and blind girl, but Bragg was unable to obtain a labor permit in England.

Upon returning to the United States, Bragg acquired a managing office, Bay Area Productions, and he performed in legendary nightclubs around San Francisco, such as "The Backstage," "the hungry i," and "The Outside-Inside," both wearing the traditional mime costume with striped shirt and painted face, and his own improvisations, where he responded to requests from the audience for such performances as an interpretation of "By Love Possessed." Like Marceau, he had certain "classic" routines, including his portrayals of a tightrope walker harassed by a bee and a boy blowing spitballs. For this club work, he was nicknamed the "Houdini of Pantomime." Bragg was chosen by *Life* magazine as one of the best small nightclub performers of the year, appearing in the February 3, 1958 issue. In addition to his performances in San Francisco, he also toured the United States and Puerto Rico, receiving positive notices and critical attention. Under the title "The Language of Silence," he appeared on the Sylvania award-winning series *Expression*, a rather unusual experience for many viewers used to television with sound. Bragg also taught pantomime to

Bernard Bragg, American actor. Photo courtesy of Bernard Bragg.

hearing students at the Mara Alexander Gilbert's Actors Lab in San Francisco—through the pure use of pantomime.

During this period as a teacher and actor, Bragg was also studying for his master's degree in special education at San Francisco State University, graduating in 1959 with a thesis on ''The Nature of the Intellectual Achievement of the Deaf.'' For the next five years, he appeared regularly on the San Francisco television show, *The Quiet Man*, on which he performed mime and drama based on telephoned requests, prompting *TV Guide* critic Carolyn Auspacher to call Bragg the ''most eloquent performer on television today'' in 1961. The televised performances in San Francisco ranged from *A Christmas Carol* to

Shakespeare's *Hamlet*. During these years, he also traveled to Europe, appearing on television and the stage in England, Yugoslavia, France, and Spain.

Bragg presented many workshops in the early 1960s, including lecture-demonstrations for the *Now See This*, in which he pooled his creative acting talents with the inventive lighting and camera work of Gene Bunge to show the visual power of theatre of the deaf. In 1966, he also directed the convention show "Moments Preserved" for the National Association of the Deaf, bringing "sign-mime," a combination of sign language and pantomimic expressions, to a larger segment of the Deaf community.

In 1967, Bragg was invited by David Hays to appear on an NBC-TV network special to introduce the National Theatre of the Deaf (NTD) to a national audience. As one of the founding members, Bragg began to adapt the scripts to sign-mime, a form fundamental to the creation of NTD's aesthetic. On NTD's first tour of twenty cities in five weeks, Bragg performed William Blake's *Tyger, Tyger*, a sophisticated visualization of the "fearful symmetry," the hands and body sculpting the stern ferocity of the tiger. By 1971, NTD had completed its fourth tour abroad, performing in Holland, Yugoslavia, France, and Israel. That year also marked NTD's ninth national tour, beginning with *My Third Eye* at the National Technical Institute for the Deaf (NTID) at the Rochester Institute of Technology (RIT). Bragg became the company's first deaf director, responsible for the third episode, "Manifesto."

In 1968, Bragg collaborated as a founding member of the Little Theatre of the Deaf, joining Linda Bove,* Mary Beth Miller, and Richard Kendall in addressing the cultural needs of children. He taught creative dramatics to hearing children in inner city schools, and sign-mime and mime in summer schools. Bragg traveled to Moscow in 1973, where he served as artist-in-residence with the Russian Theater of Mimicry and Gesture as part of a ground-breaking cultural exchange. This theatre had been established after the Revolution and was the first professional theatre of the deaf in the world. After his appearance as "Hermes" in the Aeschylus tragedy *Prometheus Bound*, which was warmly received by Russian audiences, *Soviet Life* noted that Bragg was the first American to perform with Russians in over one hundred years, the last being the African-American actor Ira Frederick Aldridge. At every entrance or exit of his performance, the cast raised their thumbs toward him, a universal sign of praise. His international experience from multiple tours has served the Deaf community well. He was the recipient of the International Medal Award from the World Federation of the Deaf and was appointed the Consultant on Cultural Affairs for the National Association of the Deaf.

In 1977, Bragg was invited to serve on the U.S. Information Agency's Overseas Speakers Program. In this program, sponsored jointly by the U.S. Department of State, Ford Foundation, International Theatre Institute, and National Association of the Deaf, he had the opportunity to perform across multiple cultures. In 1978, this tour reached thirty-eight cities in twenty-five countries with the purpose of encouraging the development of creative arts and enhancing worldwide recognition of sign-mime as a powerful medium for cross-cultural communication. That year he also accepted a position of artist-in-residence at NTID. There, he performed as an artist-teacher in NTID's production of Molière's *The Would-Be Gentleman*, repeating the performance later at the National Association of the Deaf convention in Rochester. Bragg then began lecturing on theatre and drama in a position at Gallaudet College. In 1979, he wrote and directed the romantic comedy *That Makes Two of Us*; and, the following year, he joined with Eugene Bergman* to write *Tales from a Clubroom* (1981) which satirized issues of class and Deaf culture in the American Deaf community. In addition, he was the leading actor in the play *The White Hawk*, which John Basinger wrote for him. In 1989, he completed an autobiography titled *Lessons in Laughter* (as signed to Eugene Bergman), and, in 1993, he coauthored with Jack Olson a book titled *Meeting Halfway in American Sign Language*. Bragg has been awarded an honorary doctorate in Humane Letters from Gallaudet University in recognition of his extraordinary service to deaf people of the world in theatre, education, and communication.

Television shows in which Bragg has appeared include *A Child's Christmas in Wales*, *And Your Name Is Jonah*, *My Third Eye*, and *Can Anybody Hear Me?* "The amount theater can contribute to education is infinite," he believes. Bragg as artist and teacher has earned the title conferred on him by his mentor, Robert F. Panara: "Prince of Players on the Silent Stage."

References

Bowe, F. (1972). The DA interview: Bernard Bragg. *The Deaf American, 24* (11), 5–8.

Bragg, B., & Bergman, E. (1989). *Lessons in laughter: The autobiography of a deaf actor*. Washington, DC: Gallaudet University Press.

Bragg, B., & Olson, J. (1993). *Meeting halfway in American Sign Language: A common ground for effective communication among deaf and hearing people*. Rochester, NY: Deaf Life Press.

Gitlits, I. (1975, February). Theatre of the deaf: An American "Signs In." *Soviet Life*.

Panara, R. F., & Panara, J. (1983). *Great deaf Americans*. Silver Spring, MD: T. J. Publishers.

Powers, H. (1972). *Signs of silence: Bernard Bragg and the National Theatre of the Deaf*. New York: Dodd, Mead and Company.

Scott, D. S. (1960). Bernard Bragg: Master of mime. *The Silent Worker, 12* (11), 3–5.

JOHN BREWSTER (1766–1854), American Folk Artist.

John Brewster, Jr., was born on May 30, 1766, in Hampton, Connecticut, the son of a physician. He appeared from relative obscurity, having taken some early lessons in painting from a retired minister and self-taught portrait painter, the Reverend Joseph Steward. He established himself as a freelance artist in Massachusetts and Maine during his early years. With no formal schooling available for U.S. deaf children during his childhood, Brewster was largely self-educated. His ability to vary his medium of communication was once described in the diary of a friend of the family, the Reverend James Cogswell of Scotland

Parish, Windham, grandfather of Alice Cogswell, whose deafness lead Thomas
Hopkins Gallaudet and Laurent Clerc* to found the American School for the
Deaf. On December 13, 1790, Cogswell wrote, "Doc^{tr} Brewster's Son, a Deaf
& Dumb young man came in in the Evening, he is very Ingenious, has a Genious
for painting & can write well, & converse by signs so that he may be understood
in many Things, he lodged here." The Connecticut Asylum for the Education
and Instruction of Deaf and Dumb Persons (now the American School for the
Deaf), the first permanent school for deaf children in the United States, was not
opened in Hartford, Connecticut until 1817. Brewster, fifty-one years old at the
time, was, nonetheless, the seventh pupil enrolled. There, he learned the sign
language brought to America by the eminent Laurent Clerc, the first deaf teacher
in America. Brewster remained at this school for three years, probably tutoring
and teaching as well as studying.

Prior to his enrollment in the school, Brewster had been producing folk art
for several decades. *Dr. and Mrs. John Brewster*, a large portrait of his father
and stepmother, was painted between 1790 and 1795. Around this time, he also
painted a pair of portraits of Mr. and Mrs. James Eldredge of Brooklyn, Connecticut, which critics noted for his concept of portraying couples on separate
canvasses, giving a sense of space, and also for his use of decorative backgrounds. In November, 1795, Brewster's brother, Royal, married and settled in
Buxton, Maine, and the deaf artist seems to have settled there also, calling
Buxton home when he was not on painting excursions.

At about the turn of the century he completed *The Boy and the Finch* and
Girl in Green, both now in the Abby Alrich Rockefeller Folk Art Collection in
Williamsburg, Virginia; and one of his best works, a portrait of Sarah Prince of
Newburyport, Massachusetts, which is now in a private collection. Sarah was
the sixteen-year-old daughter of James Prince, a businessman and politician.
Brewster lived for some time in the luxurious Prince mansion, where he also
painted James Prince and three of Prince's other children. He was particularly
talented in painting children. Among his attractive full-length portraits were of
three of his half-sisters, completed in Hampton, Connecticut, around 1800, and
of the two-year-old Francis Osborne Watts. Brewster remained in Newburyport,
advertising his services in the January 22, 1802 Newburyport *Herald*, with the
Prince portraits available for examination as "specimens" of his work.

The gifted folk artist's life-size painting of Sarah Prince received much praise
in 1969 when it was selected for a "Collectors' Choice" exhibition at the Museum of American Folk Arts in New York City. The respect for his work as an
example of the best of American folk art was shown in its location on the wall
facing the entrance to the museum. Some critics have interpreted the pianoforte
in the painting and the partly completed song sheet of "The Silver Moon" held
by Miss Prince to reflect Brewster's thoughts on the absence of music in his
own life; but the dearth of personal information on Brewster in these years
makes such suppositions highly speculative.

During the busy first decade of the nineteenth century, Brewster executed *A*

Gentleman, depicting a somber man in his thirties. The dark-hued painting was sold in 1977 for $8,600, exciting private collectors who had rediscovered the deaf primitive artist. A few years later, a portrait of a rosy-cheeked girl sold for $67,500. At least eleven portraits have survived from this period, most from Kennebunkport and Saco. After leaving the American School for the Deaf in 1820, he then traveled to Saco, Maine, completing at least ten portraits that year. The darkness of his work appears to have increased during this period of his life. At the same time, however, Brewster's paintings are often termed "photographic," and they display unusual depth for their time.

In 1960, forty of Brewster's portraits were exhibited at the Connecticut Historical Society headquarters in Hartford. His surviving works are representative of the paintings of the talented itinerant artists who traveled America in its early days and recorded life in these times. Many of his other works have been lost. Like many artists of the period, Brewster seldom signed his paintings. One characteristic of Brewster's works is his inclination to paint his subjects life-size, and this very consistent pattern has led critics to reject several works attributed by others to the deaf artist. Brewster's subjects also often had particularly rosy complexions and robust forms. Their poses convey stillness and quiet. By the 1980s, more than one hundred of his paintings had been located. While several miniatures also had been attributed to him, it was not until the discovery of the atypically signed miniature of Benjamin Apthorp Gould (1809) on ivory, encased in a gold locket, that a touchstone for evaluating other works of Brewster could be found. Art critics have continued to search for his works in the coastal regions of Massachusetts and Maine, in particular, where he completed considerable freelance portrait painting.

Certain periods of his life are unaccounted for and undocumented. In 1983, Joyce Hill published a report on Brewster's works, describing how the deaf itinerant artist had advertised that he had "commenced his business" in Poughkeepsie, New York, in December, 1799, yet no paintings or miniatures have been positively identified as originating during his stay there. In describing the ledger of a Danbury, Connecticut, storekeeper Comfort Starr Mygatt, however, Hill sparked further interest. Art experts searched for five years, ultimately finding one of his masterpieces. *Comfort Starr Mygatt and his Daughter Lucy* was completed in 1799 and sold for less than $500. The painting brought more than $800,000 at a Sotheby's auction in 1988.

In 1980, the Whitney Museum of American Art in New York City held an exhibition titled "American Folk Painters of Three Centuries." Among the 140 works by thirty-seven artists were six of Brewster's paintings prominently displayed. *Sarah Prince* was accompanied by portraits of Henry James Prince and his son William, painted in 1800, and Henry James Prince, Jr. (1801). Also included in the exhibition was the somber portrait of Colonel Cutts and another of Cutts' wife, Elizabeth Scamman (1795–1800), and one of a round-faced girl holding a bird. Brewster's latest work was dated 1832, portraits of Mr. and Mrs. William Pingree of Denmark, Maine. His oil portraits are held by the Connecticut Historical Society, Dyer-York Library and Museum in Maine, and, in Massachusetts, the Historical Society of Old Newbury, Museum of Fine Arts, and at the Old Sturbridge Village. He is considered one of the best primitive artists of post-Revolutionary America.

Like William Mercer* and Augustus Fuller,* two other deaf portrait painters of this era, Brewster never married. He died August 11, 1854, in Buxton Lower Corner, Maine, and was buried in Tory Hill Cemetery.

References

Golladay, L. E. (1961, January). Historical society features work of deaf artist who entered ASD aged 51 when school opened. *The American Era*, 36–38.

Hill, J. (1983, Spring/Summer). Miniatures by John Brewster, Jr. *The Clarion*, 49–50.

Little, N. F. (1980). John Brewster, Jr. In J. Lipman & T. Armstrong (Eds.). *American folk painters of three centuries* (pp. 18–25). New York: Hudson Hill.

Swain, R. L., Jr. (1968). John Brewster, Jr . . . 18–19th century deaf artist, accorded recognition. *The Deaf American, 20* (5), 9–10.

Swain, R. L., Jr. (1969). Exhibition pays tribute to deaf artist of early America. *The Deaf American, 22* (2), 5–6.

MORRIS BRODERSON (1928–   ), American Artist.

Morris Broderson was born deaf on November 4, 1928, in Los Angeles, California, and attended two residential schools for deaf students. At the age of fourteen, he executed a pencil sketch of his aunt, Joan Ankrum, playing the piano. It impressed her enough to guide him using a book of drawings by Leonardo da Vinci and another by Nicolaïde on *The Natural Way to Draw*. Broderson soon came to the attention of Jarvis Barlow, director of the Pasadena Art Museum, who enrolled Broderson in a life drawing class under Francis de Erdely, a Hungarian artist who had immigrated to the United States. Broderson's family was amused by the special releases that had to be obtained for the young man in his early teens to attend classes with nude models. When de Erdely was offered a position at the University of Southern California, he was able to convince officials there to admit Broderson as a special art student. There, Broderson's anatomical renderings were viewed as technically perfect and out of the ordinary. Musculature was a particularly strong point. After four years, Broderson enrolled at the Jepson Art Institute in Los Angeles, where he studied under William Brice and Howard Warshaw. At Jepson, Broderson began to lose enthusiasm for technical and anatomical perfection and ''ideal'' bodies. His new teachers nurtured a strong romantic vein in his work.

When Jepson closed, Broderson began to work independently and portray a distinctly nonconformist style. He rejected the abstract expressionism then prevalent in the art world. He experimented with new techniques, including media in silk screen and mixed media such as watercolor and pencil, pastel and pencil, or all three at once. Coffee grounds added texture to his oil; a squeegee was used at times to apply watercolor. These applications were a temporary diversion, however. Working for several years as a janitor at local race tracks, and in the darkroom of a photographer, he continued to practice painting and drawing in oils and watercolors on his own time. For many years, his health suffered from his urge to create, by night if necessary.

Broderson was twenty-eight when he held his first one-man show at Dixie Hall Studio in Laguna Beach. The success of the exhibition was a high point in a turbulent time, however. He took a two-year hiatus from painting during a period of emotional turmoil. As he told friends and colleagues later, it was an exceedingly painful time for him as he explored his own identity and professional direction. He isolated himself from family and friends, feeling that he must live through that episode alone and find his strength. He meditated, investigated possibilities, and worked through this difficulty. After he returned to painting, his work soon gained national recognition. Partly based on his personal experiences and to an extent on his affinity with his mentor de Erdeley, Broderson expanded his work to embrace humanity in the face of suffering, loss, and alienation. In 1957, his solo exhibition at the Stanford Museum of Art attracted the attention of Mackinley Helm, the art biographer, who helped Broderson plan for an exhibition at the Santa Barbara Museum of Art the following year. Helm also wrote the introduction to Broderson's 1959 La Cienega exhibition at the Bertha Lewinson Gallery. At this time, he worked in a small house in Hollywood, with doors widened to accommodate some of his larger paintings. *The Death of Christ*, for example, measured six and a half by eleven feet, and *The Shadow of the Cross* seven feet by six, both completed for showing at the C. H. de Young Memorial in San Francisco. In 1960, he won awards at the Municipal Gallery in Los Angeles and the Los Angeles County Museum of Art. The inclusion of his painting *Chicken Market* in the "Young America U.S.A. 1960" exhibition at the Whitney Museum of American Art brought his work to the attention of Joseph H. Hirshhorn. Hirshhorn purchased three of his paintings immediately and many more through the years as he provided continuing support for the deaf painter.

As Henry J. Seldis wrote in *Art in America* in 1960, "since much of the art world seems to be groping for a 'new image,'—having been exhausted by the Action Painting holocaust—Southern California imagists with their spirit of continuous re-invention are belatedly achieving national and international fame." Among these "vigorous artists" Seldis included Morris Broderson and his "poignant beings." When the Ankrum Gallery opened in December, 1960, Broderson's work was successfully exhibited for the M. H. de Young Memorial Museum in San Francisco. Broderson then left for Europe to spend the winter.

Upon his return to the United States, Broderson had new paintings for a 1961 Ankrum Gallery exhibition. He continued to paint for several years before he opened his own studio in Los Angeles. He preferred watercolor as a medium as he began to work with delicate, intricate patterns and colors, but also used oil when he felt it necessary. He began many of his paintings by drawing in pencil on raw canvas or illustration board, sometimes working on several paintings at once. The detail he includes in his watercolors requires a long time frame for each work. *Of All Time* took eighteen months to complete. His work also became more complex as travel informed his interests. He was fascinated, for example, by the hand gestures of Japanese Kabuki, which led him to a series of Kabuki paintings. "It is not surprising that Broderson had an affinity for hand gestures," wrote Diane Casella Hines in the *American Artist*, "since sign language was his first means of communication." *The Rape*, a painting in a series in which Broderson incorporated Kabuki hand gestures, won the 1963 Whitney Annual. Broderson translated the sign language as "The Rape of Dokuro Ni" and represented the dramatic incident as a trap, where the vanquished victim cannot escape evil warriors, and, implicitly, war.

Between 1964 and 1969, Broderson continued to exhibit his paintings at major galleries, including the Phoenix Art Museum, the Ankrum Gallery, the Downtown Gallery in New York City, and the Fine Arts Gallery of San Diego. In 1963, he was offered a permanent membership by Edith Gregor Halpert at the Downtown Gallery. His humanistic, thematic, and haunting work was notable in its consistent rejection of minimalist and abstract trends. The curator and critic Halpert made no secret that independence and individual vision were what made Broderson attractive to her and many others. When Halpert died in the early 1970s, Broderson joined the Stemple Gallery as a permanent artist.

Broderson continued to mine varied creative sources. He based a series of paintings on Agnes De Mille's ballet, *Fall River Legend*, which gave him the opportunity to experiment with his formal use of color and shape accentuated by movement. Flowers and plants appear in many of Broderson's works. In Mexico, Federico García Lorca's poem "Death in the Afternoon," written about the tragic death of the toreador Ignacio Sanchez, led him to a series of paintings commingling the images springing from blood and red roses left in a slain bull's wake. In *Window*, his own image is reflected above a white bloom. In *Memories*, sketches of plants are posted on a wall with other souvenirs. His "Sounds of Flowers" series was inspired by a friend who mused on the special, simple relationship children have with things of nature. In *Life Story*, petals drift past an inert mask.

The movement characteristic in much of Broderson's dream-like work is apparent in his use of sign language and fingerspelling imagery, where the hands float across the canvas in much the way the flower petals do. Broderson's use of hands and faces is highly complex and unsettling to many viewers of his work.

Broderson is quick to point out that his deafness is not the reason for the unique expression in his art. He has great feeling for the universality of certain human experiences. Some critics have argued, however, that the beautiful world of his paintings comes from a very separate inner world of Broderson. In 1975, Broderson's particular spiritual vision, evidenced in his work *Angel and Holy Mary after Leonardo da Vinci*, was included in the inaugural exhibition of the Hirshhorn Museum in Washington, D.C. In 1981, he exhibited his works at

Gallaudet College in Washington, D.C., including *Of All Time*, one of his favorite paintings. Love, beauty, and peace, he explained during his visit to the Gallaudet campus, were the qualities he sought most to blend into his brushstrokes. He also painted a series of works based on the life and writings of Anne Frank displayed in a later Gallaudet exhibit on the Holocaust. Broderson also presented a slide show of his works to young deaf students at the Model Secondary School for the Deaf.

In 1993, several of his self-portraits were exhibited at the Switzer Gallery at the National Technical Institute for the Deaf at Rochester Institute of Technology. They are complex in imagery and psychological suggestion. In *Portrait*, he appears beneath a cracked and flaking painting of a semi-nude. Broderson has superimposed Christian symbols in a number of paintings, such as the crucifixion of Christ. His works also are reminiscent of medieval tapestry.

Broderson's work is presently represented in the permanent collection at the Guggenheim Museum, the Whitney Museum of American Art, the Smithsonian Institution's Hirshhorn Museum and Sculpture Garden, and the San Francisco Museum of Modern Art.

Broderson steadfastly has held to a vision of beauty, and beauty represented in the arts in particular, as salvation. The loneliness and spiritual crisis he endured as a young artist have served to remind many of the creative bursts that can follow such events; and the cultural world maintains consistent interest in his work.

References

Casella Hines, D. (1980, October). Morris Broderson speaking through his art. *American Artist*, 46–51, 97.

Morris Broderson. (1975). University of Arizona Museum of Art. Tucson, AZ.

Seldis, H. J. (1960). Southern California. *Art in America*, No. 4, 57–59.

Snyder, C. (1970, May 10). Without sound. *California Living*, 9–10.

Steadman, W. E. (1971). In *Morris Broderson*. New York, NY: Staempfli, 13–18.

C

EARNEST ELMO CALKINS (1868–1964), American Writer/Advertiser.

Earnest Elmo Calkins was born on March 25, 1868, in Geneseo, Illinois, and was deafened by an attack of measles at the age of six. The family moved to the cultured and quiet town of Galesburg, where his father became city attorney. Unfortunately, his father's reputation was chiefly built around pool halls and betting parlors, and his absenteeism put the family's well-being into peril on more than one occasion. Calkins attended a public school in Galesburg. He graduated from Knox College in 1891, although he later reported that he did not benefit much from classes, since he was unable to follow the lectures or hear well enough to participate in class discussion. He depended primarily on his own reading. He would, thirty years later, receive an honorary Lit.D. degree from Knox College.

Calkins set out to be a printer and journalist. While editing the school paper at Knox College, however, he published a story about a magazine, and, as a result, was rewarded with a free promotional subscription. This experience attracted him to advertising. He soon read about a copywriting contest and entered it. He won first prize, and, at the age of twenty-three, was offered a $15-a-week job in New York. While editing a trade paper, *Butchers' Gazette and Sausage Journal*, he met Ralph Holden, who was to become his partner. While he found friendships and enjoyed New York, he worked for an unscrupulous and insensitive publisher. When he found out that the man was advertising Calkins' position behind his back, he left.

For a time, Calkins returned to Galesburg as a columnist for the *Galesburg Evening Mail*. In 1894, he received his first job as an advertising manager with a Peoria, Illinois department store. Meanwhile, he shared samples of his advertising work with Charles Austin Bates, who ran an agency in New York City. Bates hired him. In 1902, after a period of writing and further study at the Pratt School of Design where he learned to work collaboratively with artists, Calkins joined Ralph Holden in founding the Calkins and Holden advertising agency, which later became Fletcher, Richards, Calkins and Holden. Calkins and Holden is widely regarded as the first modern advertising agency. Where early agencies merely acted as brokers to place ads, Calkins and Holden advanced the concept of the advertising campaign, the thematic co-creation of advertising displays and campaigns by teams. Calkins and Holden set up a typographical department, whereas earlier agencies simply sent the material to newspapers for them to arrange and typeset. The agency also pioneered new ideas in merchandising, packaging, and layout. Calkins and Holden devised symbols and trademarks such as ''Phoebe Snow'' of the Lackawanna Railroad who rode ''the road of anthracite.'' Calkins came to be known as the ''Dean of Advertising.''

In 1905, Calkins published *Modern Advertising* with Holden, acknowledged to be the first real textbook in advertising and its associated processes. In 1908, he was the primary organizer of an exhibit of advertising art at the National Arts Club in New York City. This was a completely new concept: the notion of advertising art as a legitimate art form. He was the first recipient of the Edward Bok Gold Medal for distinguished service to advertising in 1925.

Calkins' partner Holden died in 1926. Calkins' firm was then merged into the Interpublic Group of Companies, Incorporated. Calkins retired from the advertising business five years after Holden's death. He recalled later that his decision was precipitated by the advent and popularity of radio. As a deaf person, Calkins felt he would not have the intuition for what would work in radio advertising.

A rare book collector, Calkins pursued a wide range of personal interests, including art, sculpture, natural science, and model boat building. He himself was the author of numerous books, including *The Business of Advertising*, *The Advertising Man*, *Printing for Commerce*, and *Business the Civilizer*. In his 1924 autobiography *Louder Please*, and later in his book *And Hearing Not—Annals of an Adman* (1946), he set out to illustrate the ''disadvantages of being deaf by way of personal experiences and anecdotes, concluding that the assets far outweigh the liabilities.'' In *They Broke the Prairie* (1937), he fulfilled a forty-year-long dream of writing about the settlement and growth of the Upper Mississippi Valley, focusing on the town of Galesburg and Knox College. While writing this book, he constructed a wooden model of the original town. Woodworking was one of his many hobbies, along with gardening, beekeeping, and numerous others, as he described in still another book, *On the Care and Feeding of Hobby Horses*. He often remarked that his deafness led him to pursue many areas of interest, and that he found pleasure in anything his eyes and hands could behold.

Calkins published many articles in periodicals as well. In ''Deaf, But Not Dumb,'' which was one of more than fifty articles he published in *Atlantic Monthly*, he wrote a humorous essay on deafness in July, 1939, including the challenges of socializing with hearing people, and a list of others he drily called the ''underhearing'' who had made their mark in a variety of fields. He also published on food, European travel, and fine printing. In the letter columns of the *New York Times*, he wrote on traffic lights, wise investing, and numerous other areas. He served as a biographer in the *Volta Review*, a journal for educators and parents of deaf children, with his column "Lives of the Deafened," featuring such individuals as *Harper's Weekly* writer Edward Sandford Martin, British author Harriet Martineau,* and the eminent artist Sir Joshua Reynolds, many of whom were hard-of-hearing or progressively deafened and who faced challenges in adjusting to life as late-deafened individuals. He gave many lectures to civic and community groups on the subject of deaf people and deafness. A title from a 1921 lecture, typical of his whimsical style, was called "The Technique of Being Deaf." A friend said that until his death at the age of ninety-six, he was still sitting up, writing humorous letters and notes on his own typewriter.

He died on October 4, 1964, in New York City.

References

Calkins, E. E. (1924). *"Louder, please!" The autobiography of a deaf man*. Boston: The Atlantic Monthly Press.

Calkins, E. E. (1946). *"And hearing not"—Annals of an adman*. New York: C. Scribner's Sons.

Carson, G. (1981). Earnest Elmo Calkins. In J. A. Garraty (Ed.). *Dictionary of American biography* (Suppl. 7, pp. 101–102). New York: Charles Scribner's Sons.

Davies, L. A. (1923). Successful deaf people of today: Earnest Elmo Calkins. *Volta Review*, 25 (1), 1–4

"Earnest Calkins, ad pioneer, dead." *New York Times*, October 6, 1964, L39.

ANNIE JUMP CANNON (1863–1941), American Astronomer.

Annie Jump Cannon was born in Dover, Delaware, on December 11, 1863, the oldest of three siblings. Her father, Wilson Lee Cannon, was a shipbuilder and Lieutenant Governor of the state of Delaware. Annie's mother, Mary (Jump) Cannon, was herself interested in astronomy and had taken a course in astronomy at the Friends' School. She and the child Annie spent many hours studying the constellations using the attic of their house as an observatory. By candlelight, Annie studied an old astronomy book to learn to recognize the stars. As a student at Wellesley College from 1880 to 1884, she became further enamored of physics and astronomy. One of the foremost women scientists of the nineteenth century, Professor Sarah F. Whiting, was her mentor, and it was she who interested Cannon in the science of spectroscopy.

Cannon's deafness was commonly believed by contemporaries to have resulted from exposure to the harsh winter cold during her first year at Wellesley. She experienced a progressive loss of hearing, but she accommodated and appeared to have a natural ability in speechreading. Her deafness became very severe by middle age, and, coincidentally or by hereditary disposition, her brother at Yale also lost his hearing following a cold. They were the only two deaf members of the Cannon family. At astronomical conventions, which she loved to attend, Cannon's deafness steered her primarily toward one-to-one conversations, but did nothing to discourage her from making many friends. Fellow scientists noted that she was almost completely deaf without a hearing aid and suggested that this fostered her great power of concentration.

After graduation, she spent a decade at home and she established reading clubs in Dover. She was a beautiful young woman, and her family and friends had expected one of her many courtships to end in marriage. The fact that she never married may have been related to the death of an intelligent young man whom she was seeing while at Wellesley. She continued to refer to him and memorialize him until her own death.

In 1893, her first intellectual companion, her mother, died, leaving her disillusioned, unable to read or find meaning in those things that had previously been a source of pleasure in Dover. The following year, she returned to Wellesley to assist in physics, most of her time being spent with X-ray experimentation. Following the advice of Edward Pickering, the director of the Harvard College Observatory, she continued her studies at Radcliffe, and he appointed her to the observatory staff in 1896. She spent her entire career there.

Cannon quickly became a popular collaborator; the staff found her a pleasure to work with. She soon realized that deafness was no barrier in the field of astronomy—the stars were fascinating company. During her early years at the Observatory, she sharpened her skills in studying variable stars. She became curator of astronomical photographs in 1911 and continued with this responsibility for several decades.

One of the most extensive efforts to classify the stars is Pickering's *Henry Draper Catalogue*, which provides the positions, magnitudes, and spectra of 225,300 stars. That invaluable reference for astronomers covers the heavens from pole to pole for all stars brighter than the eighth magnitude and many fainter stars, and provides data on distances, distributions, and motions. Scientists investigating the colors, temperatures, sizes, and compositions of stars frequently refer to the *Henry Draper Catalogue* for its spectral information. Development of the *Catalogue* was a colossal challenge—nearly a quarter of a million stars had to be classified. After the equipment was readied in both hemispheres, Pickering chose Cannon as the principal investigator for the project. In this capacity, she not only identified, recorded, and indexed the data on the stars, she also supervised the publication of all nine volumes. Cannon examined every single one of these spectra.

When Cannon began her classification of the stars, she revised the symbols used for the spectral types. Originally, Williamina Fleming had used letters of the alphabet and Antonia C. Maury employed Roman numerals. Cannon reordered the classes in terms of decreasing surface temperature. The "Draper Classification" scheme she devised was first introduced in her *Catalogue of the Spectra of 1122 Stars* and it was adopted internationally. Only slight modifications have been made to the system since. Cannon's use of the spectral image

Annie Jump Cannon (far right) and Henrietta Swan Leavitt* (third from left), American astronomers. Photo from *New England Magazine, 6* (1892).

was remarkably efficient. She was capable of classifying more than three stars per minute. Improved observational techniques made it possible to photograph fainter stars and Cannon eventually added another 10,000 in the *Henry Draper Extension.*

Cannon was the first woman to receive the Henry Draper Medal for "notable investigations in astronomical physics." Cannon's contributions in the field of spectroscopy are unsurpassed in quantity. Probably no other single observer in the history of science gathered so great a mass of data on a single system. Cecilia H. Payne-Gaposchkin (1941) complimented Cannon in this way: "The system of the spectral classification of the stars that it [*Henry Draper Catalogue*] contains represents a work comparable to the system of classification of living things that was made by Linnaeus." Patience, not genius, was responsible for her success, Cannon countered modestly. Many view Cannon's pioneering work forever upheld for its thoroughness in the *Henry Draper Catalogue.*

Cannon labored for years at the 6-inch telescope at the Harvard College Observatory and at the facilities established by Harvard in Arequipa, Peru, where she photographed the stars near the South celestial pole not visible from the United States. In the process, Cannon discovered many variable stars and novae. Her love for her work was revealed in her writing and in her presentations. She wrote the biography of her colleague Solon Irving Bailey for the National Academy of Sciences.

Cannon not only classified one-third of a million stars, but she discovered more than 300 variable stars, five novae, and many stars with peculiar spectra. One nova was found while she was at the Arequipa observatory in 1922, the year after Pickering died.

Cannon won many honors for her work. Campbell (1941) called her the "world's most notable woman astronomer." In 1925, she received an honorary Doctor of Science degree from Oxford University, the first woman to receive one in its 600-year history. Other honorary degrees were conferred upon her from the University of Groningen in Holland, University of Delaware, Oglethorpe University, and Mount Holyoke College. Wellesley presented her with the degree of Doctor of Laws in 1925. She was active in many professional organizations, including the American Philosophical Society, the American Astronomical Society which she served as treasurer for many years, the International Astronomical Union, and the American Association of Variable Star Observers, from which she received the Nova Medal in 1922. Cannon was an honorary member of the Royal Astronomical Society in England, one of only six people ever to receive such a status since the Society's establishment in 1820. In 1938, she was appointed William Cranch Bond Astronomer for her distinguished service at the Harvard College Observatory. When she was awarded the Ellen Richards Research Prize in 1932, she used the money to establish the Annie Jump Cannon Prize presented to women astronomers by the American Astronomical Society.

The hard-earned honors received by Cannon came primarily from outside the

Harvard College Observatory. Although she encountered the same discrimination that challenged other women of her time, Cannon was a deaf woman during the heyday of Social Darwinism, and she faced additional attitudinal barriers to her advancement and professional recognition; in particular, her status as a "defective," as discussed in the correspondence of several leading eugenicists in the early 1920s [see Lang (1994)], seems to have prevented her from being nominated as a member of the National Academy of Sciences. Pickering did everything in his power to gain her recognition. In addition to crediting her work in his reports, he wrote to President Lowell in 1911, encouraging him to appoint her Curator of Astronomical Photographs, replacing Williamina Fleming, and to give her a corporation appointment. Lowell did not give Cannon the appointment. Harlow Shapley, Pickering's successor at the Observatory, also felt strongly that Cannon deserved greater recognition at Harvard. To gain her further visibility, Shapley encouraged other universities to award Cannon honorary degrees. Her six honorary degrees, Draper Medal of the National Academy of Sciences, and several women's awards highlighted an embarrassing status inconsistency and put pressure on Harvard.

It was not until 1938, three years before her death, that Cannon received the William Cranch Bond Astronomer Award and a corporation appointment from Harvard.

In a 1941 issue of *The Telescope*, Cecilia H. Payne-Gaposchkin paid her the ultimate compliment: "Miss Cannon has mapped the field; and if the view that we see is distant and splendid, it is because we stand upon her shoulders."

Annie Jump Cannon, the "Dean of Women Astronomers," died on Easter Sunday, April 13, 1941.

References

Campbell, L. (1941). Annie Jump Cannon. *Popular Astronomy, 49* (7), 345–347.

Hoffleit, D. (1971). Annie Jump Cannon. In E. T. James, J. W. James, & P. S. Boyer (Eds.). *Notable American women, 1607–1950: A biographical dictionary* (Vol. II). Cambridge, MA: The Belknap Press.

Lang, H. G. (1994). *Silence of the spheres: The deaf experience in the history of science.* Westport, CT: Bergin & Garvey.

Payne-Gaposchkin, C. (1941). Miss Cannon and stellar spectroscopy. *The Telescope, 8,* 62–63.

Yost, E. (1943). Annie Jump Cannon (1863–1941). *American women of science* (pp. 27–43). Philadelphia: Frederick A. Stokes.

JOHN CARLIN (1813–1891), American Painter/Writer

John Carlin was born on June 15, 1813, in Philadelphia and deafened in infancy. His brother, Andrew, born a few years later, was similarly deaf. At the age of seven, the abandoned Carlin was picked up with a group of fifteen deaf street children by David G. Seixas, a Philadelphia crockery dealer, who fed and clothed them and organized a private school. The school became the Pennsylvania School for the Deaf, the third such program established for deaf pupils in the United States. Carlin graduated in 1825, then began a thorough study of drawing at John R. Smith's academy, and portrait and genre painting at the Artist's Fund Society in Philadelphia. His father, a sometime cobbler, was unable to support him; and Carlin secured employment as a sign and house painter for seven years in order to pay for his art education. He also studied portrait painting under John Neagle in New York City.

In 1838, Carlin traveled to London to study objects of antiquity in the British Museum, and to Paris for further study of portrait painting under Paul Delaroche. Despite his deafness, he was able to use the French he had learned earlier to assist Delaroche in communicating with another American who knew little of that language. Under Delaroche, he illustrated in outlines such works as *Paradise Lost* and *Pilgrim's Progress*. He practiced his own verse while illustrating these epic works, although he described himself as discouraged by what he saw as discordance. He often discussed this difficulty with hearing writers and concluded that it was a result of his profound deafness: "I was convinced that I could never be what I so ardently desired—a correct writer of verses."

Carlin returned to America in 1841 to set up a studio in New York. In the winter of 1842 he traveled to Springfield, Massachusetts, where he met the Reverend B. O. Peabody, who took an interest in Carlin's pursuit of poetic writing. Peabody directed him toward rhyming and pronouncing dictionaries, while the poet William Cullen Bryant personally advised him to read the renowned English poets. Carlin found such advice a valuable guide, producing poetry that was widely published in the newspapers. "A Scene on Long Island Sound," published in *The American Reader*, was described by Edward Miner Gallaudet as "remarkable for a certain majesty of movement."

In 1841, Carlin established himself as a painter of miniatures with his own studio in New York City. In 1843, he married a deaf woman and eventually raised a family of five children. His miniature portraits on ivory brought him success, with many diplomats from the nation's capitol commissioning him for paintings. Jefferson Davis, then Secretary of War under President Pierce, requested that Carlin paint his son's portrait. Carlin developed friendships with Pierce's wife and many men of renown, including ˙William H. Seward, Thurlow Weed, Horace Greeley, and Hamilton Fish.

Carlin's poetry and articles on architecture were published in the *Philadelphia Saturday Courier*. A number of his educational writings were published in the *American Annals of the Deaf*, including his poem "The Mute's Lament" in the journal's first issue in 1847, prompting Luzerne Ray, the editor, to remark that a deaf poet was such a rarity in this time that it may be compared with a man born blind who paints a picture. William Cullen Bryant even congratulated Carlin on his success. Carlin is also known for a novel, *The Scratchside Family*, a book written for children. He lectured on subjects ranging from geology to New York Central Park, and published many columns in leading periodicals in the Deaf community, often using the pseudonym "Raphael Palette," especially

John Carlin, American painter and writer. Drawing from *Harper's New Monthly Magazine, 68* (406), 1884.

when he argued with others on teaching methods. Possibly a result of his frustrations in attempting to learn from teachers who used their individual invented signs during the earliest days in the formal education of deaf children in the United States, Carlin was opposed to sign language in teaching, preferring fingerspelling and speechreading. Despite this attitude, he nevertheless signed many of his lectures in what he described as a "simple, yet forceful, manner." He was in demand for such presentations. Active in the Deaf community, he helped raise $6,000 for St. Ann's Episcopal Church for the Deaf in New York City; and, later, he assisted in raising funds for the Gallaudet Home for Aged and Infirm Deaf.

Carlin's works of art have been exhibited throughout the Northeast. He contributed a side panel in the monument to Thomas Hopkins Gallaudet, representing Gallaudet teaching fingerspelling to young deaf children. When photography made the painting of miniature portraits an obsolete and unprofitable art form, Carlin turned to portraits and landscape subjects. His oil on canvas, *After a Long Cruise* (1857), was purchased by New York's Metropolitan Museum of Art in 1949. The painting shows the drunken antics of a group of sailors on leave from their ship. Other important works by Carlin include *The Flight into Egypt, Dolce far Niente, The Admirer of Nature, The View of Trenton Falls, The Orphaned Grandchild,* and *The Village Gossips,* several which were exhibited at the 1934 International Exhibition of Fine and Applied Arts by Deaf Artists at the Roerich Museum in New York City. For many years, one of his best works hung on a wall at the old Fanwood School for the Deaf before the school moved to White Plains. It is a large painting of a Roman sentry tempted to conceal the resurrection of Christ by blocking the empty tomb. His portrait of Laurent Clerc,* the first deaf teacher in the United States, which Carlin painted around the time of the Civil War, was acquired by the Kentucky School for the Deaf for their chapel. Carlin was the only artist considered by the school to paint the revered Clerc.

Carlin delivered an address in sign language at the inauguration of the National Deaf-Mute College (Gallaudet University) in Washington, D.C. This was a special moment in his life. He had actively encouraged Gallaudet to establish this program in higher education, publishing on this in the *American Annals of the Deaf*. At the inauguration, he began, ''Mr. President, ladies and gentlemen: On this day, the 28th of June, 1864, a college for deaf-mutes is brought into existence. . . . I thank God for this privilege of witnessing the consummation of my wishes—the establishment of a college for deaf-mutes—a subject which has for past years occupied my mind.'' At the ceremony, Carlin received the first honorary degree granted by this institution.

In 1864, Carlin also had founded the Manhattan Literary Association of Deaf Mutes, whose purpose was to stimulate thinking and promote social intercourse among deaf scholars. He, James Nack,* John Burnet, and Charlotte Elizabeth Tonna* were pioneer deaf poets—founders who helped to break down the formidable attitude barrier of the day. They clearly proved that being a deaf person was no obstacle in the creation of powerful texts.

Carlin died of pneumonia on April 23, 1891.

References

''Death of John Carlin.'' (1891). *The Silent Worker*, *4* (31), 2.

Domich, H. (1946). John Carlin: A biographical sketch. *The American Era*, *32* (4), 37–40.

Hills, P. (1974). *The painter's America: Rural and urban life, 1810–1910*. New York: Praeger Publishers.

GEORGE CATLIN (1796–1872), American Painter/Writer.

George Catlin was born on July 26, 1796, in Wilkes-Barre, Pennsylvania, the son of Putnam Catlin, who served in the colonial forces during the Revolutionary War. When George was one year old, his adventurous and resilient mother carried him in her arms as the family traveled by horseback over an Indian trail to Ona-qua-gua Valley, Broome County, New York, where they settled. He was the fifth of fourteen children. Catlin grew up in a cultured home, surrounded by friends who were hunters, trappers, Revolutionary War soldiers, and explorers. Through their stories, he developed a romantic lifelong attachment to Native American culture. He studied law in 1817–1818 in Litchfield, Connecticut, continuing in Pennsylvania, but a passion for painting attracted him to Philadelphia in 1823. There, he joined such artists as Thomas Sully, John Nagle, Charles Willson Peale, and Rembrandt Peale. Catlin studied at the Pennsylvania Academy of Fine Arts and was quite successful as a miniature painter on ivory. Among the subjects of his portraits were Mrs. Madison in a turban, as well as De Witt Clinton, Governor of New York and commissioner of the Erie Canal. Catlin married Clara B. Gregory in 1828, who supported his work tirelessly, often to the consternation of her wealthy family.

The following year, Catlin began a nine-year adventure and painting excursion in the West, living among Native Americans, traders, trappers, and hunters. In 1830, he accompanied Governor Clark, Superintendent of Indian Affairs, to discuss treaties at meetings held with the Winnebagoes and Menomonees, the Shawnees, Sacs, and Foxes; it was at this time that he began the series of portrait paintings for which he is renowned. His portraits included Black Hawk and his warriors, while they were still prisoners of war in 1832. While visiting and painting ten tribes during a two-thousand-mile canoe trip, he discovered the red pipestone, now called *Catlinite* in his honor by the Smithsonian Institution. He traveled to Fort Laramie, painting the Pawnees, Omahas, and Otoes; and accompanied a regiment of mounted dragoons to the Comanches and other tribes. Along the Mississippi, he painted members of the Sioux and Ojibway nations. In 1837, he was on the coast of Florida with the Seminoles and Euchees, then went on to Charleston to paint Osceola and other Seminoles. Members of at least thirty-eight tribes sat for more than 600 portraits by Catlin, most of them in a collection now in the United States National Museum (the Smithsonian Institution).

Catlin was as much a source of curiosity to many Native Americans he visited as they were to him. His intensity as he worked on canvas and his skill in reproduction were much admired. His ability to capture expression and movement in the eyes of his models was a source of discussion. He was honored by the Mandans as ''Te-ho-pe-nee Wash-ee,'' or ''Medicine Man.'' Similar names were given him by the Sioux at Fort Pierre.

Catlin supported himself by painting portraits and by the sale of his books. His wife accompanied him on his 1834 expeditions and for three years after that, and she aided him in research for his books. In 1838, he recorded the last moments of the Seminole warrior *Os-ce-o-la* as he made signs on his deathbed to his wives and children. In this year, a resolution was introduced in the U.S. Congress to purchase the unfortunately named ''Catlin Collection of Indian Portraits & Curiosities,'' but it was not passed. Through the years, however, he had made friends with such important men as Henry Clay, Daniel Webster, and William H. Seward. He left for England with his Indian Gallery in 1839 and he rented gallery rooms in Egyptian Hall, Piccadilly, where he exhibited his paintings and met with visitors throughout the day to answer questions.

Catlin's experiences and observations during his years in the West were documented in his first book, *Letters and Notes on the Manners, Customs and Conditions of the North American Indians* (1841), which went through many editions in the years to follow. He regarded his own goal in his work as introducing Native American people to mainstream culture in the most carefully observed way. He wanted his representations to capture moods, relationships, and everyday life, not simply ceremonial or colorful subjects. He hoped that his notes as well as his paintings would make some contribution.

In the late 1840s, both his beloved wife and his son died. His in-laws removed his three young daughters from his care. By 1848, he himself was nearly completely deaf. Catlin was bankrupted in London in 1852, from which he never recovered. Because of his deafness, his acquaintances in London, who formerly enjoyed his wit and companionship, began to drift away. Ill, isolated, and depressed from a decade of misfortune, he mysteriously disappeared from his home in Paris, and biographers feel that he experienced some type of breakdown. He sought refuge in the wilderness. Between 1852 and 1857, the deafened artist traveled through South and Central America with an escaped slave from Havana, but the native people he wished to study there often resisted his invitations to sit for portraits. Nevertheless, he was able to make sketches of members of more than thirty tribes.

In the meantime, his friend, von Humboldt, encouraged him to pursue some questions relative to the origin of the Gulf Stream, which the great geographer was then too old to investigate himself. Catlin published a book on this subject, *The Lifted and Subsided Rocks of America, With Their Influence on the Oceanic, Atmospheric, and Land Currents.* The rather convoluted treatise was a complete failure, receiving withering criticism by scientists who, logically, questioned why an artist was reporting on geological formations. Catlin also wrote the two-volume *Eight Years' Travel and Residence in Europe* and a small book on Native Americans and sleep, *The Breath of Life* (1865). *Life Among the Indians* (1867) and *Last Rambles Amongst the Indians of the Rocky Mountains and the Andes* (1867) were considerably more well received. Catlin has also been credited for choosing the Yellowstone region for a park.

In 1871, after thirty-two years out of the United States, he returned. His dream of having his collection hung in the National Museum was realized only after a long struggle. Joseph Henry at the Smithsonian Institution invited him to exhibit his work, with the purpose of having the Government purchase the entire collection of more than 1,200 paintings and sketches. The George Catlin Indian Gallery of the United States National Museum included his first collection of pictures and other articles given to the Smithsonian Institution by Mrs. Joseph Harrison, Jr. Her husband had advanced the funds to purchase Catlin's collection, which had been seized for debt in London. Finally, all the paintings were hung. Unfortunately, Catlin's remuneration was still being debated in Congress, and, old and ill, his time was running out.

Catlin died in Jersey City, New Jersey, on December 23, 1872, finally reunited with his daughters. McCracken (1959) described him as the ''Pioneer and dean of documentary artists.'' His detailed depictions of Native Americans, as well as his notes, provided invaluable information for ethnographers who followed.

References

Catlin-Roehm, M. (1966). *The letters of George Catlin and his family: A chronicle of the American West.* Berkeley: University of California Press.

McCracken, H. (1959). *George Catlin and the Old Frontier.* New York: The Dial Press.

Youmans, W. J. (Ed.). (1896). George Catlin. In *Pioneers of science in America: Sketches of their lives and scientific work* (pp. 336–346). New York: D. Appleton.

PAUL-FRANÇOIS CHOPPIN (1856–1937), French Sculptor.

Paul-François Choppin was born on February 26, 1856. His father was a lawyer. Choppin was deafened at the age of two, when a nurse accidentally dropped him. He was enrolled in the Paris Institution for the Deaf at the age of nine, where he applied himself and was considered a model student. In 1873, he left the Paris Institution and began study in the School of Decorative Arts, where he won two medals He then studied under Jouffroy and Jean-Alexandre Falguière at École des Beaux Arts, where he won three more medals in different competitions. His rise to success as a sculptor was meteoric. Choppin was a regular contributor at the annual Salon exhibitions in Paris from its establishment in 1877. He was commissioned to execute a bust of the celebrated lawyer Guy-Coquille, which adorns the facade of the Faculté de Droite in Paris.

At the Paris Exhibition of 1886, thirteen deaf artists exhibited their works, prompting critic Théophile Denis to remark in *Revue Français* that the proportion of successful artists among deaf people appeared to be four times greater than that among the hearing population of France. Choppin won honorable mention at the Exhibition for *The Genius of Arts*, which was later purchased by the museum in Poitiers. In 1888, *A Conquerer of the Bastille* won him a medal. This sculpture in bronze was later erected in one of the Parisian public gardens. He was given the purple ribbon and the title of Officier of the Academy. The following year, he won a bronze medal at the Universal Exposition for *A Volunteer of 1792*, later erected in a public park in Remiremont.

In the competition for the execution of the statue of Sergeant Bobillot, who fell at Tonquin, Choppin won honorable mention, as he did in the competition for the monument of Lazare Carno at Wattignies. Moreover, he was one of the finalists for the monument to Danton in Paris. For the natural pose he had suggested for Danton, Choppin received much praise by the critic J. Cardane in an 1888 issue of *Le Soleil*. While he did not receive the Danton commission, Choppin was soon unanimously awarded the contract over sixty competitors for the erection of the statue of Paul Broca, the great anthropologist. Broca's statue was erected on Boulevarde St. Germain in Paris with the legend, "Man is Mortal—Science Endures." An engraving of his statue of Broca was subsequently included in *Salon Illustré* and *Revue Français*.

In the 1889 Paris Salon, Choppin entered a bronze statue of Commander Marchand and a religious portrait sculpture titled *Feu Soeur Dorothée*. At this time, he began to produce more work with religious overtones in addition to the historical memorials for which he was famous. In 1890, he exhibited a marble statue of St. Cecile. His fame was increasing at the rate of his productivity, and he was becoming internationally renowned. In the United States, Alexander Graham Bell wrote to Edward Miner Gallaudet in October, 1893, encouraging Gallaudet to approach Congress with a proposal to have a work of Choppin's placed in a public location in the United States.

In 1899, Choppin's plaster bust of the late Monsieur Lartigue was exhibited at the Paris Salon; also exhibited was a plaster vase with a mythological theme, *The Nereids*, a massive but beautiful sculpted work, populated by sea nymphs, gods, and dolphins playing among crashing waves. The imposing and very decorative monument to Lartigue was erected in the town of Givet, and Choppin was praised for the scholarly preparation and research that captured the personality of Lartigue. In 1900, he exhibited a small terra cotta bust titled *Cupidon* at the Paris Salon, and in 1902, his allegorical figure *La France Militaire* was exhibited. The following year, he was represented by *Ondine*, a terra cotta bust, and *Châtelaine Henri II*, a terra cotta statuette. At that time he was also promoted to Officier of Public Instruction in the Academy. *Portrait of M. Adolphe Deslandres, Musical Composer,* a bronze bust, soon followed in 1904. At the Paris Salon of 1906, he exhibited a bust of General Fournier-Sarlovèze and a small terra cotta statue titled *Bacchus Enfant*. Ironically, Choppin often hid the fact that he was deaf, out of fear that his rivals would claim that he won by virtue of the sympathy of the judges, rather than for his talents. In 1907, Choppin's statue of Jacobo Pereire teaching a young deaf boy was exhibited. In the United States, the eminent American sculptor Douglas Tilden* described Choppin's success in the *American Annals of the Deaf*, writing that "if France does not boast a college for the deaf like ours [Gallaudet], art education among the deaf certainly rises correspondingly high."

Other Choppin sculptures are also found in museums in Roanne and Dieppe, a public garden in Montsouris, and the School of Medicine in Paris. The museum at the National Institution for the Deaf in Paris, from which he graduated, holds many of his works, including busts of Ladreit de Lacharrière and Ernest Javal, and statues titled *La France Militaire* and *Châtelaine Under Henry II,* as well as one of Etienne Dolet.

Choppin died in 1937.

References

Boyer, A. (1909). Paul Choppin. *Revue Générale de L'Enseignement des Sourds-Muets,* *10* (10), 205–208.

Halbertsam, L. (1940, March). Paul Choppin—Deaf sculptor. *Digest of the Deaf,* 28–31.

JOHN LOUIS CLARKE (1881–1970), American Wood Sculptor.

John Louis Clarke was a Blackfoot Indian born on January 20, 1881, in Highwood, Montana, not far from Great Falls. Clarke's grandfather, Captain Malcolm Clarke, was a European-American graduate and classmate of William

T. Sherman at West Point. Malcolm Clarke married the daughter of a Blackfoot chief and was later murdered by the Piegans. His father, Horace Clarke, was shot and left for dead at the time of Malcolm Clarke's death; he later lived on the Blackfoot lands, devoting his life to advocating for the rights of his tribe. Horace Clarke married Margaret Spanish, whose Blackfoot name was First Kill, the daughter of Chief Stands Alone.

Clarke was deafened at the age of two by scarlet fever. His first communication was through Indian sign language and drawings when he studied at the Fort Shaw Indian School. As a child, he modeled wild animals from clay found in the river beds of the Highwood Mountains. Clarke entered the North Dakota School for the Deaf at Devil's Lake at the age of thirteen. After three years there, he transferred to the Montana School for the Deaf, where he first began to show his talents in woodcarving. He completed his education at the St. Francis Academy for the Deaf in Milwaukee, Wisconsin. His Blackfoot name was "Catapuis," or "Man-Who-Talks-Not," reflecting the fact that he preferred never to use his voice. By then, Clarke had learned American Sign Language, which he used to communicate with family and friends throughout his life. He also studied for a short time at the Chicago Art Institute, where he became thoroughly bored sketching fruit in still life drawing classes. He quit. In about 1900, he was employed in a Milwaukee factory, where he carved altars for churches.

Talented in oils, charcoals, pastels, and clay, he found particular interest in wood. In 1913, Clarke set up a studio in East Glacier Park, where he would often be found riding his jeep around East Glacier, searching for burled wood and interestingly twisted branches. His ability had first been discovered by Louis Hill, son of a railroad builder, who found Clarke carving a grizzly bear out of wood. His wife assisted Clarke in setting up exhibitions and hosting tourists at their studio home.

Clarke's love for wildlife inspired him to carve their likenesses in maple, walnut, and especially cottonwood. Some pieces he stained or painted; on others he took advantage of the natural characteristics found in the wood. The imperfections became humps, paws, ears, and tails. In 1916, he held his first exhibit in Helena, Montana. His reputation quickly spread to the East when Mary C. Wheeler, a Helena art teacher, sent one of Clarke's animal groups to Dr. Maria M. Dean in New York. The composition attracted the attention of W. Frank Purdy of the American School of Sculpture, who made many connections for the artist. In 1918, Clarke won a gold medal from the American Art Galleries of Philadelphia for a carving of a bear, which included such detail as hair. His three wood carvings in the thirty-fifth annual exhibition of American paintings and sculpture at the Chicago Art Institute on November 2, 1923, was praised by the Associated Press as a notable feature of the exhibit. These carvings included a mother bear, with her cub nestled in her arms, and a puma's dramatic battle with a grizzly bear. The following year, John D. Rockefeller, Jr., purchased four of Clarke's carvings; one of a walking bear was sent to the permanent exhibit at the Chicago Art Institute. The sculpted animal was about three

John L. Clarke, American wood sculptor. Photo from *The Silent Worker,*
2 (2), 1949, courtesy of Gallaudet University Archives.

feet high and weighed nearly 150 pounds, requiring many months to complete.
President Warren G. Harding had already acquired a carving by Clarke of an
eagle holding an American flag. In 1925, Clarke won a gold medal from the
American Art Gallery of Philadelphia, and he exhibited at the Palace of Fine
Arts and the New York Academy of Design. In 1927, his works were shown at
the Biltmore Salon at Los Angeles and at galleries in Chicago and Tulsa,
Oklahoma. Howard H. Hays, president of the Glacier Park Transport Company,
purchased one of Clarke's Rocky Mountain goats in 1932, which he later presented to the Museum of the Plains Indian at Browning.

Occasionally, Clarke would follow his whims, abandoning his sculptures to
build a boat for fishing on Two Medicine Lake. As with his artistic pieces, he
would work on everyday chores and recreational projects to the point of ex-

haustion. Some of his sculptures were based on his own experiences with animals in the wild; others were produced after his father told him stories, such as his carving of a lion and a bear fighting. In 1933, he carved a bust of his friend the Blackfoot Chief Two-Guns-White-Calf.

As Clarke was known internationally as a leading sculptor in wood, carvers came from around the world to study his techniques. In 1934, he joined deaf artists from all over the world in the International Exhibition of Fine and Applied Arts by Deaf Artists at the Roerich Museum in New York City. Clarke showed three watercolor paintings, including *Rising Wolf Mountain* and *Goat on Mountain*; and seven wood carvings, among them *Grey Wolf, Mother and Cub*, and *Big Horn Sheep*. Upon his death, unfinished pieces and his tools were helpful in understanding how Clarke approached the carving of anatomically accurate animals. Among his friends was the hearing western artist Charles Russell, who was also skilled in Indian sign language, and the two of them would often converse comfortably. Clarke's work in wood has often been compared to Russell's on canvas in terms of the realistic portrayal of animals. Clarke once attended a convention of deaf people and fascinated a large crowd with a presentation on Indian sign language with his Native American friends dressed in tribal costumes.

Some of Clarke's works are in a permanent collection at the Montana Institute of the Arts. At the fifth annual meeting of this institute in 1953, Clarke exhibited his work and conducted a workshop. Museums in Chicago, Kansas City, Boston, Los Angeles, New York, London, and Paris have displayed his works, and his western wildlife pieces can now be found in the Art Institute of Chicago, Montana Historical Society, and the Museum of the Plains Indian. Clarke's wood-carving career lasted for fifty-seven years. Unfortunately, in 1962, a fire broke out in the historic East Glacier dwelling of the late Helen P. Clarke, John L. Clarke's aunt, destroying many of his wood sculptures.

Clarke carved sculptures until the end of his life. His eyes clouded with cataracts in his last year, he produced mostly through the sense of touch a large grizzly springing itself from a trap.

The variety of media employed by Clarke was demonstrated in an exhibit at the Museum of the Plains Indian and Crafts Center in Browning, Montana, from August 30 until October 15, 1970. Sixteen of Clarke's sculptures and paintings were shown, including wood sculptures such as *Walking Bear*, wood reliefs (*Buffalo Hunt*), monochromed cast stone (*Reservation Man, Blackfoot Warrior*), watercolors (*Tree*), and oil on masonite (*Confrontation at Lake Josephine, Mountain Goats and Elk*).

He died on November 20, 1970, at Cut Bank, Montana, and was buried at East Glacier Cemetery, Glacier National Park. A year-long exhibit of his work was opened on December 4, 1993, by the Montana Historical Society in Helena, whose staff felt Clarke deserved more recognition than he had received during his lifetime. He is receiving overdue acclaim as one of the most innovative portrayers of Western wildlife.

References

Catapuis: John Clarke, Indian woodcarver. (1938). *Digest of the Deaf, 1* (1), 8–9.
Jokerst, G. (1994, April). The man who talks not. *Silent News,* 25.
Randles, A. R. (1949). John L. Clarke—The man who speaks not. *The Silent Worker, 2*
(2), 3–4.

LAURENT CLERC (1785–1869), American Educator.

Laurent Clerc was born in LaBalme, France, on December 26, 1785, the son of a notary and mayor. His parents believed he was deafened from a fever, which followed a fall into a fire during his first year of life. It is possible that he was born deaf. When Clerc was twelve years old, he was placed in the Royal Institution for the Deaf in Paris, the first government-sponsored school in the world. There, he was taught by the brilliant deaf teacher Jean Massieu under the superintendency of the Abbé Roch-Ambroise Sicard, successor to Abbé de l'Epée. Sicard was in prison when Clerc arrived at the school. As a priest, Sicard was expected to be beheaded with other followers of the old order during the Terror at the heat of the French Revolution. Jean Massieu and a cadre of students took a letter to the court, describing Sicard's worth as a teacher of deaf pupils, thus saving Sicard's life.

Upon completion of his studies, Clerc became an assistant teacher at the Royal Institution and was responsible for the advanced class. In 1815, Sicard, still a royalist, took temporary self-exile in London with Clerc and Massieu, as Napoleon planned to overthrow the king of France. It was in London that they met Thomas Hopkins Gallaudet in May of that year. A neighbor of Gallaudet's in Hartford, Connecticut, Dr. Mason Fitch Cogswell, had been very impressed by Gallaudet's rudimentary successes in teaching Alice Cogswell, his young deaf daughter. Cogswell subsequently helped to find funds to support Gallaudet's voyage to Europe for the purpose of examining methods of instruction then used by European educators of deaf pupils. Admiring Clerc's talents as a teacher, Gallaudet invited him to accompany him and embark on the major challenge of establishing a school for deaf pupils in the New World. Bidding farewell to his parents and other family and friends, Clerc left on a pioneering adventure. During the fifty-two-day-long voyage on the *Mary Augusta,* he taught Gallaudet signs; and his American friend reciprocated with lessons in reading and writing English.

Clerc is revered among the American Deaf community as the nation's first deaf teacher. With Gallaudet, he opened the American School for the Deaf in Hartford, Connecticut, organizing the courses and evaluating and placing the first pupils. The sign language Clerc taught Gallaudet, which was used in this school, eventually evolved into American Sign Language (ASL). With Gallaudet voice-interpreting as he read Clerc's signs, Clerc presented many demonstrations of teaching methods he had found effective with deaf students in France. Through their efforts, great gains were realized in the education of deaf students in the United States.

Clerc worked tirelessly to seek funding for the school, since it was over-crowded with uneducated deaf children whose families could not afford tuition. Nor could the school pay the teachers' salaries. After eight months of speeches and demonstrations, Clerc had helped to raise about $5,000, and the Connecticut General Assembly provided another $5,000, the first U.S. appropriation for the education of children with disabilities. Clerc then met President James Monroe and Speaker Henry Clay of the House of Representatives, conversing with them in both French and English; and he was able to convince Clay to help sponsor an 1818 Congressional bill to secure $300,000 to erect buildings and begin an endowment for income. In addition to teaching and teacher training, Clerc helped to prepare other educators to establish new schools around the country. Clerc also served as principal of the Pennsylvania Institution in Philadelphia during a period in which they sought his expertise in shaping the curriculum. During this stay in Philadelphia, a portrait of Clerc, his wife Elizabeth, and their young daughter was completed by the eminent artist Charles Willson Peale. Throughout his career, Clerc published many reports on the education of deaf pupils. His deaf pupils went on to become distinguished educators, artists, poets, and founders of other schools.

In 1846, Clerc obtained leave from the American School for the Deaf to visit France, his third and last visit to his homeland. While he visited several other schools established in Bordeaux and St. Etienne, he was especially interested in the Institution in Paris where he had studied and taught. Through publications in the *American Annals of the Deaf*, he shared with his American colleagues his perceptions during his travels, particularly his encounters with his former teachers.

In 1850, more than two hundred of Clerc's former pupils honored him with an elaborate silver pitcher with an inscription expressing their appreciation for a man who had so generously left his home in France to devote his life to the deaf people in the United States.

Clerc retired with a pension in 1858. He served America well for more than half a century. One would find the gentle old man daily on the streets or in the reading-rooms of Hartford, ever pleasant in his friendships and involved in civic affairs. Yet, even in retirement, he continued to contribute to the education of deaf students in great ways. In June 1864, for example, then at the age of seventy-nine, Clerc presented an address at the inauguration of the National Deaf-Mute College (now Gallaudet University), sharing the excitement with the Deaf community in America at the revolutionary inception of higher education for deaf persons. Clerc himself had never had the opportunity to attend a college, although he received several honorary degrees.

Clerc died on July 18, 1869, after a long illness. For weeks, as he lingered on, he was able to see and insisted on talking and holding hands with the many friends who visited. Of his six children, only two survived him, the youngest daughter having died two weeks before her father. Honored with a monumental bust in bronze at the American School for the Deaf in Hartford, Clerc's memory lives on in the hearts and minds of the many deaf and hearing persons he has inspired in the century since his death.

References

Denison, J. (1874). The memory of Laurent Clerc. *American Annals of the Deaf, 19* (3), 238–244.
Golladay, L. (1980). Laurent Clerc: America's pioneer deaf teacher. *The Deaf American, 32* (7), 3–6.
Lane, H. (1984). *When the mind hears: A history of the deaf.* New York: Random House.
Turner, W. W. (1870). Laurent Clerc. *American Annals of the Deaf, 15* (1), 14–25.

HAROLD J. CONN (1886–1975), American Bacteriologist.

Harold J. Conn was born on May 29, 1886. When he was about eleven years old, while traveling with his family in Europe for a year, he first realized he was losing his hearing. At first the condition was an "inconvenience" since his teachers knew he could not hear them and never blamed him for inattentiveness. During recitations in class, he studied lessons for the next day. In his unpublished autobiography, he explained that he did not make many friends in high school because it was too difficult to communicate without raising voices. He described an increasing frustration as lectures, music, and radio became inaccessible to him, and his social life became more and more limited. Conn was haunted by the idea that in personal interactions, he could inadvertently say something wrong and hurt someone's feelings. Speechreading was difficult for him, and he blamed himself for being too logical to master it. Looking back on his life, he philosophically evaluated the question of whether he had mostly gained or lost by the onset of his deafness. He noted that a "disability" is more often inconvenient to one's interlocutors; and remarked that his wife had had to deal with more frustration than he. Conn believed that deafened people such as himself generally classified hearing persons into two groups: those who seem motivated to take the trouble to engage, and those who avoid the deaf person and the bother of finding a communication strategy.

During his high school years he made frequent trips to Hartford, fifteen miles from his home, to visit a doctor who hoped ("a vain hope," he thought) that he could arrest the course of his increasing deafness. His father presented him with a microscope and encouraged him to go to the laboratory to make preparations of slides. To his father's surprise, he figured a way to dry the preparations more quickly with alcohol, not realizing he had conceived a technique that usually had to be taught to older students. The episode seemed significant to him when he considered how, much later in life, he made a name for himself in connection with "microtechnic."

Conn's interest in biology led to an eventual specialization in bacteriology, but there were no courses in bacteriology being offered at Boston University or Johns Hopkins University, where his father had studied. When his father began to offer a course in bacteriology at Wesleyan, it had only been a few years since

Pasteur's groundbreaking work. Theobald Smith and others had begun to specialize in applications of bacteriology to medicine, but Conn, now an undergraduate at Wesleyan, turned his interest to agricultural bacteriology and was one of the first Americans to do so. He felt that soil bacteriology was wide-open for research. He was encouraged in this direction by the offer of an assistantship at Cornell University and the opportunity to study for a doctoral degree in soil bacteriology.

Although Conn made friends at Wesleyan, he felt many students were friendly only at a superficial level and in a patronizing manner. One of his acquaintances was also deaf, and Conn made an effort, with the encouragement of a member of the faculty, to help his fellow student. Describing this experience, Conn wrote in his autobiography that he was shocked by what he considered a "defeatist" attitude. He had little patience for deaf persons who did not take responsibility for learning or else felt that a different standard of performance was expected. In the face of this student's resistance, Conn gave up trying to assist him.

A physics professor of Conn could not understand how he turned in very good papers without hearing the lectures. The professor's own son, with normal hearing, stood near the bottom of the class. According to Conn, the professor probably did not realize that his lectures followed the textbook so closely that hearing was entirely unnecessary for anyone taking that course. Conn graduated from Wesleyan *summa cum laude*.

In 1908, he obtained an assistantship at Cornell (New York State School of Agriculture), studying under the agronomist T. L. Lyon, who had observed productivity differences of certain plots in the fields. Hypothesizing a possible relation to bacterial action, Lyon assigned the responsibility of investigating this to Conn. With few people knowledgeable about soil bacteriology at Cornell at the time, Conn turned to the library, reading everything he could find in both English and German. In December 1909, he accompanied his father to the Society of American Bacteriologists. His father had cofounded the Society ten years earlier and introduced Conn to experts, including K. F. Kellerman, who later proved to be a helpful acquaintance. Yet there was little at the conference that was useful to his research. H. A. Harding, a dairy bacteriologist from the New York State Agricultural Experiment Station at Geneva, shared with him some methods that were applicable to soil bacteriology. Harding suggested that Conn not focus on the few known species of bacteria, but investigate what he called "general soil flora."

Conn's first publication drew much attention. In it, he pointed out that, under certain conditions, soil bacteria increased while the soil was frozen, rather than decreasing as naturally expected. At Cornell, he established a bacteriological club which met monthly, although his hearing loss prevented him from benefitting much from the papers presented. In 1911, he completed his studies at Cornell and was offered positions at the Department of Agriculture in Washington, D.C., working with Kellerman, and at the Agricultural Experiment Station in Geneva, New York, with Harding. He chose the latter and remained in

Geneva for the rest of his life. Harding left in 1913, and R. S. Breed, who was supportive of his work, succeeded him. Along with his father and Harding, Conn included Breed as one of the persons who most inspired him.

For over a decade, Conn continued to study soil bacteria until he realized that his line of attack was not advancing practice to the extent that bacteriologists in dairy and medical areas were. Before 1920, he had devised a successful method of staining bacteria to make them visible under the microscope. This did not lead to revolutionary changes, but inspired him to examine the use of dyes which brought him much recognition in the field. Conn was flexible enough and pragmatic enough to realize that a "side line" could enable him to make a more lasting contribution to his field than work in his primary area of study.

In 1920, the first edition of the *Manual of Methods for Pure Culture Study of Bacteria* was published in looseleaf format to allow for frequent revision. The purpose of the manual was to list approved methods of studying cultures of bacteria in order to characterize them. Through its publication, Conn gained prestige and greatly influenced the development of methods used in bacterial classification and description. This work, and correspondence with R. T. Will of Rochester, New York, encouraged him to consider forming the Biological Stain Commission a few years later. The Commission tested bacteriological stains with the hope of decreasing the dependence on the German stains that had become hard to obtain as a result of World War I. With the assistance of a cadre of about thirty volunteers, Conn's work attracted the attention of the National Research Council, which took over the responsibility of continuing the undertaking.

The establishment of the Biological Stain Commission in November, 1921, was very important to Conn. He knew it would bring him recognition among fellow scientists, many his seniors; and, in retrospect, he considered this effort his greatest service to biological science. He recalled that at the time he wanted so much to hear the discussion in the meeting that he decided to try some new hearing aids. However, he found that his increasing deafness ran parallel to improvements in technology. As he continued to experiment with the more powerful aids, he remarked ironically that he "no more than broke even." In 1923, Conn published *Bacteriology*, a general treatment of the science. Within four years, the text (to which he had assigned second authorship to his father, who had begun it before his death), had gone through its fourth edition and brought him further recognition.

Conn published a number of other works in subsequent years, including *Biological Stains* (1925). He also played a key role in founding and editing the journal *Stain Technology*. In 1933, he republished a series of articles from the journal in a book titled *History of Staining*. Another book, *Staining Procedures*, was printed in looseleaf format over a period of years (1944–1955) and then published as a completely revised edition in 1960. In 1948, he retired from the Experiment Station. He kept busy editing *Stain Technology*, traveling to Rochester, New York, weekly where many of the stains were being tested and certified; and, as late as 1957, he edited the *Manual of Microbiological Methods.*

His deafness made Conn restless in retirement. Even television was useless to him. He took up painting for relaxation, producing a large volume of work. Conn's wife died in 1963. With his doorbell connected to a series of electric lights and a helper who stopped by for an hour each day to make phone calls for him, he continued to publish, including the *Manual of Microbiological Methods* and the second edition of *Biological Stains.*

His daughter, Jean, worked as an assistant to him for twenty years and became a successful bacteriologist herself.

Conn died on November 10, 1975.

References

Conn, H. J. "A religious scientist at the turn of the century: Herbert William Conn of Wesleyan University." Unpublished manuscript at American Society for Microbiology Archives.

Conn, H. J. Autobiography. Harold Joel Conn Papers (#22/2/661), Department of Manuscripts and University Archives, Cornell University Library.

Lang, H. G. (1994). *Silence of the spheres: The deaf experience in the history of science.* Westport, CT: Bergin & Garvey.

SIR JOHN WARCUP CORNFORTH (1917–   ), British Nobel Laureate in Chemistry.

John Warcup Cornforth was born in Sydney, Australia, on September 7, 1917, a descendant of a German minister who moved to New South Wales in the year 1832. The second of four children, he lived for a while in Sydney, and then his family moved to Armidale. He was in his early adolescence when his progressive hearing loss began. In later years, Cornforth remembered a high school teacher, Leonard Basser, who had interested him in chemistry and directed him toward a career where deafness might be of minimal importance. Cornforth could not hear lectures through his high school years. He read the literature on chemistry and conducted his own experiments.

By the age of fourteen, Cornforth had his own organic chemistry laboratory at home. Two years later, he entered Sydney University, and in 1937, he graduated with honors with a bachelor of science degree in chemistry. In 1939, Cornforth received one of two Exhibition Scholarships awarded for doctoral work at Oxford University in England. Rita Harradence, also from Sydney, received the second. Cornforth and Harradence, a successful organic chemist, were awarded their Ph.D.s in 1941 and were married the same year. By this time, he was almost completely deaf, and he was communicating primarily through speechreading and writing.

Cornforth's doctoral work focused on steroid synthesis. He was especially interested in researching the chemical structure of penicillin. In 1946, he joined the staff of Mill Hill Research Laboratories of Britain's Medical Research Council, where he spent sixteen years. During this period, he collaborated with Robert Robinson in investigating the synthesis of steroids. Even before his early studies with Robinson, Cornforth had discovered the basic reaction for the synthesis. He continued to work with Robinson when he took the Medical Research Council position, and together they completed the first total synthesis of nonaromatic steroids in 1951.

In 1962, Cornforth accepted the position of director of the Milstead Laboratory of Chemical Enzymology, established by Shell Research Ltd., at Sittingbourne in Kent. In collaboration with George Popjak, a biochemist at the Milstead Laboratory, Cornforth applied radioactive isotopes and demonstrated the pattern of incorporation of acetic acid into the ring structure of cholesterol. For this work, they were awarded the CIBA Medal of the Biochemical Society in 1965, the Stouffer Prize (1967), and the Davy Medal of the Royal Society in 1968. Between 1965 and 1971, Cornforth was also associate professor at the School of Molecular Science of the University of Warwick. In 1971, he accepted a visiting professorship at the University of Sussex; and four years later, he joined the permanent faculty at Sussex as a Royal Society Research Professor.

Cornforth's preference for professional communication is the medium of writing. The scientific impact of his work is conveyed in publications rather than in lectures. Probably in part due to his deafness, he has limited his public presentations. On the other hand, his deafness has also been viewed as an advantage to concentration and an asset to diligence. Cornforth has admitted that, although he is a good speechreader with his colleagues, he is less successful with strangers. In a personal interview with a Gallaudet chemistry student from Hong Kong who was writing a term paper, Cornforth explained that he never had the assistance of interpreters or notetakers while in the universities. He viewed lectures as inessential, explaining that by this he meant that, in terms of conveying information, the spoken word is inferior to printed, symbolic languages of science. Cornforth explained his belief that the structure of organic chemistry is like a "three-dimensional language" in which, for example, a chemist *feels* what it is like to be a molecule.

Cornforth's distinguished work in chemistry won for him wide recognition in scientific bodies. Among his many honors, he was elected a fellow of England's Royal Society in 1953, a foreign associate of the National Academy of Sciences in 1978, a member of the Australian Academy of Science in 1977, and a member of the Royal Netherlands Academy of Arts and Sciences in 1978. Awards and medals have been given to him by British, American, and French societies, including the Corday-Morgan Medal from the Chemical Society in 1953 and the Flintoff Medal in 1966. In 1967, he won the Royal Society's highest honor, the Godfrey Copley Medal, for his work in stereochemistry. He held the Pedler and Robert Robinson lectureships in 1968 and 1971, respectively. The American Chemical Society presented him with the Ernest Guenther Award in 1969. In France, he won the Prix Roussel Award in 1972. Also in 1972, Cornforth was made a Commander of the British Empire; and, in 1977,

John Warcup Cornforth, British Nobel Laureate in chemistry. Photo from *The Deaf American, 30* (6), 1978, courtesy of the National Association of the Deaf.

he was knighted. A prolific author, Cornforth has published several hundred scientific articles.

Cornforth's interest in stereochemistry led him to trace the chemical steps adopted by the living cell to form the molecule of cholesterol from the acetic acid molecule. In his Nobel Prize lecture, Cornforth explained that a note by Alexander Ogston published in a 1948 issue of *Nature* started his thinking on that topic. By combining chemical, biochemical, and physical techniques, Cornforth unlocked the mystery of the nature of enzyme catalysis. Enzymes are natural biological catalysts for speeding chemical reactions. Cornforth "marked" hydrogen atoms through the use of isotopes, and examined the chemical reactions and their relationships to cholesterol. He sought to understand how cholesterol is actually synthesized in the living cell. It was for this work that John Warcup Cornforth won the Nobel Prize in 1975, shared with his friend Vladimir Prelog.

Cornforth's research required concentrated effort and much was owed to the skill and dedication of his collaborators. He singled out three for special appreciation in his Nobel Prize presentation: George Popjak, his colleague and partner for more than 20 years; Herman Eggerer, with whom he cooperated over distances of thousands of kilometers; and his wife, Rita Harradence Cornforth, who offered not only unwavering support as a spouse but also superb execution of critical synthetic processes as a colleague.

Concluding his presentation, Cornforth remembered his teacher and friend

Robert Robinson, regretting that his untimely death had prevented his witnessing his collaborator's success. Cornforth, however, celebrated Robinson's life as one filled with curiosity and wonder and a deep respect for the chemistry of nature. These attributions seem apt for Cornforth, as well.

References

Cornforth, J. W. (1976). Asymmetry and enzyme action. *Science, 193* (4248), 121–125.
Elrel, E. L., & Mosher, H. S. (1975). The 1975 Nobel Prize for chemistry. *Science, 190* (4216), 772–774.
Lo, A. H. (1978). An interview with Professor John W. Cornforth. *The Deaf American, 30* (6), 3–8.
Nobel Foundation. (1975). *Le Prix Nobel*. Stockholm: Imprimerie Royale.

D

ROBERT DAVILA (1932–), American Educator.

Robert R. Davila was born on July 19, 1932, in San Diego, California, the son of Mexican-born parents who were migrant agricultural workers. His father died when he was six years old, and his mother raised the family of seven children. Davila was totally deafened through spinal meningitis at the age of eight. He later described how this apparent disruption would eventually give his family stability. With a deaf son attending the California School for the Deaf at Berkeley, the family decided to settle permanently in Carlsbad, California, north of San Diego. Davila, who knew only Spanish, traveled hundreds of miles by train to the California School for the Deaf, where he learned English and American Sign Language. He progressed rapidly, graduating at the age of fifteen.

Davila then attended Gallaudet College. At that time, there were only two hundred and fifty students enrolled, including hearing graduate students, and he was one of about forty-five preparatory students. In addition to studying education, language, and literature courses, he was active in track and cross-country and was a feature writer for the Gallaudet periodical *The Buff and Blue*. After graduating from Gallaudet with a bachelor's degree in education in 1953, Davila earned his master's degree in Special Education from Hunter College in New York City in 1963, and a Ph.D. in Educational Technology from Syracuse University in 1972.

His own educational experiences gave him a first-hand perspective on both the education of deaf persons and other persons with learning differences and the education of students in linguistic minorities.

Davila began his career teaching high school mathematics, social studies, and English for fourteen years at the New York School for the Deaf in White Plains. He also served for three years as elementary school supervisor. In 1974, he was appointed as director of the Kendall Demonstration Elementary School (KDES) at Gallaudet College, followed by two years as acting dean of the Model Secondary School for the Deaf (MSSD). As Vice President for Pre-College Pro-grams at Gallaudet from 1978 to 1989, Davila directed both KDES and MSSD. Throughout his experience there, he appeared before Congressional Committees to discuss issues pertaining to the civil rights and education of deaf people and to help defend the Gallaudet College appropriation. He served as president of the Conference of Educational Administrators Serving the Deaf, the Convention of American Instructors of the Deaf, and the Council on Education of the Deaf, the first deaf person elected president of each organization as well as the first to hold all three of these presidencies. Davila also chaired numerous committees in organizations addressing the educational needs of deaf and hard-of-hearing people.

In 1989, in an appointment that would be termed "historical," President George Bush selected Davila to replace Madeline Will as Assistant Secretary of Special Education and Rehabilitative Services in the Department of Education, the highest ranked federal position ever held by a deaf person. In this position, Davila had the responsibility to oversee $5 billion in special education and vocational programs aiding more than four million children and adults with disabilities. Between 1989 and 1993, he also chaired the Federal Interagency Coordinating Council, an oversight group responsible for coordinating federal programs serving young children with disabilities and their families. He served on the Architectural Transportation Barriers Compliance Board, the President's Committee on Mental Retardation, and the Task Force on National Agenda for Achieving Better Results for Children with Disabilities.

In his keynote address to the National Association of the Deaf (NAD) in 1992, Davila expressed an increasing concern, which was also stated in the Commission on Education of the Deaf report. He observed that many school districts were interpreting the "least restrictive environment" provision of the Individuals with Disabilities Education Act to mean placements in or close to the regular classroom. The overgeneralization that these placements are "inher-ently" less restrictive, Davila noted, is often not the case for many deaf children, particularly when nothing is done for them to allow them to communicate and interact with other children. He encouraged the NAD to redirect some of its efforts toward helping school systems to provide appropriate support services for deaf children. He also urged that placement decisions be based on the par-ticular needs of each child. In addressing the needs of minority individuals with disabilities, Davila targeted expansion of infant and toddler programs and high school graduation rates through cultural sensitivity, increasing the number of minority individuals in careers in special education, improving outreach to mi-nority communities, and training representatives of minority institutions to adopt effective strategies to recruit members of minority groups and persons with disabilities.

When President Bush left office, Davila was hired as Headmaster at the New York School for the Deaf at White Plains, where he is responsible for all aspects of the school program he started as a teacher thirty years ago. In this capacity, he has also begun to investigate creative programs to address the growing minority student population in that and other New York state schools for deaf students.

In 1991, Davila received an honorary doctoral degree from the Rochester Institute of Technology, host institution for the National Technical Institute for the Deaf. He has also received honorary degrees from Stonehill College in North Easton, Massachusetts (1991), and from Hunter College in New York (1990). He has been honored with more than twenty significant awards for his leadership by such organizations as the National Hispanic Council of the Deaf and Hard-of-Hearing, American Speech-Language and Hearing Association, National Association of the Deaf, Alexander Graham Bell Association for the Deaf, and from his alma maters, Syracuse University and Hunter College. In 1994, he was selected as one of the ten "Newsmakers of the Quarter Century" by the periodical *The Silent News* for his contributions to the Deaf community in the area of government. As a scholar, he has presented keynote addresses and lectures all over the United States and in many other countries, including France, Japan, India, Finland, England, Italy, Argentina, Australia, New Zealand, and Spain. He served as associate editor of *Exceptional Children* from 1979 to 1982 and has authored many reports in educational journals.

Davila's story is followed by many young deaf persons. Hispanic and other minority deaf children still struggle to gain quality education, despite the opportunities that have become available over recent decades. Educational leaders who can bridge cultures and affirm ethnicities are needed at this time. Davila continues to work in this way, in the United States and internationally. Among his special honors was being the first foreigner and first deaf person inducted into La Associacion Espanola de Educadores de Sordos in Spain.

References

Alumnus. (1973). *Gallaudet Today, 3* (3), 29–31.

Cooper, K. J. (1990, February 20). Deaf official moves from advocate to insider. *Washington Post*, A19.

Davila, R. R. (1991, Spring). Goals for improving services to minority individuals with disabilities. *Office of Special Education and Rehabilitative Services News in Print*, 2–5.

Leung, P. (1991, October–December). Dr. Robert Davila: The man and his mission. *Journal of Rehabilitation*.

CLAUDE-ANDRÉ DESEINE (1740–1823), French Sculptor.

Claude-André Deseine was born deaf on April 12, 1740, the son of a highly respected bourgeois artisan. Deseine was probably one of more than fifteen children. Little is known about his childhood. Deseine's poignant life story is important to modern historians. Like his Spanish deaf contemporary Roberto Francisco Prádez, he demonstrated great artistic talents in a time when formal education for deaf pupils had yet to be established in Europe. Deseine, Prádez, and many other aspiring deaf artists met with formidable prejudice in their time. Their contributions to the arts, as well as to the education of other deaf persons, have not been adequately recognized.

In *Looking Back: A Reader on the History of Deaf Communities and Their Sign Languages*, Maryse Bézagu-Deluy provided an account of Deseine's life as a "banned sculptor." In 1777, a few weeks after his father died, Deseine, then thirty-seven years old, accompanied his mother, two of his brothers, four uncles, two cousins, and a family friend to the Châtelat de Paris, a capital supreme court, whereby, after they all took an oath and stated their opinion, Judge François Angran D'Alleray, head of the Châtelet, documented that they were "unanimously in favor of the ban of Sieur Claude Deseine, deaf and dumb from birth, as being incapable of managing and administrating his person and possessions." Interestingly, two centuries later, Bézagu-Deluy took note that on a separate piece of paper that had survived through the years, the judge had personally struck out the words "cannot know how to read or write" and replaced them with "does not know how to read or write," indicating possible indecision and some thought that Deseine could have been taught such skills. And the ruling left Deseine still capable of disposing of income; his "guardians" only oversaw management of his possessions. Thus, a single scrap of paper summarizes well the fate of Deseine and many other deaf persons of his era left to the discretion of others.

Around this same time, Deseine began to leave records of his work as an artist. In 1778, he was a student at the Royal Academy of painting and sculpture in Paris, studying with his brother Louis-Pierre under Pajou. That same year, he won a third medal, and Louis-Pierre won a grand prize. Deseine exhibited five works at the Salon de la Correspondance on the Rue Saint-André des Arts in 1782. Over subsequent years, he sculpted busts of the Baron of Besenval, the Viscount of Ségur, the Count of Argental, and the Duke of Richelieu, indicating his work was highly respected and that he received private commissions.

In 1791, the year of the French Revolution, a brother-against-brother scenario was played out, as Deseine sculpted works indicating his support for the Revolutionary heroes while his brother was a diehard Royalist. Deseine was also one of four competitors, who included the great sculptor Houdin, in a contest to complete a marble bust of Mirabeau. His plaster-of-Paris submission was awarded the Jacobin prize, judged "a perfect likeness with expression and energy." That same year, Deseine also completed a bust of the venerable Abbé de L'Epée, under whom some historians surmise the deaf sculptor may have studied as a young adult.

Deseine exhibited his *Mirabeau* at the Salon du Louvre, along with another bust of Jean-Jacques Rousseau and an allegorical representation of La Liberté. He followed this with busts of the Jacobins Maximilien Robespierre and Jérome Pétion de Villeneuvre. In a period of only a few years, the deaf sculptor completed forty works, including one of General Bonaparte in 1797.

After the death of Robespierre, Deseine, as with many other Jacobins, went underground, and his subsequent activities are shrouded in mystery. He lived into his eighties on a modest pension, ludicrously still under a guardian's watch. Deseine died on December 30, 1823.

Reference

Bézagu-Deluy, M. (1993). Personalities in the world of deaf mutes in 18th century Paris. In R. Fischer & H. Lane (Eds.). *Looking back: A reader on the history of deaf communities and their sign languages* (pp. 25–42). Hamburg: Signum Press.

THEOPHILUS HOPE D'ESTRELLA (1851–1929), American Artist/Photographer.

Theophilus Hope d'Estrella was born deaf on February 6, 1851, in San Francisco. He never met his father, whose last name was de Rutte, a Swiss immigrant and sometime wine merchant seeking fortune in the West. His mother was a Mexican native who died when he was five years old. He changed his own name to d'Estrella when he was sixteen years old.

For four years, he avoided his assigned guardian, a young, overworked, and unsympathetic woman, and he often lived in the colorful streets of Chinatown and the waterfront, making friends with sailors and stealing food and money whenever he could. Fortunately, the California School for the Deaf opened on May 1, 1860, and D'Estrella escaped the dangers of the streets. He was enrolled with two other deaf students in the makeshift schoolhouse on Tehama Street in San Francisco in the "Society for the Instruction and Maintenance of the Indigent Deaf, and Dumb, and Blind." Under the watchful eye of William A. Crandall, a deaf teacher who taught him sign language, and Warring Wilkinson, a former teacher of the New York Institution who became principal, D'Estrella received a broad education. He proved to be a natural leader in the Abbé de l'Epée Literary Society, participating in debates and staging plays in sign language. D'Estrella graduated in 1873. In this year, he became the first deaf student at the University of California at Berkeley, where he studied for three years. He excelled in rhetoric, English, German, and French. During this time, he became fascinated with the eminent photographer Eadweard Muybridge's work in photographing the Gothic stone structure of the California School for the Deaf building where he was still boarding. D'Estrella was also hired by Wilkinson to teach a class in drawing on Saturday mornings at the school. In truth, D'Estrella never left the California School for the Deaf. It was the only real home he had ever known, and his affection for the place lasted throughout his lifetime.

In 1879, he became the first deaf student at the San Francisco Art Association's California School of Design, where he studied for five years. This was not without great difficulty; for the administrator there, whose name was Virgil Williams, believed that it was virtually impossible to teach a deaf person at an advanced level. Williams soon realized his mistake, however, and became a devoted instructor, communicating by writing on scraps of paper, which D'Estrella saved and, in 1887, published in the *Overland Monthly* as "Virgil Williams' Art Notes to a Deaf-Mute Pupil." Williams also developed a habit of passing by D'Estrella's easel and tapping him on the shoulder, and D'Estrella soon learned a kind of code for the variety of moods that his instructor conveyed through the tapping, from tender encouragement to minor annoyance. On the writing pad, the deaf artist explained, Williams wrote with ease: "Sheet after sheet flies from the pencil; criticism runs into anecdote, and a dissertation on anatomy comes as easily as a description of a sunset on the beloved Naples; he scolds—which he oftenest does—and praises and encourages and cautions by turns."

Williams once explained to D'Estrella that he was severe with his criticism in order to guard students against self-satisfaction and stagnation. In the notebook, D'Estrella and Williams discussed the works of many great artists—Leonardo DaVinci, Jerome, Léon-Joseph Bonnat, and others—and the deaf painter H. Humphrey Moore.* Williams recommended a variety of readings to D'Estrella, including Hamerton's *Thoughts about Art*, the lectures of Jarvis on Grecian art, and the criticism of Oscar Wilde. "When you do a female head of an ideal character," Williams wrote, "I want you to study it so carefully that you shall not only be in love with your own creation, but that everybody else shall." D'Estrella learned well, poring over his mentor's written advice. After he had spent three months on a Venus of Milo, his teacher wrote to him, "You have one thing to congratulate yourself on, that you have learned to love this Venus." D'Estrella's book of notes from Williams was considered a unique reference on its own; for nowhere else could one find in the literature of art education such detailed descriptions and instructions in the documented dialogue between a mentor and a gifted and precocious student.

When D'Estrella took a position at the California School for the Deaf, he remained in touch with Williams, often seeking his advice. Shortly before Williams's death, the artist-mentor also became an enthusiastic supporter of D'Estrella's emerging photographic work. Using Bonnat's "La Communion" as an example, he encouraged D'Estrella to reflect upon the life at the Institution for what he quaintly described as "episodes that you alone could understand and express . . . something peculiar, interesting, and touching that all would recognize as pertaining to the deaf . . . and if you can hit upon something that is pathetic, and yet unites beauty with affliction, you are sure to make a success of it."

This D'Estrella did. Known by his students as "The Magic Lantern Man," he developed and utilized the lantern slide as an instructional medium, with special emphasis on nature, often accompanying the slide presentations with compelling storytelling in American Sign Language. He offered them as many as forty exhibits a year. His frequent hiking excursions to the Sierra Nevada wilderness with John Muir's Sierra Club were a primary source for his photographs and slides. He also explored the tidal pools and beaches of Santa Cruz. D'Estrella traveled to Paris to visit and photograph his old friend, the eminent deaf sculptor Douglas Tilden.* He was a member of the California Camera Club and documented much of the natural beauty of California while serving on the Club's lantern-slide committee. His collaborative work with other members was reviewed favorably in the San Francisco *Examiner*. During one outing, the poet Edwin Markham, who had a deaf brother, surprised him by communicating in fingerspelling. In 1901, out of 1,400 photographs submitted to the first San Francisco Photographic Salon, he won first prize for animal studies with a photograph of two cats. Following Williams' advice, D'Estrella visually chronicled life in the California School for the Deaf for over forty years. His darkroom was in the old wooden trades building on the school campus; when it burned down in 1910, all of his camera equipment and more than 2,000 negatives were destroyed. The discouragement essentially put an end to his photographic career.

As a teacher for half a century, D'Estrella won the admiration of many students. His most successful student was Granville Redmond,* who went on to distinguish himself as a landscape painter in Southern California. D'Estrella, Redmond, and Douglas Tilden were members of the Bohemian Club of San Francisco. Through the years, D'Estrella continued to produce many paintings as well, for example, exhibiting fifteen paintings with the Guild of Arts and Crafts in San Francisco in 1896. His sketches and photographs are found in many collections, including the Oakland Museum, California Historical Society, and the National Maritime Museum in San Francisco. Like many Californians of that era, he was enamored of neoclassical style and experimented with works reflecting that period. He worried about the decline of culture and viewed the advent of the movies and automobiles as potentially harmful to human intellectual progress.

D'Estrella was also an avid writer, and he wrote regularly for the school newspaper, *The Itemizer*, which became *The California News*. He published several articles in the *American Annals of the Deaf* and lectured to the Deaf community on his travels in Europe. He served as treasurer of the National Association of the Deaf and later as vice president. He additionally assisted the renowned psychologist William James of Harvard University, who was interested in the relationship of thought and language. Based in part on D'Estrella's detailed recollections recorded in their correspondence, James began to conclude that abstract thought preceded formal language development, and that moral conscience was more universal and intuitive than previously believed.

D'Estrella died of cancer in Berkeley, California, on October 8, 1929. A faithful member of the California Association of the Deaf, he bequeathed his meager estate to the organization to help establish a home for aged deaf people.

References

Albronda, M. (1985). *The magic lantern man: Theophilus Hope D'Estrella*. Fremont, CA: California School for the Deaf.

D'Estrella, T. H. (1887, March). Virgil Williams' art notes to a deaf-mute pupil. *Overland Monthly*, 285–294.

James, W. (1892, November) Thoughts before language: A deaf-mute's recollections. *Philosophical Review*, *1*(6), 613–624.

"Prominent deaf persons—Theophilus H. D'Estrella. (1899). *The Silent Worker*, *11* (8), 116.

ROLANDO LOPEZ DIRUBE (1928–   ), Cuban Artist.

Rolando Lopez Dirube was born in Havana, Cuba, on August 14, 1928. He has explained that he was completely deafened from an unknown cause while in his first year in primary school. Dirube has told the story to several interviewers that at age six, he literally went to bed one night and awakened profoundly deaf. After a year of learning to speechread, he returned to school, demonstrating his talents early with hundreds of drawings of familiar objects. His productivity in these representations signalled his desire to communicate through vision. In 1947, Dirube entered the College of Engineering and Architecture of the University of Havana, where he studied mathematics and philosophy while experimenting with his first oil paintings. This training in engineering would later be helpful to him when he began designing his large cast concrete and iron sculptures. During his college years, he also took up fencing and became fascinated with foils and swords.

After a successful first exhibition of his largely expressionistic paintings and drawings at the Havana Lyceum in 1949, he received a scholarship from the Cuban-American Cultural Institute to study under George Grosz in the Art Students League of New York. A second scholarship enabled him to study further at the Brooklyn Museum School of Graphic Arts. A dozen scholarships followed, and Dirube developed his techniques in painting, engraving, and drawing under a number of masters, including Max Beckman. Established artists, Jackson Pollock among them, took notice of young Dirube quickly.

In 1951, Dirube had his second solo exhibition at the Brooklyn Museum Art School; this was followed by exhibitions sponsored by the Cuban Ministry of Education and the Cuban-American Cultural Institute. At the Cuban Ministry of Education, he showed color woodcuts executed with the unorthodox techniques he was already developing—using fire induced by gunpowder, gasoline, and other inflammable substances with knife and gauge cut. Later, as he moved to the use of hammers and electric saws as well, his total deafness was viewed by colleagues as a distinct advantage. At the First Exhibition of Latin-American Art, organized by the University of Tampa, Florida, he won first prizes in both painting and graphic arts. After moving to Madrid with a new scholarship from the Institute of Hispanic Culture, he won still another prize for a woodcut at the First Hispanic-American Biennial in Madrid. Dirube's earliest work demonstrated his eclecticism and versatility. He moved from oil painting to engravings to abstract drawings to woodcuts to sculpture, all done in various and mixed media. He identified his chosen artistic forebears as Matisse and Brancusi for their range and iconoclasm. As he was receiving honors in Spain for his woodcuts, his graphics were touring the museums of Germany under the aegis of the Panamerican Union Exhibition of Latin-American art.

Dirube exhibited three times in 1952: woodcuts at the Estilo Gallery in Madrid, oil paintings at the Lyceum in Havana, and a variety of works, including lithographs and temperas, at the Museum of Contemporary Art in Madrid. In the repressive atmosphere of the Franco era, Dirube was arrested for subversion. This may have been connected to his work, but was also likely due to his relationship and ultimate marriage to a Basque gun-shop owner. The couple returned to Havana, where Dirube set up a workshop to experiment, at first unsuccessfully, with cast concrete sculpture. Eventually, his large-scale concrete works found an audience, and Dirube collaborated with architects and engineers to mount his sculptures, frescoes, and murals in thought-provocative and environmentally enhancing ways.

Over the next twenty years, numerous exhibitions of his works were held in Cuba, Brazil, Spain, Puerto Rico, and the United States. His own training in architecture was revealed in many of his murals and concrete and metal sculptures created for public buildings, schools, and churches in Cuba. In 1961, he and his family moved to Puerto Rico in the wake of the Cuban revolution—his works, tools, and possessions in Havana had been confiscated. He incorporated into the Puerto Rican and Caribbean scenery many new creations borrowing from the play of light, color, and shape in the sea and landscape. One of his first large sculptures done in Puerto Rico was for the atrium of the City of Silence, a center for deaf children.

Dirube's eclecticism defies easy categorization of his style. Such works as his large wood and wrought iron *Las Cadenas (The Chains)* are distinctly political; the Cuban regime blocked its initial exhibition abroad in 1960. *Antares*, a 36-foot sculpture named for the bright star in Scorpio, symbolizes the hope of political exiles like himself. Many of Dirube's other works, however, come from aesthetic and emotional response to the struggle to master materials or to sheer delight in nature's composition. He has also done significant religious work, including a wooden Christ four meters high and composed of over 300 individually sculpted pieces for the church of San Luis Rey in San Juan. He continued to exhibit oil paintings, watercolors, and ink and graphite drawings on canvas, concrete, and wood. The fusion of technology and culture is a recurring theme, but Dirube would argue that every piece is individually conceived in a particular context at a particular moment in time. He has given great care and analysis to his creative process, and he has lectured on this point. Meanwhile, Dirube has been tireless in encouraging architects to incorporate painting and sculpture into building design. Dirube's work can be found in numerous buildings in San Juan, One Biscayne Tower in Miami, and the Gulf and Western Corporation in the Dominican Republic, among others.

In 1975, Dirube held the position of visiting professor at the Art Department of the Interamerican University in Puerto Rico. The United States government commissioned him, in 1978, to complete a nine-meter-high concrete and wrought iron sculpture for a park in Perrine, Florida. A number of Dirube retrospective exhibits have been held throughout the world in the 1980s and 1990s. His work can be viewed in major museums, including the Metropolitan Museum of Art in New York City.

References

Pau-Llosa, R. (1979). *Dirube*. Santa Polonia, Spain: Editorial Playor.
Sonnenstrahl, D. (1987). Rolando Lopez Dirube. In J. V. Cleve (Ed.), *Gallaudet ency-clopedia of deaf people and deafness* (Vol. 1, pp. 304–306). New York: McGraw-Hill.

GEORGE T. DOUGHERTY (1860–1938), American Metallurgist.

Born on a farm in Franklin County, Missouri, on January 4, 1860, five years before Gallaudet College was founded, George T. Dougherty was deafened by typhoid fever at two years of age. He entered the Missouri School for the Deaf at Fulton in 1868; and, after spending some time there (the school did not award diplomas during this period), he began studies at Gallaudet College and earned a bachelor of science degree in 1882. He also studied practical and analytical chemistry in a two-year course of study at the Polytechnic School of Washington University in St. Louis, Missouri, borrowing lecture notes from his classmates and comparing them with his own reading and experimental work. Among his friends who shared lecture notes and communicated with him solely by writing was Pope Yeatman, who later became a successful general manager of the gold mines at the Transvaal in South Africa. In 1885, Dougherty earned a Master of Science degree from Gallaudet College. He married an English-born deaf woman, Annie Wicktom, in 1886.

Dougherty's first position was as an assayer and chemist for the St. Louis Sugar Refining Company. He was also a chemist and assayer for Vulcan Steel Works in South St. Louis, and for the Deering Harvester Company, where he tested and analyzed metals. In 1890, he traveled to Chicago with some of his former employers to organize the National Smelting and Refining Company. He was offered a three-year contract and a fifty-percent increase in salary. In 1895, he began employment with the Sargent Company, which became part of the American Steel Foundries. Although consolidation of many of the large industrial establishments led to changes in employment for many chemists in this era, Dougherty remained Head Chemist and Metallurgist of the American Steel Foundries Company for the rest of his career. His reputation as an authority in analytical chemistry was reinforced by his reliability and accuracy in making fine measurements. He was offered large salaries and posts in Costa Rica, and later for the government of Cape Colony at Capetown, South Africa; but he declined them. On several occasions he was called to Montana to investigate and settle disputes in assays of precious metals. The accuracy of his measurements meant thousands of dollars in valuation of the gold and silver bullion for the parties involved. While performing these analyses, he made the acquaintances of Senator William A. Clark and Governor Hauser of Montana. Dougherty regarded speechreading as "too much guess work," and conducted most of his social and business interactions in writing.

Dougherty's many publications included scientific articles in the New York *Engineering and Mining Journal*, *Chemical News*, *Journal of Industrial and Engineering Chemistry*, and *The Iron Age*. His writing ability is repeatedly mentioned and celebrated in reports found in the contemporary literature of the Deaf community, perhaps because persons born deaf or deafened in early childhood often find mastery of written English challenging. One of his articles, titled "Determination of Nickel in Iron and Steel," was published in the *Chemical News* of London. Another on a "Complete Evolution Method for Sulfur in Iron" was published in 1902 in *The Iron Age*. T. B. Stillman considered the report important enough to incorporate as a chapter in the fourth edition of *Engineering Chemistry*, a textbook widely used in the early decades of the twentieth century. Dougherty's procedure for determining the amount of nickel in armor plate steel, published in the *Journal of Industrial and Engineering Chemistry*, became the standard method by 1921. Among his other contributions were a method for evaluating the vanadium content in steel, which led to the improved design of automobile axles around 1915, the procedures for determining salt in petroleum, and the development of the Reflux Air Condenser used in a process of chemically converting oils and fats into soaps. Sir William Crookes, discoverer of several chemical elements and editor of the long-established *Chemical News* of London, reprinted Dougherty's previously-published scientific papers whenever he received them.

Dougherty was extensively involved in the Deaf community and published in periodicals for deaf readers on such topics as "Industrial Training and Fields for the Deaf." He also presented this paper at the Alumni and Alumnae Meeting of the Wisconsin School for the Deaf in 1905. Since he was one of the first successful deaf scientists who graduated from a state school for deaf children, the visibility of his work in the field of industrial chemistry served an important purpose in inspiring professional career aspirations in deaf youngsters. In reporting on his article "Determination of Salt in Petroleum," for example, *The Iowa Hawkeye* and *The Silent Worker*, popular periodicals in the Deaf community, concluded in 1923 that Dougherty had attained a place in scientific work that reflected well on deaf people of the United States; and that his achievement proved that deafness was not in itself a barrier to success in almost any endeavor.

Dougherty's portrait on the October, 1924 cover of *The Silent Worker*, with regard to a report on "Deaf Persons of Note," reflected the high esteem the Deaf community held for him. Not content to be a passive "model," he was consistently active in enhancing the lives and employment opportunities of deaf people. In 1880, while still a student at Gallaudet College, he helped to found the National Association of the Deaf (NAD); and he served as its first secretary. The organization, still active today, was the first U.S. advocacy group to be established for people with a particular disability. Dougherty later served the NAD as vice president. In 1893, he was chairman and presiding officer at the

World Congress of the Deaf and was twice elected president of Chicago's Pas-a-Pas club. He also advocated for technical education for deaf people in 1900. In the early twentieth century, he participated in the NAD's Moving Picture Committee which worked hard to preserve examples of American Sign Language in a then-new medium. Dougherty's signed 1913 lecture on the discovery of chloroform is now preserved at the Library of Congress.

Dougherty died on December 2, 1938.

References

Braddock, G. C. (1975). *Notable deaf persons*. Washington, DC: Gallaudet College Alumni Association.

Dr. George M. Dougherty. (1906, March 24). *The Missouri Record.*

Lang, H. G. (1994). *Silence of the spheres: The deaf experience in the history of science.* Westport, CT: Bergin & Garvey.

"Deaf Persons of Note." (1924). The Silent Worker, *36* (8), 360.

JOACHIM DU BELLAY (1522?–1560), French Poet.

Most scholars agree that Joachim Du Bellay was born in 1522. It is specifically known that the birthplace was in Liré, near Anjou, France, at the Château of La Turmelière on the Loire River. The Du Bellay name was well known in French history for the soldiers and clergy the family produced. Joachim's first cousins continued to make the Du Bellay name renowned, including Guillaume, who was governor of Piedmont; Martin, a military captain; and René, the bishop of Le Mans. The fourth of these brothers, named Jean, who became archbishop in 1532 and cardinal in 1535, played an important role in Joachim Du Bellay's life. Joachim Du Bellay belonged to a less-distinguished branch of the clan, the son of a country farmer, Jean du Bellay. His parents both died when he was young, and he was put under the care of an older brother who had no understanding of his love of letters and consequent need for an education. "My youth was lost like a flower deprived of rain," he later wrote in verse, "without a hand to tend it." Confined to bed for two years in ill health himself, he spent his time studying Latin. His cousin, Cardinal Jean Du Bellay, supposedly encouraged him to consider law as a profession; and it was while studying at Poitiers that he began to write his first verses, mostly modelled after Clémont Marot. This we know from records that indicate Du Bellay entered a poetry competition in Poitiers at this time and lost. In time, however, Du Bellay's lyrical impressions, love sonnets, satirical verse, and literary criticism would place him among the great French poets of the Renaissance.

Du Bellay met the deaf poet Pierre de Ronsard,* a chance meeting at a wayside inn on the Poitiers road. Some scholars believe this story of the meeting at the Inn to be pure legend, and that the two may not have met until 1543, at the funeral of Guillaume Du Bellay in Le Mans. Nevertheless, as their personal and intellectual friendship developed, Du Bellay left his study of law and in 1547 joined Ronsard in Paris, where he studied with Ronsard and Jean-Antoine de

Baïf at the Collège de Coqueret under Jean Dorat, a respected scholar from Limoges. Around 1550, Du Bellay and Ronsard encouraged Baïf and four other hearing poets to join them in the Pléiade, or "seven stars of French poetry," dedicated to writing poetry in the Greco-Roman tradition, but with a new linguistic and literary form. Although other poets were more qualified, Ronsard insisted on Dorat being included in the Pléiade.

Du Bellay's first work was a pamphlet published in 1549. In *Défense et Illustration de la Langue Français*, he argued against Thomas Sebillet's *Art Poétique*, which praised several French poets of the medieval tradition and was critical of the neoclassical work of the Pléiade. Du Bellay, probably in collaboration with his fellow students at Coqueret, advocated French as a language of poetry. *L'Olive*, also published in 1549, was his first collection of sonnets. In 1550, a second edition increased the number of sonnets from fifty to 115, forty original and the remaining either "borrowed" or verbatim translations; unfortunately, with less-than-satisfactory citations, as Keating (1971) has pointed out. *L'Olive* was a sonnet sequence in honor of a lady, the first such dedicated opus in French. The volume contained poems reflecting the literary theory of the Pléiade. *L'Olive* also has thirteen odes ("vers lyrique"), each with a dedication to Ronsard, Dorat, or a member of the court; and "Musagnoeomachie" ("War of the Muses"), a poem of 516 verses. Du Bellay also published *Recueil de Poesie* in 1549, an effort to alert the intelligentsia and patrons of the arts to the need for a "new poetry." Du Bellay was largely influenced by the work of Petrarch, and he helped to popularize the sonnet with French audiences.

Between 1550 and 1551, Du Bellay had a serious illness and lost his hearing a second time. This time, however, he was left with a significant and permanent deafness by the illness, which only occasionally improved and for very brief periods. The illness seemed to have also aged him in appearance. When his brother died unexpectedly in 1551, Joachim Du Bellay was left with debts as well as his brother's eleven-year-old son. The following year, he published his translation of the fourth book of the *Aeneid*, followed by a new edition of *Recueil de Poesie*.

In 1553, Du Bellay traveled to Rome as secretary to his second cousin, the cardinal, but the journey held much more significance in helping him to further realize his poetic talents. When the cardinal arrived in Lyons on his journey from Paris to Rome, Du Bellay learned that he had acquired international renown. Guillaume des Autels wrote several poems about his meeting in Lyons with Du Bellay, and Du Bellay appreciated this new experience of attention and intellectual stimulation, which had often been denied him. Du Bellay's deafness made it difficult for him to manage the cardinal's palace, serve as messenger, and deal with financial arrangements. Constant embarrassments in society associated with his hearing loss, which increased with each bout of illness, and a general dissatisfaction with the duties he was expected to perform over the four-year period magnified his frustration. He found therapy in poetry and poet-friends. Then, Du Bellay met Faustina, a married woman. The intimate friendship they developed was unacceptable to her elderly husband, who shut her up in a convent. Du Bellay wrote *Poematica*, a collection of poems describing this love affair, in Latin, which contradicted his argument for use of the vernacular in *Défense*.

In 1557, Du Bellay departed for France, resigning from his office to return to editing his poetry. His travels and interactions with humanists and intellectuals had greatly influenced the poetry he included in *Les Regrets*, *Les Antiquités de Rome*, and *Divers Jeux Rustiques*.

In *Divers Jeux Rustiques* Du Bellay wrote a long tribute to his dear friend Pierre de Ronsard, one deaf poet to another. Unlike his many references to how his deafness saddened him, and even his assertion that his vocation as a poet was an introverted one influenced by his deafness, the hymn praises deafness and views sensory loss as a companion to be treated with humor. "Thou hast with thee for companion gentle deafness," he wrote to Ronsard, "who commandeth silence, and taketh care that noise/Comes not near to hinder the joy of thy work. . . . In being thus deaf One is deprived of little good and much ill."

Du Bellay is credited with creating a new, vital French poetic, by applying heretofore unused meters in the French language. At the same time, there is also considerable criticism of his use of neoclassical models as unoriginal and derivative, since nearly all his work was a close translation or paraphrased from Italian and neo-Latin sources. Even the famous *Défense* parallels a defense of the Italian language written by Sperone Speroni. This was quite typical of the time, however, and cannot be regarded as merely plagiaristic. Du Bellay had a distinct personal style, and he was intent on "making French" classical forms. He was interested in an interpretation of these forms that was in keeping with his own time and culture.

DuBellay's other works include *Discours*, composed in Rome in 1555, and *Épitaphe*, which he wrote for the king upon the loss of Madam Marguerite, one of Du Bellay's patrons. His health was now declining rapidly, and his deafness had reached a point that nearly completely isolated him from others. His bitterness associated with personal as well as legal struggles surfaced in "Le Poète courtisan," which he published in 1559. He died of apoplexy on January 1, 1560, at the age of thirty-seven, and was buried at Notre-Dame.

One day soon after Du Bellay's death, Ronsard, the "Prince of Poets," walked along the Seine: "I wept Du Bellay who was of my age, my craft, my temper, my kin, who died, poor and wretched, after singing so often and so learnedly the praise of princes and of kings."

References

Bishop, M. (1959). *Ronsard: Prince of poets*. Ann Arbor, MI: University of Michigan Press.

Keating, L. C. (1971). *Joachim Du Bellay*. New York: Twayne Publishers.

Kunitz, S., & Colby, V. (Eds). (1967). Joachim Du Bellay. *European authors, 1000–1900: A biographical dictionary of European literature*. New York: Wilson.
Weinberg, B. (Ed.). (1964). *French poetry of the Renaissance*. Carbondale, IL: Southern Illinois University Press.

E

GILBERT C. EASTMAN (1934–), American Actor/Playwright.

Gilbert C. Eastman was born on September 12, 1934, in Middletown, Connecticut. In 1952, he graduated from the American School for the Deaf in West Hartford, Connecticut, and he earned a bachelor's degree in art from Gallaudet College in 1957. Eastman married June Russi, a deaf professional actress, after graduating from Gallaudet. In 1963, Eastman obtained a master's degree in drama from Catholic University in Washington, D.C., the first deaf person to earn such a degree. He studied with the National Theatre of the Deaf (NTD) in their summer programs in 1967, 1968, and 1971. One summer, David Hays invited him to teach a class in nonverbal communication at the NTD summer school, but Hays forgot to plan an interpreter either by accident or by intent. Eastman improvised and out of these efforts came a special method of teaching he called "Visual and Gestural Communication," which allows sign language students to improve their abilities to "sign like Deaf" people. Eastman summarized the essentials of this approach in his book *From Mime to Sign* in 1989. He has lectured widely on visual/gestural communication all over the world.

From 1957 until 1969, Eastman served as an instructor in Gallaudet College's Drama Department, advancing to chair the program in 1963. Over a thirty-five year period, the department expanded from one man to seven faculty and staff with a recognized performing arts curriculum.

Eastman acted in both the Gallaudet Dramatics Club and the D.C. Club for the Deaf productions of such plays as *MacBeth*, *Charley's Aunt*, *The Hairy Ape*, and *Gloria Mundi*. He took the role of "Jay" in excerpts from *All the Way Home* with the NTD on NBC-TV's *Experiment in Television* in 1967. Other NTD dramatic roles included "Horatio" in *Hamlet*, "Yeoman" in *The Tale of Kasane*, and "Rinuccio" in *Gianni Schicchi*. Eastman was the stage manager for numerous plays, including *Othello* (1959), *Our Town* (1961), *Medea* (1965), and *Cyrano de Bergerac* (1971). He has directed over forty productions, in-

Gilbert Eastman, American actor. Photo from *Gallaudet Today*, 23 (1), 1992, courtesy of Gallaudet University Archives.

cluding comedies, medieval plays, modern classics, mysteries, musicals, and several children's plays. Among his productions are Moliere's *The School for Wives*, Christie's *Ten Little Indians*, Simon's *Barefoot in the Park*, Rodgers and Hammerstein's *Flower Drum Song*, Barry's *The Philadelphia Story*, and Wilde's *The Importance of Being Earnest*.

Eastman is also a playwright. His works include a 1972 American Sign Language version of *Antigone* that was selected by the American College Theatre Festival as one of the ten finalist entries to be performed at the Kennedy Center in 1973. That year, he also wrote *Sign Me Alice*, based on Lerner and Loewe's *My Fair Lady* and George Bernard Shaw's *Pygmalion*, with a focus on a young deaf woman who is thrust into the controversy between artificial sign systems and American Sign Language. After a sabbatical in France, Eastman wrote *Laurent Clerc: A Profile*, a dramatization of the impact of the life of Laurent Clerc,* the first deaf teacher in the United States. The previous year, his play, *Hands*, was first produced. The period of Eastman's work beginning in 1973 is significant in that he began to write a corpus of work specifically aimed at deaf audiences, using Deaf themes and experiences. Today, Deaf community theatre companies regularly perform Eastman works in their repertoire. He wrote *What* in 1982 and *Aladdin and His Magic Lamp* in 1983.

Eastman's teaching experience has also included workshops for children in the fundamentals of acting, sponsored by the Mott Foundation. He assists other professionals in the various roles of sign language translator, dramaturge, acting coach, and costume and set designer. He has performed solo pieces, including *Epic: Gallaudet Protest*. He has become a familiar presence to a wider audience since the late 1980s and the expansion of cable television systems as a host of the popular news magazine program *Deaf Mosaic*.

References

Dietl, D. (1980, January/February/March). What's the "sign" for extraordinary? *Journal of Rehabilitation*, 10–12.

Eastman, G. C. (1989). *From mime to sign*. Silver Spring, MD: T. J. Publishers.

Johnstone, M. (1992). Center stage: Gil Eastman leaves a legacy of excellence in theater and entertainment. *Gallaudet Today*, *23* (1), 14–17.

Shuart, A. (1973). Eastman's "Sign Me Alice" huge success. *The Deaf American*, *26* (3), 9–10.

Silver, A. (1988). Deaf Mosaic wins 2 Emmys. *Silent News*, *20* (8), 1.

Gilbert C. Eastman: A profile. Washington, DC: Gallaudet University Archives, 1992.

TILLY EDINGER (1897–1967), American Paleoneurologist.

Born Johanna Gabrielle Ottelie on November 13, 1897, in Frankfurt, Germany, Tilly Edinger is known throughout the world as the person who essentially founded the study of paleoneurology, the study of fossil brains. This is a remarkable accomplishment when one considers the circumstances of her life. Her father, Ludwig Edinger, was a leading medical researcher who helped found comparative neurology as a science. But it was not her father who encouraged her to pursue science; on the contrary, he did not support the idea of women pursuing professional careers and argued against her goals.

Edinger was the youngest of three children. Her mother, Anna (Goldschmidt) Edinger, was well-to-do, having come from a family involved with banking. The prominence of the Edinger name in Frankfurt was apparent. Edingerstrasse was a street named in honor of her father. A large bust of her mother, who was active in social welfare programs, stood in the park. Tilly Edinger attended the prestigious universities of Heidelberg and Munich between the years 1916 and 1918. In 1921, she completed her dissertation on the investigation of the skull and cranial cavity of Nothosaurus, a fossil reptile, and she was awarded a doctorate from the University of Frankfurt. Edinger had found a Nothosaurus skull in a private fossil collection in Heidelberg and had made a cast of the cavity. She compared the brain of the reptile that had lived more than two million years ago with those of living reptiles, and her fascination with these comparisons became her life's work. She continued at the University as an assistant in paleontological work until 1927, when she was offered the position of curator at the Natur-Museum Senckenberg, also in Frankfurt. Here, she was responsible for vertebrate fossils. Working without salary, Edinger laboriously studied her specimens and published *Die Fossilen Gehirne* (Fossil Brains) in 1929, one of more than a hundred professional reports she was to publish during her career.

Edinger had begun to lose her hearing in her mid-teens. At Heidelberg University, she consulted a specialist who confirmed her suspicions of an inherited hearing impairment. She subsequently lost most of her hearing, although she continued to experiment with and use hearing aids in both Germany and the United States. As Edinger once described her hearing loss, "Without a hearing aid I am deaf" ("Ohne Hörgerät bin ich taub"), and when she wished to be alone, she would switch off the device.

Edinger conducted her scientific work under the most difficult and, ultimately, threatening conditions. With the help of Rudolf Richter, at that time the Director of Museums, she remained as unobtrusive as possible. Her name was removed from the door of the office where she worked, and, for five years, she entered the building through a side entrance. Her discovery by the Nazis in 1938, however, ended her employment at the Natur-Museum. The sign on Edingerstrasse honoring her father was torn down and the bust of her mother in the town park was removed. Her brother was later to die in a concentration camp. Fearing for her life, she escaped with much difficulty to England in May 1939. After a year of work as a translator, she learned of a program in the United States offering temporary positions to European scholars displaced from their homelands. She was one of about a dozen "displaced scientists" who were given Harvard appointments while still in Europe. After her arrival in the United States in 1940, she was given a position as assistant at the Museum of Comparative Zoology in Boston, where she remained for the rest of her life. At one point, when the Museum was under financial strain, Edinger tried her hand at teaching comparative anatomy at Wellesley College. Although she was highly respected, she found her deafness made this career challenging.

Her groundbreaking study of cranial cavities assured Edinger quick acceptance into American academic life. Half of her nearly 100 books and articles were written in German and published before her escape. After becoming a citizen of the United States, she dedicated her energies once again to vertebrate paleontology. While most of her works were paleoneurological in nature, she also wrote biographical sketches ("The Life of Three Reference Hunters," 1944) and obituaries (for example, Carl Wiman in 1946). She investigated and published on the hearing and smell of cetaceans (1955) and reported on the advances of others in brain research (1964). She published more than 1,200 reviews and abstracts.

Edinger was charming, warm, dedicated, and personable, yet challenging and opinionated. Her heavy smoking was a source of teasing by her colleagues. Among her awards were honorary degrees from Wellesley College in 1950, from Justus Liebig University, Giessen, Germany in 1957 (the only woman among thirty people thus honored up to that time), and from Johann Wolfgang Goethe University, Frankfurt, in 1964. When she received an honorary doctorate in medicine in Frankfurt, she turned to her colleague Hofer and said, "Jetzt kann ich etwas, was Du nicht kannst! Jetzt verschreibe ich mir meine Medikamente selbst!" ("Now I can do something you cannot do. Now I can write my own prescriptions!").

Edinger won a fellowship from the Guggenheim Foundation in 1943. In 1948, the Society of Vertebrate Paleontology passed a resolution to find a way for Edinger to update the comprehensive survey of the brains of extinct animals that she had published in 1929, and she won a fellowship from the American Association of University Women to complete this work in 1950. With this assistance, she was able to visit museums in London, Paris, Switzerland, Holland, and Germany and examine the specimens she had found cited in the professional journals. In the process, she corrected errors, gathered a wealth of material, and combined this with the numerous papers she had previously published to produce her classic work, *The Evolution of the Horse Brain*. In 1929, while still living in Germany, Edinger had suggested that an American should conduct an investigation of the ancestral series of endocranial casts of the Equidae, since it was on the North American continent that the 55-million-year history of the horse family occurred. Because of Hitler, she became the American to undertake this study.

Through a period of many years, she actively directed and enlarged the new edition of *Fossil Brains* at the Museum of Comparative Zoology; much of her work, including that in her homeland, culminated in the *Bibliography of Fossil Vertebrates, Exclusive of North America: 1509–1927*, coauthored with A. S. Romer (who helped bring her to the Museum in 1940), N. E. Wright, and R. V. Frank. In 1963–64, she was the president of the Society of Vertebrate Paleontology.

During this time, Tilly Edinger took several trips to Europe. In Germany, she renewed her professional relationships, and, from her friend Hofer's perspective, this was important because she brought German vertebrate paleontology out of postwar isolation. She brought together two diverse areas of scientific knowledge—paleontology and neurology—a recognizable accomplishment.

Tilly Edinger was struck by a car in Cambridge, Massachusetts. She died the following day, May 27, 1967.

References

American Association of University Women. (1967). *Idealism at work: 80 years of AAUW fellowships* (62–63). Washington, DC: AAUW.

Gould, S. J. (1980). Tilly Edinger. In B. Sicherman, C. H. Green, I. Kantrov, & H. Walker (Eds.), *Notable American women: The modern period* (Vol. 4, pp. 218–219). Cambridge, MA: Harvard University Press.

Hofer, H. (1969) In memoriam Tilly Edinger. *Gegenbaurs morphologisches jahrbuch, 113* (2), 303–313.

Lang, H. G. (1994). *Silence of the spheres: The deaf experience in the history of science.* Westport, CT: Bergin & Garvey.

THOMAS ALVA EDISON (1847–1931), American Inventor.

Thomas Alva Edison was born on February 11, 1847, in Milan, Ohio. While a young child, his teachers considered him "addled" because of the strange questions he asked, and his mother decided to teach him herself—not only the fundamentals, but also a love of knowledge. He was fascinated with making things fly and was undeterred by failure. At one point he attempted to propel a friend into the air by inducing him to swallow several doses of seidlitz powders to generate gas. By the age of ten, however, Edison had read the *Penny Encyclopedia*, Hume's *History of England*, Gibbon's *Rome*, Sears' *History of the World*, and various works on chemistry and other sciences. He worked as a trainboy on the Grand Trunk Railroad between Port Huron and Detroit, selling newspapers, magazines, toys, fruit, and other merchandise; and he began to publish his own newspaper, "The Grand Trunk Herald," with four assistants hired to help him conduct the business. His relentless curiosity led him to the Library Association of Detroit, where he undertook the challenge of reading every volume of the collection, beginning with the lowest shelf and proceeding through them one by one, devouring technical writings such as Newton's *Principia* as well as his favorites, the works of Victor Hugo. He also set up a small chemical laboratory in the freight car with his printing apparatus. Unfortunately, an accident involving spilled chemicals resulted in the end of his business as well as his job on the train.

Edison has written that his deafness began at the age of twelve while working on the train. In his diary, he described the definite advantage his deafness gave to his business transactions. He did not rely on verbal agreements and insisted everything be in writing to avoid misunderstandings. He asserted that his deafness never prevented him from earning money. He also insisted that deafness was an asset, a radical view for that time. In the heat of discussions with his fellow inventors, Edison was inclined to drive home his points by vigorously pounding on a table. Because of his deafness, it was difficult to argue with him.

Edison's hearing loss was severe enough to restrict his communication and to isolate him socially. He preferred to view his hearing impairment as "insulation" rather than "isolation," for it allowed him to contemplate, and he frequently took advantage of the silence. On his Winter estate in Fort Myers, there is a pier where he would often sit with his fishing pole for long hours. Edison used no hook on his line, for he did not wish to bother the fish any more than he wished to be disturbed by others.

Edison believed that people with good hearing become accustomed to the noise of civilization. Broadway was a peaceful thoroughfare for him and he appreciated the opportunity to concentrate. He often pointed out that he was able to sleep well and undisturbed. He was also never fond of small talk. The inventor's main residence in Fort Myers had no dining room for guests. His guest house did. He preferred to retire from the guest house dining area when he wished. As described in the November 18, 1955, Omaha, Nebraska *Evening World Herald*, one night during a party, the hostess approached Edison seated in a secluded corner and, wondering if he was sensitive about his hearing impairment, inquired why he had never invented something to improve his own hearing. Looking at the guests chattering around him, Edison responded that he would prefer not to listen to what he did not want to hear.

In regard to his work with telegraphy, Edison's contributions were invaluable. In 1862, when Edison was fifteen years old, he saved the life of a small boy on the train tracks. The boy's father had no money but offered to teach Edison telegraphy. Approaching this enthusiastically, Edison quickly became the best and fastest telegrapher in the United States. His sensitivity to his environment was notable.

Later, after his hearing loss more seriously affected his communication, Edison made use of the telegraphic code through the sense of touch for many of his general communication interactions. At the theater, his wife "interpreted" for him by tapping out on his knee the code for words spoken on stage. In fact, it was with Morse Code that Edison proposed marriage to her. Numerous accounts of the severity of Edison's deafness have been provided by those who knew him. Reuben Fleet, for example, who brought together the remnants of Dayton-Wright Company and Gallaudet Aircraft Corporation to establish his new enterprise, Consolidated Aircraft Corporation, flew with his father several times to visit Edison and celebrate their common birthday. Fleet told others of the difficulty of communicating with the deaf inventor. Messages would often have to be written, and Edison would respond with a somewhat distorted voice quality. The nephew of the electrical inventor Charles P. Steinmetz also recalled how Edison and his uncle communicated through Morse code by tapping the messages on each other's knees to compensate for Edison's deafness.

Thomas Alva Edison, American inventor. Drawing from J. Louis Young (1890), *Edison and his Phonograph* (Bournemouth, England: *The Talking Machine Review*).

Edison's work with the telegraph machine naturally led to his career as an inventor. An often-told event occurred during an 1869 job interview in New York City. A telegraph machine broke down while Edison was waiting to be interviewed. He was the only one in the office who could repair it and was immediately offered a better position than the one to which he had applied. Not long after Edison began with the company in New York City, he decided to start his own business. He kept fifty workmen busy on his various inventions day and night. It was in New Jersey that he developed numerous devices for telegraphy. The quadruplex, a device used for sending and receiving four messages at the same time over a single wire, was one important invention. Another was his high-speed automatic telegraph. Between 1870 and 1876, he received about 120 American patents, and most of them were for telegraphic inventions.

As early as 1875, he was on the track of wireless telegraphy, noting mysterious sparks that oscillated. He built his famous "black box" with two carbon points separated by a gap. Through a window, the sparks could be seen crossing the gap. Edison did not fully understand the nature of his discovery. Heinrich Hertz later proved the existence of electromagnetic waves. Edison received many offers from rivals of the Marconi Company, but he sold his rights to the Marconi Company in 1903.

Edison's contributions in physics went beyond his device for generating electric waves. He also conducted research on Roentgen rays and devised a method for astronomers to safely study the solar corona. But of all his experiments, one purely scientific discovery was of particular merit. In 1883, while working toward improving the light bulb, he inserted into an evacuated glass bulb an electrode plate in addition to the filament and observed the flow of electricity from the hot filament across the gap. Although it had no immediate use to Edison, he patented it and published his observations. His tube was basically the first "diode," and the phenomenon he observed is known to scientists as "thermionic emission," or the "Edison effect." Because of the demands of the electric light industry during this period, Edison had no time to devote to the phenomenon. Other scientists, including J. J. Thompson and Sir John Ambrose Fleming,* did further research on the Edison effect, and the electronics industry arose from their work.

As for Edison's work on the phonograph, he believed the general defect was in rendering the overtones of music and the high-frequency hissing sounds in speech. With his staff, he worked for more than one year, twenty hours a day, including Sundays, to produce the word "specie" perfectly. When this was accomplished, he knew that everything else could be done. The phonograph soon became useful in many ways besides entertainment. In one example, it was reported that a London coster, having lost his voice, used an Edison phonograph to cry his wares while he waited on trade, perhaps a prelude to today's radio and television commercials.

In 1878, Edison's thirst for knowledge led him to join the ranks of those striving for a practical incandescent lamp. Many experimental incandescent lamps were in operation before 1878, when Edison began to design one that was commercially viable. The arc variety, with its flame crossing an air gap between electrodes, was too powerful for ordinary indoor use. As refractory metals began to appear commercially, it became clear that the days of the carbon lamp were numbered. The controversy over who actually invented the incandescent lamp still rages today. Unquestionably, though, Edison developed a practical lamp and a complete generation system using parallel-wire distribution with constant voltage. This approach earned him international acclaim.

Edison began to entertain the idea of motion pictures while in West Orange in 1887. His goal was to invent a device that would entertain the eye in the way that the phonograph brought pleasure through hearing. Within two years he had developed and patented several devices that graphically recorded movement and operated on the principle of "persistence of vision." He also organized the first film studio. His kinetoscope, a box with a peep hole, was used to view the first films produced. He had artists paint every frame of a film reel in 1890 and thrilled viewers with his prediction that color movies would some day be a reality. The first two thousand films were produced in "Black Maria," a studio in Edison's backyard, and included the first picture of man in motion ("The Sneeze"), the first with two people ("The Kiss"), and the first with a plot ("The Great Train Robbery").

Edison was elected to the National Academy of Sciences in 1927, awarded the Congressional Medal of Honor in 1928 for illuminating the path of progress by his inventions, and posthumously was elected to the Hall of Fame of Great Americans in 1960. Edison died in West Orange, New Jersey, on October 18, 1931. In an effort to erect a momentary monument to the deaf inventor, President Hoover put out the White House lights for one minute on October 22, 1931.

References

Crowther, J. G. (1937). *Famous American men of science.* Freeport, NY: W. W. Norton.
Palmer, A. J. (1984). *Edison: Inspiration to youth.* Milan, OH: Edison Birthplace Association.
Roe, W. R. (1917). *Peeps into the deaf world.* Derby, England: Bemrose.
Runes, D. D. (Ed.). (1948). *The diary and sundry observations of Thomas Alva Edison.* New York: Philosophical Library.

ANDERS GUSTAF EKEBERG (1767–1813), Swedish Chemist.

Anders Gustaf Ekeberg was born at Stockholm, Sweden, on January 16, 1767. His father was a shipbuilder in the royal Navy and later became a construction captain. His mother was the daughter of a manufacturer in Stockholm. At ten years of age, Ekeberg was sent to a school at Kalmar where he stayed for two years. At twelve, he entered another school in Söderakra. While staying in the home of a clergyman, he developed a strong interest in Greek literature, an interest throughout his life. It was during this time that he suffered a severe cold that left him partially deaf, and his hearing progressively decreased as time went on. In 1781, Ekeberg went to Westervik. On his own initiative, he learned much during his few years there, demonstrating unusual talent for his age. In 1784, he studied mathematics and other subjects at the Academy in Uppsala. With special support from a professor of economics, later named Bishop Lostbom, Ekeberg completed his doctor of philosophy degree at the University of Uppsala in 1788. In time his thesis on "Oils Extracted from Seeds" was to play a role in the revolution taking place in chemistry.

With the help of a scholarship, Ekeberg then traveled through Germany for several years. In 1787, Antoine-Laurent Lavoisier published *Methods of Chemical Nomenclature*, in which each chemical was assigned a name indicating its composition. Ekeberg introduced the modern names for such elements as hydrogen, nitrogen, and oxygen into the Swedish language, thus eliminating the obscure names assigned the elements by early alchemists. His reports were published anonymously, however. Ekeberg preferred to avoid conflicts with Johan Afzelius, his superior, who distrusted the new theory based on the role of oxygen, a theory that overturned the long-held belief in "phlogiston," a hypothetical substance released as flame during combustion.

Following a period of successful mineral studies and public demonstrations, Ekeberg was promoted to professor of chemistry in 1794. By 1796, he had become Sweden's foremost chemist. He served as demonstrator in the laboratory of Torbern Olof Bergman, who had studied under Linnaeus. As an early public-interest scientist, Ekeberg lectured on the theory of combustion and published on such topics as "On the Present State of Chemical Science" and "The Advantage Which Medicine Gains from the Most Recent Discoveries in Chemistry." His familiarity with many aspects of natural history led him to be considered for other positions at the university. In 1799, he was elected a member of the Royal Academy of Sweden; and, three years before his death, he was admitted to the Academy of Sciences in Uppsala.

Ekeberg became deeply interested in the minerals found in the quarries of Ytterby and Falun, in Sweden, and began to analyze them. The Finnish chemist Johan Gadolin had several years earlier examined a mineral from the Ytterby quarry, which was later found to contain over a dozen different "rare earth" elements, one named in Gadolin's honor. Ekeberg worked extensively on his own mineral samples between 1797 and 1802. In 1801, he lost an eye when a flask filled with gases exploded in his laboratory. Neither his deafness nor his vision impairment, however, impeded his work. His subsequent chemical analyses confirmed Gadolin's earlier discovery.

In 1802, Ekeberg isolated a new metal in a mineral found in Ytterby. It was not a rare earth. He precisely defined the metal, and his extensive analyses brought credit to him as the discoverer of the element tantalum. The name tantalum comes from the element's failure to dissolve in any acid. Ekeberg's love for Greek literature is revealed in the name he chose for the element. In the Greek myth, Tantalus was not able to drink, although he stood in water up to his chin.

The discovery of tantalum was controversial. Charles Hatchett, an English chemist, claimed to have discovered a new metal in a sample he had received from Connecticut that he named "columbium." Eight years later, Hatchett's fellow countryman, William Wollaston, erroneously declared columbium to be identical to Ekeberg's tantalum. In 1809, Ekeberg supplied Thomas Thomson with samples of tantalite for examination, but the ship that contained Thomson's highly valued Swedish collection sunk in the Baltic. It was not until 1865, half a century after Ekeberg's death, that Jean Marignac used spectroscopic analyses to confirm that tantalum and columbium were distinct metals. Eventually, columbium came to be called niobium (Niobe being the daughter of the mythical Tantalus).

Ekeberg's student, Jacob Berzelius, defended Ekeberg's discovery of tantalum after the deaf chemist had died. Berzelius corresponded with Thomson and explained the difference between the tantalum and columbium oxides. Berzelius later went on to discover the elements selenium, silicon, thorium, cerium, and zirconium; and he is credited with having started the serious investigation of catalysis. Berzelius was devoted to his deaf mentor, and his own considerable contributions have led scientists to credit Ekeberg with masterful teaching as well as careful scientific investigation.

Tantalum was later used in the manufacture of rayon, in electrodes for neon signs, and in fine jewelry with iridescent colors. In the early days of radio, the metal was useful as an electrode in rectifiers for converting alternating current to direct current and found its way into the homes of many people.

Ekeberg was also an artist and poet, and his love for Greek literature provided him with joy throughout his life. His poetry, in particular, provided pleasure when he felt isolated by his deafness or poor health. In 1790, when Sweden and Russia signed a peace treaty, Ekeberg demonstrated his talents, writing a beautiful poem about this event. In 1792, he similarly expressed the Academy's loss of its great supporter, King Gustaf III. Later, when the royal family of Sweden came to visit Uppsala in 1801 and an exposition of chemical knowledge was planned in their honor, Ekeberg composed a three-stanza poem for the King written with invisible ink. When the King warmed the paper, the poem appeared in blue letters. The poem revealed Ekeberg's love of both science and art, and his personal wishes for a world without war.

Ekeberg was a frail man who suffered with tuberculosis in addition to partial blindness. Upon Ekeberg's death, Johan PehrLindh from Stockholm described him in the journal published by the Swedish Academy as charming, kind, and attentive to students, despite his considerable difficulties. He was positive and hopeful.

Ekeberg died in Uppsala at the age of forty-six on February 11, 1813. As his student and friend Berzelius wrote of his former master in a letter to the Swiss chemist Alexandre Marcet, the poet-scientist Ekeberg was a "most lovable" man.

References

Konglia Vetenskaps Academiens Handlingar. (1813). Biography of Magister Anders Gustaf Ekeberg, teacher of the academy and laboratory chemist in Uppsala. Stockholm: Tryckte Hos Joh. Pehr Lindh.

Lang, H. G. (1994). *Silence of the spheres: The deaf experience in the history of science.* Westport, CT: Bergin & Garvey.

Weeks, M. E. (1956). *Discovery of the elements.* Easton, PA: Journal of Chemical Education.

F

ROBERT J. FARQUHARSON (1824–1884), American Civil War Surgeon.

Robert James Farquharson was born in Nashville, Tennessee, on July 15, 1824. His father was a Scotsman and an early settler of the state. His mother was a native of Kentucky. Little is known about his childhood, except that he was very bright. He entered the University of Nashville at the age of fourteen and graduated in 1841 at the age of seventeen. One of his professors there encouraged him to take an extra course in higher mathematics, and the president spoke of him as an exemplary student. At one point in his adolescence, Farquharson joined a survey of the state of Tennessee as an assistant to the Dutch geologist Gerard Troost, a man who had great influence on him. He first became interested in medicine while reading books in the office of Dr. Jennings of Nashville. Farquharson then moved to Philadelphia, the seat of medical education in the United States. He graduated from the medical department of the University of Pennsylvania in 1844. While working for a year at Blockley Hospital, where he also earned a diploma from the Obstetric Institute, he made the acquaintance and earned the esteem of many great physicians of the time, including Paul Goddard, Robert Morris, George B. Wood, Richard Ashurst, and Samuel Jackson. In 1845, he entered private medical practice and hospital service in New Orleans; two years later he enlisted in the United States Navy, with which he traveled the world as an assistant surgeon. Farquharson was profoundly deafened while serving on the schooner *Taney* off the coast of Africa. He continued his work as an assistant surgeon, despite "so great an affliction." In 1855, he resigned from the Navy and was married to Lydia Smith.

Although he personally felt great opposition to the secession movement in Tennessee, Farquharson served as a surgeon in the Civil War. His friend Andrew Johnson appointed him surgeon of his own regiment, the Fourth Tennessee Infantry, but Farquharson's deafness led him to an 1863 decision to move to Nashville and take charge of a hospital. In 1868, he left Nashville for Davenport, Iowa, where he held the office of president of the Academy of Sciences, which he had helped to found. While serving on various committees for six years, he was able to pursue many scientific interests. In 1875, he represented the Iowa Academy at the American Association for the Advancement of Science meeting in Detroit. There he presented his lecture entitled "Recent Explorations of Mounds Near Davenport, Iowa," in which he described the work of Reverend Gass and four theological students who had examined aspects of the culture of Native American "Mound Builders." During the lecture, however, the audience was unable to hear him and repeatedly requested a louder voice. Farquharson, reading from his paper, neither heard nor saw the commotion and completed his entire lecture despite the screaming participants. The humorous incident was subsequently reported in the *New York Tribune*, and Farquharson's lecture was repeated the following day by his friend, the naturalist J. Duncan Putnam.

Most of Farquharson's work in medicine thereafter was as a consulting physician. With a retiring disposition and a "singular sensitiveness" he displayed with regard to his deafness, Farquharson was nevertheless successful in his career and maintained a breadth of interests. He published a number of medical reports in the *Proceedings* of the Iowa Academy of Sciences, which ranged in topical content from studies of the burns caused by rifle balls when entering the body of an animal to the postmortem examination of a boa constrictor. He also wrote an analysis of the skulls and long bones from mounds in Illinois and the formation of ground ice on the rapids of the Mississippi. As a close friend of Putnam, he became increasingly interested in ethnology and was appointed a member of the French Société Ethnographique in 1880.

As an elected member of the staff of Mercy Hospital, he established St. John's Ward for contagious diseases. He devoted a great deal of his energy to the prevention of disease and involved himself with the Board of Health at Rock Island in its analysis of diseases. He was active in the Sanitary Council of the Mississippi Valley and the American Public Health Association, and published reports in the proceedings of the Iowa State Medical Society, including one on "Leprosy in the State of Iowa" that attracted much attention. In 1880, he felt honored to accept the position of Secretary of the Iowa State Board of Health.

Farquharson often described to his friends how his deafness had provided him with greater ability to concentrate on his work. Without external disturbances, he had become an avid reader, with a special love for Thackeray. He was known and respected for his high standards of professionalism and scientific accuracy. His death on September 6, 1884, was a great loss to his associates, who had learned to appreciate his administrative talents and his high regard for quality services in the health field.

References

Lang, H. G. (1994). *Silence of the spheres: The deaf experience in the history of science.* Westport, CT: Bergin & Garvey.
Middleton, W. D. (1885). Biographical sketch of Dr. Robert James Farquharson. *Pro-

ceedings of the Davenport Academy of Natural Sciences. Davenport, IA: Davenport
Academy of Natural Sciences.

ANGELINE FULLER FISCHER (1841–1925), American Writer.

Angeline Fuller Fischer was born on August 11, 1841, in Savanna, Illinois.
Her parents had been early midwestern settlers. The family lived by the Mississippi River for her first nineteen years, and it was by the river that she first
learned to read. Fischer attended a local school until the spring of 1854, when
a severe attack of whooping cough and typhoid fever left her profoundly deaf.
For five years, she drifted in isolation and loneliness, unaware of any special
state-run programs for deaf students; but in 1859, an article in the *Northwestern
Christian Advocate* led her to apply to the Illinois School for the Deaf in Jacksonville. There, "Angie's" instructors soon realized her poetic talents and encouraged her to pursue them. Fischer had fallen in love with the musicality of
poetry during the years after she first became deaf. Severe eye problems, however, caused by her earlier illness, plagued her throughout life; and after only
two years in the school, traumatic spells of blindness forced her to leave.

Around 1875, Fischer became interested in the Deaf community. She helped
raise funds for St. Ann's Church for the Deaf. Her own experiences with hearing
and vision loss also likely played a motivating role in her subsequent efforts to
instruct a young deaf-blind girl. In 1880, she served as matron, a kind of residential dean's position, at the Texas School for the Deaf in Austin; but poor
health again forced her return to Savanna. During this period, she also began to
submit articles to the *Deaf-Mutes' Journal,* which offered social and career
advice to deaf women through a wide range of cultural, religious, literary, and
critical discussions. Within five years, she became the leading feminist in the
American Deaf community.

In 1880, the National Association of the Deaf (NAD) was organized partly
as a result of the Edict of Milan, which suppressed the use of sign language in
the education of deaf pupils. Fischer advocated persistently for the participation
of deaf women in the first NAD convention. At the convention, she met her
future husband, George E. Fischer, the deaf editor of a county newspaper in
Maine; they were married in 1887.

Fischer's next cause was the admission of deaf women to Gallaudet College,
which had already been graduating men for several decades. Through a satiric
letter in a leading periodical in the Deaf community, she argued that the funds
being used for a gymnasium at Gallaudet ought to be better applied to a building
for deaf women, pledging five dollars to build a college for deaf women far
from Gallaudet. But such was not necessary. Within a few years, under mounting
pressure, Gallaudet College opened its doors to deaf women.

Her first volume of verse, *The Venture* (1883), was 232 pages long, containing
about half the poems she had written over a period of twenty years. As one
reviewer wrote in the Omaha, Nebraska *Rising Tide,* "Hearing no sound she
sings with faultless rhythm and pleasing euphony, and taste and power of

thought are manifest in every verse.'' The hearing writers Ella Wheeler Wilcox and Alonzo Hilton Davis admired Fischer's beauty of expression and Fischer's closer friends, Oliver Wendell Holmes and John Greenleaf Whittier, reviewed the collection favorably. In an 1883 personal letter to her, Whittier wrote, ''I have read thy little book, and find much in it to like and which is calculated to do good, and comfort and encourage others. The temperance lyrics are excellent, especially the 'Plea,' 'Our Friend,' 'A Soliloquy,' and 'When I Shall Be Satisfied,' are fine poems.''

In 1884, Edward Miner Gallaudet, then the first president of Gallaudet College, presented an extract of Fischer's sonnet ''The Semi-Mute's Soliloquy'' in an article in *Harper's Monthly Magazine* titled ''The Poetry of the Deaf,'' and twenty-one of her pieces were included in *Women in Sacred Song*. Fischer was given honorable mention in the anthology *Poets of America*. She was one of the leading deaf writers of her era, publishing numerous articles in *The Wisconsin Times*. ''Poems and Fancy Needlework'' was the title of her 1885 exhibit at the World's Industrial Exposition in New Orleans. She and her husband contributed verse and other writings to the *Omaha Monitor* and other newspapers. She also helped him manage the Fischer Distributing Agency.

Her husband died in July 1904, and Fischer moved to Rockford, Illinois, to live with her older sister. Her poetry appeared in newspapers wherever she traveled, and her articles in periodicals in the Deaf community continued to address important issues of the day. In 1908, a former mayor of Savanna sent her a copy of the *Thorold Post* of Ontario, in which one of her poems, ''The World and Human Life,'' had been reprinted along with a biographical note. During her final years, Fischer enjoyed such reminiscences of events that compelled her to write verse.

A feminist to the end, her final piece of writing in *The Silent Worker*, in 1915, was a call for a memorial to Sophia Fowler Gallaudet, the ''Mother of the American Deaf,'' to remind young deaf men and women of her influence that had pervaded Gallaudet College for so many years, and of her contributions to its early growth as an institution of higher education.

Fischer died on April 2, 1925, at the age of eighty-three.

References

Gallaher, J. E. (1898). *Representative deaf persons in the United States of America.* Chicago: Gallaher.
Interesting letter from Angie Fuller Fischer. (1915). *The Silent Worker, 27* (6), 108.
One of America's greatest deaf poets. (1908). *The Silent Worker, 21* (2), 1.
Terry, A. T. (1921). A visit to Angie Fuller Fischer. *The Silent Worker, 36* (6), 193–194.

DOROTHY CANFIELD FISHER (1879–1958), American Writer/Educator.

Dorothea Frances Canfield was born on February 17, 1879, in Lawrence, Kansas. She grew up in an uncommonly educated and sometimes chaotic household. Her father, James Hulme Canfield, was a professor at the University of Kansas. He would later become president of Ohio State University, but when Canfield was young, her father's job security and chances for career advancement were sometimes in doubt. He was an outspoken advocate of women's rights and championed a variety of other controversial causes. Her mother, Flavia Camp, was a progressive school teacher, who took her daughter to Paris for a year when Canfield was ten. Her paternal grandfather had taught French at the University of Kansas, and the family went to France on study trips throughout her teens. Given the bustle of her home life, Canfield appreciated the quiet summers spent with relatives in Vermont, which also became the background for some of her stories.

At the age of fourteen, for reasons she steadfastly refused to write about or discuss, she became deaf. She took speechreading lessons and turned her attention to preparation for entry into the University of Nebraska the next year. She had hoped to study music; her deafness forced a re-evaluation, and she majored in literature. At this time, she also changed her first name to Dorothy. After a year, she transferred to Ohio State University and completed her bachelor's degree there in 1899. Thinking that she would like to pursue a professorship in languages, she continued her studies at the Sorbonne; and, after a year there and four years in New York, she became the first woman to earn a Ph.D. in Romance languages from Columbia University. She taught for a year at the Horace Mann School, where she had been a secretary.

In New York, she met John Redwood Fisher, who dropped out of law school and took on editorial work following their May 7, 1970 marriage. They settled in Arlington, Vermont, and raised two children. The births of her son and daughter rekindled a longstanding interest Fisher had in child development. In 1911, she traveled to Rome for a year of study with Maria Montessori. From 1912 until 1916, Fisher wrote four books on child development, based both on her studies of Montessori theory and her meticulous observations of her own two children. She was selected to serve on the Vermont State Board of Education in 1921, as well as on a number of commissions.

World War I provided the backdrop for profound changes in Dorothy Canfield Fisher's life. She was basically a pacifist, but her fear of imperialism persuaded her to become involved in the war effort. In 1916, the entire Fisher family moved to France for three years. John Fisher volunteered for the ambulance service; Dorothy coordinated brailling services for blinded soldiers and ran the commissary for the Soissons training center. She also was in charge of a home for refugee children in the Pyrenees toward the end of the war. The work frequently put her in close proximity to the action. The experience was at once intense, disturbing, and exhilarating. Fisher returned home severely depressed for a time, but she recognized the profound humanity in the darkness she had experienced. She became remarkably productive in both creative and academic writing following the war.

During the war, Fisher published two volumes of short stories about France.

Her 1921 novel, *The Brimming Cup,* about a woman torn between her love of her husband and another man, was a best seller. In 1923, she translated Papini's *Life of Christ,* and the edition sold 350,000 copies. While critics sighed about the "undue" length of her books, *Rough Hewn* (1922), *The Home Maker* (1924), and *Her Son's Wife* (1926) were also hugely popular. All were about the delicate interrelationship among family members and were informed by her study of human psychology. *The Deepening Stream* (1930) traced a woman's maturation from her life as a midwestern girl to womanhood in France. The stress of academic life and the impact of marital discord on children are dominant themes in this novel, and they appear in much of her other work.

Despite the generally accepted autobiographical motifs in her fictional work and her nonfiction interests—strong families, the Midwest, France, blind soldiers, academic circles, and human development—Fisher never wrote about being deaf. Asked about this, she replied candidly that she found her deafness "a hindrance in every way." Her blind characters probably give her viewpoint indirectly. One of them states: "Our senses are not ourselves. . . . The use one makes of what he has; that is the formula."

From 1926 until 1950, Fisher was a member of the selection committee of the Book-of-the-Month-Club, a formidable reading task. In the 1930s, her writing interests shifted back primarily to education, which she viewed as the salvation of the future.

Dorothy Canfield Fisher died in Arlington, Vermont, on November 9, 1958. Annual awards established in her memory are given by the Book-of-the-Month Club to public libraries in small communities.

References

Basset, T.D.S. (1980). Dorothea Frances Canfield Fisher. In J. A. Garraty (Ed.). *Dictionary of American Biography* (Suppl. 6, pp. 202–203). New York: Charles Scribner's Sons.

Davies, L. A. (1922). Successful deaf people of today: Dorothy Canfield Fisher. *The Volta Review, 24* (5), 148–150.

Kunitz, S. J., & Haycraft, H. (Eds.). (1942). Mrs. Dorothea Frances (Canfield) Fisher. In *Twentieth century authors: A biographical dictionary* (pp. 457–458). New York: H. W. Wilson.

JULIANNA FJELD (1947–   ), American Actress/Producer.

Julianna Fjeld was born deaf on June 1, 1947, in Minneapolis, Minnesota. When she was a very young child at the John Tracy Clinic for Deaf Children in Los Angeles, she was thrilled when Spencer Tracy, whose son John was deaf, would visit and play with the children. Fjeld attributed part of her motivation to become an actress to his visits, particularly when, at the age of eight, she saw Tracy star in *The Mountain.* After Tracy died in 1967, Fjeld wrote a long letter to Katharine Hepburn, and they developed a poignant friendship based on their memories of the beloved actor.

As the daughter of a U.S. Army colonel, Fjeld moved from school to school, attending the Kendall School in Washington, D.C., the Kansas School for the Deaf, the Percy M. Hughes School in Syracuse, New York, and the California School for the Deaf in Berkeley. She grew up in what she has humorously called the "Dark Ages" for deaf people, when the notion of a deaf actor on television or in film was just a dream. In 1955, however, her mother showed her a newspaper clipping about the pioneering deaf actor, Bernard Bragg,* starring on television. She began to watch him as he acted and directed, her mind set on following in his footsteps.

In 1961, at the age of fourteen, Fjeld attended experimental summer classes offered by Gallaudet College. She graduated from Gallaudet in 1970 with a bachelor's degree in English literature. From 1971 until 1976, she toured as an actress with the National Theatre of the Deaf (NTD) and the Little Theatre of the Deaf. Fjeld also served as a consultant to the Tony Award-winning Broadway production of *Children of a Lesser God*, while serving as understudy for the central role of "Sarah Norman" on Broadway. She also appeared at the renowned Mark Taper Forum in Los Angeles, conducting "visual workshops," and she portrayed the "Spirit of Christmas Present" in *A Christmas Carol* at the Taper. She starred in the award-winning production of *Trojan Women* as "Hecuba" at the Los Angeles Actors' Studio.

Increasingly concerned with access for deaf and hearing audiences, Fjeld helped to create Project D.A.T.E. (Deaf Audience Theatre Experience), a Los Angeles project developed to offer sign-interpreted performances and related workshops and discussions. She traveled to Paris to co-found the International Visual Theatre as well. She has lectured on script selection and analysis, acting, and sign language at the Claude Kipnis Mime School and at Hunter College in New York City.

On December 17, 1975, Fjeld wrote to Joanne Greenburg, author of *I Never Promised You a Rose Garden* and *In This Sign*, the best-selling novel about two deaf parents who raise a hearing child during the Depression. Through this letter, Fjeld struck up a lasting friendship. She expressed her strong feelings that *In This Sign* should be made into a film—and immediately emphasized to Greenberg the importance of casting deaf actors: "Your novel is very powerful and I'm afraid that if hearing actors do the Abel and Janice roles, they may not understand what deafness is really like." Greenburg agreed completely, responding on December 28, "I would never have Abel or Janice played by anyone but a Deaf person. I can think of no one in the world I would more wish to see in the role of Janice than you." Fjeld bought the rights to the book for one dollar to produce the story for a wide audience. When she was named an associate producer at Warner Brothers TV, the first deaf person to attain a position of that stature in a major production company, she worked on the film adaptation for television of Greenberg's novel. In 1985, as co-executive producer of the Hallmark Hall of Fame drama *Love is Never Silent*, she won the Emmy Award for the best drama/comedy special. *Love is Never Silent* was the first television movie to star deaf actors in three principal roles. The story is about "Margaret Ryder," who grew up during the Depression and served as her deaf parents' bridge to the world of hearing people. Fjeld herself portrayed "Barbara," a family friend.

Fjeld took the Emmy with her during visits to deaf school children so they could touch it. A twelve-minute videotape about the making of the film helped her promote self-advocacy as a lesson for the children. Fjeld met Marlee Matlin* in Portland in 1986, and they have shared concerns about the struggles of deaf actresses. She experienced a shared sense of celebration when her friend Matlin won the Oscar for best actress for the film version of *Children of a Lesser God*.

Fjeld's television credits include *Johnny Belinda* and *Hear No Evil*. She also appeared on *Dallas*, *Sesame Street*, and in a special feature on visual language for deaf people, with narrator Timothy Near, on the *Captain Kangaroo* CBS-TV series, which won an Emmy Award. She has been involved in the production of a number of specials for the Public Broadcasting Service. She had a role in the Hollywood film, *Golden Girl*, with Susan Anton. She has performed in the play *A Child's Christmas in Wales*, a National Theatre of the Deaf classic, shown on both BBC and CBS. She is the subject of an award-winning documentary, *Julianna: A Portrait*.

In 1987, she directed Gilbert Eastman's* *Sign Me Alice* at the California School for the Deaf, giving the children the chance to work with a professional artist-in-residence. The play is about a deaf woman seeking personal identity, a particularly apt choice for young people in a multicultural society.

In 1991, Fjeld was appointed Co-Artistic Director of the National Theatre of the Deaf. Along with NTD founder David Hays, she led NTD through its twenty-fifth anniversary year. Fjeld enjoys the challenge of promoting increased understanding between deaf and hearing people through art. Performances offered by NTD during her co-directorship included an adaptation of Robert Louis Stevenson's *Treasure Island*. She also arranged for the Little Theatre of the Deaf to tour such places as Thailand, India, Scandinavia, and the Far East. Fjeld's imagination, vision, and collaborative spirit have literally extended to all corners of the globe.

References

Brooks, D. E. (1986, October 6). Producer able to break silence of Hollywood in film about deaf. Fremont, California *Argus*.

Carroll, C. (1992). New directions: NTD'S Julianna Fjeld makes her presence felt. *Gallaudet Today*, *23* (1), 5–6.

Cowan, R. (1987, February). Banners greet Emmy winner. Salem, Oregon *Statesman-Journal*.

Moore, M. (1991). Julianna Fjeld: A heart full of joy and faith and patience and hope. *Deaf Life*, *3* (12), 10–22.

SIR JOHN AMBROSE FLEMING (1849–1945), British Electrical Scientist. John Ambrose Fleming was born in Lancaster, Lancashire, November 29,

1849, the son of a Congregational minister. In school he did poorly in Latin, but was quick at mechanics and science. He graduated from University College in London in 1870, and he entered Cambridge University. There, he worked for James Clerk Maxwell, repeating the experiments of Henry Cavendish. According to acquaintances, as Fleming's hearing loss increased, his impatience in manner grew proportionately. Whether in reality his deafness can be directly blamed for his moodiness is debatable.

While Fleming served as a consultant to Thomas Alva Edison's* company in London, the firm was combined with the Bell Telephone interests. His attention was turned to photometry after the carbon filament lamp was improved by Edison and Swan; and this eventually led to a close connection with Marconi and his Wireless Telegraphy Company. Fleming was also an advisor on electrical generation and distribution networks. His work with the generating plant for the Atlantic transmission from Cornwall to Newfoundland reached fruition in Marconi's successful reception of Morse telegraph signals in December 1901. Fleming saw the value of the potentiometer, an adjustable resistance device, and he contributed toward its development, encouraging R.E.B. Crompton to market it in a practical form. Among other uses, the potentiometer is the common control switch used to adjust the volume on a television or radio.

Fleming was a devoted scientist. He participated fully in scientific discussions. As his deafness increased, he would take an assistant with him to take notes, allowing him to follow more effectively. The first paper ever presented to the Physical Society, founded in 1874, was a discussion of a form of voltaic cell read by Fleming. Sixty-five years later, he read his *last* professional paper to the same organization. He worked constantly throughout this period on a variety of electrical experiments—transmitters, receivers, wireless telegraphy, and the rectifier tube (thermionic valve). He served as president of the Television Society until his death at ninety-five years of age. He provided much support to John L. Baird, a brilliant inventor. Fleming's mental powers and clarity of expression, as well as his individual concentration, were admired by colleagues.

As a teacher Fleming had a sterling reputation. He was highly organized, designed attractive plans, and was a motivating speaker. He did not digress or ramble, choosing words and examples carefully. Despite Fleming's deafness, he remained an excellent lecturer. It was not, however, easy to get Fleming to understand questions in class. Fortunately, when he did, he was uncharacteristically amiable and encouraging to students. Because of his deafness, as years went on, he became less involved with the actual supervision of students in their laboratory work.

Fleming's deafness may have hindered him at times, but, as Professor MacGregor-Morris (1954) points out, it also enabled him to isolate himself from outside disturbances and concentrate on the subject in a way that would have been more difficult for a person with normal hearing. Fleming worked at home virtually every evening on writing and scientific problems. This ceaseless work, too, appeared to colleagues to increase with more profound deafness. Yet, he also appeared to take pleasure in a broad array of challenging questions. His day-to-day life at University College tested his limited communication and bothered him more. In the 1920s, Fleming is described as having developed a microphone, to which earphones were attached, to assist his hearing. He would sit behind his desk and direct his visitor to sit in front of him, next to the microphone. On one visit, Crowther (1970) started by explaining the object of his visit, and Fleming's first comment was: "How much do you propose to pay me for this advice?" Crowther was dumbfounded as Fleming went into a tirade on how scientists "are always expected to do something for nothing. Now, if I were a lawyer, there would be a proper fee." When Crowther attempted some reply, Fleming roared: "Don't speak to me! Speak to the microphone!" Crowther was concerned about not looking at Fleming, but turned and responded. When Fleming abruptly finished the interview, Crowther jumped up, and ran out of his laboratory and the department. About twenty years later, Crowther received a "charming" unsolicited letter of congratulations from Fleming. He had just read the Pelican edition of Crowther's book *British Scientists of the Nineteenth Century*, which contained lives of Maxwell and Kelvin. Fleming had been a student of Clerk Maxwell and had known Kelvin well. He told Crowther that he was very appreciative of what he had written, particularly with regard to critical comments on Kelvin's character which Fleming said he had directly experienced. Thus, Crowther had a rather interesting direct experience of his own with Fleming's contradictory nature.

Fleming proceeded to combine the knowledge he had gleaned from the two masters—Edison and Marconi. He took up the Edison effect around 1883 while an advisor to the Edison companies. In his many years of investigating the unidirectional passage of electricity from a hot filament to a cold plate within an evacuated bulb, he found it to be due to the passage of the newly discovered electrons leaving the hot filament. Fleming found that these electrons would travel only when the plate was attached to the positive terminal of a generator; and, by 1904, he realized that this meant that in alternating current, the electricity would pass only half the time. AC would then enter the device and DC would leave it. He had developed the rectifier which he called a "valve," since it turned on for current in one direction and off for current in the other. In the United States, the valve came to be called a "diode vacuum tube." In his memoirs, however, Fleming wrote that he regretted that some authors prefer to denote it by the unmeaningful name of "diode."

The value of this contribution was at once recognized. Lee De Forest's addition of a grid made the tube an amplifier as well as a rectifier. This led to practical electronic instruments. Shortly after this, the detection of radio waves in receivers followed, and then from these inventions of Fleming and De Forest came the television, radar, and computer industries.

Fleming received many honors. In 1892, he was elected Fellow of the Royal Society; and in 1910, it awarded him the Hughes Medal. The Institution of Electrical Engineers presented him with the Faraday Medal in 1928; and he was given the Gold Medal of Honor of the Institute of Radio Engineers five years later, an honor bestowed on that person who had made public the greatest advance in the science or art of radio communication. In 1929, Fleming was knighted.

Fleming died on April 18, 1945, in Sidmouth, Devon, England.

References

Crowther, J. G. (1970). *Fifty years with science*. London: Barrie & Jenkins.

MacGregor-Morris, J. T. (1954). *The inventor of the valve: A biography of Sir Ambrose Fleming*. London: The Television Society.

MacGregor-Morris, J. T. (1959). John Ambrose Fleming. In L. G. Wickham Legg & E. T. Williams (Eds.), *The dictionary of national biography 1941–1950* (pp. 258–260). London: Oxford University Press.

ANDREW FOSTER (1925–1987), American Educator/Missionary.

Andrew Foster was born in Birmingham, Alabama, on June 27, 1925, the son of a coal miner. He was totally deafened through spinal meningitis at the age of eleven. At the time, he was in public school in Fairfield, Alabama. For several years, he attended the Alabama School for the Colored Deaf in Taladega. When he was seventeen years old, at the height of World War II, his family moved to Detroit, Michigan, where he worked in a factory manufacturing equipment for the war effort while studying in the evenings. As a young teenager in Detroit, he attended a presentation by a missionary who described the neglect of deaf people in Jamaica. The experience inspired him at this early age to consider a religious vocation and evangelical work.

Foster first pursued interests in business administration and accounting. Several years after World War II ended, he enrolled in the Detroit Institute of Commerce, earning a diploma in 1950. A correspondence course earned him a high school diploma from the American School in Chicago. In 1951, he became the first African American to enter Gallaudet College since its 1864 authorization to grant college degrees. During his years there, he found his life's work. He began to search actively for young deaf African Americans who needed inspiration and guidance. Heretofore, very few deaf African Americans had received an education adequate to prepare them for professional work in any field. Foster also learned that in all of Africa, only twelve schools served deaf children. Recalling the pleas of the missionary from Jamaica he had met years ago, he set his own goal to effect change in Africa. While a student at Gallaudet, Foster also took summer courses at the Hampton Institute in Virginia. He graduated from Gallaudet with a bachelor's degree in education in 1954, then earned a master's degree in special education from Eastern Michigan University in 1955 and a degree in Christian Missions from Seattle Pacific College in 1956.

With the assistance of his friends in Detroit and encouraged by Leonard M. Elstad, president of Gallaudet College, Foster founded the Christian Mission for

Andrew Foster (far right), American missionary and educator. Photo from *Gallaudet Today, 4* (3), 1974, courtesy of Gallaudet University Archives.

Deaf Africans. Its goal was to bring both religious and general education to several hundred thousand deaf people in Africa. In 1957, he began his crusade in the newly independent Ghana; he gathered more than fifty deaf people in a seventeen-room rented public school in Accra and offered classes to both children and adults. When he arrived there, the nation had no facilities whatsoever for teaching deaf people. By 1959, Foster's school had twenty-five boarding students, another twenty day students, and a waiting list of one hundred children. He trained seven assistants to help him educate these children. Within five years, there were 113 children in the school and a waiting list of three hundred more. Ironically, Ghana had first resisted Foster's proposal, responding that there were not enough deaf children to justify his efforts.

As the school's primary teacher, administrator, and public relations specialist, he was extremely busy during those years, returning to the United States to give fundraising speeches. His pioneering efforts resulted in the eventual establishment of the Ghana Mission Center for Deaf Youths and Adults and the Ghana Mission School for Deaf Children, which were ultimately accredited and funded by the national government. He was also asked to investigate and make recommendations to the Ghanaian government for a comprehensive national rehabilitation scheme for people with disabilities. This success in Ghana motivated Foster to attempt to train teachers in Nigeria, where he established three schools in the early 1960s—in Ibadan, Kaduna, and Enugu. Meanwhile, he also studied further at the Wayne State University in Detroit to prepare himself more completely in teacher education, and at the Detroit Bible College for his evangelical work.

In 1961, Foster married Berta Zuther, a deaf woman, who became his dedicated partner. Together, while raising five children, they founded schools in Togo, Ivory Coast, Chad, Senegal, Benin, Congo, Central African Republic, Gabon, Kenya, Niger, Sierra Leone, Upper Volta, and Zaire. They also founded the Africa Bible College for the Deaf. Foster served on the governing boards of all of these schools. In 1965, he organized the first All-Africa Conference on the Education of the Deaf at the University of Ibadan in Nigeria. For this pioneering work, he was elected president of the multinational Council for the Education and Welfare of the Deaf in Africa. Civil war and political unrest, however, made the organization short-lived. In 1970, Gallaudet College awarded Foster an honorary doctoral degree and, in 1975, the Gallaudet College Alumni Association Award. Eastern Michigan University named him an Outstanding Alumnus in 1980. This period was also one of worry. Amid all the relentless activity, Berta Foster contracted cancer. Fortunately, treatment was successful.

In addition to twenty schools for deaf people, Foster also established many churches, camps, and programs. Through training African-born leaders among deaf persons, he had prepared a significant number to enter Gallaudet College and return as change-agents to their respective countries. By 1974, there were more than seventy schools for deaf pupils on the continent of Africa. All through these years, Foster conducted fundraising tours in forty-seven states, across Canada, and in Mexico, the Caribbean Islands, nearly all of Western Europe, and twenty-five African countries. Over the next decade, he established and taught intensive teacher training courses in both English and French in many countries while continuing his evangelical work.

On December 3, 1987, Foster accepted an empty seat on a chartered airplane carrying twelve other persons from Kenya. During the twenty minutes the Cessna was in the air, it struggled to gain altitude and the passengers were seen waving in despair and tossing their briefcases from the windows to aid in identification. Reverend Andrew Jackson Foster and all of the passengers died when the plane crashed in a mountainous area in East Africa near the town of Gisney in Rwanda. As Foster's many friends and coworkers gathered at Gallaudet College to eulogize him at a memorial service in January, 1988, among them could be found the "second generation" of Foster's students, including Gabriel Adepoju, who summarized that "Andrew Foster is to Africa what Thomas Hopkins Gallaudet is to the United States of America."

References

Brenner, B. (1981, June 13). Deaf man began mission 25 years ago. *The Flint Journal*.
Dr. Andrew Foster. (1974). *Gallaudet Today, 4* (3), 23–24.
Dr. Andrew Foster eulogized on campus. (1988). *Gallaudet Alumni Newsletter, 22* (4),
   1.

Panara, R. F., & Panara, J. (1983). *Great deaf Americans.* Silver Spring, MD: T. J. Publishers.

Sanders, R. S. (1987, December 5). Crash victim left mark in Africa by creating 20 schools for deaf. *The Flint Journal,* A1, A11.

ROBERT FREIMAN (1917–   ), American Artist.

Robert Freiman was born deaf on March 16, 1917, in New York City, the son of Viennese and Russian parents. His father, a woolen merchant, had a business in Manhattan. Freiman attended the Wright Oral School at the age of two and a half, then at the age of six, he entered the Lexington School for the Deaf in New York City. He stayed at that school for twelve years, followed by a year at the New York School for the Deaf (Fanwood School). Noting the artistic abilities displayed in his sketching and designing at an early age, his parents hired private tutors to work with him after school and on weekends. He also attended classes on Saturdays at the Art Students' League, Parsons School of Art, and the Pratt Institute.

When Freiman was nineteen years old, he chose art school full time over the two more years of academic education and, although ranked third on Regents examinations administered at Columbia University, decided against attending college. He felt that his artistic development was dependent on a full-time commitment to in-depth study. In 1939, during his fourth year at the National Academy of Design, he decided to leave that program. During subsequent years, he found it effective to study independently under other artists, including Howard Steiger, Robert Brackman, Eliot O'Hara, Jerry Farnsworth, and Wayman Adams. Freiman had the impressive capability to speechread in both English and French. From all of the artists with whom he worked, he developed technique, incorporating what he learned into a style of his own; he experimented continuously, particularly with mixed media in crayon, oil, charcoal, pen and ink, and pencil. Freiman also began to do larger seascapes and florals, notable for strong use of color, in watercolor, lithograph, oil painting, and sepia conté. Tony Sarg, the illustrator of children's books, invited him to his home and served as a critic-mentor during his early years.

Serendipitously, when a passerby saw Freiman sketching on the street in Boston, he helped arrange an exhibition of his work. Several shows were subsequently held at art galleries in Boston. Guided by what he termed an "inner voice," Freiman painted his portraits and landscapes, the latter often scenes of the French Riviera, of Nantucket, and New York, with emotion. In 1938, for example, while painting boats and fisherfolk in Nantucket under the guidance of Frank Chase, his friends held a private reception, which brought further recognition to his work. *A Nantucket Street* and *Water Front, Nantucket* were included in a short sketch of Freiman, "The Story of a Young Artist," published in the *Digest of the Deaf* in 1940. During the 1930s, Freiman's work was exhibited at the source of much of his inspiration—Nantucket and Martha's Vineyard. He also showed in such prestigious galleries and exhibitions as the

Whitney Museum of American Art, International Exhibition of Fine and Applied Arts by Deaf Artists at the Roerich Museum, the Associated American Artists galleries, and the National Academy of Design. Through the 1940s, he had numerous exhibits at Doll & Richards.

Freiman studied further under Lucien Fontonarosa at the Ecole des Beaux-Arts at Fontainebleau, where he won a first prize from the French Republic in both 1950 and 1951. In Paris in 1954, he exhibited at the Galerie Cardo Matignon. In 1955, he was elected a member of the American Water Color Society and held exhibits at the Galleries of Doll & Richards in Boston; in Oxford and Otley, England; in New York at the Barzansky and Roerich Galleries; and at the National Academy of Design. The following year, he exhibited oils, watercolors, and a self-portrait in silver point at the O'Hana Gallery in London.

Many reviewers have commented that Freiman's deafness had led him to see *through* otherwise conventional subjects, often with some humor. In 1962 in Paris, for example, friends remarked on the born-deaf artist's active, searching, restless eyes. His work was reviewed in 1971 by the Paris-born professor of French literature at New York University, Madame Lamont. She attributed the openness of Freiman's work to the attention to visual interest deafness demands.

Freiman's engaging personality and increasing renown has given him access to worlds of power and privilege. He has completed portraits of a number of prominent citizens, including college presidents and British rear admirals. In the New York *Daily Mirror*, Harry Hershfeld wrote that "Freiman's pastel of Msgr. Fulton J. Sheen is the talk of the art world." He has worked to remain focused and creative in a high-pressure atmosphere, however. In 1973, fifty-seven of his works in oil, watercolor, mixed media, and pen and ink were exhibited at Gallaudet College. The titles reveal his love of the ocean, and particularly the areas of Saint-Paul de Vence and Nantucket, where he typically spends half the year: *Fleurs au Soleil*; *Morning Crimson, Nantucket*; *Au March de Poisson à Nice*; and *Twilight in South Beach Harbor, Nantucket*. Freiman's works have also included landscapes from Italy and Greece. Portraits in the Gallaudet exhibition included those of Youssef Riz Kallah of Cairo, Tanya of Tunisia, Tahir Qadri of Kashmir, Zoubeida Barmania of India, and Prince Doan Thai of Laos.

The sketchbooks of Robert Freiman reveal many other fascinating personalities whom he painted. In Paris, the noted Russian sculptor Ossip Zadkine sat for him on the terrace of the Cafe des Deux Maggots, praising the completed portrait. When he met Picasso, the great artist autographed Freiman's tennis shorts. Freiman painted James Baldwin, Tennessee Williams, and James Joyce. In Saint-Paul, he painted the artist Georges Braque, the director Henri-Georges Clouzót, the poet Jacques Prévert, and actor Peter Ustinov. Prominent actors, including Simone Signoret, Anne Bancroft, and Dirk Bogarde, have commissioned his work.

In 1977, an exhibit entitled "The Silent World of Robert Freiman: His Paintings and Portraits" was held at the Edward J. Brown and Associates Studio in New York City. He has been awarded many honors; perhaps the most significant accolade has come from the critic Pierre Rouve in the London *Art News and Review*, who called Robert Freiman the best American watercolorist since John Marin. In addition to many private collections, his paintings are found in permanent collections of the Boston Fine Arts Museum, the Connecticut Museum at New Britain, the Kenneth Taylor Galleries at Nantucket, and Le Musée Municipal de Saint-Paul de Vence.

References

Kowalewski, F. (1973). Robert Freiman—Artist of two worlds. *The Deaf American, 26* (3), 3–4, 8.
Simon, A. B. (1947). A young deaf artist. *The Volta Review, 49* (7), 313–315, 348, 350.

PHYLLIS FRELICH (1944–   ), American Actress.

Phyllis Frelich was born on February 29, 1944, in Devil's Lake, North Dakota, the daughter of deaf parents and the first of nine children all deaf from birth. Her father was a struggling farmer for the first thirteen years of her life; he later turned to printing to support his family. Frelich inherited her parents' independence, observing their refusals of assistance as they managed to provide for the family. She was enrolled at the North Dakota School for the Deaf and later studied at Gallaudet College, where she developed an interest in theater, participating in the lead role in *Medea* and in a second Greek play *Iphigenia at Aulis*, for which she won the Best Actress of the Year award. She graduated from Gallaudet in 1967.

Frelich joined the National Theatre of the Deaf (NTD) as a founding member in 1967. She married NTD stage manager and set designer Robert Steinberg, and over the next decade she focused on her craft while raising two young children. She first appeared on Broadway in *Songs From Milkwood* with the Tony Award-winning NTD. Touring in Europe with NTD, she acted in such roles as "Marie" in *Woyzeck*, "Canina" in *Volpone*, and "Fonsia Dorsey" in *The Gin Game*.

Frelich began her association with the playwright Mark Medoff in the New Repertory Project at the University of Rhode Island, where she was an artist-in-residence. Medoff's play, *Children of a Lesser God*, was developed in 1979, based in part on Medoff's friendship with Frelich and Steinberg. The play describes the inevitable communication challenges in a deaf-hearing marriage, as well as in intimate relationships between teacher and student, man and woman. By the time of the play's completion, Medoff was chairperson of the theater department at New Mexico State University and, after further developing the play with the advice of his friends Frelich and Steinberg, he presented it in a workshop with them as the principal characters, "Sarah Norman" and "James Leeds." From there the play went to Los Angeles, directed by Gordon Davidson at the Mark Taper Forum. Davidson made a number of changes in the writing, and he replaced Steinberg with John Rubinstein. Steinberg became the understudy there and later on Broadway. Frelich was described in this performance

Phyllis Frelich and Patrick Graybill* in "The Gin Game." Photo courtesy of the National Technical Institute for the Deaf.

as a remarkable actress who made the audience see language through her graphic talents and elegance. *Children of a Lesser God* opened in the Longacre Theatre on Broadway on March 30, 1980, receiving critical acclaim and culminating in Tony Awards to Frelich for Best Actress and Rubinstein for Best Actor. Frelich was praised by the Outer Critics Circle for her Broadway debut. On April 13, *New York Times* critic Walter Kerr wrote that the play was "the season's unexpected find, a play unlike any other and immensely likable in its self-assertion." The Deaf community, too, viewed it as a breakthrough—a deaf actress in a major Broadway production—"a play in which sign language is the mode!" The honor she received was also regarded as an honor for the National Theatre of the Deaf, which from its inception ten years earlier had advocated that deaf performers could communicate effectively to the general theatre audience.

While Frelich continued on Broadway, the National Tour Company then took the play throughout the United States and Canada. Frelich was further honored in 1981 with the Roosevelt Rough Rider Award by the state of North Dakota. In 1984, Medoff's *Hands of Its Enemy* featured Frelich in a lead role as "Marietta Yerbt," a deaf playwright. When this play was taken to Los Angeles, again by Gordon Davidson, Richard Dreyfuss starred as Yerbt's director, "Howard Bellman."

Among Frelich's other television acting roles were appearances on an episode of *Gimme a Break* that NBC cast in 1985 and a satirical *Barney Miller* episode. She was nominated for an Emmy for her portrayal of Janice in *Love is Never Silent*, an adaptation of Joanne Greenberg's novel, *In This Sign*. She also appeared on *New Love American Style*, *Night of 100 Stars*, and *Spenser: For Hire*. In 1988, she played a deaf nun with a mysterious past, "Sister Sarah," in the soap opera *Santa Barbara*.

In 1991, Frelich was elected to the ninety-member Screen Actors Guild (SAG) Board in Hollywood, the highest policy-making body in the entertainment industry. She was the first deaf actor to be so recognized. That year, she also starred with Patrick Graybill* in *The Gin Game*. D. L. Coburn's play was adapted to American Sign Language and directed by Linda Bove,* with Ed Waterstreet* as artistic director. *The Gin Game* was a successful inaugural selection for the newly formed Deaf West Theatre Company in Los Angeles. Frelich and Graybill were praised for their ability to "move the audience with their language of the heart" (*The Angeles Reader*). A reporter for *The Drama-Logue* wrote, "There is no more of an intently watchable actress than Frelich."

Phyllis Frelich's colleagues and acting students consistently admire a simple fact of her life: in a competitive and often ego-involved profession, she has sought opportunities not only to showcase her own talent, but to open new doors to other deaf actors, directors, and playwrights.

References

Daniels, R. (1992). Making history: Phyllis Frelich continues to be a role model for deaf actors. *Gallaudet Today*, *23* (1), 10–11.

Deaf West's "Gin Game" scores aces in Hollywood!!! (1991). *Silent News, 23* (7), 1, 31.

Kakutani, M. (1980, April 1). Deaf since birth, Phyllis Frelich became an actress—and now a star. *New York Times,* C7.

Kroll, J. (1980, April 14). Songs without words. *Newsweek,* 105.

Panara, R. F., & Panara, J. (1983). *Great deaf Americans.* Silver Spring, MD: T. J. Publishers.

Strassler, M., & Carter, M., Jr. (1980). Phyllis Frelich: Actress extraordinaire. *The Deaf American, 33* (4), 2–6.

AUGUSTUS FULLER (1812–1873), American Folk Artist.

Born on December 9, 1812, in Deerfield, Massachusetts, Augustus Fuller was deafened in early childhood. Fuller was enrolled at the American Asylum for the Education and Instruction of the Deaf and Dumb (now the American School for the Deaf) in Hartford, Connecticut. He also studied painting briefly under Chester Harding. Immediately commencing his career upon returning from Hartford, he traveled through Massachusetts, New York, New Hampshire, and Vermont to find subjects for portraiture and pursue various apprenticeships. By 1832, he had begun to work as an itinerant artist. In April of that year, he was in Chatham, Connecticut, where records indicate he had received commissions for paintings. That summer, he also traveled to Clinton, New York, and spent the fall in New York City working briefly for the lithographers Thayer and Pendleton. In December, he was back in western Massachusetts, advertising his services in the *Hampshire Gazette:* "Portrait Painting, Augustus Fuller, although deaf and dumb, asks for a share of public patronage in his profession." His brother George had attended one of the first demonstrations in Boston of Daguerre's invention and had become interested in photographic portraits. After realizing that his brother Augustus could paint a full color portrait in oil for the same price of a daguerreotype, George gave up the idea after a few months. However, the arrival of the daguerreotype may have been an early harbinger of the end of Fuller's career.

Prints of four of Fuller's works can be found in *Somebody's Ancestors: Painting by Primitive Artists of the Connecticut Valley* (1942), published by the Springfield Museum of Fine Arts: *The Twins—John and Frank Fuller, with their Mother; Portrait of a Lady, Wearing a Red Pompon; Portrait of a Man;* and *Portrait of a Lady.*

Upon returning home for visits, he continued to paint portraits, including that of his stepmother, *Fanny Negus Fuller and Her Sons Francis Benjamin and John Emery.* The medium he most frequently used was oil on canvas. *Mercy Bemis Fuller* was a portrait of Augustus Fuller's grandmother, most likely painted by him during one of his visits to Fitchburg, in western Massachusetts, where she and her husband Azariah and several of their dozen children lived. The grandparents were asked by the Fuller family to help watch over the peripatetic itinerant painter, as the family found it difficult to chart his movements.

Fuller's paintings of Edwards Whipple Denny and Elizabeth Stone Denny are typical of the symmetrical folk-primitive style of that era. More careful analysis of these paintings held at the Worcester Historical Museum, however, reveals Edwards holding a pencil and Elizabeth a slate, indicating both their deafness and their literacy. Critics have interpreted these props given the deaf couple-subjects as representative of Fuller's generation of deaf people, the first to receive formal education in America, and among the first in the world. Edwards Denny and Elizabeth Stone, in fact, were both former classmates of Fuller at the American School for the Deaf. With financial support from the state of Massachusetts, which had no school for deaf pupils at the time, the children of that state were able to enroll at Hartford. Fuller seemed to maintain friendships despite his nomadic life. Visits with old friends brought him pleasure, as he found communication with them in American Sign Language much less demanding than that with his hearing subjects.

Fuller's correspondence with family members is candid in its expression of loneliness and forced independence. Despite the adventure of itinerant art work, he often longed for the commitment and sense of home he saw among the Dennys, or of his deaf brother Aaron and his deaf sister-in-law Sophia, the latter two also having met as students at the American School for the Deaf. His letters home also indicate that he struggled with the English language, and more than once he had been taken advantage of in transactions involving payments for his portrait work. Members of the family sometimes accompanied him to assure that the negotiations were fair and in good faith. During one period in which his stepbrother George, also a painter, traveled with him through New York, Augustus Fuller felt greatly productive and at ease, largely because George acted as an agent, freeing Augustus to paint and create. Fuller estimated his income as $1,000 between that January and May. At other times, his father supervised some of his business dealings.

Another painting by Fuller was an oil portrait on wood panel of Elihu Hoyt, a founder of the Franklin Agricultural Society and an important member of the state legislature. While Fuller was a student at the American School for the Deaf, his father came upon financial difficulties and was unable to afford the $115 tuition. Hoyt heard of the problem and obtained state support for Fuller through the Massachusetts legislature. Writing to Augustus Fuller's father on February 20, 1826, Hoyt summarized that "I hope the little fellows will improve their priviledges & succeed in their education to the extent of our most sanguine expectations." Fuller may have later painted Hoyt's portrait as a form of appreciation, but this is not known.

Fuller apparently also struggled with alcoholism, causing his family much worry. He was jailed at the age of forty-two, in Springfield, Massachusetts, for disorderly conduct. A letter to his brother describing the ordeal of not being able to protest his innocence in court is one of the first documented incidents of a deaf person in America confronting a legal system without benefit of an interpreter. In his letter to George Fuller on November 8, 1855, he concluded in despair, "God pity this poor ignorant and deaf mute for the world is sin suffering and death.'' Recognizing his increasing despondency, his family insisted on his returning home. A breakdown appears to have ensued. After 1855, Fuller signed documents as ''Cranberry Cultivator,'' instead of ''August Fuller—Portrait Painter.''

Fuller shares with William Mercer* and John Brewster, Jr.* the prestige of being one of the earliest noted deaf artists in America. Little of his work survives, however, for forty percent of Fuller's work was in miniatures, a highly personal and fragile, easily lost form. His commissions for these ran from $5 to $30, and gradually, he became unable to support himself with these delicate mementos.

Fuller died in Deerfield on August 13, 1873.

References

Groce, G. C., & Wallace, D. H. (1957). *The New-York Historical Society's dictionary of artists in America (1564–1860).* New Haven: Yale University Press.
Sloat, C. F. (Ed.). (1992). *Meet your neighbors: New England portraits, painters, & society, 1790–1850.* Sturbridge, MA: University of Massachusetts Press.

HORACE HOWARD FURNESS (1833–1912), American Shakespearean Scholar.

Horace Howard Furness was born in Philadelphia on November 2, 1833, the third of four children. He graduated fifth in the class of 1854 from Harvard College and then spent two years with his friend, Atherton Blight, studying languages in France, Germany, Italy, and other countries. In Spain, he visited the Escurial as a scholar and actually met the Queen. He was in Constantinople a month after the Crimean War ended, touring the battlefields. Back in America, he spent two years preparing for the Philadelphia bar, but the Civil War was imminent, and its issues were at the forefront of the young man's mind. The Furness family was strongly abolitionist. On May 28, 1854, he wrote angrily and passionately to his father with regard to his intense hatred for slavery and the decision to return the escaped slave Anthony Burns to his owner in Virginia. In his first month as counsellor-at-law, Furness passionately followed the events surrounding the raid at Harper's Ferry and the hanging of John Brown. Furness, however, was rejected for service in the Civil War because of his deafness. Disappointed, he joined the sanitary commission, a precursor of the modern Red Cross, and he remained with it until the war's end. Traveling from town to town, he described in letters to his wife the battle scenes he witnessed. He assisted army surgeons attached to McClellan's army at Sharpsburg and at a hospital in Frederick.

Furness had been admitted to the bar in November 1859. In the midst of the solemn events of the following year, he married Helen Kate Rogers and was elected a member of the Shakespere Society of Philadelphia; and he nurtured a dream through the War years to pursue this interest further as a scholar. Furness had been first captivated by Shakespeare's work in his youth, through the reading of plays by his friend, Fanny Kemble. This Shakespearean actress was also a member of his father's parish. Shakespeare's supposed stage gloves had been handed down from William Shakespeare, a poor glazier and relative of the great dramatist, to John Ward, David Garrick, Mrs. Siddons, and her daughter, who bequeathed them to Fanny Kemble. Kemble gave them to Furness in 1874, continuing the long tradition of the gloves being owned by dedicated students of Shakespeare's art.

At the war's end, Furness turned his youthful interest in Shakespeare into a lifelong career. Though he remained a counsellor-at-law until 1880, he found it difficult to continue this work because of his deafness. The Shakespere Society of Philadelphia welcomed his initial work with the variorum edition of *Romeo and Juliet* in 1866. Very little attention had been paid to Shakespeare by American scholars until then. Furness chose this first play, he confessed, because he loved it, and he held doubts at the time that he would ever edit another. Over the next fifty years, he nevertheless produced a series of volumes which included *Macbeth* (1873), *Hamlet* (1877, two volumes), *King Lear* (1880), *Othello* (1886), *The Merchant of Venice* (1888), *As You Like It* (1890), *The Tempest* (1892), *Midsummer Night's Dream* (1895), *The Winter's Tale* (1898), *Much Ado About Nothing* (1899), *Twelfth Night* (1901), *Love's Labour's Lost* (1904), *Antony and Cleopatra* (1907), and *Cymbeline* (published posthumously in 1913). Furness was unique as an editor in noting the adoption or rejection of contested readings by other scholars. Even the 1863 Cambridge edition had not done this. While he was sometimes criticized for failure to specify or confirm dates, his prefaces to the fourteen plays were widely admired for their rigorous scholarship. He was encouraged by W. J. Rolfe, editor of the *Rolfe Shakespere*, and Francis J. Child, Professor of Rhetoric at Harvard. After an initial argument with William Aldis Wright of Trinity College, Cambridge (coeditor with W. G. Clark of the *Cambridge Edition of Shakespere*), a lifelong friendship developed. In 1877, Harvard honored Furness with a degree of Master of Arts.

Furness averaged ten hours per day in his library, surrounded by his beloved cats. He also translated Julius Wellhausen's *Psalms* (1898) from German into English. His *Records of a Lifelong Friendship* (1910) presented the correspondence between his father and Ralph Waldo Emerson. He was also a trustee of the University of Pennsylvania and, as acting chairman of the University's Seybert Commission to investigate the phenomena of spiritualism, he published the *Preliminary Report* in 1887.

Through the years, his silver ear trumpet became a trademark, much like that of his contemporary Harriet Martineau,* although Furness was less disposed to socializing with others outside his home at Lindenshade. He seldom broke his "vow" to limit his social life to his own residence, turning down invitations by many notables who wished to make his acquaintance. When, in 1898, W. Aldis Wright invited Furness to Cambridge University to honor him with a degree, the deaf author responded with a confession that "has palsied my hand and kept me from answering that delightful letter of yours. . . . I do not believe

Horace Howard Furness, American Shakespeare scholar. Photo from *The Letters of Horace Howard Furness* (Boston: Houghton Mifflin, 1922).

that you know that I am frightfully deaf,—so deaf that ordinary conversation across table is utterly impossible.'' Furness was proud of the honor, but preferred that Wright not have to ''stand godfather to a deaf moon-calf'' (Furness, Jr., 1922, p. 30).

Furness was shattered by the death of his wife in 1883. In the spring of 1884, he began to immerse himself in the variorum once again, completing *Othello* (1886), *As You Like It* (1890), and *The Tempest* (1892). Although a voracious and highly respected writer, he was nevertheless sensitive and self-critical with regard to his hearing loss. Indeed, it must have been difficult for such a devoted lover of Shakespeare not to have been able to enjoy stage performances. In writing about *The Taming of the Shrew* in 1887, he stated that it was ''more gorgeous than I have believed it possible for the stage to produce. . . . Of course, a deaf man's criticisms are worthless & I therefore freely remark that I think John Drew scarcely perhaps rises to the level of Shakespearean Petruchio, in that he seemed at times a little too rough with Katherine'' (Furness, Jr., 1922, pp. 243–244). He laughed at his ''infliction,'' as in his letter to Ellen Olney

Kirk, where he remarked on her kindness and her tender words; impishly noting how difficult it would be to shout them through an ear-trumpet. And, in 1910, he wrote to Ben Greet, "If I could hear the loudest thunder that heralds your 'Tempest,' I should need no invitation to attend a performance; but, of my own notion, I should be in the front row, prepared, with ungloved hands, to applaud to the echo. But I know that your tender heart would never ask an even Christian to endure the torment of *seeing* music, and not hear one word of it. . . . Don't ask me, dear Ben Greet, for, if I yielded, you would be responsible for a lost soul" (Furness, Jr., 1922, pp. 223–224).

Furness died on August 13, 1912, characteristically while working in his library at Lindenshade.

References

Calkins, E. E. (1926). Lives of the deafened. *The Volta Review, 28* (3), 114–117.

Furness, H. H., Jr. (1922). *The letters of Horace Howard Furness* (two volumes). Boston: Houghton Mifflin.

Johnson, A., & Malone, D. (1931). Horace Howard Furness. *Dictionary of American biography* (Vol. 7, pp. 78–79). New York: Charles Scribner's Sons.

Repplier, A. (1912). Horace Howard Furness. *Atlantic Monthly, 110* (5), 624–628.

G

GERTRUDE SCOTT GALLOWAY (1930–), American Educator/Deaf Community Advocate.

Gertrude Galloway was born deaf in Washington, D.C., on November 11, 1930, the daughter of deaf parents and grandparents. Her brothers and sisters were also deaf. Consequently, Galloway grew up in an environment where American Sign Language was the first language. She attended the Kendall School on the Gallaudet College campus for both her elementary and secondary education, graduating in 1947. She completed her bachelor's degree at Gallaudet College in 1951 and was married. After raising a family for two decades, Galloway, encouraged by the psychologist and advocate McCay Vernon, began studying for a master's degree in education at Western Maryland College, completing the program in 1972. She earned a Ph.D. in Special Education Administration from Gallaudet University in 1993.

Between 1951 and 1973, Galloway worked part time as a substitute teacher. While serving as Assistant Principal on the Columbia Campus of the Maryland School for the Deaf from 1973 until 1990, she also lectured at Hood College in Frederick, Maryland, taught sign language at Western Maryland College, and mathematics at the Maryland School for the Deaf. During the seventies, Galloway began to assume key leadership positions; and in so doing, significantly advanced the role of Deaf women in community activism. She served as president of the Free State chapter of the Gallaudet College Alumni Association, vice president of the Maryland Association of the Deaf (1975–1977), and vice president of the Gallaudet College Alumni Association (1973–1979). In addition, she was chairperson of the Volunteer Committee at the Seventh World Congress of the World Federation of the Deaf in 1975. Throughout these years, Galloway presented numerous talks on the education of deaf students, the rights of deaf children, sexism, and the roles of Deaf women. She was selected to serve as a delegate to the National White House Conference on the Handicapped in 1977 and on the White House Planning Advisory Board. She was also on the advisory boards for the Maryland Commission for the Hearing Impaired (1976–1978), Deafness Research Foundation (1977–1980), Kendall Demonstration Elementary School (1980–1984), the Mental Health Center for the Deaf, and the Independent Living Association. She promoted legislation to provide funds for the Mental Health Center for the Deaf and for a program for multihandicapped deaf people.

In 1982, Galloway made history when she was elected the first deaf woman president of the more than a century old National Association of the Deaf, an organization that has served to advocate for the social, political, and educational welfare of deaf persons in the United States. During her term, she worked toward the establishment of a stronger political network by coordinating services and disseminating information, increasing the role of Deaf women in the organization; and addressing the complex issues associated with federal legislation, including Public Law 94–142 (the Education of All Handicapped Children Act) and Section 504 of the Vocational Rehabilitation Act. Galloway has given particular attention to the implications for language rights in such legislation. She subsequently served on many important committees, especially the National Commission on Education of the Deaf, which made landmark recommendations to the federal government to enhance education for precollege deaf students.

Galloway made history once again in 1990 when she became the first deaf woman to hold the position of superintendent of a residential school for the deaf, the Marie Katzenbach School for the Deaf in West Trenton, New Jersey, founded in 1883. At the time, there were only nine deaf superintendents in all of the schools in the country. In this leadership position, Galloway has served as a model for many deaf children around the country. "Role models are very important," she explained, "not only to deaf children, but to their parents— who need to see more of deaf adults so that they can visualize what their deaf children can grow to be." She has worked to make the Marie Katzenbach School a resource center for the State of New Jersey. In addition, Galloway has continued to advocate for the rights of deaf children, believing that it is critical that deaf children have access to interaction with other deaf children as well as hearing children in the context of excellent educational and cultural programs.

In 1994, Galloway was elected President-Elect of the Conference of Educational Administrators Serving the Deaf, the first woman to hold that office.

References

Leusner, D. (1991, March 4). First deaf superintendent: Pupils feel special bond at school for hearing impaired. *The Star-Ledger*, 7.

Robb, J. (1992, April 27). Woman's fair draws storyteller; deaf educator gives keynote. *Frederick Post*.

Van Tassel, P. (1990, December 23). Finding new paths in education for deaf. *New York Times*, 3.

WALTER GEIKIE (1795–1837), Scottish Painter.

Walter Geikie was born on November 9, 1795, in Edinburgh, Scotland. At the age of two, a fever left him profoundly deaf. Efforts to cure his deafness did not succeed and, isolated from other children his age, he found solace in drawing chalk figures on floors, doors, and any other smooth surface he could reach. He also showed his creative abilities by representing objects with paper modeling. After years of drawing on a slate, Geikie received a drawing book and set of pencils from his father, a pharmacist and perfumer. At the age of nine, the child progressed on his own to landscapes and still lifes.

Ever-vigilant regarding his son's talent, Archibald Geikie heard of Thomas Braidwood, who had established the first school for deaf pupils in Great Britain; the father began instructing his son to read and write. Dr. Charles Stuart, a philanthropist from Dunearn, suggested the use of fingerspelling, which he had heard was being used by Dr. Watson, Braidwood's follower in London. Watson's book, with its engravings of common objects, was instrumental in Geikie's early general education at home. The father devoted himself diligently to applying Watson's methods. His success with Walter soon led to an offer to Archibald Geikie to establish a new school. When he declined, Braidwood's grandson was invited to start the school with Walter Geikie as one of the first pupils. John Braidwood soon found Walter more useful as a teacher than as a pupil. Within a short time, however, Braidwood left for the United States and the school closed. Geikie then attended a nearby academy to learn arithmetic and penmanship. His younger brother Archibald sat beside him and provided some assistance through notes and interpreting.

At the age of fifteen, Geikie was privately instructed by Patrick Gibson, a highly respected landscape painter. Daily sketching excursions were made with his brother to the city and the lovely nearby countryside of the Scottish Borders. In May 1812, Geikie was admitted into the Drawing Academy established by the Honorable Commissioners of the Board of Trustees, a school known for producing many great Scottish artists. At the Academy, he studied under John Graham, who had earlier educated the artist David Wilkie. Geikie excelled there and built a reputation as one of the school's finest artists.

Geikie's first etching was an illustration of David Laing's "John Barleycorn." Laing subsequently ordered other etchings from Geikie for the Bannatyne Club. There, Geikie often entertained other artists through mime, imitating people at various trades. Beginning around the year 1815, he made hundreds of sketches of cattle, cottages, and scenes from the city markets; and from these collections, he carefully selected those he wished to etch on copper. Some he sold during his lifetime, but most were sold after his death. He was particularly taken by images of Scottish country life and customs of the working-class Scots. Geikie's etchings became precious records of Scottish costumes of the early nineteenth century. He was called the Teniers of the Scottish school of artists; some rural scenes had the same delicacy as that of the earlier Flemish artist, David Teniers. Geikie was particularly noted for his portrayal of the comic side of daily life. He preferred etchings over engravings and printed many works in copper on his own press. Geikie's illustrations were published in such works as the Scottish national poet Robert Burns' *Tam o'Shanter* and *The Jolly Beggars*.

In 1838, Thomas Dibdin published *A Biographical Antiquarian and Picturesque Tour in the Northern Counties of England and Scotland*, in which he described Geikie's work. Geikie's observation of human nature, according to Dibdin, was striking. His *Drunken Man Led Home by the Wife and Child*, for example, depicted a man with a foolish expression on his face and hands and legs in uncoordinated, constant motion. Geikie conversed with his contemporary Dibdin by means of a slate. Dibdin later wrote that he came to be a friend to the artist as well as a documenter of his work.

In 1830, with Matthew Burns and Alexander Blackwood, Geikie gathered some forty deaf friends to receive the Scripture from his brother, a preacher. These Sunday meetings eventually became the Edinburgh Adult Deaf and Dumb Benevolent Society, which evolved into the current Edinburgh Centre for the Deaf. Geikie also visited these community members regularly at their homes to encourage their attendance. He delivered Sunday sermons based on a favorite book, Barnes' *Notes on the Gospels*, in sign language. Shortly before his death, these friends presented him with a gift in appreciation of his labors.

Geikie's volume *Etchings Illustrative of Scottish Character and Scenery* was published posthumously. In the introduction, his friend Sir Thomas D. Lauder, Baronet of Grange and Fountainhill, explained that Geikie had such an accurate memory that he could walk past an interesting person, capture the individual's features and character, and return to his sketching pad to record his observations. He would sometimes pursue more challenging subjects on the run. On one occasion, the deaf artist sketched a pompous and self-important porter until the annoyed man chased him into a nearby house. From the window of the attic, Geikie completed the sketch, feeling that the expression provoked by the altercation added to the overall effect of the work.

Geikie's oil paintings were not considered as good as his etchings, although a collection of his paintings was purchased by the Earl of Hopetoun. One of his etchings, *Cottage Scene*, is in the National Gallery of Scotland.

Geikie died of typhoid fever on August 1, 1837, at the age of forty-one, and he was buried at the Greyfriars' Church in Edinburgh. He left behind more than one thousand sketches, many now held by the Royal Scottish Academy. He had been elected as an Associate to the Academy in 1831, and a Fellow in 1834. Left unfinished was a sketch of the upper portion of the High Street in Edinburgh, which he had promised to his beloved brother. His brother later wrote Geikie's biography.

Geikie had drawn and painted up to the moment of his death and was buried on the day he had planned another of his sketching excursions.

References

Braddock, G. C. (1975). *Notable deaf persons*. Washington, DC: Gallaudet College Alumni Association.

Dibdin, T. F. (1838). *A biographical antiquarian and picturesque tour in the northern counties of England and Scotland* (Vol. 2., pp. 568–571). London: C. Richards, St. Marin's Lane.

Geikie, A. (1855). Brief sketch of the life of Walter Geikie, Esq., R.A.S., Edinburgh, Scotland. *American Annals of the Deaf, 7* (4), 229–237.

Stephen, L., & Lee, S. (Eds.). (1917). Walter Geikie. *The dictionary of national biography, from the earliest times to 1900* (Vol. 7, p. 989). Oxford: Oxford University Press.

ELLEN GLASGOW (1873?–1945), American Author.

Ellen Glasgow was born on April 22, 1873, in Richmond, Virginia. In her autobiography *The Woman Within*, she explains that the recorded birth year may have been in error and that she was actually born in 1874. The ninth of ten children to survive infancy, she was frail and subject to frequent illness, nearly dying of diphtheria and scarlet fever during one year alone. Her mother, "the sun in my universe," taught her to sing. Her father, a stern Calvinist, offered his wife and children every provision and opportunity, but Glasgow remembered him as severe and unloving. Even though she suffered from frequent illness, she looked back at the period when she was between three and seven as the happiest years of her early life. Glasgow taught herself to read at a very early age, beginning with *The Waverly Novels*, spelling out the words letter by letter. Her nurse Lizzie Jones, who had cooked General Lee's supper on the night before the surrender, became a friend, and Glasgow always regretted not having shared more reading with Lizzie.

Obsessive shyness and constant headaches isolated her from other children throughout her early years. She developed a love for nature and would often go off into secluded gardens and woodlands to experiment with writing. "In my seventh summer," she wrote, "I became a writer." Her father often read aloud in the evenings, and the well-stocked library in their house provided opportunity to read widely. In adolescence, she read works by Adam Smith, Malthus, John Stuart Mill, and Henry George. By the age of seventeen, she studied the great Victorian scientists, closely reading Darwin's *The Origin of Species*. For two years, she borrowed books by Schopenhauer, Fichte, Schelling, and Kant, all of which shaped her perspectives and modeled techniques for her own writing.

Emotionally shattered by her mother's sudden death when she was about seventeen years old, she destroyed her first manuscript for *The Descendant*. Trouble with her hearing at about the same time led her to seek professional help, but she was told not to be concerned. Within a short time she submitted a new draft of *The Descendant* to Macmillan's publishing company, only to have it rejected—a decision the publisher's president later told her was one of the two gravest mistakes he had ever made. Glasgow soon found a representative from University Publishing Company, who claimed he had not been moved as much since he had read Victor Hugo as a boy. Glasgow reminisced that upon hearing of the acceptance in New York, she stayed up watching for the dawn, relatively unaffected by the incipient deafness that was beginning to make itself noticeable to her.

A sharp attack of influenza quickly increased her hearing loss. She wrote that "morbid sensitiveness was tracking me down, like a wolf waiting for spring." She felt suffocated by melancholy and panicked by not being able to understand the words spoken to her. The image of the wolf stalking her appeared again and again in her writing. She could not bear to even see the word "deaf" in print, and frankly described deafness as a "terror."

The Descendant, published anonymously in 1897, was moderately successful. Glasgow, interested in developing her technique further, read Henry James, Flaubert, de Maupassant, Tolstoy, and Chekhov. Next came her second novel *Phases of an Inferior Planet* (1899), where she felt she had a genuine grasp of technique. Critics characterized her style as a mixture of George Meredith and Charlotte Brontë. Over the next few years, she wrote a variety of novels. *The Voice of the People* (1900) examined the Reconstruction period. *The Battle-Ground* (1902) dealt with war, as did *The Deliverance* (1904), which also took place in the reconstruction era and focused on a carpetbagger embezzler who robbed a family of their plantation in Virginia. *The Miller of Old Church* (1911) depicted small farmers, who had been largely neglected by other Southern writers. *Virginia* (1913), one of the best of her early works, critically evaluated the tradition of the Southern lady. Some experts consider Glasgow's novels as excellent sources by which readers may gain insight into "the southern mind" in this period of history. At the same time, Glasgow's work was viewed as liberal and realistic. She shunned romantic and nostalgic views of the South and of life in general.

Much of this writing was done in the solitude forced upon her by her deafness. She began to avoid social activity systematically and would only see company in the presence of her sister, Cary, who would alternately interpret and "cover" for her older sister in conversation. Glasgow viewed the sensitive shyness that was exacerbated by her hearing loss as an incurable illness itself, causing her to avoid even those she loved for fear of embarrassment in asking them to raise their voices. As her income increased, her efforts to find help did too; and she likened them to medieval pilgrimages to find a miracle cure.

In 1899, a brother supported her travel abroad for a year, and she found great delight in visiting Egypt, Asia Minor, Italy, Switzerland, France, Norway, and the Isles of Greece. In England, she walked the moors of Haworth and reconnected its dark, brooding atmosphere to her love for the passion and social conscience of the Brontës. Upon her return to America, she completed the final chapters of *The Voice of the People*, followed by *The Ancient Law* (1908) and *The Romance of a Plain Man* (1909). The latter dealt with the working man in the South. *The Wheel of Life* (1904), she later admitted, was partly autobiographical. She wrote the novel as catharsis over a seven-year relationship that ended in her lover's death from an inoperable ailment, a period in which she lived mechanically and numbly, but nonetheless productively. Glasgow completed four additional novels between 1911 and 1923.

Voices that she could hear were becoming rarer and she became extremely nervous in her struggle to simply understand others. She railed against the ever-presence of deafness, refusing to make peace with her condition. By the age of thirty-five she experimented with "an electric device," but such technology was unsatisfactory for many prospective users in the first decade of the twentieth century. Her favorite sister, Cary, died after a protracted illness, emotionally shattering Glasgow's will to continue writing or even to read. She left Richmond for New York with the hope of losing herself in a crowd.

Despite her deafness, her increasing fame brought her into contact with many notables. She traveled and visited with such prominent authors as Joseph Conrad, John Galsworthy, and Walter Page. On a voyage back to America, Colonel Theodore Roosevelt, returning from his last African trip, looked after her as a favor to her chaperones, the Walter Page family. Always finding deafness difficult to manage, however, Glasgow did not attend more than a half dozen "literary teas" in her life. She preferred the company of a select few friends who were intimates and who could adapt well to her communication requirements. Nonetheless, she could be assertive where her work was concerned.

Barren Ground, considered by many to be her most mature work, was taking form in her imagination as World War I escalated; it was finally published in 1925. During the decade following the war, she published two "comedies of manners," *The Romantic Comedians* (1926), which critics judged a flawless work of its kind, and *They Stooped to Folly* (1929). In the 1930s, Glasgow published *The Sheltered Life* and *Vein of Iron*. She considered these five works her best. Glasgow turned down a $30,000 offer by *Good Housekeeping* to serialize *The Sheltered Life*. Later, she provided a more detailed analysis of her writing in a self-criticism titled *A Certain Measure* (1943). She also courted critics to have the chance to present her literary case personally and to make perfectly clear what the vision and intent were in her work.

A heart failure in 1939 delayed the publication of *In This Our Life*, but Glasgow was able to continue work on it over the next few months, never more than fifteen minutes at a time, and published it in 1941.

In addition to a number of other novels, Glasgow published *The Freeman and Other Poems* in 1902, nearly a dozen short stories, and a variety of articles and essays in such periodicals as *Saturday Review of Literature*, *Western Humanities Review*, and the *New York Times*. Her first love was the novel, however, for this form, she believed, was where realistic depictions of the human condition could be best achieved. Her productivity demonstrated her complete conviction that being a novelist was her destiny.

Glasgow died on November 21, 1945. Nine years later, her literary executors published *The Woman Within*, which provides many autobiographical insights on her lifelong struggle as a deaf person.

References

Auchincloss, L. (1964). *Ellen Glasgow*. Minneapolis, MN: University of Minnesota Pamphlets on American Writers.

Glasgow, E. (1954). *The woman within*. New York: Harcourt, Brace and Company.

McDowell, F.P.W. (1963). *Ellen Glasgow and the ironic art of fiction*. Madison, WI: University of Wisconsin Press.

Raper, J. R. (1971). *Without shelter: The early career of Ellen Glasgow*. Baton Rouge, LA: Louisiana State University Press.

EVELYN GLENNIE (1965–   ), Scottish Percussionist.

Evelyn Glennie was born in Aberdeen, Scotland, on July 19, 1965. In her childhood, she took an interest in percussion music, causing some understandable tension with other family members trying to read and listen to the record player in the farmhouse on the "Hillhead of Ardo." She seldom left home until adolescence. For years, Glennie joined other children in the harvesting of potatoes at nearby farms.

Glennie took an early interest in music, practicing with two fingers on a piano as soon as she was able to climb onto the piano stool. By the age of eight, however, she noted in her diary that she had begun to have difficulty hearing things. Nevertheless, she also began to play a guitar, mouth organ, and, later, the clarinet.

Glennie attended the Cairnorrie Primary School, two classrooms of five-to-eight- and nine-to-twelve-year-olds in a school separated by a partition. When the powerful clang of a school bell was replaced by an electric bell, Glennie was unable to hear it. She realized that she had been responding to the vibrations of the building induced by the old bell. With the help of hearing aids, however, she completed six years of piano lessons by the time she reached secondary school.

At the age of nine, Glennie received the highest mark in the United Kingdom on the Trinity College of Music Grade One Exam. Shortly after this, she was invited to perform with other awards recipients at Aberdeen's Cowdray Hall. Unable to hear her own name being called, she had to depend on another person to tap her on the shoulder when it was her turn to perform. She nevertheless advanced through subsequent music exams. By the age of twelve, her hearing had so deteriorated that the family was counselled to send her to the Aberdeen School for the Deaf. Glennie wrote in her autobiography, "I was looking at the prospect of being classified for life as disabled, and cut off from the music that was beginning to seem vital to my happiness."

Fitted with ever-more powerful hearing aids, she enrolled at the Ellon Academy. She put away her clarinet for good and began to pursue percussion. Her music teacher naively advised her that she had no hope, unaware of her previous musical experience. After some years, Glennie felt that wearing hearing aids had become a "waste of time." She had to learn to compensate for balance problems and to adjust to visual methods of relating to fellow musicians. She took speechreading lessons; and, although she did not learn to sign, she felt that signing and speechreading together constituted an effective communication method for deaf and hard-of-hearing children.

Now profoundly deaf, Glennie had developed an ability to judge the quality of her musical notes entirely by feeling them—through her feet and lower body, as well as through her hands. For hours and hours, she practiced the identification of pitches with her hands on a wall while her music teacher played notes or discussed how music translated into vibrations she felt while her feet were on the pedals. Later, she gave concerts for deaf people who would hold balloons while sitting on wooden benches. At one point during her school years, she chaired an eight-hour piano marathon to raise funds for a phonic ear for another deaf student who could benefit from it. Contrary to everyone's expectations, Glennie's involvement with music actually increased in proportion to her deafness.

At Ellon Academy, Glennie became a regular member of the percussion group, playing such pieces as Mozart's *Rondo allo Turca* arranged for the xylophone by her teacher, Ron Forbes. More and more, she realized the potential of adapting pieces originally composed for piano for her solo percussion work. She also joined Forbes' group outside school, at the Cults Music Centre in Aberdeen, which later became the Grampian Schools Percussion Ensemble. With this group, she played festivals in England, France, Holland, and other countries. Earlier, she had studied briefly under Roderick Brydon, director of the Scottish Chamber Orchestra, playing such pieces as Mendelssohn's *Scottish Symphony* and Kodály's *Háry János Suite*. As her work became increasingly appreciated, she would avoid situations where her deafness was emphasized, wishing her musical composition, arrangement, and technique to be judged for their own sake. Glennie at first even made special efforts to make sure her deafness was not mentioned on concert programs. She found that highlighting her deafness in reviews tilted them toward sentimentality, and this frustrated the disciplined professional musician. Her exasperation was increased when Glennie was invited to perform for Ezra Rachlin, a well-known conductor in London, and his wife, Ann, who had founded the Beethoven Fund for Deaf Children. The excitement of possibly gaining their support was countered with simultaneous advice from a leading audiologist to pursue music only as a hobby and to consider accounting as a career.

On September 19, 1982, Glennie began studying at the Royal Academy of Music in London under Nicholas Cole with such instruments as the xylophone, vibraphone, marimba, and snare drums. Her application, in which she was forced to explain her deafness, caused "quite a row" at the Academy, but she was given the audition. Once in the Academy, she replaced aural tests with studying keyboard skills, and she passed up the listening rooms by strengthening her music theory and by learning to *read* music "like a book." The Rachlins continued to support her during the next few challenging years, as she worked to master many percussion instruments. For the first time in her life, she paid to attend concerts given by other people in order to observe conductors and orchestras and, in particular, the techniques of other percussionists. Bringing the musical scores along with her, she focussed on the visual cues and familiarized herself with the written music.

As a professional solo percussionist, Glennie has traveled to Japan, America, and throughout Europe. She was voted "Scot of the Year" in 1982 by BBC Radio Scotland, and subsequently appeared on talk shows and in magazines. In 1984, she also performed in the "Night of 200 Stars" show in Blackpool to raise funds for audiology clinics, and on the radio in her "Music for Deaf Ears" interview with Donny B. McLeod. She also won the Gold Medal in the Shell/LSO Percussion Scholarship competition, receiving a telegram from Prince Charles who was "thrilled" over her success. She is active in more than forty organizations for the deaf in Britain, although she downplays her charity work in general.

Performing more than one hundred concerts each year, Glennie visits schools, prisons, and other institutions, and has performed on radio and television shows; she has supported many fund-raising efforts for cancer, AIDS, and disaster funds, auditioned young percussionists, and won many honors along the way. She was chosen "Scotswoman of the Decade" (the 1980s), sharing the honor with Sir James Black, the Nobel laureate in Medicine (1988), who was selected "Scotsman of the Decade." Her pioneering work in bringing percussion a central role in the classical repertoire is unique. As a full-time percussion soloist, Glennie is the only one in the classical field who draws large, devoted audiences.

Glennie is married to a recording engineer, Greg Malcangi. Among the works she has commissioned herself are James MacMillan's *Veni, Veni, Emmanuel*, which she premiered in Washington. She won a Grammy Award in 1989 from the National Academy of Recording Arts and Sciences and continues to record. During a 1994 American concert tour through Cincinnati, Washington, and Cleveland, she performed barefoot. She explained to a *Time* magazine reporter that she does not think in terms of loud or soft, but as colors and emotions in her own thoughts, as she closely watches the conductor and orchestra. With the Cincinnati Symphony, she performed *Concerto for Percussion*, subtitled *Figure in a Landscape*, with cymbals, marimba, Japanese bells, a pair of gongs, two congas, a vibraphone, four small drums, four wood blocks, and several boobams (tuned cylindrical tubes open on one end and covered by a small drumskin at the other). The acrobatics and choreography involved in managing such a variety of instruments are yet another reason audiences are drawn to hear and see the energetic work of Evelyn Glennie.

References

Glennie, E. (1990). *Good vibrations*. London: Hutchinson.
Rockwell, J. (1993, October 3). A percussionist gives pluck new meaning. *New York Times*, H31.
Walsh, M. (1994, March 21). A different drummer. *Time*, 72.

ANTONIO GÓMEZ FEU (1907–1984), Spanish Artist.

Antonio Gómez Feu Morales was born in the Andalusian region near Ayamonte, Spain, on November 27, 1907. Born deaf, his protective family and friends kept him at home for some time, where his early predisposition to create art became obvious very quickly. The bright child drew picture upon picture in order to communicate with and engage those around him. He also observed and absorbed the customs and colors of Andalusian life, and these effects would emerge in much of his later work. The absorption of the visual elements of culture in general and Spanish cultures in particular began in these formative years.

When he was nine years old, the decision was made that young Antonio would go to Valencia, where the School for the Deaf and Blind was established. His rapid progress in sign, spoken, and written language development put to rest any concerns for his late start. Throughout his life, Gómez Feu's extraordinary communication abilities were noted by patrons, clients, and interviewers. He was offered professorships and was routinely requested to do lecture-demonstrations.

In 1926, Gómez Feu enrolled in Valencia's San Carlos Academy of Fine Arts. There, he began to work in a greater variety of media. In addition to drawings in crayon and charcoal, he began to do watercolors and oil paintings in earnest. In 1931, he moved to Madrid, where he attended the San Fernando Academy of the Fine Arts, where he was able to experiment with new techniques and to study illustration in greater depth. In Madrid, he also received licensure as a professor of art.

He left Spain at the height of the Spanish Civil War. Having his childhood home and family ties in Huelva, on the border of Portugal, Gómez Feu decided to go to Lisbon for a time to work. He was able to find substantial experience designing, illustrating, and doing layout for several magazines and poster companies. He also took the opportunity to study part time in Lisbon. He received commissions to do some portraits, and he began to direct more energy toward portrait painting, particularly after he received first prize for his portraiture in a major exhibition. Gómez Feu received considerable attention at this time. He was also offered a professorship in Lisbon, but a condition of the contract was renunciation of Spanish citizenship. This forced a re-evaluation of his situation, and, with the civil war over, Gómez Feu decided to return home in 1943.

He was offered a teaching position in Seville at the School of Fine Arts. The School gave him access to gallery space, and he held a one-man show there in 1944. After other exhibits across Spain, he decided to settle in Barcelona, with its attractions of great natural beauty and a vibrant art community. He mounted more exhibitions and received portrait commissions from military and business leaders, several well-known Spanish actors, and his fellow painter, Segrelles.

Gómez Feu's portraits are viewed by many critics as genuinely psychological. In interviews with reporters, he described his colleague Segrelles as ''genial,'' but the portrait of his fellow painter also reveals, through line and angle, a formidable gentleman. Such complex and sometimes contradictory impressions made Gómez Feu very popular and much in demand.

He was comfortable with the realism portraiture allows, but Gómez Feu also produced colorful and light-dappled landscapes and still life drawings. He was influenced by impressionist work, but he enjoyed experimenting with unconventional and contrastive composition, angles of vision, and light. He drew on his early experience in Andalusia for the colorings of these works.

Gómez Feu also remained true to his initial experiences as a professional illustrator. He executed a series of drawings depicting Cervantes' story of *Don Quixote*, now in the Museum of Denia, Alicante, and a number of fantasy works. Between 1953 and 1956, he produced forty drawings to document an ancient Catalan section of Barcelona that was razed. These are on permanent exhibition at Barcelona's Municipal Museum.

Throughout his career, Gómez Feu was an accessible and open artist, who freely expressed his preference for classical forms and romantic themes. He characterized himself as a realist but pushed realism to its limits with the element of surprise and the innovative application of impeccable technique.

Gómez Feu died on his seventy-seventh birthday, November 27, 1984.

References

Ayamonte prepara un homenaje con una gran exposicion antologica a su pintor Antonio Gómez Feu. (1980, July 1). *Odiel*.

Loe, E. F. (1987). Antonio Gómez Feu. In J. V. Van Cleve (Ed.), *Gallaudet encyclopedia of deaf people and deafness* (Vol. 1, pp. 471–472). New York: McGraw-Hill.

Marin, B. (undated). Gómez Feu, el pintor de la luz. *Arte*, 3–4. Gallaudet University Archives.

JOHN GOODRICKE (1764–1786), British Astronomer.

John Goodricke was born on September 17, 1764, in Groningen, the Netherlands. He may have inherited royal blood going back to William I and Alfred the Great. But, for some reason, he was not buried in the family vault, and there have been few remarks about him in the family chronicles. Kopal (1986) has conjectured that the astronomer's grandfather may not have approved of his father's marriage, and this may be why the Goodrickes had remained in Holland. Goodricke's deafness, too, may have been seen at that time as a stigma. This is difficult to believe, however, in view of the fact the Royal Society of London bestowed the prestigious Copley Medal on the young deaf man.

The secrecy surrounding Thomas Braidwood's instruction allows us to merely speculate on the deaf youth's progress. The Braidwood Academy prepared deaf students well. *The Monthly Repository (1813–1815)* included a brief report on Goodricke's progress there: "He lost his hearing by a fever when an infant, and was consequently dumb: but having in part conquered this disadvantage by the assistance of Mr. Braidwood, he made surprising proficiency, becoming a very tolerable classic, and an excellent mathematician." After Braidwood's school,

Goodricke entered the Warrington Academy, a "dissenting academy" established in protest of the schools controlled by the clergy.

It is not known when Goodricke's family moved to York, England; and we know little about John's life until we read the first entry in his astronomical journal, dated November 16, 1781. A neighbor of the Goodrickes, Nathaniel Pigott, an accomplished amateur astronomer, had moved from Wales to a house just a short distance away in York in 1780. Pigott's interests focused on comets, eclipses, and the transits of known planets. Wishing to spend the remainder of his life in York, Pigott had obtained a model of the well-equipped Greenwich observatory of the noted astronomer William Herschel (discoverer of the planet Uranus in 1781, as well as several satellites of Uranus and Saturn). Nathaniel Pigott's son, Edward, was also enthusiastic about astronomy.

Edward Pigott welcomed Goodricke's companionship, although his personal correspondence indicated that he had some difficulty conversing with the deaf astronomer. Others have reported Pigott's dismay that he had no one to converse with, despite Goodricke's astute presence. Communicating side by side at night during observations was also nearly impossible. On the other hand, they rarely, if ever, argued.

Goodricke and Pigott frequently gave credit to each other in their personal journals. The only reported conflict that occurred between the two young men was a disagreement in July 1783, when Goodricke noted with chagrin that they had overreacted in the course of an argument over whether one of the Cygnus novae had appeared the previous year. Apparently, some furious and rapid note-writing preceded Goodricke's realization that Pigott had probably been right.

Their spirited, lasting partnership in astronomical pursuits was based on both friendship and professional interests. Goodricke's first words in his journal, on November 16, 1781, bear witness to this friendship: "Mr. E. Pigott told me that at 9 o'clock P.M. yesterday he discovered a Comet with a small nucleus & coma near the neck of Cygnus." Edward Pigott, eleven years older than John Goodricke, was in many ways a mentor to his seventeen-year-old deaf friend. It was he who first encouraged Goodricke to watch for variable stars and introduced him to Algol's variability. Pigott's information was based on the Italian astronomer Geminiano Montanari's observations in Bologna in the early 1670s, but Pigott had no measurements to support his own conjectures. He was also curious about the roots of the name Algol. The Arabic name *al Ghul* means "the ghoul." In other sources it is called "the demon." This hinted to him a peculiarity which bore further investigation. Algol is known by contemporary astronomers as Beta Persei in the constellation Perseus.

During this early period, Goodricke used crude opera glasses and a small perspective glass with a magnification of only 10 or 12 to observe comets and stars, including William Herschel's recent discovery of a "comet" (later to be named the planet Uranus). In April of 1781, Goodricke acquired an achromatic telescope with greater magnification, modified it with cross wires, and continued to study Herschel's "comet."

Goodricke's *Journal of astronomical observations begun in Novr 1781* is housed in the North Yorkshire County Council Chambers. His entry for November 12, 1782, indicates his own astonishment at having found the brightness of Algol changed. Only a week before, he had observed Algol of second magnitude. On November 12, it was of the fourth magnitude. He wrote in his journal:

This night I looked at β Persei & was much surprized to find its brightness altered—It now appears of ab^t the 4th magn^d . . . .I observed it diligently for ab^t an hour & upwards— I hardly believed that it changed its brightness because I never heard of any star varying so quick in its brightness—I thought it might perhaps be owing to an optical illusion or defect in my eyes or bad air but the sequel will shew that its change is true & that I was not mistaken. (p. 7)

It is apparent that Goodricke told Pigott of his discovery, for the journal entries of both young men clearly show the excitement the following night as they kept close watch on Algol. What puzzled Goodricke was not the change in brightness, but the suddenness of this variation. It was completely unexpected. Many more observations followed as he attempted to confirm the period of Algol's changes. By mid-April, there was sufficient evidence accumulated to publish the results. Edward Pigott contacted Nevil Maskelyne, the Astronomer Royal and author of the *Nautical Almanac*, expressing his confidence in the period of Algol and its explanation. Pigott asked Maskelyne to inform Sir William Herschel of the discovery. Among the excited reactions to the Algol finding was that of Sir Joseph Banks, President of the Royal Society, who wrote to his loyal friend Herschel on April 30, erroneously attributing the discovery to Pigott. On May 2, he corrected himself, noting that the discovery had been made by a young deaf man named Goodricke.

Herschel had made his own observations and reported them on May 8 at an evening session of the Royal Society. Learning of this, Goodricke believed Herschel had attempted to take credit for the discovery; but after hearing of this from Edward Pigott, Herschel explained to the deaf astronomer the course of events that had led to the misunderstanding. Goodricke was pleased with the contents of Herschel's letter, and he continued to correspond in a friendly manner with the distinguished Herschel for years following the incident. For example, while Herschel was forming his conception of the Milky Way as one nebula among many, Goodricke wrote to him that "I have read your curious paper on the construction of the Heavens with great pleasure. It seems as if all the riches of the heavens are now opened to us by means of your large telescopes and I heartily wish you success in the farther pursuit of the subject." In the York University Library is a draft of another letter, written by Goodricke to Herschel, this on September 2, 1784, dealing with the prediction of an Algol brightness minimum. In this letter, Goodricke tells Herschel, as an aside: "Dr. Shepherd informs me that you have observed 200,000 stars [in] the field of your

20 feet [sic] Telescope in an hour. This indeed gives us a just idea of the immense number of fixed stars, that are scattered over the vast abyss of space.''

In regard to his own measurements of the brightness of Algol, Goodricke wrote a letter to Anthony Shepherd, Plumian Professor at Cambridge, which was subsequently read to the Royal Society on May 12, 1783, and published in the *Philosophical Transactions* as ''A series of observations on, and a discovery of, the period of variation of light of the bright star in the head of Medusa, called Algol.'' Goodricke began by citing a reference to an observation of Algol in Du Hamel's *Historia Regiae Scientiarum*. He followed by commenting that this description was vague and general; but that the star's variations indeed were regular and periodic. Goodricke also wrote that Pigott's observations, independently recorded, had validated his own.

Goodricke's estimate of the period of Algol was two days, 20 hours, 45 minutes. This differs only *4 minutes* from modern figures. It is remarkable that with such a crude telescope, and through the cloudy skies of the Yorkshire moors, John Goodricke was capable of this accuracy. Also difficult for modern astronomers to believe were Goodricke's observations of ''spots or such like matter''on Algol. Even with today's sophisticated telescopes and the statistical analyses of irregularities in the light curves of the stars, this observation on Algol is difficult. More amazing is Goodricke's conjecture as to the cause of the changes in brightness. He noted that Algol appeared to have a companion, and that the system eclipsed itself at regular intervals:

If it were not perhaps too early to hazard even a conjecture on the cause of this variation, I should imagine it could hardly be accounted for otherwise than either by the interposition of a large body revolving around Algol, or some kind of motion of its own, whereby part of its body, covered with spots or such like matter, is periodically turned towards the earth. But the intention of this paper is to communicate facts, not conjectures; and I flatter myself that the former are remarkable enough to deserve the attention and farther investigation of astronomers. (Goodricke, 1783, p. 482)

With his letter to the Royal Society, Goodricke included a table of his observations that contained the dates, times, and number of revolutions. The speculation of a periodic eclipse by a large, dark body remained unproven for nearly a century until the German astronomer Hermann Vogel used spectrographic analysis to confirm that Algol was indeed a binary star. More recent research has again verified Goodricke's conjecture, with the correction that the other star is faintly luminous rather than dark.

Goodricke's discovery led to great interest in Algol's periodicity among other astronomers who sent confirmations of the deaf amateur's observations to the Royal Society. Some grabbed the opportunity to use Goodricke's paper to prove the existence of planets outside the solar system. John Goodricke joined the ranking of his well-known contemporaries—Herschel, Priestley, Watt, and

Volta, to name a few—when only nineteen years old. The Royal Society awarded him Britain's highest scientific honor, a Godfrey Copley Medal.

In August 1784, Goodricke began to study the constellations Lyra, Capricorn, and Aquarius and to compare his measurements with the data found in Flamsteed's *Atlas*. On September 10, 1784, he discovered that Beta Lyrae, too, was a double star with an eclipse occurring a little more than every twelve days. After several months, he wrote to Sir H. C. Englefield (who communicated his letter to the Royal Society on January 27, 1785). Goodricke explained that he had found the star less bright than he expected the previous September; and he had begun to track Beta Lyrae, suspecting that it might be a variable star.

A month later, Goodricke found a third variable, *Delta* in the constellation Cepheus. He noticed that Delta Cephei behaved differently from Algol, reaching its brightness and then immediately beginning to fade, brightening again after its lowest magnitude had been estimated. He wrote to Nevil Maskelyne and described the strange quality in the fluctuations of brightness in Delta Cephei. In this letter published in *Philosophical Transactions* in 1785, Goodricke again revealed the enthusiastic companionship and assistance of Edward Pigott.

Limited by the quality of their telescopes, all attempts by Goodricke and his contemporaries to explain such changes failed. Improved telescopes and the science of spectroscopy later enabled astronomers to see the "dark" companions of other stars, but Delta Cephei remained an enigma. An annoying fact to many astronomers who followed Goodricke was that not only did the star change its brightness, it also changed its type. In his paper, the young deaf astronomer promised to provide detail through further observations. But Goodricke did not live to fulfill that promise.

On April 20, 1786, two weeks after he was elected a Fellow in the Royal Society, a most prestigious and coveted honor, John Goodricke, now only twenty-one years old, died of exposure to the cold night air.

The deaf astronomer has been honored by historians of science. His achievements are highlighted in many books and journals, and at York University can be found a memorial tablet mounted on a wall:

> From a window in Treasurers House near this
> tablet, the young deaf and dumb astronomer
> JOHN GOODRICKE
> 1764–1786
> who was elected a Fellow of the Royal Society
> at the age of 21, observed the periodicity of
> the star ALGOL and discovered the variation
> of δ CEPHEI and other stars thus laying the
> foundation of modern measurements of the Universe.

References

Gilman, C. (1978). John Goodricke and his variable stars. *Sky and Telescope, 56* (5), 400–403.

Golladay, L. E. (1962). John Goodricke story includes locating of his observatory; memorial fund will honor him. *The American Era, 48* (4), 33–35, 37.

Goodricke, J. (1783). A series of observations on, and a discovery of, the period of the variation of the light of the bright star in the Head of Medusa, called Algol. *Philosophical Transactions* lxxiii, 474–482.

Hoskin, M. (1982). Goodricke, Pigott and the quest for variable stars. In M. Hoskin (Ed.), *Stellar astronomy: Historical studies.* Chalfont, St. Giles, Bucks, England: Science History Publications.

Kopal, Z. (1986). *Of stars and men: Reminiscences of an astronomer.* Boston: Adam Hilger.

Lang, H. G. (1994). *Silence of the spheres: The deaf experience in the history of science.* Westport, CT: Bergin & Garvey.

FRANCISCO JOSÉ DE GOYA Y LUCIENTES (1746–1828), Spanish Artist.

Francisco Goya was born on March 30, 1746, in Fuendetodos, a small town in Saragossa. His parents were peasants who survived on several acres of land. Goya spent his childhood in the country. Around the age of sixteen, he developed a love for landscape drawing, which attracted the attention of a monk near Saragossa. Goya then began to study in the studio of José Luxan Martinez of Saragossa, an artist educated in Italy. In 1771, he won second prize at the Academy of Parma.

Goya's many realistic genre paintings soon made him popular. After engaging in one of the street riots involving painters and confraternities, however, he feared the Inquisition. This mixture of enthusiasm and paranoia would be a pattern throughout his life. The monk Felix Salvadora encouraged him to take no chances and flee to Madrid, where he spent four years. Goya's recklessness again brought him to grief, in an incident where he was stabbed in the back. Fortunately, friends saved his life. He then hurried off to Rome, where he developed a friendship with Jacques-Louis David, the founder of the French Neoclassical school of painting. Goya, however, became involved in an unsuccessful abduction of a young girl from a convent. After studying under the Spanish artist Francisco Bayeu, who became a stabilizing mentor, he returned to Madrid with him. He married into the Bayeu family and produced twenty children.

More turbulent years followed, with Goya nonetheless completing many paintings and portraits, which earned him membership in the Academy of San Fernando in 1779. By 1795, he was director. Raphael Menges also employed Goya to design "cartoons" and satiric drawings for tapestries. His new relative, Bayeu, was responsible for the decorative frescoes for the rebuilt Cathedral of Saragossa, and Goya was recruited to assist him. Goya's pride, however, was intense and he exploded in anger when Bayeu returned several designs for retouching. Once again, Goya's friend, the monk Felix Salvadora, was called upon to minimize the falling out with increasingly impatient church officials. Goya's painting of the King, however, brought him into favor with the Spanish court, and the personality of the Queen excited the humorous side of Goya. He became the king's chief painter.

The onset of Goya's deafness was characteristically dramatic, although the exact cause has never been ascertained. His good friend, the Duchess of Alba, had been sent into exile to her estate at Luca. While accompanying her in the winter of 1792–1793, the chaise broke down and Goya's insistence upon singlehandedly mending the broken axle brought on a chill and fevers. The complications appear to have resulted in complete deafness. He learned how to speechread and took instruction in Spanish Sign Language.

Goya was never a serenely happy individual, and deafness coupled with side effects such as tinnitus emphasized his dark side. He became prone to taking out his frustrations on his ever-suffering loved ones, who remained steadfast in their support. More of a real change took place in his art, however. Formerly, Goya's genres had been realistic landscapes, portraits, religious, and satirical drawings. His subjects following the onset of his deafness took a disturbing, grotesque, and often-allegorical turn. Now his paintings and etchings were populated by demons, torturers, victims, and monsters. When the court recalled its favorite painter, Goya successfully lobbied for his favorite, banished Duchess of Alba, to return as well. She had been particularly kind and helpful in his illness and adjustment. He was further saddened, though, when she died prematurely soon afterward.

In 1819, Goya bought a twenty-acre estate near the River Manzanares, where he later settled and began to fill the walls with his "Black Paintings," demonic works and hellish images of human war. One can only surmise the reactions of dinner guests used to neoclassical, ornate splendor. Many of Goya's portraits show the influence of Velázquez. Among Goya's notable works are *Adoration of the Name of God*, *Family of Charles IV*, and *Naked Maja*.

Goya's character was the subject of consternation and gossip in the court. His instability was legendary. Not only had he the honor of being painter in ordinary to Charles IV, but he was the official painter for the royal family of Spain for about four decades. Goya transformed the evils of eighteenth-century Spain into brushstrokes that portrayed interestingly, in satirical and metaphoric ways, the miseries and disillusions of this period of Spanish history. When Joseph Bonaparte took the Spanish throne by usurpation (1808–1813), Goya changed his allegiance immediately; and when King Ferdinand VII, the rightful heir, returned to power, he freely acknowledged Goya's disloyalty yet granted him clemency, probably because of Goya's age and infirmity. Goya was again made the royal painter.

Goya's wife Josepha and friends were by this time all dead, and he sought voluntary exile in France in the early 1820s to escape his sense of loss and loneliness. In Paris, he found friendship with Madame Weiss, sharing her home and providing instruction in drawing to her daughter.

While Goya could himself be deceitful, he was not treacherous; and he shrunk from the human cruelty of tyranny and war. He portrayed the inhumanity and folly of violence mercilessly, as an object lesson to his viewers. Perhaps he was partially motivated by horror at his own violent streak. An instance of his evil temper is given when he painted the portrait of the Duke of Wellington. Angered by a casual criticism of his manner of working, Goya grabbed a sword from the wall and nearly killed the hero of Waterloo. He could not tolerate the presence of a third person in his studio and could barely remain civil to his models. His self-portrait is noted by critics, and inexperienced viewers as well, to be the self-evaluation of a bitter and ill-tempered old man. Other works of art of his late period, such as *On the Balcony*, show human beings muffled, distant, and alienated from one another. Wernick (1989) and other critics describe Goya as both a "magician of color" who turned out bright portraits and beautiful scenes, and an embittered isolate who visualized the hatred of a world rushing toward chaos and madness. Works such as the unsettling *Disasters of War*, however, point to Goya's humanism and concern for the true cost of violence.

Goya died at Bordeaux on April 16, 1828.

References

Gassier, P. (1955). *Goya*. New York: Skira.

Richardson, J. (1989). The dark side of Goya. *House and Garden, 161* (2), 106–111, 164.

Wernick, R. (1989). Out of dark dreams and bright hopes, the blazing art of Goya. *Smithsonian, 19* (10), 56–67.

WILSON H. GRABILL (1912–1983), American Statistician.

Wilson H. Grabill was born on December 13, 1912, in Evansville, Wisconsin. His father was a Congregational minister. Progressive deafness began at the age of five and led to profound deafness within a few years. Although Grabill attended public schools for several years, he transferred to the Wisconsin School for the Deaf in Delevan, and graduated in 1929. At Gallaudet College, he advanced through all of the mathematics courses offered, and took additional courses at George Washington University and a correspondence course at the University of Wisconsin. Grabill graduated from Gallaudet College in 1934 and earned a master's degree in statistics from American University in 1942 while working with the Federal Emergency Relief Agency as a junior statistical clerk. He also studied at the Department of Agriculture Graduate School and the National Bureau of Standards. He did so after negotiation, however. As Crammatte (1987) explained, Grabill was the "first deaf person to demonstrate the irrelevance of the then current requirement that every applicant [of the civil service examination] be able to hear a watch tick at 15 feet."

Grabill's career at the Bureau of Census began in 1934, when he took the position as a junior statistical clerk in the Division of Special Tabulation; he continued at the Bureau until his retirement. Using pioneering methodology for which he was praised, Grabill helped produce the Bureau's first ten-year census report on fertility in 1940. Within six years, he rose from a clerk/operator's position to that of chief of the Bureau's Fertility Statistics Branch, with supervisory responsibilities. In this branch, he was also involved with sample surveys and reports on households, families, inmates of institutions, marital status, dissolution of marriage, fertility, and childspacing. Grabill used predictions derived from fertility research to provide an "early warning system" of demographic changes and fertility patterns influencing population dynamics. Such information is valuable to the fields of family planning and education, as well as to demographers, sociologists, and anthropologists.

In addition to many published reports on child spacing and differential fertility in such journals as *Eugenics Quarterly, Demography*, and the *American Journal of Sociology*, Grabill authored, with Clyde V. Kiser and Pascal K. Whelpton, *The Fertility of American Women* (1958), which was hailed by reviewers as a landmark publication. The book contained 448 pages and 243 tables and figures summarizing census data pertaining to fertility. Donald Bogue's *The Population of the United States* (1959) included a chapter by Grabill. In 1962, Grabill became chief of the Family and Fertility Statistics Branch of the Population Division. That year he also received the Department of Commerce Silver Medal Award. Work in the Family and Fertility Statistics Branch led to the publication of *Trends and Variations in Fertility in the United States* in 1968 (with Clyde V. Kiser and Arthur A. Campbell), and *Differential Current Fertility in the United States* in 1970 (with Lee J. Cho and Donald J. Bogue). In the later book, he included a detailed analysis of the offspring of deaf parents, finding that in 176 cases of fertile deaf-by-deaf matings examined, 147 produced only hearing children (294 such children). Grabill concluded that prenatal influences such as rubella and other viruses, trauma, hypoxia, infections, head injuries, and drug toxicities are much more prevalent causes of early deafness; that, in fact, heredity plays a relatively minor role in the etiology of deafness. This, of course, was directly counter to the earlier eugenics-rooted arguments against the intermarriage of deaf persons.

Grabill was invited to present lectures on fertility statistics to many organizations, and he served on the boards of directors for the Population Association of America, Milbank Memorial Fund, the Technical Advisory Committee for Population, the American Statistical Association, Institute of Mathematical Studies, and the U.S. National Committee of the International Union for the Scientific Study of Population. In 1971, his influence became even more far-reaching, as he presented the Population Census Tabulation Programs at the East-West Population Institute in Honolulu, Hawaii. In addition, Grabill served as a member of the U.S. Board of Civil Service Examiners for statisticians and on several *ad hoc* committees of the U.S. National Committee for Health and Vital Statistics, which reported to the Surgeon General.

Grabill was notable as a person with a strong quantitative and statistical bent who additionally was committed to a tireless social activism and advocacy. He was deeply involved in enhancing the lives of deaf people, serving on the Board of Directors of Gallaudet College and its Laurent Clerc Cultural Fund committee, and helping to found the National Health Care Foundation. He actively participated in the National Fraternal Society of the Deaf and as a treasurer of the Episcopal Conference of the Deaf. In 1972, he founded Deaf-REACH with Otto Berg. Deaf-REACH grew from one program in Washington, D.C., with six members, to a multi-program social service organization benefitting deaf adults who are mentally ill, mentally retarded, low-income, or who have additional disabilities. The Grabill Center, named in his honor, provides a home-like atmosphere for participants seeking psychosocial and vocational rehabilitation.

Grabill retired from the Census Bureau in 1973 after forty-one years of service. He was honored that year with the Gold Medal Award from the Department of Commerce. He died of cancer on January 30, 1983, in Clinton, Maryland.

References

Alumni News: Recording the population explosion. (1972, Spring). *Gallaudet Today, 2* (3), 28–29.
Crammatte, A. B. (1987). Wilson H. Grabill. In J. V. Van Cleve (Ed.), *Gallaudet encyclopedia of deaf people and deafness* (Vol. 1, pp. 477–478). New York: McGraw-Hill.
Deaf-REACH to honor founders on anniversary. (1992, April). *Silent News, 24* (4), 17.

PATRICK GRAYBILL (1939–   ), American Actor.

Patrick Graybill was born on August 29, 1939, in Overland Park, Kansas. He was one of seven children; three of his sisters and one brother were deaf, and he had two hearing sisters, one of whom became a certified sign language interpreter. His mother, a former teacher who had learned sign language from Pat's deaf sisters, taught him to read and write at an early age. His father, however, never learned signs, which Graybill attributes more to the interpretation of gender roles at the time than to lack of desire. Graybill graduated from the Kansas School for the Deaf in Olathe in 1958, where he was inspired by an elegant deaf teacher, Mrs. Ayers. Her storytelling ability made him think seriously about teaching for the first time. He also saw his older sister in a dramatics production of *Tom Sawyer*, which planted the idea of acting in her admiring brother's head.

He graduated from Gallaudet College with a bachelor's degree in English in 1963 and a master's degree in education in 1964. Active in the Dramatics Club at Gallaudet, he was a three-time winner of the Best Actor Award—in 1961 for his role of "Judge Wargrave" in *Ten Little Indians*, in 1962 for "Dr. Haggett" in *The Late Christopher Bean*, and in 1963 for "Algernon Moncrieff" in *The Importance of Being Earnest*. Graybill was also involved in the Ballard Literary Society and was the only senior in his class to win listing in the 1962–1963 *Who's Who in American Colleges and Universities*. Nonetheless, he encountered his first serious barrier when he signed up for the teacher certification program. He was told that because he could not speak and be a model for speech and speechreading, he should choose another career path. Terribly upset, he and other students who had been so advised petitioned for a probationary trial. He did so well in his course work and practicum at West Virginia School for the Deaf that he was immediately offered a job at Kendall Demonstration Elementary School.

In December 1962, Graybill presented a Christmas reading in sign language on WRC Channel 4's program "Inga's Angel." He had top TV billing on WTTG–5 the following week when he played the role of the devil in "Don Juan in Hell," a portion of George Bernard Shaw's play *Man and Superman*. While teaching at the Kendall School for three years, Graybill directed *Morning's at Seven* and *Boy Meets Girl* through the Frederick H. Hughes Memorial Theater, a local community theatre. While he enjoyed the cultural stimulation and opportunities for part-time acting in the Washington, D.C. area, he became restless and felt his life should be taking another direction. He resigned from Kendall in 1967. Then, he enrolled at Catholic University of America to study theology. He began the seminary training in earnest to prepare for the priesthood. The challenge of interacting with 200 hearing students in classes with no notetakers or tutors was somewhat allayed by the friendships he formed with some enthusiastic candidates who did their best to learn ASL. But his third career path was waiting in the wings.

Graybill joined the National Theatre of the Deaf (NTD) as an actor in 1969. For ten years, he performed on stage in such roles as "Mosca" in *Volpone*, "Ivan Ivanovich Nyoukhim" in *On the Harmfulness of Tobacco*, "Rabbi Azrielki" in *The Dybbuk*, and "Woyzeck" in *Woyzeck*. He also joined the NTD cast for the CBS Special *A Child's Christmas In Wales* and for the WGBH show *Who Knows One*. While with NTD, he studied theater for ten years at the annual Professional School for the Deaf Theatre Personnel, administering the program himself from 1972 until 1976, and perfecting his acting skills. In the Professional School he also taught the course "Resources for the Artist." Graybill conducted many workshops on creative interpretation of drama. He served as associate director of NTD in 1978 and 1979. In 1978, with the cast of the National Theatre of the Deaf, he received the Tony Award for Theatre Excellence.

In 1979, Graybill accepted a position as artistic consultant at the National Technical Institute for the Deaf (NTID) at the Rochester Institute of Technology (RIT). During the next twelve years, he taught advanced acting and creative translation into American Sign Language for NTID. He directed *One Flew Over the Cuckoo's Nest*, translated into ASL such productions as *Fantastiks* and *Once Upon a Mattress*, and appeared as guest actor in the role of "Arnolphe" in *The School for Wives* and as "Prospero" in *The Tempest*. The move to Rochester also allowed him to complete the studies for his diaconate at St. Bernard's Institute.

Graybill has reflected on his "luck" in being a person who has never stopped learning. He maintains the delicate balance among three distinct, yet related career areas with real enthusiasm and anticipation of the future. Currently, he continues to teach at Gallaudet University as an adjunct professor and develops instructional materials at Sign Media, Incorporated. He starred with Phyllis Frelich* in the Theatre In Sign production of *The Gin Game*, playing the lead role of ''Weller Martin,'' and they reprised their pairing in the highly experimental and well-received 1992 Deaf West production. One can predict that students and audiences will never stop learning from Patrick Graybill.

References

Deaf culture autobiographies on video: Patrick Graybill. (1990). [Videotape]. Salem, OR: Sign Enhancers.

Walworth, M. (1992, February). There were no losers at *The Gin Game. NAD Broadcaster, 14* (2), 16.

H

ELIZA HAIGH-VOORHIS (1865–?), American Painter.

Eliza Haigh was born on April 12, 1865 in Brooklyn, New York, the daughter of a prosperous owner of a wire factory, and one of five children. She was profoundly deafened by meningitis at the age of two. When she was about six years old, she was enrolled in a school to learn to speak. After notably unsuccessful attempts, her father took her out of school and hired a private teacher, Miss Abbie Locke, who had trained as a pupil with Alexander Graham Bell. When she was only fifteen, Haigh's mother died, and she spent her adolescence in Boston, Buffalo, and in her family home in New York City, taking lessons in riding and dancing. Her protective and anxious father wanted his daughter to have the best of everything, and Eliza lived a life of privilege productively. For about six years, she spent the summers in South Bristol, Maine, at her sister's home, where she camped alone most of the time, sketching and thinking. Back in New York City, she took formal lessons in drawing and painting from such notable artists as Carol Beckwith, Kenyon Cox, and William Chase. She followed these lessons with a tour of Italy and France, studying the works of masters in such museums as the Pitti and Uffizi.

Over the next two years, she spent her winters at the Academy Vitti and the Academy Colarossi, taking lessons from such great painters as Merson, Aman Jean, Mac Mounier, and Raphael Colin. In Europe, she made many friends among her fellow painting students and traveled with them. She remained in Paris for eight years, producing many landscapes, still lifes, and portraits. *The Meal* and *A Reading Woman* were accepted at the Paris Salon; her reputation led to further commissions and private gallery showings. After another two years in Etaples, on the Channel, where she continued painting striking seascapes, she traveled to Amsterdam, Holland, where she stayed with a family while studying Dutch art. Both deaf and hearing models sat for her paintings there. She enjoyed other deaf people, and she regretted that she did not have many opportunities to interact with larger Deaf communities. When World War I began, Haigh was in Veer, Holland. She returned to the United States for eleven years.

In Winsted, Connecticut, at a home owned by her brother-in-law, she volunteered to assist with the Red Cross, knitting, sewing, and rolling bandages for wounded soldiers. A light connected to the doorbell allowed her to know visitors were at the door. Distressed by the war and her concerns for people she knew in Europe, that period was soon made even more difficult by a fire which destroyed Haigh's studio.

In 1925, Haigh returned to France, overjoyed to see Paris, especially the Louvre, again. She produced landscapes during her visits to the Alps, Brittany, the convent of Grande Chartreuse, and the Riviera. Unable to read lips in French, she often resorted to writing in order to communicate while traveling alone through France or Holland. Haigh was remarkably fluent in French and Dutch. Although very sensitive about her deafness, she was a resourceful and flexible traveler. In 1928, two of her open-air paintings, *The Country Road in Litchfield, Connecticut*, and *Old Curiosity Shop in Nantucket*, were highlighted in *The Volta Review*, a periodical for the teachers of deaf pupils. Both paintings had been exhibited at the Salon des Indépéndants in New York. A critic in *La revue du vrai et du beau* wrote, "These two works are well composed, brilliantly colored. . . . Miss Eliza Haigh excels in creating an atmosphere, giving to her landscapes air and light, making them vibrate and live. . . . She is a very remarkable artist." While based in Europe, she retained membership in the New York Art Students League and Connecticut Association of Fine Artists. As a woman artist of her era, she enjoyed uncommon success and a life of quiet adventure.

References

Opitz, G. B. (Ed.). (1983). *Mantle Fielding's dictionary of American painters, sculptors & engravers*. Poughkeepsie, NY: Apollo Book.

Pitrois, Y. (1928). An American artist. *The Volta Review, 30* (4), 196–201.

ERNEST E. HAIRSTON, JR. (1939–   ), American Writer/Deaf Community Advocate.

Ernest E. Hairston, Jr., was born on March 1, 1939, in Stotesbury, West Virginia, a mining town near Beckley. He was deafened at the age of five from spinal meningitis. At first, his mother Dorothy resisted the idea of sending the little boy to the West Virginia School for the Colored Deaf and Blind near Charleston. She felt it was too far from home. Ultimately, however, she and young Ernest's father decided it was the best way to assure a better life for their active son. During Hairston's sophomore year, in 1954, the U.S. Supreme Court ruled such segregated schools unconstitutional. The African-American students from his school were transferred to the West Virginia School for the Deaf and Blind in Romney. Hairston has looked back at his experience in these schools as one of the best things to ever happen to him. Not only did he receive a solid elementary and secondary education, but the West Virginia School for the Colored Deaf and Blind was located a short distance from the West Virginia State College. Many African-American students in this strong teacher preparation program practice taught in Hairston's classes and, although they were less familiar with deafness, they provided him with a challenging learning environment. Hairston scored high on the academic placement tests. Having also studied several trades, though, he expressed interest in becoming a barber. However, his senior English teacher at the West Virginia School for the Deaf and Blind was Malcolm Norwood,* who wisely counseled him to consider higher career aspirations. Hairston completed his bachelor's degree in education from Gallaudet College. While there, he received the George M. Teegarden award for creative poetry and was a member of the Gallaudet Dance Troupe and wrestling team. He received a bronze medal in wrestling at the 1961 International Games for the Deaf in Helsinki.

Hairston began teaching English and social studies in 1961 at the Governor Morehead School for the Deaf in Raleigh, North Carolina. Although the school was composed of an all-black student body, he was the first deaf African-American teacher in that school's history. Three years later, he was offered a teaching position at the Michigan Association for Better Hearing and Speech in Lansing, where he focused on assisting deaf people with other disabilities develop independent living skills. He then held positions as coordinator and supervising teacher at the State Technical Institute and Rehabilitation Center in Plainwell, Michigan, and as director of the Diagnostic, Evaluation, and Adjustment Facility (Project D.E.A.F.) in Columbus, Ohio. During these years, Hairston also studied at Michigan State University and the California State University at Northridge Leadership Training Program, from which he received a master's degree in special educational administration in 1967. Through these years, he and a colleague, Linwood Smith, were often asked to present on the subject of black deaf people. At the 1972 Fourth Biennial Conference of Professional Rehabilitation Workers with the Adult Deaf, he and Smith served on a panel of black deaf persons and emphasized the importance of addressing problems associated with undereducation and underemployment, communication skills, and self-identity. Their continued advocacy role culminated in the publication of a much-needed book, *Black and Deaf in America: Are We That Different?* The book addresses issues of the black deaf child and the family, education, rehabilitation, and highlights the accomplishments of a number of deaf black professionals. Sadly, his co-author and friend, Linwood Smith, an accomplished poet and writer, died in an accident in November 1982, shortly before the book went to press. Hairston summarized the issue at heart: "To dismiss the racial aspect of deafness would be naive and presumptuous because the Black deaf person is already at a disadvantage from the time he is born . . . attitudes die hard. . . . We live in a 'hearing' and 'color-conscious' society."

In 1971, Hairston's mentor and friend, Malcolm Norwood, now in the U.S. Department of Education, encouraged him to apply for a position as an Education Program Specialist with the Office of Special Education and Rehabilitative Services (OSERS). By the time of Norwood's retirement in 1989, Hairston had advanced through the ranks and was ready to take over Norwood's responsibilities as chief of the Captioning and Adaptation Branch of the Division of Educational Services within OSERS. In this position, he has been responsible for coordinating research and development related to media and captioning services, developing policy and creative strategy for assuring support for such projects, and promoting innovative and creative programs for deaf students and adults. Throughout his years under Norwood, Hairston published many reports on multimedia, career education, multicultural services, captioning, microcomputer, videodisc, and telecommunication technologies.

Dr. Hairston continues to serve as a leader in the Department of Education. He is also an active participant and driving force in the National Black Deaf Advocates.

References

Bowe, F. (1972). Ernest Hairston, A Conversation With Frank Bowe. *The Deaf American, 24* (8), 7–9.

Hairston, E., & Smith, L. (1983). Black and deaf in America: Are we that different? Silver Spring, MD: T. J. Publishers.

Johnstone, M. (1990–1991). Making an impact: Ernest Hairston influences the lives of deaf people nationwide. *Gallaudet Today, 21* (2), 44–48.

ANTHONY A. HAJNA (1907–1992), American Bacteriologist.

Anthony A. Hajna was born in Chicopee, Massachusetts, on March 21, 1907, and lost his hearing when he was five years old, a result of meningitis. After his family moved to Bridgeport, Connecticut, a coal peddler who had a deaf nephew found Hajna playing on the street and convinced his parents to enroll him in the Mystic Oral School for the Deaf in Connecticut. After his graduation, he worked there for several years as a supervisor of boys until he was admitted to Gallaudet College, where he finished his bachelor's degree in 1930. During the Great Depression, he obtained a Rockefeller fellowship and studied at Johns Hopkins University School of Hygiene and Public Health in Baltimore. The head professor there was at first reluctant to admit him into the program and they agreed to allow him to study as a ''special student.'' Within a month, however, he had proven his abilities and became a candidate in the program for the Master of Science in Hygiene degree.

Hajna quickly became one of the nation's authoritative scientists in enteric bacteriology, authoring many papers and designing laboratory procedures for identifying epidemic type forms of bacteria. In 1932, following the completion of his master's degree, he was appointed assistant bacteriologist in the central laboratory of the Maryland State Department of Health, where he remained for seventeen years. Taking the competitive state examination covering various topics in protozoology, immunology, helminthology, and pathology, he won that position over twelve other applicants. Over the next few years, he gained increasing recognition for his development of a medium for isolating typhoid bacteria. His new "TSI" medium was an improvement over the widely used "Russell" medium at that time, in that it expedited the classification of bacteria in a shorter and more economical manner. Large orders for the medium from the Naval Procurement Board immediately followed. In 1935, Hajna published several studies on the isolation of typhoid bacilli in sewage and the development of a procedure for bacteriological examination of oysters. Other studies followed on the examination of bacteria of the coliform group.

In 1949, Hajna accepted an offer from the Vermont State Board of Health, training workers in the state laboratories; he then joined the U.S. Public Health Service in Cincinnati, Ohio, where he was involved in membrane filter studies. This work prepared him for his position as bacteriologist-in-charge at the Indiana State Board of Health. Here, he spent many years researching techniques to accurately and quickly identify epidemic-type bacteria, especially those found in spoiled food and contaminated water. Hajna's research skills were called upon numerous times. One case occurred when an outbreak of food poisoning sickened many people who had gathered for a conference. The state board of health conducted numerous tests, but found nothing in the milk and food. Hajna examined the conditions that led to the food poisoning and discovered that one of the workers hired to prepare the food was carrying the typhoid bacteria. A similar incident at an Amish picnic involved salmonellosis. Hajna's thorough understanding of this bacteria led him to suspect poultry as the source. No eggs were found to be contaminated, but his investigation identified one of the persons who had prepared the food as having handled eggs covered with the salmonellosis bacteria.

Hajna served on the Editorial Board for *The Laboratory Digest*, publishing many of his studies in that journal as well. These reports included summaries of his work with polyvalent salmonella "H" agglutination, and simplified and reliable gram staining techniques. In 1956, he developed a new enrichment broth medium for gram-negative organisms of the intestinal group for the Air University School of Aviation Medicine. He was also the principal assistant to Samuel R. Damon in developing the report to the Commission on Enteric Infections of the Armed Forces Epidemiological Board. By 1965, he had authored more than thirty articles on advanced laboratory techniques for the identification of enteric infections associated with typhoid, salmonellosis, and related diseases. His description of the "G.N. Broth" is on file in the National Archives in Washington, D.C. He was an active member of the American Society for Microbiology, the American Public Health Association, the New York Academy of Sciences, and the American Association for the Advancement of Science. He enjoyed visiting schools and promoting science as a career for deaf persons, taking films with him to attract the interest of the students.

Hajna was active in the Deaf community, serving as president of the Baltimore division of the National Fraternal Society of the Deaf, the Indianapolis chapter of the Gallaudet College Alumni Association, and the Indiana Association of the Deaf. In 1961, he received an honorary doctoral degree from Gallaudet College and, in 1965, he was the recipient of the Indiana State Achievement Award by the Executive Audiological Rehabilitation Society for outstanding achievement. In an exchange of letters with the developers of a careers program for Gallaudet College, George Beauchamp, leader of the Washington Ethical Society, said: ''[Hajna] is becoming recognized as one of the outstanding scientists in his field any place in the world.''

Hajna died on March 14, 1992, in Springfield, Massachusetts.

References

A life worth while. (1956, April 29). *Indianapolis Times.*

Anthony Hajna, 84; noted bacteriologist. (1992, March 15). Springfield, Massachusetts *Sunday Republican.*

Smith, J. M. (1967). Dr. Anthony A. Hajna: Hoosier bacteriologist. *The Deaf American*, *19* (10), 3–6.

FERNAND HAMAR (1869–1943), French Sculptor.

Fernand Hamar was born deaf at Vendome, France, on July 15, 1869. At the age of twenty, he entered the École des Beaux Arts, where he was a student of P. J. Cavelier and Schüler von E. Barrias for ten years. He also was instructed by the deaf sculptor Paul Choppin.* Hamar then opened his own studio where he took commissions for monuments.

Hamar's works have been exhibited many times at the Salon des Champs Elysees. The bust entitled *The Falconier*, one of his most important works, won a medal there, and the allegorical group titled *Triumph of Truth* is now in the museum at the National Institution for the Deaf in Paris. In 1893, he received honorable mention for a bust at the Salon. In the 1899 Salon, Hamar exhibited a bronze bust of an unnamed gentleman, *Portrait de M. B . . .* , and a statuette in bronze representing the French physicist, Joseph-Nicéphore Niepce, who had produced the world's first photograph in his work with Louis-Jacques Daguerre. Niepce was portrayed as standing by his apparatus in 1830, seemingly interrogating the future.

In 1900, Hamar received honorable mention at the Universal Exposition. He was also commissioned by a committee to sculpt a statue in memory of Conte de Rochambeau (Admiral Jean-Baptiste-Donatien Vimeur), who had aided the Americans in defeating Cornwallis at Yorktown. Rochambeau's statue was erected in his native Vendome, where Hamar had also been raised. In the Salon of 1901, the sculptor exhibited a marble bust of *Mille J. Monnet* and a second statue of Rochambeau, this one on a horse. Hamar was honored with an invitation to complete the eight-foot-high statue of Rochambeau for the U.S. government to be erected on the southwest corner of Lafayette Square facing the White House in Washington. In 1902, the deaf sculptor's masterpiece was unveiled in Washington with its large pedestal adorned with an allegorical figure of *Victory and the American Eagle*. Attending the ceremony were President Roosevelt, the Diplomatic Corps, General Brugyere, Admiral Fournier of the French navy, and representatives of the Rochambeau and Lafayette families. Dinners with Ambassador Jules Cambon at the French Embassy and with President Roosevelt and his wife at the White House followed. During a visit on that same trip to Gallaudet College, Hamar met with a number of deaf people. While he did not know English, his French signs were generally comprehended by his American friends. Both sign languages have French roots (see Laurent Clerc*).

In 1904, Hamar exhibited a plaster statuette *Amour lutinant un crabe* and a portrait bust in plaster of *Jacquot Grooters*. *The Triumph of Truth* was shown in the Salon of 1905. In 1906, he showed a marble portrait bust of *M. Riverain* and a bronze portrait of *Senator M. Henry David*.

Among Hamar's other significant works were *Fortune Rewarding Labor*, a large, graceful panel in high relief for the Savings Bank at Vendome. In this work, a reaper is shown pausing for a brief rest as "Fortune" passes across the field and shares her bounty.

As with many other artists, Hamar was too distraught during World War I to produce new pieces. When peace came, he began to sculpt war memorials, unveiling several in great ceremony at or near Vendome, the headquarters and flying field for British aviators during the war. The memorial erected at Vendome in 1921 was a large, irregularly-shaped shaft of stone with a Gallic cock in bronze on the summit and a German double-headed eagle at the back. In 1921, he also exhibited *Diana in Repose* at the Salon of French Artists. At the soldiers' cemetery at Freteval in 1923, his monument portrayed France paying homage to its war dead. Hamar's bronze bas-relief of Abbé Goiselot was dedicated at the chapel at the National Institution for the Deaf in Paris in 1925, as well as busts of Henri Gaillard and Gabriel Herouard, leaders in the French Deaf community. *The Shadow of Remembrance*, completed in 1925, depicted the strength and sacrifice of the French people during World War I and was inspired by Hamar's visits to the grave of the unknown soldier beneath the Arch of Triumph in Paris. Hamar's smaller sculptures, many in bronze, of cupids, swans, doves and other decorations for mantelpieces, clocks, and tables were in a considerably lighter vein, and they often followed the eighteenth-century style.

In 1930, Hamar exhibited a bronze group *Lévriers* and *Portrait de M. Vigier*. Another of his hero Rochambeau's statues was erected in Newport, Rhode Island. In 1934, Hamar showed *Rochambeau* and a second bronze statue titled *Greyhound* at the International Exhibition of Fine and Applied Arts by Deaf Artists at the Roerich Museum in New York City. This collaborative exhibition with other deaf artists was the culmination of his successful career. He died in 1943.

References

International Exhibition of Fine and Applied Arts by Deaf Artists, New York City, July 21–August 11, 1934.
Stevens, K. H. (1927). Fernand Hamar, sculptor. *The Silent Worker*, *39* (9), 322–324.

JEAN HANAU (1899–1966), French-American Painter.

Jean Hanau was born in Paris on June 2, 1899. Sensing his potential, his wealthy family provided the budding artist with private tutoring at an early age. The young Jean also made the acquaintance of the illustrator Pierre Brissaud, who advised him to study under Corman at École des Beaux Arts in Paris. After his studies were completed there, he took further private lessons from such distinguished artists as Bernard Naudin, Charles Guérin, Picard-le-Doux, and Louis Billoul; he became known as the best of Billoul's impressive stable of students. Hanau intrigued his teachers and viewers by combining classical with emerging contemporary expressionistic forms.

In 1925, Hanau opened a studio on the Boulevard Saint Michel, spending time each summer in the Midi in southern France, at Toulon, Cannes, and other coastal cities. He favored seascapes with warm colors, seaport traffic and street scenes. He held regular exhibits at the Salon d'Automne, in the Salon des Independants, and in galleries with colleagues who called themselves the "Group of Eleven." The French government purchased two of his paintings for the national collection, and the city of Paris bought one for its municipal collections.

Hanau traveled to the United States in 1928; he remained for six months painting landscapes in New Jersey and Pennsylvania. He also visited the Southwest, where he was able to apply the full range of his masterful use of warm, bright colors. He particularly enjoyed studying the culture of Native Americans in New Mexico. His paintings of that period show cacti and hollyhocks in adobe-walled gardens and mountain landscapes. He incorporated Native American designs into much of this work. Back in New York, he continued to demonstrate his versatility with a series of city scenes.

Upon returning to Paris in 1929, he exhibited his paintings from his American tour at the Bernheim Jeune Galleries, practically selling out the entire collection. His work was also exhibited at the galleries of Devambez, Drouant, and Simonson. This American experience deeply impressed him, and he continued to paint Native American ceremonies (*Festival Day, Santo Domingo*) and dances. He completed this work from sketches brought back from the United States. The French public enthusiastically received this series at another 1930 exhibit.

Around 1931, Hanau experienced a transformation in his technique and in his choice of subject matter. He abandoned sketching excursions and the use of models in favor of drawing upon psychological perceptions and memory. He also began to favor a tiny palette knife over the brush. With this, he could mix colors partly on the palette and partly on the canvas to achieve interesting texture and glaze. His enormous painting, *The Birth of Venus* (1932), represents this evolution. Venus rises from the waves of the sea and floats on draperies. On either side of her are two groups of five figures each representing the friends of the artist. All are portraits of Hanau's noted literary and artistic friends, including the African-American poet, Countee Cullen. Hanau maintained his desire to combine the classical and the contemporary in a unique way.

After completing *The Birth of Venus*, Hanau applied his new technique to a series of portraits and still life paintings. At a 1934 exhibit at New York's Roerich Museum, a critic in the *New York American* wrote that Hanau had a "rare feeling for delicate and sensuous coloring." The Roerich Museum subsequently displayed these paintings in a number of galleries in the northeastern United States.

In the 1930s, Hanau also pursued decorative murals, screens, and porcelain pieces. The National Manufactury of Sevres accepted many of his designs, which were exhibited in Paris. Simultaneously, he was invited by a wealthy individual from Paris to design a mirrored decorative panel for an apartment. From this work, he began to experiment with a technique for designs in gold, silver and colors on the back of mirrors, leading him to exhibit many such works for which he was praised by critics for his versatility in media.

Hanau's gold leaf on mirrors and lacquered panels were found in the Hotel Plaza, the Countess Mara boutique, lobbies of Mahattan apartment buildings, and commercial offices. His one-man shows were at many galleries, including those of Devamberg and Druot. He also exhibited in New York at the Penthouse and IBM galleries. In 1942, he settled in the United States and later became a U.S. citizen.

Hanau died on November 17, 1966, in his West 55th Street studio in New York, where he had lived and worked for twenty-five years. After his death, a number of unstretched canvases were discovered under his living room rug. They were restored for an exhibition in May 1968, titled "Jean Hanau: Retrospective."

References

Jean Hanau: Retrospective. May 16–19, 1968. Park Avenue, New York City.
Stevens, K. H. (1937). Jean Hanau, French modern. *The Pelican*, *58* (4), 1–3, 18–19.

EUGENE E. HANNAN (1875–1945), American Sculptor.

Eugene Elmer Hannan was born on July 26, 1875, in Washington, D.C, the son of a successful businessman and a social worker. He was deafened at the age of two and a half through scarlet fever. At the age of seven, his parents placed him in the Kendall School for the Deaf, where he remained for six years. He also attended St. Mary's School for the Deaf in Buffalo, New York, and St. John's Institute near Milwaukee, Wisconsin. It was about this time that he first learned to carve wood.

Hannan entered Gallaudet College in 1896, where he studied for one year. He then studied at the Corcoran School of Art in Washington, D.C., taking courses in anatomy, charcoal drawing, and other fundamentals for three years. At the Art Institute of Chicago, he studied under Lorado Taft and J. C. Mulligan, completing, while still a student, a bust of the Reverend Thomas Gallaudet, son of the cofounder of the first formal school for deaf pupils in the United States and pastor of St. Ann's Church for the Deaf in New York City. Hannan then joined the Art Students League of New York City, and studied under the sculptors Herman MacNeil, Richard E. Brooks, and Gutzon Borglum. Following this, Hannan worked in studios in France, Italy, and Spain, developing friendships with the deaf sculptor Paul Choppin,* the deaf painters Valentin* and Ramon de Zubiaurre,* and the hearing American sculptor Jo Davidson. One of the de Zubiaurre brothers subsequently painted his portrait, which was given to Hannan for his home.

In 1917, Hannan presented Clifford D. Perkins, manager of the Hotel Heublein in Washington, D.C., a handcarved medallion with Thomas Hopkins Gallaudet's profile. He also sculpted a bronze memorial tablet of Sophia Fowler Gallaudet, which was unveiled in Guilford, Connecticut. As the wife of Thomas Hopkins Gallaudet, cofounder with Laurent Clerc* of the American School for the Deaf, and as the mother of Edward Miner Gallaudet who founded Gallaudet College, Sophia Fowler Gallaudet played an important role in helping Edward solicit support in Congress to establish Gallaudet College.

Hannan accepted a position as a modeler at the U.S. National Museum in Washington. He enlarged models of statues, medallions, and busts for special exhibits. His portrait busts, which he sculpted on his own time, included college presidents, Governor Sulzer of New York and Governor Atkin of West Virginia. At the American Museum of Natural History in New York, he modelled various groups for the St. Louis and San Francisco Expositions and decorative art work for several expositions at Baltimore. He assisted Gutzon Borglum in sculpting the bronze equestrian statue of the Civil War General Philip H. Sheridan located at Sheridan Circle in Washington. Hannan had his own studio there, and the Gallaudet College class of 1926 commissioned him to sculpt a bust of Edward Miner Gallaudet, who had until then declined sitting for others. Gallaudet sat for him five times, for one hour each session. The bust was placed in Gallaudet College's Chapel Hall.

One of the great honors paid Hannan by the Deaf community in America was the selection of his design, in a competition with deaf and hearing sculptors from the United States and Europe, for a statue of the benevolent Abbé de l'Epée, founder of the first public school for deaf pupils in France in 1760. Hannan traveled to Paris in 1929 to complete this work. Epée's statue was unveiled before representatives of the French Embassy and about three thousand delegates to the third World Congress of the Deaf at St. Mary's School for the Deaf in Buffalo on August 7, 1930. The following year, Hannan married Helen Constance Price. They moved to Westport, Connecticut, where he contributed a number of sculpted works to the town. Among Hannan's best-known sculptures in the Connecticut area are the bust of the late E. T. Bedford in the Bedford Elementary School, two large mural panels in plaster in the Staples High School depicting the retreat of the British at Cedar Point and the Battle of Compo Hill, and sixteen bronze medallions on various walls of the building with bas relief portraits of the Founders of Connecticut, including such distinguished men and women as John Winthrop, Thomas Hooker, Samuel Huntington, Oliver Woolcott, Nathan Hale, Israel Putnam, Sarah Pierce, and Noah Webster.

In 1934, Hannan showed a plaster bust of F. P. Gibson, a statuette titled *Curve Ball*, and a copper medallion of Thomas Hopkins Gallaudet at the International Exhibition of Fine and Applied Arts by Deaf Artists at the Roerich Museum in New York City. He joined artists from around the world in this highly praised exhibit of the talents of deaf men and women.

Hannan died on February 7, 1945, and was buried in the Willowbrook Cemetery in Westport.

References

Higgins, F. (1980). Eugene Elmer Hannan—American deaf sculptor. *On the Green, 10* (25), 4.
International Exhibition of Fine and Applied Arts by Deaf Artists. International Art Center of Roerich Museum, July 21–August 11, 1934, 20.

OLOF HANSON (1862–1933), American Architect.

Olof Hanson was born on September 10, 1862, in Fjelkinge, southern Sweden; his father was a prosperous farmer, member of the local legislature, and railroad director. In 1874, the family purchased a farm in America. They planned to immigrate after a short while, but the father died suddenly from fever at the age of forty-three, and plans were postponed for a year. Hanson was totally deafened in one ear during a severe snowstorm while still in Sweden, and in the other a few weeks after arriving in America, at the age of thirteen. For three years he did not go to school. Knowing no English, he read Swedish newspapers. Then, Olof Norling, a deaf neighbor, heard of him, and soon convinced Hanson to enter the Minnesota School for the Deaf in Faribault, where a new world opened for him. With the help of several Swedish-English dictionaries, he studied eagerly. He graduated in 1881; he then attended Gallaudet College, graduating in 1886 at the head of the class. While a roommate of young Cadwallader Washburn,* who was destined to greatness in the field of dry-point etching, Hanson decided on architecture as a life pursuit. Washburn's father, a senator, had arranged summer work for Hanson at the E. T. Mix architectural company in Milwaukee, Wisconsin. There, he was inspired by the positive attitude of his mentor. He entered the office of Hodgson & Son, an architectural firm in Minneapolis, where he remained until 1889. He was one of the first deaf Americans to enter the field of architecture.

Hanson spent ten months abroad for professional study, first in England and Scotland, where he studied the cathedrals and was impressed by the classical

Greek style. At École des Beaux Arts for five months, he learned ornamental design. There, he met daily for dinner with Douglas Tilden,* the deaf sculptor. Hanson then traveled through southern France and Italy to study architecture, painting, and sculpture, stopping in Milan, Pisa, and Florence. Next, he went to Switzerland, Germany, Denmark, Norway, and Sweden, where he visited with friends. All along the way, he visited schools for deaf children, communicating in both writing and sign languages. He returned to New York in July 1890, then went on to Philadelphia, where he found a position with Wilson Brothers & Company, a firm then designing the buildings for the new Pennsylvania School for the Deaf at Mt. Airy. During the business panic of 1893, he tried his hand at teaching at the school in Faribault. Hanson then opened his own office, where his first major assignment was to design buildings for the North Dakota School for the Deaf. Over the next six years, he designed twenty-four residences, eighteen store buildings and hotels, two churches, and ten school and institutional buildings. These included the Minnesota School for the Deaf, a dormitory for Kendall Green on the campus of Gallaudet College, a hotel for the Orinoco company in Venezuela, the beautiful rectory of the Episcopal Church on the shore of Lake Superior, and the house for Jay C. Howard, a banker in Duluth, Minnesota. In 1899, Hanson married Agatha M. Tiegel, the first woman graduate of Gallaudet College.

Meanwhile, architect Frank Thayer from Mankato invited Hanson as a partner, and he moved there in 1901. One of his first responsibilities was to design plans for the U.S. Court House in Juneau, Alaska. When Thayer became ill, Hanson continued on his own for some time, then joined other firms. In Seattle, he designed another twenty-four residences, eight schools, ten stores, and other structures.

Hanson moved to St. Paul, Minnesota, during World War I, returning to Seattle in 1918 to work as a draftsman for the University of Washington. He was ordained a minister in January, 1929, working exclusively with deaf people on Sundays while maintaining his position as an architect during the week. In the Deaf community, he was an active member of the Puget Sound Association of the Deaf, the Washington State Association of the Deaf, the National Fraternal Society of the Deaf, and the National Association of the Deaf, for which he served as president following in the footsteps of George W. Veditz.* He continued Veditz's insistence on the use of the combined method (sign language, speechreading, and writing) in schools for deaf children.

Olof Hanson died in Seattle on September 8, 1933. In 1988, Governor Rudy Perpich signed a bill to honor him by having State Highway #299 named Olof Hanson Drive.

References

Bahl, D. D. (1987–1988, December–January). Olof Hanson, architect & clergyman. *The Companion*, 1–5.
Cloud, J. H. (1916). Public opinion. *The Silent Worker*, 28 (10), 181–183.

Hanson, O. (1932). Olof Hanson: An autobiography. *The Companion*, *57* (16), 1–4.

OLAF HASSEL (1898–1972), Norwegian Astronomer.

Olaf Hassel was born on a farm at Upper Sandsvaer on May 12, 1898, a few miles from the town of Kongsberg, Norway, and was completely deafened at the age of one. In his autobiographical notes, Hassel reminisced that "some people have written and spoken about the bright years of my childhood. But for me, without hearing, my childhood years were the worst and darkest of my life. I soon noticed that I was different from other children and adults who could hear and talk, and I was of course disconsolate with my heavy destiny." From 1907 until 1915, Hassel studied at the Christiania Public School for the Deaf in Oslo, where he received training as a designer. During his final year in the school, the principal arranged for him to begin additional training in the Museum of Art; and an instructor encouraged him to become a lithographer. When offered a position as a copper etcher, he came close to accepting it, changing his mind only because his parents preferred that he stay at home. He worked on his parents' farm for twenty years, until his mother's death.

Hassel took an interest in astronomy while in his final years at the school for the deaf. He busied himself learning the names of the constellations and identifying known comets, and he became proficient enough to point them out to others. The astronomer Sigurd Einbu's monthly articles in a local newspaper further roused Hassel's interest. In 1918, one report in particular, a description of a large nova discovered by a Swedish student, started him dreaming of discovering one himself. Upon Einbu's suggestion, Hassel joined the Nordic Nova Society; and he was subsequently assigned observational areas near the constellation Gemini. His responsibility was to monitor the region for new stars or comets, and to warn astronomers of any findings. He was also encouraged to study variable stars in his field of observation. Hassel soon felt disappointed, though, with the limited area assigned him. He purchased books on astronomy and began to expand his territory. At the end of World War I, he was delighted to see his father have electric lights installed in the farmyard. Now he could study college textbooks in the early hours of the morning. He used a borrowed collapsible telescope, his father's old binoculars, and opera glasses to experiment with his own observational techniques.

Hassel became particularly fascinated with the numerous dim stars in the Milky Way region. On September 2, 1919, he discovered a dim Bronson-Metcalf comet; and, in the following year, he discovered a star of second magnitude in Cygnus, "the Swan." In 1921, he discovered a dim Reids comet without a tail, also in Cygnus. Einbu described Hassel's discovery in one of his monthly articles, noting that the deaf youth had found the star with only a spectacle lens.

Hassel and the geophysicist and mathematician Fredrik Carl Størmer, a professor at the University of Oslo, accumulated an enormous amount of observational material on altitude, size, shape, and periodicity of the auroral displays. On the subject of nacreous ("Mother-of-Pearl") clouds alone, Størmer published no less than seventeen papers between 1927 and 1951; and Hassel assisted in preparing the photographs found in many of Størmer's reports.

It was during a study of binary stars that Hassel made one of his most exciting discoveries. After spotting the Reids comet in 1921, he spent the next eighteen years exhaustively observing the heavens finding no new undiscovered celestial bodies. It was thus with no great sense of expectation that he looked through his telescope on Sunday night, April 16, 1939, to observe R Trianguli, a binary star system. Looking out over the firmament, he was surprised to see the tail of a bright comet between two clouds. The comet was in the constellation Andromeda. Unable to use the telephone because of his deafness, Hassel ran to find someone at the local telephone office to call the Oslo observatory. The office was closed when he arrived, and he rapped on the door. Still no one answered. He then tapped on a window in the back of the house and awakened a startled woman to explain the circumstances.

The next morning, the telephone operator called Einbu who then contacted the observatory at Copenhagen, but the Northern Lights made it difficult to spot the comet that night. The clouds at Oslo and at home thwarted his own efforts to watch the nameless comet. For several days Hassel waited, and finally Einbu sent him the message that no other Norwegian astronomer had identified the comet. It was his.

Anxiously, Hassel waited for days until a confirmation arrived from Copenhagen that he was the comet's discoverer. Congratulations for discovering ''Comet Hassel 1939'' poured in from around the world, and the amateur astronomer experienced the true joy that accompanies such a finding. The comet passed its perihelion on April 10, and it distanced itself from the sun and Earth, its glow decreasing. As it traveled in a path across the constellation Perseus and into Gemini, observations again became difficult because of glare. Preliminary calculations estimated the period of Olaf Hassel's comet at about 330 years. The comet was later renamed ''Comet Jurlof-Achmarof-Hassel'' when it was learned that two Russian astronomers had also sighted it.

Hassel worked at the Meteorological Institution of Oslo from 1941 to 1968 and continued to study the heavens. While photographing the Northern Lights for Fredrik Størmer, he nearly discovered another comet of the seventh magnitude in the Dragon, but an observer in South Africa had beaten him by a short time. Hassel was awarded several grants from the Nansen Foundation, including one for a solar eclipse expedition in 1927. He planned to make several films simultaneously through two telescopes using a homemade device. The weather, however, ruined his expedition. It rained very hard, and he was unable to complete the project. On a similar expedition eighteen years later, this time to Nordland, the same thing happened. Then, nine years later, his third attempt to photograph a solar eclipse was also rained out. Another Nansen Foundation grant provided him the opportunity to take depth and temperature measurements of a number of inland lakes, including Eibern and Fiskum Lake, of which little was known at the time.

Hassel was a dedicated astronomer and carried a camera wherever he went. He frequently brought his photographs with him, too, to share his adventures with others. He was a kind and gentle man, extensively involved with the Norwegian Deaf community, and always had time to visit the old and infirm. He was fluent in Norwegian Sign Language. He communicated with other astronomers predominantly through writing and lipreading. Throughout his life, he shared his knowledge of astronomy with the Deaf communities of Norway and other nations. At the Nordic exhibition of deaf people's work in Copenhagen in September 1934, Hassel displayed a model of the relative distances of stars in light-years, using white pearls suspended in a large, dark cabinet measuring more than ten feet in length, width, and height. King Christian X of Denmark personally complimented him on the exhibit, and many astronomers praised it. In Paris for a convention of deaf people, Hassel visited a planetarium and found an error in the positions of the stars in one of the displays. At another convention for deaf people in Italy, he took special pleasure in observing stars that were not visible at home in Norway.

Hassel made his second significant discovery, a nova, on March 7, 1960. He found the new 5th-magnitude star near the boundary of Hercules and Aquila, slightly west of Zeta Aquilae. That morning, his wife woke him up earlier than usual; and since there was still some time to observe the sky before dawn's light, he went up to his loft and opened the skylight. As Hassel wrote in his autobiographical notes:

I happened to raise my prism telescope a little too high over the brightest part of the . . . horizon. Then I made a fantastic discovery! In the telescope I caught sight of a star of the 5th magnitude which I had never seen before. I realized it was a nova and immediately informed Professor Rosseland.

Photographs by a Japanese astronomer a few days earlier did not show the nova among the dim stars. All over the world astronomers turned their telescopes to the star. It was first called "Nova Hassel" because it was thought to be between Hercules and the Eagle. Later, it was decided that the new star belonged to Hercules and it was assigned the astronomical name "Nova Hercules 1960 (Hassel)."

A decline in visual brightness of the nova discovered by Hassel was reported over the next few weeks. On March 9, A. F. Jones in New Zealand estimated the nova as magnitude 5.2. By March 19 it was 5.8 according to A. V. Nielsen in Denmark. German astronomers, however, reported it as 6.2 on March 21 and 22. These measurements were confirmed by the American Association of Variable Star Observers which also reported a magnitude of 6.8 on March 29. At Kitt Peak Observatory on March 12, D. Crawford measured the nova at 5.49 at 11:00 Universal time using the photoelectric photometer of a 16-inch reflector telescope. Also at Kitt Peak, Helmut A. Abt obtained a spectrum of the nova, using the 60-inch Mount Wilson reflector. Dr. Abt explained that most of the star's light came from the emission lines of hydrogen, ionized calcium, iron, and titanium. His measurements indicated that the star was a "fast nova," one that runs rapidly through its sequence of spectral changes, declining quickly in brightness. Olaf Hassel's star was estimated to be about 3,000 light-years from Earth. He acknowledged his wife's role in his discovery: "In my opinion, my deaf wife Marie deserves the main credit for the first Norwegian nova discovery. If she had not wakened me ten minutes earlier, it would have been too late to watch it in the morning light."

Hassel was a member of Amatørastronomen, a group affiliated with the Norsk Astronmisk Selskap (Association of Amateur Astronomers). He was given the Fridtjof Nansen award and the American Association of Variable Star Observers' award for his discovery of Nova Hercules 1960. The latter award was presented to him by the American Ambassador to Norway. He was elected an honorary member of the Norwegian Astronomical Society in 1969. The deaf astronomer's most important contributions were in the general observations of variable stars over a fifty-year period. In 1970, the King of Norway's gold medal of service was conferred upon Olaf Hassel for his contributions to astronomy.

Between the years 1970 and 1972, three of Hassel's brothers and two sisters-in-law died. He became very depressed and fell ill himself. His niece, Mrs. Reidun Guldal, went to visit him and found the door locked. Finding Hassel ill in bed, she brought him to her home to take care of him. After several days his health worsened and he entered a hospital. During the final week of his life, Hassel discussed the subject of life after death with his good friend who was a clergyman for the Deaf community in Oslo. "When I die," Hassel signed, "I shall ask the Almighty God to make me a star which will twinkle for you." He died soon afterwards, on August 15, 1972.

References

Hassel, O. (1960). Amatør-astronom med internasjonalt ry. *Forskninqsnytt*, No. 2, 2–5.
La Comète Jurlof-Achmarof-Hassel (1939, May 19). *Société Astronomique de France*, 193–201.
Lang, H. G. (1994). *Silence of the spheres: The deaf experience in the history of science*. Westport, CT: Bergin & Garvey.
Nova Herculis 1960. (1960, May). *Sky and Telescope, 19*, 414.
Ringnes, T. S. (1979). Olaf Hassel. *Aschehoug og gyldendals store Norske leksikon*. Oslo: Kunnskapsforlaget.

VILEM J. HAUNER (1903–   ), Czechoslovakian Artist.

Vilem J. Hauner was born in June 1903, the son of a scholar and scientific writer; he was deafened at the age of six months. His mother taught him his own language as well as English and French. A private tutor was also hired to provide Hauner with lessons in the home. At the age of eight, Hauner attended private classes in drawing under a Mr. Ebert at the Normal School, learning floral designs and producing drawings highly praised at local exhibitions. He then began studying bookbinding under L. Bradec at the National School of Graphic Arts in Prague, then later Bradec taught him artistic bookbinding and suggested that he study in Paris. Arriving in Paris, however, he had much difficulty in acquiring further training. Even with Bradec's recommendations and certificates from the National School of Graphic Arts, his deafness was a factor in his being turned down by a number of master bookbinders as he applied for study in their studios. After working in Paris for fifteen months in a commercial bindery of Mr. Engel and in the Taupin Bindery, he enrolled at the Stadium Pagnier-Meyrueis and studied artistic bookbinding and gilding. He also took advantage of the Parisian museums and galleries, especially the Exposition of Modern Decorative and Industrial Art in 1925.

Hauner returned to Prague in 1925, worked for a bookbinder named Nozicka for one year, then completed the highest classes under Solar and Hessel at the School of Graphic Arts. He won several prizes in competitions held that year. Hauner held exhibitions at Prague, Pilzen, and Brunn, Czechoslovakia, in 1926 and 1927. He also exhibited in Copenhagen, Chicago, Trenton, New Jersey, and Amsterdam in the late 1920s. His works were exhibited at the Salon des Artes Silencieux in Paris (1927) and Madrid (1928). Photographs of his highly praised work appeared in the periodicals *Cesky Svet, Graficka Prace,* and *Vyrochni Zpravy.* In 1929, the American Deaf community learned of Hauner's talents when the deaf artist Kelly H. Stevens* provided samples of his work in the April issue of *The Silent Worker,* including illuminations in the Persian style designed for the covers of Voltaire's romance *Zadig,* illuminated diplomas for a ceremony to honor Pedro Ponce de Leon in Madrid in 1926, and bindings for such works as Anatole France's *The Seven Wives of Bluebeard* and Gustave Flaubert's *Salammbo.* Hauner was also commissioned by the Republic to complete a leather-covered casket with the Czecho-Slovak arms and colors to contain important state documents. At the International Exhibition of Fine and Applied Arts by Deaf Artists held at the International Art Center of Roerich Museum in New York City in July and August 1934, Hauner exhibited five leather book covers and six leather bindings, including *Lecon d'Amour dans un Parc, Les Bains de Bade, Les Sept Femmes de la Barbe Bleue,* and *The Basques and Their Country.* Upon his return to Czechoslovakia, he wrote to Margaret E. Jackson* describing his impression of how well educated the deaf Americans were in comparison to his fellow deaf Czechoslovakians.

During World War II, his friends heard nothing from Hauner. Czechoslovakia came under German occupation, and many citizens were killed or starved to death. His father, Dr. Wilem Julius Hauner, a military writer, had been tortured to death in a Nazi concentration camp at Mauthausen, Austria, in 1941, and his younger brother, a lawyer, was executed by the Gestapo the following year. His mother had fallen ill with grief. In a letter to his friend Jackson in July 1946, he explained his silence during the war years: ''I write this to you, that you should know that my present life is quite unlike . . . my happy life in 1924–1938.'' Hauner struggled during the years following the war as well. Suffering financially and confined to a hospital for seven months with pneumonia, he was barely able to support his wife and two children by filling orders for bookbinding. The Iron Curtain again cut him off from his friends in the American Deaf community.

References

Jackson, M. E. (1948). Czechoslovakia's Vilem Hauner. *The Silent Worker, 1* (4), 5.
Stevens, K. H. (1929). William B. Hauner: Deaf master bookbinder of Czechoslovakia. *The Silent Worker, 41* (4), 111–114.

MORRISON HEADY (1829–1915), American Poet/Novelist.

Morrison Heady was born in Spencer County, Kentucky, on July 19, 1829. He was blinded in one eye by a chip from a woodcutter's axe when he was a child. At the age of sixteen, he was totally blinded in the other eye from another accident while playing. Two years later, his hearing, which had begun to fail after a fall from a horse when he was younger, progressively worsened until he was totally deaf at the age of forty. As Heady wrote, the loss of both senses, one traumatically and one progressively, was "like the slow swinging . . . of the prison door, when the prisoner is left alone in his cell." The statement would evoke great sympathy in readers, but Heady had no intention of remaining in solitary confinement.

Heady began his education in a small country schoolhouse. Through the eyes of his many friends, he read everything he could find. Transferring to the Kentucky School for the Blind, he learned to read embossed print. He also designed a cotton glove with the letters of the alphabet marked at different positions, which his friends touched in conversation with him. Those close to him learned to use the glove as readily and rapidly as a typewriter. Largely self-educated through these means, he slowly developed the literary tastes and creative powers that enabled him to begin his own career as a writer. Throughout his life, Heady assembled one of the largest private collections of books in raised type in the country, which he later presented to the Louisville Public Library.

Heady developed a close friendship with Laura Bridgman, the deaf-blind woman educated at the Perkins Institute. He later made the acquaintance of Helen Keller.* The poet John Greeleaf Whittier and his sister were among the friends who read to him, as were Abraham Flexner of the Carnegie Foundation, Simon Flexner, Director of the Rockefeller Institute, and Lewis N. Dembitz. Heady regularly read such periodicals as the *Matilda Ziegler Magazine* and others printed in embossed print and was able to remain current with the major issues of his time. Friends would visit him and converse with him through his glove on such topics as the cost of the Panama Canal, or information about river tunnels, airplanes, and radium. In his obituary in the December 23, 1915 *New York Times*, it was reported that "there was scarcely a schoolchild in Louisville to whom the tall, white-haired and white-bearded man was not a dear and familiar sight, as he swung sturdily through the streets, tapping his heavy cane with a sound as cheery as his smile.'' His memory was excellent, and he could recite long verses without hesitation. The children in Louisville would clamor around "Uncle Morrie," eager to hear his stories such as "The Tom Cats" or "The White Stone Boat.'' Often less inhibited than their elders, the children were his friends, and they gladly helped him navigate the streets on his way back home, the third floor of a red brick building where his sister and her family lived.

In his room, one would find volumes from floor to ceiling, including the Bible and ten large volumes in Roman print, an old English printface that was used for some time before the invention of braille. He enjoyed Shakespeare, Dickens, Walter Scott, Milton, and Homer, and the more "experimental"works of Swedenborg and Byron. On the other side of his room was a model of the Louisville Library, a typewriter, and an invention of his own which typed raised letters in braille. A chessboard with black squares raised and red ones sunken and in each a peg hole to keep the pieces steady during his games with friends was always set up, ready for the next game. Family members and friends recollected the poignant times when, thinking no one was home, Heady sat at the piano and displayed his earlier talent for music by playing old melodies.

Through the years, the children whom he delighted with stories had grown into adulthood. It was this generation of his fans who encouraged him to write for a larger audience. Heady's work was first recognized in 1869 when the volume *Seen and Heard* was published in Baltimore. George D. Prentice presented an account of the deaf-blind scholar in "Poets of America" in the *Louisville Journal*. Some of Heady's poems then appeared in the *Deaf-Mutes' Journal*, an organ of America's Deaf community.

Among his other works were *Burl, The Farmer Boy, The Red Moccasins*, and *The Double Night and Other Poems*. Critics believe *Burl*, a story of pioneer life, showed a fertile imagination and remarkable descriptive power. The style was occasionally peculiar, but charming: so much of Heady's language was acquired through print that his representations of dialogue and conversation seem to belong to the page, rather than to spoken language. A writer in the *American Annals of the Deaf*, in reviewing this book in 1884, mentioned that the style seemed to reflect that Heady had lost his hearing at an earlier age than reported, "before idiomatic language was perfectly acquired," but that the "peculiarities" added to the interest of the book, particularly in view of the author's deaf-blindness. Heady's book of verse, *The Double Night and Other Poems*, was described by the *Unitarian Review* in 1881, which reprinted the title poem "The Double Night," as his most powerful work. Victorian readers responded emotionally to this autobiographical poem on the loss of senses. One reviewer melodramatically summarized that Heady's poems would be valued both for their literary merit and for the "deathless courage and perseverance which have impelled so sad a prisoner to cling persistently to the pen which a cruel fate endeavors to wrench from his grasp." Heady himself was puzzled by portrayals of his life as one of pathos, for he wrote poetry in several genres, with many other themes. "Cecilia," for example, is a piece of elaborate romantic verse. "DeProfundis" addresses philosophical and religious issues. "As I have only had experience of this life," he once explained, "I prefer it to any I know about, and, furthermore, it will answer my purpose as long as it lasts." The sentimentality of the times predisposed readers to those works that were accounts of his struggle, but his own attitude belied an overemphasis on his fate.

Always a charming storyteller for children, he completed at the age of eighty-six, a book of juvenile tales and a novel, for which friends were seeking a publisher when he died on December 19, 1915.

References

A blind-deaf poet. (1916). *American Annals of the Deaf, 61* (2), 194–195.
Anagnos, J. R. (1881). A blind poet. *Unitarian Review, 15* (5), 424–434.
Famous deaf-blind poet issues new books at 84. (1914). *The Silent Worker, 26* (7), 136–137.
Morrison Heady. (1884). *American Annals of the Deaf, 29* (2), 140–141.

OLIVER HEAVISIDE (1850–1925), British Electrical Scientist.

Oliver Heaviside was born in Camden Town, London, on May 18, 1850, the youngest of four sons. His mother, Rachael Elizabeth West, may have provided him with some of his early education. She had established a private school for girls to bring in supplemental income. Heaviside's father, Thomas, a talented wood-engraver and painter in watercolor, struggled to support the family. Thomas's violent temperament and his use of the strap for discipline may have had some influence on Oliver's later attitudes and behaviors.

The eminent electrical scientist Charles Wheatstone, Oliver's uncle, encouraged him to pursue his studies. Wheatstone had maintained an interest in the science of speech production, designing a "talking machine," and devising and copatenting (with Sir William Fothergill Cooke) an electric telegraph in 1837, based on Joseph Henry's research. Fortunately for the world of science, Wheatstone's nephew uncharacteristically followed his advice and remained with his books. In addition to studying Danish, German, and the natural sciences, Heaviside taught himself Morse Code and conducted experiments on electromagnetism. In 1868, he obtained, with the influence of Wheatstone, a position as a telegraphic operator in Denmark.

Heaviside's hearing had begun to give him problems during his early twenties. He soon left the telegraph company; but it is not clear whether the hearing loss or the fact that he was not given a salary increase was a factor in his leaving. Since he was familiar with the practical aspects of telegraphy and radio, Heaviside immediately delved into mathematical theory when he began his research at home. He pursued the writings of Jean-Baptiste Fourier and extended James Clerk Maxwell's work in electromagnetism. Heaviside and Heinrich Hertz struck up a friendship through writing. Their correspondence was sufficiently relaxed so that Hertz felt comfortable in advising Heaviside to make his papers easier to read. Perhaps because of Heaviside's self-education, he employed notations in his mathematical writings that were unconventional, frustrating many scientists who wished to learn from his work. In his address at the Heaviside Centenary Meeting in 1950, a quarter of a century after Heaviside's death, Sir Edward Appleton related an anecdote that not only reveals this frequently-mentioned unorthodox style, but also his crisp sense of humor: "You know, Mr. Heaviside," said a colleague, "your papers are very difficult indeed to read." Heaviside's piercing eyes stared back at the fellow as he replied, "That may well be, but they were much more difficult to write." His work was frequently rejected by other mathematicians because he did not follow the standards of rigorous mathematical proofs then in vogue. He had the seeming ability to work intuitively with complex mathematics. Heaviside invented what is today called "operational calculus," a mathematical process used to obtain solutions of differential equations. He anticipated the later use of Laplace and Fourier transforms in electrical theory and devised a vector notation similar to that of Josiah Willard Gibbs. He also was the first to develop the "telegrapher's equation" relating voltage to distance, time, and resistance.

As a result of correspondence with Heaviside, John Ambrose Fleming* was able to place before the Institution of Electrical Engineers (IEE) definitions of the terms "permittance," "inductance," "conductance," and "admittance," which Heaviside had coined. The genius of Heaviside provided scientists with the distinction between "electro-motive force" and "potential difference." In his Inaugural Address as the first IEE president on January 10, 1889, Sir William Thomson paid tribute to Heaviside as the person responsible for accentuating through mathematical theory the importance of electromagnetic induction in carrying electrical current. The first volume of Heaviside's great work *Electromagnetic Theory* was published in 1893, the second volume in 1899, and the third and concluding volume in 1912. Heaviside was the first to provide a theory of the steady rectilinear motion of an electron (which to him meant an electric charge) and the first to predict the increase in mass of a moving charge at a very great speed. Heaviside also suggested a system of electromagnetic units similar to the presently used mks (meter-kilogram-second) system.

In 1922, Heaviside was chosen as the first recipient of the Faraday Medal for his outstanding work in the field of telegraphic science. J. S. Highfield, then President of the IEE, called upon him several times in Torquay, but he had difficulty in making Heaviside hear the knock at the door. For Heaviside, such honors as the Faraday Medal mattered little. The short, red-headed Englishman grew increasingly eccentric. He lived in relative isolation for most of his life, never married, and refused to pay his bills, even if it meant that he would live without gas heating for a year at a time. Once the police had labelled his furniture for removal and sale, but the bank allowed him some accommodation. Friends helped him with his bills. Others fixed his gas mantles or brought him candles. He needed spectacles but refused to go to the shop. A friend guessed at the appropriate power of the lenses and brought them to his house. Three members of the Royal Society's Scientific Relief Fund wrote to him for his consent that they pursue an honorarium for him in recognition of the value of his contributions to science.

Oliver Heaviside has been compared to both Newton and Einstein in attitudes and lifestyle. He did not agree with his contemporaries that everything must be proven rigorously. He asked the learned societies to publish his papers as work in progress, much in the way Einstein later did.

Heaviside published his first article in *The English Mechanic* in 1872, which introduced the electrical world to his talents. He was only twenty-two years old at the time. The report was titled "Comparing electromotive forces" and made use of algebra. During the following year, he published a discussion of the Wheatstone Bridge, his uncle's ingenious invention, in *Philosophical Magazine*. Heaviside worked out the mathematical symbols and analytic methods for alternating current circuitry more than a decade before alternating current came into commercial use. By the age of twenty-four, he had seven papers published. But it is in Heaviside's private notes that we acquire a feeling for his interactions with other great men of his time. For this latter article, for example, he had discussed his ideas with Sir William Thomson (Lord Kelvin) and shared them with James Clerk Maxwell. In that same year (1873), Maxwell had published his crowning work, *A Treatise on Electricity and Magnetism*, which greatly inspired Heaviside. But Heaviside's strange shyness deprived him of many other such opportunities to meet and converse with these scientists. In January 1889, for example, the distinguished electrical engineer Silvanus P. Thompson wrote warmly to Heaviside, inviting him to a quiet dinner for the purpose of discussing electricity with himself and Oliver Lodge. Thompson wrote again in early March, further enticing Heaviside, but, by all accounts, Heaviside never attended the proposed dinner. Years later, in 1902, Thompson was still attempting to make "personal acquaintance" with the reclusive Heaviside.

Many more of Heaviside's publications appeared in the *Electrician* between 1885 and 1887. His most important work, from a practical perspective, was in laying the foundation of the modern theory of telephone transmission. In this analysis, he described the distortion and attentuation of signals, including speech and the existence of echoes in telephone circuits. He watched curiously as Alexander Graham Bell and Thomas Alva Edison* perfected the telephone, and he followed by formulating the mathematical laws governing the propagation of telephone and telegraph signals in wires and cables. Many of the great breakthroughs in telephone theory development, including the early concept of loaded lines by inserted coils at intervals, were Heaviside's creations.

During the early years of Heaviside's publications, editors repeatedly rejected his work because they were not in accord with the views of William H. Preece and H. R. Kempe at the General Post Office. Several other scientists who supported Heaviside's views actually lost their positions. Heaviside never forgave Preece for rejecting his early papers submitted to the Society of Telegraphic Engineers.

In 1899, the Irish physicist George Francis FitzGerald wrote to Heaviside and inquired whether he had done any work on the propagation of electromagnetic waves. Although Heaviside had not, he boldly suggested the existence of some kind of waveguide in the atmosphere that would make long-distance transmission possible. He theorized that there might be a conductive layer in the upper atmosphere. Heaviside's name thus became immortalized in the "Kennelly-Heaviside layer," the ceiling sixty or more miles high that reflects radio waves back to the earth, now called the "ionosphere." Heaviside received many other honors. Besides the Faraday Medal, he was awarded an honorary membership in the IEE in 1908 and in the American Institute of Electrical Engineers in 1918. He declined the Hughes Medal from the Council of the Royal Society in 1904. The following year the University of Göttingen, where Weber and Gauss conducted their studies, conferred on him an honorary doctorate.

Yet, even with these honors being bestowed upon him, Heaviside often poked fun at his own eccentricities, both of a social and technical nature, and his introversion. In a letter to his friend FitzGerald on June 19, 1897, for example, Heaviside described his next door neighbor, an "awfully deaf" grocer, whose deaf wife offended him by going around the streets without a bonnet—then drily remarked that he was, of course, more liberal in principle than in practice, which was easier. From about 1918, he called himself "the Worm" and signed his letters Oliver Heaviside, W.O.R.M. He took pleasure if a correspondent interpreted this as some kind of distinction and addressed him as "Oliver Heaviside, W.O.R.M." His residence was referred to by contemporaries as "the Cave." He was a legend in his own time.

Heaviside died on February 3, 1925, in Paignton, Devonshire.

References

Appleyard, R. (1931). A link with Oliver Heaviside. *Electrical Communication, 10*, 53–59.

Institute of Electrical Engineers (1950). *The Heaviside centenary volume.* London: Institution of Electrical Engineers.

Lang, H. G. (1994). *Silence of the spheres: The deaf experience in the history of science.* Westport, CT: Bergin & Garvey.

Nahin, P. J. (1988). *Oliver Heaviside, sage in solitude: The life, work, and times of an electrical genius of the Victorian age.* New York: Institute of Electrical and Electronics Engineering.

Russell, A. (1925). Obituary of Oliver Heaviside. *Nature, 115* (2885), 237–238.

FRANK P. HOCHMAN (1935–   ), American Physician.

Frank P. Hochman was born deaf on December 26, 1935, in New York City, and at the age of three he was placed in the National School for Speech Disorders there. Two years later he enrolled in the New York School for the Deaf (P.S. 47), where he graduated in 1953. He attended Stuyvesant High School and graduated from the then City College of New York with a bachelor's degree in biology in 1958. After taking additional courses, he was also accredited as a chemist and physicist. Between 1955 and 1966, he held various positions as a research chemist or physicist in several hospitals and medical centers in New York City. At Mount Sinai Hospital, Hochman was involved in research on the effects of gamma globulin on immunities in children, and at the Veterans Administration Hospital in New York City, Hochman investigated structures of blood proteins. He also held the position of Chief Clinical Chemist at St. Joseph's Hospital in Queens. As a biochemist for the New York City Department of Health, he was in charge of several different divisions, examining and evaluating clinical laboratories and blood banks, and serving as technical consultant. Between 1969 and 1972, Hochman was Chief Medical Technologist at Somerset Hospital in Somerville, New Jersey, where he was responsible for administration and technical management of the laboratory and School of Medical Technology. Despite this impressive list of accomplishments and promotions, however, Hochman felt restless and unfulfilled.

When Hochman received the Edmund Lyons Memorial Lectureship Award at the National Technical Institute for the Deaf in Rochester, New York, in 1986, he reminisced about the various attitudinal barriers he faced in pursuit of what he really desired—a medical degree: ''I always wanted to be a doctor. I was always told that I could not. . . . It was decided (for me, of course) that I would become a printer. My mother was given the school's very excellent reason for this, ' . . . he spells very well.' Never mind what I wanted.'' Hochman's college guidance counselor also discouraged him from a medical career. Fortunately, he did not follow their advice.

In *Silence of the Spheres: The Deaf Experience in the History of Science*, Lang (1994) has provided an account of the long struggle of deaf men and women in the United States and other countries to gain admission to medical schools. Among the notable cases were Donald L. Ballantyne,* who, although disappointed with the rejections, went on to become an international authority in transplantation techniques and a teacher of medical students; and Judith Pachciarz who, with a Ph.D. in biochemistry, was still rejected by nineteen medical schools until she was finally accepted to one and earned her M.D. Over the past few decades, federal legislation and increased awareness by university officials have opened some doors to deaf persons. Noting a modest change of attitude in 1971, as some medical schools began to accept more women, African-American, and Hispanic-American students, Hochman decided to apply. Although his Medical College Admission Test scores were excellent, the attitudinal resistance he encountered was nevertheless formidable. Many who interviewed him were openly negative about his deafness. Persevering and bolstered by a letter-writing campaign among his friends and colleagues, he was accepted to Rutgers Medical School in 1972 at the age of thirty-seven, one of the oldest medical students in the country.

At Rutgers, Hochman sat in the front row in classes, and with the financial assistance of the rehabilitation department he photocopied the notes of his classmates. He completed his masters degree in 1974 and his M.D. in 1976. Since then, other medical schools have sought advice from Rutgers when deaf men and women have applied for study. Hochman felt that his sense of humor won him friends and helped him get through the difficult times during his studies in medical school. He was continually challenged in attempting to speechread his medical school professors because they often turned their faces away from him. He once modified a "deaf peddler's card" and handed it to the physician/professors, who often missed the point entirely. On one side of the card was the manual alphabet (fingerspelling) he hoped would encourage them to learn so that communication would be facilitated. On the other side of the card was the following message: "Dear Doctor: I am a deaf medical student who is anxious to learn from you—so if you continue to speak softly and do not look in my direction so that I may lipread you—I may end up selling these cards for a living. Thank You." When asked how he has learned to speak so well, Hochman deadpans, "I fake it."

Hochman served his residency at the University of California at San Francisco, San Francisco General Hospital, and Stanford University. After he completed his medical degree, he was also a resident for one year in family practice at San Jose Hospital and Health Center/Family Practice Center, then decided to settle with a family practice in the East Bay area to serve the large Deaf community attracted to the California School for the Deaf in Fremont. He has also been the physician at the California School for the Blind. Once Hochman entered practice, he experienced much less prejudice. His hearing patients have been undisturbed by his deafness and, he says, gladly repeat for his benefit. He used a stethoscope attached to an oscilloscope so that he would be able to *see* the heart sounds and murmurs with precise visual patterns corresponding to what other physicians heard. Candid discussions with patients about his deafness were critical so that there were minimal concerns or misunderstandings. Asked whether he had any limitations, Hochman responded, "Forty hours a week." He is skilled in both speechreading and sign language. He is paged through the use of an electronic beeper, the vibrations of which he can feel. Flashing phone signalers alert him to the ringing telephone when he is on call at a hospital.

In addition to being a physician and surgeon, over the years, Hochman has lectured many times on medical and educational topics, chaired the Department of Family Practice at Washington Hospital in Fremont, and served on the National Board of Medical Examiners. Through his visits to schools, he has inspired numerous young deaf students to consider medicine as a profession. Hochman was the first born-deaf American to become a physician. Today, there are several dozen deaf men and women with medical degrees in the United States, but attitudinal barriers remain formidable.

References

Hochman, F. P. (1986, April). Breaking new ground in careers for the hearing impaired. Edmund Lyon Memorial Lectureship Presentation. National Technical Institute for the Deaf, Rochester Institute of Technology.

Lack of hearing hasn't meant lack of success. (1988, March 15). *San Jose Mercury News*, 3D.

REGINA OLSON HUGHES (1895–1993), American Scientific Illustrator.

Regina Olson Hughes was born on February 1, 1895, in Herman, Nebraska, where she attended public schools. In childhood, she developed an interest in drawing and took private lessons. Simultaneously, she became fascinated with the world of plants and flowers. At the age of ten, Hughes began to lose her hearing and was deaf by the age of fourteen. She made the decision to pursue her college education at Gallaudet College, then the only postsecondary program for deaf students. Hughes graduated from Gallaudet College with a bachelor's degree in 1918 and a master's degree in 1920. For a time, she taught at the Mississippi School for the Deaf. During World War II, she had the distinction of serving as a translator for the U.S. Department of State, one of only two non-French women employed by the U.S. Office of Translation. She married Dr. Frederick H. Hughes, a deaf professor who distinguished himself for forty years in dramatics at Gallaudet College, and she lived with him on the Gallaudet campus for thirty years. He died in 1956.

Hughes was primarily self-educated in botany, working closely with taxonomists and other scientists as she illustrated the flowers, weeds, plants, and seeds they collected and categorized from all over the world. She has had thousands of her scientific illustrations appear in textbooks and publications. Her botanical paintings and drawings are exhibited in many museums and galleries, including the Brookside Gardens (Maryland), the Selby Botanical Garden (Florida), the Hunt Institute for Botanical Documentation at Carnegie-Mellon University in Pittsburgh, and Gallaudet University. A collection of forty watercolors of orchids was exhibited in the Rotunda Gallery of the Museum of Natural History of the Smithsonian Institution. In the fall of 1986 alone, she had three overlapping exhibitions for the Smithsonian Institution at Selby Botanical Gardens in Sarasota, the Eastern Orchid Congress in Alexandria, and at Gallaudet University. She is the only deaf artist to have a solo exhibition at the Smithsonian Institution, the one at Selby Botanical Gardens being her third. Six thousand of her illustrations appear in one work alone, *Economically Important Foreign Weeds: Potential Problems in the United States*, a U.S. Department of Agriculture Handbook, published in 1927, which took her two and a half years to complete. For all of these illustrations, she also wrote the plant descriptions.

Hughes' experience has included years of honored illustration work for the Agricultural Research Service and the U.S. Department of Agriculture. She has also been a resident illustrator in the Department of Botany at the Smithsonian Institution. Her illustration of a bromeliad was on display in an exhibit of the research of Lyman B. Smith and Robert W. Reed. In 1979, the new species illustrated in this painting was named in her honor by the Smithsonian Institution, *Billbergia reginae*. Hughes received the singular honor of having both a plant genus and species named for her—*Hughesia reginae*. It is not unusual for

Regina Olson Hughes, American botanical illustrator. Photo from *Gallaudet Today, 18* (1), 1987, courtesy of Gallaudet University Archives.

one to have a species named in one's honor, but it is rare to have a new genus. Other honors include the U.S. Department of Agriculture's Superior Service Award for botanical illustration and technical translation, the Woman of the Year award by Phi Kappa Zeta, and an honorary doctorate from Gallaudet University.

Hughes' formal education focused on the arts and languages; her interest in botany led her to rigorous self-education. Her lived combination of arts and sciences emanated from her passion for flowers, and she became adept at illustrating seeds, weeds, leaves, and mosses. In addition to developing her scientific and illustrative skills, she became familiar with technical Latin, which was the means by which most specimens were described diagnostically. She also became proficient in Spanish, Portuguese, Italian, and German, in addition to French, both to find further descriptions in foreign journals and to summarize scientific papers.

In *Common Weeds of the United States* (1971), Hughes illustrated 224 species of the more prevalent weeds in croplands, grazing lands, noncroplands, and aquatic sites. She prepared the drawings from herbarium specimens loaned by the National Arboretum, the U.S. National Herbarium, and the Reed Herbarium, using a legend to show relative size. Another book with her illustrations, *Selected Papers on Floral Evolution III*, by E. E. Leppek (1968–1976), was a true rarity (only twenty-two copies were printed, one owned by her); it was distributed to the principal libraries of the world. She also produced all of the plates for *Flora of Ecuador, No. 13—138: Melastomataceae*, by John J. Wurdack of the Smithsonian Institution (1980). Other works in which her botanical illustrations appear include *Flora del Uruguay IV: Bromeliaceae* (1972), *The Agaves of Baja California* (1978), and many issues of the U.S. Department of Agriculture (USDA) *Technical Bulletin.*

Regina Hughes also had a gregarious professional life. She was a member of the Guild of Natural Science Illustrators, the National League of Pen Women, and the Washington Watercolor Association. In addition to an honorary doctoral degree from Gallaudet College (1967), Hughes received the USDA Superior Service Award for excellence in botanical illustration and technical translation of foreign publications (1962) and the Amos Kendall Award (1982), and she appeared in the sixth edition of *Who's Who of American Women.* Talented in poetry as well, she published verse and articles in magazines, newspapers, and periodicals.

She was disarming, open, and free of competitiveness. She described the pleasure of seeing her work used in various publications: "Many of my drawings are in the public domain now and they turn up like old friends. A couple of weeks ago, there was one in the *Post.* I've seen them on pesticide labels and many other places, from a small-town newspaper in Montana to the *New York Times.*" Perhaps her years of working on projects alone for long periods of time reinforced her natural freedom from pretension. While she had received numerous honors and accolades, she tended to turn attention away from herself systematically.

In "retirement," when she was over ninety years old, she continued to work five days a week without a salary. "I don't believe in retirement," she told the reporter of the Omaha, Nebraska *World-Herald.* "I hope to die with a brush in my hand." When asked by the authors of this biography if she had any anecdotes about how she pursued a demanding career as a deaf woman before many women were in such professions, she responded, "I guess I do the best I can—angels can do no more."

Hughes died on August 12, 1993.

References

Crammatte, F. B. (1987). Regina Olson Hughes. In J. V. Van Cleve (Ed.), *Gallaudet encyclopedia of deaf people and deafness* (Vol. 2, pp. 77–79). New York: McGraw-Hill.

Langrall, P. (1987, January). Regina Hughes lends her skills to SI botanists. Smithsonian Institution *Torch*, 5.

Peterson, C. (1987, October 11). A brush in her hand. Omaha, Nebraska *World-Herald*, 12, 14.

GEORGE HYDE (1882–1968), American Wild West Historian.

George Hyde was born on June 10, 1882, in Omaha, Nebraska, the son of a policeman. As a young boy, Hyde developed a friendship with a son of E. L. Eaton, a photographer who had known Custer, Buffalo Bill Cody, and the Brulé Chief Spotted Tail. While playing in the attic of the Eaton house, Hyde was fascinated with the glass plate negatives of these historical figures; and the tales he heard from the senior Eaton about the Duke Alexis buffalo hunt and other frontier experiences inspired him toward a lifelong career as a Western historian. The friendship he himself developed with Native Americans during the 1898 Trans-Mississippi Exposition in Omaha deepened this interest. By this time, however, Hyde was totally deaf and had lost much of his vision in both eyes. Determined to pursue the career to which he aspired, he obtained strong corrective lenses and a powerful magnifying glass; and, using his "good right eye," he read everything he could find to prepare him for his research. Unable to travel or to use the local library without great difficulty, he cultivated professional relationships and depended on the Omaha Public Library staff, to whom he expressed more than sincere appreciation in his book acknowledgments. Personal communication with him was accomplished rather laboriously through handwritten notes, aided by his magnifying glass. He would respond by voice with speech progressively influenced by his profound deafness. He reminisced that he had really turned to writing as a vocation, feeling that it was the best way that he could express himself. He said that Native American life was a natural subject for his writing because of his closeness to several tribes and his admiration for the Native people he knew.

Hyde began corresponding with various experts, among them George Bird Grinnell, who hired him in 1912 as an assistant to collect data for his book *The Fighting Cheyennes*. He not only gathered information, but he contributed a significant amount to the writing of the early drafts of Grinnell's manuscript. Hyde's responsibilities were to seek out Cheyenne informants and collect oral history and eyewitness testimony. This work quickly developed into a primary research focus of his own. Being profoundly deaf, he developed unconventional techniques through laborious letter-writing and notetaking and a network of Native American friends. He became lifelong friends with many of his informants, including George Bent, the son of William Bent and Owl Woman, a Southern Cheyenne. Their correspondence formed the basis for Hyde's last published volume, coauthored with Savoie Lottinville and titled *Life of George Bent, Written from His Letters* (1968). The book was called a "treasure" by Oliver Knight in *The Saturday Review*. Working alone most of the time with the Blackfeet, Brulé Sioux, Oglala Sioux, Southern Arapahos, and other tribes, Hyde tried to record multiple perspectives in his work, including tribal history as well as using public documents. First came *Corn Among the Indians of the Upper Missouri* (1917), which Hyde wrote with George F. Will.

Living with his half-sister, Mabel Reed, a schoolteacher, and running a secondhand bookstore in his home to bring in a steadier income, he never allowed his vision problems or his deafness to discourage him. In 1933, Hyde published two monographs in J. Van Male's Old West Series. *Rangers and Regulars* summarized Spanish, Texan, and American military history. *The Early Blackfeet and Their Neighbors* reviewed French and English reports on the geographic distribution and travels of the Blackfeet and neighboring tribes in the seventeenth and eighteenth centuries.

Having only completed eighth grade, Hyde was always sensitive to not being conventionally educated. He openly and appreciatively sought counsel and critique. Hyde did not try to excuse any of the limitations others saw in his research, but asked questions to learn new methodologies. He was so nondefensive that it amazed certain critics, acknowledging that his work might be supplemented by that of other writers who found research material he could not access. He added, however, that he believed his theories and research findings would stand up to scrutiny over time.

In *Spotted Tail's Folk: A History of the Brulé Sioux* (1961), Hyde was aided by Stephen Spotted Tail, the grandson of the famous chief, as well as other Native Americans named Knife Scabbard and Sore Eyes. *Spotted Tail's Folk* marked the completion of Hyde's trilogy on the history of the two southern Teton Sioux tribes, the Oglalas and Sichangus or Brulés. The other members of the trilogy were *Red Cloud's Folk: A History of the Oglala Sioux* (1937) and *A Sioux Chronicle* (1956). While these two provided a chronology from the early days in Minnesota until the Ghost Dance incident of 1890, *Spotted Tail's Folk* was primarily a biography of the chief from the 1820s until 1880. Hyde's works on the Sioux were praised as engaging reading as well as reliable sources. His pioneering reliance on Native American informants led him to an appreciation and understanding of their culture and tradition not always seen in the work of his contemporaries.

In *The Pawnee Indians* (1951), Hyde also examined tribal history, cultural characteristics, and military patterns of the Pawnees in an exciting text. Hyde was still, on occasion, criticized for his lack of precision in scholarly documentation, but nearly always was acknowledged as accurate in his own way of recording information. He supported his writings with numerous illustrations and maps. To complete *The Pawnee Indians*, he spent nearly a quarter century of collecting materials and information from both Native Americans and European Americans, including Grinnell, Captain L. H. North of the Pawnee Scouts, Pawnee trail-agent John W. Williamson, and George H. Roberts, the son of Rush Roberts, the head of the Nasharo or Pawnee Council of Chiefs.

Hyde's *Indians of the High Plains: From the Prehistoric to the Coming of the Europeans* (1959) unearthed historical and archaeological records to provide a comprehensive picture of Native American life on the western high plains from the fourteenth through the nineteenth centuries. *Indians of the Woodlands: From Prehistoric Times to 1725* (1962) moved East. In this book written with George F. Will, he documented the movements and politics of tribes living in the region north of the Ohio and stretching from the Hudson west to the Mississippi in the years up to 1725. These more general demographic works were less-favorably reviewed.

Hyde was averse to publicity and personal recognition, viewing his work as essentially collaborative. He even resisted filling out forms to help biographers develop a sketch for the *Contemporary Authors* index. Nevertheless, he has been honored by National Park Service author-historian Merrill Mattes as the "Dean of American Indian Historians."

Hyde died of cancer on February 2, 1968. His writings still employ methodologies and standards for ethical research practices that historians of the West emulate.

References

Hyde, G. E. (1951). *The Pawnee Indians*. Norman, OK: University of Oklahoma Press.
Hyde. G. E. (1961). *Spotted Tail's folk: A history of the Brulé Sioux*. Norman, OK: University of Oklahoma Press.
McDermott, J. D. (1975). A dedication to the memory of George E. Hyde, 1882–1968. *Arizona and the West, 17* (2), 103–106.

J

MARGARET E. JACKSON (1902–1986), American Museum Curator.

Margaret E. Jackson was born on February 13, 1902, in Wilmington, Delaware, and was totally deafened by meningitis at the age of three and a half. She attended the Pennsylvania School for the Deaf at Mt. Airy, Philadelphia, and the New Jersey School for the Deaf (now the Marie T. Katzenbach School), where she founded a reading club. She graduated from Gallaudet College in 1925 with a bachelor's degree. During her studies there, she was often consulted by fellow students for help with French. In 1927, Jackson found a position at the Hispanic Society of America in New York City, which was founded by philanthropist Archer Huntington. The library and museum, free to the public, contained literature and artifacts related to the culture of Spain and Portugal dating from the Neolithic Age. Huntington had called the Fanwood School for the Deaf in 1919 to explain his personal interest in hiring deaf people to work in the Society. Among those who joined the staff were Eleanor Sherman Font and Sara Tredwell Ragna. The Society's photographic collection included more than 70,000 negatives, and Jackson applied the Dewey decimal system to categorizing them. She was also responsible for photographing the Society's collection of art objects, paintings, books, and manuscripts, and for preparing photographs to be used in scholarly publications around the world. In the process, Jackson developed an international reputation for her expertise in micrography and macrography. Jackson's work with shadowgraphing was particularly valuable to collectors of paintings, etchings, and tapestries. Hollywood studios and actresses such as Katherine Cornell contacted her for photographs of gowns for period costumes. Using X-ray shadowgraphy, she assisted in the analysis of artists' brushstrokes of such great painters as Velasquez, Murillo, and Goya;* and once, she was able to identify an underpainting on a work that verified that the painting attributed to Goya was a fake.

Fluent in Spanish, Portuguese, and French, Jackson traveled frequently to collect information for the Hispanic Society. She joined Font, Florence Lewis May,* and other deaf colleagues at the Hispanic Society, as well as a dozen other deaf people, in helping to organize the 1934 International Exhibition of Fine and Applied Arts by Deaf Artists held in New York City. Through these experiences, she became close friends with deaf artists around the world, such as Valentin de Zubiaurre,* Jean Hanau,* Kelly H. Stevens,* and Robert Dessales-Quentin, and she published biographical sketches of such artists as the Czechoslovakian bookbinder Vilem Hauner.*

Over the next decade, Jackson also became increasingly involved in raising funds to help deaf children left orphaned by war in France and England. Prior to the United States' entry into World War II, she was secretary of the Committee of the New York Deaf for the British War Relief Society. In 1945, she worked extensively with the deaf artist Kelly H. Stevens and other deaf and hearing people in the American Deaf community in assisting Marguerite Colas of France in the Societé Centrale D'Education et D'Assistance Pour Les Sourds-Muets en France. They raised funds and collected materials, as well as arranged placement of deaf children into schools. After the war, Jackson continued to actively assist with relief efforts, chairing a national committee called the French Friendship Fund to help manage thousands of dollars collected from the sale of stamps commemorating the Abbe de l'Epee, the first teacher of deaf pupils in France. The money was used to reopen French schools for deaf pupils and find homes for the orphans. Jackson also translated letters of gratitude from the French to the American Deaf community in various periodicals and articles on the French deaf people under German occupation. She was cited for her work by the governments of England and France.

In the early 1950s, Jackson was promoted to Assistant Curator of Photography at the Hispanic Society. In 1954, she coauthored, with Alice J. McVan* and Florence Lewis May, *A History of the Hispanic Society of America, Museum and Library, 1904–1954, With a Survey of the Collections.* Over the next two decades, she continued to study the Society's collection of sculpture, glassware, fabrics, gold and silver artifacts, handmade rugs, poetry, and paintings. Among the valued historical documents was a copy of a seventeenth-century book by the revered Spanish monk Juan Pablo Bonet about the teaching of deaf pupils.

In the Deaf community, she continued her remarkable efforts to enhance the lives of other people. In addition to serving as director of the Gallaudet College Alumni Association and as secretary of the New York Chapter, she was president of the Gallaudet Home Society, which worked with the Empire State Association of the Deaf to establish a home for aged deaf persons.

Jackson died on September 11, 1986, in Danvers, Massachusetts.

Reference

Jackson, M. E. (1947, January). Fund for France tops $1,000 mark. *The Cavalier*, 1.
Ward, M. S. (1988, June 9). Deaf Delawarean made world listen. *Brandywine Cross-roads*, 2.

DAVID JAMES (1950–   ), American Mathematician.

David James was born on August 1, 1950, in Chicago and became profoundly deaf after a bout of meningitis when he was four years old. Education was valued highly by James' family. His father, a lawyer, and all of his siblings attended college. When his parents learned that he was deaf, they went to great lengths to procure the best possible education for him, sending him first to a day school for deaf children; then, when James had made a solid start in learning to read, he was transferred to St. Bernard's, a parochial school his siblings also attended. At St. Ignatius High School, James' teachers were able to instruct him without any significant accommodations. James attributed his success in school to his flexibility in communication. He was also one of six African-Americans in a graduating class of 240 students at St. Ignatius. He reflected that his minority status was neither easy nor painless. There were many semesters when he found that maintaining a respectable academic average was difficult; and he felt that he would have done much better if he had had normal hearing and experienced less racial tension. He does not blame the school he attended for these difficulties, but viewed his schooling as simply a manifestation of two realities: the status of deafness as a disability and race relations in the United States. James named and faced these issues squarely, and he lauded choices his parents made, arguing that he was, as a result, equipped to live in a world of ambiguities, contradiction, and raw prejudice.

In high school, James also discovered that he was capable of much more than just getting by in his mathematics courses. Where he felt that he struggled in other courses, he was fully competitive with and superior to many hearing peers in that subject. He attributes the direction of his career to that realization.

James received his B.A. in Natural Sciences from Shimer College in Mt. Carroll, Illinois, in 1969. The coping strategies he had developed at St. Ignatius proved effective in undergraduate school, where he functioned well with no support. At the University of Chicago, James earned an M.S. in 1971 and a Ph.D. in 1977, both degrees in Mathematics. He had no interpreting, notetaking, or private tutoring throughout his university study. He described feelings of inadequacy in his first year, but managed to turn his initial depression into intense diligence. If he were to fail, he was determined that it would not be because of a lack of application. Deafness became an explicit issue only at the very end of his formal education, when his Ph.D. was assured, and he became interested in pursuing teaching at the college level. No one knew whether a deaf person was capable of a professorship. His advisor procured him a teaching assignment at Indiana University, however. In his courses at the Gary campus, and at Rutgers University as the Hill Assistant Professor of Mathematics from 1977 until 1979, James learned how to deal with questions from his students and other classroom dynamics. At first, he felt himself to be out of his element, a raw beginner. He soon realized that giving a lecture was only half the issue; dialogue with students demanded interaction and learned anticipation. It was not long, however, before he realized that doctoral preparation in a content area did not teach *anyone* to teach; and he came to understand that hearing junior faculty were as apprehensive and awkward as he—or more so. His attentiveness to pedagogical study, initiated because he was deaf, gave him an ironic head start on the always-challenging first few years of university teaching.

James is currently a tenured Associate Professor of Mathematics at Howard University in Washington, D.C. He also conducts research on differential topology and computer modeling. James has been at Howard University since 1984, except for a two-year leave-of-absence. During this leave, in 1987, he was awarded the Martin Luther King and Rosa Parks Visiting Professorship at Wayne State University in Detroit, Michigan. In 1988, he held the position of Associate Research Scientist at the Courant Institute of Mathematical Sciences at New York University.

James has published numerous technical reports on his mathematical and economic research, including technical writings with Rodney D. Green on the use of spatial interaction modeling and applications of statistical analyses to forecast local development activity around rapid transit systems. He co-authored a book on the economic effects of Washington, D.C.'s subway system with Green. His mathematical interests related to "free circle actions on homotopy nine-spheres" and "smooth circle actions on homotopy complex projective four-spaces" have led to publications in prestigious mathematics journals, and James has also been Associate Editor of the journal *Mathematics*. He has received funding support from the National Science Foundation for projects on geometric and differential topology, for development of an environmental data management system for the Pacific Region Mineral Management Service (U.S. Department of Interior), and for increasing the participation of minority undergraduates in energy analysis.

James was chosen the District of Columbia Disabled Individual of the Year in 1989, and presented the Thirty-sixth Annual Jackson Science Lecture at Eureka College, Illinois, in April, 1990 on the topic "Topology." In a 1988 issue of the newsletter for the Bell Association International Parents Organization focusing on deaf people in scientific careers, James characteristically minimized his own tenacity in the face of challenge, explaining that, "Hearing simply does not matter in much of my work, especially the research."

Reference

A profile of David James: Professor extraordinaire. (1994, November/December). *Volta Voices, 1* (6), 29.

JACK JONES (1923–1983), American Writer/Social Critic/Philosopher.

John "Jack" Timmins Jones was born in Dallas, Texas, on September 28, 1923, the younger of two children. He was raised in Scarsdale, New York, with his sister, who was hard-of-hearing. Jack, who was profoundly deaf, attended the Dwight School in New York City, from which he graduated in 1942.

While attending Swarthmore College, New York University, the New School for Social Research, and the Vassar Summer Institute over the next few years, he began to publish poetry and fiction regularly in such periodicals as *The Village Voice* and *Harvard's Cambridge Review*. His work came to the attention of notable literary critics, such as the famed Mark Twain scholar, Maxwell Geismar. Despite his early success, however, he began to lose interest in creative writing. He had embarked on an intensive reading program in cultural history and political science, and what had once been a secondary interest became primary. The turmoil of the McCarthy era may have heightened the sense of urgency with which he pursued his new direction.

Jones had always been fascinated by Marxist thought, and he subscribed to Marxism in his early years. He became increasingly distressed, though, when Stalin's regime and its aftermath set a course of repression and self-destruction from which the Soviet Union would never recover. In 1955, he published in the *Cambridge Review* under the pseudonym "John Jurkan." The piece, which became the seminal text for a longer version of *To the End of Thought* (also the title of the published essay), was a rationale for Jones's own disillusionment. He argued that Marxism began with a reasonable set of assumptions, but that its essential pragmatism in the pursuit of economic "good" for all persons came to rationalize repression and totalitarianism. This "ends-means" orientation, Jones further asserted, allowed for considerable abuse. Moreover, Western liberal thinkers were tentative in their responses to the terrors perpetrated in communist regimes. Jones was critical of the inadequacy and superficiality he saw in half-hearted defenses of totalitarian regimes. As he developed his thinking on this subject, Jones took an increasingly psychobiological position. The ultimate societal crisis, he concluded, did not lie in the connection of economic interests and class, as the Marxists believed, but in intellectual failure to define key constructs and their role in human and societal experience.

Jones began to focus relentlessly and particularly on freedom and its limits. He observed that Westerners assume that freedom is developed through the rational form of consciousness. This rationalism, indeed, was a cornerstone in the conceptualization of the American Revolution, at the height of the eighteenth century. In the next century, this was, according to Jones, a fundamental principle of Marxist thought. For Marxism, the maximum rational, social control would result ultimately in maximum freedom for the workers. But Jones argued that freedom is more than rational; it must be conceived of not only in relation to power, but in the biological, physical, and psychophysical sense, in the removal of artificial restrictions to human functioning. Without a set of limits placed on rational power and social control, the loss of freedom is inevitable. Jones expanded his theory to point to how the limits to power should be assessed.

Jones's writings became more encompassing, dealing with religious as well as political history. While *To The End of Thought* was never published, he used sections of the book for many articles. He published commentaries on the work of Otto Rank and Herbert Marcuse, and he was invited to write for *The International Encyclopedia of Social Sciences*.

Jack Jones published and wrote under great stress. He was declared legally blind, after lengthy struggles with cataracts and a detached retina. He persisted in his research and writing, aided by magnification and a large-print typewriter. His diaries in the Gallaudet University Archives reveal his tenacity in day-to-day living. Remarkably, from 1975 until 1982, he continued to publish major theoretical and research articles.

He died of cancer on January 10, 1983, and was buried in King David Cemetery in Putnam Valley, New York.

References

Jones, J. Unpublished diaries. Washington, DC: Gallaudet University Archives.
Seifert, G. F. (1987). Jack Jones. In J. V. Cleve (Ed.), *Gallaudet encyclopedia of deaf people and deafness* (Vol. 2, pp. 112–113). New York: McGraw-Hill.

IRVING KING JORDAN (1943–   ), American Educator.

Irving King Jordan was born on June 16, 1943, in Glen Riddle, Pennsylvania, a small town outside of Philadelphia. After finishing high school, he served four years in the Navy. At the age of twenty-one, while stationed in the Pentagon as a clerk with the Joint Chiefs of Staff, he was driving his motorcycle back to the barracks when an automobile turned into his path. The nerves in both of his ears were severed, leaving him profoundly deaf and seriously injured. At first he thought the deafness may be a temporary condition. When he realized it was not, however, he was fortunate to have a solid friendship structure to help him through the initial adjustments. A year in the hospital gave Jordan plenty of time for ''soul-searching'' and planning his future. In retrospect, he has reflected that becoming deaf provided him more opportunities to grow personally and professionally than he ever would have had as a hearing person.

Jordan then enrolled at Gallaudet College, where he graduated in 1970 with a bachelor's degree in psychology. Both his master's degree and his Ph.D. were from the University of Tennessee, also in psychology. In 1973, he joined the Department of Psychology at Gallaudet, advancing to the rank of full professor in 1982, and becoming the chairperson one year later. In 1986, he was appointed dean of the College of Arts and Sciences.

Jordan was thrust into the international spotlight during the historic protest at Gallaudet University in 1988. The ''Deaf President Now!'' movement began when Gallaudet's board of trustees appointed its seventh hearing president, Elizabeth Ann Zinser, who had not yet learned American Sign Language. The campus erupted in anger, shutting down the University for a week (March 6–13) and launching a civil rights movement of deaf people that would have powerful ramifications—not only in increasing awareness worldwide of the potential of deaf persons to take leadership roles in the educational arena, but also in instilling in young deaf men and women a realization of the positive effects of self-advocacy.

When Zinser stepped aside, Jordan, one of the finalists, was chosen as the first deaf president since the college received its federal charter in 1864. In his inaugural address, he stressed the campus battle cry, "Deaf people can do anything—except hear." The effect of the protest and Jordan's appointment has been particularly visible in the subsequent increase of deaf administrators in other schools.

Jordan's professional journey, which culminated in his presidency, has become a metaphor for the aspirations of deaf people around the world. More than five thousand people flocked to Gallaudet University for the historic inauguration on October 21, 1988, with thousands more watching around the country by satellite television. Dignitaries participating in the ceremony included Iowa Senator Tom Harkin, who presented his address in sign language, and Justin W. Dart, Jr., chairperson of the Congressional Task Force on the Rights and Empowerment of Americans with Disabilities, both of whom were instrumental in introducing to Congress the Americans with Disabilities Act (ADA); many distinguished leaders in the American Deaf community, including Lawrence Newman (National Association of the Deaf), Gerald Burstein (Gallaudet University Alumni Association president), and the Gallaudet Student Body Government president Greg Hlibok, who played a crucial leadership role during the "Deaf President Now!" movement, also participated.

"King's" subsequent status as a public figure and spokesman for the Deaf community has resulted in a flood of engagements since 1988, including trips to Poland, Scotland, France, England, and other countries. He has access to respected members of Congress. The message woven throughout his many speeches and interviews is the building of stronger bridges between hearing and deaf people. Jordan encourages deaf people to serve as ambassadors in communicating to others that deafness does not stop people from doing anything.

Jordan has served on numerous commissions and boards, including as vice chairperson of the President's Committee on Employment of People With Disabilities and as education expert on Washington, D.C. Mayor Sharon Pratt Dixon's transition team. He has served on advisory councils and committees for many organizations, including the Junior League of Washington, D.C., Electronics Industries Foundation, Deafness Research Foundation, National Science Foundation, and the American Association of State Colleges and Universities. He was a member of the U.S. Presidential Transition Committee for the Appointment of Persons with Disabilities and the Task Force on the Rights and Empowerment of Americans with Disabilities. He also served as an editorial reviewer for *Sign Language Studies* and as a member of the administrative committee for the *American Annals of the Deaf.* Jordan was a Visiting Research Fellow in Edinburgh, Scotland, and a Visiting Scholar in Toulouse and Marseilles, France.

Jordan's scholarly interests have included studies of attitudes and experiences of foreign deaf signers, intelligibility, word meaning, facial characteristics, and other features associated with American Sign Language, cultural and social orientation of deaf persons, and issues associated with access to technology. On

Irving King Jordan, President of Gallaudet University. Photo from *Gallaudet Today*, 23 (4), 1993, courtesy of Gallaudet University Archives.

these topics he published more than thirty reports in a wide range of periodicals, including *Applied Psycholinguistics, General Psychology, American Annals of the Deaf,* and *Sign Language Studies.* His chapters in books include essays on patterns of sign language used among deaf students in *Deaf Children in America,* which he edited with M. A. Karchmer in 1986, and on ethical issues in the genetic study of deafness, published in *Genetics of Hearing Impairment* by the New York Academy of Sciences (1991).

Among Jordan's many honors are included the Washingtonian of the Year Award (1989), the Courage Award (1991) from the Courage Center in Golden Valley, Minnesota, a national award to a person who has made a significant contribution to the health, welfare, and rehabilitation of individuals with disabilities; the Washington, D.C. City Council's Leadership and Dedication Award for Civil and Human Rights for All Mankind; and the Washington Times Corporation Freedom Award (1992). He has also received eight honorary doctoral degrees.

References

Adelman, K. (1991, March). Loud and clear. *The Washingtonian,* 37–40, 46.

Ayers, B. D., Jr. (1990, December 18). Gallaudet carries standard in revolution for the deaf. *New York Times,* A18.

Gannon, J. R. (1989). *The week the world heard Gallaudet.* Washington, DC: Gallaudet University Press.

Gannon, J. R. (1993). The shaping of deaf America. *Gallaudet Today, 23* (4), 6–13.

Silver, A. (1988). Let us begin together. *Silent News, 20* (12), 1, 4–10.

K

HELEN KELLER (1880–1968), American Writer.

Helen Keller was born on June 27, 1880, in Tuscumbia, Alabama, the daughter of Captain Arthur H. Keller, who fought with the Confederate army at Vicksburg. An illness at the age of one and a half resulted in both blindness and deafness. For several years, her parents struggled to find a way to communicate with her; at best she had developed about sixty gestures to indicate her basic wants. When Keller was six, she accompanied her father to visit Alexander Graham Bell in Washington to discuss how she might be best educated. Bell then referred the Kellers to Michael Anagnos at the Perkins Institute who, in turn, contacted Anne M. Sullivan. Mr. Keller offered Sullivan board, twenty-five dollars per month, and an environment that would treat her as one of the immediate family—if she agreed to accept the formidable challenge of educating his daughter. In *The Story of My Life*, Keller described the long and tedious struggle to learn from ''Teacher'' the association of such physical objects as a doll, a piece of cake, or water with their English words. Through Sullivan's repeated attempts to fingerspell these words, Helen Keller finally made the connection. From then on she learned rapidly, first a broad range of vocabulary, and then sentences. She wrote her first letter—to her father—during that first year of Annie Sullivan's instruction. Through time, she developed a passion for letter writing and recording her thoughts, which certainly accelerated her language development immensely. Moreover, during this period, she had to learn, in her own way, how she was different from other children. As Teacher rewrote stories to help broaden Keller's understanding of the world, the news of the ''miracle'' of her instruction introduced constant distractions.

After two years of daily work together, Sullivan left Keller for several months to seek medical assistance with her own eye trouble, which was to plague her throughout her life. With the exception of that hiatus, the two were separated only twice in nearly half a century.

Keller attended the Wright-Humason School in New York City, then enrolled in the Gilman School for Young Ladies in Cambridge, in order to prepare for Radcliffe. Through Anne Sullivan, contact with the Perkins Institute was maintained to provide additional support. In Gilman School, Helen exceeded expectations in comparison with sighted, hearing girls, particularly with regard to her English. Arthur Gilman learned to fingerspell in order to help instruct her, and it was through his fingers in her hand in 1899 that he, as a member of the Harvard corporation, communicated the contents of the entrance examination. She then responded in the allowed time using a typewriter. During these years, she met such notables as John Greenleaf Whittier, Laurence Hutton, Mark Twain, and Oliver Wendell Holmes.

In 1900, Keller entered Radcliffe. It was a period of growth and challenge in higher education for all women. ''Teacher'' accompanied her to all classes, with the exception of examinations, in the evenings reading her assignments through fingerspelling into her hands. This continued throughout the more than seventeen courses required for a bachelor's degree. In 1902, *Ladies' Home Journal* contracted with Keller to write a five-part autobiography, which subsequently led Edward Everett Hale to comment that Helen Keller's book and Rudyard Kipling's *Kim* were the ''two most important contributions to literature which 1902 [has] given us.'' In 1903, this writing was combined with other letters written by Keller, as well as Harvard instructor John Macy's contributions, in *The Story of My Life*, acclaimed worldwide. While she was writing and studying at Radcliffe, she continued to respond to appeals to assist others interested in the welfare of people who were both blind and deaf. Upon graduation in 1904, Keller's sense of elation at her achievement was tempered, however, by a nagging sense that adequate recognition had not been bestowed on Annie Sullivan for her own accomplishments and singleminded devotion to a student.

The public thronged to see Keller at each of her speeches, with lines of admirers sometimes numbering more than three thousand. People sought her merely to shake her hand. In 1908, Keller published *The World I Live In*, which included a frank plea to editors, journalists, and the general public to look beyond blindness and deafness and judge her on her own accomplishments and desire to change the world. This statement was a breakthrough challenge to ''charitable'' instincts, and one echoed decades later by modern organizations of persons with disabilities. Keller herself opened such doors when, in 1909, she independently followed John Macy in joining the Socialist party; and, unlike Teacher, she supported the women's suffrage movement. Her impact on social reform issues was made all the more effective by the fact that she numbered among her admirers so many great people of her time and was something of an icon. Keller was pragmatic enough to acknowledge this reality and seize the opportunity it presented.

Not everyone believed that Keller's achievements were real. There appeared in Germany in 1908, for example, a brochure by Rudolph Brohman, a teacher of deaf pupils at Weissenfels, entitled ''What Should One Think of Helen Keller?'' in which he questioned the authorship of Keller's books, believing there to be some deception. Although Brohman reconsidered after a time and publicly retracted his earlier statement, questions he posed reemerged for years, causing both Keller and Anne Sullivan much distress despite Brohman's apology. In an attempt to refute the injustice to Keller, Julius Gensel, a scholar from Leipzig, published a 72-page pamphlet, ''The Truth about Helen Keller.'' Gensel presented meticulous text analysis of Keller's writings and his own recollections of a seven-hour meeting with her. He also drew on the work of John Dewey in making the case for thoroughgoing conceptually based education of deaf-blind students. Keller herself managed critics well and with great charm when they wrote reviews challenging her ability to write descriptively. She simply responded that *she* felt she had had a very complete life and was compelled to share it.

Through World War I, Keller continued her lecture tours, often challenged for her pacifist views, and making acquaintance with such noteworthy individuals as Thomas Alva Edison,* Henry Ford, Enrico Caruso, and Maria Montessori. In 1919, Hollywood produced *Deliverance*, a biographical motion picture story highly praised for its educational value which, however, lacked commercial appeal and failed to bring Keller and Teacher the financial security for which they had hoped. Following this, they traveled on a vaudeville circuit, where they achieved unlikely popularity and success in a half-programmed, half-spontaneous question and answer format.

The early 1920s saw the death of Keller's mother, with whom she had grown increasingly close in the later years of her life; and the death of her devoted friend, Alexander Graham Bell. The traumatic events were exacerbated when Keller received a proposal for marriage, which she declined; partly, her biographers believe, because she saw the marital difficulties of her parents and of Teacher and John Macy, and partly because she felt her deafness and blindness would pose too great a burden on any man she might marry. She also survived resiliently a lifetime of highly complex, possessive, and sometimes jealous relationships, particularly with Anne Sullivan and Polly Thomson. Helen may have experienced the transformation of love into control more often than most people. She turned her energies, instead, to campaigning further for the American Foundation for the Blind as she continued to write, collaborating with Nella Braddy Henney on *My Religion* in 1927 and ending the decade with the publication of *Midstream: My Later Life* (1929). Though somewhat tired of writing, she nevertheless published three more books before World War II.

Anne Sullivan Macy died on October 20, 1936, and for some time, Keller felt that she, too, had died. Fortunately, Polly Thomson, who had been part of their household since about 1914 and who had been taking on increased responsibilities as Teacher's health declined, began to accompany Helen Keller. Together, they moved from their Forest Hills, Long Island home to a house in Westport, Connecticut, where Keller lived until her death.

During World War II, Keller supported President Roosevelt's policies. Her own desire to find a meaningful experience associated with the war was fulfilled when she toured the nation's military hospitals to visit with the wounded soldiers, "the crowning experience of my life." The decade following the war was filled with tours of countries around the world.

Keller published fourteen books and hundreds of articles, letters, and speeches. She received many honors during her lifetime, including honorary degrees from the Universities of Glasgow, Berlin, and Delhi, as well as Howard and Temple University. To her great satisfaction, she shared the Roosevelt Medal with Anne Sullivan Macy in 1936 for "Cooperative Achievement of Unique Character and Far-Reaching Significance." President Johnson conferred the highest civilian honor, the Presidential Medal of Freedom, on Helen Keller in 1964.

In 1957, *The Miracle Worker* was produced on Broadway, starring Anne Bancroft as Annie Sullivan and Patty Duke as Helen, a smashing success subsequently made into a motion picture. At the time of the making of the film, *Life* magazine photographed the elderly Keller and teenaged Duke in an animated conversation through tactile fingerspelling.

Keller died on June 1, 1968. Her ashes were placed alongside those of Teacher and Polly in the columbarium of the National Cathedral in Washington.

"A new spirit is growing in us," Keller once wrote, "No longer are we content to relieve pain, to sweeten sorrow, to give the crust of charity. We dare to give friendship, service, the equal loaf of bread, the love that knows no difference of station."

References

Keller, H. (1968). *Midstream: My later life.* New York: Greenwood.
Keller, H. (1976). *The story of my life.* New York: Andor.
Lash, J. P. (1980). *Helen and teacher: The story of Helen Keller and Anne Sullivan Macy.* New York: Delacorte Press/Seymour Lawrence.

DONALD J. KIDD (1922–1966), Canadian Geologist.

Donald J. Kidd was born on June 9, 1922, in Nordegg, Alberta, at the foothills of the Rockies. He was deafened from pneumonia at the age of nine months. His schooling experiences were remarkably varied. He attended the Wright Oral School in New York City for five years, then transferred to the P.S. 47 day school. When his family returned to Toronto in 1933, Kidd enrolled in a class for deaf students at the Clinton Street School. In 1936, he began Grade 10 at a new continuation school at Red Lake, travelling by dog team and trudging on snow shoes through blizzards to attend classes. Then, for Grade 13, he flew to the high school at Kenora, 130 miles to the south, and boarded with the sheriff there for a year. In 1941, Kidd entered the University of Toronto on an H. R. Bain Scholarship from Kenora High School, majoring in chemical engineering; he completed his bachelor's degree in 1945. He received his master's degree in Economic Geology and Physical Chemistry in 1946 and earned a Ph.D. from the University of Toronto in 1951. His thesis was titled, "The Geochemistry of Beryllium." Kidd was notable then as the first deaf person to earn a doctoral degree in Canada. In addition, he studied x-ray crystallography, statistics, and Russian at the University of Alberta.

After a period of conducting research in geochemistry at the University of Alberta, he took a position as a research geologist with the Geophysical Engineering and Surveys Company in Ontario and as a consultant geologist for the Arctic Institute of North America. Kidd joined the ill-fated expedition to Baffin Island in 1953, exploring the Cumberland Peninsula on foot and on skis. The original group of thirteen scientists, headed by Colonel Patrick D. Baird, director of the Montreal office of the Arctic Institute, studied glaciology, geomorphology, botany, and zoology. W.R.B. Battle from McGill University drowned on July 13 while exploring a glacial stream.

Kidd himself met danger several times during the expedition. During one exploration, he turned the corner of a glacier morcune and nearly walked into the arms of a huge polar bear. The deaf geologist and the polar bear stared at each other for several frightening seconds, then Kidd pursed his quivering lips and attempted to say, "shoo." To his surprise, the big animal ambled off, but before the bear went far from view, Kidd managed to snap a photograph.

Active in the Association of Professional Engineers of Ontario, Geological Association of Canada, Geochemical Society, Edmonton Geological Society, and the Arctic Institute of North America, Kidd published in *American Mineralogist*, *Arctic*, and other journals, on such topics as "Hematite-Geothite Relations in Neutral and Alkaline Solutions under Pressure" (with F. G. Smith), "Geology of Cumberland Peninsula, Baffin Island," "Iron Occurrences in the Peace River Region, Alberta," and "Industrial Sands from the Pleistocene Deposits of Alberta." In the 1950s, Kidd's experiences in geological prospecting in the Yukon Territory in Canada involved staking 110 claims in a two-year period in regions accessible only by hydroplane. With a crew of bushmen and students, he spent many months examining asbestos deposits in the Cassiar-Woodchopper Creeks area, copper and gold near the Teslin River dam, and other minerals.

Kidd was also active in the Deaf community. In 1943, he met a deaf former classmate who introduced him to sign language, fingerspelling, and other deaf people. Among his first acquaintances was the famous deaf dry-point etcher, Cadwallader Washburn.* Kidd became director of the Ontario Association of the Deaf, served as secretary of the Toronto Division of the National Fraternal Society of the Deaf, and was Director of the Canadian Association of the Deaf. In a paper titled "Impressions of Orally Taught Deaf Varsity Graduate on Problems of Educating Deaf Children," Kidd provided an autobiographical account in which he described how he visited the Rochester (New York) School for the Deaf and St. Mary's School for the Deaf in Buffalo, and based on his observations, recommended that the Royal Commission on Education in Canada adopt the "combined method" of communicating in sign language, speech, and speechreading.

After nearly two decades in geology, Kidd began to consider a teaching career. He wrote to experts in the United States, Mexico, the Soviet Union, England, and Italy, inquiring about methods and possible positions. "I enjoy my [geological] research here very much in essence," he wrote to Professor Fidel Lopez in Mexico in February, 1961, "but my isolated role is beginning to wear me down and I have been realizing a great need for daily communication with the other deaf and for the stimulation that comes from teaching."

In 1961, Kidd joined the faculty of Gallaudet College as an instructor of mathematics. He was promoted to Assistant Professor of Physics there and taught physics until 1966, when he was stricken by a heart attack and died at the age of forty-four.

References

Kidd, D. J. (undated). Testimony of D. J. Kidd. Gallaudet University Archives.
Kidd, D. J. (1955). Geological-Prospecting in Southern Yukon. Gallaudet University Archives.

HENRY KISOR (1940–   ), American Writer/Book Editor.

Henry Kisor was born on August 17, 1940, in Midland Park, New Jersey, the second of three children. He was deafened from a combination of encephalitis and meningitis at the age of three and a half at a time when, as his parents recollected, he was quite precocious. Young Henry experienced a difficult adjustment, learning to accommodate for the balance problems that often accompany deafness and ceasing completely to use his speech. His parents provided loving support to help him develop the fortitude to face these challenges. They were reluctant to send him away or pursue a special school, and they became convinced that private tutorial and home instruction were the wisest course of action for their son. They responded to an advertisement and found a brilliant teacher, Doris Irene Mirrielees, who worked privately—her unconventional methods marginalized her somewhat. Ms. Mirrielees believed that printed English and symbols were a prerequisite and corequisite to learning speech and speechreading. She also viewed parents as the primary teachers and taught them formal teaching methods. Kisor responded well to her system—so well that he says "Printed English is really my first language." He also discovered in himself a love of words and literature that allayed the normal loneliness he experienced. Private tutoring also started him with speechreading, and he has highly valued continued speech lessons through the years. His teenage years were very typical, complicated by the social challenges of being the only deaf student in his classes. Kisor attended the Evanston Township High School in Evanston, Illinois, serving as managing editor of the student newspaper.

At Trinity College in Hartford, Kisor continued his literary pursuits, encouraged by a family friend to enroll in journalism. He graduated from Trinity with a bachelor's degree in 1962 and was offered a graduate assistantship at the Medill School of Journalism at Northwestern University. He began to write and do editorial work for a magazine on sailing on a part-time basis. He earned his master's degree with distinction from Northwestern in 1964.

Kisor went to work for the Wilmington (Delaware) *Evening News* briefly. Lonely for friends and family in the Chicago area, however, he was delighted to find a copy desk position with the *Daily News* in May 1965. In March 1973, Kisor was promoted to book editor of the *Daily News* and remained in that position until the newspaper was closed down in 1978. He then joined the *Chicago Sun-Times* as a book editor, interviewing many well-known writers. Because of his deafness, he sometimes requested assistance from his wife, friends, or colleagues. In one area, this probably saved his life. "Drinking was part of the newspaper culture," he has remarked. "I thought it was part of my job to socialize at literary cocktail parties. I got drunk at almost every one of them." He realized that much of his problem was connected to the anxiety he felt fending for himself. His wife or friends began to accompany him, and he regained his sense of control.

Over the years, Kisor has distinguished himself, primarily writing criticism and interviews. He interviewed such literary giants as Bernard Malamud ("the easiest to lipread"), Tom Wolfe, William Styron, Joseph Heller, and, interestingly, the blind writer Ved Mehta. He also writes travel articles for the *Sun-Times* newspaper on occasion, as the company's resident railroad buff.

In 1981, Kisor was selected as a finalist for the Pulitzer Prize for criticism. From 1983 to 1986, he was selected to write a weekly syndicated column on personal computers that appeared in newspapers across the United States. The winner of numerous awards from the Illinois Associated Journalists' Association, he won the first James Friend Memorial Critic Award from the Friends of Literature in 1988. He chaired the general nonfiction nominating committee for the 1989 Pulitzer Prize.

In 1990, Kisor published the book titled *What's That Pig Outdoors? A Memoir of Deafness*. The title is a spoof on what he saw one day when attempting to read lips as a person actually was asking "What's that big loud noise?" Kisor's humor in the face of challenge is evident throughout the book. Deaf and some hearing critics have been concerned that his choices have been tantamount to an explicit rejection of Deaf community. Kisor disagrees, however, saying that the book is one deaf person telling his story, that it is not prescriptive. Asked by an interviewer to advise deaf children, he said, "Do your best. If it is sign, go for it. If it is speech, do the same. And if one or the other doesn't work, don't despair. Get an education. . . . We are all different. I think we should celebrate our differences rather than letting them divide us."

References

Brauer, B. (1990). Book review: What's that pig outdoors? A memoir of deafness. *Gallaudet Today, 21* (1), 30–31.

Holmes, V. A. (1990). Celebrating differences: A look inside Henry Kisor. *Deaf Life, 3* (3), 12–16.

Kelly, T. (1990, May 31). Deaf editor: His life and work speak volumes. *Washington Times,* E1, E6.

Kisor, H. (1990). *What's that pig outdoors? A memoir of deafness.* New York: Hill & Wang.

Lake, C. (1990, June 3). Book Review: The tough got going. *New York Times,* 14–15.

JOHN KITTO (1804–1854), British Biblical Scholar.

John Kitto was born on December 4, 1804, in Plymouth, England. He was totally deafened in a fall from a ladder at the age of twelve. Kitto was self-educated, reading every book he could find. At the age of fifteen, he was placed in a workhouse in Plymouth to learn the trade of shoemaker after his parents went bankrupt. Here, Kitto began a personal journal that still serves as a useful resource for historians and educators today.

Kitto's remarkable perseverance while spending two years in the workhouse saved him from a vagabond life. He was subsequently hired out to a shoemaker who mistreated him. After returning to the workhouse, he began to publish essays in Nettleton's *Plymouth Weekly Journal.* By 1823, Kitto's writing attracted the interest of a mathematician and member of the Royal Society of London, George Harvey, who became his friend. A Mr. Nettleton, proprietor of the *Plymouth Weekly Journal,* invited Kitto to submit essays that soon motivated others in the town to support him in his literary pursuits. In Exeter, Kitto was sponsored by A. N. Groves for several years, first as a student of dentistry, then later for his study of the scripture and participation in the Church of England Missionary Society. His *Essays and Letters* (1825) brought him further recognition and led him to the Missionary College at Islington where he taught printing.

Kitto's wish to serve as a foreign missionary was realized in 1827 when he was sent to Malta, although ill health brought him back to England two years later. Upon his arrival, the Church Missionary Society supported him in establishing himself in some permanent situation. In May, 1829, he and Groves traveled to Persia with a party of nine persons. His diary documents his travels to Jutland, Copenhagen, St. Petersburg, and Bagdad. Kitto served as tutor to Groves' two sons who communicated with their teacher through writing and fingerspelling.

Back in England on August 10, 1833, Kitto began the first of a series of papers about his travels in *The Penny Magazine* on many topics ranging from ornithology to manual alphabets. He developed a friendship with the editor, Charles Knight, who suggested the idea of a "Pictorial Bible" which Kitto began immediately. This was also the year Kitto married; and, thrilled over the occasion and unable to hear others, he eagerly jumped ahead of the minister. Kitto and his wife socialized very little. She told friends candidly that Kitto's comfort and ease were a priority to her, and that his work and deafness dictated that they minimize time with groups of friends.

Within two years, Kitto completed the *Pictorial Bible*, followed by *Uncle Oliver's Travels* (1838), a child's book based on his experiences traveling through Persia. Learning of the success of a deaf American poet, James Nack,* Kitto wrote supportively, underscoring his sense of connection to another deaf scholar and asserting that deaf persons need not be excluded from any scholarly or artistic endeavor. Kitto next published a Biblical commentary based on his familiarity with Oriental customs, the *Pictorial History of Palestine and the Holy Land, Including a Complete History of the Jews* (1839–40). The Reverend Edward Robinson requested an interview with him. Kitto's speech being not very intelligible, Kitto responded that Robinson should first learn fingerspelling, otherwise "the profit would be all on my side." He wrote that he believed sign language to be the natural language of deaf people and encouraged schools to promote sign and written language. Kitto's financial condition was at this time very desperate, and his family was forced to leave their home to live in a smaller one in Woking.

Kitto's *History of Palestine* and *Thoughts Among Flowers* came out in 1843, followed by *The Pictorial Sunday Book* in 1845, the year he was elected a fellow of the Royal Society of Antiquaries. A new edition of *The Pictorial Bible* was published in 1847, a decade after the first anonymous version. This time his name was on it, and it was immediately popular for its clarity of language and its descriptions of the sources of key passages. Working hard to finish the *Cyclopaedia of Biblical Literature*, his financial woes worsened, and he again had to move, this time to the outskirts of Camden Town. The *Cyclopaedia* gained very favorable recognition in literary circles, since nothing of this nature had previously existed in the English language. An inexhaustible writer, Kitto edited the *Journal of Sacred Literature* until 1853, bringing further respect for his scholarship around the world. His immensely popular work, the eight-volume *The Daily Bible Illustrations* (1849), was his last. In this book, he explained the origins of many symbolic and historical texts. He also included some personal references. As discussed by Eadie, Kitto subtly alluded to his deafness several times in *The Daily Bible Illustrations*, e.g., his description of the peacocks of Solomon, noting the original name is probably onomatopoetic from the birds' cry. He comments quickly, "but we do not know, for *we* never *heard* it."

One year before his death, Kitto received an honorary Doctor of Divinity degree from the University of Giessen, a very special honor for a layman. He fell ill in 1852 and was unable to sit at his desk for any length of time. He attempted editorship of a weekly religious periodical, the *Sunday Readings for Christian Families*, but abandoned the effort after three months. He described his work as his only pleasure, and he prayed for greater physical stamina. Around the time of his youngest child's death in 1853, Kitto had a relapse of his illness and was ordered by his doctor to have nothing but absolute rest. Kitto refused, remarking that he would like to die with his pen in his hand. Finally, however, Kitto consented to a year's rest, and a circle of influential literary and religious friends formed a committee in London and Edinburgh to provide him with financial support. On August 9, 1854, the Kittos and seven of their nine children left for Rotterdam, then to Mannheim, and Stuttgart on a steamer on the Rhine river. After a brief recovery, Kitto saw his first-born child die in September. He had spent twelve days at his eldest daughter's bedside, finger-spelling as much as his strength would permit. He exhausted his own energies and died on November 25, 1854. Kitto was buried with his two children on the south side of the cemetery at Cannstatt, his tombstone erected by the publisher of his last work, and the monogram on the upper half being the final pictorial illustration he had chosen for the *Daily Bible Readings*.

References

Eadie, J. (1856). *Life of John Kitto, D.D., LL.D*. Edinburgh: William Oliphant.
Kitto, J. (1845). *The lost senses*. Edinburgh: London: C. Knight.
Ryland, J. E. (1856). *Memoirs of John Kitto, D.D., F.S.A*. Edinburgh: William Oliphant.
Thayer, W. M. (1862). *Working and winning: Or, the deaf boy's triumph*. Boston: H. Hoyt.

FELIX KOWALEWSKI (1913–1989), American Painter/Poet.

Felix Kowalewski was born on November 20, 1913, in Brooklyn, New York, the son of Polish immigrants. He was deafened at the age of six from spinal meningitis. Kowalewski attended the New York School for the Deaf at Fanwood, before the school was moved to White Plains. When his first art instructor, Michaelena LeFrere Carroll, left for a position as floral illustrator for the Brooklyn Botanical Gardens, he continued on his own, winning the senior division scholarship in the national soap sculpture contest sponsored by Procter & Gamble. The judges included the sculptor Gutzon Borglum of Mount Rushmore fame; young Kowalewski received the prize from the world-famous Lorado Taft. At the Fanwood school, in the absence of an art teacher, he also directed the Palette & Brush Club, assisting his classmates in learning how to paint murals. During his senior year, Kowalewski also studied life drawing under Harry Baker at the New York School of Fine and Applied Arts, and his interest shifted from three-dimensional to two-dimensional designs.

At Gallaudet College, President Percival Hall, recognizing Kowalewski's talent, arranged to have him study watercolor under Donald Kline in Washington. He also took a class at the Washington Art League. With a strong interest in literature and poetry as well, Kowalewski edited several of the Gallaudet publications, published poetry and sports articles in periodicals of the Deaf community, and was a reporter for the *Washington Post*. He graduated from Gallaudet College in 1937. During his college years, he exhibited at Chapel Hall on campus and in the International Exhibition of Fine and Applied Arts by Deaf Artists in 1934. Both of his watercolors for that prestigious exhibit sold on the first day.

From 1937 until 1942, he was an art instructor at the West Virginia School for the Deaf in Romney, simultaneously doing freelance work. He married in

1941. During this period of his life, he also exhibited the pastels *Beethoven's Moonlight Sonata* and *Still Life* at the Washington County Museum of Fine Arts in Maryland, and *Intermezzo*, a still life at the Corcoran Gallery of Art in Washington, D.C., which included music and violin in memory of the actor Leslie Howard. He was fascinated by portraiture, particularly with costume. Between 1942 and 1955, he taught art at the Michigan School for the Deaf in Flint and the California School for the Deaf in Berkeley. He joined the California School for the Deaf at Riverside in 1955 as an art and drafting instructor and remained there until his retirement in 1977. During World War II, he was one of a group of artists selected to sketch miniature portraits of the wives of servicemen.

Kowalewski had his work shown at the National Gallery in Washington, D.C., the American-Anderson Gallery in New York, the San Francisco Palace of Fine Arts, the Walt Disney Studios in Burbank, International Hotel in Los Angeles, Gallaudet College, and at many other museums, fairs, and art guilds. He employed a wide variety of media, including ink, watercolor, pastel, and oil. Awarded numerous prizes, he has been praised for his exceptional use of line and tone.

Kowalewski was known as a dedicated, disciplined, and very loving man. He served in many local, state, and national organizations of the Deaf community. He wrote biographies of other well-known deaf artists and published them in such periodicals as *The Silent Worker*. He also corresponded with the eminent deaf dry-point etcher Cadwallader Washburn.* As a poet, the versatile Kowalewski also won recognition, and his verse appeared in such national publications as *North America Book of Verse, Poetry Digest Annual, This Week,* and *Weird Tales*. His poetry has been noted to be consistent with his visual representations in aesthetic and style—gentle, flowing, and respectful of his subjects. He also translated poetry from French, being particularly fond of Beaudelaire. In 1983, he published *You and I,* a collection of fifty years of his verse, translations, and art work.

Kowalewski died in Riverside, California, on August 10, 1989.

References

Deaf artist to have one-man show at Gallaudet, Gallaudet College News Release, December 4, 1974.

Deafness no handicap for Flint artist. (1944, April 4). Flint *News-Advertiser.*

Kowalewski, F. (undated). Autobiographical notes. Gallaudet University Archives.

L

HENRY LAPP (1862–1904), American Craftsman/Painter.

Henry Lapp was born deaf on August 18, 1862, on a farm at Groff's Store (now Mascot) in Leacock Township, Pennsylvania. He was the son of Michael K. Lapp and Rebecca Lantz, members of a large family that had established farms in Early, Salisbury, Paradise, and East Lampeter in Lancaster County. In this region of grain and tobacco farming, Lapp became a carpenter, working in the Groff's Store area. Little is known about his childhood. Those who remembered him have noted that he communicated with others by pencil-and-paper, which he carried with him at all times. By the age of thirty-six, Lapp had established his own business as a cabinetmaker at Bird-in-Hand on the "Philly Pike," not far from the present location of The Old Road Furniture Company, which still sells reproductions of his patterns and designs. The 1899 Lancaster County Atlas shows that he owned three buildings at this time. He lived in an L-shaped house with his sister. His name was found etched on a beam inside the half-stone barn behind the house.

Using saws and lathes run by a windmill, Lapp produced many pieces of furniture characteristic of the lifestyle of the Amish community—dower chests, drop leaf tables, wall cupboards, bureaus, washbenches, cradles, tables, desks, flour chests, rocking chairs, wagons, toys, and sleighs. He often traveled by wagon to nearby Philadelphia, where he sold his pieces on Market Street. His designs were unique in that they did not use tulip bulbs and hex symbols, for the most part. The designs were subtle and restrained, more characteristic of the furniture of the Welsh country settlers who located in Pennsylvania east of Lancaster than of the Pennsylvania German style.

Lapp's chests, desks, chairs, and washstands were not generally found in Amish homes, but were designed for larger urban houses. He adapted the favored carrot-shaped foot and roundball foot for his cabinetry. One of Lapp's benches is shown in *Arts of the Pennsylvania Germans*, in which Scott T. Swank and his colleagues described how the piece was not made exclusively for domestic use, but was typically found in churches, schools, and other public rooms.

It has been documented that Lapp's deafness and his need to communicate with customers led him to draw his plans and show design samples in small booklets, which accompanied him wherever he traveled. The notebook of primitive paintings and fine colored sketches that he showed his customers, called "A Craftsman's Handbook," has been reproduced by the Philadelphia Museum of Art. He subsequently developed his talents in pencil drawings and watercolors of the Pennsylvania German genre. The fine sketches often included such subjects as horses, mice, fruit, farm animals, and flowers. His paintings, however, were not created for his furniture as much as for gifts for his friends and their children. There are many of these in the handbook, which served as a visual journal as well as a commercial catalogue. Thus, there is an enduring record of his craftsmanship and development. Although only a few of his pieces have survived, Lapp's work is still renowned in the Amish community and beyond it. The two most complete collections of his furniture and watercolors are owned by The Old Road Furniture Company and the Philadelphia Museum of Art.

In 1980, fifty-two of Lapp's extant paintings, as well as examples of his furniture, were exhibited at the special Henry Lapp Gallery at The People's Place in Intercourse, Pennsylvania. These paintings, owned by The People's Place and individual collectors, were among sixty-nine of his works sold in May 1979, at the Cocalico Valley Historical Society's annual auction. One painting of a double distelfink alone sold for $3,125. While his furniture designs were generally for people in larger towns, he was true to his Amish upbringing in bringing his skills to new, innovative designs for stepladders, reading tables, threshing machines, and mouse traps, which were more likely used within his community. Lapp's work has received a special place in the folk art history of Lancaster County.

The austere nature of Amish belief makes it hard to put Lapp's often-playful paintings in the proper perspective. At the exhibition and auction in 1980, attendees remarked that a "celebration" of his work seemed to violate his people's quiet way of life. The circus paintings present a particular puzzle. However, while the paintings may seem in contradiction to church prohibitions against such events, observers have pointed out that it is not unheard of for Amish youths to go secretly to a circus. Critics and researchers have also suggested that Lapp, as a deaf person, was allowed more freedom, as his art was his principal means of self-expression.

Henry Lapp died on July 5, 1904, from lead poisoning and was buried in Gordonsville, Pennsylvania. He never married and his simple possessions were auctioned immediately.

References

Kraybill, E. (1980, July 2). Inventive Amishman's art displayed. Lancaster, Pennsylvania *Intelligencer Journal*, 36.

Lapp, H. (1975). *A craftsman's handbook*. B. B Garvan (Ed.). Philadelphia: Philadelphia Museum of Art.

Miller, J. (1980, July 2). Rare art by Amishman goes on exhibit. Lancaster, Pennsylvania *New Era*, 23.

Swank, S. T., Forman, B. M., Sommer, F. H., Schwind, A. P., Weiser, F. S., Fennimore, D. H., & Swan, S. B. (1983). C. E. Hutchins (Ed.), *Arts of the Pennsylvania Germans*. New York: W. W. Norton.

HENRIETTA SWAN LEAVITT (1868–1921), American Astronomer.

Henrietta Swan Leavitt was born on July 4, 1868, in Lancaster, Massachusetts, one of seven children. She was the daughter of a Congregational minister, Reverend George Roswell Leavitt, and Henrietta S. (Kendrick) Leavitt. Her Puritan heritage could be traced to Jordan Leavitt, who settled in Hingham, Massachusetts, in the 1640s. In 1885, she entered the preparatory department of Oberlin College. Two years later, she entered Oberlin, where she flourished, although her hearing was, by this time, deteriorating. She enrolled at the Society for the Collegiate Instruction of Women (Radcliffe), where her kind personality made her popular among her classmates and minimized the effects of her now-profound deafness. In her senior year at Radcliffe, a course in astronomy aroused her interest and she took another course there after graduating in 1892.

Two decades earlier, in 1872, Henry Draper had taken the first astronomical photograph, the first to show that spectral lines existed in the ultraviolet and infrared as well as the visible portion of the sun. Then, in the 1880s, Edward Pickering significantly advanced the study of the spectra of stars by employing a large prism in front of a photographic plate to capture an entire field of stars at once. As director of the Harvard College Observatory, he had ambitious plans to map the heavens using this technique. For this, he needed assistance. He chose Leavitt, who had begun as a volunteer. Unfortunately, she had to leave the Observatory when a family crisis called her to Wisconsin. After two years, Pickering encouraged Leavitt to return at his expense. He offered her a pay increase and told her that if she had to leave the Observatory again she could take with her the materials and data she had collected. Pickering's offer of a raise in 1900 was an uncommon gesture. In 1902, within a short time of her appointment, she advanced to head the photometry department.

Because of Leavitt's outstanding initiative and unfailing patience, Pickering chose her to execute his ambitious 1904 plan to redetermine star magnitudes using the most up-to-date photographic techniques. The accuracy of such data was crucial to investigations of astronomers during this period, and Pickering's staff began with the "North Polar Sequence" as a standard for the entire sky. Forty-six stars were selected, and 299 photographic plates using thirteen telescopes were employed to establish this primary sequence. Leavitt and her colleagues then applied this scale to measure the thousands of stars in the heavens. Leavitt discovered 2,400 variable stars while making these stellar measurements, doubling the number of such stars known in her time. She was the first to observe and report four new stars, various asteroids, and other celestial objects and published seventeen reports of her observations in the *Annals* and *Circular* of the Harvard College Observatory. After Leavitt reported 843 new variables in the small Magellanic Cloud during one period of investigation. Charles A. Young of Princeton, in a letter to Pickering, called Leavitt a "star fiend" and expressed pleasant exasperation that he could not keep up with her many discoveries.

Her extensive investigations of star magnitudes led Leavitt to a discovery that is considered by many to be her most significant contribution to the field of astronomy. In 1908, she observed that brighter stars have longer periods. In other words, fluctuations in brightness of the fainter stars are of shorter duration than those of the brighter ones. Leavitt had discovered a mathematical relationship, a physical law, that enabled astronomers to estimate the distance from earth to particular stars based on their brightness. Scientists were able to estimate distances up to about a hundred light-years prior to her discovery. Leavitt's formulation of the period-luminosity law helped to extend this to much greater distances—galaxies up to ten million light-years away. Ejnar Hertzsprung, Harlow Shapley, and Walter Baade were a few of the astronomers who applied this discovery as a yardstick to study globular clusters of stars. Edwin Hubble used the method to estimate the distance of the Andromeda galaxy in light-years. Shapley acknowledged that Leavitt's work on variable stars in the Magellanic Clouds (galaxies of stars) was invaluable, particularly in relation to the study of stars in the Milky Way.

The photographic plates Leavitt received from Peru in 1905 would have immediately discouraged most astronomers. On each plate were hundreds of small images of stars. She knew many of them were variables. Some were stable like our own sun. Others flared up irregularly, and it was difficult to know if a star was brighter because it was more luminous than others or because it was closer. She accepted the challenge. In the dwarf galaxy known as the Lesser Magellanic Cloud, Leavitt discovered twenty-five Cepheids.

Much of Leavitt's work was with stars known as the Cepheids. They are characterized by the regularity of their changes in brightness. Of the 2,400 variable stars she discovered, she found 1,777 of them in the Magellanic Clouds while she was in Peru. The Lesser and Greater Magellanic Clouds have no counterpart in the northern sky. They are nearby companion galaxies about 170,000 light-years beyond our system. Henrietta Swan Leavitt's investigation of the Cepheids significantly helped to advance our understanding of the universe. Mounted on a wall at the Harvard College Observatory is a memorial tablet honoring Leavitt for her discovery of the period-luminosity relation for Cepheid variables.

Leavitt herself was not able to follow up on her discovery until four years later when she confirmed the relationship with a larger number of stars. Pickering believed that it was the Observatory's responsibility to collect data and it was up to others to explain them. Leavitt's "Record of Progress" indicates the large number of projects she was working on simultaneously, including an investigation of Algol variables undertaken by Henry Norris Russell, measurements of the luminosities of stars in Kapteyn's selected areas, experiments to determine the colors of faint stars, methods of transforming photographic to visual magnitudes, and, with astronomers at Mt. Wilson, determination of the exact photographic magnitudes of the North Polar Sequence of stars.

Leavitt also discovered that fainter stars are usually redder than brighter ones. This led astronomers to question whether the light was possibly reddened by interstellar absorption. Modern photoelectric techniques can now help astronomers distinguish between this absorption effect and the actual redness of a star.

The information Leavitt supplied on the magnitudes of stars in the North Polar Sequence was recognized by the International Committee on Photographic Magnitudes for the Astrographic Map of the Sky. By the time of her death, she had completed work for 108 areas. Astronomers interested in investigating the Milky Way referred to Leavitt's North Polar Sequence data for decades.

In 1925, the Swedish mathematician and member of the Swedish Academy, Professor Mittag-Leffler, sent a letter to Leavitt at the Harvard College Observatory. He wished to nominate her for the Nobel Prize in physics for her discovery of the period-luminosity relationship that had done so much in furthering our understanding of the universe. Mittag-Leffler was not aware that Henrietta Swan Leavitt had died of cancer four years earlier, on December 12, 1921.

References

Bailey, S. I. (1922). Henrietta Swan Leavitt. *Popular Astronomy, 30* (4), 197–199.
Gingerich, O. (1973). Henrietta Swan Leavitt. *Dictionary of scientific biography* (Vol. 8, pp. 105–106). New York: Charles Scribner's Sons.
Hoffleit, D. (1971). Henrietta Swan Leavitt. In E. T. James, J. W. James, & P. S. Boyer (Eds.), *Notable American women, 1607–1950: A biographical dictionary* (Vol. 2, pp. 382–383). Cambridge, MA: Belknap Press.
Lang, H. G. (1994). *Silence of the spheres: The deaf experience in the history of science.* Westport, CT: Bergin & Garvey.

MARIE LENÉRU (1875–1918), French Dramatist.

Marie Lenéru was born on June 2, 1875, in Brest, Brittany, France. Her young father, a naval officer, died of a fever during a cruise to Tenerife while Marie was still an infant. Lenéru was educated at home by her mother and a family of sailors. Consequently, it was on or near the sea where she spent the greater part of her childhood, learning many legends and folk tales. At the age of six, Lenéru was encouraged by her mother to begin a *Journal*, and it was here that she began to express herself in writing. At a precocious age, she remarked that the diary was good for her; that it was a way to "know myself."

Lenéru was twelve when an attack of measles led to progressive deafness and a loss of much of her vision. By the time she was fourteen, she was totally deaf. During a period of about four years when she was nearly completely blind as well, she learned tactile fingerspelling from her mother as they sought medical advice in Paris. Some of her vision returned in time, but it was not enough to learn to lipread. Friends and family took up fingerspelling to communicate with her and she was able to read handwriting.

Lenéru applied herself remarkably and resiliently to learning English, German, Latin, and Italian on her own, in order to be able to read dramatic works in their original forms. With her magnifying glass, she read an average of eight hours a day. She returned to Brest in 1893, the year in which her "mature" journal begins. Personal letters during this period of her life, however, confirm that she experienced isolation and sadness as a result of her deafness. Missing the beauty of music, she became obsessed over its loss in her life. Although she charmed friends and acquaintances, she shunned social interactions which proved difficult for her, and she believed that she would never find someone to love and with whom to share a life. She felt haunted by solitude: "I am forced to dwell in it. . . .There is no suffering more inhuman than deafness. As soon as voice disappears, beings become things. They are far away, trying to join us, but they can do nothing for our happiness." Lenéru's *Journal* is characterized by this despairing view of deafness, but also by pride in her own talent. In 1899, she wrote that she kept her eyes closed when she awoke in the morning, recalling the "real life . . . which was mine for fourteen years, and which has left me with more memories than the other." In November, she wrote sadly, "I have had to give up my voice; still another link broken. Not to hear it and not to know how it sounds to others, is disquieting." Then, however, she speaks disparagingly of those who consider themselves victims: "I do not love rebels who are victims and, consequently, are without strength." She observes human experience intensely, declaring in the *Journal*: "It is from scene to scene that my characters are revealed to me."

Lenéru's *Journal* meditates on aspects of illusion and reality, and the need for moral and religious anchoring. The pages reveal her sophisticated knowledge of such thinkers as Pascal and Lacordaire. Her very extensive reading included Shelly, Darwin, Spencer, and Nietzsche; the thoughts of philosophers, scientists, and poets commingle in her entries. Her entry for July 25, 1901, describes the panic she experienced when the box containing her copy-books, her personal records of her readings, and her drafts of original work was lost during travel. Pleased to have recovered it, she vowed never to travel again without every precaution.

Still able to read only with a magnifying glass, Lenéru attempted her first book in 1901, a historical novel of Saint-Just and the French Revolution. The novel created considerable controversy when published posthumously in 1922 for its violence and passion, particularly when readers found out that the delicate and socially charming Lenéru had written it.

Next came research and writing on Helen Keller. Perhaps out of affinity with the deaf and blind American who had recently published "Sense and Sensibility," Lenéru took it upon herself to communicate Keller's story of success to

Marie Lenéru, French dramatist. Photo from *Journal de
Marie Lenéru* (Paris: G. Crès,
c. 1922).

the French public. Yet, within herself she found no peace. "The life of a happy
woman is not for me," she wrote. "I must invent another."

She found some satisfaction in dramatic writing, perhaps through her need to
externalize her passionate and persistent interior dialogue. Her discovery of
Curel gave her a more liberated sense of the power of theatre; she found Ibsen
too dark and moralistic. Her first play, *Les Affranchis* (*The Liberated*), repeats
many of the themes found in the *Journal* and letters. The play elevates passion
and "liberates" her characters from false morality. *Les Affranchis* was a moral
struggle between two lovers. She sent the play to Catulle Mendès in 1907, and
he produced it and defended it against criticism for three years preceding its
immense success at the Odéon. Lenéru followed the movements of the actors
in her play with a spyglass, not able to hear the dialogue of her masterpiece.
The play was both extensively praised and criticized throughout the fifteen performances. When the curtain fell for the final time, she was moved by the
ovation of waving hands.

Lenéru also contributed to French reviews and magazines, and had several
other plays presented in Paris theaters. In 1908 she won first prize in a contest
sponsored by a Parisian daily, *Le Journal*, for a short story titled "The Awakening." Her second important dramatic work, *Le Redoutable*, was evoked from
the childhood spent by the sea. The play was a story of a traitor on a war ship,

based on old legends. Badly interpreted and disappointingly received, it was withdrawn after three performances. She authored the play *La Triomphatrice* in 1914, a story of a distinguished woman of letters forced to choose between family and success. Accepted at the Comédie-Française, the play was seemingly out of place as World War I began, and it was withheld from production until 1918.

Lenéru again cursed her deafness when she felt it prevented her from helping to nurse the wounded soldiers during the war. She found a measure of consolation in writing, publishing many pacifist articles and, in 1917, she composed her last play, *La Paix*. Always a voracious reader, one of her last discoveries and enthusiasms was Maurice Barrès.

Shortly after the performance of *La Triomphatrice* in January 1918, Lenéru and her mother returned to their native Brittany where Marie was stricken with influenza. She died from heart complications on September 23, 1918. Her admirers, especially Léon Blum, continued to produce *La Paix* and *Les Affranchis* in the years following her death. The *Journal* was published posthumously, exhumed by the mother who must have been haunted to read of the despair her gifted and successful daughter never fully shared with anyone.

References

Kunitz, S. J., & Colby, V. (Eds.). (1967). *European Authors 1000–1900: A biographical dictionary of European literature*. New York: H. W. Wilson.

Lenéru, M. (1923). *The journal of Marie Lenéru*. (W. A. Bradley, Trans.). New York: Macmillan.

Pitrois, Y. (1932). The life and work of Marie Lenéru. *The Volta Review*, *34* (11), 582–584, 602–603.

LEO LESQUEREUX (1806–1889), American Paleobotanist.

Leo Lesquereux was born in Fleurier, Canton of Neuchâtel, Switzerland, on November 18, 1806; he was the only son of V. Aimé and Marie Anne Lesquereux, descendants of French Huguenots. His father manufactured watch springs. From a very early age, Lesquereux loved nature. He took much satisfaction in frequent excursions into the mountains, fields, and woods, roaming with abandon, and frequently bringing back flowers, hazelnuts, and wild fruits for his mother. He sang to himself all the while. This communing with nature, he later wrote, was his greatest enjoyment as a child. However, it was a fall from the top of a mountain at the age of seven that deafened him.

Lesquereux spent two years at the College of Neuchâtel, where he was a classmate of Arnold Guyot and August Agassiz, the younger brother of Louis Agassiz. In 1830, after a short time in Eisenach, Saxony, where he held a professorship in French, he accepted another position as principal at La Chaux de Fonds. He married Sophie von Wolffskel von Reichenberg, the daughter of an honored general who had followed Napoleon's Saxon troops to Russia. She was, in her childhood, a favorite of Goethe, a friend of her uncle. Over the next few years, Lesquereux and his wife raised their first two children under the most difficult economic circumstances.

After a traumatic experience in which Dr. Jean-Marc Itard had attempted to cure his deafness, Lesquereux stayed with an aunt who lived in Paris. She nursed him back to health, and he returned to Fleurier to begin a partnership with his father in the watchmaking business. Continued poverty soon forced his family to move. During these hardships, Lesquereux's love for the study of nature never faded. He took advantage of every opportunity for sojourns in the fields and mountains. These trips were now without the songs once part of his life. He did not regard deafness as much more than a social inconvenience, and he shunned parties and trips to the tavern in favor of his woodland excursions.

Lesquereux developed a close friendship with a doctor who had treated him after his fall from what was later called by villagers "Lesquereux's Cliff." They shared a strong interest in the study of plants. The physician's daughter also loved botany, and Lesquereux often visited them with his microscope. During this period of his life, the deaf botanist's expertise with the flora of the locale became well-known. Great scientists such as Desmazieu, Lenormand, Scherer, Godet, and Muhlenbeck sought his guidance on expeditions to the Jura mountains. Twice, Lesquereux led the famous Mougeot to the top of the Chasseron, the highest peak of the Jura.

The spongy bogs of Europe, which evolved over tens of thousands of years, provided him with a rich variety of unique species of fauna and flora. He examined the composition of ancient Roman wooden bridges traversing the oldest bogs. Of special interest to Lesquereux were the "Red bog" and the "Devil's bog" in the Röhn mountains. Around 1844, his growing interest in mosses led him to enter a contest sponsored by the Swiss government, which was searching for methods to improve the nation's fuel supply. Local villagers who did not understand his scientific interests called him the "fool of the peat bogs." But Lesquereux's essay on the peat bogs of Jura won the prize, and the report remained the most authoritative work on the subject until after his death. It was this writing that helped him develop a close friendship with Louis Agassiz, the scientist who made a name for himself in the study of fossil fishes and glaciation.

Lesquereux visited Germany, France, Sweden, and other countries to investigate ways in which to conserve the bogs. In Berlin, the chemist Mitscherlich, recipient of the Royal Medal of the Royal Society for his discovery of the principle of isomorphism, welcomed him for a friendly discussion on the peat bogs, while the botanist Link, director of the Botanical Garden, found communication difficult—as much because of Link's advancing age as Lesquereux's deafness—but admired Lesquereux's work and presented him with a card of entrance and ordered specimens from him.

During Lesquereux's investigation of the draining of the great swamp country in Switzerland, a revolution broke out in Neuchâtel, severing the Canton from Prussia and dissolving the academy. His friends Agassiz and Guyot, along with others, went to America. Lesquereux decided that this would be best for his family as well. Traveling to America with his wife and five children, in the steerage of a ship with three hundred refugees, was a long and difficult ordeal.

They arrived in Boston, Massachusetts, in the fall of 1848; there he had much difficulty in securing a position in science. He attributed the difficulty to other people's fear of his deafness. Lesquereux could not even smoke in peace. While enjoying one of his first walks in Boston, a policeman stopped him, confiscated his cigar, and fined him several dollars. As Lesquereux drily explained, in 1850 it was forbidden to smoke in the streets of the city as this might "incommodate the Athenian ladies."

Lesquereux briefly entered the employ of Louis Agassiz, collecting and classifying plants during the "Journey to Lake Superior." In this early period of our nation's growing scientific community, William S. Sullivant of Columbus, Ohio, a wealthy devotee to the study of mosses, was the leading expert involved with the area of true mosses, peat mosses, liverworts, and other plants in that division. Sullivant was impressed by Lesquereux's work and invited him to Columbus to help prepare two manuscripts, *Musci boreali-americani* and *Icones muscorum*. Amidst his scientific work, Lesquereux began a series of "Lettres écrites d'Amérique destinées aux émigrants" as he toured the southern states for Sullivant. These "letters" were articles revealing his impressions of American life in his time and were published in *Revue suisse* during that year. In 1851, he was hired by H. D. Rogers to study coal plants in Pennsylvania. It was during this year that he became acquainted with J. P. Lesley, whose friendship culminated forty years later in a wonderful biography of the deaf paleobotanist as the first elected member of the National Academy of Sciences. Academy members remembered Lesquereux as amiable and skilled at reading their lips.

Lesquereux participated in many geological surveys, including surveys conducted in Arkansas and Kentucky (for D. D. Owen), Indiana (E. T. Cox), Minnesota (N. H. Winchell), and Pennsylvania (Lesley). In one of his reports, "Fossil Plants of the Coal Strata of Pennsylvania," he described 110 new species of plants. He began to coauthor a *Manual of the Mosses of North America* with Sullivant, but Sullivant died in 1873; and Lesquereux's eyesight was failing him. He recruited Thomas Potts James to conduct the microscopic studies and together they completed the *Manual*, published in 1884. This 447-page document described about 900 species of mosses. The volume and quality of his work is especially remarkable considering the fact that in the early 1870s, his eyesight had already seriously deteriorated. Nevertheless, the last two decades of his life were of undiminished productivity. He spent his later years naming fossils, including those in a large private collection of R. D. Lacoe of Pittston, Pennsylvania, which was later bequeathed to the Smithsonian Museum of Natural History in Washington, D.C. Even after Lesquereux's death in 1889, his work continued to be published. "Flora of the Dakota Group," published in *Monographs of the U.S. Geological Survey*, included 2,460 specimens, many of which are now at the Botanical Museum of Harvard. In all, he published more than fifty works in his field, a dozen of them considered very important contributions to the natural history of North America.

Lesquereux actually appreciated the isolation brought on by his deafness. He strived for a quality, rather than a quantity, of human relationships. Of Lesquereux's phenomenal speechreading skills, Lesley reminisced that he had been present when Lesquereux talked with three persons alternately in French, German, and English by watching their lips. The conversation would always begin by each one saying which language he or she intended to use. Lesquereux's learning of the English language after he became deaf made his pronunciation "curiously artificial and original." However, over his forty years in America, the pronunciation improved dramatically and did not differ greatly from standard dialect.

Yet, even with these speaking and speechreading skills, Lesquereux had a certain lack of confidence in himself. This attitude about his deafness and its relationship to holding a position of merit is revealed in a letter he wrote to a potential sponsor for a geological survey. In this letter, he provided some personal details about his financial struggles, but began by explaining that he was totally deaf and felt this had prevented his obtaining a permanent position.

Lesquereux's many collections of specimens are scattered since, with the exception of the period from 1867 to 1872, he did not have the security of institutional affiliation. Many of his specimens became the property of interested individuals, often amateurs. In the British Museum of Natural History, as well as other museums around the world, one will find hundreds of preserved flowering plants that are mementos of Leo Lesquereux's work. His publications included monographs on carboniferous fossils of Pennsylvania (1854) and Illinois (1863). Between 1867 and 1872, he classified and named fossils for the Harvard Museum of Comparative Zoology, work which led to three volumes of *Coal Flora of Pennsylvania*. He was frequently called to Cambridge to help determine the specimens of fossil plants in Agassiz's museum.

Friends would often describe how Lesquereux's eyes would sparkle when he examined sketches and samples of new species. He became friends with the botanist Sternberg, whose letters are the source of much insight into Lesquereux's character. Sternberg told Lesquereux about a site, Sassafras Hollow, near Fort Harker, that he thought Lesquereux might find interesting. Later in 1872, Lesquereux collected fossils from Sassafras Hollow himself, securing among many specimens a large, beautiful leaf that he named *Protophylum sternbergii* in his friend's honor. They corresponded until Lesquereux's death. Lesquereux had written that he could not expect to become useful to others and to science except by hard work, patience, and a fixed purpose. "In my estimation," Sternberg wrote, "America can show no life more unselfishly devoted to science than that of Lesquereux, probably the most scholarly and conscientious botanist of his day." In his history *The Fossil Hunters*, Andrews (1980) described the deaf paleobotanist Leo Lesquereux as one of the "great founders of fossil botany in North America" (p. 186).

Lesquereux died in Columbus, Ohio, on October 25, 1889.

References

Andrews, H. N. (1980). *The fossil hunters: In search of ancient plants.* Ithaca, NY: Cornell University Press.

Lang, H. G. (1994). *Silence of the spheres: The deaf experience in the history of science.* Westport, CT: Bergin & Garvey.

Lesley, J. P. (1890). Memoir of Leo Lesquereux. *National Academy of Sciences biographical memoirs* (Vol. 3, pp. 189–212). Washington, DC: National Academy of Sciences.

Orton, E. (1890). Leo Lesquereux. *American Geologist, 5,* 284–296.

Sternberg, C. H. (1931). *The life of a fossil hunter.* San Diego, CA: Jensen Printing.

JAMES H. LOGAN (1843–1917), American Microscopist.

James H. Logan was born in Allegheny City, Pennsylvania, on February 27, 1843. He became deaf at the age of four and a half from scarlet fever. At fifteen, he entered the Pennsylvania Institution for the Deaf in Philadelphia. Logan looked back with appreciation on this period of his life, because great pains were taken to foster his interest in the natural sciences, particularly by Llewelyn Pratt, one of his teachers. After he left school in 1863, he purchased many books and continued his studies on his own. Joshua Foster and B. D. Pettengill helped him by providing access to their books and J. Noynes, for many years the superintendent of the Minnesota School for the Deaf, tutored him. Pratt considered him an excellent student and was able to secure Logan a position as a draftsman with the U.S. Coast Survey. Logan held this position when Gallaudet College opened. He entered the advanced course of study in September 1864 under Professor Richard S. Storrs.

While working with the Coast Survey, Logan collected samples of various deep sea microbes from the dredging operations, including foraminifera, globigerina, and radiolaria. In his spare time, while a student at Gallaudet College, he examined the microbes with the crude microscopes available to him. The position with the Coast Survey sparked his interest in biology. During the early years of his college education, his days were hectic. He would rise early in the morning, attend a recitation at the College, work from 9 o'clock until 4 o'clock, then spend the evenings studying. This continued for two years. In 1865, Logan resigned from the Coast Survey to become Dr. Edward Miner Gallaudet's secretary, a position giving him more time for his studies.

Logan was not a very sociable student. He was a bookworm who shunned other college activities and seldom related to his peers. At his commencement in 1869, he presented an oration titled "A Glimpse at Science," which revealed his strong interest in and love for the unexpected aesthetic rewards in living a life of science.

A collection of correspondence between Logan and the distinguished American physicist Joseph Henry is housed at the Smithsonian Institution in Washington, D.C. The letters reveal much about Logan's scientific interests. On November 28, 1868, Logan asked Henry, the Smithsonian Institution's first secretary, for assistance in forwarding a Smith and Beck monocular microscope from Europe "to aid me in studies to which I am specially devoting myself." Logan offered to pay for all expenses if the Smithsonian would help bring the instrument to Washington safely with its shipping services. In this letter he wrote: "I have been devoting some of my leisure time to studying the construction of microscopes and have been endeavoring to make some improvements therein."

Under the encouragement of Dr. Curtis of the Army Medical Museum, Logan attempted to reduce vibration in the microscope caused by turning the fine adjustment screw. Henry invited the young deaf scientist to demonstrate his improvement of the microscope, but Logan was unable to come in person on the specified date. Logan sent Henry his drawings and a description of how vibrations could be reduced by flooring a room with sand and Henry responded with suggestions. Logan was awarded a patent for his improvement of the microscope in 1869. As described in the July 10, 1969 issue of *Scientific American*, his basic construction of his single microscope consisted of mostly wooden parts with no sacrifice in efficiency, together with "a new and improved" method of effecting the focal adjustment.

While a teacher at the Illinois School for the Deaf in Jacksonville, Illinois, Logan requested from Henry a soil sample and a copy of the Smithsonian Institution's Annual Report. In 1870, only a year after Logan had graduated from Gallaudet College, he advocated improved science education for deaf students in the *American Annals of the Deaf*, describing the amusement and educational value pupils may find in a microscope.

In April 1875, he sent another letter to Henry, this time asking for information on the most recent knowledge of the fossil foramanifera. Henry responded a week later and provided the names of several scientists who have given attention to this fossil, but Logan replied on May 6 that he had already been in communication with them. Logan wrote: "I cannot find that anything systematic has been done, so it would appear that there is a fine field for research in this direction. Such is the opinion of Count Pourtales."

Logan's interest in foramaniferous materials continued with him when he moved on to accept the position of principal of the Pittsburgh Day School for the Deaf, which had been founded seven years earlier as the Presbyterian Mission Sabbath School by Reverend John G. Brown. Archie Woodside, another deaf man, was at that time giving lessons to deaf youth and adults in this first "day school" for deaf persons in the United States. Woodside then started a rural school in Alleghany City, and the Pittsburgh Day School was moved to a new site, an abandoned hotel in a small town named Turtle Creek where Logan became Principal. Shortly after this, Archie Woodside's school was combined with Logan's school and the Western Pennsylvania Institution for the Education of the Deaf and Dumb came into being. The position Logan held was later renamed "Superintendent," and Logan is considered the first Superintendent of what is now the Western Pennsylvania School for the Deaf.

From Turtle Creek, Logan corresponded with the notable paleontologist F. V. Hayden, who encouraged him to check with the Smithsonian Institution for the specimens he sought. He wrote to Henry on February 25, 1876: "Nothing has been done as yet in regard to making a systematic study of the North American fossil foramanifera. It is very difficult at present to get any material to work on, as it seems that little effort has been made to collect this kind." Henry's note to himself, written on Logan's letter, however, indicates "Have received nothing of the kind from Hayden." Whether Logan's search for samples of this material was ever satisfied is unknown.

At the school in Turtle Creek, Logan began to publish a collection of children's stories, *The Raindrop*. The book began on schoolroom slates and was passed around by teachers to be read by the pupils. Famous literary masterpieces and fairy tales were adapted using language structures that the young children could read with less difficulty. Logan acquired a printing press, and for about a year he published *The Raindrop* as a monthly magazine, stopping because he found himself spending more than his annual salary on the publication. Encouraged by many others, however, he reprinted the material in book form. In 1910, the Volta Bureau reprinted *The Raindrop*; and Alexander Graham Bell was one of its enthusiastic supporters. Today, copies of this book may be found in the libraries of many schools for deaf children.

Logan was dismissed from the Western Pennsylvania Institution in 1880. His scientific interests beckoned once again and, while enthusiastically pursuing further investigations in microscopy, he offered himself through his own business as a metal broker for several Pittsburgh manufacturers, and as an optician and producer of scientific instruments. A decade later, when an economic depression hit hard, Logan was forced to close his business and find employment in Pittsburgh with the Department of Agriculture, where as a microscopist, he was responsible for supervising five assistants in safeguarding the city's pork supply from *trichina spiralis*. In 1893, Logan acquired a position at the Western Pennsylvania Medical College as a "demonstrator" in biology and zoology classes. His work must have attracted the attention of those in the Biological Laboratory of the Western University of Pennsylvania; for he was transferred there in 1894, and served as an assistant to the professor of biology. While employed at the Western University, Logan sent specimens of animal and vegetable life to Gallaudet College for the benefit of deaf students interested in biology.

Logan's assignment as an instructor was prestigious from the perspective of the Deaf community. Few deaf professionals held positions at universities for hearing students until recent times. Logan approached his teaching by writing his presentations. His speech was never totally lost, but he found more comfort in expressing himself by writing and preferred that method of communication with hearing people. He taught five or six students at a time, continuing this for three years until Western University ran out of funds for his class.

Logan, however, held no special joy in his teaching at the University. According to his friends, the professor of biology was getting all of the credit for demonstrations and discoveries that Logan worked diligently to prepare.

Logan was next hired by Chancellor Holland of Western University to experiment with the microscopical analysis of molds, spores, algae, and other plant growths. His reputation led him to be invited to serve on the City of Pittsburgh's Water Commission. He was called upon to provide expert advice in microscopical examinations in legal cases; and he published articles in various scientific journals, illustrating them with his own sketches. In 1907, Logan was involved in a commission business in metals, insurance, and real estate. As noted by an old friend, John B. Hotchkiss, one of Logan's two classmates who graduated from Gallaudet in 1869, Logan begrudged the time he had to take from his scientific work to earn his living.

Logan was a founder and for several years corresponding secretary of the Iron City Microscopical Society. He also published several articles in the Pittsburgh newspapers on the uses and value of fingerspelling and sign language. He died of pneumonia on December 9, 1917, in Pittsburgh, at the age of 74.

References

Braddock, G. C. (1975). *Notable deaf persons*. Washington, DC: Gallaudet College Alumni Association.

Gallaher, J. E. (1898). *Representative deaf persons of the United States of America*. Chicago: Gallaher.

Lang, H. G. (1994). *Silence of the spheres: The deaf experience in the history of science*. Westport, CT: Bergin & Garvey.

Smithsonian Institution Archives, Record Unit 26, Correspondence between James H. Logan and Joseph Henry.

M

EUGENIE MARLITT (1825–1887), German Writer.

Eugenie John was born on December 5, 1825, in Arnstadt (Thüringen), Germany. She was the daughter of an unsuccessful tradesman, who in his own bitterness offered no support for her interest in becoming an artist. John was talented in singing as a child and captured the interest of a local choir leader, who helped her develop her voice. At the age of sixteen, her parents, whose primary interest in her singing was economic, asked for help from Duchess Mathilde von Schwarzburg-Sondershausen, known for her patronage of the arts. The Duchess invited the young girl to visit, and there she learned to play the piano and sing on stage. After two years at the Vienna Conservatoire, John returned to Leipzig to make her debut in 1846. She was appointed a private court singer in Sonderhausen and performed in many cities, including Linz, Graz, and Lemberg. On her tours, she was afflicted with almost-paralyzing stage fright, which no amount of experience or number of positive reviews seemed to allay. She may have had a premonition that her stellar career was slipping away rapidly. After she developed fevers from a chill while traveling, her hearing plummeted. A progressive deafness begun in childhood forced her to abandon music. John was heartbroken, and the Duchess sought medical help from specialists all over Europe. The experience was a nightmare for the sensitive young woman, who, fully trained for operatic singing, was forced to abandon a promising profession.

The kindly Duchess nevertheless continued to provide steadfast support for her friend, taking her into her home and encouraging her to accompany her while traveling. In this capacity, John served as a reading companion. The life of the court, society gossip, and meeting the rich and famous stimulated John's imagination. She began to construct plots and invent stories in the romantic atmosphere of the medieval town and castle. After years developing her own writing skills while serving with the court, John moved in with her brother, Alfred. She requested leave of the Duchess and began to devote herself to writing. In 1859, encouraged by another writer named Bodenstedt, as well as her brother, she completed her first manuscripts for *The Schoolmaster's Daughter* (1859) and *The Twelve Apostles* (1865). *The Twelve Apostles* was published under the pen name ''Eugenie Marlitt'' in *Die Gartenlaube*, a popular family magazine. The editor, E. Keil, sensed her potential immediately, and he contracted with her for exclusive rights to her publications. Marlitt's financial security was assured, to the relief of her father and brother. The novel *Gold Elsie* (1867) was published next, and her reputation led to an impressive increase in subscriptions, with *Die Gartenlaube* doubling its original printing of 175,000 copies. Marlitt's work became so popular among readers that by 1890, *Gold Elsie* had reached its twenty-third edition in German alone. Her novels *Bluebeard* (1866), *Old Mamselle's Secret* (1868), and *Thüringer Stories* (1869) brought her further fame. Her Gothic style led many to compare her work to Charlotte Brontë's *Jane Eyre*, but Marlitt denied ever having read Brontë's work. One of her plays, *Fay*, was copyrighted in the United States in 1871. That same year, she moved in with her father to her childhood home. Calcification of joints, which had begun many years earlier, eventually confined her to a wheelchair, but over the next decade she continued to produce more novels, including *Countess Gisela, The Second Wife, The Little Moorland Princess, At the Councillor's*, and *The Bailiff's Maid*, which were translated into many languages, including French, English, Russian, Italian, Polish, and Spanish; later they were printed in Chinese and Japanese.

Marlitt could tell archetypal stories creatively and with excitement. Many were variations of her own favorite story, Cinderella. Social and economic problems were raised, but true love defeated them in the world Marlitt created. There are different perspectives on her work and its meaning. On one hand, some critics see her romanticism as a nineteenth-century form of ''kitsch.'' On the other hand, her work has been classified as a significant representation of women's light fiction of that period. The content of popular fiction in general has been debated for years as serious or trivial. Marlitt's own stories were often simple, but held social implications.

With the death of her father in 1873, and that of her editor and friend, E. Keil, in 1878, Marlitt's heart was heavy. It was not until 1884 that she published her next work, *The Lady with the Rubies*, and for the next two years she made progress on *The Owl's Nest* (*Das Eulenhaus*).

Eugenie Marlitt died on June 22, 1887. *Das Eulenhaus*, completed by Wilhelmine Heimburg, was published the year after John's death. After the trauma of losing her first career, Marlitt had the fulfillment of extraordinary overnight success as a writer and the satisfaction of knowing she brought pleasure to readers around the world.

References

Buchanan-Brown, J. (Ed.). (1973). Eugenie Marlitt. In *Cassell's encyclopedia of world literature* (Vol. 3, p. 125). New York: William Morrow.

Sarter, E. (1938). Career woman—nineteenth century. *Volta Review, 40* (9), 515–518, 540.

THOMAS SCOTT MARR (1866–1936), American Architect.

Thomas Scott Marr was born on October 20, 1866, in Nashville, Tennessee, the son of a banker. He was deafened by scarlet fever shortly after birth. As a six-year-old child, he sat for hours watching the stonemasons construct the Old Federal Building on Eighth Avenue, dreaming of one day becoming an architect. Marr attended public schools, but made little progress. He had the frustrating experience of remaining in the second grade for three years. At the age of eleven, when he first enrolled in the Tennessee School for the Deaf in Knoxville, he had not yet learned to add; but he quickly caught up with other children his age, studying such courses as algebra and Latin. He then attended Gallaudet College, where he graduated in 1889; he started his career one week later as a draftsman with a small architectural firm. While at Gallaudet, he roomed with and befriended Cadwallader Washburn* and Olof Hanson.* He took additional courses at the Massachusetts Institute of Technology in 1892, but financial difficulties the following year forced him to leave. Within several years, Marr had saved up $500, which he used to establish his own firm in Nashville. His deafness and preference not to speak at first made it a challenge to communicate with his clients, and most of his early business was residential in nature.

In 1904, Marr met a thirteen-year-old boy selling *Saturday Evening Post*s, and he hired him as an office boy. Joseph W. Holman, Sr., worked in Marr's office for years, learning architectural work and business management. In 1910, Marr established a partnership with Holman. Together, they were commissioned to design the Broadway National Bank, the Cotton States Building, and the Sam Davis Hotel, all in Nashville. Governor McAllister of Tennessee and members of the board chose Marr and Holman as architects for the State Supreme Court Building. By 1936, the firm had designed numerous hospitals, school buildings, a county jail, the Nashville Post Office, the Warner Building, the twelve-story Andrew Jackson Hotel, the War Memorial Building, and the James Robertson Hotel. They were also the builders of the West End apartments, the Knickerbocker Theatre, the Princess Theatre, and an office of the Ford Motor Company. Marr and Holman also designed many buildings in Columbia, Clarksville, Fayetteville, Chattanooga, and Sewanee, Tennessee. While the firm became known for its elegant, contemporary Art Deco style, Marr displayed versatility and adaptability to different environments. Marr's Colonial design for the Tennessee School for the Deaf was particularly admired.

The U.S. Post Office designed by Marr and Holman was approved soon after Franklin D. Roosevelt entered the White House. The building required one hundred carloads of Tennessee rose and black marble and granite. President Roosevelt and Secretary Ickes personally visited the Post Office to see first hand the deaf architect's use of aluminum and glass panels arranged on both sides of a two-hundred-foot by twenty-five-foot lobby. The interior design depicted the progress of the nation in agriculture, industry, music, sciences, education, and other areas. Marr was content with Holman handling many of the business transactions while he concentrated primarily on the architectural design, as well as supervised draftspersons. Marr's work was recognizable for his use of stone ornaments, limestone window sills and copings, and parapet walls.

Through the years, Marr and Holman found it necessary to hire engineers to help handle the increasing volume of work. These engineers included several who eventually made names for themselves, such as Madison P. Jones and Richard S. Reynolds; Reynolds became an important part of the success of the Marr and Holman firm from 1923 until well past Marr's death. Marr spent short vacations at his cottage, "Marr's Hill," at the resort of Beersheba. He never married. Marr continued to work full days in "retirement."

Marr died of a stroke on March 2, 1936, at the age of sixty-nine.

References

Boatner, E. B. (1936). Thomas Scott Marr. *The Nebraska Journal, 65* (7), 1–2.
Chandler, J. B. (1929). Thomas Scott Marr, Architect. *The Silent Worker, 41* (5), 182–185.
Howard, J. L. (no date). History of Marr & Holman, Architects, Nashville, Tennessee. Gallaudet University Archives.
Mannes, J. P. (1987). Thomas Scott Marr. In J. V. Van Cleve (Ed.), *Gallaudet encyclopedia of deaf people and deafness* (Vol. 2, pp. 204–205). New York: McGraw-Hill.

JAMES C. MARSTERS (1924–   ), American Dentist/Inventor.

James C. Marsters was born on April 5, 1924, in Norwich, New York. The cause of his deafness was maternal rubella supplemented by scarlet fever at the age of three months. He attended elementary school in Norwich with additional instruction after school, then transferred to the Wright Oral School for the Deaf in New York City, where he graduated in 1943. Marsters entered an accelerated wartime educational program at Union College in Schenectady, New York, earning his bachelor's degree in 1947. After graduating from Union College, Marsters moved to New York City where, unable to find better employment, he took a position with a necktie fabric converting firm. After a year in this position, his employer, noting that he was bright, energetic, and enjoyed people, encouraged Marsters to consider a profession such as dentistry. During this period, Marsters was also actively involved with the Midtown Manhattan Supper Club, a group of deaf people led by the deaf artist Robert Swain, who invited such notables as Eleanor Roosevelt and author Edna Ferber to speak after dinner. The deaf members would then engage in wide-ranging, intense discussions about the topics into the early morning hours. Marsters' social nature, as well as his aspirations, suffered from an invention most people look upon as a convenience. His frustrated attempts to use the telephone for professional and social conversations through interpreters or through coding systems planted in his mind an early determination to do something about a barrier that all deaf people faced.

Marsters' attempts to apply to dental schools immediately met with resistance. He was turned down by all of them. He then took the entrance examination for the New York University College of Dentistry and his scores were so impressive that the Dental School Admissions Board immediately called him in for an interview. At first, they encouraged him to consider other fields of study, but he argued that he did not want the isolation of laboratory research. Having never heard of a deaf dentist, his interviewers still turned him down. Characteristically, Marsters persisted, and New York University admitted him on probation the following year.

Marsters met with more resistance when seeking financial help from the New York State Department of Vocations. At first they thought his chances of being accepted to the program were slim, but when he told them he had already been admitted, they agreed to pay for his tuition. During his years of study at New York University, he attended large classes, some with as many as 150 students, and at times found it necessary to pretend he was hard-of-hearing. He believed it would lessen the concern of his professors if they thought he could hear them at least a little. Using a hearing aid for effect, which did not help him, his real strategies were speechreading, the use of notes from his peers, and extra library work.

Upon graduation from the New York University College of Dentistry, Marsters passed the dental licensing examinations for the states of New York and California. Dr. Edwin Nies, the first licensed deaf dentist, offered him his office as Dr. Nies was retiring to the ministry, but Marsters preferred to practice in California. He worked in an orthodontic specialty office in Clayton, Missouri, until he was accepted for graduate work at the University of Southern California Dental School in Los Angeles. While studying there, he took over the office of a dentist who had died; and, with that dentist's very supportive nurse, he continued a successful general practice for several years. After completing a master's degree and acquiring an Orthodontic Specialty Certification, Marsters established his own office in Pasadena, where he practiced until his retirement in 1990. All through these years, he socialized with other dentists and remained active in general dental and orthodontic societies. Marsters believed socializing with his colleagues helped as much as professional meetings to keep him current with his field. He also lectured and conducted clinics at the University of Southern California and presented papers to dental societies.

Marsters valued consistent engagement in conversations on a personal level with patients and, in the case of children, their parents. He wanted to be viewed as a receptive and caring dentist who was truly interested in the health and welfare of each person who came into his office. To accomplish this as a profoundly deaf person, he felt, required extra effort and the creation of a certain environment. In his office, he had several nurses, one of whom would serve, when necessary, as an oral interpreter, standing behind the patient and carefully repeating the patient's spoken words in order that Marsters could speechread during dental work.

For several years, Marsters served as a Senior Dental Examiner on the California Dental Licensing Board. He also chaired various committees in dental societies. An accomplished pilot, he had a second office for two decades in Lone Pine, in northern California, where he would fly in his private plane and provide dental services to mostly cattle ranching people; he would then enjoy a few hours of fishing afterwards. He would also provide free services to patients in need.

Marsters visits many schools, discussing teaching methods and demonstrating through personal example how an effective education can lead to success in any career. In 1963, he established the Guy L. Marsters and Annabelle Marsters Fund, in honor of his parents, for the activation of the Oral Deaf Adults Section (now the Oral Hearing Impaired Section) of the Alexander Graham Bell Association for the Deaf, a service group which works with parents, teachers, and deaf children. In 1964, Marsters presented the keynote address at the Alexander Graham Bell Association for the Deaf biennial meeting, the first deaf person to do so in the organization's 74-year history. He was named by John W. Gardner, the U.S. Secretary of Health, Education, and Welfare, to serve on the National Advisory Committee in the Education of the Deaf and received the United Crusade's Outstanding Service Award. He is a Fellow of the American College of Dentistry and the International College of Dentistry. He has also served as a member of the National Advisory Group for the National Technical Institute for the Deaf at the Rochester Institute of Technology in Rochester, New York.

Along with a successful career as an orthodontist, Marsters is recognized in the Deaf community for his significant role as a pioneer in bringing access to the telephone for deaf people. In 1964, he recruited Robert H. Weitbrecht,* a deaf physicist working at the Stanford Research Institute, and Andrew Saks, a deaf engineer and businessman, to collaborate with him in conducting research and development of a device that would allow deaf people to use the telephone through teletypewriters. The three deaf men invested their own time and money, working for many years to accomplish a seemingly impossible dream of bringing the telephone into the lives of deaf people. The challenge involved bringing together various factions of the Deaf community, representatives of major corporations such as AT&T and Western Union, and hundreds of volunteers from the Telephone Pioneers of America and other groups, to rebuild and distribute discarded teletypewriters, train people to maintain them, establish networks, and convince reluctant disbelievers that the task could be accomplished. Today, thanks to the impetus provided by Marsters, Weitbrecht and Saks, these obsolete machines have been replaced by compact electronic devices, and federal legislation has assisted in providing a range of services so that the telephone is much less a barrier in social and work environments for deaf people.

Reminiscing on his fulfilling career as a dentist and advocate, Marsters said, "I look back with pleasure and satisfaction at time well-spent serving the public and fellow men."

Reference

Myhers, J. (1961, March 6). Pasadena dentist refused to let deafness hamper his active life. *Independent Star News*.

FÉLIX MARTIN (1844–1917), French Sculptor.

Félix Martin was born deaf on June 2, 1844, in Nevilly-sur-Seine. His grandfather was a Deputy and his uncle a Mayor of Orleans. He was at first provided some instruction at home, then enrolled in the National Institute for the Deaf in Paris at the age of eleven. He then studied at the School of Fine Arts, where he was a pupil of Duret, Larson, and Cavelier, and showed great ability. Martin won many medals and prizes, and began to exhibit his sculptures in the Paris Salon at the age of twenty. In 1865, he won Le Grande Medaille Pour LaTete d'Espression. In 1869, he won the Second Grand Prix de Rome for his bas-relief *Alexander the Great* and his *Doctor Phillipe*. In 1873, in an open competition Martin was selected one of the laureates for his statue of Figaro. By the time he was thirty years old, he was made a Chevalier of the Legion of Honor by the French Government. The Order of Isabelle la Catholique was also conferred upon him by the Spanish Government. In 1889, he was again decorated with a medal at the Paris Exposition.

The French State purchased many of Martin's statues and presented them to museums in Rouen, Senlis, and other towns. Other sculptures by Martin were erected at public parks, squares, and town halls in many large cities of France, including Paris. Among these are the marble bust of Picare in the foyer of the National Theatre of the Opera, and a bronze statue of him in the foyer of Odéon. Seven of his works are in the Museum of the National Institution for the Deaf in Paris.

Many consider Martin's masterpiece to be the statue of the Abbé de l'Epée teaching a young deaf boy, which he donated to the Court of Honor of the National Institution for the Deaf in May, 1879. The deaf biographer Yvonne Pitrois* called it "the most popular monument in the silent world." As with many other French deaf people, Martin felt a spiritual affinity to Epée, as well as a personal debt, as a successful deaf artist. Since Epée was extremely modest, accurate likenesses of him were scarce, and painstaking research was required. Martin began studying available portraits of the Abbé—a miniature in color and several sketches, a large painting by Ponce Camus, and Claude-André Deseine's* bust. Three bas-reliefs on the pedestal portray episodes of Epée's life. One represents the twin sisters who became Epée's first pupils after Father Vanin had tried to educate them. The second panel illustrates Epée's resistance to leave his school to serve the Emperor Joseph II; and the third bas-relief on the pedestal portrays the elderly Abbé sacrificing heat in his own room during a winter when the children's hall barely had enough fuel. That statue was also exhibited at the Paris Salon in 1878, as well as at the International Exhibition. Martin's sculpture has Epée looking down at the deaf pupil, making a sign. Some critics believe it is the French sign for "God" ("Dieu"), while others believe it is merely the letter "d." After its unveiling by the French Minister of the Interior, Monsieur Le Pere, Martin was awarded the Ribbon of the Knight's Cross of the Legion of Honor. With this honor, he followed in the footsteps of the deaf leader Ferdinand Berthier.*

Martin continued to exhibit many works in the Paris Salons over the next few decades, including a bust of *Pére Didon* (1901), the celebrated Dominican, a statuette *Une Leçon d'humanité* (1903), and *Hommage á Claude Deseine, premier sculpteur sourd-muet* (1906). Two of the statues adorning the facades of the Hotel de Ville (City Hall of Paris) came from Martin's hands. Although Martin gained considerable recognition as a painter as well, exhibiting many works, he joined Paul François Choppin,* Choppin's distinguished pupil, Félix Plessis, and other Frenchmen in establishing great respectability for the deaf artists as sculptors in the Paris Salons of the late nineteenth century.

Martin died on January 4, 1917. Many of his deaf friends in the French art community, among them Choppin, Olivier Chéron, Gustave Hennequin, and Georges Ferry, paid him lasting tributes in the forms of paintings and sculpted statues and medallions.

Reference

Legrand, A. (1917). M. Felix Martin (1844–1917). *Revue Générale de L'Enseignement des sourds-muets, 18* (4), 59–60.

HARRIET MARTINEAU (1802–1876), British Writer.

Harriet Martineau was born on June 12, 1802, in Norwich, England, where her Huguenot ancestors had settled. She was the sixth of eight children, frail and nervous, and starved for affection from her mother, who was outwardly critical and harsh. Her father was a manufacturer of dress goods. Even her loving brother, two years older, did not consider her very bright or clever, although he recognized that she possessed an extraordinary power of observation. Deprived of her sense of smell and taste since infancy, her hearing having begun to deteriorate around the age of twelve, it is no wonder that Martineau remarked in her later years that her early life was sad and lacking in normal childhood joys.

Martineau's earliest writing experiences were at weekly teas on Sunday evenings at a pastor's house, where the clergyman's family and friends took time to write recollections of the day's sermons, a practice that continued for young Harriet until she grew too deaf to maintain attention. During subsequent years at these readings, she was assigned the role of reader on account of her hearing loss. Her deafness increased considerably at the age of eighteen, a result of "what might be called an accident," but about which she offered little explanation. It became so heavy a burden that she avoided visitors and parties, repelled by people shouting and gesturing at her. Later, she reminisced that she had thought of writing down "the whole dreary story" of loss of a sense. But other matters preoccupied her; although she always allowed that she might do that book, if others could benefit from it. Largely self-educated, she found her greatest pleasure and therapy in reading. Milton's *Paradise Lost* changed her life in the inspiration it provided. From Milton she turned to Shakespeare. She learned poetry by heart, and even developed an interest in arithmetic. Religion also brought satisfaction to her. When her family's fortune took a turn for the worse, and her brother, father, and a man with whom she had a relationship died within a few years' time, she pursued writing in order to make a living. Martineau remained unmarried throughout her life.

At the age of eighteen, Martineau published her first article, "Female Writers on Practical Divinity," in *The Monthly Repository*, a small Unitarian magazine; and, motivated by her brother's reaction when it came out, she immediately started her second essay. She began to publish in many periodicals, such as the *Westminster Review* and *Penny Magazine*.

Martineau found great dissatisfaction with societal expectations for a young woman her age, preferring intellectual development to the "domestic arts." As a young woman, she was assigned a position by her mother to serve as a companion to an elderly lady in London who, although pleasant, disapproved of Martineau's early morning hours spent writing when she could be learning to sew; and her mother soon called her home. Her persistence was rewarded soon after, fortunately. Around 1832, she began to write *Illustrations of Political Economy*, instructive essays that brought her instant success. One, *French Wine and Politics*, pertaining to the French Revolution, offended the French government. Another, *The Charmed Sea*, led the Czar of Russia to demand the burning of her writings; and the controversy made her popular among loyal British contemporaries, among them Robert Owens, Princess Victoria, and the Duchess of Kent. Martineau refused to be moderate or to appease. She rose quickly from obscurity to celebrity, enjoying the irony of being a little deaf woman treated as a person of consequence. Following the three controversial essays mentioned, she wrote *Illustrations of Taxation* and *Illustrations of Poor Laws*. She produced thirty-four volumes in thirty months. Importantly, one of these tales was *Demerara*, in which she discussed and portrayed slavery in British Guiana. It was time, she decided, for a holiday.

Encouraged by Lord Henley to consider America, Martineau left for the United States in August 1834, accompanied by her friend Louisa Jeffery, who could act as an interpreter and travel-planner for her distracted companion. Arriving on a warm September day in New York, she was immediately disappointed with the living conditions she observed on Broadway. She traveled to Philadelphia, then onto Washington, warned by many of her fans who had read *Demerara* that she should not visit the Southern states.

Invited to dinner by the President, the Attorney-General, the Secretary of the Treasury, and many other American dignitaries, she faced the question "How do you like America?" nearly every day for two years. Although she avoided discussion of slavery during the early months of her tour, she had been labeled

Harriet Martineau, British writer.
Photo from M. W. Chapman
(1877), *Harriet Martineau's Autobiography*, vol. 1 (Boston: J.
R. Osgood).

an abolitionist from the start and was slowly drawn into the issue as the days
passed. Finally, she spoke to one hundred and thirty women at a ladies' meeting
of the Abolition Society. There, she flatly affirmed that she considered slavery
incompatible with the laws of God—and that she had said the same thing to
every one of her southern friends. She subsequently remained indifferent to
threats she received, many with disparaging remarks about her deafness, and
she continued to write ardently even in the face of possible violence. She published two works based on this visit, *Society in America* and *A Retrospect of
Western Travel*.

Martineau's narratives of American experiences were enthusiastically received
in England. Her first novel, *Deerbrook*, came out in 1839. Among the book's
admirers was Charlotte Brontë, who later sent an autographed copy of her own
book *Shirley* to Martineau with a note about the "genuine benefit" *Deerbrook*
had brought her. Martineau also wrote stories for children, such as *Five Years
of Youth*, and travelogues, including two works on the Holy Land. She published
in Dickens' magazine (Dickens referred to her as "the little deaf woman of
Norwich"). But illness soon confined her to her house for five years (1839 to
1844), a period during which she wrote *Life in a Sick-room* and her great novel,
The Hour and the Man (1840), the story of Toussaint L'Ouverture, the slave
leader of the revolution in Haiti. This was followed by four children's stories

still widely read today, *Settlers at Home*, *The Prince and the Peasant*, *Feats on the Fjord*, and *The Crofton Boys*.

When Martineau was introduced to mesmerism, she claimed that seances helped her to recover from her illness. Her friendship with Henry Atkinson, twelves years her junior, led to the co-authorship of *Letters on Man's Nature and Development*. This work, and her *Letters on Mesmerism*, provoked world-wide criticism. Even her devoted brother, now a well-known writer himself, severely criticized her writing and the two of them drifted apart for the remainder of their lives.

Much later, she described the many ways in which deafness influenced her life, her perceptions on the education of deaf children in the school and at home, and the attendant eye fatigue, an "important truth" seldom understood well by others. In her *Letter to the Deaf*, published in 1834, she encouraged others to face the challenge with equanimity: "The worst is either to sink under the trial [of deafness] or to be made callous by it. The best is to be as wise as possible under a great disability, and as happy as possible under a great privation."

Repeated embarrassing experiences associated with her hearing loss over a period of ten years finally led her to use the ear trumpet, which became her trademark: "My deafness was terribly in the way . . . very few people spoke to me; and I dare say I looked as if I did not wish to be spoken to." All this changed when she moved from Norwich to London and learned to use her trumpet more effectively. Nonetheless, she never fully accepted the ear trumpet. Practical vanity held sway, for example, when, at the coronation of Victoria Regina, Martineau would not use the trumpet for fear that it would disarrange her lace cap.

In her middle years, Martineau designed her first home in Ambleside with a beautiful garden and view of the countryside. Here, on "The Knoll," she wrote *Game Law Tales*, which brought her profit and further fame. She chose her servants carefully and educated them. Constantly harassed by her fans and unable to hear their approach, she would sometimes look up from her writing to find their faces pressed against the window glass staring at her.

She responded to a flood of letters from working-class readers who admired her liberalism. Wealthy friends invited her to travel and this, too, expanded her writing interests. After eight months in Palestine in 1848, she wrote *Eastern Life, Past and Present*. *Letters of Political Interest in Ireland* came after her tour of that country and documented her concern for the troubles there. She translated Auguste Comte's six-volume *Positive Philosophy* into two smaller volumes; and this English version was so appreciated by Comte that he wrote and expressed his gratitude. Her *Autobiography* was written during her last years and was perhaps influenced by her trying period with heart trouble. Martineau's final years were spent writing to local children, telling them stories, and providing support to others in need.

Martineau died in Amberside, England, on June 27, 1876.

References

Bosanquet, T. (1927). *Harriet Martineau: An essay in comprehension.* London: Frederick
   Etchells & Hugh Macdonald.
Chapman, M. W. (Ed.). (1877). *Harriet Martineau's autobiography* (Vol. 1–2). Boston:
   James R. Osgood.
Martineau, H. (1834). Letter to the deaf. *Tait's Edinburgh Magazine* (reprinted in *The
   Volta Review,* *15* (5), 1913, pp. 219–227).
Nevill, J. C. (1973). *Harriet Martineau.* London: Frederick Muller.

MARLEE MATLIN (1965–   ), American Actress.

Marlee Matlin was born on August 24, 1965, in Morton Grove, Illinois. She
was deafened by roseola at the age of eighteen months. Matlin attended public
schools and took private lessons in Hebrew from Rabbi Douglas Goldhammer
at Bene Shalom of the Deaf. She also performed in children's theater as early
as seven years old with the Center on Deafness in Chicago. She played "Dorothy" in *The Wizard of Oz* (1974), and performed in *Mary Poppins* and *Peter
Pan* as the small company traveled through Illinois, Nebraska, and Indiana. At
the age of thirteen, Matlin won second prize in the Chicago Center's Annual
International Creative Arts Festival for an essay titled, "If I Was a Movie Star."
In the precocious essay, she set her goals, pragmatically including a huge house,
letters from fans, limousines, and giving everyone her best smile on stage. The
competitive world of acting, however, disillusioned her and she planned a career
in criminal justice as she began attending Harper Junior College in Palatine,
Illinois.

Matlin was playing the secondary role of "Lydia" in Mark Medoff's *Children
of a Lesser God* on a Chicago stage when she was invited to audition for the
screen adaptation. The deaf actress Phyllis Frelich* had won a Tony Award in
1980 for the Broadway version. During the international search for an actress
to play "Sarah," thousands of photographs were rejected. Although Matlin's
photograph was one of them, she was discovered standing in the background in
the videotape of the Chicago performance. She was then flown to New York
for an audition with William Hurt and hired after additional readings in Los
Angeles. In 1986, Matlin became the youngest Academy Award winner in the
Best Actress category at the age of twenty-one, as well as the first deaf Oscar
winner. She won over such stars as Jane Fonda, Sigourney Weaver, Sissy Spa-
cek, and Kathleen Turner.

Reviews of *Children of a Lesser God* varied. In the *Chicago Tribune,* Dave
Kehr summarized Matlin's "intense, burning presence" in a film that he considered a failed attempt to accurately demonstrate how deaf people feel and act.
In the *Chicago Sun-Times,* Roger Ebert felt the film fell short in giving hearing
viewers the same experience deaf people have in seeing scenes as members of
a silent world. Some deaf people expressed disappointment that much of the
sign language was cut off by the cameras. Only ten of the 215 theaters in the
country carrying the film had subtitled versions for deaf viewers. The film was

generally highly praised by many critics for the metaphors used to symbolize the barriers people experience in realizing successful relationships. Matlin's fiery performance as a rebellious deaf woman, moreover, was universally lauded. Matlin and Hurt continued a relationship for some time after the film.

Matlin's film success opened the doors for other deaf actors. She also visited with school children, including at the Chicago Center on Deafness, where she had started her acting career. In May 1987, she left for Nicaragua for the filming of *Walker*. William Walker was a nineteenth-century American adventurer who invaded Nicaragua in 1855 with fifty-eight men, became president of the country, and in 1860, was executed by a Honduran firing squad. The film, based on true historical events, starred American actor Ed Harris as Walker. Matlin played Walker's fiancee, "Ellen Martin," a deaf woman who died of cholera early in the story. Her death contributes to Walker's emotional instability.

In the 1989 CBS movie *Bridge to Silence*, Matlin portrayed "Peggy Lawrence," an assertive deaf woman whose husband dies in an automobile accident and whose parents are entrusted with the care of her four-year-old daughter while she herself recovers from the accident. Her mother, played by Lee Remick, attempting to gain guardianship over the child, is the source of the conflict in this film, which emphasizes the ignorance that leads many people to stereotype deaf individuals. Matlin served as consultant on the original script. Her idol, Phyllis Frelich, appeared in it as her close friend.

In September 1991, the NBC series *Reasonable Doubts* made its debut with Matlin starring as "Tess Kaufman," a deaf lawyer playing opposite Mark Harmon as "Richard Cobb," a police investigator. The script originally did not include a deaf woman, but producer Robert Singer revised his plans to accommodate Matlin, including making Cobb the son of deaf parents so that he would know sign language and be able to interpret at times. The series maintained moderate ratings and Matlin was nominated for a Golden Globe Award for best actress in a dramatic series. Some viewers were concerned that the too-perfect speechreading ability of "Tess Kaufman" might create false expectations. Others felt the show provided a visible role model, helping young deaf men and women to aspire toward such a career.

Matlin has been a strong advocate for the rights of deaf people, accepting television roles only if producers commit to caption the films, remaining open-minded and respectful of both signed and spoken communication preferences, and promoting telephone equipment specially designed for deaf persons. She has testified before the Senate Committee on Labor and Human Resources in support of the establishment of the National Institute on Deafness and Communication Disorders. Matlin has also been active in the fight against AIDS, the "Victory Awards" for the National Rehabilitation Hospital, and other causes.

In 1991, Matlin received the Bernard Bragg* Young Artists Achievement Award at the Annual International Creative Arts Festival sponsored by the Center on Deafness in Chicago. In 1993, she married Kevin Grandalski, a Los Angeles policeman. The same year, she starred in the film *Hear No Evil*. She

Marlee Matlin, American actress. Photo courtesy of the National Technical Institute for the Deaf.

was nominated for two Emmy awards for guest appearances on programs in the 1993–94 television season. And, on the June 9, 1994 episode of *Disney's Adventures in Wonderland*, Matlin appeared in a rabbit's nose, whiskers, and ears as "April Hare," a deaf rabbit, who teaches sign language after the Red Queen forbids talking. Jeff Silverman of the *New York Times* has written that Matlin is unencumbered as a deaf actress: "she compensates with body language and tremendous facial expression. And that comes across very strong, both on film and in life."

References

Kehr, D. (1986, October 3). Director keeps world of the deaf at arm's length. *Chicago Tribune*.

Moritz, C. (Ed.) (1992). Marlee Matlin. *Current biography*, *53* (5), 41–45.

Sanoff, A. P., Hawkins, S., & Quick, B. (1987, April 5). Vital new roles for hearing impaired actors. *San Francisco Chronicle*.

Silverman, J. (1992, January 5). Marlee Matlin, conquering reasonable doubts. *New York Times*, 31–32.

Walker, L. A. (1989, April). Marlee Matlin: Breaking the silence. *Ladies' Home Journal*, 42–44, 48.

FLORENCE LEWIS MAY (1899–1988), American Writer/Curator.

Florence Lewis May was born on December 9, 1899, in Fairfield, Connecticut. She was deafened from spinal meningitis when she was five years old. May entered the American School for the Deaf in West Hartford, Connecticut, in 1906 and graduated in 1915. She then enrolled at Gallaudet College and earned a bachelor's degree in 1921. During her college years, May was active in dramatics. She also took three years of library training, which she found of inestimable value in her later work. She would advocate for greater attention to library education throughout her life.

Immediately following graduation from Gallaudet, she found employment as an assistant in the museum department of the Hispanic Society of America in New York City. The Society, established by philanthropist Archer Huntington, had been particularly interested in hiring deaf women for several years. Huntington's efforts were rewarded, when May, Eleanor Sherman Font, Alice McVan,* Margaret Jackson,* and other deaf women distinguished themselves in the Society and their respective fields over the decades to follow. May herself spent her entire career at the Society, retiring in 1981 after sixty years of service. She had advanced from her first position as an assistant to First Museum Cataloguer, Assistant Curator, and then to Curator of Textiles.

May completed her first book, the *Catalogue of Laces and Embroideries*, in 1936. In this work, she presented the terminology and history of Spanish lace. In an issue of *The Museum Journal* that year, G. F. Digby described the wealth of material as scholarly and well-documented.

In 1938, May contributed two sections, "Textiles" and "Laces and Embroideries," to the *Handbook: Museum and Library Collections.* She also published numerous articles and book reviews over the years in *Pantheon*, *Apollo*, and *Notes Hispanic.* That year, she was also listed as one of seventeen translators (with her deaf colleagues Alice J. McVan and Eleanor Sherman Font) in *Translations from Hispanic Poets.* Her second book, *Hispanic Lace and Lace Making*, was published in 1939. In this work, she included 432 illustrations on 417 pages, tracing the history and technique of the art in a detailed and comprehensive manner. To write this book, May mastered the Spanish language and traveled several times to Spain, touring the great museums and studying in depth the crafts of small villages. In 1940, she was temporarily distracted from her scholarly work at the Society when she was invited by the producer of the original Broadway play *Johnny Belinda* to teach sign language to actress Helen Craig. May was actually offered the leading role herself. Although she had been attracted to acting in college, performing in nearly every production during her stay at Gallaudet, she declined the offer, happy to have steady employment at the Hispanic Society.

May contributed to *A History of the Hispanic Society of America*, published by the Society in 1954. Her third book, *Silk Textiles of Spain: Eighth to Fifteenth Century*, was published in 1957. The work combined a history of silk fabrics in Spain from the Umaiyad conquest through the reign of the Catholic kings. May described in detail the weaves and patterns found in the fabrics she studied in the United States, Canada, and Europe, including the silver and gold weaves of Burgos, Toledo, and Sevilla. Her scholarly chronology traced the sources of patterns, sericulture, weaving centers, and regulations for manufacturing and selling textiles. She published "The Textile Collection" in *Apollo* in 1972; in 1977, she published *Rugs of Spain and Morocco*; and, at the time of her death, she was at work on a second volume of *Silk Textiles of Spain.* In addition, she published *The Life of Johannes Brahms* in 1981.

As with several other deaf women at the Hispanic Society, most notably Alice J. McVan, May loved poetry throughout her life, publishing essays and verse such as "Time's Healing," "Masks," and "Winter" in the periodicals of the Deaf community. May also published a biographical sketch of the eminent deaf drypoint etcher Cadwallader Lincoln Washburn.* She and her husband William lived for many years in Garden City, New York, where they raised two children. She was elected a Member of the Hispanic Society of America in 1949, won the Silver Medal of Arts and Literature in 1958, and the Silver Membership Medal in 1971.

May died on September 6, 1988, in Elmira, New York.

References

Collins, E. (1956, January 26). Village Vignettes. *The Garden City News.*
Fischer, M. (1941, March 20). Gallaudet graduate coaches star of "Johnny Belinda," Broadway hit. Gallaudet College *Buff and Blue.*
Florence Lewis May (1988, September 8). [Death Notice]. *Star-Gazette.*

May, F. L. (1940). The deaf woman and books. *American Annals of the Deaf*, 85 (2), 159–163.

GERALD M. McCARTHY (1858–1915), American Entomologist.

Gerald M. McCarthy was born in Ottawa, Illinois, in November 1858, and was totally deafened by meningitis at the age of sixteen. The disease, a leading cause of deafness, also left him with visual and physical disabilities. He completed his high school education at the Illinois School for the Deaf at Jacksonville in 1880, where he communicated personally through writing. Not yet skilled in American Sign Language and unable to participate in athletics due to his disabilities, he turned to reading with a passion. On many occasions, other students were sent to the library in search of the absent-minded youth who frequently missed classes, engrossed in one of the school's 13,000 volumes.

After his graduation from the Illinois School, McCarthy moved for health reasons; and a year later, he found a position as a florist at Shaw's Botanical Gardens in St. Louis, Missouri. This experience opened him to the idea of botany as a career. He entered Gallaudet College, where he completed his Bachelor of Science degree in 1887. At Gallaudet, he became something of a legend, spending his evenings exercising alone in the dark, since the artificial light bothered his eyes. He also avoided social activities and even lectures, when possible.

McCarthy's senior year, 1887, was a very busy one. Based on his research during previous summer vacations and the analysis and categorization of boxes of ferns and other plant specimens he brought back to Gallaudet each fall, he published a book with Thomas F. Wood entitled *Wilmington Flora: A List of Plants Growing about Wilmington, North Carolina, with Date of Flowering, and a Map of Hanover County*. Some of these rare botanical specimens were donated to the Smithsonian Institution; others were sold to foreign societies.

McCarthy was offered a position at the Agricultural Experiment Station at Raleigh that same year. He was the State Botanist for North Carolina until 1893, when he was nearly killed by a train. His leg was broken in two places, and he injured his back. During this period of U.S. history, people often chose to walk along railroad tracks to avoid the mud of unpaved roads. Many deaf people lost their lives when they failed to hear the oncoming trains. Fortunately, McCarthy recovered from his train accident and continued to sell his collections to correspondents in many countries in Europe, and to publish his papers on seed tests.

McCarthy was offered a similar position as state botanist of Virginia, but declined. He was elected to several scientific societies in Europe in honor of his work. By 1895, as secretary of the North Carolina State Horticultural Society, he had published in its *Annual Report* such topics as "The Peach and Its Enemies" and "Some Injurious Insects." Through the following years, the Gallaudet College *Buff and Blue* reported on some of his other publications, for example, on "The Wild Onion or Garlic" in 1900. Papers by McCarthy appeared on mosquitoes as carriers of disease and on the digger wasp. In a report on "Silk Culture" found in *Bulletin No. 181* of the North Carolina Agricultural Experiment Station in November of 1902, McCarthy provided a description of the history of silk production in the United States, including the natural history, food, and treatment of the silkworm and cocoon. The demand for the article was so great that the Experiment Station asked McCarthy to make a more complete study on the subject.

Shortly after a Republican victory at the polls in 1897, McCarthy and several experienced colleagues were ousted. McCarthy's replacement was apparently unqualified for the position; and the farmers in North Carolina, who had grown to appreciate the deaf scientist's studies of diseases of cotton and tobacco, were indignant at McCarthy's dismissal. But by the time the Democratic party regained control two years later, McCarthy had gone on to work for other government projects. Meanwhile, McCarthy fought fruitlessly for back wages due him. He divided his time between the Boards of Agriculture and Health. For the Board of Health, he conducted monthly analyses of the quality of drinking water. He built up a laboratory, developing new methods of analysis, and providing physicians and citizens free analyses of suspected drinking waters, most likely saving the state much sickness. He also determined the value of water samples for various technical and manufacturing purposes, and assisted physicians with urinalysis and other pathological work. Yet, through the ensuing years, an unbelievable sequence of mistreatment and corruption led him to write a lengthy complaint to the General Assembly. The complaint, which he filed in 1909, was entitled "A Memorial Concerning Thefts and Malpractices of Two North Carolina Boards." He claimed the State owed him his remaining salary and accused the North Carolina Board of Agricultural Trustees and the North Carolina Board of Health of having "broken the good faith of the State, violated contracts, stolen private property and degraded the ermine of the State." In even stronger terms, he continued, "The Board put into my place a worthless character who has since served, or is now serving a term in the State penitentiary."

In this "Memorial," McCarthy detailed the value of his role in the laboratory. In December of 1907, for example, he was out for two weeks, having a surgical operation. Upon his return, he found that the new man who had been placed by the secretary of the Board had analyzed only one sample of water, which he had reported as safe to drink. McCarthy found the sample and, wondering how anyone could analyze it with only a few drops, repeated the analysis, which proved the water to be grossly polluted. He requested a duplicate sample, and his analysis was confirmed. The physician, H. H. Harrison of Mayodan, North Carolina, had submitted the samples, suspicious that the water may have been the source of several cases of typhoid. As he wrote angrily to the Assembly: "The scalawag whom the agricultural Board put into my place in 1897 is today in the State penitentiary; the scalawag and charlatan whom the medical Board put into my place in 1908, deserves to be in the penitentiary, unless the statutes of the State prescribe a heavier penalty for manslaughter!"

McCarthy had earlier succeeded in bringing the Board to court for breach of contract, but the Board pleaded it had no funds to pay the claim. Judge Starbuck, who officiated, could not enforce payment, declaring the violation of the deaf scientist's contract a "piece of rascality." Fortunately, as McCarthy's acerbic and colorful letters of complaint demonstrate, he did not accept the role of a passive victim.

In 1904, McCarthy was listed as being a resident of Illinois. With the exception of his battle with the North Carolina Board, his last decade was largely undocumented, until Ernest Gallaher wrote to the Director of the Department of Agriculture in North Carolina in 1913 and learned that McCarthy was at Skowhegan, Maine. McCarthy died there on September 8, 1915.

References

Braddock, G. C. (1975). *Notable deaf persons.* Washington, DC: Gallaudet College Alumni Association.

Character sketches of prominent deaf persons: Gerald M. McCarthy. (1896). *Alabama Messenger,* 5 (28), 1.

Lang, H. G. (1994). *Silence of the spheres: The deaf experience in the history of science.* Westport, CT: Bergin & Garvey.

ALICE J. McVAN (1906–1970), American Poet/Museum Curator.

Alice J. McVan was born on July 25, 1906, in Pittsburgh, Pennsylvania. Her family moved to Buffalo, New York, when she was eight years old. McVan attended public schools until her early teenage years, when she experienced a severe hearing loss. She then enrolled in St. Mary's School for the Deaf in Buffalo for two years, followed by Gallaudet College, where she graduated in 1928. At Gallaudet College, McVan was a top student, demonstrating her writing talents as the first woman editor of the *Buff and Blue* and winning the prize for the best story of the year. It was known that she had the highest IQ recorded at the College at that time. Nevertheless, she was a modest and very shy person, who shunned public speaking and performance. She was popular, however, both for her humor and for her social conscience.

After graduation from Gallaudet College, McVan taught at St. Mary's School for the Deaf in Buffalo until 1930, when she was offered a position of Assistant Curator of Publications at the Hispanic Society of America in New York City. That year, she was listed with her deaf colleagues Florence Lewis May* and Eleanor Sherman Font as one of the translators in the book *Translations from Hispanic Poets.* She married Karl Bernard Stein in 1938, but the marriage ended, and she preferred to remain single thereafter.

McVan was able to benefit enough from a hearing aid that the device helped her in her interviews with the Society members. During World War II, McVan taught English and citizenship to deaf refugees from Europe in the program sponsored by the New York State Division of Vocational Rehabilitation. Active in the Deaf community, she also published articles in *The Silent Worker* and other periodicals.

McVan traveled to Spain and Portugal in 1952, 1957, and 1963, collecting information for the Society. She published articles on such topics as "The Villafranca Family and a Portrait by Esteve," "The Alameda of the Osunas," and "Spanish Dwarfs." In 1953, McVan published her first book of poems, *Tryst, and Other Poems.* The first ten of the forty-six poems in the book have Spanish themes, such as "Ballad of the Bullfight," and they reveal the love for the Spanish culture she developed over several decades of scholarly study in the Hispanic Society. Over this period of time, McVan delved into the art, history, and literature of Spain and Portugal, translating numerous works for publication, and rising to the rank of Curator. One project, her translation of Gabriela Mistral's poem "Night," was published in the *New York Times* in January 1957. Her translations have also appeared in Hubert Greekmore's *A Little Treasury of World Poetry.* In Barcelona in 1957, the Spanish Deaf community expressed its appreciation for her work by honoring her with a "Ball a la Placa," based on the theme of her poem, "Sardanas en la Plaza San Jaime." The celebration included a program in which some of her poetry was translated into both Spanish Sign Language and dance.

McVan was elected a corresponding member of the Hispanic Society in 1958 and a member in 1966. Among those she interviewed were Dámaso Alonso, Ramón Menéndez Pidal, and Ángela Figuera Aymerich. In 1959, she published *Antonio Machado*, an insightful analysis of the life and works of one of Spain's major poets.

In 1966, poor health forced McVan to retire quietly from the Society. She lived with her sister in St. Louis for a while and died in a nursing home on September 2, 1970.

References

Catuna, D. (undated). Alice Jane McVan, 1906–1970. Gallaudet University Archives.

Kowalewski, F. (1984). Alice Jane McVan: Gifted poet. *The Deaf American, 36* (4), 26–29.

THOMAS MEEHAN (1826–1901), American Botanist.

Thomas Meehan was born deaf in England on March 21, 1826. He was the son of a gardener and began to learn botany from his father at the age of twelve. Within a year, he published his first article and hybridized the Fuchsia, a flowering plant, which he named "St. Clair." He was only fifteen years old when he published his first scientific discovery, "Irritable Stamens in the Flowers of Portulaca grandiflora." Studying late into the night, he advanced his understanding of botany, as well as mastering Greek, Latin, and French. His experiments with plants led to his being elected to membership in the Royal Wernerian Society of Edinburgh while still a young man. Meehan's botanical studies at the Royal Gardens of Kew were complicated by the politics of his day. Sir William Hooker, Director of the Gardens, suspecting that Meehan was associated with the Chartists, workers who called for social and political reform in the late

1830s, subjected the deaf botanist to annoyances such as consigning him to duty in the cactus greenhouse. Meehan refused to leave until he was awarded a certificate. This he received in the year of his departure to America at the age of twenty-two. During this experience, however, Meehan acquired much knowledge about cacti, and later in his life he attributed his becoming friends with another naturalized American and world authority on cacti, George Engelmann, to Hooker's "act of disfavor."

Meehan arrived in the United States a few months before the great deaf paleobotanist, Leo Lesquereux.* In Philadelphia, he quickly found the position as a gardener at the nurseries of Robert Buist, then as superintendent of John Bartram's Garden owned by Andrew M. Eastwick. In 1852, he moved to Holmesburg, Pennsylvania, where he was responsible for the grounds and conservatories of Caleb Cope. There, Meehan became especially interested in growing the *Victoria regia* from seed obtained from Kew Gardens. He married Catherine Colflesh, the daughter of a farmer and florist in Kingsessing, and they raised a large family. Over the next year, with encouragement from William Darlington to extend the scope of his work, Meehan published *The American Handbook of Ornamental Trees*, most of the book written in an old potting shed in Bartram's Garden. He lost everything during the Civil War, but he eventually succeeded in expanding his own nurseries and edited the *Gardner's Monthly*, *Meehan's Monthly*, *Forney's Weekly Press*, and other magazines.

In general, Meehan did not let deafness stop him from involvement in scientific societies. He was a man of powerful build and left his mark through hundreds of contributions, many of which provoked controversy as well as further researches. Charles Darwin himself, in criticizing an article by Meehan, wrote on May 13, 1878 to tell him "Such a manner of treating the work of other observers did not appear to me the way to encourage truth." While Meehan's views may have antagonized many botanists, however, he was acknowledged for his philanthropy and public-spiritedness.

Meehan's correspondence with Darwin generally was a courteous exchange of scientific views interspersed with disagreement. In 1874, Darwin wrote to Meehan and encouraged him to continue his "interesting researches" on the colors of dioecious flowers. But, when Meehan published a paper in 1875 on his views denying the importance of fertilization of plants by insects, Darwin and others differed. Even when Meehan felt he had adequately changed his perspective, Darwin did not agree, and they had a more serious falling out. Seven years later, though, Meehan presented a paper titled "Variations in Nature: A contribution to the doctrine of evolution, and the theory of natural selection" at the annual meeting of the American Association for the Advancement of Science, in which he expressed strong support for Darwin's theory and emphasized that there was no conflict between the theory of natural selection and the doctrines of Christianity.

In 1860, the Academy of Natural Sciences of Philadelphia elected him to membership. In 1868, he was elected a member of the American Association for the Advancement of Science and made a fellow in 1875. Meehan was also made a member of the American Philosophical Society and was active in many other learned societies as well. In 1877, he was appointed to the Pennsylvania state board of agriculture as state botanist. His greatest work, *The Native Flowers and Ferns of the United States*, appeared in four volumes between 1878 and 1880. He later served as Vice President of the Academy of Natural Sciences; and in 1900, he published in the Academy *Proceedings* a series titled, "Contributions to the Life History of Plants" and, shortly before his death, another paper, "Bending of Mature Wood in Trees," appeared in the *Proceedings*. He was the third American to be awarded the Veitchian medal for distinguished services in horticulture. Prominent in public life as well, he nevertheless boasted of having never held a salaried office.

Thomas Meehan, the venerable "Dean of American Horticulture," died on November 19, 1901, in Germantown, Pennsylvania. At his funeral, sprays of George Engelmann's spruce were placed at the head of the casket, an enduring symbol of friendship. The sprays were taken from a tree grown from a sprig that Meehan had used for his bed during an expedition in the Wahsatch mountains, when the deaf scientist had discovered the Engelmann Canyon.

References

Burkhardt, F., & Smith, S. (Eds.). (1985). *A calendar of the correspondence of Charles Darwin, 1821–1882*. New York: Garland.

Darwin, F., & Seward, A. C. (Eds.). (1903). *More letters of Charles Darwin: A record of his work in a series of hitherto unpublished letters*. New York: D. Appleton.

Harshberger, J. W. (1899). *The botanists of Philadelphia and their work*. Philadelphia: T. C. Davis & Sons.

Lang, H. G. (1994). *Silence of the spheres: The deaf experience in the history of science*. Westport, CT: Bergin & Garvey.

McGourty, F., Jr. (1967, Autumn). Thomas Meehan, 19th century plantsman. *Plants and Gardens, 23*, 81, 85.

FIELDING BRADFORD MEEK (1817–1876), American Geologist.

Fielding Bradford Meek was born in Madison, Indiana, on December 10, 1817, where his father, a prominent lawyer, had moved after marrying. His grandparents were from County Armagh in Ireland and had immigrated to Hamilton County, Ohio, around 1768. Meek had two sisters and a brother. His father died when he was about three years old. Meek's pursuit of an education and a career in natural science was at times difficult. He endured delicate health throughout his lifetime, and this influenced his education. After failing in a mercantile business in Owensboro, Kentucky, and again in Madison, he dabbled as a portrait painter, supporting himself until 1848 when he was able to find a position in a geological survey. The offer from David D. Owen to serve as an assistant in the U.S. Geological Survey of Iowa, Wisconsin, and Minnesota was important to him. His failure in business may have been largely due to his greater devotion to collecting fossils. He finally had a position commensurate with his interests.

Meek's earlier experience as a portrait painter helped him develop etching skills needed during his first assignment in geology with Owen. The zest with which he approached the illustration work accompanying his geological reports was appreciated by those who hired him, as well as those who read his work in the professional journals. From 1852 to 1858, James Hall employed him to assist in a number of projects. His work for Hall and several summers with other surveys during this period included paleontological and geological studies in the states of New York, Nebraska, Kansas, and Missouri. A variety of publications resulted from his extensive analyses, most notably his report on Cretaceous fossils from Nebraska. Meek's discovery of Permian fossils was a significant one. Hall apparently claimed credit for it, one of a number of conflicts that led to bitter feelings between them. Throughout this period of time together, Hall was observed by others to dominate and tyrannize Meek, who was shy and unassuming.

Meek's hearing loss began when he was young; and, in adulthood, he was totally deaf. It is possible that a congenital syphilis infection was responsible for the deafness. Meek was candid in describing his preference to ''spend my evenings with the books and specimens. I can hear and understand what they say, and they require neither small talk nor formalities.'' Human communication was daunting and exhausting for Meek, who never developed skills in either speechreading or sign language. Charles A. White, a physician-turned-paleontologist, described his friend as an introvert who seldom complained about his deafness. Meek avoided social gatherings whenever possible, however.

A revealing conversation with White began one day with Meek looking up from a collection of fossils the two of them had been classifying together for the Smithsonian Institution. Meek told White about a dream he had the night before in which he had heard his sister singing a song while playing the piano. ''She has been in her grave for thirty years,'' Meek said, ''and my deafness is so complete that I have not heard a sound of any kind for a long time.'' White quickly grabbed the opportunity to encourage Meek to talk more about himself. This interview and written communication between Meek and James Hall are critical primary sources. Meek died two months after his dream.

To portray Meek as a sickly man who rarely socialized would do him an injustice and provides a very incomplete picture, however. While this conclusion regarding his personality and inclination to isolate himself with his scientific work is easy to form from his biographies, Meek's correspondence reveals another side. His letters not only provide further insight into the deaf geologist, but also give the reader a wonderful glimpse into the adventurous life of a nineteenth-century fossil hunter. One trip took place in the spring of 1853, a steamboat ride on the Missouri to the Bad Lands, or ''Mauvaises Terres.'' During the excursion, Meek had been placed in charge of the party because of his experience and relative seniority. Men were paid $25 per month. Horses cost between $60 and $75.

After finding that Major Stevens was offended at Hall for planning his expedition, Meek and Hayden attempted to explain that Hall knew nothing of their intention to explore the Bad Lands. Meek was unable to reach Hall by telegraph, and submitted the matter to Agassiz and Engelmann to be governed by their advice. The advice was not to Meek's liking, however; and, after additional discussions with all concerned, Meek went on with the expedition as originally planned. On May 22, he wrote to Hall and explained that he had found it necessary to purchase guns, and that his inquiries revealed that large quantities of bones may be collected over the Bad Lands.

On May 25, Meek described in another letter a fire that had occurred on the boat the night before which, had it not been immediately extinguished, might have cancelled the entire expedition. Some of the men had dropped tobacco pipe ashes into a hold where 10,000 pounds of gun powder was stored. Three days later, he described sighting Native Americans along the shore, young men and boys of a Kickapoo village relaxing by the river's edge.

One can imagine how, on a given night, when the boat had stopped to gather firewood, Meek and F. V. Hayden made a large bright fire in the woods, the light of which attracted thousands of insects. The pair quickly went to their supply of bottles and chased specimens. By June 2, they had also collected more than 250 species of plants, many of them by candlelight. Here, again, Meek had many opportunities to apply his artistic talents, drawing the landscapes as he enjoyed them. While floating down the Missouri River, Meek described the beauty of the countryside and his fascination with the Native Americans he encountered. On that expedition, Meek estimated that he traveled between six and seven thousand miles. By June 19, 1853, they had arrived at Fort Pierre. Meek described another adventurous incident to Hall. A tornado nearly sunk the boat in the midst of negotiations with Native chiefs to allow the boat to proceed beyond Fort Clark. He concluded, coolly: ''I hope you will excuse this incoherent letter for I am in a great hurry and have to write on a table in the cabin with about two hundred Indian chiefs and braves seated in rows on each side of me. They have come on board by invitation from the captain to a feast. They are elegantly dressed. . . .'' He nevertheless adds a note on science: ''P.S. We walked across the great bend and collected some fine cretaceous fossils—Baculites, Inoceranus, Circullea, Ammonites, Fusus, etc.''

In 1858, Meek went to Washington where he resided and worked in the north tower of the Smithsonian Institution until his death. This was a brand of hospitality extended by the Smithsonian at this time to promising scientists, particularly those without family. He was in good company at the Castle. Living there in 1861, for example, were his friend F. V. Hayden; Thomas Egleston, later professor of mineralogy at Columbia University; the explorer Robert Kennicott; William Stimpson, who at the time was working on the invertebrate of the North Pacific Exploring Expedition under Ringgold and Rodgon; August Schönborn, a talented artist who produced beautiful silverpoint drawings of Stimpson's crustaceans; and Professor Matile, an assistant of Joseph Henry and friend of Agassiz. The noted ethnologist Frank Hamilton Cushing also stayed at the Castle. During the Civil War, many of Meek's published reports were written and laid the foundations for the science of determining the age of rocks in the Great Plains. His writings at this time helped to establish him as a leading authority in the study of fauna at the Mesozoic-Cenozoic boundary.

Meek was involved in many projects during the years he resided in the Smithsonian "Castle," including the preparation of instructions for Charles F. Hall's Third Arctic Expedition, the voyage of the Polaris. In the winter of 1869–1870, Congress had passed an act authorizing the organization of the expedition. Simon Newcomb developed the astronomical instructions, and Louis Agassiz prepared the glacier-related instructions. J. E. Hilgard addressed the subjects of magnetism, gravitation, ocean physics, and meteorology; and S. F. Baird did the same for natural history. Meek's geological expertise was highly respected.

Meek's name lives on in his many published works and the organisms named in tribute to him (e.g., "Meekia," "Meekella striato-costata," and the generic type "Meekoceras"). His health, though, forced him to assume staff roles on scientific teams, rather than leadership ones. Nonetheless, the originality of his work was recognized and, ultimately, appreciated.

When Meek died in Washington on December 21, 1876, the funeral was held in the Smithsonian's hall. Professor Joseph Henry, the institution's first secretary, delivered the funeral oration. And Meek's friends recounted the numerous ways he had systematized and advanced geological science.

References

Lang, H. G. (1994). *Silence of the spheres: The deaf experience in the history of science.* Westport, CT: Bergin & Garvey.

Merrill, G. P. (1924). *The first one hundred years of American geology.* New Haven, CT: Yale University Press.

White, C. A. (1896). Biographical sketch of Fielding Bradford Meek. *The American Geologist, 18* (6), 337–350.

WILLIAM MERCER (1765–1839), American Painter.

William Mercer was born in Fredericksburg, Virginia, in 1765. He was the son of a Revolutionary War hero, Hugh Mercer, who had been appointed Brigadier General in the armies of the United Colonies by President Hancock on June 6, 1776. Stabbed by British bayonets in the Battle of Princeton while assisting George Washington, Hugh Mercer died in the arms of Major Lewis. George Weedon, who fought valiantly at the Battle of Brandywine, then became a "second father" to the five Mercer children. Generals Weedon and Mercer had met at Fort Pitt in the early 1760s. Hugh Mercer married Isabella Gordon, and Weedon married her sister, Catherine. Upon the death of Mercer, Weedon was appointed by the Court as the Mercer family's guardian, taking responsibility for financial affairs and schooling of the children. One of William Mercer's brothers, George, was also deaf, but although Congress had pledged to educate many children of war officers, it appeared that only William had the opportunity to study away from home.

Mercer studied painting under the distinguished Philadelphia artist Charles Willson Peale from 1783 until 1786. During this period, Weedon and Peale corresponded regularly. As the second student Peale had accepted, the young deaf man was loved in his new home. Peale wrote to Weedon that he and Mrs. Peale considered him an adopted son and pledged life-long love and devotion to him. In 1783, there was an incident in Philadelphia where a huge crowd of spectators celebrating the peace after the war had become riotous and many robberies occurred. Rembrandt Peale reminisced many years later in *The Crayon* that William came home, "wild with terror, being divested of his watch, and gold sleeve and knee buckles." The boy was so afraid that the family could not persuade him to go to his bed, as he argued he would be more safely hidden in the stable. Rembrandt Peale, in the same memoir, also noted that Mercer would later become an "excellent" portrait painter.

After this traumatic experience, the natural watchfulness of the Peales and Weedons probably was heightened. Mercer, in his early teens, was then regularly accompanied to and from Philadelphia by Jack Morimer, a friend of Weedon's. Peale on more than one occasion described Mercer as nervous and timid, but cheerful.

In his first few months under Charles Willson Peale's tutelage, Mercer assisted him in erecting a large arch in celebration of the end of the Revolution, brightened with eleven hundred lamps and illuminated paintings, including one for which General Washington had posed. Unfortunately, during the same raucous outburst when young Mercer was robbed, fireworks set the arch on fire while Peale was working forty feet above ground. This upset, as well as the frostbite Mercer suffered while working in the bitter cold on the structure, most likely made the young deaf artist reticent about rebuilding the arch with Peale. On February 21, 1784, Peale wrote directly to Mercer, encouraging him to reconsider assisting him, not knowing fully the reason of his refusal and return to Virginia, and offering Mercer steadfast support in his education. "Dear Billy," Peale concluded, "I give you this to weigh, and consider well, and would have you to believe that you have found a real Friend in [me]." Mercer did return and, in Peale's next letter to Weedon, he reported that "my pupil is now very deligent [*sic*] and in a fair way of becoming very clever."

Peale continued to instruct Mercer in miniatures and oil painting over the next two years. In 1786, Mercer returned home to Virginia, although only for a brief visit; for shortly after, he was back in Philadelphia completing the painting of his own father at the Battle of Princeton. Weedon wrote to Peale, anxious to have the painting of the death of Hugh Mercer, which evoked strong emotional connections, for William was said to be the picture of his father. Peale portrayed Washington on the Battlefield of Princeton. On the ground behind him lay the fallen General Hugh Mercer, and William Mercer had posed for this portrait of his dying father. Weedon wrote with great gratitude to Peale, both for the sensitivity of his depiction of the Battle of Princeton and for his kindhearted mentoring of the younger Mercer. In 1821, Peale, who incidentally much later viewed his own age-related deafness as "very mortifying," painted a portrait of the eminent Laurent Clerc,* the first deaf teacher in the United States, Clerc's wife, and their infant daughter.

While Mercer was a student, he copied another picture completed by Charles Willson Peale's son, James Peale. This painting was presented to the Historical Society of Pennsylvania by William Mercer's niece in 1887. In 1947, the Society ordered a copy made of Mercer's version, which they presented to the aircraft carrier "Princeton."

After Mercer returned home to establish himself as a self-described "Limmer," an archaic term for one who makes drawings and illuminations, he led a relatively quiet life. The American Deaf community has recognized Mercer as the first known congenitally deaf individual in the United States to become a distinguished artist. Sadly, with the exception of the painting of the Battle of Princeton, and the oval miniature on ivory of Edmund Pendleton of Virginia, now held by the Virginia Historical Society of Richmond, Mercer's other works have been lost. The Historical Society of Pennsylvania also holds a portrait of Mrs. John Gordon, William Mercer's grandmother, which some critics believe to have been the work of the deaf painter. Among the lost works is a miniature of Benjamin Franklin, which Peale mentions Mercer having completed by copying from a larger portrait of his own.

Mercer continued to paint until his death on August 20, 1839, after a protracted illness. His obituary in the *Fredericksburg Political Arena* that month described him as an "amiable and tractable" man, having a "quiet and gentle disposition" with a "retiring and unobtrusive diffidence and pure benevolence." On the subject of the American Revolution, Mercer was said to be an acknowledged expert, probably both from formal study and from knowledge of his family's tradition. Augustus Fuller* and John Brewster, Jr.* soon followed him as early deaf American artists of renown.

References

Egbert, D. D. (1952). General Mercer at the Battle of Princeton as painted by James Peale, Charles Willson Peale, and William Mercer. *Princeton University Library Chronicle, 13* (4), 171–194.

Higgins, F. C. (1983). William Mercer: Deaf artist of the post-Revolutionary War era. *Gallaudet Today, 13* (4), 28–32.

Ogden Kohler, J., & Hodge, L. L. (1988, March). William Mercer, the deaf-mute artist. *Fredericksburg Times*, 1–4.

Peale, R. (1855). Reminiscences. *The Crayon, 1* (24), 369–371.

BETTY G. MILLER (1934–   ), American Artist/Educator.

Betty G. Miller was born deaf on July 27, 1934. Both of her parents were also deaf. Her father, a commercial artist, illustrated books for children, and his daughter demonstrated an early aptitude for art. Miller attended Northbrook High School in Illinois and graduated from Gallaudet College in 1957 with a bachelor's degree, having received the Charles R. Ely Award for general scholarship.

For several years, she worked as an illustrator for the Reuben Donnelley Corporation in Washington, D.C., before she joined the faculty of Gallaudet College as an instructor. She completed a Master of Fine Arts degree at the Maryland Institute College of Art in Baltimore in 1963 and a Doctorate in Art Education at the Pennsylvania State University in 1976. Interested in drama as well as design, Miller attended summer sessions of the National Theatre of the Deaf (NTD) in 1967, 1969, and 1970, receiving training in acting, directing, set design, costume, lighting and construction. She supervised the design and construction of settings for the Gallaudet College Dance Group in the 1960s. Miller received the Best Director Trophy for the one-act revival scene of the play *Dark of the Moon,* presented in October 1968, which was praised by Richard L. Coe, a drama critic for the *Washington Post.* She designed the set for the play *Journeys* for the NTD repertory in 1970. In 1977, she played the role of the mother in the SPECTRUM Deaf Theater production *A Play of Our Own,* about the prejudices concerning hearing people held by a deaf family as the daughter announces she is engaged to a hearing man. Other plays Miller has acted in include *The Philadelphia Story* (1963) and *Wet and Wild* (1967) with Phyllis Frelich.*

In 1966, Miller joined two colleagues and four students of art history from the Gallaudet Department of Art who traveled to study art history with other students in Apulia, Rome, Siena, Florence, Naples, and other cities. She served as Co-director of the Board of SPECTRUM, Focus on Deaf Artists, a unique, multidisciplinary Deaf artists' collaborative. She is a member of the National Art Education Association. Some of her works were exhibited in a Deaf artists' group show in Los Angeles in 1971. Her first one-woman show was also in 1971 at the Washburn Art Center at Gallaudet College. "The Silent World" included fifteen pieces in oil and acrylic that, she explained, revealed her relationship to the world as a deaf child. In the *Washington Post*, Andrea O. Cohen admired Miller's soft and warm colors and light, but firm, lines: "The paintings are expressive but not shrill. An appealing whimsical quality pervades the semi-abstract creatures and plants in her nondidactic work."

Miller continued to incorporate the experiences of deaf people into her art to communicate messages to others. One of her sculptures described in the *Washington Evening Star* in September 1972, a mask of a boy with a wired jaw, included a legend that revealed the frustration experienced in learning to speak. While a deaf child often learns an idea or word within a short time, hours may be spent in teaching that child to speak the word. Miller's sculpture was part of her effort with Frank Del Rosso to advocate American Sign Language as the official language of deaf people. At a lecture to the Salisbury Branch of the American Association of University Professors, she described in detail how visual language is essential for deaf children to express themselves. Her doctoral thesis in art education at Pennsylvania State University, "Deaf Students as Artists," was an analysis of the self-image and communication of deaf students through art, including perceptions about their deafness. For example, she reported that in one student's completed drawing, a packaged ear carried a sticker price of $7,000. Another student communicated an overprotective mother in her drawing. A third student demonstrated how he used drawings as a child to communicate with his parents. Miller found through her research that art enhanced deaf students' abilities to solve qualitative problems. Studying how the students whom she videotaped expressed themselves in art and American Sign Language, she concluded that the combination was an effective educational tool.

Miller won first prize in drawing in 1974 and the Best in Show of the Exhibit in 1976 at the Charter Day Art Exhibit at Gallaudet College. In 1975, she held a one-woman show at Western Maryland College in Westminster, Maryland, and in 1976, her work was exhibited at the Martin Luther King Library in Washington, D.C. She has also illustrated the books *Say It With Hands* by Lou Fant, and *Signs for Instructional Purposes* by Kannapell, Bornstein, and Hamilton.

References

Cohen, A. O. (1972, February 16). Art for the deaf. *Washington Post*.
Deaf students express themselves through art. (1976, September 14). *York Daily Record*.
Dr. Betty Miller's research boosts combination of art/sign language. (1976). *The Deaf American, 29* (3), 11–12.

GIDEON E. MOORE (1842–1895), American Chemist.

Gideon E. Moore was born in Philadelphia in 1842, the son of a wealthy merchant of Philadelphia. He was progressively deafened as an adolescent and was profoundly deaf by the time he entered Yale College. His younger brother, H. Humphrey Moore,* was deafened at the age of three and distinguished himself as an artist. Gideon Moore graduated from Yale in 1861 and from the University of Heidelberg, Germany, in 1869, where he became the first American to earn a Ph.D. *summa cum laude*.

On his return to the United States, Moore worked for the government as an assayer in California, then later spent time assaying mines in Nevada. It was a heady and prosperous time to pursue such work. A perusal of the issues of the *American Journal of Science* at this time reveals numerous articles published by Moore. In 1870, for example, Professor Hermann Kolbe suggested that Moore investigate the phenomenon attending the electrolysis of monocyanacetic acid. Moore subsequently sent a report on this study to the Chemical Society of Berlin on May 22, 1871. His fluency in German is revealed in his continued contact with the scientific community in that country. His 1872 investigative report in the *American Journal of Science,* ''On the Occurrence in Nature of Amorphous Mercuric Sulphide,'' was reprinted from a German journal of chemistry.

When Moore received a specimen of a mineral discovered at Camden, New Jersey, he traced its origin to Avis Island in the Caribbean Sea. He analyzed it carefully and learned that the mineral was in the form of small but very perfect and brilliant crystals. After studying the hardness, specific gravity, color, direction of cleavage, and other properties of the mineral when dissolved and heated, he sent a sample to James D. Dana at Yale College who undertook a study of its crystallographic character. Moore dedicated his new mineral discovery, ''Brushite,'' to Professor George J. Brush of Yale as a tribute to that man's ''efficient labors'' on behalf of American Mineralogy.

Moore's friend, J. D. Whitney, the chief of the State Geological Survey of California, also directed his attention to a peculiar black mercury ore that he had found during a journey through Lake County, California. After undertaking the investigation, and with Whitney's permission, Moore made the results public. He detailed its composition and chemical characteristics, and proposed the name *Metacinnabarite* for the mineral. In still another study, he repeated the work on distinct isomeric modifications of mercuric sulphide conducted earlier by Berzelius, the student of the deaf Swedish chemist Anders Gustaf Ekeberg.*

Moore returned East in the late 1870s and established a chemical laboratory in New York City. He later moved to one of the largest and best-equipped private laboratories in the United States at the time, and he employed a cadre of assistants. During the Civil War, there had been a serious scarcity of sugarcane throughout the country; and the saccharine products of sorghum were in great demand. This led to an interest in the varieties of sorghum after the war was over. In 1881, Peter Collier, a chemist of the United States Department of Agriculture, read a paper at the National Academy of Sciences (NAS) meeting in Philadelphia on the results of Moore's studies. President W. B. Rogers responded to this report by establishing a Committee on Sorghum Sugar to investigate the possibility of producing sugar from sorghum on a large scale at low cost. NAS members Benjamin Silliman, Samuel W. Johnson, Charles F. Chandler, and J. Lawrence Smith were selected to conduct the chemical investigations, along with the deaf chemist Gideon E. Moore.

Not much is known about Moore's personal life. During his stay in Europe, he married the daughter of Baron Sznacz, a general in the Austro-Hungarian army. He did not appear to be very fond of high society, preferring to spend his time with a select circle of friends or his well-stocked library. Friends joked that he was unimpressed by status and rank, but was more than willing to entertain a close friend with a gourmet meal, vintage wine, and a fine cigar. He was a Renaissance man in his interests and loved to converse on travel, art, science, literature, and philosophy. In regard to communicating with hearing people, Moore ensured the accuracy of his business interactions by always giving contracts in writing. He could speechread, but did not wish to risk legal and professional agreements. He appeared to live on the border of several worlds. In the Deaf community he was not fully accepted because of the age of onset of his deafness, despite his early education and deaf brother. Among hearing people, though, it was a constant challenge for him to communicate. In describing the success of Moore and his deaf brother (an artist) in an 1870 issue of the *New York Tribune*, later reprinted in the *American Annals of the Deaf*, one reporter marveled that "The elder [Gideon] . . . passed through the rigid and extended scholastic curriculum of Heidelberg, acquiring ease and elegance in German and French, and a perfect understanding of Greek, Latin and Hebrew, enabling him to pass an oral examination in those tongues with marked ability, and to receive, at the age of 28, the unusual honor of the degree of Doctor of Philosophy, in addition to the usual degree of Master of Arts."

Moore also had a gift for poetry; and shortly before his death, he translated the German epic poem "Ahasver" of Julius Mosen, based on the legend of the Wandering Jew.

Moore died of pneumonia on April 13, 1895, at the age of 53. In his final hours, he called upon the Reverend Thomas Gallaudet, the son of Thomas Hopkins Gallaudet, and Rector of St. Ann's Church for Deaf-Mutes in New York, to be by his bedside and provide him with spiritual assistance. Moore made his marks in the annals of Deaf heritage as one of the first deaf persons to earn a Ph.D., and in the annals of science with his chemical contributions. But his obituary in the May issue of the *American Journal of Science* was as simple as his life was unpretentious: "Dr. Gideon E. Moore of New York City died on April 13th at the age of fifty-three. He was a well known chemist, who had made some valuable contributions to the science, particularly in the line of mineral analyses."

References

Braddock, G. C. (1975). *Notable deaf persons.* Washington, DC: Gallaudet College Alumni Association.

Dr. Gideon E. Moore. (1895). [obituary]. *The Silent Worker, 7* (9), 8.

Highly educated deaf-mutes. (1871). *American Annals of the Deaf, 16* (3), 207–208.

Lang, H. G. (1994). *Silence of the spheres: The deaf experience in the history of science.* Westport, CT: Bergin & Garvey.

H. HUMPHREY MOORE (1844–1926), American Artist.

Born in New York City in 1844, Henry Humphrey Moore was deafened at the age of three. His brother, Gideon E. Moore,* also was deaf and became the first deaf American to earn a Ph.D. Humphrey Moore was placed in a private school for deaf and hearing children run by David E. Bartlett, followed by the Pennsylvania Institution and the American School for the Deaf (then known as the American Asylum) in Hartford, Connecticut. With few opportunities to pursue his early interest in art, Moore was fortunate to have a supportive father, a banker, who contacted Professor Louis Ball in New Haven to set up private instruction in the basics of perspective, then arranged oil painting tutelage under Professor Waugh in Philadelphia. At the Academy of Fine Arts, Moore studied with Thomas Eakins, an American friend who later also reached eminence as a painter and sculptor. Moore also studied anatomy for human figure drawing under W. O. Ayres in San Francisco.

In 1866, Moore traveled to Dresden, Germany, where his success on a competitive examination led to his plan to further his studies at École des Beaux-Arts in Paris. His whole family stayed with him during the period of his application. On the day that Moore and his uncle went to the school, "Harry," as he was affectionately known by his friends, was so nervous about being refused that he had lost his pad and pencil. Once he located the paper, it was Thomas Eakins, his friend from Philadelphia who had been recently accepted, who used the pad to inform Moore that he had been admitted as well. Eakins accompanied Moore to visit Jean-Léon Gérôme, explaining his friend's deafness. Moore's advanced professional studies in the École des Beaux-Arts continued until 1869 under Gérôme, as well as Adolphe Yvon and Gustave Boulanger. "All I have to say is that I am proud that you have been my pupil," Gérôme once wrote to him after Moore had distinguished himself.

Moore then traveled to Seville, Spain, with Thomas Eakins, who had learned sign language; and together, they enjoyed the Spanish culture and people. William Sartain, an American genre painter, joined them for horseback riding excursions in the Spanish countryside. After some time studying architecture there, Moore traveled to Granada, where he developed a friendship with the eminent artist Mariano Fortuny y Carbó, whose works, and possibly instruction, greatly influenced the deaf painter's own style. There, he also met Isabella de Cistue, a lady of Spanish nobility, whom he married in 1872. Among the distinguished nobles in attendance were Isabella's father, Colonel Cistue, and her grandmother, who had held the position of a lady of honor to the revered Queen Maria Louisa. It was with her elderly grandmother that she had been walking in the beautiful gardens of the Alhambra, the old palace of the Moors, when she met H. Humphrey Moore in a secluded spot. There, he was painting his *View of Granada*. Having learned sign language through several deaf friends in the past, she found great happiness in making his acquaintance, and their marriage remained strong until her death.

Some of Moore's paintings of the Alhambra were particularly cherished, since they depicted parts that had been since destroyed by fire. In Tangier, Morocco, for several years, he intimately studied Moorish architecture, metal work, fabrics, and customs—perhaps too intimately. During one Moroccan feast, Moore enthusiastically began sketching a mountain chief who turned his gun on the deaf artist and fired. Fortunately, Moore's attendant pulled him away in time, the bullet grazing his head. His friendship with the Grand Shereef was a more fortunate encounter. The Shereef had supplied a guard of soldiers from the Pasha's army to provide safe passage to Moore on his painting excursions. On one occasion, Moore wore a woman's dress and full-length veil in order to verify the colors and details of dignitaries' households, including the designated women's areas. Throughout his later years in Paris, he proudly displayed in his studio a saddle presented him by the Sultan of Morocco—a reminder of adventurous days.

In 1880, Moore traveled to Japan where he was praised by leading art critics for his understanding of Japanese culture, which he incorporated in his work. A year later, he returned to New York—and to tragedy. The huge warehouse on Fourth Avenue in which he had stored his collections of Moorish fabrics and metal work, and many of his own great paintings from the early years of his career, was destroyed by fire. Gone was the *Almeh*, for which he had received a medal at the American Centennial Exposition in 1876 and praise in the New York *Nation* for its extraordinary use of color.

Moore then returned to Japan for eighteen months, where he specialized for years in Japanese life and scenery. Acclaimed by critics around the world, his work appeared in galleries and salons in Paris, Nice, London, and other cities. Moore's works touched upon a wide array of subjects reflected in such titles as *Saracenic and Moorish Armor*, *Mauresque Pottery*, *The Mandolin-Player*, *A Japanese Corner*, and *Japanese Woman Tinting her Lips*. For these and other works he was called "The Meissonier of Japanese Subjects" by a French critic, after the French genre painter known for his artistic delicacy. When, in 1890, some of the greatest French artists became dissatisfied with the management of the Salon in Paris, forming "The New Salon," with its president the distinguished Jean-Louis Meissonier, Moore was invited to send paintings to their exhibition. He sent eleven, hoping one or two might pass their rigid examination. To his surprise, Meissonier wrote to him to inform him that all eleven were to be included in the exhibition, evidence of the growing esteem for Moore's work. All were Japanese paintings, with such titles as *Street in Yokohama*, *Japanese Coffee Saloon*, *Garden of the Emperor*, *Tomb of the Mikados*, and *Village of Nikko*. In that same year, one of his paintings alone was sold to the California millionaire Charles Crocker for $4,000.

Moore was decorated by the Queen mother of Charles III of Spain. He won a medal in the Universal Exhibition at Paris in 1898 for his Japanese painting, and was a member of the Cercle de L'Union Artistique of Paris after 1886. He lived for a while at Nice on the French Riviera, then moved again to Paris where he painted a number of portraits, including that of Don Jaime, the deaf son of King Alphonso. When Isabella died, Moore married a Polish countess, who was also a devoted friend and willing interpreter for him in social situations.

In 1916, foreigners were asked to leave France when World War I escalated. Moore returned to Philadelphia, leaving about sixty of his best paintings in the vaults of a Parisian bank. Fifty years after their friendship began, Moore looked up Thomas Eakins, who still lived in a half-story red brick house on Mt. Vernon Street. Together, they ventured around New York, where they sought subjects for their paintings.

Besides the *Almeh*, Moore is well-known for the *Blind-Guitar Player*, *Gypsy*

Encampment, Granada; *Moorish Bazaar*; *A Bulgarian*; and *Let Me Alone!* His last years were spent painting portraits of prominent persons of Europe, including the Countess of Grendulain (niece of Queen Isabel), the Countess of Chateaubrand, the Duke of Madrid, and Madame Santa Marina; as well as the wives of steel magnates and Pennsylvania Railroad executives in the United States.

After an extraordinary professional life and a series of unbroken and supportive personal relationships, Moore died in his beloved Paris on January 1, 1926.

References

A deaf-mute artist's romance. (1892). *The Silent Worker, 5* (2), 1.

Artists renew friendship of Paris here in Philadelphia. (1916). *The Silent Worker, 28* (5), 94.

Henry Humphrey Moore. (1893). *The Silent Worker, 6* (1), 2–3.

McHenry, M. (1946). *Thomas Eakins who painted.* Privately printed for Margaret McHenry.

Stevens, K. H. (1927). Harry Humphrey Moore, a retrospect. *The Silent Worker, 39* (5), 258–262.

DALE L. MORGAN (1914–1971), American Wild West Historian.

Dale L. Morgan was born on December 18, 1914, in Salt Lake City, Utah, the son of an office equipment sales representative. Athletic throughout his early years, he was totally deafened at the age of fourteen by a disease that also affected motor control and coordination. With the support of his teachers and parents, he adjusted to his new challenges, replacing his favorite sports with interests in chess, art, and writing. Morgan soon found himself a position as a high school reporter for a Salt Lake City newspaper, and he won the state championship in chess twice. Unable to hear his own voice, his speech progressively lost clarity; and he found oral presentations trying. He was most comfortable with writing as a medium of communication, and this became a passion.

Morgan enrolled in the University of Utah after finishing high school. He graduated with a bachelor's degree in commercial art in 1937, but it was hard enough to obtain an advertising job during the Depression years, without the added challenge of applying for a position in an agency as a deaf person with mobility problems. With help from friends, however, he landed a position with the Federal Records Survey of the Works Progress Administration in Utah, advancing from clerk to editor, and then to supervisor for the Utah Writers' Project. There, his interest in history flourished as he began to write guides for use of county archives. Between 1940 and 1942, Morgan was state supervisor, a period during which he published "The State of Deseret" in the *Utah Historical Quarterly* and his first book, *Utah: A Guide to the State* (1941). The book was praised by scholars and subsequently was published in three editions. As with the deaf historian George Hyde,* Morgan found correspondence to be an extremely useful method of communication and information exchange. The detail to which he approached scholarly analyses made him highly appreciated by others who requested his feedback on manuscripts for publication. Although his own formal study of history was minimal, so comfortable was Morgan with writing and research that he had no inhibitions about debating in writing with such notable historians as Bernard DeVoto. Morgan also published numerous reviews in the *Saturday Review of Literature.*

In 1943, he published *Humboldt, Highroad of the West* for Farrar and Rinehart's Rivers of America Series. The book contains stories of the Donner party, fur traders, the Mormons, the Pony express, and Nevada folklore, receiving praise by *New York Times*, *Saturday Review of Literature*, and other periodicals as one of the better volumes in the Rivers of America series. The following year, he found a position in the Office of Price Administration in Washington, D.C.; and, believing that scholarly work on the subject of Mormonism would not be possible without a comprehensive bibliography, he began such a project which lasted thirty years, publishing articles on this along the way. While Morgan was not the most committed Mormon himself, he recognized the critical role of the Latter Day Saints in the history of the American West. His letters express serious doubts about his early religious training; but out of deference for his devout mother, he never formally left the church.

Even with a Guggenheim grant to conduct his research, he nevertheless found it difficult to access information without a university appointment. His part-time editorship and archivist connection with the Utah State Historical Society following World War II helped somewhat. He published *Great Salt Lake* (1947) and *Jedediah Smith and the Opening of the West* (1953) while with the state historical society, and prominent historians registered very positive reviews of these works. After 1954, his new position as editor and author at the Bancroft Library at the University of California at Berkeley opened doors for Morgan; and he had freer access to multiple sources. During the next few years he published two books and edited three others. The edited volumes include *The Overland Diary of James A. Pritchard from Kentucky to California in 1849* (1959), *California as I Saw It: Pencillings by the Way of Its Gold and Gold Diggers, and Incidents of Travel by Land and Water* (1960), and *Overland in 1846: Diaries and Letters of the California–Oregon Trail* (1963), the latter over eight hundred pages. His two coauthored shorter works were *Jedediah Smith and His Maps of the American West* (with Carl I. Wheat in 1954) and, in 1966, *Captain Charles M. Weber: Pioneer of the San Joaquin and Founder of Stockton, California.* Morgan's final publication was a 430-page volume edited with Eleanor Towles Harris, *The Rocky Mountain Journals of William Marshall Anderson: The West in 1834*, published in 1967.

In 1963, Morgan completed *The West of William H. Ashley.* Like his work on Jedediah Smith, this book reflected his love of words and interpretive skill, as well as solid research methodology. His honors for historical scholarship included the Fellow Award from the Utah State Historical Society (1960), Henry R. Wagner Memorial Award from the California Historical Society (1961), and its Fellowship Award (1962), Distinguished Alumni Award from the University of Utah (1964), Award of Merit from the American Association for State and Local History (1965), and the Silver Buffalo Award from the New York Westerners (1966).

Morgan received a second Guggenheim Foundation fellowship in 1970 to complete a volume on the fur trade in North America. Unfortunately, he died of cancer in Baltimore on March 30, 1971, shortly after he began research for the manuscript.

Reference

Cooley, E. L. (1977, Summer). A dedication to the memory of Dale L. Morgan: 1914–1971. *Arizona and the West, 19*, 103–106.

N

JAMES NACK (1809–1879), American Poet.

James Nack was born in New York City on January 4, 1809, the son of a poor merchant. He was taught by his sisters at home and, by the age of four, he was able to read. Within a few years, Nack was demonstrating an ability to write verses, the earliest a couplet he had written while attending church. At this time, an accident suddenly changed the course of his life. During a fall from a stairway while carrying a young playmate in his arms, a heavy fire screen struck his head, leaving him unconscious for several weeks and causing complete deafness. Nack attended the New York Institution for the Deaf between 1818 and 1823. Through his poetry, he found an outlet for the loneliness and poverty he was experiencing at such a young age, writing a tragedy at the age of twelve, and a second one at the age of fifteen. These works, written in a cold room without a table, were destroyed by him along with other early writings. He acknowledged, though, that they probably did him much good at a time that he was in crisis, and that they gave him the opportunity to experiment and find a voice as a writer.

At the age of fourteen, Nack produced numerous romantic poems; most of them were lost with the exception of "The Blue-Eyed Maid," "The Grave of Mary," and "The Gallant Highland Rover," which he included in a later volume. The following year, he wrote a third tragedy that was subsequently lost as well. "The Minstrel Boy," written in his sixteenth year, was later praised for its emotive power. It was at this time that Abraham Asten, a clerk of the city and county of New York, particularly impressed with "The Blue-Eyed Maid," found young Nack a position with a lawyer. The lawyer's library was complete with works on history, philosophy, fiction, criticism, and theology. Diligent reading enabled Nack to later translate works from French, Dutch, and German. During this period, Nack also wrote several manuscripts of verses. When the lawyer left for Europe, Nack began working for Asten. This association opened

James Nack, American poet.
Drawing from *Harper's New
Monthly Magazine, 68* (406),
1884.

new doors for him yet again, when Asten invited him to events where prominent writers, poets, and literary critics socialized with the fledgling deaf poet.

In 1827, his first volume, *The Legend of the Rocks and Other Pieces*, was published, causing a sensation. This book, a collection of more than sixty poems, holds special honor as one of the earliest writings by a deaf person in America. Still in his teen years, he was recognized for his precocity and talent. The New York *Critic* praised him for the musical quality of his verse, the more noteworthy because of his deafness; and he was befriended by Colonel Samuel L. Knapp, who was particularly enthused over Nack's talent and personal creativity, characterizing his critical pieces as mature works that challenged those of critics far older than he. Others were complimentary of the sheer tenacity with which he performed his work. General Wetmore, for example, praised the feeling of his work and wondered at how it could be so human when Nack was "cut off" from human society.

In 1830, Ignatius L. Robertson published *Sketches of Public Characters* in which he stated that the American public had lost its taste for war heroes, preferring instead to read of artists and poets. He then profiled leading artists and writers of that generation. His chapter on poets included a discussion of Nack's work, singling it out as a particularly sophisticated poetic language.

Nack's next work was a pamphlet, "Ode on the Proclamation of President Jackson," published in 1833. In 1838, he married a hearing woman who had been his dear friend since childhood, and his verses to her reveal a happy, warm, and close relationship. They raised a family of three daughters. Despite the new demands of family life, he continued to be productive. In 1839, he published *Earl Rupert, and Other Tales and Poems*, which was dedicated to Washington Irving, the whimsical American author from his own hometown. This work also included some prose. However, after a decade, illness caused his departure from the County Clerk's office and he was bankrupted. He reached out to friends for assistance; and, by 1850, he had recovered, publishing *The Immortal, a Dramatic Romance*, with poems dedicated to Charles Dickens. *The Romance of the Ring, and Other Poems* was published in 1859. This volume included several long poems, "The Romance of the Ring" and "The Spirit of Vengeance," fifteen romantic verses under "Love's Young Dream," and a variety of personal verses such as "To My Wife," "My Little Daughter's Welcome," "My Childhood," and "On the Death of a Young Sister." One reviewer of that day ranked Nack's volume of verse above the youthful writings of Chatterton and Byron.

Nack saw many of his verses reprinted throughout his life. He was one of four distinguished deaf poets of the early American Deaf community to be included in the *Dictionary of American Biography* in 1928. The editor summarized his work as that of a more "period" variety, which would be read as imitative and sentimental by contemporary readers.

Nack spent his final years earning a living by translating French, German, and Dutch writings. Since formal schooling for deaf students in the United States had not begun until 1817, Nack represented one of the earliest success stories. Educators of deaf children were proud to describe his accomplishments, for it served the useful purpose of also informing a naive public about the potential of education to prepare deaf men and women for the arts and sciences, heretofore a rare occurrence. In 1854, for example, Nack's name was used by John Carlin* in his argument in the *American Annals of the Deaf* for the establishment of a national college for deaf students (now Gallaudet University), "if proofs be needed to give conviction of the truth . . . that [deaf persons] of decided talents can be rendered as good scholars." While Nack's work is dated, it is important in having provided opportunities for other deaf writers to argue their case for access to a wider audience.

He died on September 23, 1879.

References

Johnson, A., & Malone, D. (Eds.). (1934). *Dictionary of American Biography* (Vol. 13, pp. 377–378). New York: Charles Scribner's Sons.

Morris, G. P. (1859). Memoir of James Nack. *Romance of the ring, and other poems*. New York: Delisser & Procter.

Robertson, I. L. (1830). *Sketches of public characters. Drawn from the living and the dead with notices of other matters*. New York: E. Bliss.

JUAN FERNANDEZ NAVARRETE (1526–1579), Spanish Painter.

Juan Fernandez Navarrete was born of noble parents in 1526 at Logroño in Spain. He was deafened through disease at the age of three. At this time, there was no formal schooling for deaf children, the famous Juan Pablo Bonet and Pedro Ponce de Leon having not yet begun their pioneering work. Navarrete was left to educate himself and find his own path to greatness. Early on he showed an interest in drawing, using sketches to communicate his needs. His father, noting his talents with charcoal or chalk, entered him into the tutelage of Friar Vincent de Santo Domingo, an artist-monk of the order of St. Jerome at the Monastery of the Star near Logroño. Friar Vincent, who had studied painting at Toledo, not only taught the young deaf boy everything he knew about drawing, but encouraged his parents to send him to Florence, Rome, Milan, and Naples, hypothesizing that travel and the expansion of experience would enrich Navarrete's mind further. In Italy, the boy studied the works of famous painters and began to dream of imitating them. Some biographers have reported that Navarrete actually studied for awhile under Titian at his school in Venice. However, the artist Pellegrino Tibaldi, admiring Navarrete's work at the Escurial, remarked that the deaf artist had painted nothing worth notice while he was in Italy as a student.

Upon his return to Spain, in 1568, Navarrete (known as ''El Mudo'') was invited to Madrid by Don Luis Manrique, Grand Almoner (dispenser of favors) at the court of Philip II, King of Spain. On March 6, 1568, he was offered an appointment as the king's painter with an unusually generous allowance, in addition to the price of his artistic works. Navarrete brought with him a small painting he had completed in Italy, *Our Lord's Baptism*, which was praised by the Spanish historian Cean Bermudez and liked enough by the king to have it admitted to the Prior's cell in the Escurial. Among his early works at the court of Philip II were many paintings on religious subjects, including a black and white painting of prophets on the folding doors of the altar, and a painting of *The Crucifixion*, which was placed in the royal chapel in the woods of Segovia. During a three-year stay at Logroño, he painted portraits of St. Michael, St. James the Great, St. Philip, and St. Jerome. The picture of St. Michael was, according to Cean Bermudez, one of the finest of that often-represented Archangel in Castile. The King himself looked on with amused approval as El Mudo painted the face of Santoys, the royal secretary whom the deaf artist disliked, on the shoulders of one of the torturers of St. James. These works were placed in the sacristy of the Escurial.

Navarrete was once described as having similar techniques in shading and anatomy to those of Rubens. His exquisite coloring, experimentation with light, and uniqueness of design, especially his adherence to the great master, earned him the honor of being called ''the Spanish Titian.'' Indeed, Titian was revered by Navarrete; and when the King asked that Titian's *Last Supper* be cut shorter in order to fit into a planned space for it in the Escurial, Navarrete pleaded with him not to damage the original. Through an interpreter, El Mudo begged in signs to be permitted to make a quality copy of the painting to fit appropriately into the Escurial, thus saving the master's original, but King Philip would not wait several weeks. It is reported that the deaf artist was unable to contain his grief and anger.

Navarrete's friends reported that he delighted in history and in mythology, played shrewdly at cards, and expressed his meaning by signs with clarity. His works continued to draw upon aspects of the Gospel, with such titles as *The Nativity of Our Lord*, *Christ Scourged at the Column*, *The Assumption of the Virgin*, *Repenting St. Jerome*, *The Martyrdom of St. James the Great*, *St. Philip*, and *St. John Writing the Apocalypse*. *The Nativity of Our Lord* has been especially admired for the manner in which Navarrete painted in three sources of light, from a candle, the heavens, and the form of the Christ Child Himself. El Mudo was disappointed with his *Assumption*, believing that the Blessed Mary, whose head was a portrait of the painter's own mother, had nearly vanished in the crowd of angels, but the king would not allow him to destroy his work. A head of one of the apostles in this painting was also a portrait of El Mudo's father. *St. John Writing the Apocalypse*, *St. Philip*, and *The Assumption of the Virgin* were all later destroyed in a fire.

In 1576, he painted *Abraham Receiving the Three Angels*, one of his most famous works and one for which King Philip had paid a formidable sum of money. This painting, with life-size representations of Abraham and the heavenly visitors, was hung over an altar in the Convent of the Escurial. In his description of the Escurial, Friar Andres Ximenes wrote that the deaf master's *Abraham Receiving the Three Angels*, although the first to meet the visitor's eye in the entrance to the Escurial, "might for its excellence be viewed the last, and is well worth coming many a league to see." De Amicis spoke of Navarrete as one of the leading painters of his time, after Titian, Velasquez, Murillo, and Ribera. John Hay, in *Castillian Days*, called him "that marvelous deaf-mute."

Navarrete died on March 28, 1579, in Toledo. At the time of his death, he had been working on a series of thirty-two altar pictures for the Church of the Escurial in contract with Prior Julian de Tricio, of which he had completed only eight. The curate of the parish of Santo Vincente later described El Mudo's final confession, in which he communicated in signs as intelligible as speech. With pen and paper on his death bed, he appointed an executor and bequeathed his money to a number of people. Among them were his brother, Friar Bautista, a four-year-old daughter in Segovia, directing that she enter the convent, and his friends at the Monastery of the Star at Logroño. El Mudo was buried at Toledo, in the church of San Juan de los Reyes. Among his unfinished paintings at the time of his death were portraits of the Duke of Medina Celi, Giovanni Andrea Doria, and one of a beautiful unknown woman.

Upon the death of Navarrete, the renowned Spanish dramatist and poet Lope de Vega composed an ode in *Laurel de Apolo* in tribute to the fellow artist who "lent Canvas a voice."

References

De Haerne, D. (1881). Two Spanish painters: "El Mudo" and "El Sordillo." *American Annals of the Deaf, 26* (3), 179–182.

Northcote, J. (1830). *The life of Titian: With anecdotes of the distinguished persons of his time* (Vol. 1, pp. 251–261). London: Henry Colburn and Richard Bentley.

Stirling, W. (1848). *Annals of the artists of Spain* (Vol. 1). London: John Ollivier.

ALBERT NEWSAM (1809–1864), American Lithographer.

Albert Newsam was born deaf on May 20, 1809, the son of an Ohio River boatman. His father, William Newsam, was drowned in an accident, and an innkeeper in Steubenville, Ohio, William Hamilton, took the young child in for a time. The child preferred to express himself by drawing pictures, and he amazed local residents and patrons of the inn with his precocious accuracy and eye for detail. It is unclear what happened to Newsam's mother. One story has her dying at childbirth; another shortly after Newsam's adoption by Hamilton. When Newsam was ten, a traveller named William Davis lodged at Hamilton's inn. Davis may have been deaf, or, more likely, pretended to be, and he immediately took notice of Hamilton's remarkably talented deaf ward. Davis persuaded Hamilton that he was sincerely interested in the boy based on their common experience. He told Hamilton that he would care for the child and have him educated in the East.

As soon as they left Steubenville, Davis began to exploit the child. He had Newsam draw pictures in sidewalk shows, telling bystanders that he was collecting money to have his "little brother" educated. He had already collected considerable money this way when the two arrived in Philadelphia. Davis was one day telling his story while Newsam made a chalk drawing of Market Street on an unused city watch box, when Bishop William White happened by. The bishop was the President of the Board of the newly founded Pennsylvania Institution for the Deaf and Dumb, and he immediately brought some staff members to the scene to query Davis. The older man told them that he had been educated by Abbé Sicard; that he and his young brother were on their way to Virginia to find relatives; and that they had faced numerous hardships after a series of family misfortunes. The staff members gave Davis some money to go to Virginia, but persuaded him to leave the boy in their care. Davis thanked them and promised to return. He never did.

"Albert Davis" continued in school as a state ward for a few years when a Mr. Wright, a visitor from Steubenville, came to tour classes. Suddenly, Albert showed great excitement. The boy motioned the visitor to the blackboard where, to Wright's amazement, he saw a rapidly sketched facade of his own home appearing before his eyes. Then Albert drew a street plan and another house, and he indicated that he had once lived there. Wright finally remembered the deaf child who had disappeared from the Hamiltons, and he was able to supply the school with the name Newsam and a few other details of the boy's early life.

Newsam's early talent was so extraordinary that school administrators sought professional tutoring for him with George Catlin,* the well-known portrayer of Native American life, who would himself later become deaf, and Hugh Bridgport, a fine miniaturist and engraver. Newsam left school in 1826 and became apprentice to Cephas Childs, a copper engraver.

Mr. Childs made a decision to add lithography to his business, and he brought Mr. Peter S. Duval over from Europe to establish a lithographic department. Duval became a mentor and supportive colleague. Newsam demonstrated an immediate and unusual ability to execute portraits on stone. Newsam was considered the first man in the United States to achieve a reputation as a lithographer. He was most brilliant as a copyist, eliciting uncanny detail from books, paintings, and engravings. Live portraits were problematic for him. Duval theorized that, because Newsam was a shy man, unable to engage his subjects in conversation, he had more difficulty in execution from life. Some critics argue that this may be an overstatement, however; it is hard to assess, since most of his live work was destroyed. For many years, however, Newsam was acknowledged as unsurpassed in the drawing of portrait lithographs from copy. According to contemporaries, he also had a photographic memory and could render detailed portraits of anything he had once seen on a page. He earned a comfortable living and made many supportive friends. He did not save or invest much, though; most of his money went for art prints, rare books, and illustrated music sheets. Since he never had the opportunity to go to Europe, he resolved to bring as much reproduction from the great galleries into his own home as possible.

Newsam's reputed magic touch brought inquiries to the Childs and Inman, and later Duval establishments from everywhere. His portraits of DeWitt Clinton, Henry Clay, Andrew Jackson, and Zachary Taylor were exceptionally popular and are still reproduced. Childs began a project to publish a lithographic portrait series of distinguished Americans, and Newsam was its principal artist. He also reproduced paintings lithographically in the French Style, and these were favorably received. In 1841, Newsam attended a dance performance by Fanny Elssler. He described himself, writing to a friend, as "moved to applaud, for I understood every one of her movements. If everyone expressed themselves as clearly as Fanny, the world would no longer be veiled for us deaf-mutes." Inspired by her work, Newsam's *Elssler* became what is probably the first lithograph from a daguerreotype.

Newsam's enormous professional success relieved a lifetime of misfortune. He married and was deserted by his bride one week later. A "friend" who had insinuated his way into Newsam's circle stole most of his collection of rare books and prints and sold them. In 1856, a fire destroyed many of his lithographs and virtually all of his life paintings. He lost vision for a time in one eye. Finally, he suffered a paralytic stroke. Without regular work, or savings, he was discharged from the hospital to a poorhouse. His loyal friends, including Duval, rescued him, raised money, and cared for him until they could secure a placement for him in a genteel care facility, the Living Home at Wilmington, Delaware.

Newsam died on November 20, 1864, and is buried in Laurel Hill Cemetery, Philadelphia.

In 1934, five of Newsam's engravings were shown at the International Exhibition of Fine and Applied Arts by Deaf Artists at the Roerich Museum in New York City. These included portraits of Thomas Jefferson, Philip Syng Physick, Bishop William White, Stephen Girard, and Charles H. Reade.

References

Pyatt, J. O. (1968). Albert Newsam. *American Annals of the Deaf, 13* (4), 255.

Reaves, W. W. (1984). *American portrait prints.* Charlottesville, VA: University Press of Virginia.

Stauffer, D. (1934). Lithographic portraits of Albert Newsam. *The Mt. Airy World, 50* (1), 1–3.

CHARLES HENRI NICOLLE (1866–1936), French Nobel Laureate in Physiology and Medicine.

Charles Henri Nicolle was born in Rouen, France, on September 21, 1866. His father, Eugène Nicolle, was a physician and professor of natural history at the École des Sciences et des Arts in Rouen. This connection likely guided the interest Charles developed in medicine. His older brother, Maurice, was also influenced in taking a scientific direction in his work. He was to become a distinguished bacteriologist and pathologist, who convinced Charles to enroll at the Pasteur Institute in Paris. For Charles, this would prove to be a turning point. Deafened at the age of eighteen, Nicolle was an intensely passionate man who intentionally hid behind an air of detachment. At Pasteur, such a mixture of enthusiasm and studied objectivity was looked upon favorably. A capable speechreader in his circle of colleagues and family members, most in the field of medicine, Nicolle found support and comfort particularly in the discourse of his field. ''Thanks to you,'' he said to his friend Georges Duhammel, ''the concert of the world starts again.''

In 1893, he completed his doctoral dissertation under the supervision of Émile Roux on the subject of a venereal disease caused by Ducrey's bacillus. While in charge of a bacteriology laboratory back in Rouen, Nicolle was an assistant professor at the medical school there, a member of the hospital staff, and a developer of inoculating techniques for a serum to fight against diphtheria. But disappointed that he was unable to establish major medical research facilities at Rouen, he accepted the directorship of the Pasteur Institute division at Tunis in 1902, where he developed the institute into a leading center for research and production of vaccines.

It was at Tunis that Nicolle's most significant medical breakthrough was made. Noting that an outbreak of typhus did not appear to spread within the wards at the hospital there, he investigated the reason, and eventually discovered the louse as a carrier of the disease. Nicolle noticed that typhus did not appear to spread within the hospital wards as it did in the city. He then experimented, emphasizing that the lice were responsible for transmission of the disease; and he reported his results to the Académie des Sciences in 1909. Subsequent development of the procedures for fighting this disease, including systematic delousing, then followed. If Nicolle had not made this contribution to the understanding of typhus prior to World War I, innumerable lives would have been lost. With this discovery, he was said to have joined the ranks of major benefactors to humanity. His friend, Germaine Lot, reminisced about the moment when Nicolle was awarded the ultimate recognition—a Nobel Prize for this work in 1928: "I reflected on Beethoven leading his Ninth Symphony without hearing the acclamation of the crowd."

Another important contribution by Nicolle, accepted unquestioningly in the present day although novel at his time, was his discovery that an infectious disease can be carried in an organism through its life cycle without external manifestations. His research with C. Lebailly on guinea pigs illustrated how an organism inoculated with typhus may remain healthy even though a germ may complete its entire life cycle, a theoretical notion that was to have important implications for epidemiologists. Nicolle's research included major investigations of infectious diseases in the Mediterranean and African regions, and in Mexico. He studied diseases in the dogs of India, rodents in Tunisia, and the role of ticks and flies in transmitting diseases in general. He is credited with having discovered *leishmaniasis* in the dog, and he developed a culture media to study related diseases further. With L. Manceaux, he isolated *Toxoplasma gondii*, a previously undiscovered parasite, in Tunisian rodents. In addition, Nicolle's research contributed significantly to the understanding of the role of ticks in epidemics involving spirochetes and that of flies in the transmission of trachoma, a viral disease of the eye. His work advanced the study of murine typhus in Mexico, and he also helped to verify the viral nature of influenza. Nicolle worked closely with E. Conseil in the area of preventive medicine, and they made significant advances in the battle against measles. In 1932, Nicolle was nominated to the chair of experimental medicine at the Collège de France where he lectured and experimented until shortly before his death in 1936.

Nicolle developed his other talents as well. He enjoyed creative writing, and authored several novels and collections of stories. His intense interest in the moral responsibilities of scientists was the focus of many of his later lectures, which took an increasingly philosophical turn. These published papers became very popular among members of the French scientific community.

He died on February 28, 1936, in Tunis, Tunisia, back in the country where he had found much fulfillment professionally and personally. Both of Charles Nicolle's children, Marcelle and Pierre, also became physicians.

References

Grmek, M. D. (1978). Charles Jules Henri Nicolle. In C. C. Gillispie (Ed.), *Dictionary of scientific biography* (Vol. 15, Suppl. I, pp. 453–454). New York: Charles Scribner's Sons.

Lot, G. (1961). *Charles Nicolle et la biologie conquérante*. Paris: Pierre Seghers.

Nicolle, C. (1930). *Naissance, vie et mort des maladies infectieuses*. Paris: F. Alcan.

Nicolle, C. (1932). *Biologie de l'invention*. Paris: F. Alcan.

Nicolle, C. (1961). *Destin des maladies infectieuses suivi de l'expérimentation dans l'étude des maladies infectieuses*. Paris: Alliance Culturelle Du Livre.

FREDA NORMAN (1945–   ), American Actress.

Fredericka (Freda) Norman was born deaf on August 15, 1945, in Alexandria, Virginia. Her parents and older sister Jane were also deaf. Norman graduated from the Virginia School for the Deaf in Staunton. She attended Gallaudet College. There, she performed as "Betty Chumley" in Mary Chase's *Harvey*, among other plays. In 1969, Norman won the Best Supporting Actress award in a one-act play, the revival scene of *Dark of the Moon* directed by Betty Miller.* She then joined the National Theatre of the Deaf (NTD), with which she performed for nine years. Norman acted in such roles as "Cunegonde" in *Candide*, "Leah" in *The Dybbuk*, "Milady" in *The Three Musketeers*, and as the leading lady in *Sganarelle*. She also performed in *Under Milkwood*, *Woyzeck*, and *Four Saints in Three Acts*. The National Theatre of the Deaf toured through the United States, Europe, Australia, and Israel.

In 1978, Norman started a touring company with Rico Peterson, Frederico Productions, in Oakland, California, where she directed and starred in several productions. When she was invited to be the understudy for "Sarah Norman" in *Children of a Lesser God*, she explained that she was several months pregnant. Gordon Davidson, producer-director of the Mark Taper Forum in Los Angeles, took the news in stride, hired Norman, and advised the costume designer accordingly. In the early 1980s, she starred as "Sarah" in appearances with Peterson across the country. Norman performed with the National Touring Company and acted in plays for the First Bus and Truck Company, the Frozen Dinner Theatre, and the Little Theatre of the Deaf.

On television, Norman appeared on *Sesame Street*, *A Child's Christmas in Wales* (with Sir Michael Redgrave), and on the *Dick Cavett* and *Today* shows. In 1979, she starred in the role of "Supersign" on the Children's PBS special *Rainbow's End*, a five-part series developed to enhance the self-identity of deaf children and to improve their language skills. "Supersign" is a heroine-type transformed from the shy, mild-mannered secretary "Penny." Norman's sister, Jane Norman Wilk, was artistic director and executive consultant for this series. Funded by the Bureau of Education of the Handicapped and the Charles Stewart Mott Foundation, the popular series won an Emmy Award for outstanding achievement in children's television programming and was aired nationally.

At one point in her life, Norman took a hiatus from acting to do advocacy work, raising the consciousness of others about deaf people and deafness. Her experiences in a deaf family enriched the workshops she conducted for social service organizations. She has also assisted the Salk Institute in La Jolla, California, in research studies on American Sign Language.

In 1987, Norman played the leading role in *The Good Person of Szechuan* in Berkeley, California. That same year, she starred as "Dolly Levi" in Thornton Wilder's comedy *The Matchmaker*. In 1992, she performed as the frustrated romantic English housewife "Shirley" in Willy Russell's comedy *Shirley Valentine*, produced by Deaf West Theater Company of Los Angeles and directed by Ed Waterstreet.* The play opened at the Fountain Theatre in Hollywood. In this story of a woman's trip of self-discovery, Norman ingeniously modified her sign language to provide a "British flavor." For this role she received a Dramalogue Award. Such commitment to experimental work and new interpretations is characteristic of her career. Norman also appeared in *Our Town* in the Milwaukee Repertoire in 1992 and in Siberia, Russia, in 1993. In 1994, she received a second Dramalogue Award when she performed in *Night, Mother* for Deaf West Theater. She is currently acting in Deaf West Theater and translating English scripts to American Sign Language.

References

Baldwin, S. C. (1993). *Pictures in the air: The story of the National Theatre of the Deaf.* Washington, DC: Gallaudet University Press.

Finston, M. (1972, February 2). Actress wins silent applause for lines that she'll never hear. Newark, NJ *Star-Ledger*.

Jackson, L. (1982, May 14). Freda Norman: "People have the right to be different," actress asserts. New York *International*.

Marsh, B. (1981, October 10). Silent stage determined life. Cincinnati, Ohio *Enquirer*.

AUDREE L. NORTON (1927–   ), American Actress.

Audree L. Norton, née Bennett, was born on January 13, 1927, in Great Falls, Montana. She was deafened from spinal meningitis at the age of two. Norton attended the Faye Allen School in Faribault and the Agassiz School in Minneapolis, where her acting debut included performances as a male. Norton was then enrolled at the Minnesota School for the Deaf, followed by a year at the Model Secondary School for the Deaf in Washington, D.C. At the Minnesota School for the Deaf, she finally had the opportunity to perform in a female role, without a mustache. While at Gallaudet College, she continued to participate in drama mainly out of love for theatre, but she was concerned about the lack of available professional opportunities for deaf actors. In 1952, she received a bachelor's degree in English Language and Literature.

Bernard Bragg* suggested her name to the National Theatre of the Deaf (NTD) when it began in 1967. NTD completed five plays on three tours to forty cities in its first year, followed by seven plays in thirty-five cities the second year, including a Japanese Kabuki play, *The Tale of Kasane*, in which Norton played the leading role in a challenging production. With a Japanese director for this adaptation of a seventeenth-century fable, two interpreters were needed to communicate in Japanese, English, and American Sign Language. Other NTD plays Norton performed in include *Gianni Schicci, The Critic*, and *Tyger! Tyger!* Norton appeared with fellow NTD actors Bragg, Gilbert Eastman,* June Eastman, Howard Palmer, Ralph White, and Phyllis Frelich* on the NBC-TV *Experiment in Television*, a one-hour special demonstrating NTD's new art form of sign-mime.

In 1968, Norton was in her kitchen in California when the phone rang and her fourteen-year-old daughter Nikki answered. It was Hollywood, and Norton was offered an appearance on *Mannix*. In September, she starred in a groundbreaking episode titled "The Silent Cry" as a deaf woman whose ability to speechread made her the target for a murder. She helped Mike Conners as "Mannix" solve a crime. This was one of the first guest appearances of an adult deaf actress on a regular series.

While her family was spending the summer in Houston, a friend encouraged Norton to do Royal Crown cola commercials with voice-overs. She then enrolled in a modeling school in Houston specializing in training for television commercials and eventually added dozens of television commercials to her credit, for such companies and products as Neiman Marcus, Pepsi Cola, Dr. Pepper, Lux soap, Cadillac, and Ford. She was pictured on the cover of the June 1974 issue of *Today's Film Maker*, part of a story about the production of an Eastman Kodak commercial by the prestigious J. Walter Thompson Company.

Her television credits include *The Streets of San Francisco*. In 1970, she was a featured player in Family Affair in an episode titled "The Language of Love" on CBS. In the 1971 ABC show *The Man and the City*, Norton starred in an emotion-packed episode called "Hands of Love." She also pursued a master's degree in rhetoric at the University of California, graduating in 1975.

Norton's acting career was sidetracked when she turned her attention to advocacy for deaf actors and actresses. Her politicization began in urgency when she was involved in a protest over the *ABC Afterschool Special*, "Mom and Dad Can't Hear Me," produced by Daniel Wilson Productions. Turned down for the lead role, she wrote letters to the Screen Actors Guild in San Francisco, charging that Daniel Wilson Productions had discriminated against her. Deaf actresses had already been incensed over the choice of Amy Irving, a hearing actress, for *Voices*, a major film about a deaf woman. Norton, who is called unassuming and humble by colleagues, felt that the personal injustice she experienced needed to be addressed as a broader systemic problem and viewed in a larger context. She has devoted her time since the protest to working for change as an educator. She wrote, produced, and directed at the Ohlone (California) Sign Theater and retired from Ohlone College as professor emeritus in 1992.

References

Fields, S. (1968, September 11). Silent Theater. *New York Daily News*.
Riste, T. (1971, September 17). Emotion takes over on "Man and the City." *Arizona Daily Star*.
Strassler, B. (1992, June). An applause for Audree. *Hearing Health*, 14–15.

MALCOLM J. NORWOOD (1927–1989), American Media Specialist.

Malcolm J. Norwood was born on March 6, 1927, and deafened at the age of five from the combined effects of measles and scarlet fever. After several years in public schools, in Hartford, Connecticut, he found communication a struggle. A school nurse convinced his mother to enroll him at the American School for the Deaf in West Hartford. "For the first time since my deafness, communication became free and easy," he once reminisced. "This has made all the difference, and I have often wished I could find that nurse and thank her for what she did." He graduated with a bachelor's degree from Gallaudet College in 1949. There, he was Editor-in-Chief of the *Buff and Blue* in his senior year. His fellow students remembered him for turning the Tower Clock back an hour and disrupting the campus; he would never outgrow his love for a good joke. His master's degree was earned at the University of Hartford in 1957. He taught for eleven years after graduating from Gallaudet, first at the Texas School for the Deaf in Austin, then at the American School for the Deaf and the West Virginia School for the Deaf in Romney. In the West Virginia School, he was promoted to director of curriculum and supervising teacher of the intermediate and advanced classes.

In 1960, Norwood became the first deaf professional to hold a position in the U.S. Office of Education. By 1965, he had received the Health, Education and Welfare Superior Service Award. Over the next twenty-eight years, he served as Program Specialist for Captioned Films for the Deaf, Education Officer, Chief of the Media Services and Captioned Films Branch, and Chief of the Captioned Films and Telecommunications Branch. In these positions, he authored many publications and presented many speeches on deaf people and deafness, media-related issues, and captioned films for deaf people. In 1970, he was invited to moderate the session "Audio Visual Communication and the Education of the Deaf in the U.S." at the International Congress on Education of the Deaf in Stockholm, Sweden.

Norwood established a nationwide distribution system of captioned films. He was responsible for securing Hollywood films and educational films for later captioning and distribution to deaf Americans. For more than a decade, he fought for the rights of deaf people to caption entertainment. Television networks were initially reluctant to respond, as were electronic equipment manufacturers. Norwood was influenced greatly by Edmund Boatner and Jules Rakow at the American School for the Deaf, pioneers in the captioned films movement. For his leadership in implementing this important technological breakthrough, Norwood is recognized as a "father of captioning." He saw the potential to improve learning as well as to provide entertainment. "As we progress toward achieving this objective," he said about captioned television in 1972, "it becomes increasingly clear that the educational possibilities for deaf children and adults have never been brighter."

Norwood also worked with the Civil Service Commission to establish official government interpreters for deaf people, making many more federal positions available to deaf persons. He developed materials and programs to train deaf drivers in defensive driving. Active in the Deaf community, he served as president of the Tri-State Council of Virginia, the District of Columbia, and Maryland State Associations of the Deaf, vice president of the Maryland Association of the Deaf, and vice president of the Gallaudet College Alumni Association. Norwood, his wife Marjorie, and their five children resided in New Carrollton, Maryland.

In addition to his work with captioning, Norwood was responsible for developing assistive devices for persons with physical disabilities as well as for blind people. He became a key promoter of new technologies, since grants from the public sector were, at the time, a primary source for the development of assistive devices.

In 1971, he was appointed Liaison Officer for the National Technical Institute for the Deaf at the Rochester Institute of Technology in Rochester, New York, while continuing to serve as chief of Media Services and Captioned Films.

Norwood received a commendation from the U.S. Commissioner of Education in 1970. In 1972, Gallaudet College presented him with an honorary doctoral degree. He received the Distinguished Service Award from the U.S. Department of Health, Education, and Welfare in 1976 "for outstanding services and dedication rendered to the handicapped population in the area of educational technology and television programming."

In 1972, Norwood earned his doctoral degree in education from the University of Maryland. He retired from his position as Chief, Captioning and Adaptation Branch, in 1988.

Norwood died of a heart attack on March 22, 1989. A memorial service attended by 250 people was held at Gallaudet University the following week.

In 1990, the Dr. Malcolm J. Norwood Memorial Award was established by the National Captioning Institute in Falls Church, Virginia, to provide scholarships to deaf or hard-of-hearing students studying for careers in communication and/or media technology. In 1991, the Malcolm J. Norwood Center was dedicated in Baltimore to house the Community Support Services for the Deaf.

References

In memory of Malcolm J. Norwood. (1989). *NAD Broadcaster, 2* (5), 1, 3.
Mac Norwood Quotes. Undated document, Gallaudet University Archives.

O

WYN OWSTON (ETHEL SHARRARD) (1919–   ), British Physician.

Wyn Owston (née Ethel Sharrard) was born on December 26, 1919, in Lincoln, England, and was deafened by meningitis at the age of eighteen months. Both of her parents were physicians practicing in Lincoln; her mother was a specialist in Obstetrics and Gynecology. They determined that Owston should have a typical education, and enrolled her in Lincoln Girl's High School; but in spite of her hard work and special help from teachers, she did not do well. With unintelligible speech and an inability to communicate with anyone except her family (whom she rarely saw), Owston found solace in religion at the age of fifteen, and she attributed her renewed strength to this faith. After only six weeks' preparation, she passed the Matriculation examination, the general university entrance requirement in England. "Deafness has its advantages," she wrote in her letter to the authors, "when one needs to concentrate really hard!"

When authorities at Sheffield University opposed Owston's entrance into the medical course of study, her physician parents argued her case. The Dean of Sheffield was extremely unwilling and rude about taking any woman student, let alone one who was deaf and had unintelligible speech. Since both of her parents were well-known in the medical community, her father was able to argue convincingly; and Owston was allowed to pursue the degree, providing she passed both the Pre-Registration and "1st M.B." examinations in one year, a condition the dean obviously thought impossible since the latter exam was usually taken after two years in medical school. The Pre-Registration examination required for entry into medical school included chemistry, physics, and biology. The 1st M.B. examination included these subjects as well as zoology. "My parents supported and encouraged me unsparingly," she reminisced, "and I knew nothing of their doubts until many years later." They, too, had thought the dean's requirements to be impossible.

Her first hearing aid was a box about eighteen inches long, fifteen inches wide, and four inches high, which she set up on the desk in front of her. With huge earphones, the device was used only to bring her into contact with sound and help her to control her own voice more naturally. She took continuous speech lessons and depended on lipreading. More often than not, it was impossible to speechread in the medical school lectures, she explained, so she brought knitting and other diversions she could do under a desk. Each evening she borrowed a friend's notes and wrote her own while studying the textbooks.

She passed the examinations at the first attempt in June 1938, and began the medical course proper, continuing her studies for the next two years. In August 1939, Owston visited the World's Fair in the United States with her family and, while staying with a great-aunt in North Carolina the following month, she learned that England had declared war. Her family encouraged her to remain in the United States to finish medical school, but she insisted on returning, eventually embarking on a dangerous journey after finding passage in an American ship.

Owston passed the 2nd M.B. examinations in March 1940, and began clinical work. She found that she could manage quite well communicatively when talking to individual patients, tutors, and nurses, using lipreading and a new hearing aid that had the amplifier and two large batteries fixed to a wide waist-belt. Once in awhile, however, the strong local dialects of Yorkshire, Lancaster, and the Pottery areas presented a challenge. The problem was less one of speechreading pronunciation variations than of being presented with entirely new vocabulary items—especially for certain parts of the body. The resourceful Owston went to her closest friend and demanded a tutorial on nonmedical anatomical terms. Later, they became husband and wife.

With the war in full progress, hospitals were short on staff and Owston found herself spending most of her time giving anesthetics, assisting in operations, and supervising treatment, desperately hard work, often for eighteen hours a day. Thus, very early in her career, she experienced a diversity of roles and communication situations, which provided invaluable experience.

She graduated with her medical degree in March 1943. In the middle of the oral examination in Medicine, the External Examiner, Sir Leonard Parsons, a national authority in Child Health at that time, asked Owston to work as his House-Physician in Birmingham, an unusual honor. After some discussion, Owston decided that she should first gain experience in General Medicine and Surgery before specializing. She also declined an offer of a research post with the Professor of Bacteriology, preferring to do clinical work. In one letter to her parents, a physician and friend cautioned about the perceived difficulty Owston's deafness may present in medical practice, arguing that her intellect better suited her to research than to day-to-day work with patients. The friend feared that her "physical infirmity which cannot be hidden" would be "blamed rightly or wrongly whenever misunderstandings occur and some scapegoat is required."

Owston did not allow the fears of others to concern her. She began working as House-Physician and then became House-Surgeon at Sheffield Infirmary for nine months. Unable to use the telephone, her main difficulty, she arranged with a nurse to come to her room to take the calls, a practice that was normally forbidden. Operating rooms, with attendees cloaked and wearing masks, were also less-than-ideal speechreading situations. Owston minimized the difficulty by being very alert and anticipating every step. At times, too, she had patients with moustaches so long that she could only lipread them by lifting the hair covering the lips.

In February 1944, Owston went to a war-time annex of the Birmingham Hospitals as Senior House-Physician. Civilians were moved to the city, and casualties from the Normandy war front were taken in. With a staff of only three taking care of more than one hundred patients every few days, the work was hectic. Their first supply of penicillin arrived (none of the staff had ever used it before), and they were amazed to see patients who were dying of gas-gangrene cured by small doses. In October, 1944, she moved to Birmingham Maternity Hospital, where she served on the resident surgical staff until the promised post at Birmingham Children's Hospital finally materialized in March 1945; but after only three months she herself became ill. She decided to return to Lincoln and work with her parents in general practice. With many physicians away at war, the number of patients was overwhelming. In addition to the usual medical work, she had an average of thirty obstetric cases each month, driving all over the coutryside and delivering in the houses. During this time, she also studied for the Diploma in Obstetrics of the Royal College of Obstetricians and Gynaecologists which she obtained in 1949.

When her eldest child began school, Owston took up part-time work in Family Planning clinics. She helped to start several new clinics in North Wales. She continued Family Planning work until her retirement in 1984 and has found rewarding work in personal counseling over the past few years.

Reference

A medical degree for a deaf woman. (1946). *The Volta Review, 48* (12), 785.

P

ROBERT F. PANARA (1920–), American Educator/Writer.

Robert F. Panara was born on July 8, 1920, in the Upper Bronx area of New York City. He was profoundly deafened through spinal meningitis at the age of ten. While he was recovering from his illness, his cousins brought him stacks of books, and he soon became a voracious reader. Even at this early age, his readings reflected the romantic and adventurous, which gave him the sense of style that endeared him to thousands of students and colleagues in the years to follow. From *Treasure Island* and *The Three Musketeers* to books on poetry and the Wild West, Panara was practically self-educated while attending public schools through his high school years. Without the assistance of note takers or interpreters, he carried his neverending supply of novels and verse with him and read them during ''classes.''

Upon graduation from De Witt Clinton High School in 1938, Panara moved with his family to Fall River, Massachusetts, where he worked for a clothing factory. Tiring of this quickly, he soon learned about Gallaudet College; and, after learning sign language at the American School for the Deaf in Hartford, Connecticut, Panara enrolled at Gallaudet in 1940. There he majored in English and literature under the special influence of Powrie Doctor, a hearing professor, and Frederick Hughes, a deaf professor of drama and economics. Panara was drawn to Hughes' visual and dramatic teaching style and ''that became my trademark from the very beginning of my teaching career.'' After graduating from Gallaudet College in 1945, he took a position at the New York School for the Deaf in White Plains, where he was an instructor in English, American history, literature, and algebra. Even in those early days, he exerted a motivating influence on his young students, among them Bernard Bragg* and Eugene Bergman,* who would become masters of dramatic arts and literature. While teaching in White Plains, Panara also studied for his master's degree in English at New York University, which he received in 1948. The following year, Panara accepted a position as instructor at Gallaudet College, where he taught English and served as faculty advisor to the Literary Club, Dramatics Club, and the campus newspaper and literary magazine. He also assisted in adapting and translating into sign language such classic plays as *Oedipus*, *The Trojan Women*, *Macbeth*, *Hamlet*, and *Othello*.

Panara's writings also inspired many of his students. In his first year as a teacher at the New York School for the Deaf, he immediately set out to share his enthusiasm over "Deaf Studies," publishing "Poetry and the Deaf" in the major periodical for educators of deaf students in the United States (the *American Annals of the Deaf*). He was the first recipient of the Teegarden Poetry Award from Gallaudet. His articles over the next two decades filled a major need in the field with such titles as "The Literary Achievements of the Deaf," "Teaching Literature to the Deaf: Creative Techniques and Approaches," "Poetry as a Language Learning Tool for the Deaf," "The Deaf Writer in America: From Colonial Times to the Present," and "Deaf Characters in Fiction and Drama."

Panara also published many poems in periodicals. In 1988, his classic poem, "On His Deafness," won a $1,000 first prize in the World of Poetry contest, and has been performed worldwide by the National Theatre of the Deaf and reprinted in many books and periodicals. After retirement, he continued to write, including coauthoring with Harry Lang an article on "Deafness and Deaf Characters in Science Fiction."

A story about Robert Panara has become part of the "lore" of the American Deaf community. In 1957, *Life* magazine invited Panara and a Gallaudet student to lipread Queen Elizabeth II through high-powered binoculars while she attended the Maryland-North Carolina football game. Reporters were not allowed near the Queen; so they were asked to "eavesdrop," recording her comments on a tape recorder. Under police escort, they were then rushed to a private plane, which took them to New York City to complete the story. The most frustrating thing about "Operation Lipread," the sports enthusiast Panara recalled with dry humor, "was that I had to keep my eyes glued to the Queen's face and couldn't watch the game!"

In 1967, Panara became the first deaf professor at the National Technical Institute for the Deaf (NTID), a college of the Rochester Institute of Technology (RIT) and a federally funded program with the goal of state-of-the-art technical education for deaf students on a hearing college campus. During his years at NTID, he established the English Department, won the NTID Student Association Outstanding Staff Award (1975) and the RIT Eisenhart Award for Outstanding Teaching (1975). Upon his retirement, NTID established the Robert F. Panara Scholarship Fund, and named the college theatre in his honor. In 1981, he was honored with the Service Award for Contributions to the Humanities by the Deaf Hollywood television and film production company Beyond Sound. He has received honorary doctorates from MacMurray College (1985) and Gallaudet College (1986). Panara was also honored by B.O.C.E.S. (New York State)

Robert F. Panara, American writer and educator. Photo courtesy of the National Technical Institute for the Deaf.

when the Support Service Personnel organization established an annual Robert F. Panara Award for their contributions to helping deaf people realize their full potential.

Panara's first book was published in 1960, *The Silent Muse: An Anthology of Poetry and Prose of the Deaf*, which he coedited with Taras Denis and J. B. McFarlane. He published *Great Deaf Americans* with his son, John Panara, in 1983. The book is a collection of thirty-three biographies of deaf persons from various walks of life, including athletes, aviators, and artists. He served as Associate Editor of the *Gallaudet Encyclopedia of Deaf People and Deafness* for four years, and contributed entries on poetry, fiction, nonfiction, Deaf culture, and the performing arts. Panara also authored the entry "Education of Deaf" in the *New Catholic Encyclopedia*. His development of a videotape collection of lectures on education and interviews with "Famous Deaf Americans" highlighted his long-time advocacy for an effective "Deaf Studies" curriculum. The interviews included such notables as Bernard Bragg;* Frances Woods* and Billy

Bray, the "Wonder Dancers;" Donald L. Ballantyne,* Director of the Micro-surgery Training Program at the New York University; and Eugene "Silent" Hairston, a former professional prize fighter. Panara, who also established the Performing Arts Department at the National Technical Institute for the Deaf, was a founding member of the National Theatre of the Deaf and a faculty fellow at their annual Summer School Program (1967–1983). During his sabbatical (1975–1976), he was a Visiting Professor in English and Drama at California State University, Northridge (CSUN), teaching both deaf and hearing students. This gave him the unique distinction of being the only person to teach full-time at each of the three major postsecondary programs for deaf students in the United States. In 1976, he was honored by the World Federation of the Deaf (WFD) when he received their Medal of Merit for his contributions to education and culture.

In retirement, Panara continues to be extremely active, presenting workshops, lecturing, and publishing. *Deaf Life* magazine featured a cover story, "A Tribute to Bob Panara," in September 1988 and, in 1994, Panara was chosen as "Educator of the Quarter Century" by *Silent News*, the major news periodical of the American Deaf community. Many students and colleagues who have observed him teach, and many others who have not, continue to feel his presence in the education of deaf students.

References

Edstrom, E. (1957, November 16). Lip readers by telescope recorded chats by Queen at Terp grid game. *Washington Post.*

First deaf professor proud pioneer of NTID's beginnings on campus. (1993, September 16). Rochester Institute of Technology *News & Events*, *25* (4), 3.

Levitan, L., & Moore, M.S. (1988). A tribute to Bob Panara. *Deaf Life, 1* (3), 14–21.

ROBERT BAARD PETERSON (1943–   ), American Painter.

Robert Baard Peterson was born in 1943 in Elmhurst, Illinois, and was deafened by rheumatic fever at the age of four. His family moved to Albuquerque, New Mexico, when he was eight years old, and he was enrolled in the New Mexico School for the Deaf. Peterson was twenty-five years old when he began to paint full time. His first exhibition of note was at the Willard Gallery in New York City in 1972, where he included paintings of highway construction in the Southwest, labyrinthine designs constructed from ramps, bridges, and over-passes. He also uses found objects, such as garbage cans, in his paintings. His work has commanded a significant amount of critical attention. "No matter what his source of inspiration," summarized *New York Times* critic David L. Shirey on January 8, 1972, "the artist marshals his subject matter into a rigorous pictorial composition where formal structure is of primary importance."

Although he is primarily a figurative painter, reviewers, such as Stroh in *Artspace*, have described his work as including a "sensuous abstraction" with an intense vision "distilled into forms of light, shade, space and mass of such precision and tension as to create an exact balance between the subject the work is based on and the abstract structure that is necessary to give any work of art a life of its own.'' Peterson always shows interest in emphasizing the relationship of positive and negative space in his composition, juxtaposing starkly simple objects against highly contrastive backgrounds. While often called formalistic, the drama of his images can evoke emotional reactions in the viewer of his work.

Peterson's early works demonstrate the energy with which he approached visualization. He began to use large machines at rest, but somehow conveying motion—machines such as bulldozers. *Red Tractor* (1970) was one of his first in this genre. Critics noted the latent strength in these ''still objects.'' Some viewers theorize that the eye of the deaf artist is particularly drawn to these giant constructions when they are not at work. He also plays with shape, and his still life paintings with gourds and eggs demonstrate, through use of subdued color, a strange, almost eerie, quiet. Peterson's use of color has been fairly restricted, but his use of light is dramatic. In *Nine Pipes*, he demonstrated an unusual quality, using browns and blacks. ''I like to choose from a situation perceived as the artificial and natural in opposition, coexistence, or isolation,'' Peterson explained in *Artspace*. In *Shop Towel Over Box*, however, the image of the burnt red towel on the open box is a unique one. Peterson's favoring of isolated images is not alienating but often forges new, unexpected relationships.

Peterson has shown his paintings in many exhibits. In 1982 alone, he exhibited at the Eason Gallery in Santa Fe, at Gallaudet College in Washington, D.C., and at the Valley House Gallery in Dallas. His paintings are in many private collections as well as museums, including the Anschutz Collection in Denver, Museum of Albuquerque, Museum of New Mexico in Santa Fe, University of New Mexico Art Museum in Albuquerque, and the First City Bank of Chicago. Peterson received the Purchase Prize and Honorable Mention at the Southwest Fine Arts Biennial in 1970, the Purchase Prize at the Fuller Lodge Competition in Los Alamos (1970), Jurors Award at the Southwest Fine Arts Biennial in Santa Fe (1972), and the Purchase Award at the October Show in Albuquerque in 1981.

References

Mannes, J. P. (1987). Robert Baard Peterson. In J. V. Van Cleve (Ed.), *Gallaudet encyclopedia of deaf people and deafness* (Vol. 2, pp. 283–284). New York: McGraw-Hill.
Shirey, D. L. (1972, January 8). Review, *New York Times*, A23.
Stroh, E. (1983, July). Robert Peterson. *Artspace*, 32–33.

YVONNE PITROIS (1880–1937), French Writer.

Yvonne Pitrois was born in Paris on December 14, 1880, and lived with her family in Tours, France. She was deafened at the age of seven through severe sunstroke, which also impaired her sight until she was twelve. During these years in darkness and silence, her mother told her stories by writing with the finger on the palm of her hand. Through her mother's patience and inventiveness, she learned both French and English. Her early aptitude and talent for language subsequently manifested themselves in her career as a writer. When Pitrois was young, she wrote to the famed deaf poetess Helen Marion Burnside, naïvely suggesting that they establish a "correspondence club" for all the deaf people of the Western world. Although Burnside responded, probably with some amusement, that she did not have time for such, sixteen years later Mrs. James Muir, a deaf woman from Australia, proposed the same idea, and a "Cosmopolitan Correspondence Club" was established in 1912. Through this club, Pitrois made the acquaintance of the deaf sculptor Douglas Tilden* and Helen Keller* in America, among others, and in France the celebrated deaf-blind poetess Bertha Galeron de Calonne, as well as Coppée, Daudet, Pierre Loti, and other men of letters. To Helen Keller, she wrote encouraging her friend to consider publishing a magazine exclusively for deaf-blind Americans.

Pitrois, following in her mother's footsteps as an authoress, published her first book when she was eighteen years old. *Nobles Vies* was published in three editions. Among her more than twenty-five scholarly works were biographies of such notables as Helen Keller and Abraham Lincoln, as well as persons less well-known to her American readers, such as Bertha Galeron de Calonne, who was christened by Victor Hugo as "The Great Seer" and whose book of verses *Dans Ma Nuit* (*Into My Night*) was highly recommended to "readers of souls" by Elizabeth, the Queen of Roumania. Her biography of the Abbé de l'Epée, the founder of the world's first government-sponsored school for deaf children in Paris in the late eighteenth century, was written in time for the World Congress of the Deaf in Paris in 1912. The Congress commemorated the 200th anniversary of Epée's birth. Pitrois also translated English and American books and published articles—some as early as when she was seventeen years old—in the periodicals of France, England, Switzerland, and the United States. She wrote a regular series of letters to *The Silent Worker* entitled "From the Old World." In these, she informed the American Deaf community of histories of institutions in Europe. As an early deaf feminist, she also highlighted the works of other deaf women in this series. In April, 1918, for example, she described the work of the French dramatist Marie Lenéru, the English novelist Jessie D. Kerrnish, and the French artist Berthe Larue-Girard.

By 1912, she and her mother had moved to LeMans, in the province of Sarthé. After writing an open letter published in a magazine of the Y.W.C.A., she was told of a lonely deaf girl in the country with whom she might correspond. The next stage of her life work had begun. In 1913, she began a periodical for young deaf women, *La Petite Silencieuse* (*The Little Silent Girl*), which offered advice. More than nine hundred "little sisters" were soon subscribing, and Pitrois knew them all, writing to nearly every one personally. Each issue of *La Petite Silencieuse* included an inspiring editorial, news of interest to deaf and hard-of-hearing readers, and letters filled with human interest and compassion. Now, at the age of thirty-two, she had already authored more than two hundred articles in periodicals.

In 1928, she began *Le Rayon de Soleil des Sourds-Aveugles* (*The Sunbeam of the Deaf-Blind*) in French Braille, in which she shared her own experiences; but most of the periodical's issues were devoted to exchanges of ideas among the deaf-blind readers themselves. Noting that Helen Keller was likely too busy in America to pursue the idea she had earlier suggested, Pitrois set out to do this for her own friends in France. Not only did the deaf-blind readers exchange ideas, but Pitrois frequently found gifts in the mail offered to one another— knitted stockings, gloves, rag dolls, and pearl necklaces and chains. "Dear Big Sister," one correspondent wrote, "I have made this pair of stockings. Will you forward it to a sister who is totally in darkness and silence and among the most lonely ones?" In addition to this circle of friendship, Pitrois also organized a fund to provide a modest sum of money to some of her "sisters" several times a year to make their lives more comfortable.

Pitrois wrote a variety of popular books. *Jeunes Vies* was composed of stories about humble life. *Cherie* was an idyll for young women and *Ombres des Femmes* was a collection of biographies of famous women. Other works of note include *Petits Enfants* and *Grands Examples*. Many of her books were translated into other languages.

Pitrois was instrumental during World War I in helping many deaf people with necessities of life. She helped to locate deaf refugees, provide them with money, and find their families, placing the deaf children in school programs. Known to many of her friends as their "Grande Soeur," she often found them employment. After the death of her mother, Pitrois welcomed destitute deaf girls to her cottage by the sea in Brittany, giving them a rural retreat in which to reflect and find direction in life. In short, as an American writer once commented, she *alone* organized and performed the same work that charitable organizations were managing with staffs of trained workers.

For this work, she was decorated with the high order by the king of Belgium, and she received the Medal of Honor in 1920 from the French Société National d'Encouragement au Bien (National Welfare Society) for her devotion to humanity. She was also a member of La Société des Gens de Lettres. In 1929, she received from the French Academy the Prix Montyon for her lifelong devotion to enhancing the lives of deaf and deaf-blind people; and, for her literary work, the Academy made her an officer.

Pitrois died on April 23, 1937; and many readers of *La Petite Silencieuse* and *Le Rayon de Soleil* lost that sunshine in their lives, as her publications stopped with her death.

References

Golladay, L. E. (1987). Yvonne Pitrois. In J. V. Van Cleve (Ed.), *Gallaudet encyclopedia of deaf people and deafness* (Vol. 2, pp. 294–295). New York: McGraw-Hill.
Hance, M. L. (1928). Yvonne Pitrois. *The Volta Review, 30* (7), 360–362.

Lamarque, A. (1923). Mlle. Yvonne Pitrois, Officier d'Académie. *Revue Générale de l'Enseignement des Sourds-Muets, 24* (8), 131–132.
Montague, H. (1937). Yvonne Pitrois. *The Volta Review, 39* (7), 409, 421.

MAURICE PRENDERGAST (1859–1924), American Painter.

Maurice Brazil Prendergast was born on October 10, 1859, in St. John's, Newfoundland. When he was two years old, his family moved to Boston, Massachusetts, and New England became his home and his inspiration for most of his life. Prendergast's father was an Irish importer who operated a trading post, and his mother, Mary Malvina Germaine, was descended from a French Huguenot family who had settled in Boston. When the trading post failed, the family moved to be closer to the Germaines, and Maurice, Jr., and a gifted artist-brother, Charles, earned the family's living by performing a variety of odd jobs. Maurice Prendergast's first job was in a dry goods store, where he had the opportunity to sketch the barrels, sacks, and customers surreptitiously. He and Charles were largely self-taught; the family did what it could to support the purchase of materials or occasional lesson. Prendergast's father connected him to a painter of show cards, and as an apprentice, he concentrated mostly on lettering and washing brushes. It was not long before he was supporting himself painting show cards, stealing weekends sketching landscapes on the nearby greens and local countryside south of Boston. His brother, in an oft-quoted reminiscence, remarked that Maurice's excursions were "hell on cows."

Charles Prendergast was always an important anchor in Maurice's life. A respectable artist himself, he recognized and cultivated Maurice's more-than-respectable talent with whatever means he possessed. Charles actually had better luck in his initial employment with the art dealers Doll and Richards on Park Street in Boston. He persuaded Maurice to accompany him working passage on a trading ship to Europe in 1886, and they had a sketching excursion to Wales, London, and Paris the following year. The work done at this time is agreed to be rather conventional by critics; the young men probably did not have the time to pursue training during this trip abroad.

Very little is known of Prendergast's deafness, except that it is remarked upon frequently in passing by contemporaries. He appears to have had a progressive hearing loss, and his deafness was profound in later life. His brother Charles' role as mediator for him in a variety of situations may point to the early need for Maurice to have had an interpreter/agent, especially in the course of business transactions. Contemporaries also characterized Prendergast as charmingly child-like and protected, qualities that emerge repeatedly in his mature work. Whether those attributes were merely the function of personality or in part the result of living in a quiet world with little formal education and social life is a matter of speculation, for Prendergast did not write his own perspectives on his deafness.

In 1891, Prendergast took a second, longer trip abroad. He studied in Paris at the Julian Academy, where he worked under Benjamin Constant, Joseph Blanc, and Jean-Paul Laurens. He also struck up a close and productive friendship with the more experienced Canadian painter James Wilson Morrice. The pair took drawing trips together, and Morrice introduced Prendergast to such expatriates on the Paris scene as Aubrey Beardsley, Arnold Bennett, and Somerset Maugham. With Conder and later, Beardsley, they journeyed to paint in St. Malo, Dinard, and Dieppe. The association with this stimulating group proved to be the turning point in Prendergast's life. He expanded his horizons and his use of media, and began chiefly to use watercolors. His distinctive, "holiday"-oriented styles and themes began to emerge.

Prendergast returned from France to Boston in 1895 with an impressive portfolio. He immediately received a commission to do 137 illustrations for Sir James Barrie's *My Lady Nicotine*. In 1897, an exhibition of his paintings was held at the Chase Gallery. There, his work came to the attention of the Montgomery Sears family and the impressionist painter Mary Cassatt. The Sears became enthusiastic patrons, and they helped send Prendergast to Europe again. This time, Prendergast spent time in Italy, visiting Rome, Padua, and Florence, and painting in Siena, Naples, Capri, and Venice. Despite a two-month illness, he produced an amazing volume of work there. Upon his return, he exhibited his Italian work at the Chase Gallery and fifteen watercolors at the Art Institute of Chicago. The well-known watercolor *Market Place, Venice*, with its colorful shoppers and Japanese influences, is representative of Prendergast at this period.

In addition to his watercolors and some oil paintings, Prendergast produced 200 monotypes. These were highly experimental copper landscape prints, and only he and a student of his knew the complete process. He exhibited them in Cincinnati, Chicago, and Boston, where reviewers remarked that works such as *Orange Market* emulated the boldness of Toulouse-Lautrec.

The Sears and other influential Bostonians were all the while collecting and promoting Prendergast's work. In 1901, he received a medal for *The Stony Beach* at the Pan-American Exposition, and he continued to exhibit in notable galleries, such as the MacBeth in New York and Kimball in Boston. He began to make the acquaintance of the other artists who would come to be known as "The Eight," or the Ash Can School, for their attraction to common places and everyday themes. He exhibited as one of The Eight in New York, Chicago, and Detroit and took three more trips to Europe in search of renewal. His art developed a less representational character after 1909, and he increased his studio work in oils, developing a new, swirling brush stroke.

In 1914, Prendergast moved to New York City, reserving his summers for time in New England. While he and Charles had established a comfortable quarters and a quasi-salon in Boston, the move to New York brought Prendergast closer to many dear friends and gave him a greater sense of freedom and flexibility. The story is told that his decision was cemented when a police officer in Boston asked him to stop sketching women in a restaurant. The Prendergasts reasoned that such activity would be less suspect in New York.

Prendergast continued to be a force in major exhibitions and a winner of major awards, such as the William Clark Prize and the Corcoran Medal in 1923.

He returned to his seascapes and holiday scenes, but with a greater, broader, more abandoned sensibility. The gentle, deaf artist and his faithful brother were now financially secure, and a sense of freedom pervades works such as *Sunday Promenade* and *Acadia*, the latter displayed in the Museum of Modern Art.

In 1922, Prendergast's health took a serious decline. He was compelled to stay in bed much of the time, and his out-of-doors sketching and watercoloring ceased. Tenaciously, however, this man, for whom painting was life, continued to work in his studio. He died on February 1, 1924.

References

Breuning, M. (1931). *Maurice Prendergast*. New York: Whitney Museum of American Art.

Pach, W. (1934). Introduction. *Maurice Prendergast memorial exhibition*. New York: Whitney Museum of American Art, pp. 5–7.

Rhys, H. H. (1960). *Maurice Prendergast, 1859–1924*. Cambridge, MA: Harvard University Press.

RENÉ PRINCETEAU (1843–1914), French Painter/Sculptor.

René Princeteau was born deaf on July 17, 1843, in the family-owned castle of Pontus in Libourne, Gironde, near Bordeaux, France. His mother began to tutor him early in reading and writing; and later, he was a pupil of the well-known instructor Valade-Gabel at the school for deaf pupils in Bordeaux. Princeteau preferred from an early age to communicate in sign language.

His artistic interests first led him to drawing, then to sculpture, and his family provided him with private tutoring under a master from Bordeaux. At the École des Beaux-Arts, he often sculpted in the studio of Augustin-Alexandre Dumont. This early work was in marble, based on mythology, earning him, at the age of twenty-two, several second and third medals for composition in an exhibition in Paris. Princeteau was one of the first of many deaf artists in this period of French history to exhibit at the Paris Salon. In his footsteps were to follow over the next few decades such great artists as the sculptors Paul Choppin,* Félix Plessis, and Fernand Hamar;* the skillful painter of marine views, Olivier Cheron; and his talented fellow painters Georges Ferry, Albert Mille, and Armand Berton.

Princeteau's morning rides in the woodlands of Boulogne with hearing and deaf friends, the latter including the American artist H. Humphrey Moore* and his fellow Frenchman, Félix Martin,* provided him with settings, positions, and potential compositions for his paintings. His first work was an equestrian statue entitled *Pilote*, a stallion mounted by M. De Lodge, which he exhibited in 1868. That initial use of the horse as a subject would characterize much of his later work. He then turned to two-dimensional work, translating his marble horses to canvas. In 1872, he exhibited a painting entitled *A Patrol of Uhlans Surprised by French Sharp-Shooters*, and, in 1873, a marble bust of Dr. Ambroise Tardieu and another sculptured group in plaster entitled *Halte!* Between 1874 and 1878, he exhibited *Marshal MacMahon, The Punishment of Brunehaut, The Return from the Promenade,* and another equestrian portrait, a portrait of Count Chapflour. His awards included a medal at Philadelphia in 1876, where he exhibited a portrait of George Washington on a white horse and another painting titled *Horses Frightened by a Railway-Train.* Over the next decade, his works included various equestrian portraits and other paintings, including *Vedette* (1879), *Relais* (honorable mention in 1880), a painting of the interior of a stable for which he received a medal from the 1883 Paris Gallery, *Labourage* (1884), *Equipage de chariots d'engrais* (second place in 1885), and *Arrival at the Press* (1889). During this period, Princeteau also taught; his most notable student was young Toulouse-Lautrec.

Following trips to Germany, Holland, Belgium, and England during the Franco-Prussian war, Princeteau gained considerable recognition with his portrayal of events during that conflict. The tragic scene *German Soldiers Taken by Surprise,* which he exhibited at the Paris Salon, was a particularly masterful and striking work that brought him many subsequent offers. He also developed a following among sports enthusiasts and was a member of the Jockey Club, where he had the opportunity to document on canvas many great and emotional races. The town of Bordeaux purchased a number of his paintings, including *Hors-Concours.* The Duke of Aumale frequently invited Princeteau to join his French aristocrats in hunts at the castle of Chantilly. Sometimes in collaboration with hearing artists, he painted large panels representing steeple chases and views of battles that included hundreds of horses and soldiers. One such panoramic painting included twenty-two carriage horses of Baroness Rothschild. Princeteau's painting of *The Balaclava Charge* was an expanse that included 160 horses, and another work included seventy horses of the Reichoffen.

Princeteau's equestrian portraits became so popular that princes and other notables, including the President of the Republic, requested his service. Those who posed for his portraits included the Duke of Bressas, the Duke Decazes, Count de Passage, General Princeteau, and Count de Raban. He painted portraits of non-human subjects alone as well: Frountin, winner of the Grand Prize de Paris in 1883; Etville, winner of the Bordeaux Derby in 1883; Boissy, winner of the Grand Steeple-Chase, Paris, 1884; and Relnesant, winner of the Derby at Chantilly, 1885. Passionately fond of horses and dogs, they were his constant companions. The American Deaf community followed his work with great interest, publishing photographs of such paintings as *Marshal MacMahon* and *Ox Labourant* in *The Silent Worker,* its major periodical. He continued to exhibit after the turn of the century.

Princeteau appears to have mysteriously changed in his later years. He left Paris and returned to the castle of Pontus, and his remaining years were marked by increased melancholy. According to his friend Yvonne Pitrois,* Princeteau's lively horses were now replaced by oxen pulling wagons, their heads bent, eyes distressed, and slowed by muddy furrows. Whether some great disappointment caused this change we will never know, for Princeteau did not leave biographical notes. Some writers believe he may have experienced a failure in romance or in family finances. Princeteau was known to be careless with his masterpieces, selling them at very low prices and misplacing others. Princeteau's horses and other four-legged creatures always evoked feeling. Drawn to the strength and beauty of animals, he bestowed human emotion and reaction upon them; and, as Pitrois suggests, their transformation from dashing to depressed in his later body of work is striking. But, because of his carelessness in records keeping, it is difficult to reconstruct his emotional state through the catalogue of his work.

Thin and frail in old age, never having married, and living with his sister, Princeteau continued to welcome visitors to his gallery, where he still possessed some of his best work. He died peacefully on January 30, 1914, at Pontus-Fronsac and his close friend, the deaf writer Yvonne Pitrois, turned her essay on him, which had delighted him in his last days, into an obituary and tribute.

References

Famous Deaf Artists and Sculptors: René Princeteau. (1897). *The Silent Worker, 9* (10), 155–156.

Legrand, A. (1914). René Princeteau. *Revue Générale de L'Enseignement des Sourds-Muets, 15* (9), 176–179.

Pitrois, Y. (1914). René Princeteau. *The Silent Worker, 26* (9), 166–167.

R

GRANVILLE SEYMOUR REDMOND (1871–1935), American Artist/Silent Film Actor.

Granville Seymour Redmond was born in Philadelphia, Pennsylvania, on March 9, 1871. He was totally deafened from scarlet fever at the age of two and a half. His father, a Civil War veteran, returned the family to San Jose, California, in about 1874. In 1880, Redmond was placed in the California School for the Deaf at Berkeley where, after a slow start, he made progress in writing. Pantomime, however, became his primary means of expression in social situations, and he gained popularity with his entertainments in the school chapel. The deaf art instructor Theophilus Hope d'Estrella* quickly recognized Redmond's artistic talents and mentored him in the visual arts as well. After graduation in 1890, Redmond took additional art lessons from D'Estrella. With funds awarded him by the California School for the Deaf's Board of Directors, he then studied under Arthur Mathews in the San Francisco Art Association's California School of Design (later, known as the Mark Hopkins Institute of Art). There he won several honors, including the W. E. Brown Gold Medal Award for best drawing from life in 1891.

Following a measure of success in art contests, he was motivated to accept State support for his study at the Julian Academy in Paris, where he studied under Benjamin Constant, Jean Paul Laurens, and other masters. Within ten days of his arrival, he won second place in a competition, completing a painting of Achilles defeating Hector in the battle of Troy. While in Paris, Redmond roomed with Douglas Tilden,* the deaf sculptor of note, also an alumnus of the California School for the Deaf. Tilden's friendship also provided artistic direction and inspiration. In 1895, his massive painting *Matin d'hiver* was accepted for the Paris Salon; and, in 1896, he exhibited *Winter on the Seine*, which he later gave to the California School for the Deaf in appreciation for its role in his education. His miniature of Julia Marlowe on porcelain and a larger painting, *The Miraculous Draught of Fishes*, were also produced while in Paris.

In 1898, Redmond returned home and within a short time, he married Carrie Ann Jean, a deaf woman from Illinois. In 1903, he painted at Laguna Beach with Elmer Wachtel and Norman St. Clair, all three exhibiting their works with Laguna Beach titles in the annual Spring Exhibition in 1904 at the Mark Hopkins Institute of Art. One of his proudest accomplishments was having five of his paintings selected for the main exhibition in the 1904 Palace of Fine Arts Gallery at the Universal Exposition in St. Louis, Missouri. *California Landscape* was exhibited at the Louisiana Purchase Exposition in 1904 and was purchased by the Jonathan Club of Los Angeles. Redmond's earliest works showed the influence of, and his love for, Impressionist painters and their technique. Local newspapers praised Redmond's work as a bold colorist and leading landscape painter. Critics described Redmond's distinctive style as reminiscent of pointillists such as Georges Seurat. Redmond's own assessment of his skills and techniques was simpler and somewhat at odds with many other artists': he believed the artist should work while thinking positively, unencumbered by stress. Also talented in figure painting, Redmond preferred, instead, the peaceful California coastal landscape; and most of his works were from Laguna Beach to Tiburon, on Catalina Island, and Monterey County. Field poppies and lupines were common in his paintings, although he was criticized for this. The criticism did not deter him.

In 1906, Redmond held a solo exhibition at Steckel's Gallery in Los Angeles, receiving accolades by leading critics. Thirty of his new paintings were exhibited at the Kanst Gallery in Los Angeles in 1908, another thirty in 1909. The year culminated with his earlier painting, *Restful Song of the Deep*, winning a silver medal at the Alaska-Yukon Exposition in Seattle, Washington; it was then purchased by the Governor of Washington for the State Capitol.

Redmond preferred not to use speech. Nevertheless, he was active in the California Art Club, the San Francisco Art Association, and the Bohemian Club, where he made the acquaintance of such notables as Paderewski, Jack London, and Buffalo Bill. The eminent etcher and muralist Gottardo Piazzoni, Redmond's lifelong friend who had studied in San Francisco and later in Paris with him, had learned sign language in order to communicate with him comfortably. Piazzoni later interpreted for Redmond when the deaf artist was honored at a formal dinner in 1913 for his contribution, "God of Fear," at the Bohemian Grove annual play. On that occasion, Piazzoni had the opportunity to translate a presenter's remarks that Redmond "speaks not with tongues of men, but with the hands of Art."

Redmond's patrons included the tycoon Henry Huntington. Encouraged by patrons in Santa Clara Valley, Redmond moved north again, receiving numerous commissions and contracts with leading galleries and enjoying continuous acclaim. Over the next decade, he exhibited works at the opening of the Museum

Granville Redmond, American painter and silent film star. Photo from *The Silent Worker, 30* (9), 1918, courtesy of Gallaudet University Archives.

of History, Science, and Art in Los Angeles (1913 and 1914) and the Panama-Pacific International Exposition in San Francisco (1915).

Redmond's early talents at pantomime resurfaced around 1913, when he appeared in several plays in the Bohemian Grove, Sonoma County, including *The Fall of Ug*. From there he began to audition for roles and appear as a bit player in silent movies. In San Francisco, in 1915, he performed with Dick Hotaling in *In an Art Studio* at the Bohemian Club. He also acted with Eric Frances in *Fearless Ferguson* (1916) and with Charlie Chaplin in *A Dog's Life* (1918). Other films in which he appeared were *A Day's Pleasure* (1919), *The Kid* (1921), and *The Three Musketeers* (1921), *A Woman of Paris* (1923), and *He's a Prince* (1925). Charlie Chaplin practiced advanced pantomime with Redmond, learned some signs from him, and personally hired him for a number of small roles. Unfortunately, many of these old silent films made with nitrate have been lost. The few that have survived with Redmond acting include *A Woman of Paris* and *You'd Be Surprised* (1926) with Raymond Griffith. His most memorable role was as a sculptor in *City Lights* in 1929. Still painting at a productive rate, he exhibited at the Harry Lindner Gallery in Long Beach in 1930, the Beverly Hills Hotel Gallery on Sunset Boulevard in 1931, and the Ilsley Gallery in the Ambassador Hotel in 1933.

Redmond spent many years painting in the atelier in the Chaplin Studios, with Charlie Chaplin's permission, painting scenery pieces for the movies, as well as easel paintings. Many of his best works were purchased by Chaplin for his private collection. "You know," Chaplin once said, "Sometimes I think that the silence in which [Redmond] lives has developed in him some sense, some great capacity for happiness in which we others are lacking. He paints solitude as no one else can convey it, and yet, by some strange paradox, his solitude is never loneliness. It's some sort of communion with Nature, I suppose."

Redmond also introduced other deaf men into silent films as extras and generally enjoyed these fulfilling experiences to the end. He died in Los Angeles on May 24, 1935.

References

Albronda, M. (1982, December). Granville Redmond: California landscape painter. *Art and Antiques*, 46–53.
Ballin, A. V. (1925). Granville Redmond, artist. *The Silent Worker*, 38 (2), 89–90.
Schuchman, J. (1983). Granville Redmond lives! *The Deaf American*, 36 (1), 2–4.
Westphal, R. L. (1982). *Plein air painters of California: The Southland*. Irvine, CA: Westphal Publishing.

EMERSON ROMERO (1900–1972), American Silent Film Actor.

Emerson Romero was born in Havana, Cuba, on August 19, 1900, and was deafened by a fever from whooping cough at the age of six. The second of three sons born to a South American exporter, he was enrolled in the Wright Oral School in New York City in 1907. There, he won the Metropolitan Wrestling Championship in the 135-pound class. After completing the program at Wright, he attended Stuyvesant High School in New York in 1915, followed by short stays in schools in Indiana, and in New Jersey, where he graduated in 1920. He began to study pre-engineering at Columbia University and, after one year, he transferred to Lafayette College in Easton, Pennsylvania. Two years later, Romero left school when his father ran into financial difficulties. He was working for the Federal Reserve Bank in New York City when his brother, Dorian, came from Cuba to introduce him to a career as a silent film actor. Dorian was president of Pan-American Film Corporation, then producing films for the Cuban government. Cuba was then interested in using films to promote tourism, and he had a feeling that Emerson's obvious talent in movement, developed for both communication and for his athletic interests, would make him a "natural."

Ever since he was a child, Romero had wanted to act in motion pictures. Dorian started him with a lead role in a six-reel comedy he had written, *A Yankee in Havana*. After this, Romero took on the stage name "Tommy Albert" when film distributors, typical of that era, told him they wanted a name that was more "American-like" and easy to pronounce. Although the films were not that successful, his talents were recognized, in particular, by Richard Harlan, a director who subsequently formed a new company, La Chica del Gato.

Before the era of strict specialization, Romero not only acted, but helped to shoot on location, cut the film, and write subtitles. "When we are not titling," he explained, "we are writing another story, and gagging it." Romero was able to speechread Harlan fairly well. He synchronized his acting with the tempo of the cameraman's cranking. In one silent film, *Sappy Days*, his leading lady was the deaf Cuban silent film actress Carmen del Arcos. Romero had convinced Harlan to give her a chance when the director was looking for a new lead. The Pan American Picture Corporation produced the films while Cranfield and Clark in New York distributed them.

In 1926, Romero went to Hollywood, where "Tommy Albert" starred in more than twenty-four two-reel comedies, such as *Beachnuts, The Cat's Meow, Great Guns,* and *Hen-Pecked in Morocco.* His short-lived marriage ended in divorce that year as well. Romero attended Charlie Chaplin films several times each to carefully study his technique. He also won many prizes with his own comic impersonations. He developed his skills even further by working closely with such stars as W. C. Fields, Louise Fazenda, and Mark Swain. Enjoying his own fan mail for years, he had the opportunity to watch such actors as Janet Gaynor, Bobby Vernon, and Victor McLaglen. He also made the acquaintance of the deaf actor and artist Granville Redmond,* who was a friend of Lon Chaney and Charlie Chaplin, and had many stories to share.

Romero, whose cousin was the film star Cesar Romero, is also remembered as a pioneer in captioned films for deaf people. When the "Talkies" arrived around 1927, deaf people felt the loss of one of their principal means of entertainment and information, as the subtitles were dropped. Romero left Hollywood shortly after. Working as a bank analyst during the Depression years, he saw his brother die at the age of thirty-two. Nevertheless, he managed to earn a promotion to junior statistician and remained with the bank for four more years. With Sam Block and John Funk, he established the Theatre Guild of the Deaf, in which he acted and directed more than twenty deaf people in the company. The Guild performed on and off for twenty years, with several productions each year, including comedies, drama, and pantomime.

Romero married Emma Corneliussen in 1936. He began a new career as a sheet-metal and template worker for Republic Aviation Corporation in Suffolk County, helping to produce the P–47 fighter planes during World War II. For several years, he also served as editor of the *Digest of the Deaf.*

Using his own money, Romero began to experiment with "captioned" films by purchasing feature films, documentaries, and short subjects; and, on his own time, he spliced subtitles and rented the films to schools and clubs for deaf people. Romero's efforts were rather primitive, for in the process of splicing in captions, the sound track was ruined. Nevertheless, his work sparked the interest of Edmund B. Boatner, the superintendent at the American School for the Deaf (ASD) in Hartford, Connecticut, and Jules Pierre Rakow, who visited with him to study his techniques. Rakow and his wife, with the support of the Hartford Junior League members, then began to caption pilot films at ASD. Boatner helped bring the appropriate bills before Congress. Consequently, Romero has been recognized as a pioneer whose work led others to establish the government's Captioned Films for the Deaf program.

In 1959, Romero established his own small business to market alarm clocks and other signaling devices for deaf people, many of which were his own inventions. In 1965, he retired from Republic Aviation, after twenty-five years of service. And, in 1970, the New York City Civic Association of the Deaf presented him with its Civic Achievement Award for outstanding volunteer service to the Deaf community.

Romero is notable, perhaps, for three distinctive facts about his life. As a pioneering deaf actor, he collaborated with hearing actors in perfecting his craft by studying acting and movement techniques in ways that continue to be emulated. Later, he made a significant contribution to the quality of life in the Deaf community through his experiments with captioning. Between those two stages of his life, he turned the potentially devastating loss of a career to a mere lesson in life, as he formed companies and kept his own creative force alive.

Romero died in 1972.

References

Penn, J. E. (1927). A deaf movie star. *The Silent Worker, 39* (6), 162–165.

Romero, D. (1965). That's my pop. *The Deaf American, 17* (11), 9–10.

Rosenholz, E., & Sturm, R. B. (1972). Emerson Romero: Man of a thousand lives. *The Deaf American, 24* (5), 7–10.

PIERRE DE RONSARD (1524–1585), French Poet.

Pierre de Ronsard was born on September 11, 1524, in his family home, the Château de Possonnièrea Poissonier on the river Loire. His father was a noble Hungarian serving as steward to King Francis I. Young Ronsard seemed destined for the life of a soldier. At the age of nine, he was sent to the Collège de Navarre in Paris, but his father removed him after six months upon learning that the regent there was excessively harsh. Between 1536 and 1540, Pierre served as a page to the children of Francis I. Traveling extensively with the royal family, Ronsard proved to be a prodigy, and was soon entrusted with missions of importance, meeting with ambassadors to foreign lands and learning to speak their languages. It was while serving in the train of Mary, Queen of Scots, that Ronsard was deafened. When Mary was forced to return to her native land, Ronsard and several others were shipwrecked on the rugged coast of Scotland; and an illness soon left him deaf, his dreams of diplomatic life shattered. Like Joachim Du Bellay,* whose public service was also somewhat limited by the onset of deafness, Ronsard's romanticism and spirit created new horizons to explore and express.

Ronsard spent seven years at the Collège de Coqueret in Paris where he studied with Jean-Antoine de Baïf under Jean Dorat. With six companions, including Du Bellay, he formed the Pléiade, named after the constellation and representing the dream these young men held of creating an eternal French literature. Ronsard's poetry was immediately successful, beginning with *Les Odes, Les Amours, Les Folâtries,* and *Le Bocage* in the early 1550s, and followed by *Les Mélanges* (1555), *Continuation des Amours* (1555), and *Les Hymnes* (1555–56). In *Odes* a long poem is dedicated to his deaf friend, Joachim Du Bellay. The story is told that the young sister of Henri II, Margaret of Savoy, upon hearing a courtier mocking Ronsard's poetry, demanded the book and read it aloud to an admiring court. Ronsard also published a series of sonnets, reflecting his admiration for a young maid of honor named Cassandre Salviati in *Amours de Cassandre* (1552), followed by those to a woman named Marie (*Amours de Marie,* 1555), and later to Helène de Surgères (*Sonnets pour Helène,* ca. 1571). None of these ladies, however, appeared to have responded to these elaborate overtures. One hundred and eighty-three of Ronsard's sonnets, most telling of his longing for Cassandre, appeared in *Les Amours de P. de Ronsard, Vendômois,* with an appendix which contained the song settings composed by his more musically inclined friends, including Claude Goudimel, Clément Jannequin, and Marc-Antoine de Muret.

When Charles IX succeeded Henry II, Ronsard became court poet, and the King bestowed him with property and money in gratitude, naming him his "Father of Apollo." Ronsard joined King Charles in hunts, playing tennis, and in composing poems. Ronsard enjoyed these favors and demonstrated his appreciation. He was also shrewd and level-headed, however; and he was able to avoid the petty politics and diplomatic snares of the court.

Court life did not blind Ronsard to those less privileged. Shocked by the wretched living conditions of the working class, Ronsard courageously composed poems of social responsibility: in particular, "Discourse on the Misery of the Times" and "The Remonstrance with the People of France." His own success did not bring him an untroubled happiness. Rather, he was often overwhelmed by his deafness and the solitude it brought to him, the jealousy of courtiers over his fame, his failed efforts to find love, and a fear of poverty: "Wealth! Poetry will not bring you thereto, nor praying to Phoebus, who has gone deaf. You must pray to the great Gods of the Court, follow them, serve them, be at their table, tell them funny stories, court them, see them, solicit them often, else your labor will be only wind, and all your learning pass in smoke. Poetry is a headache, and frenzy is its name!" When Ronsard's deaf companion Joachim Du Bellay died at the age of thirty-seven, he was led to reflect additionally on his own life of "wandering, solitary and pensive."

During the reign of Henri III, Ronsard retired to his estates at Crois Val, in his native province where he could write in a tranquil setting. Mary, Queen of Scots, who admired his work, supported his effort to collect a complete edition of his poetry. Queen Elizabeth, who otherwise agreed on very little with her cousin Mary, expressed her appreciation for his work with the gift of a diamond. Along with his writing, he spent his remaining days working, gardening, and walking on his pastoral estate.

The turmoil in France escalated, and many of Ronsard's friends were won over to the teaching of the Huguenots. Ronsard anxiously observed the Guises, Condés, and Protestants prepare for war. Ronsard attended one rally in a temple, led by his old friend Théodore De Bèze, who spoke for the Protestants. Ronsard watched De Bèze and appreciated the gestures he used and the charisma he projected. But, he told friends, he was happy for his own deafness, as a means to resist De Bèze's persuasion. Ronsard privately visited De Bèze, however, and urged him to moderate his increasingly dangerous position. In May of 1561, Ronsard wrote ''Discourse on the Misery of the Times,'' an appeal to Catherine de Medici to intercede in France's troubles, to which the Huguenots responded with personal attacks on his reputation.

Ronsard's main work, *La Franciade*, went to press in 1572, only a few months after the assassination of the Protestant leader Coligny near the Louvre. The work received negligible attention amid the strife and turmoil. Ronsard received a minimal royal gift of 600 livres.

Regarded as France's greatest poet of the Renaissance, Ronsard was the most intense star of the Pléiade, the recognized leader of the seven, who strove to be unique in enriching poetic expression. Praised by kings and queens for his lyrical genius, his paeans to life, nature, love, and death, have lived on for centuries.

Shortly before his death on December 28, 1585, at Saint-Cosme, Ronsard asked a monk to record two final sonnets which he dictated, one a trumpet call to his soul, the second a farewell to life. At his burial, his friends celebrated his life in verse.

References

Bishop, M. (1959). *Ronsard: Prince of poets*. Ann Arbor: University of Michigan Press.

Boase, A. M. (1964). *The poetry of France: 1400–1600*. London: Methuen.

Steele, A. J. (1961). *Three centuries of French verse: 1511–1819*. Edinburgh: Edinburgh University Press.

Weinberg, B. (Ed.). (1964). *French poetry of the Renaissance*. Carbondale, IL: Southern Illinois University Press.

ROSLYN ROSEN (1943–   ), American Educator/Deaf Community Advocate.

Roslyn Rosen was born deaf to deaf parents on February 22, 1943, in Bronx, New York. Her brother, Harvey Goodstein, a professor of mathematics at Gallaudet University, was also born deaf. She attended the Lexington School for the Deaf in New York City, graduating in 1958. She earned a bachelor's degree in art education from Gallaudet College in 1962 and a master's degree in the education of the deaf in 1964. In 1980, she completed her doctorate in education at Catholic University with a 4.0 grade average. Her dissertation was entitled ''Recommendations on Educational Placement and Services for Hearing-Impaired Students by Four Types of Administrators.'' She married Herbert Rosen and raised three children, a son and a daughter who became attorneys and a second son who became an engineer.

Between 1964 and 1966, Rosen served as a rehabilitation counselor for the Department of Vocational Rehabilitation in Washington, D.C. She then taught English in the Adult Education Program for that department and was a sign language instructor for the Bureau of Education of the Handicapped. Over the next decade, she worked as a films specialist for Captioned Films for the Deaf, communications specialist for the Model Secondary School for the Deaf, and then as Area Coordinator, supervising and training faculty and staff, and coordinating the student exchange program. In 1977 and 1978, she was also the coordinator of Gallaudet College's program to educate people about Public Law 94–142, the Education of All Handicapped Children Act (now known as the Individuals with Disabilities Education Act). In this capacity, she worked with the Model Secondary School for the Deaf and the Kendall Demonstration Elementary School for the Deaf, both on Gallaudet's campus and many other schools, to implement processes to comply with the law and to provide workshops for others to learn about the law. In 1978, Rosen became the director of The Special School of the Future, sponsored by the W. K. Kellogg Foundation in collaboration with Gallaudet College, responsible for working with demonstration schools and seventy-five affiliated school programs in coordinating activities related to parent involvement, community education, and continuing education.

In 1981, Rosen was appointed dean of the College of Continuing Education at Gallaudet College. She has published many papers in professional journals and presented others at conferences on topics such as Deaf Women, creating learning environments, advocacy of rights for deaf people, and effective communication in classrooms for deaf students. She has served on boards of the National Association of the Deaf, the International Association of Parents of the Deaf, National Center for a Barrier-Free Environment, the World Organization of Jewish Deaf, and the National Captioning Institute. She also served as the chairperson of the National Consumer Action Network and as a member of the Clinton Transition Ad Hoc Task Force on Persons with Disabilities.

As the second deaf female president of the National Association of the Deaf (NAD), she has presented many talks around the country—at conferences, workshops, commencements, and other gatherings. As the key spokesperson for the American Deaf community, she has had to advocate for the rights of deaf people with regard to many issues. When the CBS program *60 Minutes* aired a report on the sensitive issue of cochlear implants (November 8, 1992), for example, Rosen was interviewed by Ed Bradley, and she expressed her concern over the limitations, risks, and cultural implications associated with the implants. Her monthly articles in the NAD *Broadcaster* were often quoted and reprinted.

In 1993, Rosen was named Vice President for Academic Affairs at Gallaudet University. As the chief academic officer there, she provides leadership to the College of Arts and Sciences, the School of Communication, the School of Education and Human Services, the School of Preparatory Studies, the School of Management, the College for Continuing Education, the Gallaudet University

S

JOSEPH SAUVEUR (1653–1716), French Physicist.

Joseph Sauveur was born in La Fleche, France, on March 24, 1653, the son of Louis Sauveur, a notary. According to Pratt (1935), Sauveur was a "deaf-mute from infancy." However, there is so little information handed down to us about Sauveur's hearing loss that it is uncertain whether he was functionally deaf or, perhaps, experienced a central auditory processing disorder such as the inability to discriminate or localize sounds of different frequency, duration, or intensity. The fact that he also had a "lifelong difficulty" with his speech may indicate that he was not able to hear his own voice and monitor its quality. From the short biographical sketches available, we have learned that Sauveur was not able to speak until he was about seven years old, and that the speech problem never left him. Throughout his life, he was hesitant to give public presentations. He turned down the opportunity to become a professor of mathematics at the Collège Royal in Paris because of the requirement of a test in elocution; but a decade later, in 1686, he achieved this honor. There is no explanation for why Sauveur had changed his perspective on accepting this position and, as with his mastery and invention of the science of acoustics, one may conclude that Sauveur possessed great fortitude.

Sauveur attended the Jesuit school of La Flèche, quickly becoming fascinated with the study of mathematics. He traveled to Paris in 1670; and, under an agreement with his uncle that his expenses would be paid in full, he studied for a degree in divinity. When Sauveur's interests shifted to medicine, he lost his uncle's support; and he turned to teaching mathematics in order to earn a living. With practical interests, he prepared tables for calculations and conversions of weights and measures. When a nobleman requested private tutoring in Cartesian geometry from him, a subject with which he lacked familiarity, Sauveur spent a week mastering Descartes' work, many nights without sleep, and effectively met the obligation to which he had committed.

It was at this time, in the late 1670s, that Sauveur was offered the professorship at the Collège Royal. Required to prepare a speech and deliver it effectively, Sauveur was reluctant to accept this challenge due to his speech difficulties. Instead, he studied problems in probability.

Sauveur's life was rich with experiences, nonetheless. He tutored mathematics to the pages in the house of Madame la Dauphine. He investigated hydraulics with Mariotte at Chantilly and, while writing on the subject of military fortifications, he actually took part in sieges with his acquaintance, Prince Louis de Condé. He became examiner for the Engineering Corps in 1703.

In 1686, at the age of thirty-three, Sauveur became professor at the Collège Royal in Paris. He became *académicien géometre* in the Royal Academy of Sciences in 1696, and *associe mecanicien* at the reorganization of the Academy in 1699. After 1696, he delved into the science of acoustics, with the help of "musical assistants," who helped him to evaluate the sounds generated from his experiments. As Lang (1994) explains, this was analogous to the color-blind chemists John Dalton and Ferdinand Reich, who made great discoveries with the help of assistants with normal vision. Sauveur examined the vibrational character of sounds and the phenomena of vibrating bodies. Most often, he consulted with the Duc d'Orléans, one of his former mathematics students, who helped him analyze those sounds he was unable to evaluate. In 1713, Sauveur developed the mathematical equation relating the frequency of a vibrating string to its mass. His work with the theory of beats provides evidence that he may have been one of the first scientists to understand the principle of superposition. Isaac Newton checked Sauveur's experimental results from his work on organ pipes and performed his own mathematical calculations. In the preface to a dissertation on sound intervals and musical instruments, Sauveur proposed the term *acoustique* for a *science* of music, having as its object sound in general, distinguished from the aesthetics and related theory of music. Musical practice was to certainly benefit from his systematic investigations, however, in his establishment, for example, of a reproducible standard of pitch.

Searching the *History of the Royal Academy of Sciences* for the year 1700, Raman (1973) found the following note about Sauveur's definition of this term, a meaning which has not changed to the present day:

The science which is concerned with the sense of hearing is perhaps not any less extensive than that which is concerned with the sense of sight, but it has been much less explored until now. . . . Thus, M. Sauveur has thought that this is a field which is little known, and the farther he has explored it, the vaster he has found it to be; hence he believes that it deserves, exactly as Optics, a name for itself, and he has called it Acoustics. It is for future discoveries to justify the new name. (p. 161)

Sauveur sought to define the new field of acoustics as a study of purely physical phenomena, which he believed to be in part, subordinate, and, in part, wholly separate from the field of physics. He coined such terms as "harmonics," "fundamental," and "node," and described their properties. Although such great scientists as Euler, D'Alembert, and Lagrange referred to Sauveur's work in the eighteenth century, his name slowly disappeared into obscurity. Only occasionally has his name been mentioned in the literature of the Deaf community. He died in Paris on July 9, 1716, and very recently has reemerged to receive the credit he deserves as the "founder" of the science of acoustics. That an individual unable to distinguish musical tones laid the foundations for later work on the theory of harmonics by Rameau, Helmholtz, and others is a story of tremendous perseverance and success, shrouded in many unanswered questions.

References

Deaf founder of the science of acoustics. (1936, February 8). *Deaf Carolinian.*
Dostrovsky, S. (1975). Joseph Sauveur. In C. C. Gillispie (Ed.), *Dictionary of scientific biography* (Vol. 12, pp. 127–129). New York: Charles Scribner's Sons.
Lang, H. G. (1994). *Silence of the spheres: The deaf experience in the history of science.* Westport, CT: Bergin & Garvey.
Pratt, W. S. (1935). *The history of music: A handbook and guide for students.* New York: G. Schirmer.
Raman, V. V. (1973). Sauveur, the forgotten founder of acoustics. *The Physics Teacher, 11* (3), 161–163.

FREDERICK C. SCHREIBER (1922–1979), American Educator/Deaf Community Advocate.

Frederick C. Schreiber was born on February 1, 1922, in Brooklyn, New York, the son of Russian immigrants. Four successive bouts with spinal meningitis at the age of six left him deaf and with a curvature of the spine. A plaster cast from his neck to his knees and a brace he wore for several years helped to straighten the spine. Schreiber attended a school for children with physical disabilities until the age of ten, when he enrolled in the Lexington School for the Deaf. He remained there for three years, transferring to the New York School for the Deaf (the "Fanwood School," as it was known to the Deaf community), and, academically prepared at the age of fifteen, he entered Gallaudet College, where he graduated with a degree in chemistry in 1942. At Gallaudet, Schreiber was popular, working for the student newspaper and becoming increasingly aware of educational and employment issues faced by the Deaf community. In addition, during World War II, his father lost his vision and subsequently his business. Schreiber learned still another lesson with regard to the barriers faced by people with disabilities. Wanting to be near his father to provide assistance, he joined many other deaf people who worked at the Firestone Company in Akron, Ohio, supporting the war efforts. He personally faced the prejudice of this era, the controversies over the use of signed and spoken communication among deaf people, and the special plight of deaf blue collar workers. When he was turned down once in an application for a position as a machine shop inspector because he was deaf, he argued to the effect that it is "what's between the ears that counts, not the ears themselves," which became a motto of his through his many years as a leader in the Deaf community. Working seven days a week, he spent many evenings at club meetings and other events held by the Deaf community of Akron. He married Kathleen (Kit) Bedard in 1944 and began a family.

Schreiber became involved in the National Association of the Deaf (NAD) in the late 1940s. It was a time when the organization, now over sixty years old, was addressing pressing issues involving the rights of deaf people. Some states still did not grant deaf automobile drivers the same privileges as hearing drivers. There were no deaf superintendents in schools serving deaf children, and few deaf principals. Schreiber, noting the inefficacy of existing channels of communication, actively supported the revival of the periodical *The Silent Worker* (later changed to *The Deaf American*). He earnestly pursued the establishment of a home office for NAD with a staff to give new life to this important organization. After his father's death, he remained in Akron until 1947, when he accepted a teaching position at the Texas School for the Deaf in Austin. Returning to New York City the following year, he worked as an instrument maker and as a printer for several years. He then took a position with the International Typographers' Union, spending his free time as an English-language tutor for deaf applicants at the New York State Office of Vocational Rehabilitation and as a member of the Brooklyn Association of the Deaf. Observing the need to include women, he helped to establish the association's Ladies Auxiliary which functioned well enough to break down any remaining barriers to admitting women in that organization. He was elected president of the Hebrew Association of the Deaf at the age of twenty-eight.

For the next fourteen years, Schreiber worked as a printer in the Washington, D.C. area, at the *Washington Evening Star* and then the U.S. Government Printing Office. Meanwhile, in the Deaf community, he continued active participation in the District of Columbia Association of the Deaf. In 1966, he became the first full-time Executive Secretary of the National Association of the Deaf, while continuing to edit the monthly periodical of the District of Columbia Club of the Deaf. This provided him a forum for many years to experiment with communicating various political strategies and positions. His dedication to the welfare of the Deaf community became increasingly evident in his efforts to address rehabilitation issues. Despite some criticism, he proudly supported the NAD's stance against an extra income tax exemption for deaf people, similar to that given blind taxpayers. While struggling to make the NAD financially solvent, he worked to implement and collaborate on many grant programs funded by such agencies as the Vocational Rehabilitation Administration. These included starting programs to teach sign language to hearing adults, establishing the Registry of Interpreters for the Deaf, carrying out the National Census of the Deaf Population, and evaluating contracts with Captioned Films for the Deaf. He also negotiated contracts with the Defense Department's Office of Civil Defense and the Labor Department's Job Corps. With each effort, he turned the government's attention to the NAD as a viable advocacy organization. Schreiber helped to expand the literature on deafness and deaf people through NAD's publications of many books, most notably *A Basic Course in Manual Communication*, but also including children's books. His influence was also felt internationally. Under his leadership, the NAD membership quadrupled to more than 17,000 members.

In 1970, Schreiber had an operation for cataracts in his eyes, and eye trouble plagued him henceforth. In 1973, a heart attack sidelined him, followed by surgery for a kidney disorder in 1976 and, in 1978, a diagnosis of advanced diabetes. Nevertheless, he remained active in the politics of the Deaf community until his death on September 6, 1979, at the age of fifty-seven. Schreiber died one year before the centennial celebration of the National Association of the Deaf, which he had greatly helped to revitalize.

Schreiber's commitment to the welfare of deaf people in the United States was unstinting. For decades, he traveled across the country, presenting lectures and workshops to federal, state, and local agencies, school programs, the Leadership Training Program at San Fernando Valley State College (now California State University at Northridge), New York University Deafness Research and Training Center, and many other organizations for both deaf and hearing persons. With candor, he fearlessly challenged people to change their ways of being with each other and to examine their assumptions.

Schreiber did much to help establish sign language interpreting as a profession and inspired many deaf youths toward leadership goals of their own. His presentations and publications on such topics as "Priority Needs of Deaf People" and "Potentials for Employment of the Deaf at Levels in Keeping with Their Intellectual Capabilities" had a profound impact on improving the quality of education and employment of deaf people. Four hundred of his hearing and deaf friends came to pay tribute to him at a memorial service held on September 9, 1979, at Gallaudet College, which had awarded him an honorary Doctor of Laws degree.

In his honor, the Golden Rose Award was established as an incentive for others to follow his example of providing, on a volunteer basis, distinguished service of lasting benefit to the Deaf community.

References

Lattin, D. (1979). Frederick C. Schreiber: A legacy that will last. *Disabled USA, 3* (1), 21.

Luft, P. (1976). NAD executive secretary: Frederick C. Schreiber. *The Deaf American, 29* (4), 9–13.

Newman, L. (1973). A man for all seasons. *The Deaf American, 25* (11), 7–8.

Schein, J. D. (1981). *A rose for tomorrow: Biography of Frederick C. Schreiber.* Silver Spring, MD: National Association of the Deaf.

CHARLOTTE ANGAS SCOTT (1858–1931), British Mathematician.

Charlotte Angas Scott was born on June 8, 1858, in Lincoln, England. She was the second of seven children, and a cherished older sister died while they were in their teens. Her father, Walter Scott, was a minister of the Congregational Church. Based on the sound education she received through tutoring at home, she won a scholarship to attend Girton College, the first college for women in England and only recently opened. Scott was one of eleven young women in her entering class. Girton College was located three miles from Cambridge University, and its women students were allowed, if chaperoned, to attend the lectures of twenty-two out of thirty-four professors at Cambridge. At that time, the Tripos examinations were given to determine which Cambridge graduates would graduate with honors. In the first few years of Girton College's history, prior to Scott's enrollment, three "Girton Pioneers" had passed the Tripos, although it was not until 1948 that Cambridge would grant a degree to a woman.

In 1880, Scott took the fifty-hour, nine-day mathematics Tripos. Her result equaled that of the eighth man at Cambridge. The reaction to her accomplishment was swift and extended well beyond the banks of the River Cam. The news traveled across England that a woman had mastered a "man's" subject. Scott, and all woman students, were barred from the awards ceremony, where the names of women passing the Tripos were never mentioned. However, that year, the rank "eighth" was announced; and before the dean could say the name of the eighth-ranking man, all the undergraduates called out "Scott of Girton," and cheered tremendously, chanting her name and tossing their hats.

Had Scott been permitted to attend this dramatic ceremony, she would likely have had little difficulty hearing the shouting, although Scott's contemporaries reported that her deafness was increasing during her college years.

Scott was crowned with laurel leaves by her Girton classmates that evening, and her accomplishment was the cause for numerous parties into the night. When news spread about her marks on the Tripos, public pressure mounted on Cambridge University to administer all university examinations to female resident students as a matter of policy, not just special privilege, and to announce their names with those of the male students. On one petition advocating the admission of women to Cambridge examinations, circulated by Mr. and Mrs. W. S. Aldis of Newcastle, eight thousand signatures were recorded. The Girton College deans, while delighted, were apprehensive about the publicity alienating the Cambridge faculty. However, on February 24, 1881, the vote at Cambridge on revision of the policy passed, 398 to 32. At the American Mathematical Society in 1922, James Harkness, who was a young boy at the time of Scott's notable achievement and remembered its impact, referred to this turning point in British history when the theoretical feminism of Mill and others began to yield educational and political power.

Among the Cambridge professors supportive of Scott was Arthur Cayley, whose lectures on Modern Algebra, Abelian Functions, Theory of Numbers, and Theory of Substitutions she attended. Cayley mentored her through her graduate studies, from the time she was finishing work toward her "external" bachelor's degree (1882) through her doctoral degree (1885), both "First Class" from the University of London. She taught at Girton during this period. Cayley also recommended Scott for a position as Associate Professor at Bryn Mawr College in Pennsylvania, to which she applied in 1885, the year the college opened. Based on observations and impressions gathered by an American visitor to Girton who was considering Scott for the position, the Bryn Mawr Executive Committee had recorded in its minutes on July 7, 1884, that she was a popular teacher, friendly and personable, who further organized the mathematics department at Girton. However, they noted that "with these admirable qualifications, C. A. Scott has two defects,—she is decidedly hard of hearing, and is in delicate health. Yet neither of these has thus far proved a bar to her being a really able teacher."

At Bryn Mawr, Scott became the first mathematics department head. She was also the only woman with a Ph.D. in mathematics whose native language was English. Although her hearing was progressively worsening, and she generally struggled at first with organizing effective lectures, her classes soon grew in size, and she devoted her time to helping her students individually. Three of the nine American women who earned doctorates in mathematics before 1900 studied under her. She argued vehemently against lessening the rigor of intellectual pursuits and the adoption of lower standards for women. Scott even fought for one of her students who was dismissed due to tuberculosis, advocating on the premise that the young woman's illness would make intellectual work all the more important; and that a dismissal was the heaping of one tragedy upon another. Her attitude was thus remarkably ahead of its time with regard to the real needs of students with differences. She also argued for funding for a mathematics library and recruited two mathematicians from Cambridge to join her at Bryn Mawr. Prompted by Scott, young Bertrand Russell and his wife Alys came to lecture at Bryn Mawr in 1896.

By the first years of the twentieth century, Scott was completely deaf. However, Dr. Marguerite Lehr recalled that Scott continued to lecture "perfectly well," training graduate student protegés to answer the questions from undergraduates. If the protegé had difficulty, she would be practiced in communicating with Scott, who would then answer the question. The Executive Committee even approved $600 to pay for a "reader" who helped her communicate in class and to correct papers as her eyesight worsened. Ordered to get outside exercise to gain strength, she enthusiastically took up gardening, and even developed a new strain of chrysanthemum. She also frequently returned to England, providing forging links between the new mathematical community in the United States and the historic European societies. She was a member of the London Mathematical Society, the Edinburgh Mathematical Society, the Deutsche Mathematiker-Vereinigung, the Circolo Matematico Di Palermo, and an "honorary member" of the Amsterdam Mathematical Society. Social interactions were, of course, challenging.

In 1901, her efforts contributed to the establishment of the College Entrance

Charlotte Angas Scott, British mathematician. Photo from *The Mathematics Teacher* (September 1982), courtesy of the National Council of Teachers of Mathematics.

Examination Board, and she served as the Chief Examiner in Mathematics in 1902 and 1903. Scott helped to organize the American Mathematical Society (AMS) in 1891, serving for seven years on its council, and for two years as its vice-president. Of the thirty people honored at the fifty-year celebration of the AMS, she was the only woman.

In 1899, Scott was named coeditor of the prestigious *American Journal of Mathematics*, the beginning of a twenty-seven-year tenure. Only a year after arriving at Bryn Mawr, she had published her first paper in that journal, on the subject of binomial equations. Her primary field was algebraic geometry, and she published numerous papers on such mathematical phenomena as plane, adjoint, and linear curves, plane and equianharmonic cubics, and the treatment of cones and polygons, in such journals as the *American Journal of Mathematics*, *Quarterly Journal of Pure and Applied Mathematics*, *Philosophical Transactions of the Royal Society of London*, *Mathematische Annalen*, and *Nieuw Archief voor Wiskunde*. Probably her most important paper, published in 1899, was "A Proof of Noether's Fundamental Theorem." Max Noether's theorem had been developed thirty years earlier, but the theorem had only algebraic proofs until Scott provided a geometric one. Scott may even have been an influence on Noether's own daughter, Emmy, who changed her field from languages to mathematics. Scott was known as a particular inspiration to women, who received three times the percentage of American Ph.D.'s in mathematics before 1940 (in her immediate footsteps) than they did in the 1950s. Her accessibility as a teacher, her willingness to counsel prospective students, and her preparation of many women professors clearly had a profound impact on the numbers of women in academic circles in America.

Scott's book, *An Introductory Account of Certain Modern Ideas and Methods in Plane Analytical Geometry* (1894) was reprinted thirty years later and acclaimed, especially for its distinction between a general proof and a particular example. She also published a "school" book on plane geometry in 1907, which was not well received, a result of her emphasis on lines instead of points.

Immediately after retiring in 1925, she purchased a house in Cambridge and spent her remaining years in England. She had maintained many ties, including her church membership, there. While she enjoyed her work in the United States, she had grown increasingly lonely and homesick.

Spending her final years gardening and betting on horse-racing, she even found an area for further mathematical research—on the statistics of previous race winners and the mathematics of horse-breeding. Among her many honors, Rebière in Paris in 1897 called her "one of the best living mathematicians," and she appeared in *American Men of Science* and *Notable American Women, 1607–1950*.

Scott died on November 10, 1931, and was buried in the St. Gile's Churchyard in Cambridge. Professor Patricia Kenschaft, who interviewed Marguerite Lehr, Scott's last doctoral student, remarked to the authors that "few *people* . . . have contributed significantly to research mathematics, making it especially remarkable that one was a deaf woman."

References

Charlotte Angas Scott: An appreciation. (1932). *Bryn Mawr College Alumnae Bulletin, 12* (1), 9–12.
Kenschaft, P. C. (1987). Charlotte Angas Scott, 1858–1931. *College Mathematics Journal, 18* (2), 98–110.
Kenschaft, P. C. (1987). Charlotte Angas Scott, 1858–1931. In L. S. Grinstein, & P. J. Campbell (Eds.), *Women of mathematics: A biobibliographic sourcebook* (pp. 193–203). Westport, CT: Greenwood Press.
Putnam, E. J. (1922). Celebration in honor of Professor Scott. *Bryn Mawr College Alumnae Bulletin, 2* (5), 12–14.

HOWIE SEAGO (1953–   ), American Actor.
Howie Seago was born on December 5, 1953, in Seattle, Washington. An

older brother, David, is hard-of-hearing, and a younger deaf brother, Billy Seago, is also a professional actor. His two sisters and mother are hearing, while his father discovered that he had a hearing loss in an Air Force physical. Seago jokes about the male-female, deaf-hearing "balance" in his family. Young Howie's first experience was in a church play that his mother directed, using mime with a voice-interpreted narration. Seago went to an "oral" school, and then was mainstreamed with four or five other deaf students, during his high school years. He was still learning American Sign Language (ASL) when he entered California State University, Northridge, which has a major postsecondary program for deaf students. He was very comfortable being with other deaf people and soon elected a major in psychology.

His brief success in the church basement aside, it was not until the early 1970s that Howie Seago began acting in earnest. He had been encouraged by his roommate, the deaf linguist Ted Supalla, to participate in Supalla's original play in American Sign Language, *The Feast*. Initially reluctant, Seago caught the acting fever, and he began to sense the power of sign drama. He took a minor in theatre arts and began to contemplate his choices. He also became involved in the Happy Handfuls, a children's theatre that toured the west coast, and he taught a course at Northridge, Introduction to Deaf Theatre. Following his graduation, Seago spent a year with Washington State Educational Services as an Artist-in-Residence, working on Deaf theatre and arts for disabled students' programs throughout that state. In 1977, he experienced a major break when he joined D.E.A.F. Media in Oakland, California, to produce, direct, and write the Emmy Award-winning PBS children's television series "Rainbow's End." The multifaceted experience of direction, production, and writing bolstered his confidence. He simultaneously continued his stage training with the American Conservatory Theatre, and he taught at San Francisco State University and Ohlone College.

Seago joined the National Theatre of the Deaf (NTD) as their workshop coordinator from 1980 until 1982, and he performed major roles in *Gilgamesh*, *The Ghost of Chastity Past*, and *The Iliad: Play by Play*. He performed the latter one night while seriously injured, when the football-game metaphor for this interpretation of the epic became a little too real. His teaching career in theatre took him to the Hawaii Department of Special Education, New Mexico State University, and the National Technical Institute for the Deaf.

In the 1980s, Seago became known for three creative achievements that have markedly expanded the opportunities for deaf people in mainstream performing arts. First, the visionary director Peter Sellars cast Seago in the title character's role in the American National Theatre production of *Ajax*. The play, a "Vietnamized" version of the Greek tragedy, was controversial, a Sellars trademark. But critics such as Mike McIntyre and Jack Kroll were in complete agreement in their praise for Seago's powerful performance as the isolated, crazed general and for Sellars' brilliance in casting a signing deaf actor. In an interview where they reflected together on the production, Sellars pointed out that he was compelled by his sense that a deaf actor has an "extra edge in the desire to communicate." Seago mused on how the ancient Greek theatres used dance to communicate, a form of dance that highlighted the hands as well as the feet, and called his performance "my Greek dance."

In 1988, partly at the urging of his wife Lori, an English and drama teacher, Seago submitted a proposal for a *Star Trek: The Next Generation* episode with a deaf character. To his delight, the idea was accepted. To his consternation, he received a script that he felt portrayed deaf people naively. He was greatly impressed by the writers and the cast in their willingness to work with him to make changes, however. He was cast in the role of "Riva," a deaf mediator faced with the necessity of using his own strategy of changing a disadvantage to an advantage when his chorus of interpreter-friends are killed. "Loud as a Whisper," by Jacqueline Zambrano, was particularly innovative in its use of American Sign Language and portrayal of the distinctive integrative sides of human experience.

Shortly after the filming of the *Star Trek* episode, Seago went on to a television role in *The Equalizer* and a real-life drama. The producers cast a hearing actress in a deaf role, and Seago was faced with the dilemma of quitting in protest or working within the constraints for change. Because the show was well-written, he chose the latter despite some criticism. And he was able to influence casting decisions on the other deaf characters in the show, paving the way for other deaf actors to gain experience.

Seago's background in psychology is evident in his acting and his teaching. He is greatly concerned for children's self-esteem. At the same time, he cautions: "I do not consider myself a role model for Deaf children. I do not believe that Deaf children should be forced to copy anyone else, but just be themselves and do the best they can. . . . What I am happy to do is give the Deaf child and person a glow inside themselves."

Seago now teaches, acts, and writes in Seattle.

References

Deaf culture autobiographies on video: Howie Seago. (1990). [video]. Salem, OR: Sign Enhancers.

Deaf Mosaic. (1988, April 28). [video]. Washington, DC: Gallaudet University School of Communication.

Levitan, L., & Moore, M. (1989, April). A rising star: Howie Seago. *Deaf Life, 1* (10), 14–21.

LAURA C. REDDEN SEARING (1840–1923), American Writer/Poet.

Laura C. Redden Searing was born on February 9, 1840, in Somerset County, Maryland. Her maternal grandmother was a descendant of Sir William Waller, one of the original colonial settlers of Maryland. She was also a descendant of Edmund Waller, a poet laureate during the reign of Elizabeth I. Searing's family

Laura Redden Searing, American poet and writer. Drawing from *Harper's New Monthly Magazine, 68* (406), 1884.

moved to St. Louis while she was still a child. She lost her hearing through meningitis at the age of eleven and transferred to the Missouri School for the Deaf. Her first known poems related to the loneliness she experienced as a result of her deafness. As she progressed in school, her talent in writing quickly developed. By the age of eighteen, still a pupil in the Missouri School, she had already published "A Few Words about the Deaf and Dumb" in the *American Annals of the Deaf*, a remarkably intelligent and precocious discussion of her young perceptions of sign language and its utility. In 1859, she accepted the responsibility of editing *The Presbyterian and Our Union*, a religious paper in St. Louis. Before she was twenty, she had published numerous articles and poems in the *St. Louis Republican* under the pen name "Howard Glyndon."

Searing held fierce loyalty to the Union at the outbreak of the Civil War. Her fiery writings on the attitudes of local authorities attracted the attention of the secessionists who subsequently attacked her work as that of a schoolgirl presuming to meddle in politics. As her daughter later explained, her criticism of certain local authorities caused an investigation to be made of the pseudonymous writer. The sarcasm of the rebuttals had the opposite effect of that intended, and brought her increased respect and attention. Shortly after this, Searing traveled to Washington as the correspondent for the *Republican*, interviewing President Lincoln and several generals, and she contributed numerous newsletters and spirited war poems that were widely copied. While residing in Washington, she published her first two books, *Notable Men in the House of Representatives* (1862), a collection of well-received sketches, and *Idyls of Battle* (1864). One of these poems, "Belle Missouri," a reply to "Maryland, My Maryland," became the war song of the Missouri Unionists. The *Idyls* included more than fifty poems with such titles as "Left on the Battle-Field," "The Story of Sumter," and "Our Sacrifice." Buried among these patriotic verses is "My Story," in which she wrote of the hand of God that "fell heavily" upon her in her youth, "from thence must silence be." In the context of a nation's tears and pains, she minimized her own loss, and asked for God's forgiveness "if I groan/Beneath my lighter cross." On the proof sheets of this book, Abraham Lincoln wrote that he had found the verses "all patriotic, and some very pretty." Searing gained renown as an effective voice for patriotism to most of the Union leaders, including President Lincoln, General Grant, and General Garfield, and there are many stories of their personal friendships with her. She even accompanied General Grant to the front lines of the Union army, a privilege seldom accorded women during the Civil War.

In February 1865, Searing traveled to Europe where she remained for nearly four years, spending most of the time in France and Italy, and learning to read and write in French, German, Italian, and Spanish. She worked as correspondent for the *St. Louis Republican*, the *New York Sun*, and the *New York Times*. While in Italy, she was also employed by the Agricultural Department to investigate and report upon the subject of orange and silkworm culture; and two of these papers by her are in government records. Through these years, she kept a journal, highlighting such memorable events as her excursions to see major works of art, and her visit to the court of the Empress Eugénie of France. Upon her return to New York, she contributed to such periodicals as *Galaxy*, *Harper's Weekly*, the *Atlantic Monthly*, *Putnam's Magazine*, and *Arena*. For several years she was a leading contributor on the *New York Evening Mail* and for the *New York Tribune*. She also wrote many articles for *The Silent Worker*, the major periodical in the American Deaf community.

In 1871, Searing attempted to improve her speech at the Clarke School for the Deaf and studied further under Alexander Graham Bell in Boston while continuing to write a series of articles entitled "The Children of Silence" for the *New York Mail*. In these articles, she encouraged the teaching of speech to deaf children. She also made a translation from the French of "Memoir d'un Petit Garcon," which was published as "A Little Boy's Story" in 1869 by Hurd & Houghton. In 1874, a second volume of poems, *Sounds from Secret Chambers*, was published. This was her most successful work and, perhaps, her most personal one, with its intense, persistent voice. However, the strain of studying and maintaining her literary work led to ill health.

In Searing's later poems, compiled by her daughter Elsa Searing McGinn in *Echoes of Other Days*, one finds tributes to friends such as John Greenleaf Whittier and to "The Pioneer Women of California," sonnets and verse on nature, and poems reflecting special experiences in her life, such as the gift she received of a crystal goblet that once belonged to Lincoln. "The Reason Why" is a verse in which she responded to a challenge in a study group to provide a presentation in poetry explaining the failure of James Buchanan's administration. "The First Dog Team Over The Trail" was chosen in 1906 as the winner in a contest sponsored by the Fairbanks, Alaska *Times*. The selection of both political/historical and highly personal themes is an intriguing feature of her corpus.

She married Edward W. Searing, a New York lawyer, in 1876. Among her wedding gifts were autographed copies of works by Bayard Taylor and Whittier, the latter unable to attend due to illness. Ten years later, she and her husband moved to Santa Cruz. Struggling financially in 1886, she wrote to Edward Miner Gallaudet, president of Gallaudet College, explaining that she was selling everything she could. During this period of adversity, in 1889, Searing delivered one of her best poems at the unveiling of the Thomas Hopkins Gallaudet monument on Kendall Green. In 1894, though, her correspondence with Gallaudet revealed continued hardship. Divorced and having lost the use of her right arm to muscular neuralgia, Searing offered to sell a collection of shells to Gallaudet. A group of literary friends, including Whittier, had contributed funds to support her travel to Hawaii in order that she may recover her health—during which she had collected these shells. The following year, she again described to Gallaudet her hope to produce a volume of poetry to help fulfill her financial obligations. Houghton Mifflin of Boston, her long-time publisher, was aware of her plight, and printed five hundred copies of a booklet gratis as a Christmas present for her, which she sold for income at fifty cents apiece.

Another of her last productions was the poem, "The Hills of Santa Cruz," which Whittier said "will cling to the Santa Cruz mountain range forever." Her last verses, in April 1908, prophesied the brevity of her remaining literary life, replete with landscapes and images of death and burial.

After this, ill health prevented her from further writing, and she lived her final fifteen years in isolation with her daughter, Elsa, in California. Searing died on August 10, 1923.

References

Glyndon, H. [Laura C. Redden Searing] (1921). *Echoes of other days*. San Francisco: Harr Wagner.

Johnson, A., & Malone, D. (Eds.) (1935). Laura Catherine Redden Searing. *Dictionary of American biography* (Vol. 16, p. 534). New York: Charles C. Scribner's Sons.

Redden, L. (1858). A few words about the deaf and dumb. *American Annals of the Deaf*, *10* (3), 177–181.

GEORGE BRYAN SHANKLIN (1888–1961), American Electrical Engineer.

George Bryan Shanklin was born on September 9, 1888, in Nicholasville, Kentucky. He was profoundly deafened from scarlet fever while a teenager at the Lexington High School in Kentucky. After attempting to learn through private tutoring while continuing at the public school, he transferred to the Kentucky School for the Deaf, where he quickly mastered the skills and knowledge offered by the program. He was pursuaded by Dr. George M. McClure to enter

Gallaudet College in 1905. After two years at Gallaudet, however, Shanklin left to pursue a degree in Electrical Engineering at the University of Kentucky where he graduated with a bachelor's degree in mechanical engineering in 1911. His professors there frequently gave him written copies of their lectures to study. Shanklin's grades were so impressive at the University of Kentucky that he was recruited for employment before he graduated. He was also captain and quarterback of the championship football team.

Shanklin became one of the most prominent deaf engineers in history, contributing numerous patents in the area of electrical power and high voltage cables. In this era, there were few deaf persons entering engineering as a profession. Those who did appeared to favor civil engineering. During the first half of the twentieth century, Harris Joseph Ryan, progressively deafened and known as the "Edison of the Pacific Coast," was the only other deaf electrical engineer of note, winning the Edison Medal in 1927 for "meritorious achievement in electrical science or the electrical arts." Like Ryan, Shanklin spent years investigating the transmission of high voltage electrical energy.

In August 1911, Shanklin began working in experimental testing for the General Electric Company of Schenectady, New York, where he pursued additional training in the operations of electrical apparatus. Here, he was such an asset that the company sent him to Europe on many occasions to study the state of the art in electrical appliances. However, like many of his deaf contemporaries in scientific professions, Shanklin faced serious attitudinal barriers because of his deafness. When Shanklin was twenty-seven years old, his supervisor offered the blundering explanation that "although we had some misgivings about his doing satisfactory work, we are pleased to say that the experiment worked out very well, and his record is as good as that made by other men who are not handicapped by such a defect." Within a short time, Shanklin became head of testing at the General Electric plant in Schenectady, engaging himself in research and development work on high voltage insulation designs. He was a consulting engineer in charge of a laboratory under the eminent Charles P. Steinmetz.

Gallaudet College followed Shanklin's career as he became increasingly successful. As one writer explained in the alumni publication, *The Buff and Blue*, in 1916: "We have always regretted that the hazers of those days did not treat Bryan so as to secure his loyalty to Gallaudet, for in texture and breed he is the type of student that Gallaudet greatly needs." From 1922 until 1948, Shanklin was the chief engineer responsible for the power cable division in the central station department, managing the cable division of commercial engineering for two years. He then became manager of the wire and cable department of commercial engineering, and remained in this position until his retirement. In his retirement, Shanklin served as a consulting engineer to the hydroelectric commission in Quebec, the Canada Wire and Cable Company in Toronto, and the Potomac Power Company in Washington.

Shanklin's work with the development of oil and gas-filled high voltage cables won him many honors. He was awarded seventeen patents and twice received the Coffin Award (1933 and 1941), General Electric Company's most prestigious award to employees. In 1939, Shanklin received a citation from the Engineering Societies of New England. The deaf engineer is credited with the discovery of ionization in high voltage cables. From this discovery, he developed new ways to control that ionization, engineering most of the oil-filled cable installations in the United States. He published many technical papers on electric cables and was very active as a speaker and on committees in such engineering organizations as the American Institute of Electrical Engineers, Insulated Power Cable Engineers, and the National Electric Manufacturers Association. He was a charter member of the National Research Council.

Shanklin suffered a heart attack and died on November 21, 1961, in Schenectady, New York.

References

Lang, H. G. (1994). *Silence of the spheres: The deaf experience in the history of science.* Westport, CT: Bergin & Garvey.

McClure, G. M. (1962). Death takes George Bryan Shanklin, deaf General Electric cable expert. *The Silent Worker, 14* (6), 7.

JOSEPH HENRY SHARP (1859–1953), American Painter.

Joseph Henry Sharp was born on September 27, 1859, in Bridgeport, Ohio. His great-grandparents, William Sharp and Elizabeth Gillespie, were Irish immigrants who settled in America around 1792. His great-grandfather served with George Washington during the Revolutionary War. Joseph Henry Sharp's wife was a descendant of the colonists John Alden and Priscilla Mullins.

At the age of six, Sharp was first attracted to Native Americans while watching members of several Indian families in Bridgeport as they shot arrows at coin targets. As a child, he loved to fish and swim, nearly drowning on three occasions. On the last of these, a man pulled his body from the Ohio River and carried it to his home. His mother chased everyone away and brought him back to life by rolling him back and forth over a barrel to empty his lungs of water. A subsequent ear infection left him profoundly deaf. There were further challenges to come. Sharp's father, suffering financially in the post–Civil War depression, died when he was twelve. With no child labor laws in Ohio and no access to public schooling, Sharp began to work in a nail mill and copper shop to help his mother support their family. At the age of fourteen, he moved to Cincinnati to live with his aunt where he studied for eight years in the McMicken School of Design. He already showed promise as an artist at the age of sixteen, when Custer's defeat took place at the Little Bighorn in 1876. By this time, he had learned enough sign language and speechreading to help him communicate with those he knew personally. Sharp traveled through Europe to study under various masters, including one year with Charles Verlat at the Antwerp Academy of Fine Arts. Always with pad and pencil, he used this continuously to converse with others throughout his life.

In 1883, encouraged by the Indian painter Henry Farny, Sharp ventured west, to Santa Fe, New Mexico, to study Indian life, particularly the Klikitat, Nez Percé, Shoshone, Ute, and Umatilla tribes. Since his youthful reading of James Fenimore Cooper's *Leather-Stocking Tales*, he had a romantic attachment to the notion of Native dances and stories. Among his honors as a young artist at this time was his selection to paint a portrait of President Ulysses S. Grant, then deceased, and corresponding with General William T. Sherman to assure accuracy of the portrait.

Still not satisfied with his work, he left for Europe again in 1886, this time to study landscapes under Carl Marr and pastels under genre painter Nikolaos Gysis at the National Academy in Munich. He also studied with an American friend, the painter Frank Duveneck, in Italy and Spain, traveling to museums and developing technique by copying from the works of Goya,* Velasquez, and El Greco. Some of these works he brought home, later to be hung in his studio in Taos. The influence of this work is found in the strong technique and dark tonality of many of his later paintings. In 1890, the Smithsonian Institution purchased eleven of his portraits at an exhibit sponsored by the Cosmos Club. Sharp was instructor in life drawing and portraits at the Cincinnati Art Academy between 1892 and 1902, and it was during this period that his portraits of Native Americans first attracted interest.

After his excursion to Taos in 1893, for which he was commissioned by *Harper's Weekly*, he published in that magazine his illustration and description, "The Harvest Dance of the Pueblo Indians of New Mexico," which excited much interest. After this, he published "The Pueblo Turquoise Driller" in *Harper's Weekly* and, a while later, an article in *Brush and Pencil* titled "The Mesa from Kit Carson's Tomb, Taos, New Mexico."

In 1895, Sharp traveled with his wife Addie to Paris where he studied at the Académie Julian under portrait artist Benjamin Constant and French master Jean-Paul Laurens. Sharp also studied in night classes at the Colarossi School under Gustave Courtois and Louis-Auguste Girardot. He, Addie, and Duveneck then traveled to Spain where Sharp painted *The Alhambra by Moonlight*, *Sierra Nevada from the Alhambra*, and *Old Moorish Aqueduct—Alhambra*.

To his fellow American students at the Académie, Ernest L. Blumenschein and Bert Phillips, Sharp recounted many stories of the beautiful landscape and the culture of the Indians that had survived three hundred years of Spanish, Mexican, and Anglo rule, and he is credited with prompting these artists to establish the art colony of Taos. In 1899, on the battlefield of Little Bighorn in Montana, Sharp set up the "Prairie Dog," a shepherd's wagon studio-on-wheels that he believed would add authenticity to his work as he portrayed in oil the Crow, Sioux, and Blackfoot. In 1900, he gained further recognition when his work was exhibited at the Paris Exposition. The Cosmos Club in Washington then exhibited a selection of these portraits and, the following year, an impressed President Theodore Roosevelt directed the U.S. government to provide Sharp a cabin with a studio just south of the battlefield of General Custer's "Last

Joseph Henry Sharp, American portrait painter. Photo from *The Volta Review, 24* (8), 1922 courtesy of Gallaudet University Archives and Alexander Graham Bell Association for the Deaf, 3417 Volta Place NW, Washington, D.C., 20007.

Stand,'' where he was able to work among many Native Americans. In 1902, William Randolph Hearst's mother, Phoebe Apperson Hurst, bought seventy-nine paintings for the University of California and commissioned him to complete about the same number over the next five years. Sharp never left the West again. He settled with his wife in Taos, painting the Pueblo Indians and traveling to Montana to work with the Plains Indians. Sharp would work outside until the cold froze his paint, then warm up in his studio. In 1913, Addie died. Sharp married her younger sister in 1915. This second marriage lasted until his death forty years later.

Residents of Taos remembered Sharp as a small man with a Van Dyke beard, tattered hat, steel-rimmed glasses, and a note-pad to help him communicate. Deer Bird, the spiritual leader of Taos, called him ''Slusle-Dah-Sliedah,'' a respectful nickname that translated to ''old deaf man.'' Some writers believe that Sharp's deafness helped to establish a rapport with Indians. His many years among them helped develop an affinity, and through his brushstrokes, he incorporated the emotion and understanding he felt for his subjects. He held a sense of responsibility to record a rapidly disappearing way of life and conscientiously avoided exploitation. He remunerated his subjects and engaged in dialogue with members of the tribal communities. The accuracy of his work, and the comments he sometimes wrote on his paintings, became useful as ethnological records; and the historical value of his work, as well as the artistic value, was important to him. He was nicknamed the ''Anthropologist,'' and produced etchings, prints, and photographs in addition to watercolor and oil paintings. On the portrait of *Blackfeet Dance Chief Big Brave*, Sharp wrote, ''Very Large Man. Sense of Humor. Tremendous booming voice—when young bucks would try to shirk ceremonial dances, he'd take 'em by the belt with the hand and carry them over to the dancers, put 'em down, amid guffaws and derision of the others.'' Some of his canvases portrayed the ceremonies and traditions associated with mourning over the dead with such titles as *The Great Sleep*, *Mourning for the Dead*, *The Mourners*, and *Lament for the Dead*. Other paintings like *Watchful Waiting (Stalking Game)* illustrated hunting scenes. Portraits included *Lady Pretty Blanket*; *Chief Two Moons, Head Chief of Cheyennes in Custer Battle*; and the *Sioux Chief Spotted Elk*. His intimate relationship with Native Americans he painted led to many pleasant memories, at times captured on canvas but known only to him and told selectively through his subsequent storytelling. The smile on the face of one Sioux chief, for example, represented his disbelief over being paid to sit and pose. Sharp also painted survivors of Wounded Knee and the visionary Ghost Dances which followed. One of Sharp's portraits was of White Swan, a Crow scout wounded several times in Custer's Last Stand. As Sharp explained, White Swan was deafened from a strike of a war club on the forehead.

In addition to the Department of Anthropology at the University of California, the Bureau of Ethnology at the Smithsonian Institution was a major purchaser of his works. Sharp's interest in the American Indian lasted more than eight decades. In addition to being a founder and "Spiritual Father" of the Taos Society of Artists, he was a member of the Salmagundi Club, the Society of Western Artists, the Artists' Guild of Chicago, the Duveneck Society of Cincinnati, the Print Makers' Club of Los Angeles, and the California Art Club. He won medals at the Pan American Exposition in Buffalo in 1901 and the Panama-California Exposition in San Diego in 1915. His works are in many collections, including the Smithsonian Institution, Butler Museum in Youngstown, Cincinnati Museum of Art, the Thomas Gilcrease Institute of Art in Tulsa, Oklahoma, and the University of California at Berkeley. Private purchasers included Andrew Carnegie. Over the last four decades of his life, Sharp and his second wife traveled extensively—through Spain, Africa, across the Andes, and to the Orient. His last major painting, *Green Corn Dance*, was completed in 1949. The painting was a celebration of the life cycle, reminiscent of the style in much of his early work depicting the Pueblo community. His poetic response to a lifetime of such work is his oft-quoted expression of a desired experience: "I never heard the beat of the drum and the whoop of the dance."

Sharp died on August 29, 1953, in Pasadena, California. Back in Taos, his fellow artists and Native American friends gathered together to pay their respects.

References

Broder, P. J. (1980). Joseph Henry Sharp, Spiritual Father of Taos. *TAOS: A Painter's Dream*. Boston: New York Graphic Society.

Davis, L. A. (1922). Successful deaf people of today—Joseph Henry Sharp, Artist. *The Volta Review, 24* (8), 281–286.

Fenn, F. (1983). *The beat of the drum and the whoop of the dance: A study of the life and work of Joseph Henry Sharp*. Santa Fe, NM: Fenn.

Joseph Henry Sharp: Dedicated observer. (1978, January). *American Artist, 42* (426), 28–31, 95–97.

NANSIE SHARPLESS (1932–1987), American Biochemist.

Nansie Sharpless was born on October 11, 1932, in West Chester, Pennsylvania, the oldest child in her family. Soon after, they moved to Ferndale, near Detroit, Michigan, where her father was a research biochemist in nutrition. During World War II, Nansie's father studied the effects of different diets, since there was concern about the shortages of many daily food items, including milk. In this "scientific home," as she called it, she was raised a Quaker. Sharpless was also instilled with the notion of human suffering connected to inequality. Her parents welcomed into their home two Polish women who had undergone medical experiments by the Nazis in Germany. They also invited, in subsequent years, a man from China and a young boy from Czechoslovakia, and Sharpless's mother helped an African-American woman find an apartment in a town that was noted for its discrimination. Sharpless's brother became an invalid at the age of nine from a brain malignancy. These experiences helped her significantly to face her own adversity later and to live unconventionally. Her early interests included the piano, violin, and painting, as well as science and mathematics.

Sharpless was totally deafened from meningitis on Christmas Day in 1946. Her parents at first considered placing her in a school for deaf students, but they were advised to keep her in the local public school. She completed her junior and senior years at a Friends' boarding school, which helped her immensely in overcoming the communication and social barriers she initially experienced. Viewing deafness as a "terrible nuisance, though not a catastrophe," she enrolled in Oberlin College in Ohio, where she received a bachelor's degree in zoology in 1954, relying rather heavily on her friends' lecture notes. Her father was supportive of her interest in science. The fact that she was a woman was insignificant to him. Her sister had already entered geology and a brother became a physician. Wayne State University in Detroit admitted her on probation, with the agreement that if she could not meet the academic requirements for the master's degree, she could at least obtain registration in Medical Technology. She progressed with other students through various units in the Department of Laboratory Medicine at Henry Ford Hospital in Detroit and graduated in 1956. During this period, she reflected that she experienced few problems related to being deaf, communicating effectively with supervisors and coworkers. As she gained experience, she attended meetings and demonstrations, and visited other laboratories and institutions to learn new techniques. Sharpless also supervised several technicians. Her work in the pharmacology laboratory as a medical technologist was made more interesting with new analytical techniques to measure trace amounts of hormones in body fluids, in particular norepinephrine and adrenaline, and Sharpless assisted in examining their relationship to hypertension. In an immunochemistry laboratory, electrophoresis was applied to identify patients with insufficient antibodies in their bloodstreams.

Then, out of a need to undertake new challenges, she entered the doctoral program at Wayne State University. She immediately met with attitudinal barriers. Friends and family members were pessimistic about her chances of finding a position if she were "over-educated" as a deaf woman. The director of admissions met with her and told her that she would need to expect to be held to a higher standard, because questions would be raised about her abilities to carry out professional duties. The resistance she met only strengthened her resolve to succeed. Sharpless graduated with a perfect 4.0 grade point average.

Sharpless began her study at a very exciting time, when Dr. Arthur Ericsson at the Harper Hospital in Detroit was experimenting with L-Dopa in patients with Parkinson's disease. This followed the work of Dr. Oleh Hornykiewicz at the University of Vienna in the 1960s, who had discovered low amounts of dopamine in the brain of Parkinson patients, and Dr. George Cotzias, who reported success with oral administration of L-Dopa at the Brookhaven National Laboratory. Dr. Ericsson's collaborator was Dr. Daisy McCann, who served as dissertation advisor for Sharpless and encouraged her to examine L-Dopa metabolism in cerebrospinal fluid.

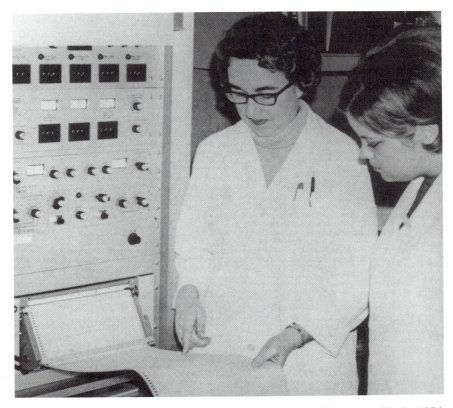

Nansie Sharpless, American biochemist. Photo from *The Deaf American, 28* (7), 1976, courtesy of the National Association of the Deaf.

After graduation, she took a position in the Department of Biochemistry at the Mayo Clinic in Rochester, Minnesota, supported by a traineeship from the National Institute of Neurological Diseases and Stroke. There she continued to study the metabolism of L-dopa in cerebrospinal fluid, plasma, and urine, and conducted investigations of the long-term effects of L-dopa treatment in rats and guinea pigs.

In 1975, she was attracted to Albert Einstein College of Medicine in New York City, where she directed a biogenic amine assay laboratory to study chemicals involved with brain functioning. Sharpless conducted research studies on the biochemical basis of neurological and mental disorders with the aim of identifying effective treatments. She was active in the Office of Opportunities in Science in the American Association for the Advancement of Science and the American Women in Science program and provided assistance to the Foundation for Science and Disability, for which she served one term as president. She also worked with the American Chemical Society to help break down barriers faced by students with disabilities who aspired to chemistry as a career. When Sharpless presented her papers at professional societies, she would always supplement her talks with visual media. A colleague or the moderator would relay the questions from the floor and she would respond. At these meetings, people seemed to remember her better because she was deaf. Sharpless saw the potential of "poster sessions" when they became popular at scientific meetings, for she felt they represented a breakthrough in communicating scientific work for deaf scientists.

Sharpless published over fifty research reports in scientific journals on metabolism and mental disorders, measurement of neurotransmitters, and the use of animal models of neurological and mental disorders. In addition, she published eleven chapters in books and review articles, and forty-five scientific abstracts. She served on numerous committees and panels for the National Science Foundation, American Association for the Advancement of Science, American Chemical Society, and the National Science Advisory Board. She was a member of the Board of Directors of the Alexander Graham Bell Association for the Deaf and received the Distinguished Alumni Award from Wayne State University in 1980.

In her paper "The Deaf Scientist as a Researcher" presented at the American Association for the Advancement of Science meeting in January 1975, Sharpless advocated scientific work for deaf people. She personally sought out other deaf women scientists, although she did not find many. Sharpless considered being deaf a much more serious barrier to a professional career than being a woman: "In addition to the real physical barrier of deafness, there are attitudinal barriers which can be devastating." Nevertheless, she overcame these barriers to contribute to the field of biochemistry.

Sharpless was on the faculty in the Department of Psychiatry at Albert Einstein College of Medicine in New York until her death on October 9, 1987.

References

Bowe, F. (1981). Nansie Sharpless. *Comeback: Six remarkable people who triumphed over disability*. New York: Harper & Row.
Brown, R. (1976). Dr. Nansie Sharpless: Biochemist. *The Deaf American, 28* (7), 3–4.

FRIEDRICH SMETANA (1824–1884), Czechoslovakian Composer.

Friedrich Smetana was born on March 2, 1824, in Litomysl, Bohemia, the eleventh child and first son to survive infancy of Frantisek Smetana, a master brewer to the households of some of the leading noblemen of eastern Bohemia. The child played a piano arrangement of the overture to *La Muette de Portici* for the Litomysl Philosophical Society when he was only six years old. In addition to learning to play the violin from his father, an accomplished violinist, he took early lessons from Frantisek Ikavec and Victorin Matocha. His music education was inconsistent, however, and for eight years, it ceased almost entirely. There were simply no teachers in the town who could play as well as the young Smetana. Finally, he left for the Academic Gymnasium in Prague in 1838. He had made fast friends with the nationalist poet Karel Havlicek prior to his time in Prague and wanted to see if the charms of the old city were all that his friend claimed. Smetana wrote a few string quartets, heard Liszt play for the first time, and otherwise had a wonderful time. His father soon intervened and sent him to an academy in Pizen. Smetana completed his scholastic education satisfactorily there in 1843. He then focused exclusively on music, frequently appearing as virtuoso on the piano in concerts. He also played on estates of wealthy clients as an accompanist for dancing. He himself was frequently partnered by Katerina Kolárova, a pianist whom he eventually married, despite frequent quarrels and separations.

Having a meager income, Smetana owned no musical instruments, playing only in the houses of friends. He studied harmony and composition under Josef Proksch and was able to meet Robert Schumann, whom he greatly admired. Unable to afford to have his compositions printed, he sent *Six Morceaux Caractéristiques op. 1* to Liszt, offering to dedicate it to him if he would help him get started. He needed seed money to start a school of music, and his concerts were not well-enough attended to augment his income from tutoring. Liszt at first resisted, but within a few years his selective interest in Smetana's work led to a lasting friendship between the two composers.

Smetana arranged a concert tour in the towns and spas of western Bohemia in order to establish his performing career. While he struggled at first, his piano and chamber concerts received considerably more attention in Prague. During the Prague Revolution, he wrote patriotic revolutionary marches. He also manned barricades.

Meanwhile, his family situation became almost unbearable. Three of his four daughters died in a three-year period, the eldest having shown talents in music herself. The grieving Smetana composed a piano trio in her memory. His wife also contracted tuberculosis and was never well again. Politics in Prague after 1848 were unstable and repressive, and Smetana's finances were again worrisome. He found an opening for a piano teacher at Göteborg, Sweden attractive.

After moving to Sweden, he gave recitals and opened a music school, while organizing and conducting choral and chamber concerts. Smetana performed in a trio with the violinist Josef Czapek and the cellist August Meissner. The response by the cultured Göteburg community was gratifying. Smetana performed pieces from *Elijah, Elverskud,* as well as Beethoven's *Piano Concerto no. 3*; in the next year he introduced choruses from *Tannhäuser* and *Lohengrin* after opening a women's music school. His own compositions included orchestral works such as *Jubel-Ouvertüre in D* and the *Triumph-Symphonie* dedicated to the Emperor Franz Josef. His first symphonic poem, *Richard III*, was composed in 1858, followed by *Wallensteins Lager* the following year.

Smetana occasionally returned to Bohemia to visit his friend Liszt, and he made the decision to return there for a time as his wife's illness progressed. He performed a series of farewell concerts and left Sweden in 1859. His wife died in April when they stopped in Dresden; she never made it home. Later, a few months after attending the silver jubilee of Schumann's *Neue Zeitschrift für Musik*, Smetana became engaged to Bettina Ferdinandová. He wrote polkas and a symphonic poem, *Hakon Jarl*; then returned to Prague when Czech nationalism led to the establishment of a national opera competition. Through the next decade, he became one of the leading personalities of Prague, producing the successful repertoire *The Brandenburgers in Bohemia* (1863), for which he received the Harrach Prize, and the opera *The Bartered Bride* (1866). While a fervent nationalist himself, he had to prove it; some critics classified him as a proponent of German style. In part, this was caused by Smetana's own tendency to use his home language, German. The Prague cultural scene was, though, noted for its jealousies and rivalries at the time. Smetana was passed over as conductor for the Provisional Theatre in favor of a lesser musician, and mischief was typical. Finally, he was made conductor of the Choral Society and elected president of the music section of the Artists' Circle.

Shortly after Smetana was appointed conductor of the Provisional Theatre, at the age of fifty, after raging disputes with its first conductor, inner ear inflammation brought on by syphilis caused nearly complete deafness. Smetana took leave for several months, during which time he was criticized by his competitors both privately and in the local newspapers. On October 30, he wrote in his diary, "I am afraid of the worst, I shall be absolutely deaf. How long will it be to the last?" He complained of whistling sounds and other noises in his ears. He then wrote to his concerned manager, "I consider it my duty to inform you of the cruel fate that has befallen me, in that I may lose my hearing entirely." Smetana consulted with Doctor Zoufal and other physicians for advice, to no avail. Countess Elisabeth von Thun, his favorite pupil, planned a concert to raise funds for him, and Swedish friends sent him money in order that he could seek medical assistance. By the fall of that year, however, his deafness was complete, and he moved into his daughter's residence a short distance from Prague. In their customary fashion, the local arts administrators found loopholes to assure that minimal royalties were paid to Smetana.

Like Beethoven, Smetana completed some of his best work after becoming deaf. He resolved to complete his career in glory, producing between 1874 and 1882 such compositions as *Dreams*, *Past Luck*, *Consolation*, and the popular *My Country*. Struggling constantly with poverty as well as physical suffering, he even took advantage of the tinnitis to transform the headnoises into music, in particular, for the symphonic poem *Vysehrad* and the string quartet *From My Life*. The biographer John Clapham wrote that the finale in *From My Life* suggests the piercing whistling sound now known as tinnitus that heightened for Smetana at evening in the first years of his deafness. As Smetana wrote to a colleague in 1877, poverty and deafness made his musical compositions less cheerful. Yet he wished to continue: "When I plunge into musical ecstasy, then for a while I forget everything that persecutes me so cruelly in my old age."

In 1881, after the opening of *Libuse*, the National Theater was destroyed by fire. Two years later, in the rebuilt Theater, *Libuse* opened once again, and an ovation of waving handkerchiefs expressed affection and appreciation for the deafened composer of Prague. But the rare moments of acclaim between infighting did little to raise his spirits. He descended into hallucinations, suicidal thoughts, and fits of violence. On April 23, 1884, he was taken to a mental hospital, where he died within weeks.

When Smetana died on May 12, 1884, Liszt said that "the death of Smetana affected me deeply. He was a real genius."

References

Clapham, J. (1980). Bedrich Smetana. In S. Sadie (Ed.), *The new Grove dictionary of music and musicians* (Vol. 17, pp. 391–408). London: Macmillan.
Rychnovsky, E. (1929). Friedrich Smetana, musician and composer. *Volta Review, 31* (3), 146–147.

KELLY H. STEVENS (1896–1991), American Painter.

Kelly H. Stevens was born on March 30, 1896, in Mexia, Texas. He was deafened from scarlet fever at the age of five. As a young boy, Stevens took an interest in drawing and painting. His sister, noticing his talents, gave him his first paint set. He entered the Texas School for the Deaf in Austin in 1907, where the widow of the distinguished Texas painter W. H. Huddle cultivated his talents further. He later attributed much of his successful use of color and love for the Texas landscape to Mrs. Huddle's guidance and instruction. Stevens graduated in 1914, then entered Gallaudet College. While at Gallaudet, he also studied drawing, painting, and composition at the Corcoran School of Art under Edmund C. Messer and Richard N. Brooke.

Upon graduation from Gallaudet College with a bachelor's degree in 1920, Stevens began teaching at the New Jersey School for the Deaf while studying further under Henry McGinnis at the Trenton School of Industrial Arts. In 1924, he spent the summer in Europe, where he studied the galleries of Italy. The following year he returned to Europe, studying at the New York School of Fine and Applied Arts in Paris and traveling through Italy and Spain to study the works of the masters. In 1926, he studied under Valentin de Zubiaurre,* the deaf Spanish painter renowned for his paintings of peasant life. Stevens published in the Deaf community periodical *The Silent Worker* several biographical and autobiographical reports of his experiences. He continued at the New Jersey School from 1927 until 1929. While leading the art department at the Louisiana School for the Deaf in Baton Rouge, he studied for a master's degree at the Louisiana State University (LSU), including classes in Italian fresco technique taught by Conrad Albrizo. He graduated from LSU in 1938.

Many of Stevens' paintings focused on the Southwest landscape, the Grand Canyon, and the ceremonial dances of Native Americans. His work, exhibited in one-man shows in Houston, Dallas, Trenton, Shreveport, and other cities, was praised for the use of light and color. Stevens traveled to Paris in 1933 and studied the theory of color and figure painting more in depth under Louis Biloul, followed by lessons in portrait and figure painting under Henri Morriset at the Académie Colarossi. In 1934, he spent much of his time in provinces of Spain, his work being subsequently exhibited at the Roerich Museum and culminating in a national tour, which brought him much recognition. He then studied under Wayman Adams in Taxco, Mexico, using his free time to paint the surrounding landscapes.

Meanwhile, Stevens had been taking an active role in the Salon International des Artistes Silencieux, exhibiting in Paris (1927), Madrid (1928), Brussels (1930), and at the International Exhibition of Fine and Applied Arts by Deaf Artists in New York City (1934). Through these associations, he had become very close friends with such distinguished deaf European artists as the sculptor Jean Hanau.* Wishing to share the contributions of deaf people to the art world, he wrote many biographical sketches for *The Silent Worker*, including H. Humphrey Moore,* Léon Morice, Fernand Hamar,* Jean Hanau,* François Crolard, Eulogio Blasco, and Vilem Hauner.* The influence of the De Zubiaurre brothers on Stevens' work is especially apparent in such paintings as *Basque Grandmother*, which was exhibited at the Roerich Museum and became one of the most popular pieces in the tour that followed. Stevens' *Enchantment*, a Native American scene, was also extremely well received.

Stevens moved to Austin in 1949. He considered one of his greatest accomplishments to be the painting titled *Holy Family Resting in Egypt* (1942), which was placed on a wall of the First United Methodist Church in his home town of Mexia. Stevens continued to paint and exhibit his works through the next few decades. Between 1961 and 1964, he traveled through Europe, organizing committees to solicit gifts of art work by deaf artists of renown for a collection to be exhibited at Gallaudet College's Centennial Celebration. In the 1970s, the University of Texas at Austin honored him by offering him a room at the Humanities Research Center in which to arrange an exhibit of deaf artists. Stevens included in this exhibit more than twenty works of the De Zubiaurre brothers, the master Goya,* the portraitist Angel Garavilla, and Jean Hanau.

Following a stroke, Stevens died on November 27, 1991, at the age of 95.

References

Dowdell, M. P. (1927). Kelly Stevens' pictures grow on one as acquaintance with them ripens. *The Silent Worker, 40* (1), 32.

Eakin, D. (1987, November 29). Works of Texas artist hang in buildings around the world. *Mexia Daily News*.

Stevens, K. H. (undated). Autobiographical notes, Gallaudet University Archives.

Thomas, M. (1937). Louisiana's new acquisition. *The Pelican, 57* (8), 1–3.

MATHIAS STOLTENBERG (1799–1871), Norwegian Painter.

Mathias Stoltenberg was born on July 21, 1799, in Tonsberg, Norway, a seafarers' town south of Oslo. He was the first of nine children. His father, Carl

Stoltenberg, was a wealthy merchant who served during Mathias' childhood as a delegate to the Eidsvold convention, where an independent Norway was first declared. In Stoltenberg Park, there now stands a monument to Carl and a second to his deaf son Mathias.

Childhood diseases claimed the lives of three of the Stoltenberg children. Mathias Stoltenberg was profoundly deafened at the age of eleven by "nerve fever," most likely spinal meningitis. His parents were unable to find the expertise they needed to educate him despite their considerable influence and their ties to the Lutheran Church. They enrolled him in the Institute for the Deaf and Dumb in Copenhagen, Denmark, when he was in his middle adolescence. There, because his father was a prominent personality, he spent many evenings at the homes of writers, churchmen, and politicians, including the Norwegian Secretary of State. The Secretary's wife noted Stoltenberg's early talent, and she spent time with him, introducing him to the world of literature and art. She also connected him to painters living in Copenhagen. Stoltenberg himself soon began to paint.

At the Institute, Stoltenberg received the standard Scandinavian curriculum of that time, with the philosophy that deaf children must be taught a skilled trade in order to support themselves. In a largely workshop-oriented environment, Stoltenberg was taught cabinetmaking, structural drawing, and carpentry, skills he used upon graduation as he sought employment under several architects and a furniture company. While in school, however, he tried to cultivate his talent in painting, and he took full advantage of his family wealth and his friendship with the Secretary's wife to commission the best painters in Denmark for private tutoring. They recognized his gifts and were uniformly helpful in encouraging him toward portrait painting; and he soon excelled in portraits of children, in particular. While many became friends and he generally enjoyed the company of these artists, he endured the negative attitudes of some who did not understand him, calling him "the crazy Norwegian rich boy." It took some time for Stoltenberg to realize that the wealth he regarded so pragmatically as a means to an end could breed resentment in others.

Stoltenberg's dream of studying in Rome or Paris was shattered. His father went bankrupt with an investment in the Vallo salt mines when the Danish government raised the duty levied on Norwegian salt. With no money to support his deaf son's education and private tutoring, Carl Stoltenberg called him home. On the passport Mathias used to return home, he listed his profession as "Portrait Painter." He arrived home to a scene that opened his eyes to exactly how much he had taken for granted. In the ten years he had been in Denmark, his parents had managed to keep their home, but that was about all. Stoltenberg failed to find employment as a carpenter in order to help support his family. At home, he recorded the emotional state of his family in his first series of portraits in Norway. His mother, Karen Stoltenberg, is shown to be an attractive, pleasant, and still-elegant woman. The portrait also captures exhaustion and depression around her eyes, however, from what must have already been a very difficult life. He also painted two portraits of his father and two of his brothers and a sister.

Stoltenberg painted a number of portraits over the next few years, but was unable to sell his work in Tonsberg or Oslo. His landscape paintings and his portraits were considered highly unconventional with their use of bright and primary colors. He soon began the life of an itinerant portrait painter, carrying with him his carpentry tools as well, living from week to week. He often worked only for shelter and food. In 1830, his father died broken from the loss of his business, and his family lost their home. His mother moved into the home of her second son, a pastor, where she remained until her death at the age of eighty-four. For the last decade of her life, she was blind and unable to see her children. Often in ill health himself, Mathias Stoltenberg traveled the country. Despite his discouraging prospects, he appears to have known that his paintings would some day be valued by collectors, for he carefully signed each one. Through time, he returned to his early love of painting children. Unfortunately, when photography made its debut, he struggled even further to find employment as a portrait painter.

Stoltenberg lived the final years of his life in poverty in a small red cottage in a remote part of rural Norway. Unable to communicate because of his deafness, he became increasingly isolated. The artistic community does not seem to have reached out to him in any way. He retreated into his painting to relieve the loneliness. He also became quite resourceful. Unable to afford canvases for his landscapes and his many portraits of children, he searched for substitutes. He once even completed a painting on the bottom of a zinc tub.

At least twenty-three landscapes and 146 portraits painted by Stoltenberg have been identified. It is now generally agreed that Stoltenberg's style of painting and now-distinguishing characteristics militated against wide acceptance of his work. He rejected the brownish, muted landscape and dark portraiture favored at that time. His bright, startling colors were considered gaudy in the circle of art-buyers. Yet, he persisted, and he does not appear to have compromised his colorful vision in his later work. Like the deaf artist Goya,* who also refused to follow the rules and ended his career largely alone, Stoltenberg was compelled to follow his own Muse and vision of the world.

Stoltenberg died in 1871 and is buried in a small churchyard in Vang, Norway.

Early in the twentieth century, his striking use of colors began to attract attention among collectors, who began to seek his work eagerly. The new wave of critics embraced Stoltenberg's vision, and young artists found a model, both in technique and in independence of thought. A cottage industry of Stoltenberg hunters emerged. The forgotten canvases were rescued from cellars and attics, easing the work of the rescuers by clearly bearing carefully placed signatures that identified the work of the talented Stoltenberg. His art can now be found in private collections and art museums all over Norway, including sixteen paintings hanging in the National Gallery in Oslo. The monument in Stoltenberg

T

HOWARD L. TERRY (1877–1964), American Writer/Poet.

Howard L. Terry was born in St. Louis, Missouri on January 4, 1877. He experienced progressive deafness throughout his childhood until he was totally deaf. His mother died when he was eleven years old and his family moved to Collinsville, a small town in Illinois. His father, a gifted writer and poet, knew little about the effects of deafness and did not at first encourage him to develop language skills. Nevertheless, Terry was only twelve when he began to type his ''Half-a-Penny-Tales'' on a toy typewriter. An entire volume of poems came two years later, and the supportive father published the verse in pamphlet form. This attracted the attention of a St. Louis newspaper reporter, who predicted a career as a poet for Terry.

Terry first attended public school, followed by Rugby Academy in St. Louis. He was bothered throughout his life with eye trouble. Later, in a letter to a friend in 1910, he looked back at his early attempts to write prose and verse as ''marred'' because he had not been adequately taught grammar and composition. He experienced what would now be called an anxiety attack when, upon accepting a publisher's offer for his first book of verse, he realized that he was utterly unprepared to produce the manuscript as expected. One literary critic was invited to provide a critique of the draft, considerately informing Terry's father that it would be ''torn to pieces by the reviewers.'' Terry nevertheless persevered, and, after undertaking intensive self-study over several months to focus on both grammar and stylistics, he submitted the work, which was received favorably by readers.

Terry's early poem ''The Old Homestead,'' written in 1886 and later published in 1916 in *The Silent Worker*, depicted scenes from his youth after his mother's death, the ''dark hour'' of his life, as he called it. A widowed aunt, Helen Bassatt, with her two daughters, moved into their unpretentious house to help raise him. Unable to make friends easily, Terry spent many evenings receiving tutoring from one of his cousins in Byron and other poets. He often climbed into the attic, where he lay on a feather bed to experiment with his own writing.

Terry began study at Gallaudet College in 1895, but problems with his eyesight led him to leave. When he entered Gallaudet, he knew no sign language and found it difficult to even follow fingerspelling in classes. At Gallaudet, however, he met Alice Taylor, a young deaf woman whom he married in 1901. They purchased a farm in Southwest Missouri where they lived for eight years. Later, in 1938, Gallaudet awarded him an honorary degree for his productive writing career.

Terry's verses appeared in issues of the Collinsville Illinois *Herald*, St Louis *Globe-Democrat*, and St. Louis *Republic* shortly after he left Gallaudet. *A Tale of Normandy* was published in 1898. Through the next few decades, he published numerous articles and verse in such periodicals as *The Mentor, Sports Afield, Out West, The Hesperian, Poetry World*, and *Wee Wisdom*, a children's magazine. Sunset Farm, where he and Alice lived, provided material for many of his writings, including the locale for his novel *Voice from the Silence*, a story about pioneer farmers. The rights to that story were sold to Selig Polyscope Company for possible filming, and the book was republished as *Man of the Soil*. The company never produced the film, however. *Waters from an Ozark Spring* was published in 1909, followed by *Our Celebrities* in 1910.

After the turn of the century, Terry kept in close contact through correspondence with Edward Miner Gallaudet and Percival Hall, who replaced Gallaudet upon his retirement in 1912 as president of Gallaudet College. In 1910, Terry wrote to Hall, enclosing a check for five dollars as a prize to "encourage English composition" among deaf students at Gallaudet College. This gift was partly made in apology for having earlier fired off a polemic denouncing the inadequacy of methods for teaching language to deaf students. Terry had followed with an autobiographical account of his own "sadly neglected and misdirected" education in the English language, with the purpose of encouraging Hall to admonish Gallaudet students to take their education in English more seriously. The harshness evoked by his own strength of feeling later appeared to have surprised Terry himself, and he was eager to repair any misunderstanding with his friend Hall.

Terry wrote seventy-five stanzas of "The Deserted Ships" at one sitting in 1910, but took ten months to bring the epic to its final form. Terry's perfectionism was always evident. He subsequently published the poem in *The Silent Worker. The Dream: A Dramatic Romance* came out in 1912. It was first written for the Open Air Theatre in Carmel, California, and although given high mention, it was too difficult to stage there and appealed to a select audience. The metrical drama was then published in serial form over seven months in *The Ohio Farmer. California and Other Poems* was published in 1917. He continued to write for both the newspaper and Sunday magazine for the Los Angeles *Times*, and for the Santa Monica *Outlook*. "Heroes of the Silent World" was written for the *Times* with his wife in May of 1920. Among the many works he wrote over the next decade, *Sung in Silence*, published in 1929, contained many of his best poems. In the preface, he described how deafness had always permeated his work, leading him to be "attracted to and impressed by things that hardly disturbed the minds of others."

For many years, he labored to organize a Guild of Deaf Writers, publishing issues of *The Guild* and, in the 1930s, published with J. H. MacFarlane and Kate Shibley, an Anthology of Poems by the Deaf. In a 1931 issue of *Social Science*, he published "The Deaf, Their Education and Place in Society," about the status of deaf people in history and the present. He was a member of Pi Gamma Mu, a social science honorary society.

Terry's wife, Alice, was also a writer, primarily for the Deaf community periodicals. Alice was a prolific essayist who studied logic at the University of California, Berkeley, and wrote articles on educational and legal advocacy. Where Howard was a more "solitary writer" in the poetic vein, Alice became an unassuming but persistent activist, a two-term president of the California Association of the Deaf. Her writer's voice was more that of a community leader, but she, too, wrote poetry; and the two writers supported one another tirelessly in the course of a nearly fifty-year marriage. Terry kept himself busy writing until his death, declining an offer to serve as editor of *Poetry World* because of his poor eyesight. He published *Peter Popcorn Pennywig and his Wonderful Village of Caliland* for children in 1949.

Terry clung to his Romantic and Victorian-bred style, as well as to a belief in poetry as a teacher and a means to self-improvement. As the Moderns revolutionized poetry and changed or discarded conventions such as metre, Terry's later poems were often viewed as sentimental and quaint, coming from another era. Nonetheless, his numerous writings reached a wide audience through major periodicals. He was not afraid to call himself a deaf writer and to attempt to convey his experiences to mainstream readers.

Terry died March 3, 1964, in Los Angeles, California.

References

Klugman, M. (1950). Howard L. Terry. *The Silent Worker, 2* (9), 3–5.

Lowman, R. Howard L. Terry. In J. V. Van Cleve (Ed.), *Gallaudet encyclopedia of deaf people and deafness* (Vol. 3, pp. 281–282). New York: McGraw-Hill.

Terry, H. L. (1940, February/March/April). A deaf writer's story. *The Modern Silents.*

Terry, H. L. (1950). Alice in silentland. *The Silent Worker, 3* (3), 3–6.

MICHAEL THOMAS (1951–), American Dancer/Choreographer.

Michael Thomas was born on May 26, 1951, in Fresno, California, and attended the Scandinavian School, the Leif Erikson School, and McLane High School. He first noticed that his hearing was failing when he was seven, probably a result of mumps and encephalitis when he was eleven months old. He decided to keep the initially mild hearing loss a secret from his parents and teachers, especially since another student in his school who wore a large body-type hearing aid was the subject of ridicule by his classmates. Intensely interested in music at a very young age, Thomas began with piano lessons, studied the clarinet, and, over a single weekend, taught himself how to play the oboe in order to join the McLane High band. His grandfather offered him one hundred dollars to learn the bagpipes—out of the house, in a nearby football field.

Thomas' particular talent in dance was also recognized early, and a special agreement allowed him to attend the Severance Ballet School while still enrolled in high school. During his first class at Severance, he was offered a Ford Foundation Scholarship by the San Francisco Ballet School. He then attended the University of Utah, one of the best dance programs in the United States. At the age of twenty, he began to have serious vertigo problems, but did not immediately associate this with his hearing loss. Attempting to accommodate for the balance problems, Thomas continued to keep his private struggle a secret, fearing that he might be rejected from dance and his dreams shattered. Some of the directors he worked under were not sympathetic to even career-threatening injuries, much less a loss of hearing and vertigo problems.

Shortly after his time in Utah, Thomas transferred to Harkness House for Ballet Arts in New York City. There, with seven other young men and eight young women he trained and competed eleven hours a day, stealing off for additional training at the American Ballet Theatre School and Martha Graham School late in the evenings. During this period, there were two markedly separate worlds of dance, ballet and modern dance; and although they are much more integrated today, his sampling of modern dance would have evoked ridicule at the Harkness School had they learned of his late-evening lessons. Thomas also studied modern dance under Jose Limon, who had instructed him in Fresno during his high school years. When the Harkness Foundation dissolved its primary dance company, one of the first companies in the world, the dancers disbanded, refusing to dance for a second company. Rebekkah Harkness then rented an entire opera house, the Grand Liceo in Barcelona, Spain, for rehearsals by the junior company. Thomas turned down an invitation to join this endeavor. On the same day, he applied for full-time study at the American Ballet Theatre School, where he was immediately offered a scholarship. With the prevailing tendency to favor Europeans for major roles, however, a young dancer like Thomas did not stand much of a chance. Nor did he have enough money to even attend the Stuttgart Ballet when it performed at the Met. He applied as a supernumerary merely to watch the professionals at work, and in this apprentice role he served for eight weeks, falling in love with that company. When he heard that they were auditioning, Thomas, with a fever of 102 degrees and his hearing loss and vertigo becoming more noticeable, nevertheless competed with two hundred other dancers and was chosen as one of two students to attend the Statstheaterschule on a full scholarship in Stuttgart. Much to his surprise, the famous director John Cranko picked him up at the airport.

The year 1971 was one of the happiest times of his life, even though the

Michael Thomas, American ballet dancer and choreographer, in San Francisco Ballet production of Béjart's "Firebird." Photo by Arne Folkadahl
courtesy of Michael Thomas.

progressive hearing loss frightened him at times, forcing him to memorize musical scores. The year was also hectic, for he danced both in opera and ballet
theatres, sometimes two different performances on the same evening. Thomas
would perform in the opera house, then rush across the street to a nearby ballet
performance while quickly changing clothes, perform there, and rush back for
the bows in the opera. He also toured the Soviet Union with Cranko's troupe.

The happy time ended on a tragic note, a turning point in his life. First,
Thomas learned that his father was in the hospital. He asked for a leave-of-
absence and was granted the leave with the agreement that he would first per-

form at a gala honoring the Brazilian ballerina Marcia Haydee. When he finally left for the airport, the mother of one of his competitors offered to take him to Frankfurt. Little did he know what events were in store. Worried about his father, and a little homesick as well, Thomas, now twenty-two years old, was vulnerable. At the airport, the woman explained to him that Cranko did not support his continued study at Stuttgart. She advised him not to return. He had a miserable flight home, fearing that his secret about his hearing loss had been detected and believing that she had inside knowledge. He subsequently resigned from the School, only to learn two years later that Cranko had felt hurt and many colleagues were angry. For years, he regretted the decision curtailing his association with the gifted Cranko, who would die prematurely. He darkly wondered, ''why I could accept my physical challenges, but not the spiritual ones.''

Thomas joined Les Grands Ballets Canadiens in Montreal under Ludmilla Cherieff in 1972, mastering a variety of styles and finding that he could be much more successful when given the opportunity to try different dances and choreography. He danced in the presence of Princess Margaret, only to be struck by another of the dancers and receive a bloody nose during the performance. An injury to a leading dancer brought Thomas into a major role in Montreal, but eight performances later he broke his ankle and left for the United States to recuperate. After six months, he began again with the San Francisco Ballet Company and, in the fall of 1976, he had the fortune of being in the right place when the famous French choreographer Maurice Béjart granted permission to the Company to perform *Firebird*. Given this most formidable soloist role, he rushed off to Brussels for a required intensive two-week training session with Béjart and with others who had performed in that role. The day Béjart took Thomas into his office and told him that he felt the young dancer understood the spiritual part of the role so well that he had his teacher's blessing even to make personal modifications, Thomas was euphoric. He felt vindicated after the experience in Germany and fully in control of the spiritual part of his dancing. Béjart himself commented that Michael Thomas had mastered the difficult *Firebird* at an age ten years younger than anyone else who had performed this role.

But the intensive training on the raked (angled) stages of Europe had taken a toll on Thomas' feet. Back in San Francisco, the director was so concerned about losing the valuable knowledge learned in Brussels that Thomas was pressured to perform the entire ballet alone and injured in front of the company while being videotaped. Later, after the performance of *Firebird* had been recorded, the production staff handed him the rehearsal videotape reel as a gift for his birthday. He took it to the Golden Gate Bridge and tossed it into the Bay.

While rehearsing for *Firebird* and performing in the *Nutcracker*, Thomas' vertigo worsened. On the night of his first performance of *Firebird*, he became violently ill from the severe vertigo. He nevertheless performed flawlessly and heroically in his solo debut before an audience of more than five thousand people. One reviewer wrote, ''I sat transfixed through the Firebird. . . . Michael

Thomas as the Bird, stopped the show receiving thunderous applause and shouts of 'bravo.' . . . It evoked a lump in my throat to see such absolute, stunning, perfection.''

''Firebird'' was a particular triumph, but Thomas by that time had performed many principal roles in major ballets around the world, including *Agon*, *Romeo and Juliet*, *Cinderella*, *The Dream*, *Triomphe Di Aphrodite*, and *Danses Concertantes*.

Now in his late twenties, he finally shared the secret of his hearing loss with his parents and sought medical attention, only to learn that nothing could be done. The Dutch Director Rudi van Dantzig, while visiting San Francisco, invited him to see better doctors in Holland, and Thomas agreed to simultaneously dance with the Dutch National Ballet in Amsterdam while on leave from the San Francisco Ballet Company. There, he exhausted his life savings and all of his salary seeking medical help. He returned to San Francisco, but found it increasingly difficult to dance. Frustrated and discouraged, Thomas left the San Francisco Ballet Company in 1979. He spent two years working for a bank, reflecting on his lost career. Then, in 1981, Mary Day invited him as a Guest Artist for the Washington Ballet. During the next few years, he cofounded the Island Moving Company in Newport, Rhode Island, where he choreographed a broad repertoire, including *Grétry Dances*, and served as Ballet Master for the Dayton Ballet, choreographing *Phases*, *The Seasons*, *Tango-San Telmo*, and *Variations for Ten Fingers and Eight Dancers*. Reviewers praised him for his innovation in both choreography and dance. During the performance of his first choreography, his hearing aid broke when he fell, and he sat through the entire performance unable to hear it. At Dayton, he also implemented a project to allow inner-city school children to study ballet.

As Thomas sought new experiences, a letter of reference he received attested to his perseverance. Mary L. Moore, president of the National Academy of Arts, wrote: ''Michael's hearing loss has disrupted what would have been a fine career as a performer and now may impede a second fine career as a teacher and choreographer. If this is allowed to happen the dance world will suffer and it will speak not of Michael's limitations but in the limitations of the way people perceive him'' (March 31, 1987). With this letter in hand, Thomas sat on a park bench in New York's Central Park on a cold snowy day. There, next to a large statue of Beethoven,* Thomas decided it was time to begin teaching other deaf persons to dance. He soon found himself co-directing the American Dance Theatre of the Deaf. He also served on the teaching staff of the Dance Theatre of Harlem under Arthur Mitchell. He quickly became recognized as a gifted and sensitive master teacher.

In 1988, Thomas was offered a position as Artist-in-Residence at the National Technical Institute for the Deaf at the Rochester Institute of Technology, where he has taught, danced, and choreographed highly praised performances, including *Symphonic Dances from West Side Story*, *Medea*, *Romeo and Juliet*, and *Cinderella*. He directs the RIT Dance Company, a unique collaboration of deaf and hearing dancers. He continues to teach students and professional dancers, and his choreography is performed by companies across the United States.

References

Levitan, L. (1988). American Dance Theatre of the Deaf. *Deaf Life, 1* (5), 8–14.

Palmer, R. V. (1991, February 17). Sounds of silence inspiring. Rochester, New York *Democrat and Chronicle.*

RIT Dance Company performance to span 50 years. (1991, February). *Silent News*, (2), 32.

ALFRED R. THOMSON (1894–1979), British Artist.

Alfred R. Thomson was born deaf in 1894 in Bangalore, India, the son of an authoritarian British army paymaster. He showed an early interest in drawing. That was largely disregarded, as his parents considered the limited options available to them. The father decided that the very young child must be educated in England, so when Thomson was only six years old, his parents boarded him at the Royal School for Deaf Children at Margate. His deeply saddened mother died shortly after her return to India. Both at Margate and subsequently at the Barber Oral School, Thomson did not fare well academically. He was a sickly youngster. His talents in art, however, were noted, particularly when he obtained the "silver star" of the Royal Drawing Society at the age of twelve. His teacher at Margate recommended that he be placed in the small academy in Earl's Court, where he studied under Sir William Orchardson, then a visiting professor. His deepening involvement in art was not agreeable to Thomson's father, who removed him from the school. The elder Thomson placed him on a farm as an agricultural student, instructing the owners not to allow the young man access to art materials. Thomson was treated harshly; he left after two years on his own. Now, at the age of twenty-two, he established himself on Redfern Road, in Chelsea. He attempted to enter the Royal Academy of Art, but was unable to pass the entrance examination. For months, he struggled to eke out an existence, sleeping in churches and terminals, as he attempted to earn enough through painting for his own survival.

Thomson began to experiment with caricatures, sending his work to the Academy. One of them was purchased by the renowned artist Sir William Orpen. Finally, Thomson's luck began to take a turn for the better when he met a wealthy woman at a club who acted as a patron and agent to him. She encouraged his more flamboyant work and renamed him "Tommy Thomson." She also connected him to advertisers. With a new image that soon intrigued others, he gained a reputation enhanced by the drawings that ultimately advertised Daimler cards and Tuborg beer. Thomson also tried his hand at decorative work. The newspapers took notice of both his commercial work and the decorative murals of London Characters he executed for the popular Duncannon Pub. He was invited to be a member of the Chelsea Art Club, where such members as Augustus John befriended him. John found him a teaching position in East

London and invited him to his own villa in southern France. From 1920, he exhibited often at the Royal Academy. In 1927, he married, but this marriage proved unsuccessful. His second marriage to Gertrude Parker in 1940 was a happy one, and they ultimately raised two children.

In the late twenties, his murals and oils were commissioned by wealthy families across Europe, and he exhibited in a number of prestigious museums in Europe and the United States. He was represented, for example, at the Carnegie Institute in Pittsburgh. In 1934, Thomson was invited to join such other deaf notables as the de Zubiaurre* brothers, Kelly Stevens,* John Louis Clarke,* Fernand Hamar,* and Cadwallader Washburn* in the International Exhibition of Fine and Applied Arts by Deaf Artists at the Roerich Museum in New York City. Thomson's canvases were particularly well-reviewed in the New York newspapers.

In 1938, Thomson won first prize painting in a contest sponsored by the Essex County Council in Chelmsford. His painting showed the departure of the Pilgrim Fathers for the New World from Plymouth, England, based on extensive analysis of records at the British Museum and a study of the scene itself. That same year, he was made an Associate of the Royal Academy and gave many sittings to such notables as the king of Greece and Lord Vansittart. Sadly, his father was never able to reconcile himself to his son's chosen path, even in the face of his astonishing success. Their relationship never improved.

Throughout World War II, Thomson painted many well-known Britons, including Wing Commander Leonard Cheshire and Matron-in-Chief Dame E. Blair, whose portraits are now at the Imperial War Museum in London and the Royal Air Force Museum in Hendon, respectively. He was named official Royal Air Force artist after the RAF initially disqualified him because of his deafness. As if to prove the point, Thomson was shot by a sentry on base when he did not hear the order to identify himself. The bullet was not removed so that his arm would not be paralyzed.

Thomson was the first painter in history allowed to capture the interior of the House of Commons and of the House of Lords. He painted both houses in session. His paintings are owned by Queen Elizabeth and several members of the royal family. Other works are purchased by the Carnegie Trust, Chantry Bequest, and the Edward Stott Trust.

Thomson continued to work, though ill, during the last days of his life. He died on October 27, 1979.

References

Dimmock, A. F. (1987). Alfred Reginald Thomson. In. J. V. Van Cleve (Ed.), *Gallaudet encyclopedia of deaf people and deafness* (Vol. 3, pp. 291–292). New York: McGraw-Hill.

Jackson, P. W. (1990). *Britain's deaf heritage*. Kippielaw, England: The British Deaf Association.

A noted deaf artist. (1942). *The British Deaf Times, 39,* 94.

DOUGLAS TILDEN (1860–1935), American Sculptor.

Douglas Tilden was born on May 1, 1860, at Chico, California. He was deafened through scarlet fever at the age of five and was educated at the California School for the Deaf at Berkeley from 1866 until 1879. The son of a physician, Tilden demonstrated an early aptitude for art coupled with a love of nature, where he drew inspiration and studied form and shape. His mother was talented in painting, and Tilden began to imitate her, making his own brushes. For one winter, he studied at the San Francisco School of Design.

After a year of study at the University of California, unable to obtain the position of mechanic to which he then aspired, he began to teach at the California School for the Deaf. He demonstrated a great natural ability in the classroom and published numerous articles in journals on the subject of educating deaf students. Under the penname "Clarence Stairly," he also published in *The Overland Monthly* a fable concerning the persistence of a deaf artist in the face of adversity, called "The Artist's Testament." Tilden and his closest deaf friend, the artist-photographer Theophilus d'Estrella,* explored the mountains of California, where they continued to pursue their love for nature and wildlife.

In 1883, a plaster sculpture modelled by his younger brother attracted his interest. After studying under the sculptor Marion Wells for a month, he moved to a laundry shed on the corner of a baseball field at the California School for the Deaf. There, he could experiment in huge forms undisturbed. Tilden also began to make inquiries concerning further study of sculpting technique. He completed his first work, a statuette entitled *The Tired Wrestler*, in 1885, which earned him support for further study.

In 1887, Tilden resigned his teaching post and journeyed to New York, where he studied under John Quincy Adams Ward at the National Academy of Design and under Henry Siddons Mowbray at the Gotham Student's League. The following year he realized his dream of traveling to Paris, where he met Paul Choppin,* a deaf Salon medalist, who also provided Tilden with guidance. For seven years, Tilden perfected his techniques by examining works in the museums, galleries, and salons of Paris, and by studying the history of sculpture and the methods of the masters.

Tilden submitted the plaster sculpture *The Baseball Player* to the International Exposition in Paris in 1889, but he was disappointed that it was not acccepted. The following year, however, he was pleased to have this work in bronze accepted at the Paris Salon des Artistes Français on the Champs Élysées.

Simultaneously, Tilden became increasingly involved in the Deaf community. He was elected vice-president at the First International Congress for the Deaf in Paris in 1889, and advocated the use of signs and speech together in the education of deaf students during a period when sign language was rejected by many hearing leaders. Meanwhile, *The Baseball Player* received honorable mention, motivating him to begin on *The Bear Hunt* (also called *Death Grip*), a large sculpture which illustrates a Native American in hand-to-hand combat with

Douglas Tilden, American sculptor. Photo from *The Silent Worker,* 7 (3), 1894, courtesy of Gallaudet University Archives.

a grizzly bear. Tilden's *The Tired Boxer* received an honorable mention at the Salon in 1890.

In 1891, the bronze *The Baseball Player* was brought to San Francisco, where it was exhibited at the Art Loan Exhibition along with the works of such masters as Rembrandt, Monet, and Delacroix. Tilden's sculpture, the only work by an American, became the principal attraction, and it was subsequently purchased by W. E. Brown of the Southern Pacific Railroad Company and presented to the Art Commission for Golden State Park. Brown continued patronage of Tilden through monthly stipends. A grateful Tilden presented *The Young Acrobat* to his benefactor, a marble and bronze statuette exhibited at the 1891 Salon. *The Bear Hunt* was also exhibited at the Paris Salon, receiving praise there as well as back home in California.

Tilden nevertheless maintained his involvement in education as well, spending considerable time preparing and presenting a paper on "The Art Education of the Deaf" at the World Congress of the Deaf in Chicago in 1892. To *The Silent Worker*, a major organ of the Deaf community in the United States, he enthusiastically submitted a detailed description of the steps he took to complete a sculptured work. He served as president of the California Association of the Deaf in 1909 and was an active member in the National Association of the Deaf.

Several of Tilden's sculptures were exhibited at the World's Columbian Exposition in Chicago in 1893. As Brown's financial fortunes changed, Tilden lost his principal benefactor, and he struggled to complete *The Football Players*, exhibited in 1893 at the Paris Salon. This was one of his most graceful works and was also included in the Pan-American Exposition in Buffalo, New York, in 1901 and the Universal Exposition in Paris in 1910. The statue was later erected at the University of California, a result of a challenge by James D. Phelan of San Francisco that the sculpture be given to the victor of the best of three football games between California and Stanford. Shortly after, Tilden returned to San Francisco, where the accolade "Michelangelo of the West" was frequently appended to his name. He set up a studio at the abandoned Woodward's Gardens. In addition to being appointed an honorary member of a committee for artistic improvement of San Francisco, Tilden taught the first sculpture classes at the Mark Hopkins Institute of Art at the University of California. He communicated to students primarily through writing, gestures, and demonstration. While a professor there from 1894 until 1900, he also helped to found the Society of Arts and Crafts.

Tilden executed many major sculptures. One, *The Native Sons' Fountain*, presented to the city of San Francisco by Phelan, depicted a miner with a pick over his shoulder commemorating the early California Gold Rush. On three sides of the pedestal of this sculpture are buffalo skulls and rattlesnakes, whose mouths form the jets of a fountain. *The Ball Player*, his friends have said, was a self-portrait. Tilden's *Mechanics*, however, is considered by many experts to be his masterpiece. Commissioned in dedication to the Pacific Coast's first foundry, the Union Iron Works, and in memory of Peter Donahue, a pioneer ship and railroad builder, the bronze sculpture includes five men working with sheet metal, a lever press, an anvil, and a locomotive driving wheel. This monument was erected at the intersection of Market and Battery Streets in San Francisco. The English poet Harrold Johnson was inspired by this sculpture and composed a poem in tribute. Tilden's other major works included *Grief* (Colma, California, 1890s), Stephen M. White Memorial in Los Angeles (1908), McElroy Memorial Fountain in Oakland, *Oregon Volunteers* of the Spanish-American War (Portland), and *Junipero Serra*, a tribute to the founder of the California missions

(San Francisco Golden Gate Park). He also completed a monument to Balboa erected in the Golden Gate park. Two of his sculptures, *Mechanics* and *The Admission Day Monument*, were still standing after the great San Francisco earthquake of 1906. *Tired Boxer* was destroyed, however.

Tilden won the gold medal in 1909 at the Alaska Yukon-Pacific Exposition in Seattle. Among his many works in plaster at the Bohemian Art Show in 1913 was *The Awakening of San Francisco.* At the Panama-Pacific International Exposition in San Francisco in 1915, he exhibited a group of highly-praised allegorical figures over seventeen feet high, representing Valor, Imagination, Truth, Morality, and Industry.

Tilden was elected a fellow of the Royal Society of Arts in London. He continued on the San Francisco Art Commission, and served on the Jury of Awards at the Chicago Exposition in 1893 and the jury on sculpture at the St. Louis Exposition in 1904. He won many other honors for his works and was selected to the Hall of Fame established in 1914 by the Native Sons of the Golden West. An eight-inch-high version of *The Bear Hunt* in gold was presented to Theodore Roosevelt in 1903. In 1980, one reporter in the *San Francisco Chronicle* wrote that ''Tilden's sculpture remains San Francisco's greatest single legacy of public art.''

Struggling financially in his last two decades, Tilden, divorced since 1926, attempted unsuccessfully to secure a post in teaching at the California School for the Deaf. After a short period assisting with modeling classes as a visiting professor of sculpture at St. Mary's College in Oakland, he worked as a machinist. Then he moved to Hollywood, where he sculpted extinct animals for educational films. When his electricity and water supply had been cut off for nonpayment of his bills, he worked with a kerosene lamp and lived on pails of water borrowed from neighbors. The proud sculptor did not share his needs with his friends. Yet, in this bleak environment, he found continued joy and fulfillment in life, sculpting new works, including a larger-than-life bust of the painter William Keith, completed from memory, which was, in 1980, part of an exhibition of his works at the M. H. de Young Memorial Museum.

Tilden died of a heart attack alone in his studio on August 5, 1935.

References

Albronda, M. (1980). *Douglas Tilden: Portrait of a deaf sculptor.* Silver Spring, MD: T. J. Publishers.

Armes, W. D. (1898, February). Douglas Tilden, sculptor. *Overland Monthly,* 142–153.

Douglas Tilden. (1894). *The Silent Worker, 7* (2), 1–4.

Runde, W. S. (1952). Douglas Tilden, sculptor. *The Silent Worker, 5* (4), 3–5.

The sculpture of Douglas Tilden. (1940). *The Silent Worker, 16* (3), 33–44.

CHARLOTTE ELIZABETH TONNA (1790–1846), British Writer.

Charlotte Elizabeth Tonna was born on October 1, 1790, in Norwich, England, the daughter of an anti-Papist, Episcopal clergyman. ''I loved silence,'' she wrote in *Personal Recollections* (1842) about her early childhood before becoming deaf. She claimed that nothing excited her sense of hearing in the way she responded to visual beauty, and this clear preference later manifested itself in her ability to imagine and describe. She did love the tones of the harp-sichord played by a composer and friend of her father's, and her father's ac-companying voice. When she was totally blinded for several months, Tonna's love for music was deepened, particularly the works of Handel and Haydn. Much deeper was her love for the Scriptures. The family Bible was the same book placed before Queen Charlotte at her coronation in 1761 and handed down to her mother. Tonna's passionate zeal for Protestantism is infused throughout her *Personal Recollections.*

Born in the period that followed the French revolution and the Irish rebellion, Tonna was by the age of six deeply engaged in discussions with her family about the antagonism between the Roman Church and the Church of England. The threat of an invasion by Napolean was another possibility, which deepened a siege mentality. The devout child and her father regularly discussed martyrdom for their faith, and Charlotte became obsessed by this fear. When her father died, she became even more religious.

Tonna was profoundly deafened around the age of ten. Treated by doctors with mercury for an illness, she nearly died. She always believed that it was the treatment, not the illness, that caused her deafness. Acutely sensitive to vibra-tions, she found some pleasure in placing her hands on the sounding board of a piano, particularly when Handel was being played, music she recalled from her childhood. Tonna attributed her abilities to compose rhythmic poems to such auditory memories. She learned sign, and her close friends and husband-to-be interpreted sermons and speeches for her in this manner. In a piece written for the *North British Review* after her death, her husband recollected how he and others were concerned for the accuracy of their signing and more-frequent fin-gerspelling. But Tonna could repeat the words verbatim, and her husband at-tributed this to the power and quickness of her eye. Her linguistic abilities probably also had a good deal to do with it.

Tonna married Captain Phelan, an officer of the British army. When sum-moned to join him in Halifax, she journeyed there and remained for two years, writing very little. Next, after a short visit to England, she traveled to Ireland, where her husband was involved in a lawsuit, and she assisted lawyers in pre-paring documents for him. With her husband often away in Dublin at this time, Tonna, encouraged by another lady to consider writing in further support of Protestantism, made a resolution to commit herself entirely to religion. The secretary of the Dublin Tract Society recommended that she mingle more with farming and working families to evangelize, believing her deafness would be no serious barrier. Then, when her husband was ordered abroad, she refused to accompany him, and she turned even further to her literary endeavors.

It is frankly disturbing for the modern reader to read the work of Charlotte Elizabeth Tonna during this period. Characterizing the Catholic Church and its rituals as "idolatrous" and "pagan" and railing against "Popery," the texts now read as fanatical at best and hate-mongering at worst. As many critics have pointed out, however, Tonna was careful to distinguish between practices and practitioners. She developed friendships with Catholics—where religion was not discussed, nor ceremonies attended. She freely admitted to having been brought up with a prejudice toward the Irish, and she reevaluated this conscientiously when she lived abroad. Nonetheless, the vitriol in her tracts is hard to read, even in context.

Amid the rising violence in the early 1820s, Tonna was invited to Kilkenny, where she stayed for three years. There, she finished *Osric, a Missionary Tale*, a three-thousand-line, epic poem. Supported by George Sandford (Lord Mount-sandford), she began to write a number of penny and twopenny books for the Dublin Tract Society, which became very popular.

In 1823, Tonna encountered an eleven-year-old deaf boy, Jack, at a convent near Vicarsfield. She taught fingerspelling to his sixteen-year-old brother, Pat, to help her instruct him. Jack was born to poor parents unable to afford an education in the South of Ireland. Tonna's first lesson focused on single words and she progressed with him over a period of seven years, using fingerspelling and writing. She also taught him religion. *The Happy Mute; or The Dumb Child's Appeal* (1833) describes her attempt to educate him and her appeal to others to follow her example. Four thousand copies sold in the first five weeks in Ireland alone, before an edition was sent to England or Scotland. Profits from the sale of the book went to Juvenile Association for the Education of the Deaf and Dumb. Tonna also conversed by signs with deaf people she met throughout her life.

After more than five years in Ireland, Tonna was summoned to England, a difficult decision for her, since she had grown to love the Irish people. Never-theless, she departed for her homeland soon after, first stopping in Clifton to meet with Hannah More, an anti-Papist writer with whom she had developed a friendship through correspondence.

Tonna's brother had fortunately survived many battles, and she was delighted to be reunited with him after a period of ten years. While he began study at Military College at Sandhurst, she pursued her literary work with anxiety. No longer feeling safe using her own name, she wrote many works anonymously. Tonna was immediately successful with the publication of nearly thirty "humble penny books," including *The System, Consistency, Allan M'Leod*, and *Zadoc*, in addition to numerous contributions to periodicals. She endured a period of legal challenges to her copyrights and the narrative of one of her many works, translated into Italian and titled *The Simple Flower*, led to angry denunciation of all of her works in Italy. Her principal prose works included *Derry, a Tale of Revolution, The Rockite, Letters from Ireland, Judah's Lion, The Flower Garden; or, Glimpses of the Past, Falsehood and Truth, The Wrongs of Women, The Deserter, Combination, Conformity, Principalities and Powers in Heavenly Places, Judaea Capta, The Church Visible in All Ages*, and *Perseverance*. She

Charlotte Elizabeth Tonna, British writer. Drawing from Harriet B. Stowe, ed. (1844), *The Works of Charlotte Elizabeth* (New York: M. W. Dodd).

also published four separate volumes of poetry: *The Convent Bell, Izram, a Mexican Tale*, the aforementioned *Osric, a Missionary Tale*, and *The Garden, with Other Poems*. Other writings include *Second Causes; or, Up and Be Doing, Passing Thoughts, Miscellaneous Poems*, and *Poems, on the Peninsula War*.

Tonna's writings were highlighted in Harriet Beecher Stowe's *The Works of Charlotte Elizabeth*. Her poetry held such important readership in America that several volumes were later pirated from Frederic Rowton's 1848 edition. In one, the anonymous editor added several of Tonna's verses. Her work was compared with Hannah More's in this volume. Tonna's *Christian Lady's Magazine*, which she founded and edited, examined serious social issues and established her as a pioneering female journalist.

Roger P. Wallins, a literary expert, examined the works of Tonna as a "social novelist." While some early nineteenth-century writers addressed social problems, such as the working and living conditions of the lower classes, from direct personal observations or experiences, others tapped, at times *verbatim*, Parliamentary Committee and Royal Commission reports (known as "blue books"). Between 1833 and 1838, for example, over one hundred articles on social conditions appeared in such periodicals as the *Edinburgh Review, New Monthly Magazine*, and *Westminster Review*. Tonna appears to have drawn heavily on these sources for fiction as well as nonfiction writing. One of the characters in Tonna's *Helen Fleetwood,* noted Wallins, points to the rather current-appearing problem that: "the facts are brought before Parliament, by having witnesses up to be examined on oath before the committee; these reports . . . are printed, and sold too: but I don't think one lady in a thousand ever looks into them, to say nothing of other classes; and if they are not read, how can the statements be known?" Tonna became as concerned in her later years for civic responsibility as for religious devotion.

Captain Phelan died in 1837, and Elizabeth married Lucius H. J. Tonna of London in 1841. Dedicated to the reform of society, Tonna ultimately saw poetry as a change agent as powerful, or more so, than prose. She also viewed poetry as a particularly strong medium for women's voices.

Tonna died on July 12, 1846.

References

Anecdote of Mrs. Tonna. (1879). *American Annals of the Deaf, 2* (2), 124–125.
Elizabeth, C. (1842). *Personal recollections.* New York: John S. Taylor.
Rowton, F. (1981). *The female poets of Great Britain.* Detroit: Wayne State University.
Stowe, H. B. (Ed.). (1844). *The works of Charlotte Elizabeth.* New York: M. W. Dodd.
Wallins, R. P. (1975). Victorian periodicals and the emerging social conscience. *Victorian Periodicals Newsletter, 8,* 47–59.

HEINRICH VON TREITSCHKE (1834–1896), German Writer/Political Publicist.

Heinrich von Treitschke was born at Dresden in Saxony on September 15, 1834, the son of a military officer. He learned to read and write at the age of four, dreaming of the life of a soldier. In the spring of 1842, a few weeks after he began in a private boys' school, he contracted chicken pox, followed by measles a few months later. A glandular infection caused swelling that affected the Eustachian tubes, eventually causing complete deafness. Tormented by a constant succession of painful treatments and the fears of living a life without hearing, Treitschke nevertheless pursued intensive education, transferring to the Holy Cross Gymnasium in Dresden in 1846, where he was enthralled by young radical teachers. Treitschke soon became a voracious reader, especially of current events in the newspapers, quickly absorbing the partisan leanings toward German unification. He graduated in 1851.

Even as a young child he had shown literary talents, mastering Latin by the age of ten, and putting into poetry his feelings about being deaf ("Krankenträume"). His devoted parents nurtured his adjustment to a world of silence. Unfortunately, their love was not enough to allay their son's continued embarrassments and disappointment in life. He became increasingly isolated in his personal activities. He also became intolerant and severe.

Treitschke was a fervent patriot, vigorously supporting the union of Germany under Prussia at the age of seventeen, and dedicating poetry to the "heroes" who fell in the rebellion of German subjects of Denmark. In 1851, he entered Bonn University, studying history and political science, especially the theory found in Aristotle's *Politics* and the writings of August Ludwig von Rochau, architect of the theory of *Realpolitik*. His deafness forced him to focus on reading, reinforced by solitary walks, where he invariably turned what he had read into his developing conception of a State. During university debates, he often caused the professors to despair when, with his loud voice, he alienated everyone with fearsome solutions and proposals. In 1852, Treitschke studied at Leipzig, then at Kiel, Tübingen, and Heidelberg, the latter university dismissing him for participating in a dangerous duel with pistols with another student with whom he had an altercation. In 1856, he was studying at Göttingen, where the writings of Machiavelli left a lasting impression. That year, he also began to publish his own perspectives, including an article entitled "The Foundations of English Liberty" for the *Prussian Year Book* (*Preussiche Jahrbüche*), and *Patriotic Songs*, a collection of militaristic verse. Oddly, also within this volume is found "Sick Room Reveries," a very personal reflection on his depression and his deafness, connected to his disillusionment during his school years.

In 1857, Treitschke completed his thesis at Leipzig on "The Science of Society," which made a case for German unity. He then spent several years writing, including a dramatization of the life of Heinrich von Plauen which, along with other literary works of his, was lost during World War II. While teaching "The History of Political Theories" in his formal appointment in 1859, he received a warning from his father that he was being watched. On every frontier, Treitschke saw enemies, yet his actions during this period became more and more public—some would say reckless. Adolf Hausrath, his friend and, later, biographer, wrote that Treitschke was often in great pain after he pursued a cure in Heidelberg that had brought about complete loss of hearing. His speech deteriorated. Nonetheless, his lectures were always crowded and, despite his efforts to ask students up front to inform him with a sign when the clock struck, often no one wished him to stop.

Treitschke wrote a letter to his father in 1861, in which he described his plans to document the "History of the German Confederation." He believed there was no power in small states, and he published and presented lectures on this. Before 20,000 student-athletes in Leipzig, he made a fiery speech, exhorting the young people to chant "Long live Germany!" The speech was reported widely, and Treitschke became an overnight sensation.

When Bismarck took power in 1862, Treitschke was turning increasingly toward autocratic strategies. He had agitated enough people in Leipzig that he felt compelled to move on to Freiburg, continuing his work on the history of the German Confederation. For the benefit of the handsome deaf professor, many Freiburg ladies learned sign language. Later, Treitschke's wife was also said to have "reported to him by finger signs." Treitschke was a capable speechreader, but pad and pencil came to the rescue many times. In 1864, he published *Historical and Political Essays*, which not only provided further explanation of his views of political freedom within the state, but also served as a warning to Bismarck with regard to his own internal policies. In 1866, Bismarck suggested that Treitschke should take part at his side and draw up the Manifesto of the German population. Treitschke refused, preferring to wait until the Constitution was re-established. He and his father had had a bitter falling-out over Treitschke's anti-Saxon rhetoric. Fortunately, they reconciled shortly before his father's death in 1867. Treitschke married a week after the funeral.

The year 1870, when Germany was established as a nation-state, should have been a joyous one for Treitschke. He and his wife, however, were plagued by ill health, and his deafness weighed on his mind as he considered running for the new Reichstag. In 1871, he was elected a deputy on the National Liberal ticket, although he soon distanced himself from that party. Adolf Hausrath, his trusted friend, served as Treitschke's secretary, sitting beside Treitschke and writing the debates down on paper for him to follow. As in his university debates, Treitschke spoke forcefully, emphasizing each syllable. He had no idea how loudly he spoke, and often, when he attempted to whisper confidential information, he would ignore efforts to restrain him. He was extremely candid and could not understand why he should say anything different from what he thought.

Treitschke's circle of political agitators during the 1870s included Herrmann, the professor of Canon Law who had learned sign language to facilitate communication when Treitschke was a student at Göttingen, the scientist Knies, historian Weber, theologians Gass, Holtzmann, and Hausrath, and the botanist Hofmeister, recognized as the "father of modern botany." In 1873, he turned down a salary of 10,000 thalers to serve as editor of the *Preussiche Zeitung*. His friends had urged him to accept, saying that being deaf would impair his functions as a lecturer in years to come. He ignored them. He accepted an invitation in 1874 to teach at the Berlin University.

Treitschke published his famous dissertation "Union of States and Single State" while at Karlsruhe in the autumn of 1868. In this work he proclaimed his belief that "the German Confederation is not a Coalition of States, but a Coalition of Rulers, that Austria cannot be called a German State, and that the Minor Powers are no States at all, lacking as they do power of self-determination . . . ." His writing was considered treasonable by some, patriotic by others. Of the German Princes he wrote, "The majority of the illustrious heads show an alarming family resemblance; well-meaning mediocrity predominates almost everywhere." His most famous work was the five-volume *History of Germany in the Nineteenth Century (1879–1894)*. The eight-hundred-page work is respected by scholars more for its literary rather than historical value, since his biases and vitriol color so many of the entries. The royalties all were spent on his wife's hospital bills in their final years.

Treitschke's formidable influence on Germany was evident in 1886, when he succeeded Leopold von Ranke, upon Ranke's death, as "The Historian of the State of Prussia," and he was invited to present a memorial address upon the death of the Emperor William. As World War I escalated, Joseph McCabe remarked that Treitschke, more than anyone, had alienated the young people of Germany against England and the rest of Europe—often by making militarism look like the moral high ground to be taken.

The extent of influence of Treitschke's experience on his interpretations will never be fully understood. He once poetically described how he, as a deaf man, relentlessly perceived "a wall between himself and his brothers which will remain there forever." Unlike countless others, he could never scale the wall. Whatever his noble intentions with regard to German unification, they were hopelessly lost in the sins of the successors who used his ideas to engineer the world's worst instance of human hatred, intolerance, and devastation.

Treitschke died in Berlin on April 28, 1896.

References

Dorpalen, A. (1973). *Heinrich von Treitschke*. New York: Kennikat Press.

Guilland, A. (1915). *Modern Germany & her historians*. New York: McBride, Nast & Company.

Hausrath, A. (1914). *Treitschke: His life and works*. London: Jarrold & Sons.

McCabe, J. (1914). *Treitschke and the great war*. London: T. Fisher Unwin.

KONSTANTIN EDUARDOVICH TSIOLKOVSKY (1857–1935), Russian Rocket Pioneer.

Born in Izhevskoye, in Ryazanskaya Province, Russia, on September 17, 1857, Konstantin Eduardovich Tsiolkovsky was the son of a forest ranger. His father was discharged from his post for obscure reasons that had nothing to do with performance. Eduard Ignatyevich Tsiolkovsky was no admirer of the Czarist regime. Tsiolkovsky's mother, Mariya Ivanova Yumasheva, was intelligent and hard-working; she needed to be in order to survive the hardships of a nomadic life.

As a youngster, Tsiolkovsky was fascinated with flight. He loved to fly kites as most children do, but his dreams rapidly moved from kites to space flight. His passengers were cockroaches in small boxes which he sent up the string. At eight years of age, his mother encouraged him further with a gift of a small collodion balloon filled with hydrogen, something which thrilled the boy who would one day author the theory of dirigibles.

A new position for his father brought the family to Vyatka, a town Tsiolkovsky loved. It was on the river in this town where he learned to swim and play. In the winter he boldly leaped from one shaky ice floe to the next as he crossed the river. But such energy and daring spirit probably made Tsiolkovsky vulnerable to a cold while playing outside when he was about ten years old. Scarlet fever then set in and left him nearly totally deaf.

His mother taught him to read and write, and enrolled him in the boy's high school in Vyatka. She inculcated in him her own determination and love of life. Unfortunately, she also believed that he would recover from his deafness, and convinced him of this possibility as well. Her death, when he was thirteen, was a tragic blow. Shortly after the loss of his mother, Tsiolkovsky left school. For the next three years, he read his brother's textbooks and the books in his father's library, especially the works on mathematics and science. When he was fourteen, he fell in love with physics, which prompted him to experiment with many inventions. His idea for a carriage driven by steam was the first of his applications of the principle of reactive motion. He also built paper aerostats and designed lathes and wind-propelled carriages.

Impressed by such precocity, Eduard Tsiolkovsky encouraged his sixteen-year-old son to travel to Moscow to continue his self-education. There, he wandered the streets of the large city, poorly dressed and hungry, until he was able to acquire a corner of a room from a laundress for a few kopecks. From early morning to late at night, he found himself reading volumes at the public library. As his imagination took flight, he studied higher mathematics, including calculus and spherical trigonometry. In *Passages From My Life*, Tsiolkovsky provided a lesson for every science teacher on the importance of having students learn by doing: ''I constructed a height-finder. Then with the help of the astrolabe, I calculated the distance between our house and the fire-tower without going outdoors. . . . I then . . . verified my calculations. This made me believe in theory.''

His first romance was with the daughter of a very wealthy man who had heard the tales of young Tsiolkovsky's eccentricity from the deaf scientist's landlady. Through correspondence their affections grew, only to have the friendship ended by the girl's father, who forbade his daughter to write to such a foolish revolutionary. Tsiolkovsky later married Varvara Yevgrapovna Sokolva. She did everything possible to help him pursue his scientific interests.

The experiments he conducted soon attracted the attention of Russia's most progressive scientists. Among those who encouraged and advised him were Dimitri Mendeleyev, the chemist who developed the Periodic System of the elements; Nikolay Zhukovsky, a founder of Russian aeromechanics; and the well-known physicist Aleksandr Stoletov, who studied the magnetic properties of iron. But Tsiolkovsky had never escaped the financial hardship of his childhood. After passing the examinations for a teaching certificate at the age of twenty-two, he began to teach mathematics in a village near Kaluga. His scientific work was thus relegated to his spare time. To add to his disappointment, much of his work was destroyed by a fire.

Tsiolkovsky very nearly became the first person ever to fly a dirigible. He made major theoretical contributions with his research on the physics of bodies with variable mass, a new subfield of Newtonian classical mechanics. Yet Tsiolkovsky experienced nothing but disappointment during the years immediately preceding the Russian Revolution. Proposal after proposal for the construction of metallic airships and other flying devices failed to result in financial support. His designs included such ingenious ideas as the capability to adjust the volume of the dirigibles to allow for altitude and weather changes. Convinced that such an airship would be forever at the mercy of the wind, the Aeronautic Department of the Russian Technical Society wrote to him in October 1891, rejecting his recommendations. Four years later, however, the German inventor Count Ferdinand Graf von Zeppelin constructed his own famous airships. Before World War I, Zeppelin carried 35,000 passengers without accident.

Between 1880 and 1892, Tsiolkovsky held another teaching position in Borovsk. It was during his stay in Borovsk that he submitted his discoveries on the kinetic theory of gases to the Russian Physico-Chemical Society at St. Petersburg. Although these findings were already long known, the brilliant mind of the deaf scientist so impressed Mendeleyev that he personally responded to Tsiolkovsky. With renewed confidence in his abilities, Tsiolkovsky pursued his scientific interests with vigor and earned membership in the prestigious Society, particularly for his work *The Mechanics of a Living Organism.*

Tsiolkovsky's thoughts about humanity and his fantastic scientific imagination led him to mentally traverse space and time. In his dreams, he populated the heavens with colonies of humans. As early as 1879, the deaf scientist had sketched details of interplanetary travel and communications. During school vacation in 1883, he completed his first work, *Free Space.* The writing was in the form of a scientific journal as recorded by an explorer in space. In *Free Space,* he demonstrated how a reactive device could overcome the pull of gravity to allow a projectile to escape earth. This was, of course, the principle of the jet engine for space propulsion, developed far ahead of its time. He also presented the first technically accurate design for an interplanetary space ship. Prior to this writing, rockets had been largely limited by black-powder formulas. Tsiolkovsky had foreseen the efficient use of liquid propellants such as hydrogen and oxygen.

In regard to the design of space vehicles, Tsiolkovsky went far beyond the space ship's construction. He delved into the necessary conditions for long voyages into space, including the concept of a closed biological cycle that made use of plant life to provide oxygen. It is no surprise that he has also been called the "Russian Jules Verne." Like the great German rocket pioneer Hermann Oberth and the American Robert H. Goddard, both born several decades after him, Konstantin Tsiolkovsky's interest in space flight received its initial stimulus from Verne. It was during his stay in Moscow that he probably read a Russian translation of Verne's *From the Earth to the Moon,* a book that was to have a pronounced influence on his life.

Tsiolkovsky's own science fiction stories, *On the Moon,* published in 1887, and *A Dream of the Earth and the Sky* (1895), still surprise readers with their prophetic quality. In the first novella, Tsiolkovsky presented a view of Earth from the surface of the moon. In the second, descriptions of aerospace flight and outer space were expanded from his original efforts.

Czarist censors were angered by Tsiolkovsky's stories of "sky dwellers." The notion of sending humans into space was in conflict with Church dogma and political views. Historian Daniil Andriyanovich Shcherbakov in his book, *K.E. Tsiolkovsky: A Great Scientist and Humanist,* described the hidden and very deliberate messages in Tsiolkovsky's writings. The unshackling of humans from the physical forces of earth was, in Tsiolkovsky's mind, a metaphor describing the unfettering of the Russian people. With gravitation on Mercury less than that of Earth, Tsiolkovsky wrote, there would be none of the discord and slavery typical of this planet. Tsiolkovsky wrote *A Change in the Earth's Relative Gravity* in 1894, but the book was not published until after the Russian Revolution.

Much of Tsiolkovsky's writing was focused on manned spacecraft. As with Goddard and Oberth, Tsiolkovsky was preoccupied with the theoretical implications of rocket technology. Radio telemetry was not applied seriously to missile research until the development of the V–2 rockets prior to World War II. For these pioneers working during the days before radio, there was no simple method of communicating information from space to Earth. Transmission of information from the moon was considered in terms of manned ships and even through the use of crude flares. In his later years, Tsiolkovsky could foresee the potential of radio. "Happy are you to deal with it," he told some young technicians. "Time will come when short waves will penetrate beyond the atmosphere and will be the means of interplanetary communications."

In 1897, Tsiolkovsky constructed Russia's first wind tunnel in order to examine the effects of air resistance. This brought him a grant for building a larger device, and his subsequent work on rocket dynamics was eventually published in 1903 in "Investigations of Cosmic Space by Reaction Vehicles." He computed a formula for attaining the velocity for a rocket to blast off into space. In his honor, it was later called the "Tsiolkovsky formula." He was also the first to calculate the efficiency of rocket engines, and his "rocket train" was the precursor of modern-day multistage rockets. It is significant that the deaf founder of the theory of space flight never said a word about the use of the rocket for war.

Tsiolkovsky was disappointed when police confiscated the periodical in which his important work was published. With this, they stopped further publication of "Investigations of Cosmic Space by Reaction Vehicles." Thwarted by the political strife of the approaching Russian Revolution and the continued struggle to find financial backing for his ideas, he lived a frustrating and angry existence. Feedback from his scientific contemporaries was seldom received, and he was regarded as a "rootless dreamer." After the Russian Revolution in 1917, the Soviet government supported his work with grants, but in reality, it was too late; Tsiolkovsky retired within three years. The pension he received did allow him to pursue his theories and to write. In all, he composed more than 500 works.

Tsiolkovsky's greatness was recognized in Oberth's *The Rocket Into Interplanetary Space* (1923). In 1927, he was honored at an international exhibit on rocket technology held in Moscow. One volume of a nine-volume encyclopedia on space travel, *Interplanetary Communications* (a term the Soviets then used to mean "space travel"), was completely devoted to Tsiolkovsky's work. And, in 1959, when the Russian Cosmic Station Lunik III photographed the mountains and craters and revealed the mysteries of the moon's far side, the Russians named the new features in honor of many great thinkers who had made it all possible. "Crater Tsiolkovsky" was named for the deaf rocket pioneer.

Tsiolkovsky has been honored posthumously with his image on stamps and medals; his life and work have been featured in film; and a heroic bust adorns the lobby of the Institute for Cosmic Research of the Academy of Sciences in Moscow, portraying the deaf scientist seated in front of a rocket blasting off into space. The accomplishments of the deaf rocket pioneer are recited by school children. More than 80,000 visitors troop through Tsiolkovsky's house in Kaluga, now a museum, where he first began to describe his ideas of space travel and rocketry. A postflight pilgrimage to Tsiolkovsky's house, 120 miles southwest of Moscow, has become a ritual for cosmonauts ever since Gagarin's historic flight in 1961. In 1974, when nine American astronauts came to Kaluga to see the modern space museum housing rocket and spaceship models and the blackened original of the Vostok 5 capsule, they also visited Tsiolkovsky's home.

Tsiolkovsky died in Kaluga on September 19, 1935, and was given a state funeral.

References

Grigorian, A. T. (1976). Konstantin Eduardovich Tsiolkovsky. In G. C. Gillespie (Ed.), *Dictionary of scientific biography* (Vol. 13, pp. 482–484). New York: Charles Scribner's Sons.

Kosmodemyansky, A. (1956). *Konstantin Tsiolkovsky: His life and work.* Moscow: Foreign Languages Publishing House.

Riachikov, E. (1971). *Russians in space.* Garden City, NY: Doubleday.

Vorobyov, B. (1940). *Tsiolkovsky.* Moscow: Young Guard Publishing House.

V

GEORGE W. VEDITZ (1861–1937), American Writer/Deaf Community Advocate.

George W. Veditz was born on August 13, 1861, in Baltimore, Maryland, the son of German immigrants. He grew up in the German community there, learning the language, and attending a school that fostered German language and culture. He was profoundly deafened by scarlet fever at the age of nine, and his parents experimented for a time with private tutoring. When he was in his early teens, he was enrolled in the Maryland School for the Deaf in Frederick, where he studied American Sign Language intently and quickly advanced through his course of study. Unable to afford tuition for Gallaudet College, he remained with the Maryland School for the Deaf, working in the print shop for two years. After graduating from Gallaudet College with highest honors in 1884, he was accepted to Johns Hopkins University, but elected to accept a teaching post at the Maryland School, where he also edited the *Maryland Bulletin*. He was also active in acquiring money for the Gallaudet Memorial Statue and helped to establish the Gallaudet Alumni Association.

Veditz moved to Colorado in 1888, where he taught at the Colorado School for the Deaf and edited the school's newspaper there. He remained in this school as a teacher and accountant until 1910; during this period he was simultaneously helping to found several organizations for deaf persons. His increasing visibility as a leader in the American Deaf community culminated in his being elected president of the National Association of the Deaf (NAD) in 1904, and in 1907. As NAD president, Veditz turned his attention to advocacy in the political arena, with particular attention to government civil service regulations. During this era in American history, deaf people were not only discriminated against, but actually classified as ''unfit'' for civil service positions. Veditz corresponded with the politician William Jennings Bryan, the Secretary of Commerce and Labor Charles Nagel, and Missouri representative to Congress Patrick F. Gill. He orchestrated campaigns to urge Presidents Theodore Roosevelt, William Howard Taft, and Woodrow Wilson to repeal the classification restrictions. In 1913, he was granted a personal interview with Wilson, winning the support of the President to assure deaf persons fair representation in government matters. Veditz did not take concessions for granted, however. He urged deaf people to apply for civil service positions whenever they became open, to assure their presence and future opportunities.

Veditz took over the reign of NAD during a turbulent period when the use of sign language, particularly in school programs for deaf children, was being challenged by organizations and individuals who believed the focus should be on teaching through the use of spoken communication only. In the wake of the International Conference on Education of the Deaf in Milan in 1880, the debate was particularly acrimonious. Veditz regarded Alexander Graham Bell, the acknowledged leader of the "oral" camp, to be no less than an "enemy of the American deaf." Cherishing his own educational experience and the turning point in his life where he learned American Sign Language, Veditz saw the withholding of sign languages from deaf children as injurious and unforgivable. He spoke out vehemently on this topic throughout the country, at conferences, and in the press. Veditz was prophetic in connecting language to culture. His fear was that the disuse of American Sign Language would be the disruption and death of the American Deaf community. His own early education in a German bilingual/bicultural program had taught him that cultures must be preserved consciously. In addition to crusading for national and international respect for American Sign Language as a language of instruction, he worked to preserve the language by establishing the NAD Motion Picture Fund, which recorded samples of ASL provided in lectures by such hearing signers as Edward Miner Gallaudet, and deaf individuals such as the distinguished chemist George T. Dougherty* and the minister Arthur D. Bryant. One of Veditz' own speeches, "Preservation of the Sign Language" (1913), was included in this project, which is still invaluable to linguists interested in the evolution and structure of ASL. About fifteen of the nearly two hundred films in the first compilation of the George W. Veditz Film Collection at Gallaudet College in 1982 were made between 1910 and 1925.

Veditz also served as president of the Colorado Poultry Growers Association. He was a writer and translator of French and German, and foreign editor of the *National Exponent* of Chicago. He published many writings in the *American Annals of the Deaf*, including "The Relative Value of Sight and Hearing" in 1937, in which he argued for the importance of vision over hearing. His articles on poetry were praised by educators, and his fascination with film led to correspondence with the inventor Thomas Alva Edison* on the potential of television during its advent. Veditz edited an eclectic collection of periodicals: *Western Poultry World, Western Pigeon Journal*, the *Deaf American*, the *Optimist* (Atlanta), and the *Silver Courier* (Chicago). His article "The Rise and Fall of a Poultry Farm" in *Country Gentleman* brought him honorary and elected memberships in every poultry association in the state of Colorado. Veditz also became a recognized authority for his work in horticulture, especially on the squab culture, dahlias, and gladioli, winning many prizes and ribbons for his flowers at state fairs. He was proud to be elected as an honorary life-member of the Dahlia Society of Colorado. In addition, Veditz was an enthusiastic chess player, joining tournaments. In one, he was the only entrant out of fifty-four who won his game against the American Chess champion Frank J. Marshall and the last survivor out of over fifty entries against the world champion Jose Capablanca of Havana.

Veditz was able to balance multiple careers and live in multiple worlds. He never lost interest in the European cultural heritage stressed in his early years, while becoming a fierce protector of Deaf community interests at a time when the community was threatened with irreparable ruptures. At the same time he was successful in professional societies. Convinced that people must work together to create change, he founded organizations such as the Maryland Association of the Deaf and the Colorado State Association of the Deaf, serving two terms each as president, where he helped to give people a place in which to collaborate for the community good. Ultimately, he never stopped fighting for the self-determination of deaf persons.

Veditz died on March 12, 1937.

References

Garretson, M. D. (1951). The Veditz Genius. *The Silent Worker, 3* (11), 18.

George William Veditz: An old timer's autobiography. (1924). *The Maryland Bulletin, 44* (4), 61–63, 72.

Veditz, G. W. (1909). The sound-memories of a semi-mute. *American Annals of the Deaf, 54* (2), 117–126.

W

CADWALLADER LINCOLN WASHBURN (1866–1965), American Drypoint Etcher.

Cadwallader Lincoln Washburn was born on October 31, 1866, in Minneapolis, the son of Senator William Drew Washburn of Minnesota. An attack of spinal meningitis left him deaf at the age of five. Washburn attended the Minnesota School for the Deaf in Faribault, and he graduated from Gallaudet College in 1890. His thesis, entitled "The Working Mind of the Spider," was received so well that the superintendent of the public schools in Washington asked him for permission to include it in an anthology for children. Washburn's special interest in entomology while at Gallaudet, including collections of insects and excursions into the country, attracted the attention of the faculty. His love for nature was shown in his papers "Experiment on the Auditory Power of Bees" and "The Psychology of a Chrysalis." The illustrations that he included with his entomological essays, however, served to attract him to drawing instead of science as a career. Possibly influenced by his friendship with Olaf Hanson,* he first pursued architecture at the Massachusetts Institute of Technology in Boston, abandoning this study when his eyes began to suffer, yet nevertheless winning a first prize in design. In New York City, he joined the Art Students League as a pupil of Henry Siddons Mowbray, and he won a place in the "Life Class" of William Merrit Chase, whom he accompanied on sketching tours during vacations. Washburn's roommate in New York was Howard Chandler Christy, who would himself excel one day as an illustrator.

When Chase left teaching to travel to Europe and North Africa, Washburn accompanied him. In Spain in 1896, they studied the work of Velásquez. Washburn then traveled to Holland to examine the works of Dutch masters, especially Frans Hals. Back in Spain in 1897, he studied under Joaquin Sorolla and became one of his favorite pupils. In 1898, he traveled to Morocco, then to Paris to study under Albert Besnard, assisting him in painting murals in many famous chapels. Between 1896 and 1904, Washburn's works were continuously accepted for exhibitions at the *Salon Elysee*. He also exhibited at the Paris Salon with other deaf artists such as Paul-François Choppin,* Olivier Chéron, and Mlle. Marthe Voulquin. In the salon of 1900, for example, he showed *Une riviére*.

While living in Venice from 1902 to 1903, Washburn began his interest in etching. There, he had planned to study the changing light effects on water, but weather conditions discouraged him; and he retreated to the Academia di Belle Art and New National Gallery of Venice to study the works of Titian, Tintoretto, Trepolo, and Dürer. But it was Whistler's etchings in the New National Gallery that attracted his attention the most, and Washburn studied them carefully with a powerful magnifying glass. He then traveled to Paris to purchase etching supplies and a small printing press, and to receive some tutoring from an American etcher living there. For a month, he struggled with the tools and temperatures needed for quality etching work, and he finished his first etchings two months later, entitled *Casa Cecchino*, *Casa d'Oro*, *Grand Canal*, and *Square in Verona*. Several additional months were needed to master the printing of plates, his model for excellence again being the genius of Whistler. "Sight and touch being my only artistic instruments," he said in the *New York Sunday Herald*, "I have been compelled to develop them beyond what might otherwise have been the case."

For the next thirty-five years, Washburn traveled the world, as far as the Canary Islands, Thailand (then Siam), Manchuria, and Tunisia. He lived in an old temple in Kyoto, Japan, while serving as a correspondent with his brother, Colonel Stanley Washburn, for the *Chicago Daily News* during the Russo-Japanese War (1904–1905). Living in the temple was one of his many adventures, for foreigners had never before been allowed in sacred buildings. When the Japanese fleet under Admiral Togo planned to capture Port Arthur, they were thwarted by Russian cruisers. No one, even the Japanese, knew where Togo's squadron was located—until the Washburn brothers found them on the Mekong River in Indochina. A newspaper "scoop" followed.

Washburn was in Mexico from 1910 to 1912, studying its architecture and culture, making the acquaintance there of a direct descendent of Omar Khayyam, who had escaped Persia when the king threatened to eliminate his heirs to the throne. When the Madero revolution broke out in Mexico, Washburn was cabled from the Associated Press to interview Madero, which he did after a month's struggle to gain access. While sending one dispatch, the Mexican railroad station in which Washburn was typing was riddled with bullets. Later, when the political conflict worsened, he managed to gain safe passage with many treasured possessions, including canvasses and fifty copperplates. However, he lost them at sea in a collision of the *Merida* on May 12. The story of his miraculous escape from the shipwreck was published in the *Print-Collector's Quarterly*. Sitting for an hour's rest at 5:00 AM in the coal bins of the *Admiral Farragut*, which had rammed the *Merida*, Washburn "thought of the many months of happy labor that were summed up on my copperplates and canvases and for a moment a regretful thought followed the lost ship. But day had come, two boats were on the horizon hurrying to our rescue, and I am sure that to the men, women and children, though shivering with cold and bereft of their possessions, life seemed very good at that moment.''

In the 1920s, Washburn traveled to the Marquesas Islands with a professor from the University of Minnesota, where they studied and sketched rare birds and insects. Washburn held a lifelong interest in entomology and oology, the latter a specialized branch of ornithology. His adventurous life recorded still another chapter during this visit to the island where Paul Gaugin had lived. Washburn stopped on a nearby island where cannibals killed his native guide, and he was stranded. He managed to make friends with a chieftain by doing his portrait. The chieftain rewarded him with a canoe; and, with his large Belgian Police dog, Washburn survived on the island for six months until the French Navy picked him up.

In 1934, deaf artists from all over the world converged on New York City to exhibit their works at the Roerich Museum. At this International Exhibition of Fine and Applied Arts by Deaf Artists, Washburn showed fifteen etchings, most of them scenes from Mexico, Japan, Venice, and Havana.

Many more trips followed over the next decade. By 1937, he had completed nearly a thousand etchings—from New Jersey landscapes to portraits of Marquesan natives. A representative review of Washburn's works was placed on exhibit at the New York Public Library in 1939. The M. H. de Young Memorial Museum in San Francisco also had an exhibition of fifty of his etchings in 1954, followed by exhibitions at the Massachusetts Institute of Technology and at Bowdoin College Museum of Fine Arts in Brunswick, Maine, where he spent years at his studio on the college campus. Washburn's early preoccupation with architecture surfaced, for example, in his plates of Japanese buildings, with emphasis on conditions of light and atmosphere. His drypoint etchings, such as the "Norland Series," which he completed between 1907 and 1910, depict scenes of woods, streams, and meadows. Picturesque views such as *Dusk*, which illustrates a plowman on a hillside, or *Summer Tranquility*, an example of his lifelong love for nature, are also characteristic of his work. A few of his portrait titles indicate the breadth of his interests and travels, often focusing on ordinary people and commonplace activities: *Old Sicilian, A Rabbi, Soudanese Chief, A Barbadan Mother*, and *French Fisherman*.

Washburn's works can be found in the Library of Congress, the Corcoran Gallery of Art, Metropolitan Museum, and in the British Museum, the Victoria and Albert Museum, Musee de Luxembourg, and the Bibliotheque Nationale in France. Among his honors were awards and medals at the Panama Exposition, National Academy of Design, Louisiana Society of Etchers, Society of American Etchers, and the American Federation of Arts. He was a Fellow of the American Geographic Society and a Trustee of the Museum of Comparative Oology in Santa Barbara, California. Bowdoin College and Gallaudet College awarded him honorary degrees. Ironically, Washburn's father, as a member of Congress, had voted against the founding of Gallaudet.

Washburn died on December 21, 1965, at the age of ninety-nine.

References

Bahl, D. D. (1988, February). Cadwallader Lincoln Washburn. *The Companion*, 1–5.
Bowe, F. G., Jr. (1970). The incredible story of Cadwallader Washburn. *The Deaf American*, *23* (3), 3–5.
Cantwell, P. (1959, March). Cadwallader Washburn—A man of many parts. *The Buff and Blue*, 3.
Holland, W. (1969, December 28). The adventures of Uncle Cad. *Washington Star Sunday Magazine*, 14–15.
Washburn, C. (1911). Notes of an etcher in Mexico and Maine. *Print Collector's Quarterly*, *1* (4), 6060–6077.

MARY WASHBURN (1868–1932), American Sculptor.

Mary Washburn was born in 1868 in Star City, Indiana, the daughter of a Civil War surgeon. Her family lived in Rensselaer, Indiana, during her childhood. At the age of sixteen, a severe fever led to deafness. After returning to high school, she graduated with her class and entered Butler College at Indianapolis, where she experienced a particularly challenging time as she attempted to adjust, focus on her academic program, and communicate with teachers and new friends. During these years, she consulted with specialists, learned to use her residual hearing as best she could, and took lessons in speechreading.

Meanwhile, Washburn became interested in drawing portraits from photographs, taking courses in drawing and commercial art in Cincinnati. She moved to Chicago and found a position for a firm in order to earn an income. After traveling through Europe and studying the works of masters, she entered the Art Institute of Chicago, constantly searching for ways to learn information she could not hear in class. She spent many hours in the library, practicing anatomy drawings from textbooks. She spent evenings in the studios, sketching from skeletons and models of organs and musculature. Charles Mulligan was one of her more influential instructors. Returning to Europe, she again studied the work of masters in courses at the Louvre.

Back in Chicago, Washburn began to send her work to exhibits, initially securing some work and seed money from her father's friends. Her first commissioned work was a statue of General Milroy in Milroy Park in Rensselaer, Indiana, unveiled before 10,000 people. Many exhibits of her work followed at the Chicago Art Institute, at artists' clubs and exhibits in Chicago, Indianapolis, Philadelphia, Pittsburgh, and other cities. In a risky decision, she resigned from her position as a commercial artist in order to pursue sculpture full time, but by then, she had acquired justified confidence in her personal resourcefulness.

In Paris during her third visit, she was a pupil of Edwin Sawyer, a master sculptor from whom she learned to sculpt medals and medallions. In 1913,

Washburn was honored when one of her sketches was accepted at the Old Salon of Paris. Over the next two years, she exhibited her works at the Paris Allied Artists Association, winning second prize in one exhibit.

In 1915, Washburn received an award at the Panama-Pacific Exposition in San Francisco. One of her medals is at the Carnegie Institute in Pittsburgh. The following year, she exhibited in the Albright-Knox Museum in Buffalo, the Indianapolis Museum, and the Carnegie Museum in Pittsburgh. She also completed the Lieutenant Joseph Wilson Memorial in Logansport, Indiana, and the Waite Memorial in Rock Creek Park, Washington, D.C. Her character sketch medallions are found in the Berkeley League of Fine Arts, and a bust of Dr. Byron Robinson is at the Medical Library in Chicago. Washburn's works may now be found in collections at Milroy Park in Rensselaer, Indiana, the Carnegie Institute in Pittsburgh, and in Logansport, Indiana.

Mary Washburn died in October 1932. Along with Dorothy Stanton Wise,* Washburn achieved the distinction of becoming a deaf woman sculptor of her era.

References

Holt, L. D. (1929, April). She would not be pushed against the wall. *The Volta Review*, 178–182.

Opitz, G. B. (Ed.). (1983). *Mantle Fielding's dictionary of American painters, sculptors & engravers* (p. 983). Poughkeepsie, NY: Apollo Book.

EDMUND WATERSTREET, JR. (1943–   ), American Actor.

Edmund Waterstreet, Jr., was born on May 5, 1943, to a farming family in Algoma, Wisconsin. He was stricken with pneumonia at the age of two and deafened. His family moved to Delavan when he was five years old, so that he could attend the Wisconsin School for the Deaf. His mother also became fluent in American Sign Language (ASL). Waterstreet graduated in 1963. He then entered Gallaudet College, where he majored in physical education. At Gallaudet, he starred in the leading role of "Mr. Peachum" in the Marc Blitzstein version of Bertolt Brecht's *The Threepenny Opera*, and as "Mr. Wilson" in *Harvey*. He graduated with a bachelor's degree in 1968.

After Gallaudet, Waterstreet joined the National Theatre of the Deaf (NTD). He appeared in eleven productions, including *Gianni Schicchi, The Critic, Our Town, The Iliad*, and *Under Milkwood*. In *Parade*, he played the role of "Mr. Silence," a deaf equivalent of "Superman." In 1975, while touring with the NTD, he starred with Patrick Graybill* and Linda Bove* in *The Dybbuk* at the International Festival of Drama, which was part of the World Federation of the Deaf meeting in Washington, D.C. Other troupes from Germany, Israel, Poland, Switzerland, and Sweden sent drama and mime groups. In addition to stage acting, he led workshops and directed productions throughout the United States, Europe, and Australia. He has also appeared with the Little Theatre of the Deaf on *Sesame Street*, along with his wife, Linda Bove, whom he met at Gallaudet

Edmund Waterstreet, Jr. (far left), American actor, with Carol Flemming, Linda Bove,* and Bernard Bragg.* Photo courtesy of the National Technical Institute for the Deaf.

College. Waterstreet appeared in television productions such as *Festival of Hands: The Silken Tent* with Jason Robards, *A Child's Christmas in Wales* with Michael Redgrave, *Road to Cordoba*, *The Miracle Worker*, *Omnibus*, and in a United Way commercial. When not touring, he also served as assistant football coach, substitute teacher, and director of several school plays at the American School for the Deaf in West Hartford, Connecticut.

In 1976, Waterstreet and his wife left the National Theatre of the Deaf to pursue other interests and opportunities. He took a position as head dormitory counselor at the Marie Katzenbach School for the Deaf in West Trenton, New Jersey, and he completed a master's degree in theater from Connecticut College in 1977.

In 1985, Waterstreet played the role of Abel, the father, opposite Phyllis Frelich* in the Hallmark Hall of Fame film *Love is Never Silent*. CBS had initially wanted bigger names in the roles, such as Paul Newman and Joanne Woodward. Marian Rees, an independent producer, took the movie with Waterstreet and Frelich to NBC, pointing out that she was bound by a contract to cast deaf actors in the roles of the deaf parents. Within a day of the viewing, there was a commitment from NBC. The story is based on Joanne Greenburg's novel *In This Sign*. The deaf actress Julianna Fjeld* spent ten years attempting to sell the story, and Waterstreet himself had tried not to be optimistic, finding it hard to believe that his deaf colleague was so persistent. When Fjeld and Rees succeeded, it was clear to Waterstreet that his career in theatre was entering a new phase.

Since the original novel takes place in the 1930s, Waterstreet and Frelich had to modify their signs. As with other languages, ASL has changed over time. The actress Mare Winningham as the hearing daughter learned to sign so well that Waterstreet and Frelich continue to regard her with affection: "And to this day I still wish she could be my daughter," he remarked.

In 1989, Waterstreet was invited by artistic director Rob Goodman to direct a production of *Children of a Lesser God* for First Stage Milwaukee at the Todd Wehr Theatre. In 1991, he founded and became artistic director of Deaf West—the only non-profit professional theatre for deaf persons west of the Mississippi, and the first to use only ASL, with an infrared sound system for hearing audience members.

References

Deaf West's "Gin Game" scores aces in Hollywood!!! (1991). *Silent News*, *23* (7), 1, 31.

Joslyn, J. (1989, February 17). Like "Children" heroine, director does it his way. *Milwaukee Sentinel*.

Stanley, J. (1985, December 8). A love story in a world of silence. San Francisco *Examiner Chronicle*.

Stratton, J. (1976). The "eye-music" of deaf actors fills stage eloquently. *Smithsonian*, *6* (12), 67–72.

ROBERT H. WEITBRECHT (1920–1983), American Physicist.

Robert H. Weitbrecht was born on April 11, 1920, in Orange, California. When his parents learned that he was profoundly deaf shortly after his birth, his mother immediately enrolled in a correspondence course to learn how to teach him to speechread. Weitbrecht was placed in a small, private class of deaf children a few years later. His father undertook some private building contracts in Glendale and was able to return home only on weekends to attend to the ranch. When his teacher left the private school for a public school position, Weitbrecht was tutored with another profoundly deaf child by a retired teacher. Not yet five years old, he was receiving lessons in reading and speech, with many side trips to orange and lemon packing houses, beet fields, rope and wine factories, and dairies. It was during these trips that his interest in science was sparked, particularly in electrical equipment, as he examined milking machines, generators, and separators and returned to his class to write about them. When his teacher died in 1931, Weitbrecht attended a public elementary school, where, although he performed at the same level as his hearing classmates, he was the subject of teasing and cruelty on account of his differences. Weitbrecht and his hearing brother George, two years younger, became increasingly rebellious in the face of this hardship.

It was a family custom to take short walks on clear nights to watch the heavens. Young Bob soon became fascinated with the moon and stars. With a sky map from his grandmother and a spyglass given to him by his father, he would use a flashlight to learn the names of many constellations. This soon evolved to private explorations, wrapped up in blankets, as he watched for meteors. In 1930, a solar eclipse was the subject of his composition in class. By the age of eighteen, Weitbrecht won the Bausch and Lomb Honorary Science Award in high school for his construction of a reflecting telescope, using a six-inch pyrex disk for the mirror and an old Ford axle for the mounting he had designed in machine shop.

Weitbrecht was nineteen years old when his father died in 1939. He was in his second year at Santa Ana Junior College, where he soon finished with honors in science. He then entered the University of California at Berkeley, where the Astronomy Department was small, enabling him to fit into the program comfortably and make many friends among faculty and students. With a modest scholarship and many odd jobs, he worked and studied with another deaf student who had taught him sign language, receiving his bachelor's degree in astronomy with honors in 1942. His master's degree, also in astronomy, was earned at the University of Chicago in 1952. Weitbrecht received no assistance in college other than occasional notes from classmates. During the time between the awarding of these two degrees, he was employed as a physicist at the Radiation Laboratory at the University of California (1942–1945), and as an electronics scientist at the U.S. Naval Air Missile Test Center in Point Mugu, California (1947–1951). There, he developed an electronics timing system for the control and photography of missiles in flight, earning him the U.S. Navy's Superior

Robert H. Weitbrecht, American physicist and inventor. Photo courtesy of Paul L. Taylor and Sally Taylor.

Accomplishment Award in 1949. He worked on the Manhattan Project under Ernest Lawrence and spent several years on Cyclotron Hill at the Radiation Laboratory. During these years, he still had keys to the observatory and spent many nights studying double stars and the planets.

Weitbrecht designed many electro-optical-mechanical instruments for nuclear physics, including geiger counters. At the Aeromedical Laboratory, he worked on oxygen safety equipment and electronics applied to air-sea-land rescue operations. He was a member of the Institute of Electrical and Electronics Engineers, the Astronomical Society of the Pacific, and was listed in *American Men of Science*. His research led to the development of the first EPUT digital frequency counters.

Weitbrecht's interest in telecommunications over the air waves was sparked in 1948 when he read a description of such a system in *QST*, a ham operator's magazine for which he subsequently wrote many articles on RTTYs and modems. Twelve years earlier, in 1936, he had passed the FCC examination for his amateur radio license. He purchased a Model 12 Teletype machine, which he subsequently used to receive signals from Japan, the Philippine Islands, Australia, South America, and many places in the United States. At Yerkes Observatory in 1951, he continued to work in his spare time on electronic equipment for RTTY operation. Weitbrecht helped to develop the worldwide WWV–WWVH Radio Time Signal adapted by the National Bureau of Standards, and petitioned the Federal Communications Commission (FCC) to permit Radio Teletype (RTTY) on the amateur radio bands. After receiving Weitbrecht's petition, the FCC established the regulations for use of teletypewriters over the airwaves. Hundreds of hams began to use them, as Weitbrecht continued to hone his skills in the technology, publishing various technical articles in radio journals.

Weitbrecht's work for the Stanford Research Institute included one of the first designs for automatic camera systems for the Dearborn Observatory, a "Stars Guide Camera" incorporating an optical transducer or "eye" that translated movement of star images into electrical error-signals used to maintain a sharp exposure by adjusting the photographic plate carriage. He also designed a high precision astrometric camera system for Lick Observatory and conducted studies on high definition photography of the ECHO satellite system.

In 1969, he left Stanford Research Institute to collaborate with Andrew Saks, a deaf mechanical engineer and business man, and the deaf orthodontist Dr. James C. Marsters* in the Applied Communications Corporation (APCOM) for the production of the Phonetype acoustic coupler. Over the years, as the experimental physicist in APCOM, he developed a variety of devices for signaling and automatic answering. Although he was the principal technical inventor, he himself credited Marsters as the "Founding Father" who brought the telephone to deaf people. Marsters conceived the idea, prompted Weitbrecht to work on it, and, with Saks, helped to bring the invention into the homes of the Deaf community. Together, these three deaf pioneers, with no financial profit for themselves, initiated a technological breakthrough that would have a profound influence on deaf people's lives. With the dedicated assistance of other deaf people such as H. Latham Breunig from the Alexander Graham Bell Association for the Deaf and Jess Smith from the National Association of the Deaf in rebuilding and distributing discarded teleprinters from Western Union and other companies, and Paul Taylor and others in establishing TTY (teletypewriter) networks around the country, the telephone soon became accessible to thousands of deaf Americans.

After forty years of radioteletype as a hobby, Weitbrecht continued to see the potential of this form of communication for deaf people. In 1977, he contacted the Federal Communications Commission to explore the possibility of a radio teleprinter broadcasting system for deaf people.

For his work on the coupler's design, Weitbrecht was recognized by the President's Committee on Employment of the Handicapped in 1969 with a Citation for Meritorious Service, the Laurent Clerc Award for outstanding social contribution by a deaf person in the interest of deaf people from Gallaudet University in 1971, the Alexander Graham Bell Association for the Deaf with an Honors Citation for Distinguished Service to the Deaf in 1971, an Honorary Doctor of Science degree in 1974 from Gallaudet, and the Certificate of Achievement award from Johns Hopkins University in 1981. He was also made an honorary member of Telephone Pioneers of America.

On the evening of May 19, 1983, Robert H. Weitbrecht was struck by a car in a crosswalk while walking his dog. His death on May 30 was an irrevocable loss to the Deaf community in America, who understood well that the invention of the acoustic telephone coupler was a turning point in the quality of their lives.

References

Lang, H. G. (1994). *Silence of the spheres: The deaf experience in the history of science.* Westport, CT: Bergin & Garvey.

Weitbrecht, W. M. (undated). Making the grade. Washington, DC: The Volta Bureau Archives.

CAROLYN WELLS (187?–1942), American Writer.

Carolyn Wells was born in Rahway, New Jersey, a descendent of Thomas Welles, the fourth governor of Connecticut. She always refused to disclose the date of her birth. By the age of eighteen months, she knew the alphabet, and she could read books and newspapers by the time she was three. The always studious Wells wrote and bound a complete book at the age of six. That year, her three-year-old sister contracted scarlet fever and died. Carolyn was infected and was left with progressive deafness, which she irreverently dismissed as the "one cherry in my bowl of black pitted Queen Annes that ought to be thrown out."

Viewing school as a waste of time, she seized every opportunity to learn informally, studying under William J. Rolfe at Amherst in the summer program, traveling to Europe, and learning foreign languages, botany, and astronomy from friends. While visiting England, Wells was invited to contribute poetry to the prestigious periodical, *Punch.* As a young American writer, she had previously published in *Puck*, Gelett Burgiss' *The Lark*, and other magazines. In 1896, she published *At the Sign of the Sphinx* and, in 1899, *The Jingle Book.* Her children's book in 1899, *The Story of Betty*, was immediately well-received. Based on the popularity of her previous works, Wells' *A Nonsense Anthology* (1902) then established her as an anthologist, and there was a clamor for other collections. Her anthologies included *A Parody Anthology* (1904), *A Satire Anthology* (1905), and *A Whimsey Anthology* (1906). This work, she once reflected, was influenced by hundreds of hours studying in libraries as a young woman. *A Nonsense Anthology* remained popular for many years. She also collected *The Book of Humorous Verse* (1920) and *The Outline of Humor* (1923); and began popular series for young girls, such as the "Betty," "Patty," and "Marjorie" books, and *Dick and Dolly.*

Wells completed more than one hundred and seventy different books, including parodies such as *Ptomaine Street* (1921). The area of her mastery, though, was demonstrated in more than seventy-five detective and mystery stories, which she began around 1910, most about her creation, the detective Fleming Stone. Her plot twists and surprise endings were rooted in her interest in puzzles and humor. Wells also wrote a critical study of the writing of mysteries, "The Technique of the Mystery Story," which was praised by other writers as an exhaustive and comprehensive discussion of the art of mystery writing.

In 1918, a heart ailment confined her to bed. With the expectation that she would die within two years, she published her thoughts on this, but she recovered and spent a decade completing such mystery series as *Beautiful Derelict*, *The Radio Studio Murder*, and *Devil's Work*. At the same time, she married Hadwin Houghton, of the publishing family. Their happy marriage was brief; he died in 1919.

Over the years, Wells tried everything she could find to help her use any residual hearing, including hearing aids, a questionable remedy consisting of running red-hot wires up her nose, "balloon-like contraptions, which, when inflated, were supposed to blow the deafness out through the ear drums," and experiments from Christian Science and Doctor Coué. None of these helped, except for the hearing aid, and even that was a "decided nuisance" she used mostly to mollify her frustrated friends, who complained of sore throats from screaming at her.

In her autobiography, *The Rest of My Life* (1937), Wells reminisced freely on a life with hearing loss. Her friend Thomas Alva Edison's* life work, she wrote, demanded solitude and silence for accomplishment, and she understood completely why he considered being deaf a blessing. Her own attitude was more complex and less sanguine, although not without humor. She wrote: "So far, by reason of [my deafness], I have lost one proposal of marriage, two invitations for trips abroad, three or four worth-while gifts, an airplane ride and a few requests for autographs." Unable to hear plays or films, she compensated by reading the stories, and concluded that one could get just as much benefit. She found herself at a disadvantage with other intellectuals in battles of wits, and her recollections of humorous anecdotes included misunderstanding Theodore Roosevelt when he had given her a golden ring made in China, returning it to him after assuming he was only showing it to her.

Wells died on March 26, 1942.

References

Kunitz, S. J., & Haycraft, H. (Eds.). (1942). *Twentieth century authors: A biographical dictionary of modern literature*. New York: H. W. Wilson.
Carolyn Wells, novelist, dead. (1942, March 27). *New York Times*, L23.
Wells, C. (1937). *The rest of my life*. New York: J. B. Lippincott.

HEATHER WHITESTONE (1973–   ), American University Student/Advocate/Miss America.

Heather Whitestone was born on February 24, 1973, in Dothan, Alabama. She was probably deafened by a reaction to the diphtheria–tetanus vaccine at the age of eighteen months. The daughter of Bill Whitestone and Daphne Gray was the focus of much attention in her early years, as her mother sought information on a communication approach that would suit Heather as an individual. After attempting a variety of methods, Gray went to Denver to take parental training in an auditory approach, intended to optimize use of residual hearing. Later, Whitestone learned sign language and speechreading as well. At the age of eleven, she attended the Central Institute for the Deaf in St. Louis, Missouri, where she graduated in 1987. The remainder of her education was in public schools, including the Alabama School for Performing Arts and Berry High School, where she graduated in 1991 with a 3.6 grade point average. "I learned social skills from hearing people and academic skills from the deaf," she told an interviewer. "It was the best of both worlds for me."

It was after graduation from high school that she learned sign language in order to benefit from sign language interpreters at Jacksonville State University (JSU). At JSU, Whitestone was also secretary of the Student Organization for Deaf Awareness while maintaining a perfect 4.0 grade point average. An accounting major interested in the possibility of teaching dance, she also considered a career as a mathematics teacher.

Whitestone's love of ballet, coupled with the practical issue of financing a college education, led her to investigate talent and beauty competitions. She participated in both the Miss Deaf Alabama and Miss Alabama contests. After being named first runner-up in the latter, she traveled to Atlantic City to watch the Miss America 1994 contest, walk the runway, and make the decision to compete further in the 1995 competitions.

The twenty-one-year-old junior from Jacksonville State University had as her platform "Overcoming Obstacles and Inspiring Our Youth." The platform featured a five-point motivational program called STARS, which was designed by Whitestone. The STARS system is drawn largely from Whitestone's own attitude in grappling with challenges. The elements of STARS involved "a positive attitude," "a dream," "hard work," "knowing your problems but not letting them master you," and "a support team." Whitestone has introduced her program in camps, programs, and schools for children with and without disabilities. One Birmingham-area school has incorporated the program into its curriculum.

In the Miss America Pageant, Whitestone was seen as an early favorite, winning the talent and swimsuit rounds, particularly earning the admiration of the judges in the 74th Miss America pageant with a classical ballet performance set to the pop-religious song *Via Dolorosa*, during which she synchronized her dance movements by counting beats.

The initial reaction of the Deaf community to Whitestone's accomplishment was generally very positive. Deaf actors and playwrights such as Bernard Bragg,* Ed Waterstreet,* and Gilbert Eastman* were enthusiastic about the potential of the young woman to make a strong impact through the media. Marlee Matlin,* the deaf Academy Award winner in 1987, sent Whitestone roses with supportive advice to "Just be yourself," and the Emmy-winning deaf pro-

Heather Whitestone, American university student, advocate, and Miss America.
Photo courtesy of *World Around You*, Gallaudet University.

ducer Julianna Fjeld* said, "That's one small step for a deaf woman, one giant
leap for deafkind!" Praise also came from the National Association of the Deaf,
the Alexander Graham Bell Association for the Deaf, the American Society for
Deaf Children, and the National Fraternal Society of the Deaf. Excitement
spread around the world as schoolchildren, parents, and teachers recognized the
potential of the new Miss America to empower other young deaf women and
men to raise public consciousness.

There is controversy, however, centered on whether Whitestone's upbringing
and educational options have minimized her contact with Deaf culture and community, making her less credible as a spokesperson. Whitestone's reaction to
these questions is disarming. She comments that she hopes to ease differences

and cautions: "What works for me may not work for others . . . every deaf person is different." While direct in her advice on building self-esteem and motivation, she steadfastly refuses to be prescriptive when asked to define "the best" educational approach for deaf children.

In her duties as Miss America, Whitestone has traveled as much as 20,000 miles each month for speaking engagements, certainly a challenge for any young woman and proof enough of her position that "Anything is Possible." When a reporter asked her, at her first press conference, how she would manage, particularly with regard to communication, she gazed at him quizzically and responded, "How hard will this be? I think we are doing fine. Look at us."

References

Feibelman, P. (November/December, 1994). Our kids grow up to be Miss America. *Voices, 1* (6), 33–36.
Neill, M., Cunneff, T., & Kemp, K. (October 3, 1994). Miss America: Loud and clear. *People, 42* (14), 48–49.
Van Biema, D. (October 3, 1994). Beyond the sound barrier. *Time, 144* (14), 66–67.
Willard, T. (November, 1994). A coming of age in the deaf community. *Silent News, 26* (11), 3.

DOROTHY STANTON WISE (?–1919), British Sculptor.

Dorothy Stanton Wise was born deaf in Dover, near London, England. With no school for deaf children nearby, she was taken to the well-known Thomas Arnold's school in Northampton. Arnold advised her mother to instruct her at home, however, and her mother received some brief training in order to accomplish this. Her instruction at home was frequently interrupted, since her father was a headmaster, and their large house was full of young boys demanding attention. By the age of five, Wise had already shown an interest in drawing and modeling, and her mother taught her anatomy drawing. Two years later, she was sent to the Dover School of Art, where she passed all the exams. Those subjects taught by lectures, such as geometrical drawing and perspective, were reinforced by her father in the evenings.

When she was seventeen years old, Wise moved with her family to London, where she gained admission to the life-modeling room at the Royal College of Art in London and studied under the Frenchman Lantéri. She won a free scholarship for three years at the College. During one of her classes in life-modeling, a visitor was impressed enough with her practice work that she received a commission to complete a long frieze, *King Arthur and the Round Table*, with many figures.

Wise's first exhibit at the Academy was a large panel sculpture of Demeter, the Greek goddess of agriculture, fertility, and marriage. The purchaser had assumed the work was done by a male artist and was surprised to meet the deaf woman when he inquired about delivery. Wise titled the panel *The Wings of the Morning*. She was then commissioned to copy one of Andrea Della Robbia's

Dorothy Stanton Wise,
British sculptor. Photo
from W. R. Roe (1917)
Peeps Into the Deaf World
(Derby, England: Bem-
rose).

bambinos on a round panel for a maternity hospital to be presented to the nurses.
In 1906, she completed her degree at the Royal College of Art, which, at that
time, was a noteworthy and unusual achievement for a woman.

For several years, Wise struggled to find work. Soon, however, she was commissioned to complete pieces for the Historical Dolls' Pageant at Westminster
and the Indian Historical Pageant at the Festival of Empire in the Crystal Palace.
For the pageant at Westminster, she had been approached by a committee concerned that they could not locate dolls to represent historical characters. Wise
then experimented in wax and, after a short time, many exhibitors liked her
work so much that she was asked to complete more than sixty heads and about
that number of pairs of hands and feet. Wise used photographs of lamas of Tibet
to sculpt life-size pieces, which included draped garments. For the pageant at
the Crystal Palace, she was asked to complete more than one hundred heads in

less than four months, and she was forced to hire two assistants to meet the demand. The three of them found her studio too small, and they worked in their living rooms, filling sideboards, shelves, and mantelpieces with limbs and heads. Her parents were not too pleased with the plaster, clay, and tools, not to mention disembodied heads, strewn throughout the house.

Encouraged by Sarah Fuller, Wise published several articles between 1913 and 1916 to share her accomplishments and education with the Deaf community in America. Her work was also highlighted by the deaf biographer Yvonne Pitrois.* During the interview, Wise explained drily that she had lost some business opportunities when purchasers "had no time to waste for speaking to a deaf person." Wise enjoyed traveling to Florence and wandering the Uffizi and Pitti Palaces, where she studied the sculpture and architecture to further her education.

One of Wise's most popular statuettes was *Spring*, which was designed as one of four electric light holders. Her medallion portrait of Catherine I. Dodd was placed in the new library of Cherwell Hall Training College in Oxford, and Dodd's former students soon asked for a replica for the women students' common room at the University of Manchester. Wise had a special talent in sculpting busts of children, such as the young boy *Bingy* and the young girl *Jessy*. She also completed statuettes of such figures as Joan of Arc as a peasant girl surrounded by sheep, and Wise was also talented in dressmaking and watercolor sketches.

In October 1914, the Worcester Cathedral unveiled before a large audience a marble medallion of Bishop John Prideaux who had led the impeachment and imprisonment of Charles I. Wise had done considerable research, copying the portrait of Prideaux from a miniature plaster medallion completed in 1638 by Claude Warin. The white marble medallion eighteen inches long was embedded in a plain slab of beautiful gray Pentelican marble with a long inscription incised below it. Shortly after the unveiling, her design for a memorial to the authoress Mrs. Henry Wood was chosen by the Mayor of Worcester to also appear in the cathedral. Wise was forced to sculpt with a harder type of marble, however, due to the shortage of Greek marble during World War I. Smaller sculptures she produced while waiting for the rough block to be cut into shape were sold to such dignitaries as Queen Alexandra and Princess Victoria. Wise entered the sculptures she did during this period in the Women's Work Exhibition in London sponsored by the *Daily Express* to assist women impoverished by the War. England was also unable to procure doll's heads from Germany during the War, and Wise enjoyed modelling patterns of doll's heads for manufacturers.

Wise was active in the British Deaf community, writing articles for the *British Deaf Times*. She joined a club for deaf people and began to study the different forms of communication her friends employed. By 1918, she stopped producing. It is believed that she may have died a victim of the influenza epidemic. She won gold medals at the Royal Academy, Manchester Art Gallery, and Liverpool's Walker Art Gallery.

After several months of ill health, during which she continued to sculpt, Wise died on Christmas morning in 1919 at her home in London.

References

Jackson, P. W. (1990). *Britain's deaf heritage*. Kippielaw, England: The British Deaf Association.

Pitrois, Y. (1916). Dorothy Stanton Wise. *The Silent Worker, 28* (7), 121–122.

Roe, W. R. (1917). *Peeps into the deaf world*. Derby, England: Bemrose.

Wilson, E. C. (1913). Note to "How I became a sculptor." *The Volta Review, 15* (9), 406–407.

Wise, D. S. (1913). How I became a sculptor. *The Volta Review, 15* (9), 403–405.

HORST WITTE (1913–1991), German Poet/Novelist.

Horst Witte was born in Brunswik, Germany, on June 5, 1913, the son of Dr. Rudolf Witte, a headmaster in a secondary school. Witte's mother, Kaethe, was the daughter of a high school teacher. Witte and his two younger sisters received a well-rounded education both at home and in school. At the age of five, he was deafened by mumps. He learned to speechread from the director of a school for deaf children in Brunswik and practiced further with local schoolmistresses and his own grandmother. He entered the public school system by first studying gymnastics and art, then mathematics, physics, German, chemistry, history, and other academic subjects. In 1933, he completed his secondary education, including English and Latin, and entered the University of Munich, where he earned his Ph.D. in 1939 with a dissertation on "The Views of James I of England on Church and State with Special Reference to Religious Tolerance."

In 1940, Witte found a position with the Brunswik City Archives. After a short time there, he joined a publishing house in Leipzig. From 1945 until 1958, he owned his own bookshop in the German Democratic Republic. He seized an opportunity to move to Tübingen in the west with his family and took a position as publicity manager in a publishing house. Witte completed his first book in 1967, *Bücherwanderung* (*A Walk Through the History of Books*), in which he traced the history of writing, printing, the book trade, and libraries from early times until the present.

In the early 1970s, tragedy struck him twice. His wife, Ruth, died of cancer in 1972. In the following year, his son Jan died in a traffic accident. These tragedies later became the substance of two of his novels. *Julie oder die Tödlichkeit* (1987) is a poignant story based on the illness and subsequent death of his first wife—a story of the physical and emotional suffering, the dreams and despair that they experienced for two years—what Witte called "a mysterious process" that finally ended in Ruth's death. In *Im Auge Behalten* (*In the Mind's Eye*), also published in 1987, Witte presented an autobiographical reflection about the experiences of a deaf man searching for full community with the world. Two friends, one deaf and the other hearing, drive through Provence in Southern France. Based on a true story, in which Witte recalled his life while

Horst Witte, German writer and poet. Photo by Ernst Schulte courtesy of John Albertini.

with his good friend, Dr. Klaus Schulte from Heidelberg, the novel received excellent reviews. One German reviewer called this novel "a book for silent hours that doesn't hold back any of the difficulties of the deaf narrator, but signals to the reader that this life was beautiful and worthwhile."

After his first wife died, Witte's daughter Ilsabe became a teacher of deaf children. In 1974, Witte traveled to Wilhelmsdorf near Lake Constance to visit her, where he met Ilsabe's colleague at a school for the deaf there, Ursula. They fell in love and married three years later. Witte left his job at the publishing house in Tübingen and moved to Wilhelmsdorf, where, for the first time, he was able to be active in a Deaf community. He felt he gained a deeper under-standing of the "mutual understanding" among deaf people, which led him to write the well-received *Im Auge Behalten.*

Over the next few years, Witte authored two more books of poetry, *Hörbare Spuren* (*Audible Traces*), and *Offenes Gelände* (*Open Country*), which reflect his love for nature and his life in silence—a "silence vibrating with my own kind of music." For Witte, "poetry is the most intensive way to understand language, to express feelings, and to transform my visual experiences into sound and the fury of life." Most of his poems attempt to transform his observations, impressions, and views into a written form of expression which has its own "melody." Several of his poems reflected on how deafness touched his daily life in mundane, yet thought-provoking ways. "Taubes Licht" ("Deaf Light"), for example, states a preference for steady light, which can withstand the "wrath of drafts." Dismissing candlelight, the poet concludes, "Bulbs transform/moderate brightness/into flowing—the Deaf join in conversation."

Witte developed a close friendship with Harry G. Lang, an educator and author at the National Technical Institute for the Deaf at Rochester Institute of Technology, the first deaf American he had met. Again, he commented and began to write on the community that deaf people achieve, even across cultures, as he and Ursula traveled and met many other members of the American Deaf community. With Professors Klaus Schulte and Christa Schlenker-Schulte from Heidelberg, the Wittes, Langs, and the Albertini family discussed a symposium planned in early May 1991 in Germany to address the needs of deaf students in universities in Germany. Professor Schulte, the organizer, invited a number of Americans, including the authors of this biographical dictionary, to participate. Along with other Americans and Germans, Horst Witte and Harry G. Lang were scheduled to address the German audience with presentations of the accomplishments of deaf persons and the need to break down attitude barriers in Germany that prevent more deaf Germans from entering the universities.

On April 30, 1991, shortly before the conference, Horst Witte suffered a heart attack and died while riding his bicycle in the town of Wilhelmsdorf. Villagers laid flowers on the street where he died. The eulogy at his memorial service touched upon his familiar presence in Wilhelmsdorf, questioning students from the school for the deaf, riding his bicycle to the library, chatting with friends at a tea house, arguing playfully with the Pastor on the merits of organized religion. In the final years of his life, it appeared that Horst Witte had fully achieved the sense of community that was the central quest of the characters in his books and poems.

References

Lang, H. G. (1992). A silence, but a silence vibrating with my own kind of music: Herr Horst Witte—German poet and author (1913–1991). *Deaf Life, 5* (3), 14–16.
Witte, H. (1987). *Im auge behalten*. Frankfurt, Germany: R. G. Fischer Verlag.

FRANCES WOODS (1907–   ), American Dancer.

Esther Richina Thomas was born deaf on March 21, 1907, in Girard, Ohio, a premature, six-month baby weighing a little more than a pound. She attended the Ohio School for the Deaf in Columbus, Ohio, playing center for the school's basketball team which had a winning record five years in a row. She graduated in 1926.

At the age of twelve, Thomas met Anthony Caliguire while he was working for Carnegie Steel in McDonald, Ohio, and teaching dancing classes in the evenings. At first, Caliguire resisted taking Thomas as a student. He considered it hopeless to teach a young deaf woman the rhythms and cadences of dance. The Thomas family, however, was well-to-do and willing to pay extra for the lessons. Moreover, after a few lessons, Caliguire was impressed by the young girl's strength and total fearlessness. Throughout his life, he would repeatedly refer to her as the bravest person he knew. Caliguire went to the Ohio School for the Deaf and learned some sign language so he could communicate with his new student. Together, they rehearsed in her father's garage, and they took further classes to see what she could do as a dancer unable to hear the music. They began to perform together.

Few people were aware that she was deaf during the initial performances, and they won many awards. Caliguire gave up his dream of a nationwide chain of dancing schools and closed his studios in Youngstown, San Francisco, and Pittsburgh to go on the road. They soon began a team known as "The Dancing DeSondos," changing their names to "Frances Woods" and "Billy Bray." It was *Ripley's Believe It Or Not* that called them "The Wonder Dancers," an appellation that remained with them for the rest of their lives.

They worked on Broadway during the Great Depression and in supper clubs. Many of their dancing acts required great risk, and both Woods and Bray had numerous slipped discs, broken ribs, torn muscles, hernias, near scalpings from mirrored posts, and splinters. Their fearlessness was a key attraction, however. Woods made all of her own costumes, one dress alone having more than 26,000 sequins which she had sewn one at a time. They were often accused of being impostors when some club owners advertised that Woods was deaf, and Bray wrote that doctors in some audiences actually requested to examine Woods. When newspaper reporters learned, after Woods and Bray had been performing for about five years, that Frances was truly deaf, the resulting publicity spread across the country. All through their career, they would also be approached by hearing aid dealers and inventors who felt they could benefit either Frances or themselves through experimentation with their products.

Their dances continued to showcase their phenomenal strength. One dance, which called for Bray to stab Woods with a rubber stiletto and carry her off the stage, caused such anger among the audience that Bray frequently had to dodge bottles thrown at him. They changed it so that Woods shot Bray with a pistol and carried him off the stage on her shoulders, evoking tremendous applause for her strength as well as talent as a dancer. During a performance in Moline, Illinois, Woods slipped from Bray's hands while whirling at full speed. She slid across the stage and ended with an unexpectedly graceful pose. It would have been a beautiful finish, had the momentum in the opposite direction not caused Bray to lose his balance and crash head first into a bass drum, turning it into a comedy.

Among the more prominent people in their audiences were Dwight Eisenhower and Wendell Wilkie. They performed on Broadway in *Being Bothered, Happy Days, Harp Fantasy,* and other shows. In the 1940s and 1950s, Woods and Bray toured the United States and Europe. After one show at the Roosevelt Theatre in Oakland, hundreds of deaf fans joined the hearing audiences, flooding the stage with roses. In sign language, Woods expressed her appreciation while

Frances Woods, American dancer. Photo courtesy of Frances Woods and Billy
Bray.

the master of ceremony voiced his to the hearing audience. Woods was always at ease with fans, often using pen and paper to communicate. She and Bray used sign language, although Bray never achieved the proficiency he desired. Bray encouraged educators in public schools to teach sign language to all students. After retiring in 1958, they maintained studios in the Hotel Pick Ohio. They held many classes in private homes as well. In a memorable trip, they even traveled to Poland to teach ballroom dancing.

In April 1973, they appeared on the Lawrence Welk Show at the Hollywood Palladium. Since 1974, after over a half century on the stage and on television, they have focused more on personal appearances, particularly for senior citizens in nursing homes. They have continued to perform dance concerts for the general public in theatres and auditoriums, dedicating an increased amount of their time to raising funds for organizations and for people with disabilities. For example, the "Wonder Dancers" performed for the Ohio Association for the Deaf in Akron and for the National Association for the Deaf convention in Youngstown, Ohio, refusing to accept the offered fee, but with the agreement that the fee would be used to pay the utility bills for unemployed deaf members.

Among their honors was the Ohio Governor's Award, citing them for their contributions to the field of dance. They received keys to cities, performed at the Friars Club in Beverly Hills with the Florenz Ziegfield Girls, at the Hollywood Comedy Club in Los Angeles, and for the Special Speakers' Series at the National Technical Institute for the Deaf at the Rochester Institute of Technology. This was remarkable given the fact that since 1968, Frances has been wearing a pacemaker, replacing it in 1971, 1975, and 1979.

In his self-published autobiography, *The Wonder Dancers*, Bray wrote not only to record the sensational career of the Woods and Bray dancing team, but also to exhort young people to pursue whatever careers they desired, even in the face of considerable challenge. Bray was convinced that that was the meaning of his work with Frances Woods.

References

Bray, B. (1974, 1981). *The wonder dancers: Woods and Bray*. Youngstown, OH: self-published.
Frances Woods, Adagio Dancer. (1940, March). *Digest of the Deaf*, 23–25.
Panara, R. F., & Panara, J. (1983). *Great deaf Americans*. Silver Spring, MD: T. J. Publishers.

DAVID WRIGHT (1920–1994), British Writer.

David Wright was born in Johannesburg, South Africa, on February 23, 1920. At the age of seven, he was profoundly deafened by scarlet fever. Following an extended period of illness, a mastoid-tonsil operation, and repeated, increasingly desperate efforts by his mother to find a cure for his deafness, Wright was provided private speech tutoring by an instructor in London.

Wright wrote that, as a resilient seven-year-old, he was unperturbed by his deafness, and puzzled at the adults trying to keep up his spirits. He was also detached from the search for a cure which preoccupied his family, convinced that he would always be deaf. However, he kept his feelings to himself out of concern for his mother. Wright and his mother then returned to South Africa, where he received additional tutoring in academic subjects. Financial difficulties associated with the depression of the 1930s led the Wright family to discontinue these lessons, and Wright turned increasingly to reading on his own over the next few years. As a day student in a preparatory school in Johannesburg, he acquired additional education, but hardly adequate for college entry standards, and he was taken to England. There, he was placed in the highly selective Northampton School for the Deaf. The school administrators forbade British Sign Language and even the two-handed fingerspelling used by many British deaf people, and Wright was taught through a combination of speechreading and pantomime. Wright found the experience of being with other deaf children a curiosity and found classroom communication tedious. He was grateful, though, for the lack of bullying and cruelty there, compared to other boarding schools. He enjoyed long walks and field trips to Stratford and London Theatres and could never master cricket or tennis. He also studied French and Latin in a local grammar school, and continued to prepare for entrance examinations to Oriel College, Oxford. His teachers were elated when Wright passed a rehearsal examination, the Oxford Junior Locals, in only his second year at Northampton. There was dismay, however, when the news came that only three student placements were available at Oriel College, Oxford. Wright also began to be a bit pessimistic when the Rector of one college declared that a deaf student would be run over within a week of arrival at Oxford. The provost brushed such concerns aside, and allowed Wright to take the Oriel College examination. And no one told the nervous young man that there were only three slots.

In preparation for Oxford, Wright wrote that he went through a period of rebellion against his mother's over-protection and other family members' concerns that his deafness made him vulnerable. He announced his intentions to travel, hike, and socialize, and, to his surprise, his mother coped.

At Oxford, Wright found the required, one-on-one tutorials with teachers to be a distinct advantage for a deaf student with regard to his ability to remain abreast with his hearing classmates. Having already developed a fascination for poetry, writing his own verse since the age of eight, he was further inspired by his meetings with such English poets as Sidney Keyes, Drummond Allison, Keith Douglas, and John Heath-Stubbs. These gentlemen, particularly Heath-Stubbs, motivated him toward the pursuit of literature as a career focus. They connected him to literati in Soho, where wartime poetry was capturing some important young imaginations.

Wright graduated from Oriel College and was confronted with the issue of how to make a living as an emerging poet. He was able, through his literary connections, to do some editing, criticism, and translation. His translation of *Beowulf* into modern English is considered one of his more important contributions to literature. This, and a similar translation of *The Canterbury Tales*, brought him income sufficient to allow him to pursue creative writing and poetry. Wright began his work, interestingly, with some collaborative projects. His first professional job as a poet was a commission of a poem for a ballet, *Minster Lovell*. Unfortunately, the ballet was not staged until 1966 (as *Ginevra*). Later, he worked on a book about Portugal with the painter Patrick Swift, with whom he collaborated on the progressive journal *X*. Other travel books also supplemented his creative work. Many of his poems have been published in such periodicals as *Ishmael*, *Agenda*, *Aquarius*, *Contrast*, and *Poetry* (U.S.A). His first poetry collection was published in 1949.

Wright published more than sixteen books over the next thirty-five years. Among the eight books of poetry were *Metrical Observations* (1980) and *To the Gods the Shades* (1976), the latter dedicated to his wife, the New Zealander actress Phillipa Reid. This collection also includes his "Monologue of a Deaf Man," where he reveals his unsentimental position: "Then do you console yourself? You are consoled/If you are, as all are." Many critics see Wright's work as taking two distinct courses—one romantic and intense, the other cool and detached. As such, there is some criticism that he does not use a true "voice" consistently. His mastery of technique and fine style are broadly acknowledged, nevertheless.

In addition to the above-mentioned volumes, he has published *Poems*, *Moral Stories*, *Adam at Evening*, *Nerve Ends*, *A South African Album*, and *A View of the North*. His anthologies include *The Mid-Century: English Poetry 1940–1960*, *Longer Contemporary Poems*, *The Penguin Book of English Romantic Verse*, *The Penguin Book of Everyday Verse*, and *The Faber Book of Twentieth Century Verse* (with John Heath-Stubbs). *Roy Campbell* is a book of biographical and critical pieces. Wright also edited several literary magazines, and has served as visiting scholar at the University of Leeds. His writings have been included in *The Modern Poets* (1963), published by McGraw-Hill, and *The Norton Anthology of Modern Poetry* (1973). His well-received book *Deafness: A Personal Account* (1969) described his experience growing up in South Africa and England, and presented a summary of the education of deaf pupils in England, in which he included many anecdotes and facts that enrich the reader's sense of history and the bond among deaf people. The book is dedicated to his parents, with a verse by the deaf poet Joachim DuBellay.*

David Wright died of cancer in London on August 28, 1994.

References

Lowman, R. (1987). David Wright. In J. V. Van Cleve (Ed.), *Gallaudet encyclopedia of deaf people and deafness* (Vol. 3, pp. 347–348). New York: McGraw-Hill.

Smith, M. S. (1973). *Guide to Modern World Literature*. New York: Funk & Wagnalls.

West, P. (1970, March 8). A poet wins at deaf man's buff. *Chicago Tribune*.

Wright, D. (1969). *Deafness: A personal account*. New York: Penguin Press.

Z

RAMÓN DE ZUBIAURRE (1882–1969), Spanish Painter.

Born deaf on September 1, 1882, in Garay, Spain, Ramón de Zubiaurre was the younger brother of Valentín de Zubiaurre,* who also became a distinguished deaf artist. Their life stories are intertwined, for they studied, traveled, and even exhibited their works together on many occasions. While they shared a studio, the brothers developed distinctive styles. The son of a talented musician who directed the Madrid Conservatory and Royal Chapel of Music under the patronage of the Dowager Queen, Ramón de Zubiaurre was educated predominantly at home with his deaf brother and hearing sister. He and Valentín developed an early interest in art, taking oaths to one another to someday be painters. His parents, ever-attentive to their three children's education, were more than pleased to provide a special private instructor, who took Ramón to the Prado in Madrid and prepared him well for the Academy of Fine Arts in San Fernando, where he won a gold medal. He also studied under Alejandro Ferrant and Muñoz Degrain. He began to collect first, second, and third place medals at the Madrid National Salon early in his career.

In 1906, his mother took him and Valentín to the Julian Academy in Paris and planned a subsequent tour of Europe. The brothers found the conventions of instruction somewhat oppressive, but Ramón particularly enjoyed studying the old masters, especially El Greco, Giotto, Fra Angelico, Hans Holbein, and Velásquez. His *Lazy Ones and Beggars*, showing the distinct influence of the Dutch masters, earned him a gold medal in Rome at the International Exhibition in 1911 and is now held by Rome's Modern Gallery. Active in the Deaf Association of Madrid, he several times provided addresses in commemoration of Spain's famous early educators of deaf students, Pedro Ponce de Leon and Juan Pablo Bonet. Zubiaurre also received gold medals in Munich in 1913, and silver medals in Barcelona, Buenos Aires, and Madrid. Zubiaurre also owed a debt to Japanese silk painters and printmakers, adapting their sense of composition and perspective. The technique he borrowed can be seen in works such as *The Victorious Rowers of Ondárroa* and *Mother and Child*.

More outgoing than his brother, Ramón often enjoyed sports and took the initiative to communicate for both of them when they traveled. His paintings reflect this personality difference. Because of the brothers' closeness in age, shared experiences, and similar training, art lovers and critics began to speak of a singular "Zubiaurre style," without regard to their clear individual distinctions. Ramón's colors are more primary and clear, favoring yellow and gold. After his father died in 1914, critics note that Ramón began to show a truly unique style and choice of subject matter. It is not known if Don Valentín's death or Ramón's winning second prize in the National Exposition of 1915 for *The Victorious Rowers of Ondárroa* amid controversy contributed to his growing independence. Ramón's paintings were often characterized by connections to the sea, both playful and dramatic. This markedly contrasts with his brother's focus on mountain folk. In 1917, Ramón de Zubiaurre married, and he increased his travels as his international fame grew. In the United States, he was a member of the Hispanic Society of America.

Zubiaurre received the French Legion of Honor in 1923 and first prize at the Madrid National Exhibition in 1924. The Zubiaurre brothers exhibited their works all over Europe, South and North America, and sold many paintings to private collectors, including royal family members in Spain and Bavaria. In Latin America, Ramón's work became extremely popular, and he lived there at various times in his life in the 1920s and 1930s and for an entire decade beginning in 1940. This became a problem upon his return to 1950s Spain, where he was suspected of communist affiliations. For a time, his work gained quicker acceptance abroad.

In the 1960s, Zubiaurre took up more drawing and worked in pastels in a more gentle manner.

Ramón de Zubiaurre died on June 9, 1969.

References

Pitrois, Y. (1915). Two great deaf artists of Spain: The Zubiaurre brothers. *The Silent Worker, 27* (7), 121–123.
Stevens, K. H. (1938). Valentin and Ramon de Zubiaurre, Spanish moderns. *The Illinois Advance, 71* (4), 1–2.
The Basque brother painters. (1926, February). *The Mentor*, 23–25.
Valentín and Ramón De Zubiaurre. (1939). *Enciclopedia universal illustrada, Europeo-Americana*, (Vol. 70, pp. 1469–1473). Madrid: Espasa-Calpe, S. A.

VALENTÍN DE ZUBIAURRE (1879–1963), Spanish Painter.

Valentín de Zubiaurre was born deaf on August 22, 1879, in Madrid, Spain, the son of Don Valentín de Zubiaurre, a Basque musician. The talented father rose from a peasant background to become one of the first composers of Spanish opera during the reigns of Alfonso XII and Alfonso XIII, as well as a director of the Royal Chapel of Music. Prominent in Madrid circles, his father was a lover of art. Valentín, as well as his deaf brother, Ramón,* who was three years younger, were educated in the home. For one year, Valentín was a day pupil at the National College for the Deaf of Madrid, but his loving parents preferred to provide private teachers, artists, and authors to tutor all three of their children, including a hearing sister, Dona Maria de Pilar, who took pleasure in working with them in signed and spoken languages. The brothers remained close to her throughout their lives. Though well instructed in science, history, literature, and poetry, Valentín de Zubiaurre fell in love with art, influenced by the beautiful Spanish landscapes and frequent visits to museums. Because of Valentín's early interests, his parents hired a teacher from Madrid named Carriedo to take the brothers to the Prado to copy the works of masters. Valentín then entered the Royal Academy of San Fernando and the Madrid School of Fine Arts, where he soon won a first prize for one of his paintings. He won fame, but also criticism, for his showing of Basque pictures at the National Salon in Madrid in 1899, 1901, and 1904.

At the age of twenty-seven, Zubiaurre accompanied his mother and brother to Paris, where the two youths studied at the Julian Academy. Disliking the techniques he was learning there, he sought independence. With his brother, he visited the Louvre, galleries in Luxembourg, and many others, spending time individually with some of the great contemporary artists of the day. Zubiaurre quickly gained prestige with his works, often painting authentic portraits of men and women of Salamanca, Segovia, Sevilla, and Madrid—peasants in their homes, working, enjoying meals, dancing, praying, and participating in the pious processions. His works included minute details with often-stern faces—colorful costumes, household furniture, utensils, and pottery. They were most often inspired by Basque traditions and customs. Despite criticism of the de Zubiaurre brothers' works in Madrid at the National Exposition, especially Valentín's for his primitivism, Valentín won second prize for *The Noon Hour*, which is now at the Museum of Modern Arts in Madrid. In Brussels in 1910, Zubiaurre won a gold medal, followed by others in Munich (1911) and Barcelona (1912). Exhibitions also followed in many towns of Spain, France, Holland, Germany, Italy, and in North and South America. Many of his works were purchased by the Chicago Art Institute, Luxembourg Museum of Paris, the Gallery of Modern Art of Roma, the Museum of Modern Arts, Buenos Aires, the Art Galleries of Amsterdam, and Carnegie Institute in Pittsburgh. Private collectors included the Dowager Queen of Spain, Infanta Isabel, and the Crown Princess of Bavaria.

More reserved than his brother, Valentín preferred the company of his sister, brother, and a few close friends. While paintings such as *Festival Day* and the *Village Fathers* use golden, masterful color schemes, there is a certain isolation and lack of communication among the characters. Other paintings, such as *The Card Players*, are done in somber browns, greys, and blacks. It should be noted, however, that *The Card Players* was literally done under fire, during the Spanish Civil War.

Much has been made of the connection between the de Zubiaurre brothers' deafness and the lack of interaction among the people they both portray. Given their history of family support and warm relationships with friends, this would appear to be a romanticized over-interpretation, however. The frontal individuality serves the purpose of highlighting Zubiaurre's favored primitivism.

In 1927, the Zubiaurre brothers exhibited jointly at various museums and galleries across the United States, selling many works to museums in San Diego, Dallas, and Louisville. In January of the following year, Valentín de Zubiaurre held a solo exhibit of eight of his paintings at the Dudensing Galleries in New York. Among these works were *The Mayor*, A *Village Fete*, and *In the Basque Country*, painted in his home village of Garay; *The Mayor of Pedraza*, influenced by the Castile region and considered one of his masterpieces; and the *Pardon of St. Anne*. In 1934, the brothers exhibited at the First International Exhibition of Fine and Applied Arts by Deaf Artists at the Roerich Museum in New York City with the other Spaniards Eulogio Blasco, Angel Garavilla, and Juan Ibarrondo. Valentín's work then increased in what some call his spiritual intensity. The influence of the master El Greco can be found in his painting.

Valentín de Zubiaurre's other honors included membership in Las Palmas Academy in the Canary Islands and the Salon d'Automne in Paris. He received the Legion of Honor award in Paris; and there, he became honorary president of the Society of Deaf Artists.

Valentín de Zubiaurre died in Madrid on January 24, 1963.

References

Pitrois, Y. (1915). Two great deaf artists of Spain: The Zubiaurre brothers. *The Silent Worker*, *27* (7), 121–123.

Stevens, K. H. (1928). Valentin de Zubiaurre's Exhibition. *The Silent Worker*, *40* (8), 334–335.

The Basque brother painters. (1926, February). *The Mentor*, 23–25.

Appendix A:
Additional Individuals

This section of *Deaf Persons in the Arts and Sciences: A Biographical Dictionary* lists some additional individuals selected for outstanding contributions to their disciplines and/or the community. Some key information about each person is included for students and scholars who wish to conduct further research.

ARTISTS

Note: Additional information on deaf persons in painting, photography, and sculpture may be found in the *Deaf Artists of America Newsletter*, Gannon (1981), and Van Cleve (1987), as well as in general dictionaries of artists.

Aaltonen, Waino; 20th century Finnish sculptor/painter; studied at Turku Academy of Fine Arts; granite monument honoring Finnish soldiers who died in World War I; statue of Paavo Nurmi; monument to poet Alexis Kivi; numerous international awards and exhibits.

Agnew, William; 19th century Scottish painter; honorable mention at Edinburgh Exhibition in 1890; *Royal Condescension*.

Alexander, Jacques; late-19th century German portrait painter; studied under Laurens and Constant in Paris; exhibited at the Kaufman Emporium and Bazaar; awarded ribbon of Officier de Instruction Publique.

Arrowsmith, Thomas; 18th century British portraitist/miniaturist; exhibited at Somerset House.

Ash, Samuel; 20th century Canadian Ojibway artist from the Osnaburgh Reserve; enclosed a short story with each painting; exhibited in Thunder Bay; Canada House Gallery in Trafalgar Square; his work is viewed as among the best of the Algonquin legend painters of Canada.

Avercamp, Hendrik; early-17th century Dutch painter; *Winterlandschaft mit Eisbelusti-*

gung; works in Dresden Gallery and in the galleries of Berlin, Rotterdam, Antwerp, as well as in private collections.

Blasco, Eulogio; early-20th century Spanish painter/sculptor; San Fernando School of Fine Arts; exhibited in Salon in Madrid, Barcelona, Seville, Paris, New York; works in major international museums.

Canter, Van Louy de; 19th century Belgian sculptor; silver medal for best work in marble, and a bronze medal in 1890; also honorable mention at the Belgian Exhibition in 1880.

Crolard, François; early-20th century French sculptor; studied under LeFevre and Le Maire; École des Beaux Arts; bust of Valentín de Zubiaurre purchased by the Spanish government to be placed in the National Museum of Modern Art in Madrid.

Davidson, Thomas; 19th century British artist; exhibited more than 20 times at the Royal Academy; 450 paintings and sketches between 1863 and 1897.

del Arco, Alonso; 17th century Spanish painter known as "El Sordillo de Pereda" (his master Antonio de Pereda); painted several arches in the royal corridor, portraits of the king; works are found in the museum at Madrid and public buildings throughout Spain.

di Betto Biagi, Bernardino; 15th century Italian painter known as *il Surdicchio*; studied with Raphaël under Pietro Vanucci; *The Miracles of Saint Bernardin* in Rome; frescoes (with Vanucci) of Moses in Sistine Chapel.

Ebstain, J.; early-20th century Algerian sculptor; active in Salons of deaf artists; won *Prix de Rome* and *Prix Osiris*; *Monuments to the Slain* and *Statue of General Damremont*.

Emerson, C. E.; early-20th century British painter; *Elterwater, Langdale* at the Royal Academy.

Font, Francisco Eulogio; early-20th century Puerto Rican caricaturist; studied under Fernando Díaz Mackenna; came to the United States in 1925; caricatures in the *Evening Post* and other periodicals.

Fortin, Henri; late-19th century French painter; studied at the School of Decorative Arts at the Academy Colarossi, École des Beaux Arts; exhibited at Rheims, Amiens, Paris; won several medals.

Frisino, Louis; 20th century American wildlife artist; studied at Maryland Institute College of Art; Peabody Award; works chosen for stamps.

Garavilla, Angel; early-20th century Spanish painter; studied in Academy Colarossi and Grande Chaumiere in Paris; portraits of Bilbao aristocrats; exhibits around the world; work praised by President Zamora of Spain.

Haeseler, Frederich C.; early-20th century American portrait painter; studied under Breckenridge and Anschutz at Pennsylvania Academy of Fine Arts; works in Philosophical Society of Pennsylvania, U.S. Appellate Court Room in Philadelphia, Pennsylvania Historical Society and numerous private collections.

Heimbach, Christian Wolfgang; 17th century Scandinavian artist; court painter to King Frederick III of Denmark, works found in galleries in Bremen, Hanover, London, and the Brunswick and Cassel Galleries of Sweden's Queen Christina.

Hennequin, Nicolas Gustave; 19th century French sculptor; studied at the Paris Fine Arts School; monument to Rector Gréard; Façade at Oceanographic Institute.

Janik, Rudolph; German-born American portrait painter; known chiefly for portrait of Kaiser Wilhelm I used widely on post cards.

Kane, Florence Breevort; early-20th century American sculptor; studied under Borglum, Art Students League; won prizes at Paris Salons; monument to poet Lamartine in Aix-les-Bains, France.

King, Frances; 20th century American painter; exhibited at Southern Vermont Arts Center; NTID Switzer Gallery; galleries in Florida, North Carolina, New Jersey; mural in the permanent collection of Texas State Senate.

LaMonto, Frederick; 20th century sculptor; exhibited at Bognar Galleries in Los Angeles, San Diego Arts Galleries, Long Beach Museum of Modern Art, and other museums.

Lopez, Jaime; 15th century Spanish painter known as "El Mudo"; decorated Hermitage of our Lady of Prado; painting of St. John the Baptist in the Church of Toledo.

Mackenzie, G. Annand; 19th century British artist; numerous prizes and medals; portraits of Sir Edward R. Russell and Dr. R. Jones; Master of Arts degree at Cambridge University.

Magoun, Priscilla; early-20th century American illuminator; studied at the Pennsylvania Museum School of Industrial Art; illustrated Annie Fellows Johnston's *In the Desert of Waiting*.

Martin, André; early-19th century painter; his works were exhibited in Brussels and Paris after his death.

Maruyama, Wendy; 20th century American crafts artist; more than 65 exhibits in the United States and Europe; her work, especially creative furniture, included in more than 40 publications.

Matosian, Peter; 20th century American painter; Art Institute of Chicago; exhibits at San Diego County Fair, Armenian Artists Guild in Los Angeles; Nexus Gallery in La Jolla, Athenaeum Gallery in La Jolla.

Montillie, Hippolyte; 19th century French sculptor; pupil of Millet, Moreau, Vauthier, Bartholdi, and Bitler; important works include decorative figures on the Pont Des Alexander (Alexander Bridge) and the bronze statue *L'Honneur dominant la Discords* on the cornice of Grand Palais des Beaux-Arts; awarded the standing of "Officer De Palme" by French government; Louisiana Exposition; medallion of Reverend Dr. Thomas Gallaudet.

Morice, Léon; late-19th century French sculptor; 129 works exhibited at the Paris Salon between 1909 and 1929; *Monseigneur Frepel* and *Dr. Montjardin* at Angens; *LePoete Lucien L'Homme*; *Chemins de Croix* at the Basilique de la Petite Soeur Therese.

Myslbek, Joseph Vaclav; late-19th century Czechoslovakian sculptor; statues of army commander Jan Zizka, poet Karel Hynek Macha; works largely in romantic style found in Museum of Modern Art in Prague.

Nazarov, Alexander; 20th century Russian painter; advanced degree in the arts; 1992 president of Russian Association of Deaf Artists.

Peysson, Frédéric; 19th century French Painter; paintings are at the museums of Versailles and Montpellier; *Last Moments of the abbé de L'Epée*.

Prádez, Roberto Francisco; early-19th century Spanish engraver/educator; studied under Fernando Selma at Royal Academy of Fine Arts of San Fernando; first prize in 1799 for rendition of Mengs' painting of the Virgin.

Quinlan, Will J.; late-19th century American painter/etcher; studied under Whittaker at National Academy of Design; exhibited in Chicago, Philadelphia, Washington, St. Louis, San Francisco; works in permanent collection of New York Public Library, Oakland Museum in California, John H. Vanderpool Art Gallery of Chicago; Shaw Etching Prize (1914).

Reid, John S.; 19th century British artist; three oil paintings at the 1880 Royal Scottish Academy Exhibition.

Reynolds, Sir Joshua; 18th century English painter progressively deafened in early twenties; painted portraits of 677 persons in 1757; knighted by George III and elected president of the Academy; appointed the Royal Portraitist; described his theories of art in *Discourses*.

Roche, Samson Towgood; late-18th century Irish artist; self taught; portrait of Mrs. Piozzi completed in 1782 shown posthumously at Brussels Exhibition, 1912; miniature of Princess Amelia, daughter of George III.

Schneider, Fritz; 20th century German sculptor; commissioned by the town of Waltenberg to execute a statue of Bismarck.

Sparks, William B.; 20th century American portrait painter; studied under L. McDaniel; works in galleries in the United States, Mexico and Brazil; portrait of Edward C. Merrill, Jr.; portrait of daughter became popular lithograph published by Bernard Picture Company.

Tavare, Fred L.; 19th century British artist; exhibited many works at Royal Manchester Institution and Whaite's Art Gallery.

Whitcomb, James H.; 19th century American silhouettist; works in New Hampshire Historical Society, Boston Museum of Fine Arts.

Wilder, Louise; early-20th century American sculptor; studied under F. Diehlman; numerous prizes in design, portraiture, sketching, sculpture.

ENTERTAINERS

Note: Additional information on deaf persons in the entertainment industry may be found in Gannon (1981), Schuchman (1988), Baldwin (1993), and Van Cleve (1987).

Arcos, Carmen de; early-20th century Cuban silent film star; *Great Guns*.

Baldwin, Steve; 20th century American playwright/teacher; numerous plays; authored book *Pictures in the Air*.

Bangs, Don; 20th century American playwright/director; Emmy award for outstanding achievement in special programming.

Brooks, Greg; 20th century American Emmy award winner for news show for deaf people in Los Angeles (1975).

Edwards, Sam; 20th century American actor/playwright/activist; *Bell*; memorialized in Sam Edwards Playwrights' competition.

Hlibok, Bruce; 20th century American actor; appeared as "Hubbell" in Broadway play *Runaways*.

Miles, Dorothy Squire; 20th century British actress/writer/playwright; authored *A Play of Our Own*.

Novitsky, Mary Lou; 20th century American TV producer; won several Emmy Awards for television show *Deaf Mosaic*.

Vreeland, Mary; 20th century American actress; winner of 1993 Helen Hayes Award for portrayal of Kattrin in Brecht's *Mother Courage and Her Children*.

Weinberg, Louis; early-20th century Silent Film Star (Stage Name David Marvel); *The Woman God Forgot*.

Wolf, Peter; 20th century American producer/director/cinematographer; two Emmy Awards for KRON Newsign 4 and the documentary *My Eyes Are My Ears*.

SCIENTISTS

Note: Additional information on deaf persons in science, engineering, medicine, and invention may be found in Lang (1994).

Andree, George K.; early-20th century American dentist; one of the first deaf persons to earn a degree in dentistry; president of Oklahoma Dental Association.

Atwood, Raymond T.; 20th century American bacteriologist; headed research work on the uses for protein materials left over from brewing operations; focused on the production of vitamins and life-saving antibiotics.

Babbitt, Lewis H.; 20th century herpetologist; published numerous reports on his studies of reptiles and amphibians; curator for Worcester Massachusetts Natural History Society.

Basch, Jay J.; 20th century American chemist; U.S. Department of Agriculture; authored numerous reports on biochemical research on concentrated milk.

Bates, Robert L.; 20th century American mathematician; U.S. Navy Bureau of Aeronautics; designed many programs for missile performance analysis, atomic shock arrival effects, and guidance systems.

Breunig, H. Latham; 20th century American chemist/statistician at Eli Lilly and Company (Indianapolis); developed statistical procedures which improved quality control.

Clark, Hubert L.; 20th century American zoologist progressively deafened; hundreds of publications on birds, insects, reptiles, and amphibians; Clarke Memorial Medal for service to Australian science.

Gavin, John J.; 20th century American molecular biochemist; Sidney S. Kramer Award for Meritorious Service to the Handicapped.

Lillie, Robert J.; 20th century American biologist; U.S. Department of Agriculture; awards for research in poultry science.

Nathorst, Alfred G.; 19th century Swedish geologist; progressively deafened; *History of the Earth*; *The Geology of Sweden*.

Neillie, Charles F.; late-19th century City Entomologist of Cleveland.

Nies, Edwin W.; early-20th century American dentist; one of the first deaf persons to earn a Doctor of Dental Surgery degree (1914); instructed at Columbia University; on staff at Knickerbocker Hospital.

Pachciarz, Judith; 20th century American physician; with a Ph.D. in microbiology, she was rejected for study at many medical schools due to deafness; graduated with M.D. in 1983 from Louisville School of Medicine.

Raykovic, Voya A.; 20th century Yugoslavian–American veterinarian; Palo Alto Medical Research Foundation; U.S. Department of Agriculture; published many reports on animal vaccines.

Ryan, Harris J.; early-20th century American electrical engineer; Edison Medal, 1927; President of American Institute of Electrical Engineers (1923).

Saks, Andrew; 20th century American engineer/businessman; co-inventor (with Robert H. Weitbrecht and James C. Marsters) of acoustic telephone coupler.

Tanaka, Yukiaki; 20th century Japanese astronomer; first Japanese astronomer to identify solar faculae (sun spots).

Taussig, Helen Brooke; 20th century progressively deafened American M.D.; president of American Heart Association; known for her work with Alfred Blalok in developing operation to save "blue babies."

Wenger, Arthur; 20th century American bacteriologist; established the Wenger Laboratories, a bacteriological-chemical firm highly praised by area doctors and other professionals.

Wenger, Ray; 20th century American bacteriologist; established the first blood bank in the state of Utah and produced the first set of anti-sera for blood matching in the state; chemist for 400 staff physicians at the Latter Day Saints Hospital.

Wiley, Averill J.; 20th century American bacteriologist; head bacteriologist for Health Department of Spokane, Washington; technical director of the Sulphite Pulp Manufacturer's Research League; authored numerous research reports on food and feed yeast, bacteriology of pulp and paper, and related topics.

Wilson, David H.; 20th century scholar; perhaps first born-deaf American to earn a Ph.D. (Harvard University, 1931).

Woodcock, Kathryn; 20th century Canadian engineer; one of the first deaf women to enter the field of engineering; served as Vice President of Hospital Services, Centenary Hospital in Scarborough, Ontario.

WRITERS/POETS

Note: Additional information on deaf writers may be found in Grant (1987), Jepson (1992), and Van Cleve (1987).

Bishop, Muriel; 19th century American writer; prolific contributor to southern newspapers and magazines.

Bourchier, James David; 19th century British writer/correspondent of *The Times* in Southeastern Europe; Office of the Order of St. Alexander of Bulgaria; authored entry "Albania" in *Encyclopedia Britannica*, 1910; correspondent in Balkan peninsula with headquarters first in Athens, then at Sofia, 1892–1918; entrusted with many secret negotiations preceding Balkan alliance, 1911–1912.

Bowe, F. R.; 20th century American writer/advocate/biographer; profiles of deaf persons in periodicals; many books; *Rehabilitating America, Changing the Rules, Handicapping America: Barriers to Disabled People.*

Braddock, Guilbert C.; early-20th century American writer/minister; biographer-author of *Notable Deaf Persons.*

Burnet, John R.; 19th century writer/editor; numerous articles and verse in periodicals; *Tales of the Deaf and Dumb, with Miscellaneous Poems.*

Burnside, Helen Marion; 19th century British writer/artist; *Driftwood—A Book of Poems*; *The Deaf Girl Next Door, or Marjory's Life Work.*

Caldwell, Taylor; 20th century British writer progressively deafened; over 50 novels; first book *Dynasty of Death.*

Cramer, Mary A. M.; 19th century American writer; contributed verse to the *Chicago Tribune* under the pen name Morna, to the *New York Citizen*, as Barbara O'Brien, and to *Good Cheer*, the *Galaxy*, and other periodicals in her own name.

Dalton, Charlotte; late-19th century American poet; *The Silent Zone*; *Flame and Adventure; The Ear Trumpet; The Marriage Music; Lilies and Leopards.*

Desloges, Pierre; 18th century French writer; one of the earliest deaf persons to publish a work, a defense of sign language.

Emery, Philip A.; 19th century American author; *Landscape of History.*

Farlow, Kate M; 19th century American writer; *Silent Life and Silent Language.*

Farrar, Abraham; 19th century British writer known for extensive early writings on the history of deaf people; one of the earliest deaf persons to pass the Cambridge University Local Examination and the London University Matriculation Examination.

Fisher, Angelina H.; 20th century American poet; published numerous verses in *Boston Transcript, Boston Journal.*

Font, Eleanor Sherman; 20th century Curator of Iconography, Hispanic Society of America; "Goya's Source for the Maragato Series" (*Gazette des Beaux–Arts*, Nov. 1958).

Gannon, Jack R.; 20th century American writer/historian; numerous scholarly publications; authored *Deaf Heritage: A Narrative History of Deaf America.*

Golladay, Loy; 20th century American writer/educator; numerous biographical sketches, poems, educational writings in periodicals; verse published in many periodicals; won several poetry prizes; book of verse *A is for Alice.*

Hanson, Agatha Tiegel; early-20th century poet/feminist; *Overflow Verses*; presented "The Intellect of Women" at Gallaudet commencement in 1893; she was the first deaf woman graduate of Gallaudet College.

Jennings, Alice; 19th century American Poet; book of verse, *Heart Echoes*; numerous poems published in *Boston Evening Transcript* and other periodicals.

Kerrnish, Jessie D.; early-20th century British novelist; *Miss Haroun at Raschid.*

Lavaud, Suzanne; early-20th century French writer; first deaf woman to earn a doctoral degree at the Sorbonne; known for her dissertation and other writings on deaf playwright Marie Lenéru.

Leisman, Arthur G.; 19th century American poet, *Old Wisconsin.*

Long, Joseph Schuyler; early-20th century writer/educator; *Out of the Silence*; *The Sign Language: A Manual of Signs.*

Lowman, Rex; Poet; AAUW poetry contest winner 3 straight years in 1930s; book of verse *Bitterweed.*

Merker, Hannah; 20th century American writer; *Listening*; *Waterborn.*

Montague, Margaret Prescott; early-20th century American author; *The Lucky Lady*; *Closed Doors.*

Muse, Helen E.; 20th century American writer; *Green Pavilions.*

Padden, Carol; 20th century writer/linguist/anthropologist; numerous scholarly publications; *ASL: A Look at Its History, Structure, and Community*; *Deaf in America: Voices from a Culture* (with Tom Humphries).

Peet, Mary Toles; 19th century American poet; *Verses.*

Pélissier, Marie Pierre; late-19th century French poet/writer; *Poesies d'un Sourd Muet*; *Iconographie des signes.*

Philbrick, Rachel J.; late-19th century American writer; romantic novel; *Desire Wentworth: A Romance in Provincial Times.*

Preston, Anna; 19th century American writer; *The Record of a Silent Life.*

Ragna, Sara Tredwell; early-20th century American author/poet; her work appeared in Braitwaite's *Anthology* and the popular *Contemporary Verse.*

Rocheleau, Corrine; early-20th century American writer; *Out of Her Prison*; *Heroic French Women of Canada*; *Those in the Dark Silence.*

Smith, Linwood; 20th century African-American writer/poet; book of verse *Silence, Love, and Kids I Know*; poems appeared in *The Gwendolyn Brooks Anthology, Soul Journey, Uptown Beat, Today's Negro Voice*; coauthored with Ernest Hairston *Black and Deaf in America.*

Smith, Marta; early-20th century American poet; pen name Hallea Stout; Governor of Arkansas officially listed her among best poets in that state.

Sollenberger, Earl; pen name Earl Crombie; 20th century American poet; *Along with Me*; *Verses*; *A Handful of Quietness.*

Sullivan, James A.; 20th century American writer; *Valley Forge.*

Von Witzleben, Margarette; 19th century German writer; *L'Helvetie, Un soupir*; *Chaineau Crois.*

Watkins, Abbie M.; 20th century American feature writer for *McCalls, Saturday Evening Post.*

Wood, John P.; early-19th century Scottish writer; wrote and edited four books.

Appendix B:
Detailed Biographies
Listed by Field

ACTORS

Linda Bove (1945–)	American Actress
Bernard Bragg (1928–)	American Actor
Julianna Fjeld (1947–)	American Actress/Producer
Phyllis Frelich (1944–)	American Actress
Patrick Graybill (1939–)	American Actor
Marlee Matlin (1965–)	American Actress
Freda Norman (1945–)	American Actress
Audree L. Norton (1927–)	American Actress
Emerson Romero (1900–1972)	American Silent Film Actor
Howie Seago (1953–)	American Actor
Edmund Waterstreet, Jr. (1943–)	American Actor

ARTISTS

Gustinus Ambrosi (1893–1975)	Austrian Sculptor
N. Hillis Arnold (1906–1988)	American Sculptor
Charles Crawford Baird (1947–)	American Painter
Albert Ballin (1861–1932)	American Artist/Silent Film Actor
David Ludwig Bloch (1910–)	American Artist
John Brewster (1766–1854)	American Folk Artist
Morris Broderson (1928–)	American Artist
John Carlin (1813–1891)	American Painter/Writer

George Catlin (1796–1872)	American Painter/Writer
Paul-François Choppin (1856–1937)	French Sculptor
John Louis Clarke (1881–1970)	American Wood Sculptor
Claude-André Deseine (1740–1823)	French Sculptor
Theophilus Hope D'Estrella (1851–1929)	American Artist/Photographer
Rolando Lopez Dirube (1928–)	Cuban Artist
Robert Freiman (1917–)	American Artist
Augustus Fuller (1812–1873)	American Folk Artist
Walter Geikie (1795–1837)	Scottish Painter
Antonio Gómez Feu (1907–1984)	Spanish Artist
Francisco José de Goya y Lucientes (1746–1828)	Spanish Artist
Eliza Haigh-Voorhis (1865–?)	American Painter
Fernand Hamar (1869–1943)	French Sculptor
Jean Hanau (1899–1966)	French-American Painter
Eugene E. Hannan (1875–1945)	American Sculptor
Vilem J. Hauner (1903–)	Czechoslovakian Artist
Regina Olson Hughes (1895–1993)	American Scientific Illustrator
Margaret E. Jackson (1902–1986)	American Museum Curator
Felix Kowalewski (1913–1989)	American Painter/Poet
Henry Lapp (1862–1904)	American Craftsman/Painter
Félix Martin (1844–1917)	French Sculptor
William Mercer (1765–1839)	American Painter
Betty G. Miller (1934–)	American Artist/Educator
H. Humphrey Moore (1844–1926)	American Artist
Juan Fernandez Navarrete (1526–1579)	Spanish Painter
Albert Newsam (1809–1864)	American Lithographer
Robert Baard Peterson (1943–)	American Painter
Maurice Prendergast (1859–1924)	American Painter
René Princeteau (1843–1914)	French Painter/Sculptor
Granville Seymour Redmond (1871–1935)	American Artist/Silent Film Actor
Joseph Henry Sharp (1859–1953)	American Painter
Kelly H. Stevens (1896–1991)	American Painter
Mathias Stoltenberg (1799–1871)	Norwegian Painter
Alfred R. Thomson (1894–1979)	British Artist
Douglas Tilden (1860–1935)	American Sculptor
Cadwallader Lincoln Washburn (1866–1965)	American Drypoint Etcher

Mary Washburn (1868–1932)   American Sculptor
Dorothy Stanton Wise (?–1919)   British Sculptor
Ramón de Zubiaurre (1882–1969)   Spanish Painter
Valentín de Zubiaurre (1879–1963)   Spanish Painter

ARCHITECTS/ENGINEERS

Olof Hanson (1862–1933)   American Architect
Thomas Scott Marr (1866–1936)   American Architect
George Bryan Shanklin (1888–1961)   American Electrical Engineer

SCIENTISTS/PHYSICIANS/INVENTORS

Robert Grant Aitken (1864–1951)   American Astronomer
Guillaume Amontons (1663–1705)   French Physicist
Donald L. Ballantyne (1922–)   Professor of Experimental Surgery

Frederick A. P. Barnard (1809–1889)   American Scientist/Educator
Ruth Fulton Benedict (1887–1948)   American Anthropologist
Charles Bonnet (1720–1793)   Swiss Naturalist
Annie Jump Cannon (1863–1941)   American Astronomer
Harold J. Conn (1886–1975)   American Bacteriologist
Sir John Warcup Cornforth (1917–)   British Nobel Laureate in Chemistry

George T. Dougherty (1860–1938)   American Metallurgist
Tilly Edinger (1897–1967)   American Paleoneurologist
Thomas Alva Edison (1847–1931)   American Inventor
Anders Gustaf Ekeberg (1767–1813)   Swedish Chemist
Robert J. Farquharson (1824–1884)   American Civil War Surgeon
Sir John Ambrose Fleming (1849–1945)   British Electrical Scientist
John Goodricke (1764–1786)   British Astronomer
Wilson H. Grabill (1912–1983)   American Statistician
Anthony A. Hajna (1907–1992)   American Bacteriologist
Olaf Hassel (1898–1972)   Norwegian Astronomer
Oliver Heaviside (1850–1925)   British Electrical Scientist
Frank P. Hochman (1935–)   American Physician
David James (1950–)   American Mathematician
Donald J. Kidd (1922–1966)   Canadian Geologist

Henrietta Swan Leavitt (1868–1921)   American Astronomer
Leo Lesquereux (1806–1889)   American Paleobotanist
James H. Logan (1843–1917)   American Microscopist
James C. Marsters (1924–   )   American Dentist/Inventor
Gerald M. McCarthy (1858–1915)   American Entomologist
Thomas Meehan (1826–1901)   American Botanist
Fielding Bradford Meek (1817–1876)   American Geologist
Gideon E. Moore (1842–1895)   American Chemist
Charles Henri Nicolle (1866–1936)   French Nobel Laureate in Physiology and Medicine

Wyn Owston (Ethel Sharrard) (1919–   )   British Physician
Joseph Sauveur (1653–1716)   French Physicist
Charlotte Angas Scott (1858–1931)   British Mathematician
Nansie Sharpless (1932–1987)   American Biochemist
Konstantin Eduardovich Tsiolkovsky (1857–1935) Russian Rocket Pioneer
Robert H. Weitbrecht (1920–1983)   American Physicist

WRITERS/POETS

Eugene Bergman (1932–   )   American Writer/Educator
Edmund Booth (1810–1905)   American Editor/Writer
Earnest Elmo Calkins (1868–1964)   American Writer/Advertiser
Joachim Du Bellay (1522?–1560)   French Poet
Gilbert C. Eastman (1934–   )   American Actor/Playwright
Angeline Fuller Fischer (1841–1925)   American Writer
Dorothy Canfield Fisher (1879–1958)   American Writer/Educator
Horace Howard Furness (1833–1912)   American Shakespearean Scholar

Ellen Glasgow (1873?–1945)   American Author
Morrison Heady (1829–1915)   American Poet/Novelist
George Hyde (1882–1968)   American Wild West Historian
Jack Jones (1923–1983)   American Writer/Social Critic/Philosopher

Helen Keller (1880–1968)   American Writer
Henry Kisor (1940–   )   American Writer/Book Editor
John Kitto (1804–1854)   British Biblical Scholar
Marie Lenéru (1875–1918)   French Dramatist
Eugenie Marlitt (1825–1887)   German Writer
Harriet Martineau (1802–1876)   British Writer

Florence Lewis May (1899–1988)	American Writer/Curator
Alice J. McVan (1906–1970)	American Poet/Museum Curator
Dale L. Morgan (1914–1971)	American Wild West Historian
James Nack (1809–1879)	American Poet
Yvonne Pitrois (1880–1937)	French Writer
Pierre de Ronsard (1524–1585)	French Poet
Laura C. Redden Searing (1840–1923)	American Writer/Poet
Howard L. Terry (1877–1964)	American Writer/Poet
Charlotte Elizabeth Tonna (1790–1846)	British Writer
Heinrich von Treitschke (1834–1896)	German Writer/Political Publicist
Carolyn Wells (187?–1942)	American Writer
Horst Witte (1913–1991)	German Poet/Novelist
David Wright (1920–1994)	British Writer

MUSICIANS/DANCERS

Ludwig Van Beethoven (1770–1827)	German Composer
Evelyn Glennie (1965–)	Scottish Percussionist
Friedrich Smetana (1824–1884)	Czechoslovakian Composer
Michael Thomas (1951–)	American Dancer/Choreographer
Frances Woods (1907–)	American Dancer

DEAF COMMUNITY LEADERS/POLITICIANS/EDUCATORS/ADVOCATES

Glenn B. Anderson (1945–)	American Educator/Deaf Community Advocate
Jack Ashley (1922–)	British Politician/Writer
Jean-Ferdinand Berthier (1803–1886)	French Writer/Deaf Community Advocate
Laurent Clerc (1785–1869)	American Educator
Robert Davila (1932–)	American Educator
Andrew Foster (1925–1987)	American Educator/Missionary
Gertrude Scott Galloway (1930–)	American Educator/Deaf Community Advocate
Ernest E. Hairston, Jr. (1939–)	American Writer/Deaf Community Advocate
Irving King Jordan (1943–)	American Educator
Malcolm J. Norwood (1927–1989)	American Media Specialist

Robert F. Panara (1920–)	American Educator/Writer
Roslyn Rosen (1943–)	American Educator/Deaf Community Advocate
Frederick C. Schreiber (1922–1979)	American Educator/Deaf Community Advocate
George W. Veditz (1861–1937)	American Writer/Deaf Community Advocate
Heather Whitestone (1973–)	American University Student/Advocate/Miss America

Selected Bibliography

Baldwin, S. C. (1993). *Pictures in the air: The story of the National Theatre of the Deaf.* Washington, DC: Gallaudet University Press.

Braddock, G. C. (1975). *Notable deaf persons.* Washington, DC: Gallaudet College Alumni Association.

Fischer, R., & Lane, H. (Eds.). (1993). *Looking back: A reader on the history of deaf communities and their sign languages.* Hamburg, Germany: Signum Press.

Gallaher, J. E. (1898). *Representative deaf persons of the United States of America.* Chicago: Gallaher.

Gannon, J. R. (Ed.). (1981). *Deaf heritage: A narrative history of deaf America.* Silver Spring, MD: National Association of the Deaf.

Grant, B. (Ed.). (1987). *The quiet ear: Deafness in literature.* London: Faber & Faber.

Holcomb, M., & Wood, S. (1989). *Deaf women: A parade through the decades.* Berkeley, CA: DawnSign Press.

Jepson, J. (Ed.). (1992). *No walls of stone: An anthology of literature by deaf and hard of hearing writers.* Washington, DC: Gallaudet University Press.

Lang, H. G. (1994). *Silence of the spheres: The deaf experience in the history of science.* Westport, CT: Bergin & Garvey.

Mirzoeff, N. (1992). The silent mind: Learning from deafness. *History Today, 42* (7), 19–25.

Panara, R. F., & Panara, J. (1983). *Great deaf Americans.* Silver Spring, MD: T. J. Publishers.

Schuchman, J. S. (1988). *Hollywood speaks: Deafness and the film entertainment industry.* Urbana: University of Illinois Press.

Van Cleve, J. V. (Ed.). (1987). *Gallaudet encyclopedia of deaf people and deafness.* New York: McGraw-Hill.

Van Cleve, J. V. (Ed.). (1993). *Deaf history unveiled: Interpretations from the new scholarship.* Washington, DC: Gallaudet University Press.

Index

Page numbers in **bold type** refer to main entries in the dictionary.

About the Authors

HARRY G. LANG is a Professor at the Center for Research, Teaching, and Learning, National Technical Institute for the Deaf, Rochester Institute of Technology. He is the author of *Silence of the Spheres: The Deaf Experience in the History of Science* (Bergin & Garvey, 1994).

BONNIE MEATH-LANG is a Professor at the Centers for Arts and Sciences/ Research, Teaching, and Learning, National Technical Institute for the Deaf, Rochester Institute of Technology. She is the author of many articles and book chapters.